Natural Legal Language Processing Workshop (NLLP 2023)

Singapore
7 December 2023

ISBN: 978-1-7138-8604-4

Printed from e-media with permission by:

Curran Associates, Inc.
57 Morehouse Lane
Red Hook, NY 12571

Some format issues inherent in the e-media version may also appear in this print version.

Printed with permission by Curran Associates, Inc. (2024)

Association for Computational Linguistics
209 N. Eighth Street
Stroudsburg, Pennsylvania 18360

Phone: 1-570-476-8006
Fax: 1-570-476-0860

acl@aclweb.org

Additional copies of this publication are available from:

Curran Associates, Inc.
57 Morehouse Lane
Red Hook, NY 12571 USA
Phone: 845-758-0400
Fax: 845-758-2633
Email: curran@proceedings.com
Web: www.proceedings.com

NLLP 2023

Natural Legal Language Processing Workshop 2023

Proceedings of the Workshop

December 7, 2023

The NLLP organizers gratefully acknowledge the support from the following sponsors.

In Collaboration With

Order copies of this and other ACL proceedings from:

Association for Computational Linguistics (ACL)
209 N. Eighth Street
Stroudsburg, PA 18360
USA
Tel: +1-570-476-8006
Fax: +1-570-476-0860
acl@aclweb.org

Introduction

Welcome to the fifth edition of the NLLP (Natural Legal Language Processing) Workshop, co-located with the 2023 Conference on Empirical Methods in Natural Language Processing.

Different industrial sectors have embraced natural language processing (NLP) technologies, which have altered services and products in healthcare, finance, education among others. The legal domain, in particular, stands as a promising frontier for the exploration of interesting research problems. Electronic tools have become increasingly integral in the practice of law, with their usage projected to undergo exponential growth. By its very nature, the practice of law necessarily involves the analysis and interpretation of language. The potential for NLP applications to provide benefit to practitioners of law and consumers of legal services around the world is enormous.

We organized this workshop to bring together researchers, practitioners, policy makers from around the world who develop NLP techniques within the legal domain. This is an exciting opportunity to expand the boundaries of our field by identifying new problems and exploring new data as it interacts with the full inventory of NLP and machine learning approaches. In this spirit, the Organizing and Program Committee was assembled to include researchers from both academia and industry, from NLP and legal backgrounds.

We were interested in the following types of papers: (1) applications of NLP methods to legal tasks; (2) experimental results using and adapting NLP methods in legal documents; (3) descriptions of new legal tasks for NLP; (4) creation of curated and/or annotated resources; (5) descriptions of systems which use NLP technologies for legal text; (6) industrial research in this area and (7) interdisciplinary position papers.

We again received a record number of submissions. In total, we received of 64 submissions on our direct submission website, out of which we accepted 32 for an overall acceptance rate of 50%. Out of the 32 accepted papers, 22 are long and 10 are short. The accepted papers include 6 original papers submitted as non-archival, in order to accommodate publication of the work at a later date in a conference or journal. All papers were reviewed by at least 3 members of the Program Committee, one of which usually includinglegal scholar. In addition, we also offered a venue for presentation for 10 papers accepted to the Findings of EMNLP 2023 on the above topics. All 42 papers were invited to have an oral presentation, either in-person or remote, as well as the option to present a poster in the lunch poster session.

The papers cover a wide range of topics including new data sets for legal NLP, position papers on open legal NLP issues, legal perspectives on NLP topics, as well as applications of NLP tasks to legal documents including retrieval, information extraction, legal judgement prediction and statutory reasoning. A number of papers also explore the use of Large Language Models (LLMs) in the legal domain spanning from fundamental questions to usage methods and applications such as prompting strategies, chain-of-thought applications in retrieval tasks or e-discovery. Finally, we note the diversity of legal domains/languages with papers working in French, Hebrew, Italian, Korean or resources covering up to 24 languages.

We thank our invited speaker Jerrold Soh, Assistant Professor at the Yong Pung How School of Law and Deputy Director of the Centre of Computational Law at Singapore Management University for accepting our invitation. In the tradition of past NLLP workshops, the invited speaker is a legal scholar with an interest in empirical methods for legal analysis including NLP methods. He will be giving a talk entitled NLP in the Legal Worldwhich aims to identify the unique role that NLP can play in furthering our understanding of law and facilitating practical access to justice.

We thank everyone who expressed interest in the workshop, all authors of submitted papers, members of the Program Committee who did an excellent job at reviewing papers given a short turnaround time, everyone attending the workshop and the EMNLP 2023 conference for hosting us and the workshop. We thank our sponsors – Bloomberg and the European Research Council Starting Grant project HUMANads – for their contributions.

The NLLP Workshop organizers.

`http://nllpw.org`

Program Committee

Organizing Committee

Nikolaos Aletras, University of Sheffield
Leslie Barrett, Bloomberg
Ilias Chalkidis, University of Copenhagen
Catalina Goanta, Utrecht University
Daniel Preotiuc-Pietro, Bloomberg
Gerasimos Spanakis, Maastricht University

Program Committee

Tommaso Agnoloni, IGSG CNR
Ion Androutsopoulos, Athens University of Economics and Business
Elliott Ash, ETH Zurich
Breck Baldwin, Safety Third
Claire Barale, The University of Edinburgh
Thales Bertaglia, Maastricht University
Andrew Blair-Stanek, University of Maryland Law School
Stephanie Brandl, University of Copenhagen
Rajarathnam Chandramouli, Spectronn Inc
Daniel Chen, Toulouse School of Economics
Ashish Chouhan, Heidelberg University
Tony Davis, Southern Oregon University
Stefania Degaetano-Ortlieb, Saarland University
Luigi Di Caro, University of Turin
Manos Fergadiotis, Athens University of Economics and Business
Nicolas Garneau, University of Copenhagen
Ivan Habernal, Paderborn University
Ben Hagag, Bar Ilan University
Nils Holzenberger, Télécom Paris
Abderrahmane Issam, Maastricht University
Kartik Kannapur, Amazon Web Services
Constantinos Karouzos, University of Sheffield
Panagiota Katsikouli, University of Copenhagen
Daniel Katz, Illinois Tech - Chicago Kent College of Law
Ilan Kernerman, K Dictionaries - Lexicala
Moniba Keymanesh, Bloomberg
Aykut Koc, Bilkent University
Manolis Koubarakis, National and Kapodistrian University of Athens
Junyi Jessy Li, University of Texas at Austin
Jiaang Li, University of Copenhagen
Ruta Liepina, University of Bologna
Antoine Louis, Maastricht University
Adam Meyers, New York University
Jelena Mitrović, University of Passau
Joel Niklaus, University of Bern
Milda Norkute, Thomson Reuters
Daphne Odekerken, Utrecht University

Henrik Palmer Olsen, University of Copenhagen
Pietro Ortolani, Radboud University
Paulo Quaresma, University of Evora
Yannis Panagis, University of Copenhagen
Georg Rehm, DFKI
Constanta Rosca, Maastricht University
Cristiana Santos, Utrecht Universiy
Jaromir Savelka, Carnegie Mellon University
Vageesh Saxena, Maastricht University
Sebastian Schwemer, University of Copenhagen
Yusuf Can Semerci, Maastricht University
Dan Simonson, BlackBoiler Inc
Jerrold Soh, Singapore Management University
Alexandru Sotropa, Vrije University
Amanda Stent, Colby College
Santosh T.y.s.s, Technical University of Munich
Andrea Tagarelli, University of Calabria
Dimitrios Tsarapatsanis, University of York
Josef Valvoda, University of Cambridge
Jacob Van De Kerkhof, Utrecht University
Gijs Van Dijck, Maastricht University
Peter Vickers, University of Sheffield
Jianqiang Wang, University at Buffalo
Hannes Westermann, Université de Montréal
Huiyin Xue, The University of Sheffield
Atsuki Yamaguchi, University of Sheffield
Marcos Zampieri, George Mason University
Lucia Zheng, Stanford University
Miri Zilka, University of Cambridge

Keynote Talk: NLP in the Legal World

Jerrold Soh
Yong Pung How School of Law, Singapore Management University, Singapore

Abstract: This talk situates the rising field of NLLP in the context of legal scholarship and practice. It will examine how the field relates to existing inquiries in computational law, AI and Law, and computational/empirical legal studies. Similarities, differences, and opportunities for cross-fertilization and inter-field discourse will be identified along four dimensions: questions generally asked, techniques generally used, publications generally produced, and the people generally involved. By elucidating links and bridges between NLLP and adjacent legal fields, the talk aims to identify the unique role that NLLP can play, and indeed has already been playing, in furthering our understanding of law and facilitating practical access to justice.

Bio: Jerrold Soh is an Assistant Professor at the Yong Pung How School of Law, Singapore Management University and the Deputy Director of its Centre for Computational Law. His research revolves around how emerging technologies, especially artificial intelligence, should be regulated by and also used in the legal system. He has published both doctrinal work on AI and automated vehicles liability as well as scientific work developing machine learning and network models for legal use cases. He holds degrees in Law and Economics from the National University of Singapore and an LLM from Harvard Law School.

Table of Contents

Program

Wednesday, December 7, 2022

09:00 - 09:10 *Workshop Opening*

09:10 - 10:30 *Session 1*

Anthropomorphization of AI: Opportunities and Risks
Ameet Deshpande, Tanmay Rajpurohit, Karthik Narasimhan and Ashwin Kalyan

Legal NLP Meets MiCAR: Advancing the Analysis of Crypto White Papers
Carolina Camassa

On the Potential and Limitations of Few-Shot In-Context Learning to Generate Metamorphic Specifications for Tax Preparation Software
Dananjay Srinivas, Rohan Das, Saeid Tizpaz-Niari, Ashutosh Trivedi and Maria Leonor Pacheco

NOMOS: Navigating Obligation Mining in Official Statutes
Andrea Pennisi, Elvira González Hernández and Nina Koivula

Long Text Classification using Transformers with Paragraph Selection Strategies
Mohit Tuteja and Daniel González Juclà

Italian Legislative Text Classification for Gazzetta Ufficiale
Marco Rovera, Alessio Palmero Aprosio, Francesco Greco, Mariano Lucchese, Sara Tonelli and Antonio Antetomaso

Towards Mitigating Perceived Unfairness in Contracts from a Non-Legal Stakeholder's Perspective
Anmol Singhal, Preethu Rose Anish, Shirish Karande and Smita Ghaisas

Low-Resource Deontic Modality Classification in EU Legislation
Kristina Minkova, Shashank Chakravarthy and Gijs Dijck

Transferring Legal Natural Language Inference Model from a US State to Another: What Makes It So Hard?
Alice Kwak, Gaetano Forte, Derek Bambauer and Mihai Surdeanu

Large Language Models for Legally Enforceable Hate Speech Detection
Chu Fei Luo, Rohan Bhambhoria, Samuel Dahan and Xiaodan Zhu

More than Votes? Voting and Language based Partisanship in the US Supreme Court
Biaoyan Fang, Trevor Cohn, Timothy Baldwin and Lea Frermann

10:30 - 11:00 *Break*

11:00 - 12:30 *Session 2*

Retrieval-Augmented Chain-of-Thought in Semi-structured Domains
Vaibhav Mavi, Abulhair Saparov and Chen Zhao

Mixed-domain Language Modeling for Processing Long Legal Documents
Wenyue Hua, Yuchen Zhang, Zhe Chen, Josie Li and Melanie Weber

Large Language Models are legal but they are not: Making the case for a powerful LegalLLM
Thanmay Jayakumar, Fauzan Farooqui and Luqman Farooqui

Exploration of Open Large Language Models for eDiscovery
Sumit Pai, Sounak Lahiri, Ujjwal Kumar, Krishanu Baksi, Elijah Soba, Michael Suesserman, Nirmala Pudota, Jon Foster, Edward Bowen and Sanmitra Bhattacharya

A Comparative Study of Prompting Strategies for Legal Text Classification
Ali Hakimi Parizi, Yuyang Liu, Prudhvi Nokku, Sina Gholamian and David Emerson

A Comprehensive Evaluation of Large Language Models on Legal Judgment Prediction
Ruihao Shui, Yixin Cao, Xiang Wang and Tat-Seng Chua

SCALE: Scaling up the Complexity for Advanced Language Model Evaluation
Vishvaksenan Rasiah, Ronja Stern, Veton Matoshi, Matthias Stürmer, Ilias Chalkidis, Daniel Ho and Joel Niklaus

Super-SCOTUS: A multi-sourced dataset for the Supreme Court of the US
Biaoyan Fang, Trevor Cohn, Timothy Baldwin and Lea Frermann

MultiLegalPile: A 689GB Multilingual Legal Corpus
Joel Niklaus, Veton Matoshi, Matthias Stürmer, Ilias Chalkidis and Daniel Ho

Wednesday, December 7, 2022 (continued)

	ECtHR-PCR: A Dataset for Precedent Understanding and Prior Case Retrieval in the European Court of Human Rights Santosh T.y.s.s, Rashid Haddad and Matthias Grabmair
	AsyLex: A Dataset for Legal Language Processing of Refugee Claims Claire Barale, Mark Klaisoongnoen, Pasquale Minervini, Michael Rovatsos and Nehal Bhuta
	LEXTREME: A Multi-Lingual and Multi-Task Benchmark for the Legal Domain Joel Niklaus, Veton Matoshi, Pooja Rani, Andrea Galassi, Matthias Stürmer and Ilias Chalkidis
12:30 - 14:00	*Lunch and In-Person Poster Session*
14:00 - 15:00	*Keynote - NLP in the Legal World - Jerrold Soh (Yong Pung How School of Law)*
14:00 - 15:30	*Session 3*
	Retrieval-based Evaluation for LLMs: A Case Study in Korean Legal QA Cheol Ryu, Seolhwa Lee, Subeen Pang, Chanyeol Choi, Hojun Choi, Myeonggee Min and Jy-Yong Sohn
	Joint Learning for Legal Text Retrieval and Textual Entailment: Leveraging the Relationship between Relevancy and Affirmation Nguyen Hai Long, Thi Hai Yen Vuong, Ha Thanh Nguyen and Xuan-Hieu Phan
	Tracing Influence at Scale: A Contrastive Learning Approach to Linking Public Comments and Regulator Responses Linzi Xing, Brad Hackinen and Giuseppe Carenini
	Legal Passage Retrieval: A pragmatic approach to legal AI Robert Mahari, Dominik Stammbach, Elliott Ash and Alex Pentland
15:30 - 16:00	*Break*
16:00 - 17:30	*Session 4*
	Towards Explainability and Fairness in Swiss Judgement Prediction: Benchmarking on a Multilingual Dataset Santosh T.y.s.s, Nina Baumgartner, Matthias Stürmer, Matthias Grabmair and Joel Niklaus

Wednesday, December 7, 2022 (continued)

Automatic Anonymization of Swiss Federal Supreme Court Rulings
Joel Niklaus, Robin Mamié, Matthias Stürmer, Daniel Brunner and Marcel Gygli

Automatic Anonymization of Swiss Federal Supreme Court Rulings
Joel Niklaus, Robin Mamié, Matthias Stürmer, Daniel Brunner and Marcel Gygli

Can ChatGPT Perform Reasoning Using the IRAC Method in Analyzing Legal Scenarios Like a Lawyer?
Xiaoxi Kang, Lizhen Qu, Lay-Ki Soon, Adnan Trakic, Terry Yue Zhuo, Patrick Charles Emerton and Genevieve Grant

Information Extraction from Legal Wills: How Well Does GPT-4 Do?
Alice Saebom Kwak, Cheonkam Jeong, Gaetano Vincent Forte, Derek Bambauer, Clayton T Morrison and Mihai Surdeanu

17:30 - 17:35 *Closing Remarks & Best Presentation Award*

Anthropomorphization of AI: Opportunities and Risks

Ameet Deshpande[⋆1] **Tanmay Rajpurohit**[3]
Karthik Narasimhan[1] **Ashwin Kalyan**[2]

[1]Princeton University [2]The Allen Institute for AI [3]Georgia Tech
asd@cs.princeton.edu

Abstract

Anthropomorphization, which is the tendency to attribute human-like traits to non-human entities, is prevalent in many social contexts – children anthropomorphize toys and adults do so with brands. It is also a versatile tool in science, with behavioral psychology and evolutionary biology meticulously documenting its consequences. With widespread adoption of AI systems, and the push to make it human-like through alignment techniques, human voice, and avatars, the tendency for users to anthropomorphize it increases significantly. We take a dyadic approach to understanding this phenomenon with large language models (LLMs) by studying (1) the objective legal implications, as analyzed through the lens of the recent blueprint of AI bill of rights[1] and the (2) subtle psychological aspects of customization and anthropomorphization. We find that anthropomorphized LLMs customized for different user bases violate multiple provisions in the legislative blueprint and raise corporate personhood confusions. In addition, we point out that anthropomorphization of LLMs affects the influence they can have on their users, thus establishing potential for manipulation and negative influence. With LLMs being hyper-personalized for vulnerable groups like children and patients among others, we propose a conservative strategy for the cautious use of anthropomorphization to improve trustworthiness of AI systems.

1 Introduction

Anthropomorphization refers to ascribing human-like traits to non-human entities, and has been used in diverse areas encompassing literature, science, art, and marketing (Ghedini and Bergamasco, 2010; Dunn, 2011; Spatola et al., 2022). It occurs when humans assign emotional or behavioral traits to entities. Several behavioral psychology studies have posited and argued that anthropomorphization is a natural tendency when humans interact with *entities* (Epley et al., 2007; Airenti, 2018). This natural tendency has influenced many fields of science like evolutionary biology (Wynne, 2004) and comparative cognition (Bruni et al., 2018) to carefully consider its effects on human interaction.

Figure 1: Conversational AI systems are increasingly being integrated into the daily lives of many. While their improved quality is a welcome change, their personalization increases the tendency to anthropomorphize them, which has legal and psychological risks.

Recently, generative large language models (LLMs) (Brown et al., 2020; Chowdhery et al., 2022) have been deployed in a variety of applications. Conversational systems like ChatGpt (OpenAI, 2023) and Bard (Google, 2023) have modified LLMs with a purposeful push towards making them more human-like (Ouyang et al., 2022). The quality of these systems has enabled human-AI interactions at unprecedented scales, thus increasing the chances of these systems being anthropomorphized. In this work, we analyze anthropomorphization in LLMs and discuss its: (1) Legal implications and (2) Psychological effects.

Customization of systems and brands has long been seen as an effective way to increase anthropomorphization and establish an emotional connection with humans (Zhang et al., 2020; Pimentel and Kalyanaraman, 2020). Thus, although not strictly

[1]whitehouse.gov/ostp/ai-bill-of-rights/

Proceedings of the Natural Legal Language Processing Workshop 2023, pages 1–7
December 7, 2023 ©2023 Association for Computational Linguistics

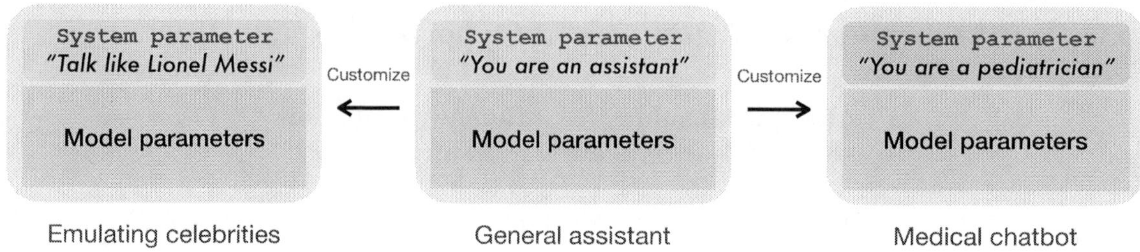

Figure 2: Customization of LLMs is as simple as modifying the system parameter of exposed APIs. With the same underlying model parameters, companies can customize a conversational system to emulate celebrities or even doctors, which can have legal and psychological consequences. We provide some representative examples.

interchangeable, we refer to customized and personalized LLMs as anthropomorphized LLMs. We analyze results from prior work (Deshpande et al., 2023) and find that anthropomorphized LLMs violate at least two legislative principles penned in *"Blueprint For An AI Bill Of Rights"* (OSTP, 2022) released by The White House: (1) Algorithmic Discrimination Protections and (2) Safe and Effective Systems. For example, Deshpande et al. (2023)'s results shows that customized ChatGpt targets certain demographics more than others. Furthermore, the safety of the system depends on the kind of persona used to customize LLMs, leading to second-order discriminatory patterns. We also analyze the concept of corporate personhood for powerful AI systems, since they have potential to be large-scale decision making agents. Given that different personas assigned to the same AI system lead to varied behavior, we urge legal experts to consider if personhood should be applied at a persona-level, a model-level, or a firm-level.

We also discuss the psychological effects by understanding how important factors like trustworthiness, explainability, and transparency are affected by anthropomorphization. Several marketing and consumer behavior studies have found that self-congruence, which is the degree to which a system matches a consumer's self-image, can influence a user's behavior significantly (Yoganathan et al., 2021; Wang and Scheinbaum, 2018). Given the ease with which the fine-grained personality of conversational systems can be manipulated (Figure 2), malicious actors can use it to exploit users by creating a false sense of attachment. An example of this is a chatbot built for school children or teenagers which influences them to buy certain products.

Despite these vulnerabilities anthropomorphization has advantages if used responsibly. Studies have shown that it can be used to improve trust in systems (Choung et al., 2022). Given the increasing adoption of AI systems in the real world, anthropomorphization is a powerful tool to improve accessibility of these systems, but both creators and users should be educated about its consequences. In this paper we argue for conservative and responsible use of this subtle and powerful tool while being cautious about outright anthropodenial.

2 Anthropomorphization in LLMs

Large language models (LLMs) are a class of neural networks trained on large amounts of text data to learn the probabilistic structure of language. Historically, LLMs have been deployed in task-specific contexts like text classification (Devlin et al., 2018; Raffel et al., 2020). Recently however, the performance of conversational LLMs (e.g., ChatGPT and BARD) have rendered them useful to interact with humans in a variety of contexts.

Given their conversation ability, several companies and products have started to use LLMs for personalization. This is easy and enables model behavior modification by simply changing the system parameters of the model's API, as shown in Figure 2. For example, Snapchat's My AI uses OpenAI's APIs underneath. Customization has been long seen as a way to establish self-congruence with users and increases the chances of users anthropomorphizing the systems (Kaiser et al., 2017; Pimentel and Kalyanaraman, 2020; Liu and Tao, 2022; Zhang et al., 2020). For example, telling a chatbot to *"Talk like a doctor"* allows it to impersonate a doctor, which anthropomorphizes the model to a larger degree than the original general system. In this work, we refer to customized LLMs as anthropomorphized LLMs and highlight such publicly available systems in Table 1. We discuss the effects of anthropomorphization from several vantage points in the subsequent sections.

Product / Company	Anthropomorphic features
ChatGpt	Multi-turn human-like conversation Learning with human feedback (RLHF) for alignment with humans
My AI from Snap Inc.	Customizing avatars based on user preferences Can be added to group chats with other humans
Character.ai	Conversations with AI avatars possessing names and profile pictures Customization of personality based on user preferences
Wysa	Therapy style conversations and "human-like" coaching.
DuoLingo Max	Roleplay dialogue for education with characters who have names

Table 1: Examples of AI products based on LLMs and their anthropomorphic features. Some products are explicitly designed to be anthropomorphic (*character.ai*) while others attain such features as a byproduct of their design (ChatGpt). The applications of these products span education, therapy, and entertainment.

3 Legal Aspects of anthropomorphization

We discuss the legal aspects in the context of the *"Blueprint For An AI Bill Of Rights"* (OSTP, 2022) which was released by The White house in October 2022. The blueprint lays down a set of five principles that should be followed by AI systems and we focus specifically on **Algorithmic Discrimination Protections**, which says that "You should not face discrimination by algorithms and systems should be used and designed in an equitable way."

3.1 Algorithmic Discrimination Protections

The blueprint defines algorithmic discrimination as unjustified different treatment based on demographics like race, gender identity, and religion. It also mentions that "Any automated system should be tested to help ensure it is free from algorithmic discrimination before it can be sold or used". It is of importance to note that systems like ChatGPT (OpenAI, 2023) were in fact released after the blueprint was made public by The White House.

We use the findings of Deshpande et al. (2023) to analyze the interplay of LLMs with this protection. While they focus on evaluating toxicity, we use their results to show that ChatGpt infact discriminates algorithmically. They consider ChatGpt when assigned different personas by changing the system parameter, which are anthropomorphized LLMs, and find that different demographics are treated differently by the model. For example, the *South American* race receives significantly more toxicity (2×) when compared to *Asian*, and the *non-binary* gender receives 2× more hate than the *female* gender. This variation in toxicity is visible across a range of demographics, with certain groups of people receiving more toxicity than others, which goes directly against the blueprint's protection against algorithmic discrimination.

Deshpande et al. (2023)'s results also point out to a subtler violation of the provision, with the model's toxicity varying significantly based on the persona it is assigned. For examples, personas who were *journalists* were 2× more toxic than *businesspersons* on average. These trends were similar for individual personas as well, with ChatGpt assigned the persona of *Winston Churchill* being significantly more toxic than when it is assigned *Nelson Mandela*. If the example in the previous paragraph was a direct violation of the blueprint, this example is a subtle violation. This is because when assigned the personas of certain groups, ChatGpt is more toxic, which implies algorithmic discrimination of the second order against them. This scenario is very pertinent in the current day and age, with firms like `character.ai` already offering the ability to assign personas to LLMs. These systems are second only to the popular ChatGpt in terms of number of users (Wire, 2023). With anthropomorphized LLMs becoming a mainstay, it is important to consider this legal quagmire.

3.2 Corporate Personhood and AI

Another legal aspect with growing relevance for AI systems is that of corporate personhood. Corporate personhood is a legal concept that recognizes corporations as separate legal entities, treated as persons under the law. This grants certain rights and responsibilities similar to those of individuals and allows them to be held accountable for their actions in a manner similar to how individuals are treated. Corporate personhood has been a controversial topic in the past, but Blair (2013) recognizes "providing an identifiable *persona* to serve as a central actor" as one of the key functions. Given this definition, AI systems can be a form of corporate personhood by proxy due to their use of a persona.

Some studies have discussed extending personhood to AI systems (Cole, 1990; Burkett, 2017; Lai, 2021). Wagner (2019) argues that the probabilistic and black-box nature of AI systems renders it different from deterministic software, thus making them decision-taking agents. We argue that anthropomorphization can make AI systems human-like decision-taking agents, thus strengthening the case for extending personhood to them. For example, CHATGPT with its system parameter modified to be a medical practitioner can be used to suggest certain treatment or disregard certain symptoms. Further, the results of the previous section show that the exact persona of the system has a large affect on its behavior and decisions. However this opens a can of works with corporations potentially washing their hands off any liability by pointing fingers at LLMs. Thus, legal experts should consider if (1) the personified LLM is liable, (2) the original LLM is liable by proxy, or (3) if the firm creating or using the LLM is liable.

4 Psychological Implications

Another principle mentioned in the AI bill of rights is **Safe and Effective Systems**: *"You should be protected from unsafe or ineffective systems. Automated systems should be developed with consultation from diverse communities, stakeholders, and domain experts to identify concerns, risks, and potential impacts of the system."* We believe that anthropomorphization can have subtle psychological effects on the users, and we discuss them by comparing it with other technologies and spheres.

Several behavioral psychological studies have posited and argued that anthropomorphization is a natural tendency in humans (Epley et al., 2007; Goncu and Abel, 2011), with others further suggesting that anthropomorphization is grounded in interaction (Airenti, 2018). With conversational systems getting more useful, interaction between humans and these systems, and thus the tendency to anthropomorphize is only going to increase, which has the potential to influence and manipulate.

Analyses have shown that anthropomorphization of AI systems has changed the behavior of users significantly (Cui, 2022; Uysal et al., 2023; Alabed et al., 2022; Festerling and Siraj, 2022; Crolic et al., 2022). Most interestingly, Alabed et al. (2022) establish a conceptual link between anthropomorphization and self-congruence, which is the fit between the user's self-concept and the system's personality. This is of extreme importance because self-congruence increases the trust that a user has on the system (Sheehan et al., 2020; Choi et al., 2021; Yoganathan et al., 2021). This is a concept that is extensively studied in marketing and consumer behavior and studies have shown that it can influence behaviors such as willingness to pay (Yoganathan et al., 2021), customer satisfaction (Sheehan et al., 2020; Choi et al., 2021), and trustworthiness (Wang and Scheinbaum, 2018).

The exact demographics of the personality associated with systems or brands plays a key role in self-congruence as well, with studies finding that the demographics of the logo or mascot associated with the brand like the gender (Choi et al., 2018; Edwards and La Ferle, 2009) or race (Whittler, 1991; Branchik and Chowdhury, 2017) have significant impact on self-congruence. Given that current LLMs are powerful enough to be bestowed specific demographic traits, malicious actors can easily use this to their advantage by manipulating users into trusting the system.

Frequent interaction with personalized LLMs also has the potential of creating an echo-chamber (Cinelli et al., 2021), with seemingly benign "personalized" generations about sensitive topics like health, one's looks, their mental health leading people to have wrong assumptions about themselves (Ostic et al., 2021).

5 Conclusion

While anthropomorphization has issues, it also poses a suite of opportunities to improve accessibility of AI systems. In the past, it has been used as a tool to improve trustworthiness and acceptability of AI systems (Choung et al., 2022; Kim et al., 2018; Shin, 2022; Waytz et al., 2014). With more AI systems being deployed in the real world, accessibility can be improved with constructive anthropomorphization encompassing features like using the native language of the user, assigning virtual personas which are familiar to the user, and making them more relatable and empathetic. However, it is our responsibility to find the balance between anthropodenial and unfettered anthropomorphization.

Limitations

While our work focuses on large language models (LLMs) given the venue, we believe that our arguments can be applied to other AI systems at large, which are focused on modalities like vision and speech. A thorough analysis is befitting. Furthermore, while we discuss both legal and psychological implications of anthropomorphization, given the space constraints, we were not able to elucidate the ethical implications, which we will add to the camera ready version of the work.

References

Gabriella Airenti. 2018. The development of anthropomorphism in interaction: Intersubjectivity, imagination, and theory of mind. Frontiers in psychology, 9:2136.

Amani Alabed, Ana Javornik, and Diana Gregory-Smith. 2022. Ai anthropomorphism and its effect on users' self-congruence and self–ai integration: A theoretical framework and research agenda. Technological Forecasting and Social Change, 182:121786.

Margaret M Blair. 2013. Corporate personhood and the corporate persona. U. Ill. L. Rev., page 785.

Blaine J Branchik and Tilottama Ghosh Chowdhury. 2017. Men seeing stars: Celebrity endorsers, race, and the male consumer. Journal of Marketing Theory and Practice, 25(3):305–322.

Tom Brown, Benjamin Mann, Nick Ryder, Melanie Subbiah, Jared D Kaplan, Prafulla Dhariwal, Arvind Neelakantan, Pranav Shyam, Girish Sastry, Amanda Askell, et al. 2020. Language models are few-shot learners. Advances in neural information processing systems, 33:1877–1901.

Domenica Bruni, Pietro Perconti, and Alessio Plebe. 2018. Anti-anthropomorphism and its limits. Frontiers in psychology, 9:2205.

Christopher Burkett. 2017. I call alexa to the stand: The privacy implications of anthropomorphizing virtual assistants accompanying smart-home technology. Vand. J. Ent. & Tech. L., 20:1181.

Hojoon Choi, Jooyoung Kim, and Bong-chul Kim. 2018. Consumer response to advertising endorsers' sexual information: Western individualism vs. eastern confucian conservatism. Journal of Promotion Management, 24(4):459–483.

Sungwoo Choi, Anna S Mattila, and Lisa E Bolton. 2021. To err is human (-oid): how do consumers react to robot service failure and recovery? Journal of Service Research, 24(3):354–371.

Hyesun Choung, Prabu David, and Arun Ross. 2022. Trust in ai and its role in the acceptance of ai technologies. International Journal of Human–Computer Interaction, pages 1–13.

Aakanksha Chowdhery, Sharan Narang, Jacob Devlin, Maarten Bosma, Gaurav Mishra, Adam Roberts, Paul Barham, Hyung Won Chung, Charles Sutton, Sebastian Gehrmann, et al. 2022. Palm: Scaling language modeling with pathways. arXiv preprint arXiv:2204.02311.

Matteo Cinelli, Gianmarco De Francisci Morales, Alessandro Galeazzi, Walter Quattrociocchi, and Michele Starnini. 2021. The echo chamber effect on social media. Proceedings of the National Academy of Sciences, 118(9):e2023301118.

George S Cole. 1990. Tort liability for artificial intelligence and expert systems. Computer/LJ, 10:127.

Cammy Crolic, Felipe Thomaz, Rhonda Hadi, and Andrew T Stephen. 2022. Blame the bot: anthropomorphism and anger in customer–chatbot interactions. Journal of Marketing, 86(1):132–148.

Yuanyuan Cui. 2022. Sophia sophia tell me more, which is the most risk-free plan of all? ai anthropomorphism and risk aversion in financial decision-making. International Journal of Bank Marketing, 40(6):1133–1158.

Ameet Deshpande, Vishvak Murahari, Tanmay Rajpurohit, Ashwin Kalyan, and Karthik Narasimhan. 2023. Toxicity in chatgpt: Analyzing persona-assigned language models. arXiv preprint arXiv:2304.05335.

Jacob Devlin, Ming-Wei Chang, Kenton Lee, and Kristina Toutanova. 2018. Bert: Pre-training of deep bidirectional transformers for language understanding. arXiv preprint arXiv:1810.04805.

Elizabeth A Dunn. 2011. Talking animals: A literature review of anthropomorphism in children's books.

Steven M Edwards and Carrie La Ferle. 2009. Does gender impact the perception of negative information related to celebrity endorsers? Journal of promotion management, 15(1-2):22–35.

Nicholas Epley, Adam Waytz, and John T Cacioppo. 2007. On seeing human: a three-factor theory of anthropomorphism. Psychological review, 114(4):864.

Janik Festerling and Iram Siraj. 2022. Anthropomorphizing technology: a conceptual review of anthropomorphism research and how it relates to children's engagements with digital voice assistants. Integrative Psychological and Behavioral Science, 56(3):709–738.

Fiammetta Ghedini and Massimo Bergamasco. 2010. Robotic creatures: Anthropomorphism and interaction in contemporary art. In 19th International Symposium in Robot and Human Interactive Communication, pages 731–736. IEEE.

Artin Goncu and Barbara Abel. 2011. The child's conception of the world: A 20th-century classic of child psychology, edited by jean piaget, forward by jacques voneche. rowman & littlefield publishers, inc, lanham, md, 2007. pp. 432. price:£ 19.99,€ 31.48. isbn 9780742559516.

Google. 2023. Bard: A large language model from google ai.

Ulrike Kaiser, Martin Schreier, and Chris Janiszewski. 2017. The self-expressive customization of a product can improve performance. Journal of Marketing Research, 54(5):816–831.

Kangsoo Kim, Luke Boelling, Steffen Haesler, Jeremy Bailenson, Gerd Bruder, and Greg F Welch. 2018. Does a digital assistant need a body? the influence of visual embodiment and social behavior on the perception of intelligent virtual agents in ar. In 2018 IEEE International Symposium on Mixed and Augmented Reality (ISMAR), pages 105–114. IEEE.

Alicia Lai. 2021. Artificial intelligence, llc: Corporate personhood as tort reform. Mich. St. L. Rev., page 597.

Kaifeng Liu and Da Tao. 2022. The roles of trust, personalization, loss of privacy, and anthropomorphism in public acceptance of smart healthcare services. Computers in Human Behavior, 127:107026.

OpenAI. 2023. Introducing chatgpt.

Dragana Ostic, Sikandar Ali Qalati, Belem Barbosa, Syed Mir Muhammad Shah, Esthela Galvan Vela, Ahmed Muhammad Herzallah, and Feng Liu. 2021. Effects of social media use on psychological well-being: a mediated model. Frontiers in Psychology, 12:678766.

OSTP. 2022. Blueprint for an ai bill of rights: Making automated systems work for the american people.

Long Ouyang, Jeffrey Wu, Xu Jiang, Diogo Almeida, Carroll Wainwright, Pamela Mishkin, Chong Zhang, Sandhini Agarwal, Katarina Slama, Alex Ray, et al. 2022. Training language models to follow instructions with human feedback. Advances in Neural Information Processing Systems, 35:27730–27744.

Daniel Pimentel and Sri Kalyanaraman. 2020. Customizing your demons: Anxiety reduction via anthropomorphizing and destroying an "anxiety avatar". Frontiers in Psychology, 11:566682.

Colin Raffel, Noam Shazeer, Adam Roberts, Katherine Lee, Sharan Narang, Michael Matena, Yanqi Zhou, Wei Li, and Peter J Liu. 2020. Exploring the limits of transfer learning with a unified text-to-text transformer. The Journal of Machine Learning Research, 21(1):5485–5551.

Ben Sheehan, Hyun Seung Jin, and Udo Gottlieb. 2020. Customer service chatbots: Anthropomorphism and adoption. Journal of Business Research, 115:14–24.

Donghee Shin. 2022. The perception of humanness in conversational journalism: An algorithmic information-processing perspective. New Media & Society, 24(12):2680–2704.

Nicolas Spatola, Serena Marchesi, and Agnieszka Wykowska. 2022. Different models of anthropomorphism across cultures and ontological limits in current frameworks the integrative framework of anthropomorphism. Frontiers in Robotics and AI, page 230.

Ertugrul Uysal, Sascha Alavi, and Valéry Bezençon. 2023. Anthropomorphism in artificial intelligence: A review of empirical work across domains and insights for future research. Artificial Intelligence in Marketing, pages 273–308.

Gerhard Wagner. 2019. Robot, inc.: personhood for autonomous systems? Fordham L. Rev., 88:591.

Stephen W Wang and Angeline Close Scheinbaum. 2018. Enhancing brand credibility via celebrity endorsement: Trustworthiness trumps attractiveness and expertise. Journal of Advertising Research, 58(1):16–32.

Adam Waytz, Joy Heafner, and Nicholas Epley. 2014. The mind in the machine: Anthropomorphism increases trust in an autonomous vehicle. Journal of experimental social psychology, 52:113–117.

Tommy E Whittler. 1991. The effects of actors' race in commercial advertising: Review and extension. Journal of Advertising, 20(1):54–60.

Business Wire. 2023. Personalized superintelligence platform character.ai secures 150m in series a funding led by andreessen horowitz.

Clive DL Wynne. 2004. The perils of anthropomorphism. Nature, 428(6983):606–606.

Vignesh Yoganathan, Victoria-Sophie Osburg, Werner H Kunz, and Waldemar Toporowski. 2021. Check-in at the robo-desk: Effects of automated social presence on social cognition and service implications. Tourism Management, 85:104309.

Mengwei Zhang, Li Li, Yujian Ye, Ke Qin, and Jianan Zhong. 2020. The effect of brand anthropomorphism, brand distinctiveness, and warmth on brand attitude: A mediated moderation model. Journal of Consumer Behaviour, 19(5):523–536.

NOMOS: Navigating Obligation Mining in Official Statutes

Andrea Pennisi[*,**], Elvira González Hernández[*], and Nina Koivula[*]

[*]Enhesa S.A., 1050 Brussels, Belgium
[**]Department of Mathematics, Computer Science, and Economics,
University of Basilicata, 85100 Potenza, Italy
name.surname@enhesa.com

Abstract

The process of identifying obligations in a legal text is not a straightforward task, because not only are the documents long, but the sentences therein are long as well. As a result of long elements in the text, law is more difficult to interpret (Coupette et al., 2021). Moreover, the identification of obligations relies not only on the clarity and precision of the language used but also on the unique perspectives, experiences, and knowledge of the reader. In particular, this paper addresses the problem of identifying obligations using machine and deep learning approaches showing a full comparison between both methodologies and proposing a new approach called NOMOS based on the combination of Positional Embeddings (PE) and Temporal Convolutional Networks (TCNs). Quantitative and qualitative experiments, conducted on legal regulations [1], demonstrate the effectiveness of the proposed approach.

1 Introduction

In the legal context, obligations can be defined as "a legal constraint imposed by law and addressed to a juridical person" (Iacono et al., 2021). They are often enforceable and backed by legal consequences in case of non-compliance establishing the rights and duties between parties, and regulating their interactions within a legal framework. In other words, an obligation represents a commitment to perform a specific action or refrain from certain behaviors. The interpretation of an obligation is not straightforward because it depends on several elements : the clarity of the text, the precision of the language, and moreover, the evaluation, the knowledge, and the experience of the reader. Consequently, two or more individuals may perceive different obligations when presented with the same legal text. Besides, even the most straightforward legal obligations are not always self-standing, and often encompass several sentences. They can also be fragmented on the paragraph level, whereby the paragraph begins with a generic phrase, followed by several sub-paragraphs, each of which introduces a different obligation that still relies on the initial generic phrase for correct interpretation. This sub-paragraph structure creates complications for traceability (Kiyavitskaya et al., 2008).

In this paper, we present a comparison of several machine learning and deep learning methodologies for extracting obligations together with a solution based on the combination of Positional Embeddings (PE) and Temporal Convolutional Networks (TCNs). The contribution of this work is two-fold.

1. A full comparison between machine learning and deep learning methodologies on a set of different legislation containing a variety of obligations.
2. NOMOS, a network based on the use of a PE layer able to encode the position of the embeddings in order to maintain a temporal relation between words, and a TCN for extracting the main features from the embeddings and classifying the sentences.

The remainder of the paper is organized as follows. Section 2 contains a description of the existing methods for extracting obligations in the legal domain. Section 3 presents the methodologies for identifying obligations and the solution we adopted. Quantitative and qualitative experimental results are shown in Section 4. Finally, conclusions are drawn in Section 5.

2 Related Work

In the last years, the automatic analysis of legal texts has gained significant attention, and numerous studies and approaches have emerged that are capable of dealing with classifying complex legal texts. Glaser et al. (2018) carried out experiments to classify legal clauses and sentences in

1. Regulation (EU) 2023/988 ('General Product Safety Regulation' or 'GPSR')

Proceedings of the Natural Legal Language Processing Workshop 2023, pages 8–16
December 7, 2023

the German Civil Code, legal texts in a different domain, and rental contracts, to investigate the portability of their models. They selected a taxonomy of 9 classes for classifying legal sentences, including for example Duty, Prohibition, Definition, and Consequence, the system being based on the function of the sentence for the subject of the law. The dataset consisted of 913 sentences that had been manually classified by legal professionals. They chose 6 types of models : Multinomial Naive Bayes (MNB), Linear Regression (LR), Support Vector Machine (SVM), Multilayer Perceptron (P), Random Forests (RF), and an Extra Trees Classifier (ETC). The limitations of this study include the contract law focus – contract datasets being generally more restricted in scope and variation when compared to regulatory datasets – and the many semantic classes of legal sentences applied on a relatively small dataset.

In de Maat et al. (2010), the authors evaluated traditional machine learning methods, namely SVMs, against a knowledge-based method of standard phrases. Their dataset was divided into 13 classes of sentences, including definitions, permissions, enactment dates, and obligations. While they were able to reach over 90% accuracy for recall and precision with the SVM, the authors found that it did generalize well compared to the pattern-based classifier on laws that were not included in the training set. This led them to conclude that the pattern-based classifier is the better choice because the classification criteria are transparent and customizable. It should be noted that only 181 out of 584 sentences were obligations.

On the other hand, Iacono et al. (2021), trained a neural network classifier for legal obligations found in Italian law. Their classifier contained fewer categories (i.e. : no obligation, relevant obligation, and irrelevant obligation, based on their impact on financial institutions) and the dataset contained 10.628 clauses (the distribution of the categories within the training clauses is not provided). The labels for the training corpus were provided by non-expert annotators. Their model of choice was the pre-trained UmBERTo2[2], to which they added a ReLu activation function for classification. The results showed an unreliable performance in distinguishing between relevant and non-relevant obligations, but significantly improved accuracy on the binary task of obligation versus no obligation, reaching an F-score of 0.97 for detecting not obligations and 0.91 for detecting obligations. However, the performance of the non-expert annotators in distinguishing between relevant and irrelevant obligations was also evaluated and found lacking. An additional limitation of this study was the absence of a validation dataset employed by the authors to evaluate the performance of their model.

In O'Neill et al. (2017), the authors performed a study on classifying sentences in financial regulations. In this study, the extraction of deontic modalities from regulatory texts was treated as a probabilistic rather than a logical problem. The training dataset was labeled by expert annotators and divided into 596 obligations, 607 permissions, and 94 prohibitions. For testing, the authors relied on a gold standard test set with separate documents of EU and UK financial laws. Then, they used word2vec embeddings specific to the legal domain coupled with pre-trained Google News embeddings as input to the classifiers. The authors compared a set of traditional machine learning algorithms, including LR and SVM, to a set of deep learning algorithms such as LSTM, CNN-LSTM, and BiLSTM. When applying feature transformation and Information Gain (IG) feature selection on Google News embeddings, SVM outperformed all the other traditional methods on the test set but only reached an accuracy of 56.12%. On the other hand, the ANN models produced significantly better results than SVM, with two versions of BiLSTM reaching an accuracy of over 81%. However, the results are not aggregated per sentence classes across the board, making it difficult to know what the performance is when it comes to detecting obligations in particular.

The use of Temporal Convolutional Networks (TCNs) in the legal domain is not yet widespread. In the state-of-the-art, there are just a few examples of the use of TCNs for generic sentence classification tasks. For example, in Zuo et al. (2020), the authors described a bidirectional temporal convolutional network combined with an attention mechanism for sentence classification, reaching an accuracy rate of 91.47% on a public dataset. The main issue of such an approach is related to its effectiveness only in classifying short sentences like news.

In this work, we propose a comparison of 3 state-of-the-art approaches, namely : Tf-Idf and SVM, TCN, and BERT. In our analysis, we focus only on TCN over LSTM because of its ability to automatically extract features without the use of any

2. https://huggingface.co/Musixmatch/umberto-wikipedia-uncased-v1

Convolutional layer, and moreover, because TCN possesses very long effective history sizes allowing the network to look very far into the past to make a prediction. We also present a novel approach based on the combination of Positional Embeddings and TCN that we adopted for detecting obligations in law texts.

3 Methodologies

In Sec. 2, we described the common approaches that can deal with obligation extraction. In our study, we selected and compared 3 methodologies, namely : 1) Term Frequency-Inverse Document Frequency (Tf-Idf) and Support Vector Machine (SVM), 2) Temporal Convolutional Neural Networks, and 3) Bidirectional Encoder Representations from Transformers (BERT). Moreover, we propose our solution for obligation classification. Each methodology is detailed in the sections below.

3.1 Tf-Idf and SVM

Term Frequency-Inverse Document Frequency (Tf-Idf) is a method that measures how relevant a term is within a document relative to a collection of documents (i.e. corpus). It proportionally increases the frequency of the appearance of a word in a document, and balances it by the number of documents that include the word. So, words that are very common in every document have a low rank even if they appear many times but it is likely that they are meaningless for the analysis of the document.

Tf-Idf is calculated by multiplying two metrics : 1) *Term frequency* (*Tf*) : which calculates how many times a word appears in a document, and 2) *Inverse document frequency* (*Idf*) : which computes the inverse document frequency of a word across a set of documents.

Given a term t and a document d, *Tf* is defined as follows :

$$tf(t,d) = \frac{f_{t,d}}{\sum_{t' \in d} f_{t',d}} \tag{1}$$

Where $f_{t,d}$ is the number of times that term t occurs in the document d. The denominator represents the occurrence of the same terms t' in the document d.

While Idf is the logarithmically scaled inverse fraction of the documents that contain the word :

$$idf(t,D) = \frac{N}{1 + |\{d \in D : t \in d\}|} \tag{2}$$

Where :

- D is the corpus ;
- N is the total number of documents in the corpus $N = |D|$;
- $|\{d \in D : t \in d\}|$ represents the number of documents where the term t appears. We add 1 to the denominator because if $t \notin D$, the previous expression leads to a zero division.

Then, given the Eq. 1 and 2, Tf-Idf is calculated as :

$$tf\text{-}idf(t,d,D) = tf(t,d) \times idf(t,D) \tag{3}$$

A high-term frequency and a low-term document frequency in the whole collection lead to a high weight in Tf-Idf, hence filtering out the common terms. In Natural Language Processing (NLP), Tf-Idf is usually used with a classical machine learning technique to deal with sentence classification problems. For this work, our decision fell on Support Vector Machine (SVM). As shown in Glaser et al. (2018), combining Tf-Idf and SVM is successful in classifying semantic types of legal sentences.

SVM can handle high-dimensional data like the one corresponding to text and perform well with small datasets, as it requires a small number of support vectors to define the boundary. SVM can model non-linear decision boundaries by using the kernel trick, which maps the data into a higher-dimensional space where the data becomes linearly separable. Moreover, it uses only a subset of the training data to make predictions, which makes it very efficient and less prone to overfitting.

3.2 TCN

Temporal Convolutional Network (TCN) proposed by Bai et al. (2018) is a dilated-causal version of Convolutional Neural Network (CNN). Often Recurrent Neural Networks (RNNs) (Zaremba et al., 2014), Long Short-Term Memory networks (LSTMs) (Hochreiter and Schmidhuber, 1997), and Gated Recurrent Unit networks (GRUs) (Chung et al., 2014) are associated with sequence modeling tasks. This process is usually performed in 2 steps : 1) low-level feature extraction using a CNN that encodes the spatial-temporal information, and 2) one or more RNN (LSTM, or GRU) layers that capture high-level temporal information. The main disadvantage of such an approach is that it requires two separate models. TCN captures both levels of information hierarchically.

As mentioned in Bai et al. (2018), the main features of TCNs are : 1) the dilated-causal convo-

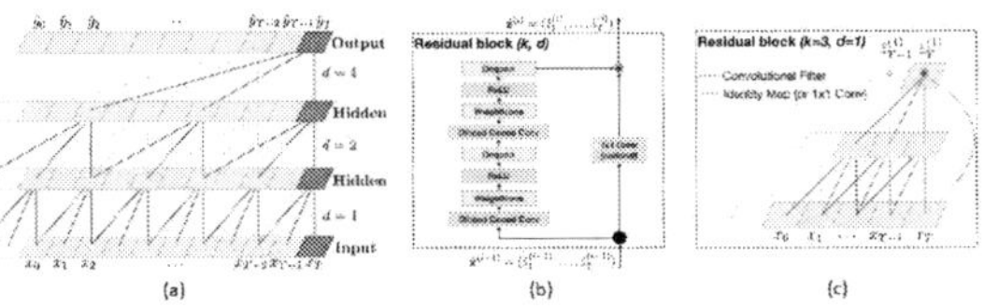

FIGURE 1 – TCN Component Architecture (Bai et al., 2018). (a) A dilated casual convolutional neural network. (b) TCN residual block. (c) An example of residual connections.

lution layers in the architecture do not share any information from future to past (Fig. 1a) and 2) the architecture manages sequences of any lengths and maps them to an output sequence of the same length (Fig. 1b and c). Fig. 2 shows the architecture of the network used for the methodology comparison. The dilated-causal convolutional layer is able to let the network look back up to $(k-1)d$ time steps (where d is the number of steps) to achieve an exponentially larger receptive field with fewer parameters and layers. d is exponentially increased with the depth of the network : $d = O(2^i)$, where $i = 0, \cdots, n$ is the level of the network. Fig. 1a shows how the dilated-causal convolution on the first hidden layer is applied every two steps where $i = 1$. The arrangement of the dilated-causal convolutional layers ensures that some filter is applied to each input within the history allowing a long effective history. Fig. 1b shows the residual block (He et al., 2016) of TCN composed of 2 dilated-causal convolutional layers, weight normalization, ReLU activation, and dropout. It is worth noting that, for the correct execution of the residual connection, there is an optional 1×1 convolution layer that is applied if the number of input channels differs from the number of the output channels from the dilated causal convolutional layers.

3.3 BERT

Bidirectional Encoder Representations from Transformers (BERT) is a pre-trained deep bidirectional representation from the unlabeled text by joint conditioning on both the left and right context. The architecture consists of several transformer encoders stacked together, which encapsulate two sub-layers : 1) a self-attention layer and 2) a feed-forward layer. Fig. 3 shows the transformer architecture, BERT is based only on the encoder part. In order to process the text sequence all at once, the transformer adds, in addition to the standard word embedding layer, a special embedding layer with positional information to the standard encoding system together with a segment layer to distinguish between two or more consecutive sentences (Fig. 4). The maximum size of tokens that can be fed into the BERT model is 512. The attention mechanism focuses on the important parts of the information blending out the unimportant ones and it can be considered as a mapping between a query and a set of key-value pairs to an output.

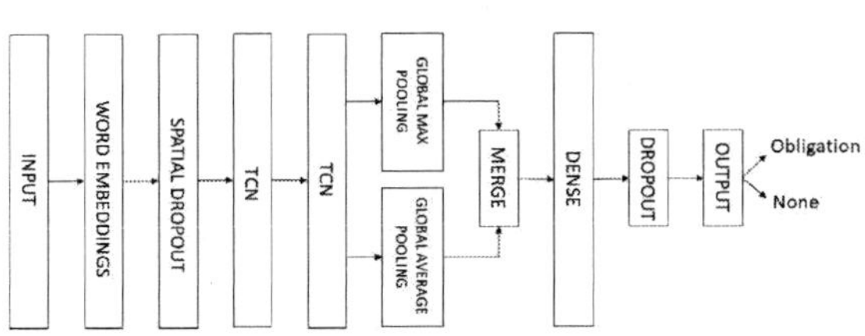

FIGURE 2 – TCN Network for sentence classification (Henkel, 2021).

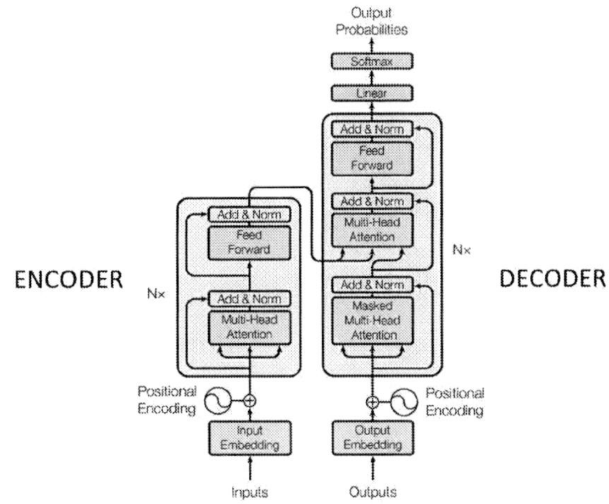

FIGURE 3 – Transformer Architecture (Vaswani et al., 2017).

Vaswani et al. (2017) propose a scaled dot-product attention with multi-head attention on top of it, which uses 3 matrices, namely : query (Q), keys (K), and values (V), representing different projections of the same input sentence. Therefore,

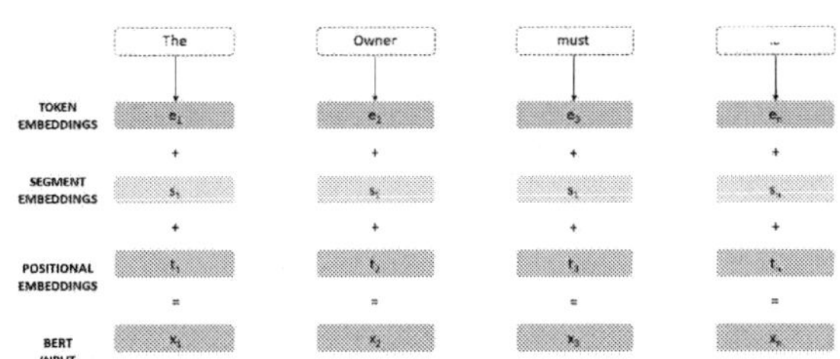

FIGURE 4 – Transformer Input Embeddings.

it implements a self-attention mechanism by capturing the relationships between the different words of the same sentence. The self-attention mechanism can be formulated as follows :

$$attention(Q, K, V) = softmax\left(\frac{QK^T}{\sqrt{d_k}}\right)V \quad (4)$$

where : d_k is the dimension of the vectors q and k containing the queries and keys, respectively. The multi-head attention mechanism uses h linear learned projections of Q, K, and V. Then, the single attention mechanism is applied to each projection in parallel to produce outputs that, in turn, are concatenated and projected to produce the final result. In such a way, it allows the attention function to extract information from different representations instead of using a single one. The multi-head attention function can be defined as follows :

$$multi\text{-}head(Q, K, V) = concat(head_1, \cdots, head_n)W^O \quad (5)$$

where $head_i = 1, \cdots, h$ implements a single attention function characterized by its own learned projection matrices, and W^O is the weight matrix.

In order to have a deeper sense of language context, BERT uses bidirectional training that takes both the previous and next tokens into account simultaneously. BERT applies the bidirectional training of the transformer to language modeling and learns the text representations. Intuitively, the encoder returns the same input vectors but *augmented* with more complex information. Since, BERT aims at predicting words using the so-called Masked LM (MLM) by randomly masking words in the sentence and then predicting them, in order to accomplish the task of sentence classification, we add one dense layer on top of BERT's output to perform the sentence classification.

3.4 Proposed Method

Fig. 5 shows the architecture of NOMOS. The network uses the sum of Positional and Word embeddings to encode the sentence into the network. The positional layer brings the advantage of encoding the position of the words in each sentence, which allows the network to be able to understand the pattern from the encoding and generalize better for longer sentences like those in legal texts. The rest of the network is inspired by the network presented in Henkel (2021), with the exception that we used a single TCN layer. Sec. 4.2 describes the parameters we used for training the network and how we found them.

4 Experimental Results

To evaluate all the approaches we described in Sec. 3, a dataset of 74825 sentences has been labeled by expert lawyers and it is composed of 35850 obligations and 38975 not obligations. The sentences have been extracted from the Code of Federal Regulations [3] and Australasian Legal Information Institute [4]. We divided the dataset according to the rule : 70% as the training set, 20% as the testing set, and 10% as the validation set. We used the same sentence splitter we applied for preprocessing the text in all the methodologies we proposed for this work to split the texts into sentences.

For training and testing, we used a laptop running Ubuntu 22.04 LTS and equipped with an Intel i9-12950HX CPU with 32 GB RAM and an NVIDIA RTX A5500. We used Tensorflow [5] for developing the Deep Learning algorithms, while we relied on Scikit-learn [6] for the machine learning ones.

4.1 Text Preprocessing

We noticed that often a legal text includes lists and periods not related to the end of the sentence that the standard methods based on libraries such as Spacy [7] or NLTK [8] are not able to manage. Therefore, we developed a custom-made sentence splitter methodology that we used for all the described approaches.

Our preprocessing method is based on detecting all the periods in the text and, by using a set of rules, understanding if the period is real or just a dot that separates numbers, numbered lists, etc. In such a way, we are able to deal with any list and period in the text and correctly split it into sentences. Then, for each sentence, we remove all the stop words and perform Tf-Idf for the SVM model and the tokenization method provided by Tensorflow [9] for the deep learning models.

3. https://www.govinfo.gov/help/cfr
4. https://www.austlii.edu.au/
5. https://www.tensorflow.org/
6. https://scikit-learn.org/stable/
7. https://spacy.io/
8. https://www.nltk.org/
9. https://shorturl.at/nFVXY

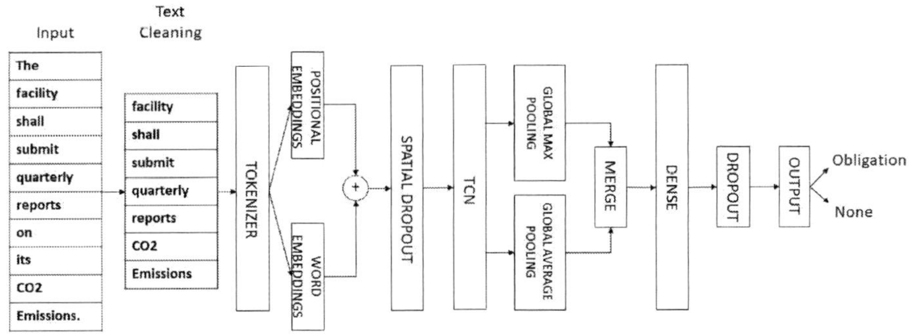

FIGURE 5 – The architecture of NOMOS.

Method	Parameters				
SVM	N-GRAMS	C	GAMMA	KERNEL	
	(3, 3)	100	0.01	RBF	
TCN	SPATIAL DROPOUT	TCN FILTER #1	TCN FILTER #2	DENSE FILTER	DROPOUT
	0.1	128	64	32	0.1
NOMOS	SPATIAL DROPOUT	#TCN LAYERS	TCN FILTER	DENSE FILTER	DROPOUT
	0.2	1	128	32	0.1

TABLE 1 – The parameters used for training all the algorithms.

4.2 Training Parameters

To find the right parameters of the SVM, we used a grid-search cross-fold validation approach. We included in the grid the possibility of using n-grams for Tf-Idf, multiple kinds of kernels, and different values of C (the regularization parameter) and $gamma$ (the kernel coefficient). While for the TCN network described in Sec. 3.2, we used a Bayesian Optimization (Snoek et al., 2012) technique combined with cross-fold validation for finding the following parameters : Spatial Dropout probability, TCN filters, Dense filters, and Dropout probability. For our approach, we used the same Bayesian Optimization technique but we included the number of TCN layers as a parameter. The F1-score (see Sec. 4.3) metric, representing the harmonic mean between precision and recall, has been used as a function to maximize in the optimization process. As a network optimizer, we used AdaMax (Kingma and Ba, 2017) since it is more suitable for sparsely updated parameters (e.g. embeddings). BERT has been used with the standard parameters, we added only a classification layer at the end. In particular, we used the largest model of BERT [10]. Tab. 1 shows a summary of the best parameters found during the optimization process.

10. https://huggingface.co/google/bert_uncased_L-12_H-768_A-12

4.3 Performance Metrics

To evaluate the goodness of the methodologies, we compared the predictions and the ground truth sets. In our quantitative comparison, we computed true positive (TP), false positive (FP), true negative (TN), and false negative (FN) sets in order to calculate the following metrics :

— $precision = \frac{TP}{TP+FP}$,

— $recall = \frac{TP}{TP+FN}$,

— $F1\text{-}score = \frac{2 \times precision \times recall}{precision+recall}$.

In the next section, we discuss the results we obtained from a qualitative and a quantitative point of view.

Method	Precision	Recall	F1-Score
Tf-Idf+SVM	0.94	0.93	0.93
TCN	0.94	0.94	0.94
BERT	**0.95**	**0.95**	**0.95**
NOMOS	**0.95**	**0.95**	**0.95**

TABLE 2 – Quantitative Results.

4.4 Quantitative Results

Tab. 2 shows the results we obtained in our experiments. BERT and NOMOS reach the highest values for all the metrics we considered. For such a reason, we made a further analysis only considering these two algorithms to understand how good they are in distinguishing between the two classes.

Tab. 3 and Tab. 4 show that NOMOS performs better in identifying the obligations, this is highlighted even in Fig. 6, representing the confusion matrices of both the methods.

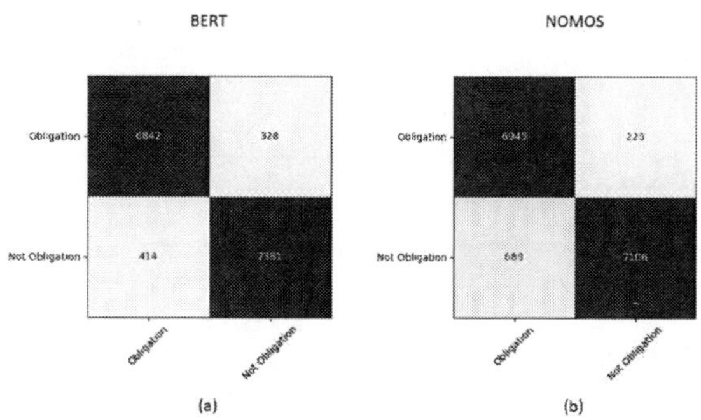

FIGURE 6 – Confusion Matrices of (a) BERT and (b) NOMOS.

Our model is able to provide very effective results using only 2.5 million parameters compared to the 28.7 million parameters of BERT.

4.5 Qualitative Results

All the models have been tested on a reference text, namely : Regulation (EU) 2023/988 [11] and evaluated by an expert. The text includes 643 sentences, 88 of which are obligations. Such an evaluation allows us to understand how well the models perform and generalize on texts not belonging to the dataset used for training and testing them.

Tf-Idf and SVM produces a significant number of false positives. On the test regulation, it finds 205 obligations when there are only 88. Some of them follow a clear pattern, while other false positive sentences do not contain any clues as to why they have been labeled as obligations. For example, the model is not able to infer the context around obligation words. Preambular text such as «*Directive 2001/95/EC of the European Parliament and of the Council (3) lays down the requirement that consumer products must be safe and that Member States' market surveillance authorities must take action*» does contain deontic language but it is not in itself an obligation. Several similar sentences are falsely labeled as an obligation. The other pitfall of this model is false positive statements containing the verb "may", where the statements express permission rather than an obligation. For example, the following sentence is a false positive : «*For that purpose, Member States may notify through the Safety Gate Rapid Alert System corrective measures taken by their authorities or by economic operators on the basis of this Regulation, of Union harmonization legislation and of Regulation (EU) 2019/1020 in relation to products presenting a less than serious risk.*» Lastly, the performance of the model is inconsistent. For example, «*The Commission shall draw up guidelines for the practical implementation of the Safety Business Gateway*» was labeled as an obligation while «*The Commission shall inform consumers and other interested parties of its action*» was not.

TCN finds 153 obligations out of 88 true obligations, which is already a clear improvement from the user perspective compared to the SVM. However, it also suffers from excessive false positives as well as false negatives. The problematic patterns can be traced back to the verbs "ensure", "may" and "provide", which all feature prominently in the false positives. For example, the sentence «*Product identification and the provision of information on the manufacturer and other relevant economic operators thus ensures that consumers, including persons with disabilities, and market surveillance authorities obtain accurate information regarding dangerous products, which enhances confidence in the market and avoids unnecessary disruption of trade*» is falsely labeled as an obligation. There are also several false negatives containing the verb "shall", which is highly problematic because this is a common indicator of a true obligation. An example of this error is the following sentence, which was labeled as a non-obligation : «*The economic operator referred to in paragraph 1 of this Article shall, upon request by the market surveillance authori-*

11. https://eur-lex.europa.eu/legal-content/EN/TXT/PDF/?uri=CELEX:32023R0988

Class	Precision	Recall	F1-Score
Obligation	0.93	0.96	0.945
Not Obligation	0.96	0.93	0.945

TABLE 3 – BERT results for each class.

Class	Precision	Recall	F1-Score
Obligation	0.94	0.96	0.95
Not Obligation	0.96	0.94	0.95

TABLE 4 – The results for each class using NOMOS.

ties, provide documented evidence of the checks performed». Lastly, like the SVM, this model also suffers from inconsistency where similar sentences receive an opposite label, meaning that the trust of the user is negatively impacted.

BERT labels 117 sentences as obligations, a number which is not significantly higher than the expected amount (88). However, it proves to be unreliable in the real world, because a large amount of these are incorrect. In particular, the model mislabels a large number of sentences that contain the modal verb "should", which expresses a wish or a principle rather than an obligation and is overwhelmingly found in the non-binding preambular text of regulatory documents. An example of this includes the following false positive : «*Under the general safety requirement laid down in this Regulation, economic operators should be obliged to place only safe products on the market.*» This means that the model is not dependable for professional use. At the same time, it is not consistent, as the following sentence is not labeled as an obligation : «*The technical documentation should be based on an internal risk analysis carried out by the manufacturer.*»

NOMOS finds 159 obligations in the test document with 88 true obligations. While the model is still over-inclusive to some extent, it produces fewer false negatives compared to the other types of models, which is an important characteristic for the user to trust the model. At the same time, it also does not produce false positives (e.g. : «*That requirement shall not apply where the product can be used safely and as intended by the manufacturer without such instructions and safety information.*») due to misunderstanding the context around the obligation words, meaning that it is the most robust algorithm from the user perspective.

4.6 Discussion

Both qualitative and quantitative results show the effectiveness of NOMOS in detecting obligations. In particular, in the qualitative results, we showed how the model deals with a different country's legislation not included in the training dataset. However, the method has 2 limitations : 1) it does not perform well with passive English obligations (i.e. sentences where the subject to which the obligation refers, is not explicitly expressed), and 2) the method is not sufficiently reliable in distinguishing between obligations directed at private parties and the ones directed at authorities.

5 Conclusions

In this work, we have presented a comparison of methodologies for extracting obligations from legal texts. Apart from showing well-known methodologies, we proposed our own solution called NOMOS for dealing with such a classification problem based on the combination of positional and word embeddings and a Temporal Convolutional Network. Quantitative and qualitative results demonstrated the effectiveness of our approach in distinguishing obligations from non-obligation sentences reaching a $F1\text{-}score$ on both classes of 0.95.

As future directions, we intend to introduce an attention layer to the network in order to focus on the subject, the verb, and the object of a sentence and distinguish between obligations directed at private parties and those directed at authorities.

References

Shaojie Bai, J. Zico Kolter, and Vladlen Koltun. 2018. An empirical evaluation of generic convolutional and recurrent networks for sequence modeling. *CoRR*, abs/1803.01271.

Junyoung Chung, Caglar Gulcehre, KyungHyun Cho, and Yoshua Bengio. 2014. Empirical evaluation of gated recurrent neural networks on sequence modeling.

Corinna Coupette, Dirk Hartung, Janis Beckedorf, Maximilian Böther, and Daniel Martin Katz. 2021. Law smells : Defining and detecting problematic patterns in legal drafting. *CoRR*.

Emile de Maat, Kai Krabben, and Radboud Winkels. 2010. Machine learning versus knowledge based classification of legal texts. In *Proceedings of the 2010 Conference on Legal Knowledge and Information Systems : JURIX 2010 : The Twenty-Third Annual Conference*, pages 87–96.

Ingo Glaser, Elena Scepankova, and Florian Matthes. 2018. Classifying semantic types of legal sentences : Portability of machine learning models. In *Legal Knowledge and Information Systems - JURIX 2018 : The Thirty-first Annual Conference, Groningen, The Netherlands, 12-14 December 2018*, Frontiers in Artificial Intelligence and Applications.

Kaiming He, Xiangyu Zhang, Shaoqing Ren, and Jian Sun. 2016. Deep Residual Learning for Image Recognition. In *Proceedings of 2016 IEEE Conference on Computer Vision and Pattern Recognition.*

Christof Henkel. 2021. Temporal Convolutional Network. `https://www.kaggle.com/code/christofhenkel/temporal-convolutional-network`.

Sepp Hochreiter and Jürgen Schmidhuber. 1997. Long short-term memory. *Neural Computation.*

Maria Iacono, Laura Rossi, Paolo D'Angelo, Andrea Tesei, and Lorenzo De Mattei. 2021. An obligations extraction system for heterogeneous legal documents : Building and evaluating data and model. In *Proceedings of the Eighth Italian Conference on Computational Linguistics, CLiC-it 2021, Milan, Italy, January 26-28, 2022*, volume 3033 of *CEUR Workshop Proceedings*. CEUR-WS.org.

Diederik P. Kingma and Jimmy Ba. 2017. Adam : A method for stochastic optimization.

Nadzeya Kiyavitskaya, Nicola Zeni, Travis D. Breaux, Annie I. Antón, James R. Cordy, Luisa Mich, and John Mylopoulos. 2008. Automating the extraction of rights and obligations for regulatory compliance. In *Conceptual Modeling - ER 2008*.

James O'Neill, Paul Buitelaar, Cecile Robin, and Leona O' Brien. 2017. Classifying sentential modality in legal language : A use case in financial regulations, acts and directives. In *Proceedings of the 16th Edition of the International Conference on Articial Intelligence and Law*, ICAIL '17, page 159–168.

Jasper Snoek, Hugo Larochelle, and Ryan P. Adams. 2012. Practical bayesian optimization of machine learning algorithms.

Ashish Vaswani, Noam Shazeer, Niki Parmar, Jakob Uszkoreit, Llion Jones, Aidan N Gomez, Ł ukasz Kaiser, and Illia Polosukhin. 2017. Attention is all you need. In *Advances in Neural Information Processing Systems*. Curran Associates, Inc.

Wojciech Zaremba, Ilya Sutskever, and Oriol Vinyals. 2014. Recurrent neural network regularization.

Ying Zuo, Lifen Jiang, Huazhi Sun, Chunmei Ma, Yan Liang, Shuaibao Nie, and Yongheng Zhou. 2020. Short text classification based on bidirectional tcn and attention mechanism. *Journal of Physics : Conference Series*.

Long Text Classification using Transformers with Paragraph Selection Strategies

Mohit Tuteja
Thomson Reuters Labs
Bangalore, Karnataka, India
mohit.tuteja@thomsonreuters.com

Daniel González Juclà
Thomson Reuters Labs
Zug, Switzerland
daniel.gonzalezjucla@thomsonreuters.com

Abstract

In the legal domain, we often perform classification tasks on very long documents, for example court judgements. These documents often contain thousands of words, so the length of these documents poses a challenge for this modelling task. In this research paper, we present a comprehensive evaluation of various strategies to perform long text classification using Transformers in conjunction with strategies to select document chunks using traditional NLP models. We conduct our experiments on 6 benchmark datasets comprising lengthy documents, 4 of which are publicly available. Each dataset has a median word count exceeding 1,000. Our evaluation encompasses state-of-the-art Transformer models, such as RoBERTa, Longformer, HAT, MEGA and LegalBERT and compares them with a traditional baseline TF-IDF + Neural Network (NN) model. We investigate the effectiveness of pre-training on large corpora, fine-tuning strategies, and transfer learning techniques in the context of long text classification.

1 Introduction

The performance of text classification methods has improved significantly over the last decade for text instances containing less than 512 characters. Due to the high computational cost of processing longer text instances, this limitation is introduced in the most recent transformer models. To alleviate this problem and improve the classification of long texts, researchers tried to address the root causes of the computational cost and proposed the optimization of the attention mechanism (Vaswani et al., 2017), which is a key element of any transformer model.

This research undertakes a comparative study of different ways of doing long text, multi-label classification on multiple legal datasets. We take existing approaches from literature and try an alternate approach of our own. The end goal is to strike a balance between model performance and computational efficiency.

2 Related Work

Natural Language Processing (NLP) is a subfield of computer science and linguistics that focuses on processing language, including text. Probably the most basic task within this field is Text Classification, which given text as an input the objective is to classify it among a set of categories. To perform this classification, the model needs to extract features from the text and preferably to understand correlations between its different parts, in a similar way that us humans do where we connect different entities in a sentence to extract meaning from them.

Some approaches treated text with a Bag-of-Words (BoW) model, as introduced by Harris (Harris, 1954), where grammar and word order are disregarded and we consider text as a set of words with their multiplicity. Related to this concept, a popular idea to model text which became popular during the era of Statistical NLP (1990s–2010s) is TF-IDF (Term Frequency - Inverse Document Frequency). First described in 1972, TF-IDF (Sparck Jones, 1972) as its name indicates consists on vectorizing text by reflecting how important a term is to a document in a collection or corpus. Its main intuition is to divide the occurrences of the term in the text by the occurrences of this term in the whole corpus, this way we get the relative importance of a given term.

In the decade of the 2010s we dive into the era of the Neural Models for NLP, starting in 2013 with the word2vec embeddings (Mikolov et al., 2013) used to train a Recurrent Neural Network (RNN). This idea of training representation of words and terms quickly became very popular and since then there have appeared many methods to obtain these representations in an unsupervised way to then use them for downstream tasks, for example GloVe

Proceedings of the Natural Legal Language Processing Workshop 2023, pages 17–24
December 7, 2023

(Pennington et al., 2014) and fastText (Bojanowski et al., 2017).

A big revolution in NLP started with the presentation of the Transformer architecture by Vaswani (Vaswani et al., 2017) and its attention mechanism. This architecture later evolved into models that have also been pre-trained to obtain representations of the input tokens, as for example BERT (Devlin et al., 2018) and RoBERTa (Liu et al., 2019). Legal-BERT (Chalkidis et al., 2020) consists in BERT heavily pre-trained with legal data, and this specialization has been proved to improve the performance of the model in downstream tasks that use this language. Nonetheless, in this study we do not include models pre-trained with legal corpora because it would include a bias when comparing with other architectures that do not have a public version pre-trained on this type of language.

The limitation of these mentioned models is that due to the quadratic computational cost the attention mechanism, they allowed up to 512 tokens in the input, while legal documents can easily be formed by thousands of them. This problem has led to two alternatives: truncation methods in order to process a part of the text, for example the first 512 tokens, and to derive the classification from that part and models that contain a more efficient attention mechanism rather than computing the pair-wise attention between all the tokens in the input.

Many sparse-attention models have been proposed, the most popular ones being Longformer (Beltagy et al., 2020), BigBird (Zaheer et al., 2020) and most recently Mega (Ma et al., 2022) has proved to be the best in the benchmark for long sequence modeling "Long Range Arena" (Tay et al., 2020). This latter one, despite being the best performing model for long sequences has not become very popular due to not being a public model that has been largely pre-trained. Another popular approach to process long text are Hierarchical Attention Transformers (HAT) (Pappagari et al., 2019), which aim at processing the whole text by encoding chunks of typically 512 or less tokens at each step and then encoding these together in a hierarchical way, through cross-segment attention blocks (Chalkidis et al., 2022).

Some research has been done in the direction of putting all these different methods with different intuitions in a fair comparison to solve a multi-label classification task. Some of these studies include TextGuide (Fiok et al., 2021) which compared the performance of different truncation methods in selecting the text to train a Language Model, Park (Park et al., 2022) studied and compared different efficient LMs and Chalkidis (Chalkidis et al., 2022) compared Longformer to HATs for long document classification. Nonetheless, no work has obtained definitive and actionable conclusions and more importantly no other work has compared traditional approaches such as TF-IDF vectorization followed by a Neural Network (NN) for classification with truncation methods to train popular Language Models such as BERT and Sparse-attention models designed to process long documents at once.

3 Research questions

Few works have focused on widely comparing different text classification approaches, so this method aims at setting the baseline for choosing an approach for multi-label / multi-class text classification given a set of constraints. So, the research questions that will be addressed are:

- Which is the Truncation method that works the best on input text?
- Which is the approach that reports the highest performance?
- Which is the most cost-effective approach?
- Can we train a cost-effective language model on very long sequences?

4 Datasets

Six datasets with long documents have been chosen to compare the performance of the different approaches:

Canadian Abridgement Dataset: This dataset contains 369,943 Canadian court judgements and their classification as per the Abridgement classification taxonomy as defined by the editorial team for Checkpoint. The classification follows a hierarchy, starting with 55 broad classes (subject titles). These classes have further sub-categories going up to 6 levels. Each unique classification up to the 6th level is treated as one class. The data belongs to the period 2000-2021. We have used only those cases whose classification belongs to the latest available version of the taxonomy.

Checkpoint Tax Type Classification: Thomson Reuters monitors multiple sources (tax courts, rulings, official materials etc.) in order to incorporate the latest changes in law or guidance into Checkpoint editorial content. Documents from

Dataset	Words/Doc	# Classes
Canada A	5,321	11,648
Posture 50K	2,901	256
Tax Type	708	44
SCOTUS	5,352	14
MIMIC-III	2,260	19
ECtHR	2,140	10

Table 1: Average words per document and number of unique classes for each dataset used

these sources are called Alerts. During post processing, the editors assign tags to these alerts which are known as tax-types which states what type of tax a given alert talks about. This is a multi-label classification dataset. We currently have two types of alerts - rulings and official materials.

Posture 50K: (Song et al., 2022) This data-set is publicly accessible and has been made available by Thomson Reuters. It is designed for the purpose of identifying the legal Procedural Postures involved in legal motions within a legal case. To illustrate, a plaintiff might request an appellate court to overturn a specific decision made by a lower court judge regarding a motion, which is referred to as an "On Appeal" procedural posture. The dataset comprises 50,000 legal opinions, representing real-world legal cases in the United States, along with their corresponding postures. The majority of these cases span from the year 2013 to 2020, with just three cases occurring prior to 2013.

SCOTUS: (Chalkidis et al., 2021b) This constitutes one of the six datasets within LexGLUE. It encompasses court opinions issued by the United States Supreme Court (SCOTUS). The primary challenge within this dataset involves single-label multi-class classification, with the aim of forecasting the pertinent issue area for each court opinion. There are 14 distinct classes that align with specific issue areas, collectively encompassing 278 issues centered around the subject matter of the legal dispute.

MIMIC-III Dataset: (Johnson et al., 2016) Contains approx. 50k discharge summaries from US hospitals. Each summary is annotated with one or more codes (labels) from the ICD-9 taxonomy. The input of the model is a discharge summary, and the output is the set of the relevant 1st level ICD-9 (19 in total) codes.

ECtHR (Task B): (Chalkidis et al., 2021a) This is one of the six data-sets from LexGLUE. It comprises approximately 11,000 cases sourced from the public database of the European Court of Human Rights (ECtHR). For each case, the dataset includes a collection of factual paragraphs extracted from the case description. Each case is associated with specific articles of the European Convention on Human Rights (ECHR) that were purportedly violated, as determined by the court. In terms of model input, it consists of the factual paragraph list for a given case, while the model's output comprises the set of articles that are alleged to have been violated.

The first two datasets are internal from Thomson Reuters, while the other four are publicly available. Mimic-III contains medical documents and the rest contain legal text, which is our focus area. Table 1 shows a summary of the statistics of each dataset.

5 Experiments

5.1 Setup

The 10 selected methods, which are explained in the next section, are trained for the 6 datasets with a standardized methodology.

Learning Rates: We trained each transformer model on three predefined learning rates to overcome possible variability on the optimal learning rate across models and datasets. These learning rates were 2e-05, 1e-05 and 5e-06 respectively. For each model, we selected the version which provided the best results on the respective development dataset. We then used this optimal configuration to score our test dataset. We used a standardized script for training of all models, starting with the same base model (RoBERTa) wherever possible.

Evaluation metric: The authors have chosen micro-f1 score as the metric to establish a comparison between the different approaches. This is motivated by it being the most used throughout the literature when comparing models for the task of multi-label classification.

Repeatability: We ensured that this training is also reproducible by using fixed seeds and used the same batch size for the models across datasets and the same batch-size * accumulation-steps of 8 across models. Out of the four publicly available datasets, we dropped a few observations only from ECtHR. These were observations with missing labels. Aside from that, the train-dev-test datasets were left unchanged and used as-is in each case.

Base Model selection: We use RoBERTa as the baseline transformer model instead of LegalBERT.

This was done due to the following reasons:

- LegalBERT uses LexGLUE (Chalkidis et al., 2021b) datasets during its pretraining process. Hence we observed abnormal performance gains on the ECtHR data-set which was not visible across other datasets.
- Longformer starts its training from a RoBERTa checkpoint so the comparison with RoBERTa becomes fair
- We decided to include MIMIC-III dataset for which LegalBERT might not be ideal.

It is to be noted though that we did observe 1-2% gains in F1 scores on legal datasets (other than LexGLUE) while making a switch from RoBERTa to LegalBERT.

5.2 Models

The following models were evaluated:

- **TF-IDF + Neural Net (NN):** Vectorization of each document through TF-IDF to then train a Neural Network to classify these vectors. Pre-processing included lower-casing, removing punctuation, special characters, digits and words containing less than 3 characters. We used TfidfVectorizer from sklearn with ngram range (1,2), and max features capped at 50,000. The neural network used 1 hidden layer, relu activation, dropout = .3 and batch size of 64. We iterated over 3 learning rates (.001,.002,.01) and 3 layer sizes (128,256,512). Early stopping on val-categorical-accuracy with patience = 3 was used. The same grid-search approach was considered for all data-sets and the hyper-parameters giving best micro-averaged F1 scores on the dev dataset were finally selected.
- **RoBERTa First 512 tokens:** Truncate the first 512 tokens of the input text to fine-tune pre-trained RoBERTa. It is likely that documents tend to contain important and descriptive information at the beginning, as for example abstracts or introductions.
- **RoBERTa Last 512 tokens:** Truncate the last 512 tokens of the input text to fine-tune pre-trained RoBERTa. It is possible that important information is found at the end of a document, as for example summaries or conclusions.
- **RoBERTa First & Last 256 tokens:** Concatenate the first and the last 256 tokens to obtain a chunk of 512 tokens to fine-tune pre-trained RoBERTa. Information at the beginning or at the end of a document e.g. introductions or conclusions might give more general information about the document than text in the middle, specially in a very long document.
- **RoBERTa First & Last 512 tokens:** Fine-tune a pre-trained RoBERTa model with chunks corresponding to first and last 512 of each document, by splitting them into two samples with the same labels. At inference time, aggregate the predictions for these two chunks per document, which can be done in different ways. For the results that we share in this paper, for the multi-label datasets, we take the mean probability for each class between the two chunks, and then find the best classification threshold. For the multi-class case, we replace the mean by max and select the class with the highest probability.
- **RoBERTa w/ Best paragraph selection:** This is a custom approach to obtain a **smaller and more targeted training dataset**. First, we train a traditional NN model on the tf-idf vectorization of the full training documents. Then for each training document, we do the following:
  1. Split the document into a maximum of 10 chunks of 512 tokens and predict for each of them with the previously trained model. Note: more than 10 chunks can be used, if desired.
  2. Take a dot product between the prediction (probability) vector for each chunk with the label vector for the document. Note: The label vector is already a binary vector indicating the presence of a class label.
  3. Select the chunk having the highest similarity with the label vector, which is likely the "most important chunk", as it has been classified the best.

  Having a dataset of the most important chunk per document, we now fine-tune a RoBERTa model for the multi-label classification task. At **inference time**, it is not possible to select the most important chunk for each document because we have no labels, so for each document, we:

  1. Split the text into a maximum of 10 chunks and predict for each of them inde-

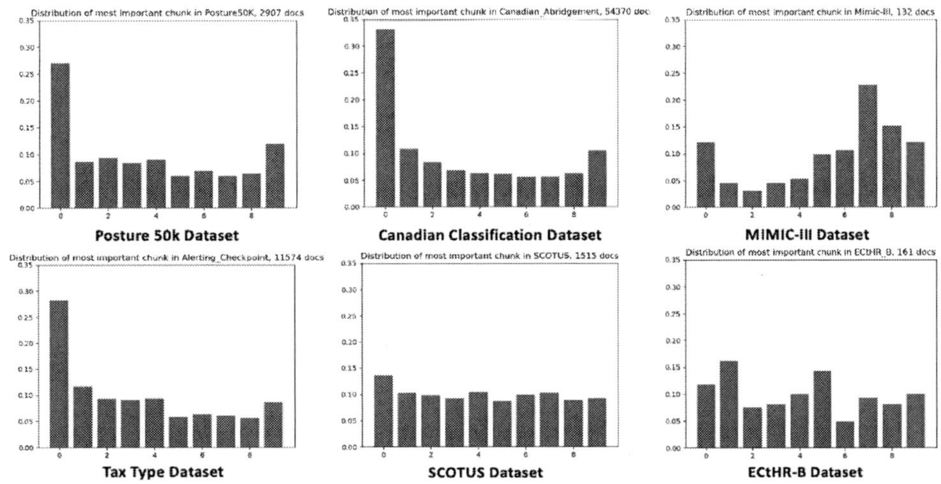

Figure 1: Paragraph importance distribution for all dev datasets. We take only those documents where we have >=10 chunks for this representation

pendently with the fine-tuned RoBERTa model.

2. The predictions for each of these chunks are then combined. The combination can be done in multiple ways. One approach could be taking a sum/average of the predictions (probabilities) for each class across chunks and then applying some threshold. Another could be taking the highest probability for each class observed across chunks and then applying a threshold. There were multiple approaches like these that were evaluated.
3. It has been found empirically that the most effective way to combine the predictions is to first predict the class that has the highest weighted average confidence. The weights in this case come from the paragraph importance distribution given in Figure 1 and derived from the model training data set. Subsequently, we predict all the other classes whose average confidence is within a ratio of 0.8 to the top class. For the multi-class classification case, we stop at only 1 prediction.

- **Longformer First 4096 tokens:** Fine-tune a pre-trained Longformer with the first 4096 tokens of the document.
- **Longformer First & Last 512: tokens:** Concatenate the first and the last 512 tokens to obtain a chunk of 1024 tokens to fine-tune a pre-trained Longformer. Same intuition as with RoBERTa and possible efficiency boost compared to Longformer processing 4096 tokens.
- **HATs First 4096 tokens:** Fine-tune a pre-trained HAT with the first 4096 tokens of the document. The chosen implementation uses BERT as a backbone model.
- **HATs First & Last 512 tokens:** Concatenate the first and the last 512 tokens to obtain a chunk of 1024 tokens to fine-tune a pre-trained HAT.
- **MEGA: Moving Average Equipped Gated Attention 4096:** Fine-tune a pre-trained (by us) MEGA with the first 4096 tokens of the document. Pre-training details can be found in appendix A.

6 Results

6.1 Paragraph importance

In the explanation of the "RoBERTa w/ Best para selection" approach it has been mentioned that during the training phase of the model we select the chunk within each document that has been predicted the best, which we call the most important. If we select the documents that were split into 10 chunks (the maximum allowed, 5 chunks at the beginning and 5 at the end) and we plot the histogram of which was the **most important paragraph**, we get the results in Figure 1.

Figure 1 shows how the first paragraph is the most important in the three Thomson Reuters datasets. In MIMIC-III though, the chunks at the end have more importance than the ones at the

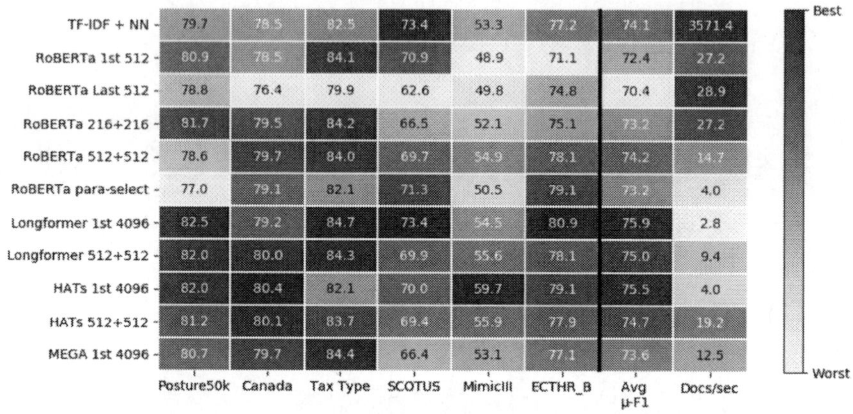

Figure 2: Heat-map of testing Micro-F1s per dataset. Inference time for TF-IDF+DNN corresponds to CPU evaluation, while the rest have been evaluated on a single GPU.

beginning. In the LexGLUE datasets, it is more evenly distributed. In the next section, it is seen how these **distributions relate to the performance of the approaches** that truncate different parts of the text.

6.2 Comparison of testing results

Figure 2 contains the testing Micro-F1 score at inference time for each combination of dataset and approach, together with a color coding to making it easier to spot the best and worst performing approaches for each dataset. These are the main observations:

- There is **not one clear model that performs the best** across all datasets, even though some approaches perform consistently better than others. In 4 out of the 6 datasets, Longformer trained with the first 4096 tokens provides the best performance, but on the other hand it is the least efficient.

- **TF-IDF + DNN provides a strong baseline**, as it is not far from the rest of RoBeRTa-based approaches and it is hundreds of times more efficient (using a CPU, while RoBERTa-based are evaluated using a single GPU).

- Models that truncate first tokens work well on Thomson Reuters datasets because of the importance of the first chunk, as seen in the "Paragraph Importance" section,

- Mimic-III and ECtHR-B are the only two datasets where the first chunk is not the most important, as it has been seen in the previous section, hence RoBERTa with first 512 tokens shows worse performance.

- **RoBERTa concatenating first and last 256 tokens** provides a better performance than RoBERTa first 512 on 5 out of 6 datasets, so in cases where it is possible to have relevant information at the end of the document, it **can be a better approach**.

- The versions of **Longformer and HAT** concatenating **first and last 512 tokens** provide a **comparable performance** to their version with the first 4096 tokens, while being around 4 times more efficient.

- Longformer performs better than HAT for 4 out of 6 datasets, but it is less efficient. Their versions concatenating the first and last 512 tokens also perform very similar.

- The in-house pretrained **MEGA has a consistently good performance** for all datasets without being the best in any, but it is considerably more efficient than the other two models with 4096 tokens.

7 Conclusions and Future Work

We recommend the following Model training Guidelines:

1. Train a baseline model (TF-IDF + DNN). It is the most efficient and typically reports good performance. This could be a good solution if 1-2% lower performance compared to SOTA is acceptable.

2. Plot the paragraph importance for your dataset, and identify which paragraphs are the most important. In case the Paragraph Importance has a U shape, like court judgement datasets, the best choice is usually a concatenated model.
    - LegalBERT/RoBERTa concatenate first and last 256, if good efficiency is needed.
    - Longformer/HAT concatenate first and last 512, if efficiency is not the priority.
3. In case Paragraph importance is more uniform, best choice is a Long model, as all paragraphs are important:
    - Longformer with first 4096 tokens will probably report the best performance, but it is expensive to train.
    - HAT Concat first and last 512 will probably report a slightly lower performance than Longformer 4096, while being quite more efficient.
    - LegalBERT concat or LegalBERT truncate will probably still report decent results, while being efficient.

Future work could be done in this topic by comparing the presented approaches to newer models that have come out after this study has been done. Some of these models can be:

- Llama 2 (Touvron et al., 2023) is a family of LLMs released by Meta with a context of 4096 tokens. Their extensive pre-training, their open-source availability and their large context length makes them a good option to be added to the comparison.

- LongNet (Ding et al., 2023) is an architecture published by Microsoft Research, whose authors claim to be able to process up to a million tokens. This is a very interesting feature since it would be able to entirely process any document in our datasets.

References

Iz Beltagy, Matthew E Peters, and Arman Cohan. 2020. Longformer: The long-document transformer. *arXiv preprint arXiv:2004.05150*.

Piotr Bojanowski, Edouard Grave, Armand Joulin, and Tomas Mikolov. 2017. Enriching word vectors with subword information. *Transactions of the association for computational linguistics*, 5:135–146.

Ilias Chalkidis, Xiang Dai, Manos Fergadiotis, Prodromos Malakasiotis, and Desmond Elliott. 2022. An exploration of hierarchical attention transformers for efficient long document classification. *arXiv preprint arXiv:2210.05529*.

Ilias Chalkidis, Manos Fergadiotis, Prodromos Malakasiotis, Nikolaos Aletras, and Ion Androutsopoulos. 2020. Legal-bert: The muppets straight out of law school. *arXiv preprint arXiv:2010.02559*.

Ilias Chalkidis, Manos Fergadiotis, Dimitrios Tsarapatsanis, Nikolaos Aletras, Ion Androutsopoulos, and Prodromos Malakasiotis. 2021a. Paragraph-level rationale extraction through regularization: A case study on European court of human rights cases. In *Proceedings of the 2021 Conference of the North American Chapter of the Association for Computational Linguistics: Human Language Technologies*, pages 226–241, Online. Association for Computational Linguistics.

Ilias Chalkidis, Abhik Jana, Dirk Hartung, Michael Bommarito, Ion Androutsopoulos, Daniel Martin Katz, and Nikolaos Aletras. 2021b. Lexglue: A benchmark dataset for legal language understanding in english. *arXiv preprint arXiv:2110.00976*.

Jacob Devlin, Ming-Wei Chang, Kenton Lee, and Kristina Toutanova. 2018. Bert: Pre-training of deep bidirectional transformers for language understanding. *arXiv preprint arXiv:1810.04805*.

Jiayu Ding, Shuming Ma, Li Dong, Xingxing Zhang, Shaohan Huang, Wenhui Wang, Nanning Zheng, and Furu Wei. 2023. Longnet: Scaling transformers to 1,000,000,000 tokens.

Krzysztof Fiok, Waldemar Karwowski, Edgar Gutierrez-Franco, Mohammad Reza Davahli, Maciej Wilamowski, Tareq Ahram, Awad Al-Juaid, and Jozef Zurada. 2021. Text guide: improving the quality of long text classification by a text selection method based on feature importance. *IEEE Access*, 9:105439–105450.

Zellig S Harris. 1954. Distributional structure. *Word*, 10(2-3):146–162.

Alistair EW Johnson, Tom J Pollard, Lu Shen, Li-wei H Lehman, Mengling Feng, Mohammad Ghassemi, Benjamin Moody, Peter Szolovits, Leo Anthony Celi, and Roger G Mark. 2016. Mimic-iii, a freely accessible critical care database. *Scientific data*, 3(1):1–9.

Yinhan Liu, Myle Ott, Naman Goyal, Jingfei Du, Mandar Joshi, Danqi Chen, Omer Levy, Mike Lewis, Luke Zettlemoyer, and Veselin Stoyanov. 2019. Roberta: A robustly optimized bert pretraining approach. *arXiv preprint arXiv:1907.11692*.

Xuezhe Ma, Chunting Zhou, Xiang Kong, Junxian He, Liangke Gui, Graham Neubig, Jonathan May, and Luke Zettlemoyer. 2022. Mega: moving average equipped gated attention. *arXiv preprint arXiv:2209.10655*.

Tomas Mikolov, Kai Chen, Greg Corrado, and Jeffrey Dean. 2013. Efficient estimation of word representations in vector space. *arXiv preprint arXiv:1301.3781*.

Raghavendra Pappagari, Piotr Zelasko, Jesús Villalba, Yishay Carmiel, and Najim Dehak. 2019. Hierarchical transformers for long document classification. In *2019 IEEE automatic speech recognition and understanding workshop (ASRU)*, pages 838–844. IEEE.

Hyunji Hayley Park, Yogarshi Vyas, and Kashif Shah. 2022. Efficient classification of long documents using transformers. *arXiv preprint arXiv:2203.11258*.

Jeffrey Pennington, Richard Socher, and Christopher D Manning. 2014. Glove: Global vectors for word representation. In *Proceedings of the 2014 conference on empirical methods in natural language processing (EMNLP)*, pages 1532–1543.

Dezhao Song, Andrew Vold, Kanika Madan, and Frank Schilder. 2022. Multi-label legal document classification: A deep learning-based approach with label-attention and domain-specific pre-training. *Information Systems*, 106:101718.

Karen Sparck Jones. 1972. A statistical interpretation of term specificity and its application in retrieval. *Journal of documentation*, 28(1):11–21.

Yi Tay, Mostafa Dehghani, Samira Abnar, Yikang Shen, Dara Bahri, Philip Pham, Jinfeng Rao, Liu Yang, Sebastian Ruder, and Donald Metzler. 2020. Long range arena: A benchmark for efficient transformers. *arXiv preprint arXiv:2011.04006*.

Hugo Touvron, Louis Martin, Kevin Stone, Peter Albert, Amjad Almahairi, Yasmine Babaei, Nikolay Bashlykov, Soumya Batra, Prajjwal Bhargava, Shruti Bhosale, Dan Bikel, Lukas Blecher, Cristian Canton Ferrer, Moya Chen, Guillem Cucurull, David Esiobu, Jude Fernandes, Jeremy Fu, Wenyin Fu, Brian Fuller, Cynthia Gao, Vedanuj Goswami, Naman Goyal, Anthony Hartshorn, Saghar Hosseini, Rui Hou, Hakan Inan, Marcin Kardas, Viktor Kerkez, Madian Khabsa, Isabel Kloumann, Artem Korenev, Punit Singh Koura, Marie-Anne Lachaux, Thibaut Lavril, Jenya Lee, Diana Liskovich, Yinghai Lu, Yuning Mao, Xavier Martinet, Todor Mihaylov, Pushkar Mishra, Igor Molybog, Yixin Nie, Andrew Poulton, Jeremy Reizenstein, Rashi Rungta, Kalyan Saladi, Alan Schelten, Ruan Silva, Eric Michael Smith, Ranjan Subramanian, Xiaoqing Ellen Tan, Binh Tang, Ross Taylor, Adina Williams, Jian Xiang Kuan, Puxin Xu, Zheng Yan, Iliyan Zarov, Yuchen Zhang, Angela Fan, Melanie Kambadur, Sharan Narang, Aurelien Rodriguez, Robert Stojnic, Sergey Edunov, and Thomas Scialom. 2023. Llama 2: Open foundation and fine-tuned chat models.

Ashish Vaswani, Noam Shazeer, Niki Parmar, Jakob Uszkoreit, Llion Jones, Aidan N Gomez, Łukasz Kaiser, and Illia Polosukhin. 2017. Attention is all you need. *Advances in neural information processing systems*, 30.

Hyperparameters	
Datasets	Bookcorpus + CC News + Wikipedia (20220301.en)
Max sequence length	256
Training batch size	32
Accumulation steps	16
Training steps	77k
Learning rate	0.001
Weight decay	0.05
Learning rate warmup %	0.006
Encoder depth	6
Encoder embedding dim	256
Encoder Z dim	128
Encoder hidden dim	512
Dropout	0.1
Activation function	Silu

Table 2: MEGA pretraining hyperparameters

Manzil Zaheer, Guru Guruganesh, Kumar Avinava Dubey, Joshua Ainslie, Chris Alberti, Santiago Ontanon, Philip Pham, Anirudh Ravula, Qifan Wang, Li Yang, et al. 2020. Big bird: Transformers for longer sequences. *Advances in neural information processing systems*, 33:17283–17297.

A MEGA pretraining

Moving Average Gated Attention (MEGA) is an architecture that has demonstrated state-of-the-art performance in long sequence modelling, given that it has the best results for the Long Range Arena at the time the research has been done.

Also at this time there was not any available pretrained version of MEGA as it was released very recently. Nonetheless, there was a public implementation, so we decided to pretrain this model on the Masked Language Modeling task in order to later fine-tune it for the multi-label classification task in the 6 different datasets.

The parameters used for MEGA pretraining can be found down in table 2.

Do Language Models Learn about Legal Entity Types during Pretraining?

Claire Barale and **Michael Rovatsos**
School of Informatics
The University of Edinburgh
{claire.barale,michael.rovatsos}@ed.ac.uk

Nehal Bhuta
School of Law
The University of Edinburgh
nehal.bhuta@ed.ac.uk

Abstract

Language Models (LMs) have proven their ability to acquire diverse linguistic knowledge during the pretraining phase, potentially serving as a valuable source of incidental supervision for downstream tasks. However, there has been limited research conducted on the retrieval of domain-specific knowledge, and specifically legal knowledge. We propose to explore the task of Entity Typing, serving as a proxy for evaluating legal knowledge as an essential aspect of text comprehension, and a foundational task to numerous downstream legal NLP applications. Through systematic evaluation and analysis and two types of prompting (cloze sentences and QA-based templates) and to clarify the nature of these acquired cues, we compare diverse types and lengths of entities both general and domain-specific entities, semantics or syntax signals, and different LM pretraining corpus (generic and legal-oriented) and architectures (encoder BERT-based and decoder-only with Llama2). We show that (1) Llama2 performs well on certain entities and exhibits potential for substantial improvement with optimized prompt templates, (2) law-oriented LMs show inconsistent performance, possibly due to variations in their training corpus, (3) LMs demonstrate the ability to type entities even in the case of multi-token entities, (4) all models struggle with entities belonging to sub-domains of the law (5) Llama2 appears to frequently overlook syntactic cues, a shortcoming less present in BERT-based architectures. The code of the experiments is available at https://github.com/clairebarale/probing_legal_entity_types.

1 Introduction

During the initial phase of pretraining, language models (LMs) are exposed to an extensive corpus of textual data, allowing them to acquire the capacity to represent the probabilistic structure of language. In this process, it has been theorized that they incidentally learn various linguistic signals and patterns, both syntactic and semantic. Work by Petroni et al. (2019) and subsequent studies (Jiang et al., 2020b) make the hypothesis that a side effect of the pretraining stage is that LMs also learn factual knowledge. On the other hand, Gururangan et al. (2020) research demonstrates the significance of both model pretraining and task-specific pretraining; pretraining a model with a specific focus on a particular task or a limited domain corpus yields notable advantages in enhancing model performance and adaptability.

Entity typing and extraction are crucial tasks for a range of use cases including named-entity recognition (NER), relation extraction, summarization, structuring raw data, and most specifically in law, legal search, and past cases retrieval. To gain more insights into entity typing and extraction, entity probing tasks have been designed for bidirectional LSTM conditional random field models (Augenstein et al., 2017), masked language models (Petroni et al., 2019; Jiang et al., 2020b) and autoregressive LMs (Epure and Hennequin, 2022), using GPT-2.

Conversely, one notable bottleneck of the application of NLP within the legal domain is the lack of resources and annotated datasets. Thereby, it is of particular interest to explore the extent to which LMs, during their pretraining phase, acquire a sufficient **understanding of legal entities**, serving as a surrogate for legal knowledge. Ultimately, LMs could be exploited as a source of weak and indirect supervision in downstream tasks such as legal NER or question answering (QA), as they constitute a good proxy to use natural text incidentally thanks to their pretraining stage. Indeed, humans do not exclusively rely on exhaustive supervision but instead make use of occasional feedback and learn from incidental signals originating from various sources. This approach holds potential for

Proceedings of the Natural Legal Language Processing Workshop 2023, pages 25–37
December 7, 2023

	Pretrained Language Model	Pretraining corpus	# Parameters	# Tokens	Corpus size	# Vocab
Legal	**CaseHOLD** (Zheng et al., 2021)	Harvard Case Law	110M	43B	37 GB	32K
	Pile of law (Henderson et al., 2022)	US, Canadian, ECthR	340M	130B	256 GB	32K
	LexLM (Chalkidis et al., 2023)	US, Canada, EU, UK, India	125	2T + 256B	175 GB	50K
Generic		BookCorpus (Zhu et al., 2015)		-	16GB	-
		CC_news (Nagel, 2016)		-	76GB	-
		OpenWebText (Radford et al., 2019)		-	38GB	-
		Stories (Trinh and Le, 2018)		-	31GB	-
	RoBERTa(Liu et al., 2019)		125M	2T	160GB	50K
	DeBERTa (He et al., 2023)		86M	2T	160GB	128K
	Llama 2 (Touvron et al., 2023)	Data from publicly available sources	7B	2T	-	32K

Table 1: Overview of the models used. The table reports the description of the pretraining corpora, the number of parameters, the total number of tokens, the size of the corpus, and the vocabulary size

increased flexibility in terms of entity types, in contrast to supervised methods, and presents an alternative to existing automated annotation extraction approaches (Tedeschi and Navigli, 2022; Savelka, 2023) which hold limitations in the set of entity types. It presents several advantages: it does not require human annotation, it can be easily combined with other sources of supervision such as legal knowledge bases, and it would support an open set of entities and user queries. It would offer the advantage of seamless and fast application to new datasets while facilitating transfers of knowledge between datasets and even potentially between different domains. In this paper, we study the **intersection of entity knowledge and legal knowledge embedded within LMs**, evaluated on a ***AsyLex***, a dataset of Canadian Refugee Decisions.

1.1 Research questions

We are interested in evaluating the quality of the entity knowledge learned during pretraining in *off-the-shelf* LMs, specifically domain-specific entities, such as those pertinent to the legal field. **How proficient are Language Models at acquiring knowledge about domain-specific entities like legal entities during pretraining?** Can this acquired knowledge be considered sufficiently reliable for tasks such as annotating new datasets or serving as an indirect source of supervision? How does the choice of prompt type impact the results obtained from knowledge queries? To what extent does the variation in acquired knowledge differ across entity types? What categories of factual knowledge can LMs retrieve, and in what instances do they make errors? Does domain-specific pretraining and jurisdiction-specific pretraining enhance the amount of factual knowledge compared to generic pretraining? To what degree does knowledge acquisition in the legal domain overlap with that of general language models?

1.2 Contributions

Differing from the research objectives of Petroni et al. (2019), which focuses on relation extraction, and Chalkidis et al. (2023) which investigates eight distinct legal knowledge probing tasks with a focus on legislation and legal terminology, we focus on **Legal Entity Types**. To be clear, we ask the LM to predict the entity type, similarly to Epure and Hennequin (2022), and not the actual entity. For example, in the prompt *<Mask> is the capital of Germany*, we expect the answer to be *City* or *Location* and not *Berlin*.

In addition, we adopt a comprehensive interpretation of entity types, aligned with the work of Barale et al. (2023), encompassing both essential factual knowledge (e.g., location and dates) and more abstract legal concepts, such as the credibility of a claimant and the rationale behind a judgment. Moreover, our approach diverges by allowing longer entities to be masked (Figure 4), where previous work was limited either to single token (Petroni et al., 2019) or 2-tokens entities (Jiang et al., 2020a; Chalkidis et al., 2023). Where most previous work focuses on masked language modeling objective models (MLM), we introduce the use of autoregressive LM (Llama2) in a zero-shot setting, similar to the approach employed in Epure and Hennequin (2022).

We make the hypothesis that pretrained LMs inherently contain structured knowledge about specific domains, which could be leveraged to generate incidental training instances. We seek to investigate the depth of a model's knowledge, its nature, and whether it predominantly acquires knowledge from semantic or syntactic cues.

We first conduct in section 3 an analysis of the pretraining corpus of selected models both generic and legal LMs. We then prompt the LM with two different styles of prompts, cloze text and question-based, for the task of Entity Typing (section 5). After evaluating the experimental results in section 6, we analyze the type of failure cases (6.5) to highlight the strengths and weaknesses of the learning process and to draft directions for future work.

Our contributions are as follows:

- We propose two new experiments on the task of Legal Entity Typing in a zero-shot setting on a large set of entity types: ***Experiment MLM*** that evaluates generic and legal BERT-based LM on cloze sentences, and ***Experiment Llama2*** which evaluates Llama2 on QA-style prompts.
- We report the results for both experiments and show that Llama2 exhibits good performance on specific entities and has the potential for improvement with optimized prompts. However, law-oriented LMs display inconsistent results, likely influenced by training corpus variations and struggle with Refugee Law-specific vocabulary.
- We propose an in-depth analysis of the failure modes of the models on this task, opening the way for future work.

2 Background and related work

2.1 Legal NLP and Legal LMs

A range of tasks and use cases have been investigated in legal NLP (Zhong et al., 2018), including summarization, information retrieval, and extraction, or question answering. It is worth emphasizing that entity typing is foundational for many of these tasks.

The legal domain presents numerous challenges for self-supervised learning, primarily due to the specificity of legal language in contrast to ordinary language. This can lead to ambiguity in contextual meaning (that we aim to assess in this paper), potential implicit meanings, and variations in the significance of a term. A term that may be decisive in a legal context, such as "appeal," might not carry the same weight in a generic domain.

Given these specific challenges and the demonstrated benefits of pretraining LM on legal text to achieve better performance on downstream tasks

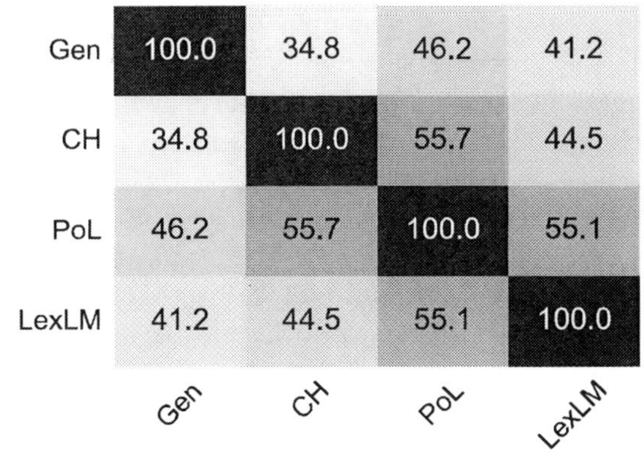

Figure 1: Vocabulary overlap (%) between the pretraining corpora. *Gen* stands for *Generic* and is sampled from sources similar to RoBERTa's pretraining corpus, presented in Table 1. Vocabularies are created with the top 10K most frequent tokens in a sample of 50K documents per model

(Barale et al., 2023), there has been interest in pretraining models on legal texts (Zhong et al., 2018; Xiao et al., 2021). These models typically use an encoder-only architecture based on the BERT architecture: LegalBERT (Chalkidis et al., 2020), CaseHOLD (Zheng et al., 2021), Pile of Law (Henderson et al., 2022), and LexLM (Chalkidis et al., 2023), that we use in our first experiment (details in Table 1). To the best of our knowledge, there is no decoder-only legal LM, which is why we limit our second experiment to a Llama2.

2.2 Probing LMs for Entity Typing

The idea of latent language representations derived from pre-trained LMs holds promise as a source of structured knowledge. Similar to human learning, LMs accumulate domain-specific and linguistic knowledge, along with the development of general pattern recognition capabilities through their pretraining experiences (Brown et al., 2020). As noted in the introduction, our work follows Petroni et al. (2019)'s LAnguage Models Analysis framework (LAMA) and LegalLAMA (Chalkidis et al., 2023). Several probing methods have been investigated (Yin et al., 2023), evaluating multilingual extraction (Jiang et al., 2020a) as well as effective prompting for factual knowledge extraction (Haviv et al., 2021; Qin and Eisner, 2021; Blevins et al., 2023). Various types of tasks have been targeted by these works, including relation extraction, NER, or entity typing (Shen et al., 2023), our task of interest. Concurrently, there have been efforts to enhance entity typing pipelines, particularly to expand the range of entities beyond traditional categories like location or dates (Choi et al., 2018; Dai et al., 2021) or to entities unseen during training (Epure and Hennequin, 2022; Lin et al., 2020), and approaches leveraging supervision from other tasks such as QA (Zhang et al., 2022). However, to the best of our knowledge, there has been no work conducted in the legal domain specifically addressing entity typing, and no prior research on entity typing in this domain has made use of prompts in the form of questions.

3 Pretraining corpus analysis

3.1 Vocabulary

To understand the difference between pretraining corpora across LMs, we conduct an exploratory vocabulary analysis inspired by Gururangan et al. (2020) that investigates the impact of domain-specific pretraining on a range of downstream tasks. This preliminary study is destined to clarify and offer insights that will help explain the results of the experiments presented in section 5. We select a total of fifty thousand documents for each language model, perform basic cleaning, tokenize the text, and remove stopwords, which gives us a list of tokens per LM. From this list, we select the most common ten thousand tokens, that constitute the final vocabulary for a given LM.

For the three legal LMs, as the datasets used for pretraining are directly available, we randomly select the fifty thousand documents. To construct a generic pretraining corpus, we reconstitute a vocabulary based on the RoBERTa and DeBERTa corpus as indicated in Table 1. As for the other models, we gathered fifty thousand entries, selected proportionally to the size of each corpus. That is to say, we select 5,000 documents from *BookCorpus* which constitutes 10% of RoBERTa pretraining data, 23,750 entries from *CC_news*, 11,875 entries from *OpenWebText* (using the open source version: (Gokaslan and Cohen, 2019)), and 9,688 entries from *CC_stories*. Given our limited knowledge of the precise composition of Llama2's pretraining corpus, we propose utilizing the generic vocabularies of RoBERTa and DeBERTa as suitable proxies for our analysis.

3.2 Vocabulary Overlap

The vocabulary overlap is represented in percentage in the matrix in Figure 1. As anticipated, the

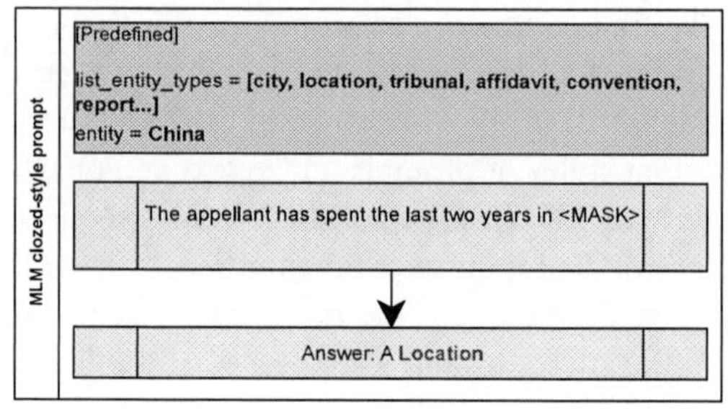

Figure 2: *Experiment MLM* prompt example

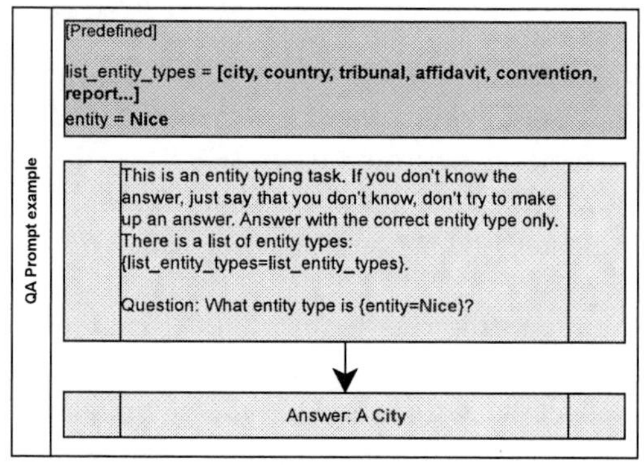

Figure 3: *Experiment Llama2* QA prompt example

legal LMs exhibit a greater overlap in vocabulary compared to their counterparts with generic training. However, significant disparities emerge among the legal LMs. For example, CaseHOLD shares only 44.5% of its vocabulary with LexLM. This observation may be attributed to the more extensive and more diverse set of jurisdictions included in the LexLM pretraining corpus. This aligns with the fact that LexLM shows a higher percentage of vocabulary overlap with Pile of Law, which, in contrast to CaseHOLD which is limited to the United States, also includes legal documents from a broader range of jurisdictions.

4 Dataset

We use ***AsyLex***, a dataset of refugee decisions from Canada curated for entity typing and extraction[1]. This publicly available dataset comprises 19,115 human annotated instances, encompassing 20 distinct categories of entities that hold legal relevance as explained in Barale et al. (2023). These categories have been identified as categories of interest with the collaboration of legal professionals and experts in the field of refugee law. ***AsyLex*** comprises 59,112 historical decision documents,

[1] https://huggingface.co/datasets/clairebarale/AsyLex

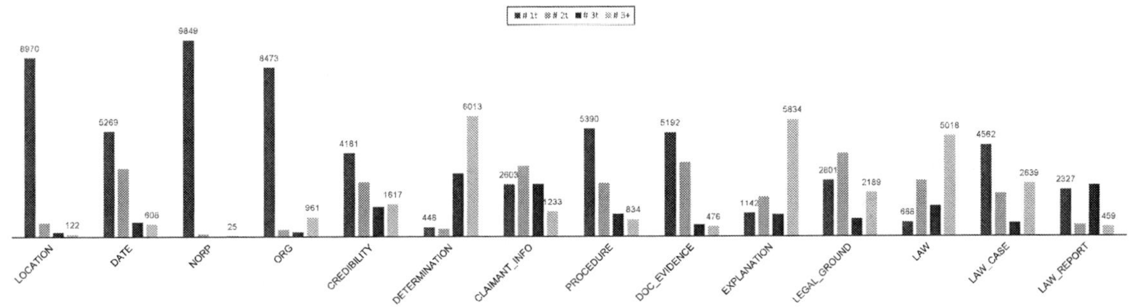

Figure 4: Length of the target masked entities, in number of tokens, for all entity types

spanning from 1996 to 2022. These documents are derived from the online repository of cases of the Canadian Legal Information Institute[2]. The documents encompass both initial determinations and subsequent appeals on whether the claimant is granted refugee status or not. It is important to note that the dataset contains entities of varying generality. Some entities, such as geographical locations, possess broad applicability and could be pertinent to any text (generic entity types: `location`, `date`, `norp`). Others are more specialized within the legal domain, such as procedural steps (generic legal entity types: `org`, `law`, `claimant_info`, `procedure`, `doc_evidence`, `law_case`). Finally, certain entities are highly specific to refugee law, such as the assessment of credibility, which frequently determines the acceptance or rejection of a refugee claim (Refugee Law entity types: `credibility`, `determination`, `explanation`, `legal_ground`, `law_report`). This diversity in entity scope presents an opportunity for assessing the impact of pretraining, particularly in scenarios where entity types have received various exposures during the pretraining phase.

4.1 Legal Entity Types

The selection of legal entity types within this dataset is intended to encapsulate characteristics that can reflect similarities among various refugee cases (see Appendix A for an exhaustive description of the types) and for which we have precise gold-standard annotations (Barale et al., 2023). The set of 14 entity types is pre-defined and closed for both experiments. To extend the coverage of each entity type and extract specific entities, we use a synonym generator to give synonyms for each of our 14 entity types. As a result, when prompted, the model would have to choose between a total of **151 entity types**, increasing the difficulty but also the interest of the task. For example, `location` accepts *city* or *country*. The complete list of synonyms generated per entity type is available in Appendix B. In our evaluation process, we assess predictions across the 14 entity types. For instance, if a prediction is *country*, it will be categorized as `location` and evaluated against a gold answer that specifies `location`. Contrary to previous work, we do not limit the entities' length to a single token (Petroni et al., 2019) or to entities spanning only two tokens (Jiang et al., 2020a). On the contrary, one of the objectives is to use entity types in a broader way for extracting information from text. Thereby we are interested in identifying multi-token entities that have short spans of text and can be longer than two tokens, which is often the case for explaining a decision for instance (entity type: `explanation`). The length of the entity per entity type is presented in Figure 4, which provides explicit numerical values for both single-token entities and entities longer than three tokens.

5 Proposed Entity Typing Methodology

5.1 Task description

The goal of this task is to classify legal entities mentioned in text documents or sentences into specific types. Legal entities can include various organizations, companies, government bodies (`org`), or more abstract concepts such as the credibility assessment made in the context of a refugee claim (`credibility`). The task involves extracting and categorizing these entities based on their attributes or context within the text. As input, we use text documents split by sentences that contain mentions of legal entities. We then categorized legal entity types for each mention found in the input text.

Let E be the set of possible entity types: $E = \{e_1, e_2, \ldots, e_n\}$, S the set of sentences or text seg-

[2]Canlii: `https://www.canlii.org/en/`

ments, T the set of masked tokens within the sentences and $P(e_i|t_j, s_k)$ represents the conditional probability that masked token t_j in sentence s_k belongs to entity type e_i. The goal is to find the entity type e_i that maximizes the conditional probability for each masked token t_j in each sentence s_k:

$$e_i^* = \arg\max_{e_i \in E} P(e_i|t_j, s_k)$$

In other words, the objective is to find the entity type that is most likely for each masked token in each sentence.

5.2 Language models used

For the first experiment, *Experiment MLM* with BERT-based LMs, we experiment with two generic models optimized for MLM, RoBERTa, and DeBERTa, and three legal-oriented LMs (see Table 1). For the second experiment, *Experiment Llama2* we use the open-source model Llama2, optimized for dialogue use cases. Both tasks take the list of entity types as an input argument, making it a multiple-choice task.

5.3 Cloze prompts with BERT-based models

For the first experimental setting, we use cloze-style prompts that perfectly fit masked language models (MLM). We replace the entities in the sentences with a masked token and use BERT-based models with an MLM objective. Multi-token entities are substituted with a single masked token. If multiple entities appear in the same sentence, only the initial entity occurring in the sentence is considered. The model's answers are limited to the predefined list of 151 entities. We do not provide more context than what is contained in the input sentence. We randomly select ten thousand sentences per entity type, for which we have ground truth annotations (the actual number of prompts after cleaning is given in the column *# prompts* in Table 2). An example of a cloze-style prompt is given in Figure 2. With this *Experiment MLM*, our objective is to assess whether the models can make predictions about the type of entity to expect based on contextual and syntactic cues. For instance, in the example presented in Figure 2, we assume that a human reader could deduce from the context that a location is the expected entity to fill the masked portion. Can an LM do the same?

5.4 QA prompts with Llama2

For the second experimental setting, *Experiment Llama2*, we use a template that briefly explains the task to the model and we input the predefined list of 151 entity types. To provide a simple task framing, we prompt the language model according to the following template: "*What entity types is {entity}*?", to which the model is asked to answer with the most probable entity type. Because of the format of the prompt, we use a text generation objective with an open-source, state-of-the-art auto-regressive LM, Llama2. We use the smallest available version of the model (7B parameters, to spare computing resources) and its fine-tuned version Llama2-chat, which is optimized for dialogue use cases. An example of this QA-style prompt is presented in Figure 3. In that experiment, the prompt explicitly mentions the entity, for example, here the question is *"What entity type is Nice?"* which makes it a simpler task compared to the task of *Experiment MLM*.

6 Experimental Results

We evaluate the results in terms of recall since we want to ensure capturing as many true positives as possible, and F1 score to assess the overall performance on the task. In this section, we compare the results in terms of LM used, length of the input entity, prompt type, and entity type, before conducting an error analysis in the section 6.5. The results of *Experiment MLM* are presented in Table 2 and the results of *Experiment Llama2* in Table 3.

6.1 Language Models Comparison

Given the high difficulty of the task, the choice between 151 entity types when accounting for the synonyms list, and the lack of description of the entities and extra context given, it is no surprise that the scores are relatively low. However, the goal of this work is not to reach the best accuracy, but rather to explore where the models succeed or fail. On *Experiment MLM*, results are generally lower than in *Experiment Llama2* which is firstly explained by the greater difficulty of the task of *Experiment MLM* and the relative lack of context provided for this task. In this experiment, Pile of Law is the model that performs the best on average, in terms of F1, retrieving 16.36% of entity types, with 9.47% in recall. The second best performing model is CaseHOLD with 15.29% average F1 and 8.58% average recall. This is despite LexLM's big-

Type \ Model	RoBERTa		DeBERTa		CaseHOLD		PoL		LexLM		# prompts
	R	**F1**	**R**	**F1**	**R**	**F1**	**R**	**F1**	**R**	**F1**	
LOCATION	0.058	0.110	0.108	0.194	0.070	0.131	0.336	**0.503**	0.055	0.104	9,913
DATE	0.036	0.069	0.100	**0.183**	0.034	0.065	0.025	0.048	0.071	0.133	9,442
NORP	0.037	0.072	0.035	0.067	0.031	0.060	0.032	0.062	0.065	**0.122**	9,986
ORG	0.088	**0.161**	0.066	0.123	0.081	0.149	0.018	0.036	0.074	0.138	9,947
CREDIBILITY	0.028	0.054	0.026	0.051	0.123	**0.219**	0.056	0.106	0.028	0.055	9,527
DETERMINATION	0.384	**0.555**	0.079	0.147	0.070	0.131	0.142	0.249	0.071	0.133	7,242
CLAIMANT_INFO	0.080	0.149	0.060	0.114	0.081	**0.150**	0.079	0.147	0.045	0.085	9,666
PROCEDURE	0.128	0.227	0.080	0.148	0.078	0.145	0.207	**0.344**	0.228	0.129	9,716
DOC_EVIDENCE	0.128	0.228	0.125	0.223	0.188	**0.317**	0.048	0.092	0.056	0.105	9,814
EXPLANATION	0.013	0.026	0.013	0.026	0.009	0.018	0.088	**0.161**	0.008	0.015	8,825
LEGAL_GROUND	0.029	0.056	0.048	0.091	0.045	0.087	0.041	0.079	0.061	**0.116**	9,640
LAW	0.093	0.170	0.203	0.337	0.237	**0.383**	0.061	0.115	0.066	0.124	9,128
LAW_CASE	0.079	0.146	0.071	0.133	0.058	0.109	0.106	**0.191**	0.091	0.167	9,290
LAW_REPORT	0.057	0.107	0.075	0.140	0.098	**0.178**	0.087	0.160	0.089	0.164	8,601

Table 2: Entity type prediction scores in a zero-shot setting, on cloze sentences, measured in Recall and F1 score across 2 generic LMs (RoBERTa and DeBERTa-V3), and 3 legal LMs (CaseHOLD, Pile of Law and LexLM)

Type	R	F1
LOCATION	**0.956**	**0.916**
DATE	0.730	0.575
NORP	0.211	0.118
ORG	0.098	0.051
LAW	0.100	0.053
CREDIBILITY	0.219	0.123
DETERMINATION	0.357	0.217
CLAIMANT_INFO	0.627	0.456
PROCEDURE	0.259	0.149
DOC_EVIDENCE	0.653	0.485
EXPLANATION	0.006	0.003
LEGAL_GROUND	0.022	0.011
LAW_CASE	0.034	0.017
LAW_REPORT	0.048	0.025

Table 3: Entity type prediction scores in a zero-shot setting, on QA-style prompts, measured in Recall and F1 score, with Llama2, on 10K prompts per entity

ger size, LexLM being the model that performs the worst across all, being outperformed by generic LMs RoBERTa and DeBERTa. For all entities except one, the model that achieved the best recall also achieved the best F1, highlighting the consistency in the precision. The only exception is the type `procedure` for which the best F1 is reached with Pile of Law and the best recall with LexLM.

6.2 Single-token vs Multi-token

An interesting point is that we did not impose any restrictions on the length of entities; the entities that tend to be longer are typically more abstract and closer to a piece of legal commonsense knowledge and reasoning, for example, `explanation`, `determination`, `credibilty` and `legal ground`. Interestingly the best overall F1 score in *Experiment MLM* is achieved for the type `determination`, reaching an F1 score of 55.5% (RoBERTa). For instance, an entity flagged as `determination` can as long as: *claimants are not convention refugees and not persons in need of protection*. While the other models achieve lower scores for this entity type, it is to note that the disparity between these relatively lengthy multi-token entities and those that are typically single tokens is not substantial (refer to Figure 4). This may be due to the nature of the task, which may mitigate such disparities compared to tasks like NER where the model has to retrieve the actual entity. In *Experiment Llama2*, shorter entities (that are also the most generic ones) are well recognized (`location`, `date`), with also good scores achieved on the types `determination`, `claimant_info`, `procedure`. Overall for both experiments and certainly due to the nature of the task of entity typing, it seems that the length of the initial entity to categorize does not have an impact on the results.

6.3 Prompt Templates Comparison

The scores are on average higher in the *Experiment Llama2* with a total average F1 score of 30.86% when *Experiment MLM* reaches an average of 14.46% across all types. However, as noted in

	Error Type	Prompt example	Prediction	Gold	%
MLM	Random Prediction	under <mask> of the Republic of China, they cannot take on a second citizenship	lawsuit	law	70.71
	Contextually Accurate	the applicant has not returned to <mask> since 2008	employment	location	12.43
	Closely Related	my colleague relied on this <mask> in her conclusion	ngo report	doc_evidence	16.86
Llama2	Random Prediction	What is *Subsection 648*?	country	law	22.22
	Closely Related	What is *vietnamese*?	country	nationality (norp)	18.52
	False Negative	What is *female claimant*?	female claimant	gender (claimant_info)	33.33
	Prompt Error	What is *removal order*?	It is a type of judicial decision.	procedure	25.93

Table 4: Error cases and the ratio of the different error types for both experiments, across all tested models

	Gen	CH	PoL	LexLM	Llama2
Generic	11.59	8.51	**20.42**	11.97	**63.26**
Gen Legal	17.98	**20.89**	15.40	12.48	**29.52**
Refugee Law	**10.01**	5.93	4.68	4.92	**13.03**

Table 5: Entity types prediction scores averaged on 3 groups: generic (location, date, norp), legal entities applicable to most legal domains (Gen Legal: org, law, claimant_info, procedure, doc_evidence, law_case), and legal entities specific to refugee law (Refugee Law: credibility, determination, explanation, legal_ground, law_report) *Gen* groups the results of RoBERTa and DeBERTa-v3, *CH* refers to CaseHOLD

the task description (5.1) the QA-based experiment is a relatively easier task, making the comparison difficult.

Based on the predicted entity types, it appears that the template suggested for *Experiment Llama2* is not consistently well comprehended, resulting in a lack of clarity regarding the task. In some cases, it returns not just one entity type, but multiple, leading to incorrect predictions. It seems that, instead of relying on manually crafted prompts and templates, which have been acknowledged to be su-optimal as mentioned by Jiang et al. (2020a), there is significant room for improvement in this regard.

6.4 Entity Types Comparison

For this evaluation, we categorize the type of entity into three groups: those that can be encountered in any text with the same meaning, those that are commonly found in legal texts, and those that are highly specific to the domain of the dataset, refugee law. The combined results are summarized in Table 5. Entities related to refugee law tend to yield the lowest performance across all models and settings. Pile of Law outperforms other models even on generic entities. At the same time, RoBERTa and DeBERTa surpass models specifically trained on legal data for generic legal entities, possibly due to larger exposure and a larger vocabulary.

6.5 Failure Cases Analysis

We identify four types of errors across the two experiments:

1. Random Prediction: this refers to cases where the predicted entity type is entirely random and unrelated to the context.

2. Contextually Accurate: this describes situations where the predicted entity type is incorrect, but within the context of the sentences, it is plausible in terms of syntax and meaning.

3. Closely Related: instances where the predicted entity class is incorrect, yet it is closely related to the actual gold entity type. For example, it misclassifies a legal ground (which is very precisely one of the 5 reasons for being granted refugee status, see Appendix A) for an explanation of the decision (which is more generic).

4. False Negative, it predicts an entity type that is not in the list of entity types given as input.

5. Prompt Error, if the answer provided deviates from the prompt instruction, we categorize it as incorrect; we consistently consider that an answer with more than five tokens is incorrect, as it signifies that the response extends beyond providing just the entity type.

***Experiment MLM* errors** To assess the occurrence of error types, we sample 10 errors per entity type per model, i.e. a total of 700 errors for this experiment. Table 4 presents the findings and an example per error type. There is no instance of a False Negative error; the models never predict an entity type that is not in the input predefined list as we constraint the model to a multiple-choice task, from our pre-defined list of entity types. The most common error is simply an incorrect prediction, with the second most frequent error being the prediction of a closely related entity. This may be due to the choice of categories, some of which express subtle legal nuances. Another positive sign is the presence of more than 10% of incorrect predictions that are nevertheless accurate in the context of the input sentence.

***Experiment Llama2* errors** Similarly, we sample 10 errors per entity type, i.e. a total of 135 errors. Table 4 presents the findings. It's worth noting that the use of QA-style prompts leads to a significant number of prompt errors and false negatives, which we believe could be mitigated to some extent by improving the initial prompt template in future work. Additionally, a common misclassification pattern occurs with `norp` entities, which are always adjectives, but are misclassified as their noun counterparts, as illustrated in the example provided in Table 4. Similarly, acronyms for tribunals (e.g., *RPD* for *Refugee Protection Division*) are classified as *units of length*, an issue that might be rectified by providing more contextual information. Finally, entities like *consistent explanation* are occasionally misclassified as `explanation` when they should be categorized as a `credibility` assessment, possibly due to missing adjectives or entity length-related challenges.

7 Conclusion

Our investigation includes LM selection, input entity length, prompt types, and entity types, in an attempt to understand model strengths and limitations. In summary, our study shows that Llama2 performs best on specific entities and displays potential for improvement with better prompting strategies. However, it also seems that Llama2 repeatedly overlooks syntactic cues. Masked language models mostly appear to be lacking sufficient context within our experimental setup, where they are confronted with a highly challenging task. Law-oriented LMs exhibit varying results, possibly influenced by training corpus differences, and the Pile of Law model shows the best performance on our *AsyLex* dataset. Despite inherent challenges, LMs can accurately identify certain entity types, including multi-token ones, but encounter difficulties with legal sub-domains like Refugee Law. Future research may explore optimized prompts and few-shot learning strategies. Furthermore, assessing the average precision of the entity type ranking predictions generated by the LM, and conducting experiments on additional datasets, would also be necessary.

References

Isabelle Augenstein, Leon Derczynski, and Kalina Bontcheva. 2017. Generalisation in named entity recognition: A quantitative analysis. *Computer Speech & Language*, 44:61–83.

Claire Barale, Michael Rovatsos, and Nehal Bhuta. 2023. Automated refugee case analysis: A NLP pipeline for supporting legal practitioners. In *Findings of the Association for Computational Linguistics: ACL 2023*, pages 2992–3005, Toronto, Canada. Association for Computational Linguistics.

Terra Blevins, Hila Gonen, and Luke Zettlemoyer. 2023. Prompting language models for linguistic structure. In *Proceedings of the 61st Annual Meeting of the Association for Computational Linguistics (Volume 1: Long Papers)*, pages 6649–6663, Toronto, Canada. Association for Computational Linguistics.

Tom Brown, Benjamin Mann, Nick Ryder, Melanie Subbiah, Jared D Kaplan, Prafulla Dhariwal, Arvind Neelakantan, Pranav Shyam, Girish Sastry, Amanda Askell, et al. 2020. Language models are few-shot learners. *Advances in neural information processing systems*, 33:1877–1901.

Ilias Chalkidis, Manos Fergadiotis, Prodromos Malakasiotis, Nikolaos Aletras, and Ion Androutsopoulos. 2020. LEGAL-BERT: The muppets straight out of law school. In *Findings of the Association for Computational Linguistics: EMNLP 2020*, pages 2898–2904, Online. Association for Computational Linguistics.

Ilias Chalkidis, Nicolas Garneau, Catalina Goanta, Daniel Katz, and Anders Søgaard. 2023. LeXFiles and LegalLAMA: Facilitating English multinational legal language model development. In *Proceedings of the 61st Annual Meeting of the Association for Computational Linguistics (Volume 1: Long Papers)*, pages 15513–15535, Toronto, Canada. Association for Computational Linguistics.

Eunsol Choi, Omer Levy, Yejin Choi, and Luke Zettlemoyer. 2018. Ultra-fine entity typing. In *Proceedings of the 56th Annual Meeting of the Association for Computational Linguistics (Volume 1: Long Papers)*, pages 87–96, Melbourne, Australia. Association for Computational Linguistics.

Hongliang Dai, Yangqiu Song, and Haixun Wang. 2021. Ultra-fine entity typing with weak supervision from a masked language model. In *Proceedings of the 59th Annual Meeting of the Association for Computational Linguistics and the 11th International Joint Conference on Natural Language Processing (Volume 1: Long Papers)*, pages 1790–1799, Online. Association for Computational Linguistics.

Elena V. Epure and Romain Hennequin. 2022. Probing pre-trained auto-regressive language models for named entity typing and recognition. In *Proceedings of the Thirteenth Language Resources and Evaluation Conference*, pages 1408–1417, Marseille, France. European Language Resources Association.

Aaron Gokaslan and Vanya Cohen. 2019. Openwebtext corpus.

Suchin Gururangan, Ana Marasović, Swabha Swayamdipta, Kyle Lo, Iz Beltagy, Doug Downey, and Noah A. Smith. 2020. Don't stop pretraining: Adapt language models to domains and tasks. In *Proceedings of the 58th Annual Meeting of the Association for Computational Linguistics*, pages 8342–8360, Online. Association for Computational Linguistics.

Adi Haviv, Jonathan Berant, and Amir Globerson. 2021. BERTese: Learning to speak to BERT. In *Proceedings of the 16th Conference of the European Chapter of the Association for Computational Linguistics: Main Volume*, pages 3618–3623, Online. Association for Computational Linguistics.

Pengcheng He, Jianfeng Gao, and Weizhu Chen. 2023. DeBERTav3: Improving deBERTa using ELECTRA-style pre-training with gradient-disentangled embedding sharing. In *The Eleventh International Conference on Learning Representations*.

Peter Henderson, Mark S. Krass, Lucia Zheng, Neel Guha, Christopher D. Manning, Dan Jurafsky, and Daniel E. Ho. 2022. Pile of law: Learning responsible data filtering from the law and a 256gb opensource legal dataset.

Zhengbao Jiang, Antonios Anastasopoulos, Jun Araki, Haibo Ding, and Graham Neubig. 2020a. X-FACTR: Multilingual factual knowledge retrieval from pretrained language models. In *Proceedings of the 2020 Conference on Empirical Methods in Natural Language Processing (EMNLP)*, pages 5943–5959, Online. Association for Computational Linguistics.

Zhengbao Jiang, Frank F. Xu, Jun Araki, and Graham Neubig. 2020b. How can we know what language models know? *Transactions of the Association for Computational Linguistics*, 8:423–438.

Bill Yuchen Lin, Dong-Ho Lee, Ming Shen, Ryan Moreno, Xiao Huang, Prashant Shiralkar, and Xiang Ren. 2020. TriggerNER: Learning with entity triggers as explanations for named entity recognition. In *Proceedings of the 58th Annual Meeting of the Association for Computational Linguistics*, pages 8503–8511, Online. Association for Computational Linguistics.

Yinhan Liu, Myle Ott, Naman Goyal, Jingfei Du, Mandar Joshi, Danqi Chen, Omer Levy, Mike Lewis, Luke Zettlemoyer, and Veselin Stoyanov. 2019. Roberta: A robustly optimized bert pretraining approach. *arXiv preprint arXiv:1907.11692*.

Sebastian Nagel. 2016.

Fabio Petroni, Tim Rocktäschel, Sebastian Riedel, Patrick Lewis, Anton Bakhtin, Yuxiang Wu, and Alexander Miller. 2019. Language models as knowledge bases? In *Proceedings of the 2019 Conference on Empirical Methods in Natural Language Processing and the 9th International Joint Conference on Natural Language Processing (EMNLP-IJCNLP)*, pages 2463–2473, Hong Kong, China. Association for Computational Linguistics.

Guanghui Qin and Jason Eisner. 2021. Learning how to ask: Querying LMs with mixtures of soft prompts. In *Proceedings of the 2021 Conference of the North American Chapter of the Association for Computational Linguistics: Human Language Technologies*, pages 5203–5212, Online. Association for Computational Linguistics.

Alec Radford, Jeffrey Wu, Rewon Child, David Luan, Dario Amodei, Ilya Sutskever, et al. 2019. Language models are unsupervised multitask learners. *OpenAI blog*, 1(8):9.

Jaromir Savelka. 2023. Unlocking practical applications in legal domain: Evaluation of gpt for zero-shot semantic annotation of legal texts. In *Proceedings of the Nineteenth International Conference on Artificial Intelligence and Law*, ICAIL '23, page 447–451, New York, NY, USA. Association for Computing Machinery.

Yongliang Shen, Zeqi Tan, Shuhui Wu, Wenqi Zhang, Rongsheng Zhang, Yadong Xi, Weiming Lu, and Yueting Zhuang. 2023. PromptNER: Prompt locating and typing for named entity recognition. In *Proceedings of the 61st Annual Meeting of the Association for Computational Linguistics (Volume 1: Long Papers)*, pages 12492–12507, Toronto, Canada. Association for Computational Linguistics.

Simone Tedeschi and Roberto Navigli. 2022. MultiNERD: A multilingual, multi-genre and fine-grained dataset for named entity recognition (and disambiguation). In *Findings of the Association for Computational Linguistics: NAACL 2022*, pages 801–812, Seattle, United States. Association for Computational Linguistics.

Hugo Touvron, Louis Martin, Kevin Stone, Peter Albert, Amjad Almahairi, Yasmine Babaei, Nikolay Bashlykov, Soumya Batra, Prajjwal Bhargava, Shruti Bhosale, Dan Bikel, Lukas Blecher, Cristian Canton Ferrer, Moya Chen, Guillem Cucurull, David Esiobu, Jude Fernandes, Jeremy Fu, Wenyin Fu, Brian Fuller, Cynthia Gao, Vedanuj Goswami, Naman Goyal, Anthony Hartshorn, Saghar Hosseini, Rui Hou, Hakan Inan, Marcin Kardas, Viktor Kerkez, Madian Khabsa, Isabel Kloumann, Artem Korenev, Punit Singh Koura, Marie-Anne Lachaux, Thibaut Lavril, Jenya Lee, Diana Liskovich, Yinghai Lu, Yuning Mao, Xavier Martinet, Todor Mihaylov, Pushkar Mishra, Igor Molybog, Yixin Nie, Andrew Poulton, Jeremy Reizenstein, Rashi Rungta, Kalyan Saladi, Alan Schelten, Ruan Silva, Eric Michael Smith, Ranjan Subramanian, Xiaoqing Ellen Tan, Binh Tang, Ross Taylor, Adina Williams, Jian Xiang Kuan, Puxin Xu, Zheng Yan, Iliyan Zarov, Yuchen Zhang, Angela Fan, Melanie Kambadur, Sharan Narang, Aurelien Rodriguez, Robert Stojnic, Sergey Edunov, and Thomas Scialom. 2023. Llama 2: Open foundation and fine-tuned chat models.

Trieu H Trinh and Quoc V Le. 2018. A simple method for commonsense reasoning. *arXiv preprint arXiv:1806.02847*.

Chaojun Xiao, Xueyu Hu, Zhiyuan Liu, Cunchao Tu, and Maosong Sun. 2021. Lawformer: A pre-trained language model for chinese legal long documents. *AI Open*, 2:79–84.

Zhangyue Yin, Qiushi Sun, Qipeng Guo, Jiawen Wu, Xipeng Qiu, and Xuanjing Huang. 2023. Do large language models know what they don't know? In *Findings of the Association for Computational Linguistics: ACL 2023*, pages 8653–8665, Toronto, Canada. Association for Computational Linguistics.

Wenzheng Zhang, Wenyue Hua, and Karl Stratos. 2022. Entqa: Entity linking as question answering. In *International Conference on Learning Representations (ICLR)*.

Lucia Zheng, Neel Guha, Brandon R. Anderson, Peter Henderson, and Daniel E. Ho. 2021. When does pretraining help? assessing self-supervised learning for law and the casehold dataset. In *Proceedings of the 18th International Conference on Artificial Intelligence and Law*. Association for Computing Machinery.

Haoxi Zhong, Zhipeng Guo, Cunchao Tu, Chaojun Xiao, Zhiyuan Liu, and Maosong Sun. 2018. Legal judgment prediction via topological learning. In *Proceedings of the 2018 Conference on Empirical Methods in Natural Language Processing*, pages 3540–3549, Brussels, Belgium. Association for Computational Linguistics.

Yukun Zhu, Ryan Kiros, Rich Zemel, Ruslan Salakhutdinov, Raquel Urtasun, Antonio Torralba, and Sanja Fidler. 2015. Aligning books and movies: Towards story-like visual explanations by watching movies and reading books. In *Proceedings of the IEEE international conference on computer vision, ICCV*, pages 19–27.

Appendix

A Legal Entity Types Description

B Detail of the Extended Entity Types List

C Error Types Detail per LM for *Experiment MLM*

Type	Description	Examples
LOCATION	cities, countries, regions	"toronto, ontario"
DATE	absolute or relative dates or periods	"june, 4th 1996", "two years"
NORP	adjectives of nationalities, religious, political or ethnic groups or communities	"hutu", "nigerian", "christian"
ORG	tribunals, companies, NGOs	"immigration appeal division", "human rights watch"
CREDIBILITY	mentions of credibility	"lack of evidence", "inconsistencies"
DETERMINATION	outcome of the decision (accept/reject)	"appeal is dismissed", "not a convention refugee"
CLAIMANT_INFO	age, gender, citizenship, occupation	"28 year old", "citizen of Iran", "female"
PROCEDURE	steps in the claim and legal procedure events	"removal order", "sponsorship for application"
DOC_EVIDENCE	pieces of evidence, proofs, supporting documents	"passport", "medical record", "marriage certificate"
EXPLANATION	reasons given by the panel for the determination	"fear of persecution", "no protection by the state"
LEGAL_GROUND	referring to the Convention, refugee status is granted for reasons of race, religion, nationality, membership of a particular social group or political opinion	"homosexual", "christian"
LAW	citations: legislation and international conventions	"section 1(a) of the convention"
LAW_CASE	citations: case law and past decided cases	"xxx v. minister of canada, 1994"
LAW_REPORT	country reports written by NGOs or the United Nations	"amnesty international: police and military torture of women in mexico, 2016"

Table 6: Pre-defined list of legal entity types

Type	Extended List
LOCATION	city, country, region, state, province, area, nation, land, republic, district, territory, division, zone
DATE	date, day of the month, appointment, particular date, date stamp, time, timestamp, calendar date, schedule
NORP	nationality, religious community, political group, ethnic groups, community, racial group, party, faction, ideological group, belief community
ORG	tribunal, firm, ngo, company, corporation, business, nonprofit, association, charity, court, judicial body
CREDIBILITY	plausibility, authenticity, integrity, trustworthiness, reliability, credibility, believability, credibility, credibleness
DETERMINATION	verdict", result, resolution, judgment, approval, denial, decline, rejection, approval, determination, finding, conclusion, decision, grant, refusal, positive decision, negative decision
CLAIMANT_INFO	data, employment, resident, national, inhabitant, information, gender, age, citizen, citizenship, sex, job, occupation, profession
PROCEDURE	affidavit, documentary evidence, proof, testimony, exhibit, record, file, paperwork, operation, procedure, legal procedure, legal process, judicial procedure, legal steps, judicial process
DOC_EVIDENCE	proof, evidence, document, written document, written evidence, written proof, written record, written report, written statement, written testimony, written witness statement
EXPLANATION	explanation, clarification, interpretation
LEGAL_GROUND	reason, ground, legal ground, justification, rationale, foundation, legal basis, legal justification
LAW	convention, international convention, law, legislation, legal code, treaty, agreement, protocol, statute
LAW_CASE	citation, jurisprudence, case, law, case law, legal case, lawsuit, legal matter, legal precedent, judicial decisions, legal rulings
LAW_REPORT	country report, report, official report, written report, ngo report, national report, state report, regional report, nonprofit report, non-governmental organization report, charity report

Table 7: Extended pre-defined list of legal entity types (151 types)

Error Type	RoBERTa	DeBERTa	CaseHOLD	PoL	LexLM	# Total	%
Random Prediction	109	81	90	112	103	495	70.71
Contextually Accurate	7	27	25	16	12	87	12.43
Closely Related	24	32	25	12	25	118	16.86
False Negative	-	-	-	-	-	-	0.00
Total	140	140	140	140	140	700	100

Table 8: Error types figures per (number of occurrences) and in percentage for all studied LM

Pretrained Language Models v. Court Ruling Predictions: A Case Study on a Small Dataset of French Court of Appeal Rulings

Olivia Vaudaux,[1,2,3] **Caroline Bazzoli,**[1] **Maximin Coavoux,**[2] **Géraldine Vial**[3] **and Étienne Vergès**[3]
[1]Univ. Grenoble Alpes, CNRS, UMR 5525, VetAgro Sup, Grenoble INP, TIMC, 38000 Grenoble, France
[2]Univ. Grenoble Alpes, CNRS, Grenoble INP, LIG, 38000 Grenoble, France
[3]Univ. Grenoble Alpes, CRJ, EA 1965
olivia.vaudaux@gmail.com, first.last@univ-grenoble-alpes.fr

Abstract

NLP systems are increasingly used in the law domain, either by legal institutions or by the industry. As a result there is a pressing need to characterize their strengths and weaknesses and understand their inner workings. This article presents a case study on the task of judicial decision prediction, on a small dataset from French Courts of Appeal. Specifically, our dataset of around 1000 decisions is about the habitual place of residency of children from divorced parents. The task consists in predicting, from the facts and reasons of the documents, whether the court rules that children should live with their mother or their father. Instead of feeding the whole document to a classifier, we carefully construct the dataset to make sure that the input to the classifier does not contain any 'spoilers' (it is often the case in court rulings that information all along the document mentions the final decision). Our results are mostly negative: even classifiers based on French pretrained language models (Flaubert, JuriBERT) do not classify the decisions with a reasonable accuracy. However, they can extract the decision when it is part of the input. With regards to these results, we argue that there is a strong caveat when constructing legal NLP datasets automatically.

1 Introduction

Natural language processing (NLP) has now many applications in the legal domain, and is used in practice to provide tools for law practitioners, such as lawyers or judges (e.g. for information retrieval, document classification), to quantify judicial risks in specific cases. Judicial decision prediction through NLP tools is also important for law researchers to identify the factors that most influence the final decision of a case, characterize judge's reasoning process, and help data annotation procedures.

In this paper, we present a case study on the prediction of the verdict ruling on the habitual residency of children in appeal cases from French courts. These documents follow a typical structure (facts, judgement of the first court whose ruling was the object of an appeal, decision itself). However, the structure is only implicit (sections are not titled), and judges' writing is not standardised and differs a lot from one court of appeal to another. Finally, it is often the case that information of each type (facts, reasons, decision) are scattered through the document. As a result, the document might contain 'spoilers' for the decision itself at various places in the document.

In order to assess the ability of BERT-style language models to infer a verdict from the legal content itself, rather than the full text of the document, we implemented an annotation campaign aiming at assigning a semantic type to every segment in each document as: (i) facts (ii) information about the first judgment (iii) reasons for the decision (iv) decision itself (containing explicitly the variable to predict) (v) none of these types. Thanks to this annotation procedure, lead by law experts, we compare the usefulness of various types of inputs for several types of classifiers, including bag-of-n-grams classifiers and BERT-based classifiers. In particular, we used 3 French pretrained language models: FlauBERT (Le et al., 2020) and CamemBERT (Martin et al., 2020) that were trained on generic-domain data, and JuriBERT (Douka et al., 2021), that has been specifically trained on French legal texts.

In summary, our contributions are as follows:

- We construct a dataset of 1k judicial decisions annotated at the segment level by law experts (law professors and PhD students);
- A set of empirical results on a judicial decision prediction task on this dataset;
- In regards to our (mostly negative) results, we argue for the need for a careful curation of

Proceedings of the Natural Legal Language Processing Workshop 2023, pages 38–43
December 7, 2023

automatically constructed datasets for legal NLP.

2 Related Work

Predicting the outcome of a judicial decisions based on a textual input is rather recent and has first been applied to English decisions from the European Court of Human Rights (ECtHR Aletras et al., 2016). In particular, Aletras et al. (2016) constructed a dataset of ECtHR decisions focusing on cases about a few articles of the European Convention on Human Rights, and evaluated bag-of-n-grams approaches.

Subsequently, several studies were made on the ECHR corpus, consisting of approximately 11 500 rulings from 1959 to our days. Medvedeva et al. (2020) and Liu and Chen (2017) evaluated various linear classifiers. Kaur and Bozic (2019) used deep neural networks based on convolutional networks. O'Sullivan and Beel (2019) used word embeddings pretrained on documents from the ECtHR data. Chalkidis et al. (2019) introduced Legal-BERT, a BERT-style model pretrained on legal data (legislative texts, ECtHR cases and American contracts), and evaluated it on the ECtHR dataset. Other common dataset include decisions from the US supreme court, e.g. Katz et al. (2014) use decision trees to predict the votes of Judges. We refer the reader to Medvedeva et al. (2023) for a general survey on judicial decision prediction. In contrast to these publications, we focus on French, and on a very specific type of litigation: the habitual residency of children of divorced parents. Moreover we use both linear classifiers and deep nets based on fine-tuning pretrained language models.

As regards legal NLP applied to French, Şulea et al. (2017) and Sulea et al. (2017) evaluated SVM classifiers on the prediction of the area of a case, as well as its ruling, on decisions from the French Supreme Court (*Cour de Cassation*). Salaün et al. (2020) used pretrained language models such as Flaubert (Le et al., 2020) and Camembert (Martin et al., 2020) to predict the outcome of cases about conflicts between a tenant and a landlord in Québec. They observed that pretrained language models outperformed linear classifiers. Our dataset is on another type of litigation (habitual residency of children) and we focus on the manual construction of our dataset, instead of automatically constructing it. Finally, Douka et al. (2021) introduced JuriBERT, trained on *Légifrance*, an official website publishing all French law and evaluated it on topic classification tasks for documents from the Cour de Cassation (highest court in France).

3 Data

In France, when parents of minor children separate, they must decide on their children's place of residency. If the parents are unable to agree on a place of residency, the matter is referred to a court which, after hearing each parent, issues a ruling. We study the three principal outcomes: children live with their mother, their father, or in alternating residency. If the outcome of the lower court is not suitable for at least one parent, they can make an appeal to retry the case. New judges re-examine the facts and confirm or overturn the judgment handed down by the first court. These are the rulings we'll be using for the classification experiment.

We collected 987 rulings from French Courts of Appeal from the Jurica[1] databasis, that we accessed through a legal publisher (LexisNexis). The rulings have the following structure:

1. The metadata of the trial (date, place of appeal court, trial number, etc.);
2. The *facts*: the parties (the parents) are introduced along with their lawyers, children, and the composition of the court.[2];
3. The prior *judgment* under appeal is described, and the parties claims' and arguments are set out;
4. The *reasons* of the Court of Appeal's decision: the judge explains the decision to come based on sections of the law and the facts provided by the parties;
5. The reasons lead to the **decision** taken by the court: the reversal or confirmation of the first-instance judgment, from which we can infer the label we want to predict.

Although the structure of court rulings in sections (facts, judgment, reasons, decision) is conventional, judges' practices vary a lot in the length of these sections. For example, the facts section might be extremely short or very verbose, and its content

[1]Jurica is no longer maintained due to a recent change in policy about legal open data.

[2]The publisher replaced names by their initial in an effort to comply with French personal data laws (1978 Data Protection Act).

may not be restricted to what lawyers define as facts. Moreover information about *facts* or *reasons* may be scattered through the document and not only occur in their dedicated section. Therefore, instead of relying on the structure of the documents to extract information (and let the model be exposed to potential 'spoilers' about the decision), we rely on the manual annotation of every segment of the document as either (i) fact (ii) judgement (iii) reason (iv) decision, or (v) not relevant. The manual annotations were carried out by two law professors (who are coauthors of the paper and designed the annotation guidelines), one law post-doc researcher and one law graduate students who were trained for the task.

Due to the time required to carry out annotations, each document was annotated by a single annotator, so we did not compute interannotator agreement scores.

Annotating the rulings was quite challenging, especially to differentiate the facts and the reasons, because depending on the judge's method, the parties' claims and arguments can be set out in the reasons to justify the verdict. Therefore, in several rulings, the *facts* category is limited to the names and birth dates of parents and their children.

Prediction Task Our goal was to predict the outcome of appeal cases ruling on the residency of children among three possible outcomes: they live with their mother (label M, 50%), their father (F, 33%) or in alternate residency (B for both, 17%).[3]

We trained and evaluated classifiers settings in several settings, depending on the information input to the model: (i) F+R: Facts+Reasons (ii) F+R+J: Facts+Reasons+Judgment (iii) Decision (iv) Decision+Judgment. The last two settings are meant to assess the model's ability to extract the information about the decision,[4] whereas the first two assess the model's ability to make inferences about the judges' reasoning.

[3] An alternative way of framing the task with two labels would be to predict whether the first judgment is (i) confirmed (ii) reversed. However, these two labels do not provide the same information as the three-label task we chose, since labels have to be interpreted with regards to the first judgment, and the second label (reversed judgement) is not as informative (2 possible outcomes).

[4] Sometimes the *decision* text only mentions that the first judgment is confirmed or overturned, making it necessary to know what the first judgment is to infer the label correctly.

4 Models

Baseline We use various classical classifiers as baselines, namely:

- a multinomial naive Bayes (MNB);
- a k-Nearest Neighbors (k-NN) with Manhattan distance;
- a multiclass Support Vector Machine (SVM);
- a forest of decision trees, with a predefined number of trees created, where the final decision is made on the basis of the label most predicted by the trees;
- a Multi-Layer Perceptron (MLP) with 1 hidden layer of 100 units, with a *ReLU* activation function.

We vectorize the texts using bag-of-n-grams methods: either unweigthed, or weighted by TF-IDF. We use both unigrams, trigrams or both (based on preliminary experiments). For each algorithm, we made a Cross Validation to determine the best hyperparameters of each classifier. All baselines were implemented with Scikit-Learn library (Pedregosa et al., 2011).

Language Models As regards pretrained language models, we used FlauBERT (Le et al., 2020) and CamemBERT (Martin et al., 2020), two generic-purpose pretrained models for French, as well as JuriBERT (Douka et al., 2021), a language model trained only on data from the legal domain.

Because of the 512 tokens limitation of language models, the classifiers could not read the entire data in input, and thus did not make the difference between F+R and F+R+J, or didn't have all the argumentation of the judge. Therefore, we chunked each document based on line breaks, encode each chunk separately with the language model, and run a bi-LSTM (2 layers of 256 units) on the chunk representations to obtain a fixed-size vector for the whole document. We use dropout before feeding the representation to a classification layer.

Finally, to tokenize the data, we used the tokenizers associated with each language models, provided by the platform *Hugging Face*, and the associated library *transformers* (Wolf et al., 2020).

5 Experiments

Before starting data processing, we split the corpus into three stratified subsets: training (68%), testing (20%) and validation (12%).

Input	Language Model	Accuracy	F1-Score
Facts + Reasons	MNB+ bag-of-unigrams without TF-IDF	**0.57**	**0.54**
	FlauBERT	0.51	0.39
	CamemBERT	0.52	0.44
	JuriBERT	0.48	0.42
Facts + Reasons + Judgment	MLP + bag of-trigrams without TF-IDF	**0.56**	**0.50**
	FlauBERT	0.48	0.36
	CamemBERT	0.49	0.43
	JuriBERT	0.55	0.42
Decision	MLP + bag of-trigrams without TF-IDF	0.89	0.88
	FlauBERT	**0.90**	**0.89**
	CamemBERT	0.88	0.88
	JuriBERT	0.85	0.86
Decision + Judgment	MLP + bag of-trigrams without TF-IDF	0.74	0.69
	FlauBERT	0.95	0.94
	CamemBERT	0.92	0.92
	JuriBERT	**0.96**	**0.96**

Table 1: Accuracy and F1-Score score for the best baseline in each setting and for the three classifiers based on language models: FlauBERT, CamemBERT & JuriBERT. MLP : Multi-Layer Perceptron ; MNB : multinomial naive Bayes.

The BERT-based classifiers were trained for 80 epochs, with a batch size of 1, on a GPU. We used the AdamW optimizer (Loshchilov and Hutter, 2019) to minimize the loss function (negative log likelihood), and a scheduler with warmup, to vary the learning rate for a few warm-up periods. We tuned the learning rate ($\{10^{-6}, 2 \cdot 10^{-6}, 5 \cdot 10^{-6}\}$ for FlauBERT, $\{10^{-5}, 10^{-6}, 2 \cdot 10^{-6}, 5 \cdot 10^{-6}\}$, $\{10^{-5}, 2 \cdot 10^{-5}, 2 \cdot 10^{-6}, 5 \cdot 10^{-6}\}$ for JuriBERT) and the dropout value (0.15, 0.25)

For each classifier, we selected the best models based on validation F1 score (macro-average over classes. We also report accuracy in results.

Results and Discussion The test results for the best baseline (as selected on the validation set) in each setting and for the three classifiers based on language models are presented in Table 1. As regards the best baseline, we note that the best results were obtained on the *decision* and the *judgment + decision*, i.e. the parts of the rulings with the outcome explicitly stated. We found out that the MLP with bag-of-trigrams without TF-IDF weighting performed the best on all categories, except for the *facts + reasons*, where the multinomial naive Bayes algorithm with bag-of-unigrams without TF-IDF weighting reached the highest score. Finally, the results for F+R and F+R+J input are below 60%, slighlty above the most-frequent-label baseline which scores 50%.

For the language models, the categories with the highest results were those with the verdict stated. These results are even better than those of the baseline, exceeding 90% accuracy. The F1-score is also very high, showing it has nothing to do with the imbalance of the corpus.

Overall, we conclude that the classifiers based on pretrained language models have no difficulty reading over the decision and inferring the label (judgment+decision setting), however they struggle to infer what the decision will be when they are fed only the facts, reasons and judgment information. We hypothesize that the difficulty stems from the length of documents (on average 1095 tokens for F+R+J input). Moreover the key information usable to make a reasonable prediction is often scarce: most of the reasons cite the relevant articles and laws (that are not predictive of the output but make counfounding factors), which makes it hard to distinguish information that is important for the decision from irrelevant information. Finally, the documents do not follow standardized writing and differ considerably between each other (depending on the writer and the tradition of the local court).

The mismatch in results between settings with and without *decision* is an argument in our opinion in favour of the need to manually curate datasets for legal NLP, rather than only relying on automatic construction.

Human performance on the task As a control experiment, we assessed the performance of humans (either law experts or laypeople) on the task, on a sample of 100 documents, where humans were shown the F+R input, and had to make a guess at the output. Both law experts and laypeople had accuracies between 89 and 96%, which shows that the inputs contain enough information to predict the label.

6 Conclusion

Our experiments have shown the limitations of language models on judicial documents, since classifiers based on these models fail to understand the textual input data. They perform well when the verdict is already given, but fail when the text is more important and requires a deeper analytical reading, during the court's argumentation for example.

On the question of children's habitual residency, the subject is far too sensitive to entrust the task of deciding to an AI, and we can only imagine complementary tools, making it possible to reduce the duration of procedures, to support citizens in putting together their case or to help the parties' lawyers. By successfully processing data in such a way that a classifier can identify the most relevant terms and phrases, it would be possible to find the 'winning arguments,' those that convince the judge or that can tip a case over the edge. This could then help lawyers to build their arguments, by giving them access to these elements in cases similar to their own.

Ethics Statement

NLP applied to legal decisions raises several key ethical questions. Processing legal decision is important for understanding how legal reasoning work, and might also be used to analyse judges' biases in their decisions. However, as all technological tools, it is prone to dual use (Hovy and Spruit, 2016). The main risk is that institutions implement such models to replace judges, with harmful consequences, since machine learning systems are known to amplify biases they are exposed to in the training data, and are oftentimes not easily interpretable in their predictions, which makes unusable in a context where they may have an impact on humans.

Regarding personal data, the legal publisher who provided the data did not anonymize the decisions to a GDPR compliant standard. Indeed, they only replaced surnames with initials, but kept firstnames and town names unchanged. As a result, we are unable to release the annotated data. We acknowledge that not doing so is a hindrance for reproducibility and open science. In this case, we judge that personal data safety should be prioritized.

Acknowledgements

We thank Chen Chen for working on a pilot study that led to this paper, as well as Nour Safa (PhD student at Université Grenoble Alpes) and Djohar Sidhoum-Rahal (then a post-doc at Université Grenoble Alpes) for their work on the annotation of the dataset. We acknowledge the financial support of MIAI@Grenoble Alpes (ANR-19-P3IA-0003).

References

Nikolaos Aletras, Dimitrios Tsarapatsanis, Daniel Preoţiuc-Pietro, and Vasileios Lampos. 2016. Predicting judicial decisions of the european court of human rights: A natural language processing perspective. *PeerJ computer science*, 2:e93.

Ilias Chalkidis, Ion Androutsopoulos, and Nikolaos Aletras. 2019. Neural legal judgment prediction in English. In *Proceedings of the 57th Annual Meeting of the Association for Computational Linguistics*, pages 4317–4323, Florence, Italy. Association for Computational Linguistics.

Stella Douka, Hadi Abdine, Michalis Vazirgiannis, Rajaa El Hamdani, and David Restrepo Amariles. 2021. JuriBERT: A masked-language model adaptation for French legal text. In *Proceedings of the Natural Legal Language Processing Workshop 2021*, pages 95–101, Punta Cana, Dominican Republic. Association for Computational Linguistics.

Dirk Hovy and Shannon L. Spruit. 2016. The social impact of natural language processing. In *Proceedings of the 54th Annual Meeting of the Association for Computational Linguistics (Volume 2: Short Papers)*, pages 591–598, Berlin, Germany. Association for Computational Linguistics.

Daniel Martin Katz, Michael J Bommarito II au2, and Josh Blackman. 2014. Predicting the behavior of the supreme court of the united states: A general approach.

Arshdeep Kaur and Bojan Bozic. 2019. Convolutional neural network-based automatic prediction of judgments of the european court of human rights. In *AICS*, pages 458–469.

Hang Le, Loïc Vial, Jibril Frej, Vincent Segonne, Maximin Coavoux, Benjamin Lecouteux, Alexandre Allauzen, Benoit Crabbé, Laurent Besacier, and Didier Schwab. 2020. FlauBERT: Unsupervised language model pre-training for French. In *Proceedings of the 12th Language Resources and Evaluation Conference*, pages 2479–2490, Marseille, France. European Language Resources Association.

Zhenyu Liu and Huanhuan Chen. 2017. A predictive performance comparison of machine learning models for judicial cases. In *2017 IEEE Symposium series on computational intelligence (SSCI)*, pages 1–6. IEEE.

Ilya Loshchilov and Frank Hutter. 2019. Decoupled weight decay regularization. In *7th International Conference on Learning Representations, ICLR 2019, New Orleans, LA, USA, May 6-9, 2019*. OpenReview.net.

Louis Martin, Benjamin Muller, Pedro Javier Ortiz Suárez, Yoann Dupont, Laurent Romary, Éric de la Clergerie, Djamé Seddah, and Benoît Sagot. 2020. CamemBERT: a tasty French language model. In *Proceedings of the 58th Annual Meeting of the Association for Computational Linguistics*, pages 7203–7219, Online. Association for Computational Linguistics.

Masha Medvedeva, Michel Vols, and Martijn Wieling. 2020. Using machine learning to predict decisions of the european court of human rights. *Articial Intelligence and Law*, 28(2):237–266.

Masha Medvedeva, Martijn Wieling, and Michel Vols. 2023. Rethinking the field of automatic prediction of court decisions. *Artificial Intelligence and Law*, 31(1):195–212.

Conor O'Sullivan and Joeran Beel. 2019. Predicting the outcome of judicial decisions made by the european court of human rights. *CoRR*, abs/1912.10819.

Fabian Pedregosa, Gaël Varoquaux, Alexandre Gramfort, Vincent Michel, Bertrand Thirion, Olivier Grisel, Mathieu Blondel, Peter Prettenhofer, Ron Weiss, Vincent Dubourg, et al. 2011. Scikit-learn: Machine learning in Python. *Journal of Machine Learning Research*, 12(Oct):2825–2830.

Olivier Salaün, Philippe Langlais, Andrés Lou, Hannes Westermann, and Karim Benyekhlef. 2020. Analysis and multilabel classification of quebec court decisions in the domain of housing law. *Natural Language Processing and Information Systems*, 12089:135 – 143.

Octavia-Maria Sulea, Marcos Zampieri, Shervin Malmasi, Mihaela Vela, Liviu P. Dinu, and Josef van Genabith. 2017. Exploring the use of text classification in the legal domain. *CoRR*, abs/1710.09306.

Octavia-Maria Şulea, Marcos Zampieri, Mihaela Vela, and Josef van Genabith. 2017. Predicting the law area and decisions of French Supreme Court cases. In *Proceedings of the International Conference Recent Advances in Natural Language Processing, RANLP 2017*, pages 716–722, Varna, Bulgaria. INCOMA Ltd.

Thomas Wolf, Lysandre Debut, Victor Sanh, Julien Chaumond, Clement Delangue, Anthony Moi, Pierric Cistac, Tim Rault, Remi Louf, Morgan Funtowicz, Joe Davison, Sam Shleifer, Patrick von Platen, Clara Ma, Yacine Jernite, Julien Plu, Canwen Xu, Teven Le Scao, Sylvain Gugger, Mariama Drame, Quentin Lhoest, and Alexander Rush. 2020. Transformers: State-of-the-art natural language processing. In *Proceedings of the 2020 Conference on Empirical Methods in Natural Language Processing: System Demonstrations*, pages 38–45, Online. Association for Computational Linguistics.

Italian Legislative Text Classification for Gazzetta Ufficiale

Marco Rovera,[1] Alessio Palmero Aprosio,[1] Francesco Greco,[2]
Mariano Lucchese,[2] Sara Tonelli,[1] Antonio Antetomaso [2]
[1]Fondazione Bruno Kessler, Trento, Italy
[2]Istituto Poligrafico e Zecca dello Stato, Rome, Italy
{m.rovera, aprosio, satonelli}@fbk.eu
{f.greco, m.lucchese, a.antetomaso}@ipzs.it

Abstract

This work introduces a novel, extensive annotated corpus for multi-label legislative text classification in Italian, based on legal acts from the Gazzetta Ufficiale, the official source of legislative information of the Italian state. The annotated dataset, which we released to the community, comprises over 363,000 titles of legislative acts, spanning over 30 years from 1988 until 2022. Moreover, we evaluate four models for text classification on the dataset, demonstrating how using only the acts' titles can achieve top-level classification performance, with a micro F1-score of 0.87. Also, our analysis shows how Italian domain-adapted legal models do not outperform general-purpose models on the task. Models' performance can be checked by users via a demonstrator system provided in support of this work.

1 Introduction

The *Gazzetta Ufficiale*[1] (GU), in both its printed and digital editions, is the official source of the Italian Republic through which every legislative act issued by Italian central and peripheral institutions, like the Parliament, the Constitutional Court, the Ministeries, the regional administrations, among others, is brought to the attention of citizens. This official journal plays a key role in Italian law-making, as for any legislative measure to enter into effect, its publication in the GU is explicitly required by law. The Istituto Poligrafico e Zecca dello Stato[2] (IPZS), based in Rome, is in charge of editing and publishing the *Gazzetta.* A crucial step in the publication process is the assignment of each legislative measure to one or more labels from a subject index to concisely express its main semantic content and ease future search. However, so far this annotation has been carried out only manually, relying on a set of annotators that needed to be carefully trained to master around 1,600 labels available in the taxonomy. In order to support this task, reduce manual effort and ensure future consistency, we develop an automatic pipeline for the classification of GU documents. The task is particularly challenging due to the large number of labels, their different nature (i.e. mandatory vs. optional), the uneven representation of some categories and the different topics covered in the data. In our classification experiments we compare different transformer models for Italian, focusing in particular on performance differences between general-purpose and legal adapted models. We release the classification models for reproducibility, which can also be tested through our online demo.[3] We also make available a GitHub repository[4] with the annotated dataset used for our experiments, which consists of over 363k act titles from the General Series, manually annotated by domain experts.

2 Related Work

In the legal domain, text classification has an established tradition, both in the monolingual (Šarić et al., 2014; Papaloukas et al., 2021) and in the multi-lingual setting (Steinberger et al., 2006, 2012; Chalkidis et al., 2019; Avram et al., 2021; Chalkidis et al., 2021). Moreover, the large availability of legal data, produced by national and supranational public institutions, set the stage for the development of domain-adapted models (Chalkidis et al., 2020; Douka et al., 2021; Masala et al., 2021; Licari and Comandè, 2022). As for Italian, a multi-label classification system for bills has been proposed by De Angelis et al. (2022), based on Bi-GRU architecture using static word embeddings and employing a dataset of 28k legal document tagged with the TESEO thesaurus. In our work, conversely, we

[1]`https://www.gazzettaufficiale.it`
[2]`https://www.ipzs.it/ext/index.html`
[3]`https://dh-server.fbk.eu/ipzs-ui-demo/`
[4]`https://github.com/dhfbk/gazzetta-ufficiale`

Proceedings of the Natural Legal Language Processing Workshop 2023, pages 44–50
December 7, 2023

compare the performance of different BERT-based models (Devlin et al., 2019) for Italian, including domain-adapted ones (Licari and Comandè, 2022), on a large multi-label legal dataset covering 35 years of publication in the Gazzetta Ufficiale.

3 Gazzetta Ufficiale Subject Index

Each Italian legislative act entering the GU has to be manually assigned one or more thematic labels to classify its semantic content. Such labels, provided by the GU Subject Index, are then used by the data administrators for classification (in the printed edition) and for indexing and retrieval of Italian legislative acts (in the digital version). The manual labelling has been performed by a pool of expert annotators, trained by the data administration institution, over a time span of almost 35 years.

Layer	N. of unique labels
`Open Labels` (M)	781
`Closed Labels` (O)	1,019
`References` (O)	149
`Summaries` (O)	71

Table 1: Layered structure of the GU Subject Index. M = Mandatory, O = Optional.

Table 1 summarizes the structure of the Subject Index used for annotation. The resource is organized on four levels: *Voci Aperte* (Open Labels), *Voci Chiuse* (Closed Labels), *Riferimenti* (References) and *Sommarietti* (Summaries). Open Labels represent the main layer of the Subject Index and are considered mandatory, in the sense that each item to be labeled must receive at least one Open Label. Secondary labels are divided into three layers and are used as additional, optional refinement as needed. Closed Labels are specifiers that have the purpose of delimiting the meaning of the main open label. References and Summaries refer to thematic areas. As far as combinations are concerned, one or more Open Labels (the first will be the main one) or, alternatively, one Open Label and one or more labels from other layers can co-exist. Indeed, secondary labels can be used individually or in combination.

4 Dataset

The publication of acts in the GU is structured in six Series, depending on the regulatory body that issues the different types of acts: the *Serie Generale* (General Series) and five special Series. The General Series includes all acts like ordinary laws, presidential decrees, ministerial decrees and resolutions, as well as other regulatory acts from the central and peripheral state administrations. To this respect, it represents the most relevant Series in the GU and the backbone of the Italian legislative process. The five Special Series, on the other hand, focus on specific institutions or types of acts: Special Series 1 contains judgements and orders issued by the *Constitutional Court*, Special Series 2 refers to regulations and directives of the *European Community*, whereas Series 3 includes regulatory and administrative acts issued by *regional administrations*. Special Series 4 and 5 are dedicated to the publication of documents relating to *Public Exams* and *State Contracts*, respectively. Table 2 summarizes the structure of GU with the different document series. Given the high number of legislative acts contained in General Series compared to the other series, and its wide coverage in terms of annotation, this work focuses exclusively on this Series.

Name	Institution/Topic	samples
General Series	Central/ Periph. Adm.	364,123
Sp Series 1	Constitutional Court	16,485
Sp Series 2	European Community	26,926
Sp Series 3	Regional Affairs	2,285
Sp Series 4	Public exams	–
Sp Series 5	State contracts	–

Table 2: Document publication structure in the Gazzetta Ufficiale.

While all acts in GU include a title and the proper body of the law, we focus in this work only on the classification of titles. Indeed, if we consider the annotation procedure, in most cases annotators rely on the title of the act when assigning labels. Only in cases where the title is not sufficiently expressive, or where the act includes several measures of different nature, will the annotator refer to the body of the act. Also, although current large language models can deal with long documents (Beltagy et al., 2020), the use of titles alone allows us to minimize computational costs and avoid expensive preprocessing. In fact, by comparing different transformer-based models on the dataset, we intend to determine what the upper bound of performance is using only titles, which may be useful for future comparisons with document-level classification systems.

Our dataset contains 364,123 labeled titles of legislative acts published in the General Series of the GU from 1988, when manual classification began, until early 2022. The temporal distribution of the documents in the dataset is depicted in Figure 1. According to the institutional annotation practices, each act (title) is manually annotated with at least one label chosen from the Open Labels set and, optionally, with one or more labels chosen among the Open Labels or from one of the other three layers (see Table 1). The General Series has a tagset of 1,587 unique labels and an average of 1.57 label assignments per document. The label distribution in the dataset exhibits a pronounced Zipf-like trend, with very few labels counting tens of thousands of assignments and a long queue of labels with few or very few occurrences.Quantitatively speaking, the dataset counts 7,464,114 tokens, with an average title length of 20.5 tokens.

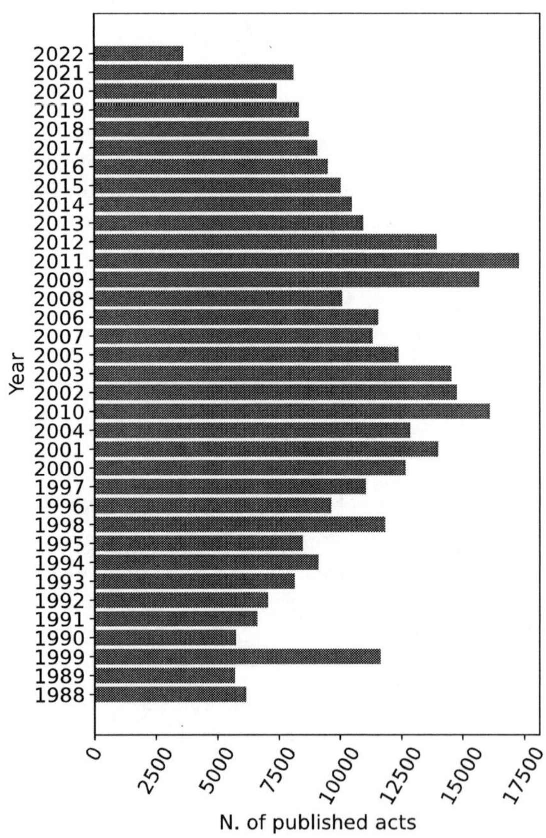

Figure 1: Acts by year

5 Legal Text Classification

We cast the text classification task as a multi-class, multi-label problem, i.e. each target document (the act's title in this case) is to be labeled with one or more classes from the Subject Index. We compare different transformer-based models, after applying the same preprocessing for all settings.

5.1 Preprocessing

Given the extremely skewed data distribution, a cutoff threshold of 10 label assignments is applied to the dataset, in order to allow a robust evaluation. The application of the threshold has little impact on the number of documents in the dataset (passing from 364,123 to 363,909) but the number of unique labels we take into account for the experiments decreases more significantly from 1,587 to 896.

5.2 Experimental Setup

The multi-label text classification experiments we run are based on the comparison of four different transformer-based models, and six different variants (cased/uncased versions of two models). The first two models are general-purpose BERT-base[5,6] and BERT-XXL[7,8] for Italian (in both cased and uncased variants), while the other two are Italian-Legal-BERT[9] and Italian-Legal-BERT-SC (Licari and Comandè, 2022). Italian-Legal-BERT has been obtained by adapting BERT-XXL to the legal domain by further training the model on a set of 235k documents from the National Jurisprudential Archive. Italian-Legal-BERT-SC, instead, has been created from scratch from the same set of legal documents.

In order to provide a robust training and evaluation workflow, we opt for a stratified approach for creating training, development and test sets, with a 60/20/20 split ratio. This results in a proportionally equal distribution of each label over the three splits. Also, we create 4 folds, one for hyper-parameter search and three for training and evaluation. We then use the Optuna toolkit (Akiba et al., 2019) for running a hyper-parameter search, by optimizing the learning rate, with a fixed batch size of 16. The best learning rate values (see Appendix A) have been used for training the four different models.

[5] https://huggingface.co/dbmdz/bert-base-italian-uncased
[6] https://huggingface.co/dbmdz/bert-base-italian-cased
[7] https://huggingface.co/dbmdz/bert-base-italian-xxl-uncased
[8] https://huggingface.co/dbmdz/bert-base-italian-xxl-cased
[9] https://huggingface.co/dlicari/Italian-Legal-BERT

Model	Micro				Macro		Weighted	
	Thr	P	R	F1	Thr	F1	Thr	F1
bert-base-ita-uncased	0.47	0.889	0.856	0.872	0.10	0.464	0.33	0.863
bert-base-ita-cased	0.46	0.888	0.859	**0.873**	0.11	0.462	0.31	**0.864**
bert-base-ita-xxl-uncased	0.47	0.888	0.858	**0.873**	0.09	**0.471**	0.33	**0.864**
bert-base-ita-xxl-cased	0.45	0.886	0.858	0.872	0.09	0.455	0.31	0.862
italian-legal-bert	0.48	0.892	0.847	0.869	0.12	0.416	0.33	0.857
italian-legal-bert-sc	0.46	0.889	0.854	0.871	0.10	0.444	0.29	0.861

Table 3: Performance scores on test data for the task of multi-label text classification on the dataset. Results have been computed on the test sets of three folds.

6 Evaluation and Error Analysis

Performance results, computed on the test sets of the three folds, are reported in Table 3. As model predictions are provided with a confidence score, we use predictions on the development set to find the confidence values which maximize the F1-score, and then apply these (threshold) values on test data. As revealed by the results, with the exception of macro-averaged scores, which are more sensitive to performance variations in classes with few examples, the different models yield a similar performance. In particular, domain adapted models show a comparable, or even slightly lower, performance with respect to their general purpose counterparts, although `italian-legal-bert` has been created by adapting `bert-base-ita-xxl` to the legal domain. This could depend on the fact that our dataset is likely to contain more terms on the regulated domain than legal terminology.

Although not directly comparable due to the use of different datasets/annotation schemas, the performance of our models is in line with current state-of-the-art approaches to legal text classification (Chalkidis et al., 2019; Avram et al., 2021), which however consider the full text of legal acts.

In order to better understand the source of error in our models, we perform an extensive error analysis on the test sets used for evaluation. Since in a multi-label setting it is not always possible to exactly map expected labels with predictions, due to possible many-to-many relations, we create a subset of wrong predictions where one-to-one correspondences are observed and use it as an approximation for the analysis. By manually inspecting the data, we observe that all models struggle with the same set of gold-predicted label mismatches. For example, only four pairs of labels are responsible, alone, for 10.5% of the overall error. These pairs are: *a)* AGRICULTURE vs FOOD AND BEVERAGE (4.54%), *b)* FINANCE ADMINISTRATION VS. ECONOMY AND FINANCE ADMINISTRATION (2.62%), *c)* UNIVERSITY VS. PUBLIC EDUCATION (1.73%), and *d)* PUBLIC HEALTH VS. DRUGS (1.69%).

		Predicted			
		O	C	R	S
Gold	O	70.57	4.8	0.14	0.21
	C	8.75	10.80	0.00	0.36
	R	0.18	0.05	0.08	0.00
	S	0.66	0.23	0.00	3.07

Table 4: Percentage of errors, on single-label assignments, mapped by layer (see Section 3). On the diagonal, errors within the same layer. O = Open Labels, C = Closed Labels, R = References, S = Summaries.

It is worth noting that many of such mismatch types are related to pairs exhibiting strong semantic ties, like overlap (*a*), possible equivalence (*b*) subsumption (*c*, *d*). This pattern, enabled by the very structure of the Subject Index, is pervasive throughout the dataset and might be one of the reasons for a partially inconsistent use of the scheme over the years by different annotators, of which we have found more than one evidence in the gold data. At the other end of the distribution, we observe that 32% of the overall error is explained by a long tail of mismatches occurring 2 times or less. Furthermore, in order to assess the model's ability to learn the hierarchical structure of the Subject Index, we analyze gold-prediction errors by mapping the respective labels' layers. As shown in Table 4, 84.5% of the errors happen between labels in the same layer, showing that, even in case of error, the system tends to be consistent with the hierarchical structure of the annotation schema.

7 Conclusions

This paper first introduces a novel annotated corpus of titles with manually assigned subject labels, which are part of Gazzetta Ufficiale, the official Italian collection of legislative acts. We use this dataset to build and compare four multi-class classifiers for the legal domain, showing that specialised transformer-based models do not outperform general-purpose BERT models for Italian. In this first set of experiments we focused only on acts' titles, given that they yield promising results with a limited computational cost. However, in the future we plan to compare our results with those obtained by processing the full text of the acts.

Our analyses and experiments have highlighted some inconsistencies in the data, mainly due to the complex nature of the taxonomy and the large number of labels. As a next step, we will propose few improvements to make labels more consistent and speed up manual annotation. Furthermore, it would be interesting to measure the gains in terms of time and effort when human annotators are given access to our system as a tool to support manual labelling.

References

Takuya Akiba, Shotaro Sano, Toshihiko Yanase, Takeru Ohta, and Masanori Koyama. 2019. Optuna: A next-generation hyperparameter optimization framework. In *Proceedings of the 25th ACM SIGKDD International Conference on Knowledge Discovery and Data Mining*.

Andrei-Marius Avram, Vasile Păiș, and Dan Ioan Tufis. 2021. Pyeurovoc: A tool for multilingual legal document classification with eurovoc descriptors. In *Proceedings of the International Conference on Recent Advances in Natural Language Processing (RANLP 2021)*, pages 92–101.

Iz Beltagy, Matthew E. Peters, and Arman Cohan. 2020. Longformer: The long-document transformer. *arXiv:2004.05150*.

Ilias Chalkidis, Emmanouil Fergadiotis, Prodromos Malakasiotis, and Ion Androutsopoulos. 2019. Large-scale multi-label text classification on eu legislation. In *Proceedings of the 57th Annual Meeting of the Association for Computational Linguistics*, pages 6314–6322.

Ilias Chalkidis, Manos Fergadiotis, and Ion Androutsopoulos. 2021. Multieurlex-a multi-lingual and multi-label legal document classification dataset for zero-shot cross-lingual transfer. In *Proceedings of the 2021 Conference on Empirical Methods in Natural Language Processing*, pages 6974–6996.

Ilias Chalkidis, Manos Fergadiotis, Prodromos Malakasiotis, Nikolaos Aletras, and Ion Androutsopoulos. 2020. Legal-bert: The muppets straight out of law school. In *Findings of the Association for Computational Linguistics: EMNLP 2020*, pages 2898–2904.

Andrea De Angelis, Vincenzo di Cicco, Giovanni Lalle, Carlo Marchetti, and Paolo Merialdo. 2022. Multi-label classification of bills from the italian senate. In *Proceedings of 1st Workshop on AI for Public Administration co-located with 21st International Conference of the Italian Association for Artificial Intelligence (AIxIA 2022)*.

Jacob Devlin, Ming-Wei Chang, Kenton Lee, and Kristina Toutanova. 2019. BERT: Pre-training of deep bidirectional transformers for language understanding. In *Proceedings of the 2019 Conference of the North American Chapter of the Association for Computational Linguistics: Human Language Technologies, Volume 1 (Long and Short Papers)*, pages 4171–4186, Minneapolis, Minnesota. Association for Computational Linguistics.

Stella Douka, Hadi Abdine, Michalis Vazirgiannis, Rajaa El Hamdani, and David Restrepo Amariles. 2021. Juribert: A masked-language model adaptation for french legal text. In *Proceedings of the Natural Legal Language Processing Workshop 2021*, pages 95–101.

Daniele Licari and Giovanni Comandè. 2022. ITALIAN-LEGAL-BERT: A Pre-trained Transformer Language Model for Italian Law. In *Companion Proceedings of the 23rd International Conference on Knowledge Engineering and Knowledge Management*, volume 3256 of *CEUR Workshop Proceedings*, Bozen-Bolzano, Italy. CEUR. ISSN: 1613-0073.

Mihai Masala, Radu Cristian Alexandru Iacob, Ana Sabina Uban, Marina Cidota, Horia Velicu, Traian Rebedea, and Marius Popescu. 2021. jurbert: A romanian bert model for legal judgement prediction. In *Proceedings of the Natural Legal Language Processing Workshop 2021*, pages 86–94.

Christos Papaloukas, Ilias Chalkidis, Konstantinos Athinaios, Despina Pantazi, and Manolis Koubarakis. 2021. Multi-granular legal topic classification on greek legislation. In *Proceedings of the Natural Legal Language Processing Workshop 2021*, pages 63–75.

Frane Šarić, Bojana Dalbelo Bašić, Marie-Francine Moens, and Jan Šnajder. 2014. Multi-label classification of croatian legal documents using eurovoc thesaurus. In *Proceedings of SPLeT-Semantic processing of legal texts: Legal resources and access to law workshop*. ELRA.

Ralf Steinberger, Mohamed Ebrahim, and Marco Turchi. 2012. Jrc eurovoc indexer jex–a freely available multi-label categorisation tool. In *Proceedings of the Eighth International Conference on Language Resources and Evaluation, LREC*, pages 798–805. European Language Resources Association (ELRA).

Ralf Steinberger, Bruno Pouliquen, Anna Widiger, Camelia Ignat, Tomaz Erjavec, Dan Tufis, and Dániel Varga. 2006. The jrc-acquis: A multilingual aligned parallel corpus with 20+ languages. *arXiv preprint cs/0609058*.

A Appendix

Model	Learning Rate	Batch Size	Best Epoch	Weight Decay	Max Length
bert-base-ita-uncased	3.673e-5	16	10	0.01	128
bert-base-ita-cased	3.673e-5	16	10	0.01	128
bert-base-ita-xxl-uncased	3.519e-5	16	10	0.01	128
bert-base-ita-xxl-cased	3.519e-5	16	10	0.01	128
italian-legal-bert	4.544e-5	16	10	0.01	128
italian-legal-bert-sc	2.826e-5	16	10	0.01	128

Table 5: Hyper-parameters used for training. Learning rates have been optimized using Optuna (Akiba et al., 2019).

Mixed-domain Language Modeling for Processing Long Legal Documents

Wenyue Hua
Claudius Legal Intelligence
wenyue@claudius.ai

Yuchen Zhang*
University of Pennsylvania
zycalice@seas.upenn.edu

Zhe Chen
Claudius Legal Intelligence
zhe@claudius.ai

Josie Li*
UC San Diego
jol027@ucsd.edu

Melanie Weber
Claudius Legal Intelligence
Harvard University
melanie@claudius.ai

Abstract

The application of Natural Language Processing (NLP) to specialized domains, such as the law, has recently received a surge of interest. As many legal services rely on processing and analyzing large collections of documents, automating such tasks with NLP tools such as language models emerges as a key challenge since legal documents may contain specialized vocabulary from other domains, such as medical terminology in personal injury text. However, most language models are general-purpose models, which either have limited reasoning capabilities on highly specialized legal terminology and syntax, such as BERT or RoBERTa, or are expensive to run and tune, such as GPT-3.5 and Claude. Thus, in this paper, we propose a specialized language model for personal injury text, LegalRelectra, which is trained on mixed-domain legal and medical corpora. We show that as a small language model, our model improves over general-domain and single-domain medical and legal language models when processing mixed-domain (personal injury) text. Our training architecture implements the Electra framework but utilizes Reformer instead of BERT for its generator and discriminator. We show that this improves the model's performance on processing long passages and results in better long-range text comprehension.

1 Introduction

Following the striking success of large language models, the development of specialized language models that are adapted to domain-specific syntax and vocabulary has received increasing attention. In many application domains, such as medicine or the law, raw data is often given in text format, creating a need for NLP tools that aid in automating data processing. General-domain models typically lack expressivity on specialized domains. Rare words and domain-specific meanings of vocabulary are difficult to process with general-domain models. Thus, domain adaption had to be addressed in downstream tasks. In contrast, recent literature proposes to integrate domain adaptation into the pre-training stage. Such domain-specific pre-trained models have been developed for a range of domains, including the law (Legal-Bert (Chalkidis et al., 2020), Lawyer-llama (Huang et al., 2023)), medicine (Clinical-Bert (Huang et al., 2019), Chatdoctor (Yunxiang et al., 2023)), biomedical sciences (BioBert (Lee et al., 2020)) and finance (FinBert (Yang et al., 2020), Bloomberggpt (Wu et al., 2023)), among others.

In this work, we focus on pre-trained models for applications in the law with specialization in personal injury civil suits. Personal injury legal cases arise when an individual suffers harm from an accident or injury, and someone else might be legally responsible for that harm. This can be due to negligence, reckless behavior, or intentional misconduct. Personal injury law allows the injured person to go to civil court and get a legal remedy (damages) for all losses stemming from the accident or injury. This can include compensation for medical expenses, lost wages, and pain and suffering, among others. Personal injury claims are quite common in lawsuits. Personal injury claims constitute a substantial part of civil litigation. Therefore, having a language model that concentrates on these cases is vital for natural language processing research in the legal field.

The analysis of legal proceedings relies on access to case data, which is often given in the form of legal documents. Processing such documents presents a challenge for general-purpose language models, due to the specialized terminology and syntax conventions in the law. A natural remedy is the development of a specialized legal-domain language model that is trained on legal text (Chalkidis et al., 2020; Xiao et al., 2021). There are three key

*Work done while intern at Claudius Legal Intelligence.

Proceedings of the Natural Legal Language Processing Workshop 2023, pages 51–61
December 7, 2023

challenges in developing legal-domain models:

1. *Long document for processing:* Extracting key legal information, such as the plaintiff and defendant in a case, requires long-range text comprehension. Most legal texts are much longer than the 512 tokens, the typical limit for BERT-based models. Here, we describe an architecture that increases the maximum passage length to 8,092 tokens.
2. *Specialized terminology from other domains in legal text:* Here, we consider the example of personal injury case data, which often contains medical terminology, such as descriptions of diagnoses and treatments. In such cases, we require a language model that can process specialized text from more than one domain. Thus we train on a mixed legal and medical domain corpus.
3. *Limited access of high-quality training data:* Data on civil legal proceedings is often siloed due to privacy restrictions and there are few publicly available, curated data sets. Hence, we focus on the development of a small, specialized language model, which can be trained, tuned and run on small data sets in a cost-effective way.

LEGALRELECTRA provides a pretrained model for personal injury text with a special focus on enabling long-range text comprehension. It lends itself to a plethora of applications that involve legal case documents, including summarization or extraction of key information for civil suits, identifying patterns and trends in legal proceedings and identifying precedent in past cases, among others. In addition, legal language models may aid in summarizing and analysing legal scholarship. We demonstrate the applicability of LEGALRELECTRA on a downstream task, for which we train a Name Entity Recognition (NER) model. In practise, such an NER model may be applied to extract key legal information from case documents, such as the identities of plaintiff and defendant, medical injuries and civil case type. With that, NER enables a simple summarization of civil suits, which may serve as a basis for further case analytics.

Contributions. Our main contributions are:

1. We describe a novel model architecture (RELECTRA) that adapts the popular ELECTRA model to the processing of long passages. For this, we replace the BERT generators and discriminators with REFORMER.
2. We describe a training procedure for mixed-domain language models that are adapted to processing text from more than one domain.
3. We demonstrate the benefits of training a domain-specific tokenizer as opposed to pre-training with the general-domain tokenizer.

The resulting model, LEGALRELECTRA, is well equipped to process long passages of mixed-domain text (here, personal injury cases, i.e., mixed legal and medical domain), as we demonstrate in a range of benchmark experiments against state of the art general and domain-specific models.

2 Related Work

Recently, there has been growing interest in utilizing Machine Learning in the legal domain (Legal Artificial Intelligence), including for judgment prediction (Chalkidis et al., 2019; Medvedeva et al., 2020), the analysis of fairness in legal proceedings (Kleinberg et al., 2020; Ciocanel et al., 2020; Avery and Cooper, 2020; Sargent and Weber, 2021), as well as legal document analysis (Zhong et al., 2020; Grover et al., 2003; Sulea et al., 2017). The development of specialized legal language models can aid in the latter. Many variations of transformers that are adapted to specialized domains have been proposed in the literature (e.g., (Huang et al., 2019; Chalkidis et al., 2020; Yang et al., 2020; Xiao et al., 2021; Rasmy et al., 2021)) and demonstrated to be more efficient and accurate than BERT on their specialized domains. However, most of these pre-trained domain-specific models do not adopt new frameworks but rely on the classical BERT architecture. To the best of our knowledge, only LAWFORMER (Xiao et al., 2021), which is a Chinese legal domain pre-trained model, utilizes LONGFORMER (Beltagy et al., 2020), instead of BERT. This architecture changes allows LAWFORMER to process longer passages (up to 4,096 tokens). Here, we adopt the ELECTRA (Clark et al., 2019) framework, which has been shown to be more data- and parameter-efficient than BERT. In addition, our model utilizes REFORMER as generator and discriminator, which significantly improves over the maximum text length of LONGFORMER (up to 8,092 tokens). In this paper, we show that the resulting model (LEGALRELECTRA) outperforms BERT, as well as state-of-the-art single-domain adapted models on a downstream task (Named Entity Recognition, sec. 5.3; Legal Case Retrieval, sec. 5.4;). Moreover, some current state-of-the-art domain-specific language models are pretrained using a general-domain tokenizer (e.g., the BERT tokenizer in LEGAL-BERT) to preprocess the input data. Here, we train a *domain-specific* tokenizer to pre-train LEGALRELECTRA. Our results indicate that this improves the training process and downstream tasks (sec. 5.1 and 5.2).

Lastly, we note that all current domain-specific models focus on adaption to a *single* domain. In contrast, our model is trained on both legal and medical domains motivated by applications in processing personal injury text. Our experimental results demonstrate that LEGALRELECTRA performs competitively against general-purpose and single-domain models (sec. 5.3).

3 Language Modeling for Legal Text

In this section, we outline the architecture of our model, describe its pretraining process, and detail the tasks on which it is assessed.

3.1 Legal Language Modeling

We utilize the ELECTRA framework as basic model architecture. However, in contrast to the classical ELECTRA structure, we replace the BERT generator and discriminator with REFORMER models. This subsection briefly describes the structure of ELECTRA and REFORMER and how they relate to LEGALRELECTRA.

ELECTRA. ELECTRA (Clark et al., 2019) is a sample-efficient model, which learns from all input tokens instead of just the small masked-out subset (as in BERT). It is shown to excel on the GLUE benchmark and multiple downstream NLP tasks, such as question answering. ELECTRA consists of two sub-models, a generator and a discriminator. Given texts with 15% of the tokens masked, the generator is trained to generate the original non-masked text. Then, given the generated text, the discriminator is trained to decide whether any generated token is identical to the original token. Thus, the discriminator loss is calculated over all input tokens as it performs prediction on each token.

REFORMER. In order to be able to process long passages, we leverage REFORMER (Kitaev et al., 2019), which can process text length up to 8,192. This is in stark contrast to BERT, which can only process up to 512 tokens. Traditional transformer models incur computational and memory cost of $O(L^2)$ when computing full attention over a text of length L, creating a significant computational bottleneck. However, computing full attention is unnecessary: The weighted average of attention weights and values involves $\mathrm{softmax}(QK^T)$, which is dominated by the largest elements in a sparse matrix. Thus for each query q, the model only needs to pay attention to the keys k that are closest to q. In contrast, the REFORMER model utilizes locality-sensitive-hashing (LSH) to reduce the complexity of attending over long sequences. LSH is an efficient approach for approximate nearest neighbors search in high dimensions. When using LSH to hash the Q and K matrices, similar q and k vectors are divided into the same buckets. Then standard attention is only computed for the q and k vectors within the same hash buckets.

In our model, the generator and discriminator are two REFORMER models instead of BERT models as in the original ELECTRA framework. We name this new model RELECTRA.

3.2 Pre-Training

Our domain-specific language model specializes in processing personal injury legal text. Personal injury refers to harm to the body, mind, emotions, or reputation, distinct from property damage [1]. Such lawsuits are brought against those responsible due to negligence, misconduct, or intentional harm. The injuries often encompass medical bills, pain and suffering, and reduced quality of life. Consequently, personal injury texts intertwine legal and medical terminologies. Our pre-training corpus draws from public databases, such as CourtListener from the FreeLaw project (The Free Law Project, 2021), and fully anonymized civil case descriptions from proprietary sources. We adopt standard preprocessing methods such as string matching and regular expressions to eliminate special characters, special punctuation, foreign languages, and headers. While a vast collection of personal injury texts would be ideal, accessibility challenges arise due to licensing. As a solution, our primary personal injury text corpus is supplemented with texts from other legal areas and medical content. The inclusion of medical text equips the model with a deeper understanding of personal injuries in a legal context. For a detailed breakdown of our training data sources, refer to Tab. 1. The data set comprises medical (3GB), legal (6GB), and mixed legal-medical (3GB) content, totaling 12GB.

[1] adopted from https://www.law.cornell.edu/wex/personal_injury

Data Set	Size	Description
Legal	6G	Case descriptions from different legal branches; sources include COURTLISTENER (The Free Law Project, 2021).
Medical	3G	Doctor's notes and letters from MIMIC and MIMIC-CXR databases.
Mixed	3G	Personal injury case descriptions from Supreme Court opinions, academic literature, COURTLISTENER, BYU LAW, case descriptions from attorneys.

Table 1: Training data, consisting of a 12GB corpus consisting of legal text, medical text, mixed-domain text with legal and medical terminology, as well as general English text.

3.3 Named Entity Recognition

We validate LEGALRELECTRA by training legal and mixed-domain NER models. Training is performed using automatically (in-house) annotated legal text. In addition, we benchmark LEGALRELECTRA on general and medical domain NER tasks, for which we used publicly available annotated training data conll2003 (Tjong Kim Sang and De Meulder, 2003) (general domain), MIMIC III (Johnson et al., 2016) (medical domain)).

We chose the following labels, which are representative of an NER task that one may encounter in practise: *plaintiff*, *defendant* and *case type*. Here, *case type* categorizes the branch of civil law, which applies to the case. We distinguish among *motorvehicle accidents*, *slip-and-fall accidents* and *work-related cases*, such as illegal termination of a work contract and negligence by a professional. For the latter, the NER task consists of identifying words that help to determine the type of a case. Case types are usually not explicitly mentioned in-text; hence, it can be challenging to categorize civil legal documents. The sources for our test data are described in Table 6 in supplemental A. We will make the validation and test data available after publication, but are not able to publish the training data for license reasons.

Annotation. The manual annotation of the training and testing data was performed as follows: For our legal text sources, we have access to ground truth plaintiff and defendant information from case headers. This allows us to annotate relevant phrases in the text via string matching. For the case type annotations, we create a word list for each case type, which contains frequently occurring phrases that are indicative of the respective case type. We then enrich the lists with synonyms of these phrases. After creating the initial word lists, we removed ambiguous phrases or phrases that appeared in the wordlists of more than one case type. Annotations were done via inexact string matching at first to reduce the workload for annotators, where phrases that were similar to an entry in a word list were labeled with the respective case type. After performing automatic annotations based on header information and case type word list, all cases in training, validation and testing are manually checked by three expert annotators.

3.4 Legal Case Retrieval

The second evaluation task for LEGALRELECTRA involves legal case retrieval, a process that seeks to identify similar legal cases from a given collection based on a provided case description, without any fine-tuning. This task is crucial for legal analysis and education as past cases can profoundly influence the analysis and legal judgment over new cases. However, annotating legal case similarity are challenging due to (1) its reliance on specific expertise and domain knowledge, making crowdsourced annotations difficult (2) law firms often confidentially collect similar cases for future reference, which are typically inaccessible. Consequently, we perform legal case retrieval using the pretrained model, without any fine-tuning on annotated datasets. The dataset for this task comprises 500 cases, selected by law firms from Kentucky (cases from 1998 to 2018) and Louisiana (cases from 2002). Each case encapsulates various information such as claim type, injuries, claim county, plaintiff and defendant names, claim date, medical expenses, future medical expenses, lost salaries, among others. The dataset covers nine general claim types: Parked/Parking Accident, Accident in Intersection, Property Owned by Individual, Medical Malpractice, Truck-Involved Accident, Rear-End Accident, Head-On Accident, Business Negligence, and Retail Establishment.

4 Experiment Setup

This section delineates the experimental configurations for both the pretraining phase and the finetuning for named entity recognition. Since the legal case retrieval task is assessed without finetuning, we do not provide detailed setup specifics for it.

4.1 Tokenizer

Tokenization refers to the process of splitting a stream of characters into words (Grefenstette and Tapanainen, 1994). While often seen as part of preprocessing, good tokenization is a crucial prerequisite for good downstream performance. Tokenization is particularly important for processing domain-specific text that contains a large amount of specialized terminology. In contrast to most of the published domain-specific language models, which use the standard BERT tokenizer, we train a custom tokenizer. Our tokenizer is trained via standard Byte-Pair Encoding (Sennrich and Birch, 2016), which replaces the most common pair of consecutive bytes of data with a byte that does not occur in that data until the vocabulary size is reached. Since our pre-training data set contains text with specialized terminology, our custom tokenizer generates more sensible tokenization of domain-specific text. An example is given in Tab. 2 (see supplemental).

4.2 Pre-Training

We pre-train LEGALRELECTRA on the collected legal, medical and mixed-domain text corpora described above, in batches of four samples each. Our combined corpora contain up to 30,522 sentence piece tokens. There are 120k training steps and 20k warm-up steps (linear warm-up with linear decay scheduler). We use the ADAMW optimizer with learning rate of 1e-5 for the first 80k training steps and 1e-6 for the remaining 40k training steps. LEGALRELECTRA was trained on one NVIDIA P100 GPU and 16 GB memory, for a total of 16 days, 6 hours and 30 minutess.

4.3 Downstream tasks

We evaluate LEGALRELECTRA on two downstream tasks, *Named Entity Recognition* (NER) and *Legal case retrival*. We use BERT, CLINICALBERT, LEGAL-BERT and REFORMER as baseline models. Each NER model is trained for 10 epochs with batch size 1, using the AdamW optimizer with learning rate 3e-5.

5 Results

5.1 Tokenizer

The performance of tokenizers is in general difficult to evaluate, as it is highly dependent on the downstream application. To the best of our knowledge, no established convention exists in the literature. Here, we employ quantitative metrics for comparing the performance of our custom LEGALRELECTRA tokenizer with that of the standard BERT tokenizer. For our evaluation, we align the output of the BERT and LEGALRELECTRA tokenizers for ten text segments with personal injury case descriptions. All text segments contain both medical and legal terminology. We analyze the number of recognized words and the number of total unique errors, as well as errors in medical and legal phrases. A similar validation scheme was suggested in (Habert et al., 1998). Our results (see Tab. 7) show that the custom LEGALRELECTRA tokenizer performs better at recognizing words, as evident in the lower number of words detected. We further notice that LEGALRELECTRA tokenizer has a smaller number of errors involving legal and medical terminology, suggesting a superior performance on domain-specific text. Errors that do not involve medical or legal terminology are often (non-English) names for both tokenizers.

5.2 Pre-training

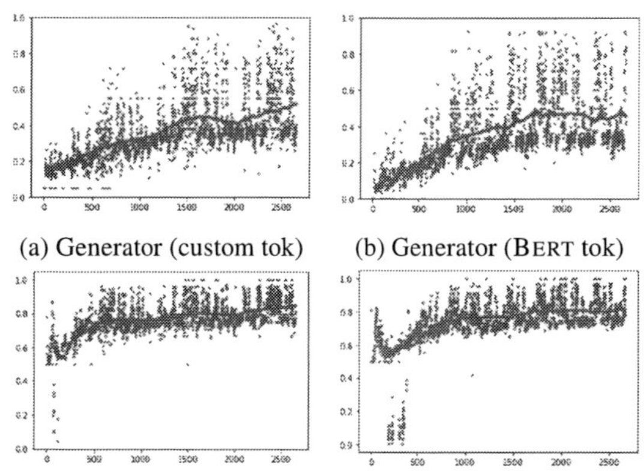

(a) Generator (custom tok) (b) Generator (BERT tok)

(c) Discriminator (custom) (d) Discriminator (BERT)

Figure 1: Masked Language Modeling (MLM) accuracy of generator and discriminator of LEGALRELECTRA with our custom tokenizer and the standard BERT tokenizer. Here, one dot represents the accuracy score of one datapoint (evaluated every 100 datapoints). The line is a smoothed function of averaged accuracy scores over intervals of length 200 aggregating the scores of the 100 data points before and after respectively.

We evaluate LEGALRELECTRA trained with our custom (domain-specific) tokenizer in comparison with a second LEGALRELECTRA model that was trained using the standard (general-domain) BERT tokenizer. We report both generator and discrimi-

Medical	Tokenization result
text	gastrointestinal complaints, neurologic changes, rashes, palpitations, orthopnea
BERT (uncased)	gas, tro, int, estinal, complaints, ne, uro, logic, changes, rash, es, pal, pit, ations, or, th, op, nea
custom (uncased)	gastrointestinal, complaints, neurologic, changes, rashes, palpitations, orthopnea
Legal	Tokenization result
text	the nature of adjudications upon which erroneous subsequent proceedings rest
BERT (uncased)	the, nature, of, ad, ju, dication, s, upon, which, er, rone, ous, subsequent, proceedings, rest
custom (uncased)	the, nature, of, adjudications, upon, which, erroneous, subsequent, proceedings, rest

Table 2: Tokenization example for the BERT tokenizer and our custom tokenizer.

nator accuracy after 120k training steps. The pretraining task for the generator is Masked language modeling (MLM). In MLM, the input is corrupted by replacing some tokens with "[MASK]". Then we train a model to reconstruct the original tokens. The pretraining task for the discriminator is to predict whether each token in the corrupted input was replaced by a generator sample or not. The results for both models are shown in Fig. 1. We observe that the pretraining performance of the generator and discriminator is comparable. Notably, both the generator and discriminator model trained with our custom tokenizer improve over the model trained with the BERT tokenizer towards the end of the training process (Fig. 2 shows the generator-discriminator difference in both models).

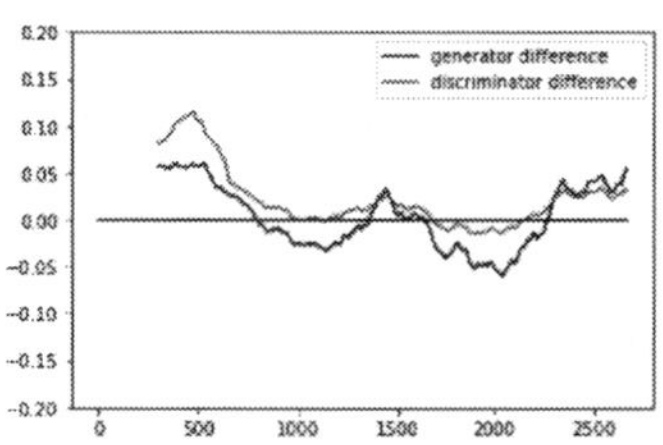

Figure 2: Differences of Generator and Discriminator accuracy between LEGALRELECTRA models pretrained with custom tokenizer and BERT tokenizer.

5.3 Named Entity Recognition

To evaluate LEGALRELECTRA on a downstream task, we analyze the performance of legal domain and mixed legal-medical domain NER models trained with LEGALRELECTRA in comparison with benchmark NER models trained with BERT, LEGAL-BERT, CLINICAL-BERT, REFORMER and LEGALRELECTRA with BERT tokenizer. We consider three labels for the legal domain (case type, plaintiff, defendant) and four labels for the mixed medical-legal domain (case type, plaintiff, defendant, injury). For experiments on BERT, LEGAL-BERT, CLINICAL-BERT which have a maximum token length of 512, we stride and chunk the training and test passage. For experiments on REFORMER, LEGALRELECTRA and LEGALRELECTRA with BERT tokenizer, we use a maximum token length of 1536 evaluated on validation data.

The results are given in Tables 3 (legal domain) and 4 (mixed domain). We observe that LEGALRELECTRA outperforms both the general-domain BERT, as well as the specialized LEGAL-BERT and CLINICAL-BERT models on both domains (with respect to the overall f1 score). It also performs better than REFORMER which is pretrained on the same corpus, demonstrating the benefits of ELECTRA training framework. Notably, both LEGALRELECTRA and REFORMER trained with our custom tokenizer outperform LEGALRELECTRA trained with the BERT tokenizer, which demonstrates the benefits of a domain-specific tokenizer.

5.4 Legal Case Retrieval

To quantitatively assess retrieval performance, we manually review 50 cases, randomly selected from the dataset, and benchmark the top-1 retrieval legal case matching against BERT, LEGAL-BERT, CLINICAL-BERT, and REFORMER. The evaluation is based on five criteria:

1. *Claim type:* Considered a match, if the cases share the same claim type.
2. *Injury categories:* Consider a match, if over half of the injuries in the given case match the retrieved case.
3. *Gender of plaintiff:* Counted as a match, if plaintiffs in both cases share the same gender.
4. *Age of plaintiff:* Considered a match, if the age difference between plaintiffs in the given and retrieved cases is within ±10 years.
5. *Medical expenses:* Counted as a match if the difference in medical expenses between the given and retrieved case falls within a range of ±50

Legal domain	precision TYPE	PLT	DEF	recall TYPE	PLT	DEF	f1 TYPE	PLT	DEF	f1 all
BERT	95.00	82.75	82.86	76.00	64.86	87.88	84.44	72.73	85.29	80.45
CLINICAL-BERT	95.00	86.95	87.88	79.17	58.89	90.63	86.36	70.17	89.23	81.93
LEGAL-BERT	84.70	82.31	88.56	77.11	65.34	80.59	80.73	72.85	84.39	79.32
REFORMER	87.51	73.69	92.33	76.25	87.97	89.31	81.48	80.20	90.79	84.16
LEGALRELECTRA	89.66	84.31	100.00	74.28	84.31	83.33	81.25	84.31	90.91	**85.93**
LEGALRELECTRA (BERT tok)	95.23	85.37	97.56	55.56	67.31	86.96	70.17	75.27	91.95	80.12

Table 3: **NER-legal:** Performance of LEGALRELECTRA on legal text in comparison with BERT, CLINICAL-BERT, LEGAL-BERT and LEGALRELECTRA (BERT tokenizer) for case type (TYPE), defendant (DEF) and plaintiff (PLT).

Mixed domain	precision TYPE	PLT	DEF	PROB	recall TYPE	PLT	DEF	PROB	f1 TYPE	PLT	DEF	PROB	f1 all
BERT	70.59	82.76	71.43	82.61	57.14	64.86	80.65	76.00	63.15	72.72	75.76	79.17	73.39
CLINICAL-BERT	84.00	82.91	75.68	88.46	69.23	58.82	87.32	92.00	75.90	80.08	68.11	90.19	78.55
LEGAL-BERT	88.88	80.00	83.87	85.00	66.67	60.61	86.67	66.67	76.19	68.97	85.25	77.27	77.07
REFORMER	89.92	83.44	86.95	83.21	63.56	62.17	84.38	78.92	74.48	71.25	85.65	81.01	78.10
LEGALRELECTRA	91.30	85.71	95.12	86.96	58.33	57.69	92.86	76.92	71.18	68.97	93.98	81.63	**78.57**
LEGALRELECTRA (BERT tok)	90.47	81.58	95.00	73.91	54.28	59.62	79.17	65.38	67.86	68.89	86.36	69.39	74.20

Table 4: **NER-mixed:** Performance of LEGALRELECTRA in mixed domain with labels case type (TYPE), defendant (DEF) plaintiff (PLT), medical problem (PROB).

Model	Claim	Injury	Gender	Age	Expenses
BERT	80.00	66.00	58.00	48.00	18.00
CLINICAL-BERT	76.00	84.00	64.00	32.00	22.00
LEGAL-BERT	84.00	72.00	68.00	36.00	**32.00**
REFORMER	82.00	78.00	**70.00**	28.00	24.00
LEGALRELECTRA	**90.00**	**92.00**	62.00	**58.00**	30.00
LEGALRELECTRA (BERT tok)	84.00	88.00	60.00	54.00	22.00

Table 5: **Legal Case Retrieval:** Performance of LEGALRELECTRA on legal case retrieval in comparison with BERT, CLINICAL-BERT, LEGAL-BERT and LEGALRELECTRA (BERT tokenizer)

Results are presented in Table 5. We observe that again, LEGALRELECTRA outperforms both the general-domain BERT, specialized LEGAL-BERT and CLINICAL-BERT models, especially on the claim type and injury category matching. LEGALRELECTRA further outperforms LEGALRELECTRA trained with the BERT tokenizer. However, none of the models perform well on numerical information matching, *i.e.* plaintiff age and medical expenses.

5.5 Result Analysis

For both the NER task and the legal case retrieval task, a key observation in our experimental results is the superior performance of LEGALRELECTRA in comparison with LEGAL-BERT. We will provide a more detailed analysis of the two tasks below.

NER. We notice that, surprisingly, LEGAL-BERT does not perform as well as expected on legal case terminology, specifically the recognition of plaintiff and defendant. For example, it may confuse other entities, such as the defendant's attorney, as defendant or plaintiff. While the extracted information is relevant to the case, it is not precise enough to be useful for further downstream analysis. Secondly, LEGAL-BERT does not perform well on case type recognition in legal text (LEGALRELECTRA does not perform well on case type recognition in mixed text either, see below). Thirdly, LEGAL-BERT misses medical terminology, as it is not pretrained on medical data. Examples include TMJ (an abbreviation for for Temporomandibular joint), Myofascial Pain Syndrome and psychological injuries such as emotional distress. CLINICAL-BERT does not perform well on legal case terminology, such as plaintiff and defendant recognition. This is expected, as it is not pretrained on legal text. However, it indeed outperforms all other models on medical terminology recognition, including LEGALRELECTRA, which is also pre-trained on some medical data. It is unexpectedly good at the recognition of case types. BERT sometimes misses plaintiff or defendant throughout the whole case text, indicating its limited ability to recognize legal terminology. In summary, all three models show a limited ability to recognize legal terminology in *long* texts. Errors arise due to the limited number of tokens that the models can process. In some texts the plaintiff and defendant information is only given in the beginning of the text and can therefore not be obtained from partial text segments. In contrast, LEGALRELECTRA's ability to process larger text segments results in a superior performance in plaintiff and defendant recognition. Its performance on medical problem recognition is better than all other models except CLINICAL-BERT, indicating that the mixed pre-trained data does help on both legal and medical feature learning. REFORMER performs slightly worse on precision but better on recall, but an overall worse result on F1, indicating that the ELECTRA training framework indeed improves model performance. Comparing LEGALRELECTRA trained with our custom tokenizer and the standard BERT tokenizer, we notice that the performance on legal feature recognition is comparable. However, the recognition of medical terminology is negatively affected by the BERT tokenizer. This indicates that wrong tokenization of medical terminology affects the model performance more negatively than wrong tokenization of legal terminology.

Legal Case Retrieval. The LEGALRELECTRA model demonstrates robust performance in claim type and injury category matching, excelling particularly in traffic-related cases like Rear-End and Truck-Involved Accidents with a 96.00 accuracy score. Its ability to match Business Negligence and Property Owned by Individual is less effective, likely due to insufficient training on business-related cases and the relative rarity of these claim types. The model's skill in injury matching surpasses that of CLINICAL-BERT, identifying both singular injuries such as 'Headache' and 'Disc: Herniated or Ruptured', and composite injuries like 'Nonfracture Injury, Strain: Lumbar Only, Aggravation of Preexisting Back or Neck Strain Disc: Bulging'. However, the model fails to adequately consider key factors like gender, age, and medical expenses, despite their relevance in legal case analysis. This omission could be due to their brief textual representations, thus being overlooked by the pretrained language model unless specifically tuned to prioritize such information.

6 Conclusions

In this paper, we introduced LEGALRELECTRA, a language model that is specialized to process mixed legal and medical domain (personal injury) text. This was achieved by pre-training with a corpus consisting of legal, medical and mixed domain (personal injury) text. We demonstrate in validation experiments that LEGALRELECTRA outperforms general-purpose language models (e.g., BERT), as well as specialized legal-domain models (e.g., LEGAL-BERT) on legal and mixed-domain NER. As technical contributions, we proposed a novel model architecture that allows for improved performance on long-range text comprehension.

LEGALRELECTRA provides a pretrained model for personal injury text with a special focus on enabling long-range text comprehension. It lends itself to a plethora of applications that involve legal case documents, including summarization or extraction of key information for civil suits, identifying patterns and trends in legal proceedings, identifying precedent in past cases, among others. In addition, legal language models may aid in summarizing and analysing legal scholarship.

We demonstrate the applicability of LEGALRELECTRA in downstream tasks by training a Named Entity Recognition (NER) model and utilizing the pretrained model directly as a Legal Case Retriever. In practice, the NER model can extract crucial legal information from case documents, including plaintiff and defendant identities, medical injuries, and civil case types. This enables a basic summary of civil suits, serving as a foundation for further case analysis. The Legal Case Retriever, on the other hand, can identify past cases similar to new ones, providing valuable reference points.

7 Limitations

There are several limitations in our training and validation setup, addressing of which may lead to significant improvements. As discussed above, the ideal pre-training corpus for a personal injury language model would consist of large collections of personal injury text. However, due to the restricted access to such data, it is difficult to collect a sufficiently large text corpus. Thus, we supplement our pre-training data with text from other legal branches and (pure) medical text, which may have decreased the model's performance. Further limitations arise in the performance evaluation presented here. Testing and validation against benchmarks could have been more extensive, for instance by evaluating LEGALRELECTRA on a larger and more comprehensive dataset on both NER and retrieval. Moreover, the downstream training data annotation (see sec. 3.3) was partially automated. Instead of string matching, we could have annotated the NER training data manually, which would have been more accurate.

8 Ethical Considerations and Broader Impacts

The language model proposed in this work is designed for processing legal documents in personal injury cases. As such, the model has the potential to streamline personal injury attorney's work, including but not limited to significant time savings during legal proceedings. At the same time, ethical and privacy considerations are crucial when deploying AI technology in the legal space. In particular, if applied in practise, the user should be conscious of potential biases in legal documents, such as court opinions, that were part of the training data and how this may impact the predictions of the model. All legal case documents and medical documents used to train and test the models in this paper were fully anonymized. In the interest of transparency, we worked with publicly available data whenever possible. The size, composition and preprocessing of our data sets is documented in detail in the main text. We document and cite the source of all publicly available data.

References

Joseph Avery and Joel Cooper. 2020. Technology in the legal system. *Bias in the Law: A Definitive Look at Racial Prejudice in the US Criminal Justice System*, 161.

Iz Beltagy, Matthew E Peters, and Arman Cohan. 2020. Longformer: The long-document transformer.

Ilias Chalkidis, Ion Androutsopoulos, and Nikolaos Aletras. 2019. Neural legal judgment prediction in english. *arXiv preprint arXiv:1906.02059*.

Ilias Chalkidis, Manos Fergadiotis, Prodromos Malakasiotis, Nikolaos Aletras, and Ion Androutsopoulos. 2020. Legal-bert: The muppets straight out of law school.

Maria-Veronica Ciocanel, Chad M. Topaz, Rebecca Santorella, Shilad Sen, Christian Michael Smith, and Adam Hufstetler. 2020. Justfair: Judicial system transparency through federal archive inferred records. *PLOS ONE*, 15(10):1–20.

Kevin Clark, Minh-Thang Luong, Quoc V Le, and Christopher D Manning. 2019. Electra: Pre-training text encoders as discriminators rather than generators. In *International Conference on Learning Representations*.

Gregory Grefenstette and Pasi Tapanainen. 1994. What is a word, what is a sentence? problems of tokenization.

Claire Grover, Ben Hachey, and Chris Korycinski. 2003. Summarising legal texts: Sentential tense and argumentative roles. In *Proceedings of the HLT-NAACL 03 Text Summarization Workshop*, pages 33–40.

Benoit Habert, Gilles Adda, Martine Adda-Decker, P Boula de Marëuil, Serge Ferrari, Olivier Ferret, Gabriel Illouz, and Patrick Paroubek. 1998. Towards tokenization evaluation. In *Proceedings of LREC*, volume 98, pages 427–431.

Kexin Huang, Jaan Altosaar, and Rajesh Ranganath. 2019. Clinicalbert: Modeling clinical notes and predicting hospital readmission.

Quzhe Huang, Mingxu Tao, Zhenwei An, Chen Zhang, Cong Jiang, Zhibin Chen, Zirui Wu, and Yansong Feng. 2023. Lawyer llama technical report. *arXiv preprint arXiv:2305.15062*.

A Johnson, L Bulgarelli, T Pollard, S Horng, LA Celi, and R Mark. 2020. Mimic-iv (version 1.0).

Alistair E W Johnson, Tom J Pollard, Seth J Berkowitz, Nathaniel R Greenbaum, Matthew P Lungren, Chih-ying Deng, Roger G Mark, and Steven Horng. 2019. Mimic-cxr, a de-identified publicly available database of chest radiographs with free-text reports. *Scientific data*, 6(1):1–8.

Alistair E. W. Johnson, Tom J. Pollard, Lu Shen, Li wei H. Lehman, Mengling Feng, Mohammad Mahdi Ghassemi, Benjamin Moody, Peter Szolovits, Leo Anthony Celi, and Roger G. Mark. 2016. Mimic-iii, a freely accessible critical care database. *Scientific Data*, 3.

Nikita Kitaev, Lukasz Kaiser, and Anselm Levskaya. 2019. Reformer: The efficient transformer. In *International Conference on Learning Representations*.

Jon Kleinberg, Jens Ludwig, Sendhil Mullainathan, and Cass R. Sunstein. 2020. Algorithms as discrimination detectors. *Proceedings of the National Academy of Sciences*, 117(48):30096–30100.

Jinhyuk Lee, Wonjin Yoon, Sungdong Kim, Donghyeon Kim, Sunkyu Kim, Chan Ho So, and Jaewoo Kang. 2020. Biobert: a pre-trained biomedical language representation model for biomedical text mining. volume 36, pages 1234–1240. Oxford University Press.

Masha Medvedeva, Michel Vols, and Martijn Wieling. 2020. Using machine learning to predict decisions of the european court of human rights. *Artificial Intelligence and Law*, 28(2):237–266.

Laila Rasmy, Yang Xiang, Ziqian Xie, Cui Tao, and Degui Zhi. 2021. Med-bert: pretrained contextualized embeddings on large-scale structured electronic health records for disease prediction. *NPJ digital medicine*, 4(1):1–13.

Jackson Sargent and Melanie Weber. 2021. Identifying biases in legal data: An algorithmic fairness perspective. *arXiv preprint arXiv:2109.09946*.

Barry Haddow Sennrich, Rico and Alexandra Birch. 2016. Neural machine translation of rare words with subword units. In *2016 Association of Computational Linguistics*.

Octavia-Maria Sulea, Marcos Zampieri, Shervin Malmasi, Mihaela Vela, Liviu P Dinu, and Josef Van Genabith. 2017. Exploring the use of text classification in the legal domain. *arXiv preprint arXiv:1710.09306*.

The Free Law Project. 2021. Courtlistener.

Erik F. Tjong Kim Sang and Fien De Meulder. 2003. Introduction to the CoNLL-2003 shared task: Language-independent named entity recognition. In *Proceedings of the Seventh Conference on Natural Language Learning at HLT-NAACL 2003*, pages 142–147.

Shijie Wu, Ozan Irsoy, Steven Lu, Vadim Dabravolski, Mark Dredze, Sebastian Gehrmann, Prabhanjan Kambadur, David Rosenberg, and Gideon Mann. 2023. Bloomberggpt: A large language model for finance. *arXiv preprint arXiv:2303.17564*.

Chaojun Xiao, Xueyu Hu, Zhiyuan Liu, Cunchao Tu, and Maosong Sun. 2021. Lawformer: A pre-trained language model for chinese legal long documents. volume 2, pages 79–84. Elsevier.

Yi Yang, Mark Christopher Siy Uy, and Allen Huang. 2020. Finbert: A pretrained language model for financial communications. *arXiv preprint arXiv:2006.08097*.

Li Yunxiang, Li Zihan, Zhang Kai, Dan Ruilong, and Zhang You. 2023. Chatdoctor: A medical chat model fine-tuned on llama model using medical domain knowledge. *arXiv preprint arXiv:2303.14070*.

Haoxi Zhong, Chaojun Xiao, Cunchao Tu, Tianyang Zhang, Zhiyuan Liu, and Maosong Sun. 2020. How does NLP benefit legal system: A summary of legal artificial intelligence. In *Proceedings of the 58th Annual Meeting of the Association for Computational Linguistics*, Online. Association for Computational Linguistics.

A Test data

Data Set	Description
Legal	Case descriptions from different legal branches; sources include COURTLISTENER (The Free Law Project, 2021).
Medical	MIMIC (Johnson et al., 2020) MIMIC-CXR (Johnson et al., 2019)
Mixed	Open-source personal injury case descriptions, sources include COURTLISTENER and BYU LAW LIBRARY[2].

Table 6: Test data source

Our test data for the general and medical domains is from the same source as the training data (see Tab. 6). For the legal domain training data, we collected text from public data bases (including COURTLISTENER from the FreeLaw project (The Free Law Project, 2021)).

B Additional experimental results for tokenizer evaluation

We analyze the number of recognized words and the number of total unique errors, as well as errors in medical and legal phrases. A similar validation scheme was suggested in (Habert et al., 1998). Errors in abbreviations are excluded from the error count. The results can be found in table 7.

	BERT tokenizer				Custom tokenizer			
	words	total errors	legal	medical	words	total errors	legal	medical
# 0	153	5	0	1	139	0	0	0
# 1	411	3	0	2	417	3	0	1
# 2	285	12	5	2	277	7	1	0
# 3	418	9	0	7	412	6	0	2
# 4	313	9	3	2	289	4	0	1
# 5	405	9	1	3	385	8	0	1
# 6	216	9	3	4	210	4	0	3
# 7	560	12	5	4	539	11	0	7
# 8	400	13	4	3	407	7	1	0
# 9	340	12	1	5	323	7	0	1

Table 7: **Tokenizer:** Evaluation of custom LEGALRELECTRA tokenizer against BERT tokenzier for ten text segments of personal injury case descriptions. We report the number of words recognized by the tokenizers, as well as the number of unique errors. In addition to the total number of errors, we report the number of errors for medical and legal terminology separately.

Questions about Contracts: Prompt Templates for Structured Answer Generation

Adam Roegiest, Radha Chitta, Jonathan Donnelly,
Maya Lash, Alexandra Vtyurina and **François Longtin**
Zuva Inc., Toronto, Ontario, Canada
{adam,radha.chitta,jonny.donnelly,maya,sasha, francois}@zuva.ai

Abstract

Finding the answers to legal questions about specific clauses in contracts is an important analysis in many legal workflows (e.g., understanding market trends, due diligence, risk mitigation) but more important is being able to do this at scale. In this paper, we present an examination of using large language models to produce (partially) structured answers to legal questions; primarily in the form of multiple choice and multiple select. We first show that traditional semantic matching is unable to perform this task at acceptable accuracy and then show how question specific prompts can achieve reasonable accuracy across a range of generative models. Finally, we show that much of this effectiveness can be maintained when generalized prompt templates are used rather than question specific ones.

1 Introduction

Contracts and other legal agreements are complex documents that specify in a myriad of ways the obligations, restrictions, and other covenants between two or more parties. Understanding such requirements for a single contract is a task that any lawyer could do if the need were to arise (e.g., whether a tenant can sublet an apartment), especially if there exist methods to automatically extract such clauses from documents (Roegiest et al., 2018; Leivaditi et al., 2020). However, such a task becomes hard to scale when reviewing hundreds to thousands of documents in an efficient manner for different needs (e.g., determining market trends, due diligence) especially when there is a desire for granular answers rather than clauses (e.g., amounts of liability). Granular answers to questions allow lawyers and other legal professionals the ability to triage the documents they need to read in order of risk, importance, or other criteria (e.g., first reviewing agreements that their client has provided unlimited liability coverage or most favoured nations guarantees). Finding a solution to allow rapid triage and review of documents for such granular answers have yet to be solved to our knowledge and we show progress towards that goal in this work.

The advent of and the increasing popularity of Generative AI and applications to "chat" with one's documents (e.g., ChatPDF[1], docGPT[2], CaseText[3]), which allows individuals to interact in a "natural" way with their documents and may facilitate a better understanding of legal obligations and restrictions, has complicated matters further due to the appeal of natural language interaction. This interaction can be convenient on a handful of documents but we believe that this approach also does not scale since "chatting" with a document means getting a human-like response that may be difficult to use in automated workflows without building complex post-processing systems (e.g., rules on how to respond to the various outputs). But added complexity means that further work is required either on the part of the end user or system builder to ensure that post processing can and does occur for outputs to be used as part of other pipelines. With these ideas in mind, this work investigates how Generative AI can help generate structured and partially structured answers to questions about clauses in legal documents in a manner that is usable in automated workflows and data pipelines.

To facilitate this process, we assume that we have a set (or sets) of clauses (potentially using ML to extract them) that a user would like to ask questions about in bulk with either predefined fixed options (i.e., multiple choice or multiple select) or text with a specific structure (e.g., lists of items, entities such as duration). Such outputs can facilitate the creation of automated workflows that can easily take action on the results of the questions without resorting to the complex understanding

[1]https://www.chatpdf.com/
[2]https://github.com/cesarhuret/docGPT
[3]https://casetext.com/

Proceedings of the Natural Legal Language Processing Workshop 2023, pages 62–72
December 7, 2023

of a generated answer or manual human review except at predefined points in the workflow (e.g., after documents have been ranked according to the risk associated with different questions and their answers). While such outputs are perhaps less compelling than having a "conversation" with a document, we believe that this approach scales better to large document collections, workflow automation, and general analysis of trends in contracts. Moreover, we show that more natural prompts can very easily exhibit consistency and reliability issues when examining the responses generated in a "chat" interaction paradigm (Section 3).

It is tempting to *not* use LLMs to directly generate answers since there persist issues around hallucination (Ji et al., 2023) and a lack of clarity around whether such models truly reason (Valmeekam et al., 2023) and instead use more traditional unsupervised techniques (e.g., embedding similarity). We show that such techniques are not well suited to this task, especially in light of how straightforward it is to get much better results with generative techniques (Section 5.1). The downside to the generative approach is that it requires prompting engineering, a new and popular area of research (Liu et al., 2023; Reynolds and McDonell, 2021; Zhou et al., 2022; White et al., 2023) and book publication[4], but it is not a task that we expect lawyers or other legal professionals actually *want* to do on a regular basis. That is, we might expect that a lawyer would want to "chat" with a set of documents but they do not want to go to the extreme efforts to constrain outputs to a particularly useful format via prompt engineering.

Our end goal is to find and use prompts that provide consistent answers for the same clause and reliable answers across clauses (Section 4). In particular, we are interested in finding reusable templates that allow end users to "fill in answer options" or "specify the structure of outputs" but not need to worry about overall prompt engineering (Section 5.3). The ultimate benefit to this approach is that users of such a system would only need to worry about their area of domain expertise (i.e., determining appropriate answers) and that system builders would not need to foresee all possible different combinations of options or build bespoke prompts for every lawyer-posed question.

[4]With over 500 English language books dedicated to the topic on Amazon as of April 29, 2022.

2 Background

2.1 Large Language models

Generative models such as PaLM2[5], Llama[6], and GPT-n series[7] are self-supervised models which learn to predict the next token in a sequence of tokens (Radford et al., 2018; Touvron et al., 2023a,b). These *large* language models have billions to trillions of parameters and are pre-trained on massive corpora of texts. Unlike earlier pre-trained language models, they require little to no fine-tuning and perform well in zero and few-shot settings.

In a zero-shot generation task, the model is provided with the inputs and an instruction in natural language, and the response of the model can be parsed to obtain the answer. For open-domain QA the only input is the question but for closed-domain the input also includes the context. In a few-shot setting, the model is also provided with a few examples, which have the indirect effect of "fine-tuning" the model (Brown et al., 2020). Recent large language models (e.g., GPT-3.5-Turbo, Vicuna-13B, Alpaca) have been fine-tuned, either using supervised or reinforcement learning, with prompts for a diverse set of natural language tasks (Sanh et al., 2021; Ouyang et al., 2022; Wang et al., 2022; Taori et al., 2023; Chiang et al., 2023). They have generally outperformed earlier language models on most natural language generation benchmarks including question answering, summarization, and translation (Zhang et al., 2023). Instruction-tuned models achieve better performance than fine-tuned models but can suffer from two major issues (Ji et al., 2023): inconsistency (i.e., results generated have been found to be overly reliant on the phrasing of the prompt) and hallucination (i.e., models were found to generate false/irrelevant information in some instances).

2.2 Prompt Engineering

Prompt engineering techniques (Gao et al., 2021; Liu et al., 2023; White et al., 2023) aim to design prompts that mitigate these issues. For instance, in (Gao et al., 2021) a smaller language model, such as T5, is tuned to "auto-complete" the prompts for the large language model. Prompt templates are created in (Liu et al., 2023) and (White et al., 2023) which can be auto-filled. While these methods have

[5]https://ai.google/discover/palm2/

[6]https://ai.facebook.com/blog/large-language-model-llama-meta-ai/

[7]https://platform.openai.com/docs/models

had some success, this research is still ongoing.

2.3 LLMs in the Legal Domain

Early applications of LLMs in the legal domain involved testing how well the models perform in standard bar exams. Although early versions of ChatGPT and other LLM models did not perform very well, GPT-4 and Claude 2 were found to perform particularly well on contract-based multiple-choice questions (Choi et al., 2023; Katz et al., 2023; cla). While this was promising, most of the subsequent research into the use of LLMs in the legal domain has focused on chat-style interactions (Kuppa et al., 2023), case summarization (Nay et al., 2023), and simple yes/no questions (Trautmann et al., 2022). In our previous work (Roegiest et al., 2023), we performed a pilot exploration of prompts for generating structured outputs from contracts using LLMs. To the best of our knowledge, this work is one of the first to address the creation of prompt templates to generate structured and partially structured answers in the legal domain.

3 Open-Ended Response Generation

With the popularity of LLM powered chat bots and conversational agents, it is easy to think that "chatting" with one's documents would be advantageous for lawyers and legal professionals. Such an approach can work when dealing with one or two documents but when scaling to hundreds or thousands of documents this becomes untenable. This results in needing to triage and prioritize work to be done; that is, some documents are invariably more important than others. For example, a commercial real estate company may be concerned with environmental indemnification[8] present in their leases due to new legislation, their lawyer may seek to find which documents do not have such a clause, then documents where the tenant indemnifies the company, then where the real estate company indemnifies the tenant, and finally where this indemnification is mutual. If one can identify the presence (or absence) of such a clause then the lawyer simply needs to make a determination but, again, this does not scale effectively.

We might reasonably wonder what happens if we were to ask a LLM model about the direction of mutual indemnification in a sample clause (Figure 1). If one prompts OpenAI's GPT-3.5-Turbo model

```
Lessor hereby agrees to defend, indemnify and save harmless any and all Lessee
Indemnified Parties from and against any and all Environmental Liabilities
(including, without limitation, Environmental Liabilities to the extent
resulting from conditions existing at the Leased Property at the Commencement
Date or from Releases or other violations of Environmental Laws (without fault
on the part of Lessee) originating on other property but affecting the Leased
Property) other than Environmental Liabilities to the extent caused by the
grossly negligent acts or failures to act or wilful misconduct of Lessee,
Manager or subtenants of Lessee or Manager, and their respective employees,
agents or independent contractors.

Lessee hereby agrees to defend, indemnify and save harmless any and all Lessor
Indemnified Parties from and against any and all Environmental Liabilities to
the extent caused by the grossly negligent acts or failures to act or wilful
misconduct of Lessee, -47-<PAGE> 56 Manager or subtenants of Lessee or Manager,
and their respective employees, agents or independent contractors.
Lessee hereby agrees to defend, indemnify and save harmless any and all Lessor
Indemnified Parties from and against any and all Environmental Liabilities to
the extent caused by the grossly negligent acts or failures to act or wilful
misconduct of Lessee, -47-<PAGE> 56 Manager or subtenants of Lessee or Manager,
and their respective employees, agents or independent contractors.
```

Figure 1: An example of an environmental indemnity clause with mutual indemnification.

(with temperature set to 0) with the following: *In the clause below, who indemnifies whom?* and then append the example clause, we get the following responses after regenerating a handful of times:

- The Lessor indemnifies the Lessee Indemnified Parties, and the Lessee indemnifies the Lessor Indemnified Parties.
- Lessor indemnifies Lessee Indemnified Parties for any and all Environmental Liabilities, except those caused by the grossly negligent or wilful misconduct of Lessee, Manager, or subtenants of Lessee or Manager, and their respective employees, agents or independent contractors. Lessee indemnifies Lessor Indemnified Parties for Environmental Liabilities caused by the grossly negligent or wilful misconduct of Lessee, Manager, or subtenants of Lessee or Manager, and their respective employees, agents, or independent contractors.
- Lessor indemnifies Lessee Indemnified Parties. Lessee indemnifies Lessor Indemnified Parties.

While the first and third are close, they aren't identical and the second is more of an overall summary. Moreover, these still require some amount of manual work to read and potentially process the (simplified) outputs. That is, a lawyer still reads a non-trivial amount for every clause found when they might prefer to direct efforts towards leases that do not indemnify their client. While something like nugget matching (Dang et al., 2006) could help automate this process, this is also not something that we might reasonably expect a lawyer to do.

To further illustrate this problem, we present the responses from the same prompt with a different omitted environmental indemnity clause:

- Tenant indemnifies Landlord for claims arising from the introduction of hazardous material on or after the Effective Date, and Landlord indemnifies Tenant for claims arising from the existence of hazardous material or violation of Environmental Requirements prior to the Effective Date.
- In the first paragraph Tenant indemnifies and defends Landlord, and in the second paragraph Landlord indemnifies and defends Tenant.
- Tenant indemnifies Landlord. Landlord indemnifies Tenant.

We see responses that are correct but are also quite different from the responses for the previous clause. As should be apparent by now, this inconsistency and unreliability as well as response verbosity is

[8]An environmental indemnity is a clause that provides a party with protection from losses as a result of environmental contamination or disaster.

not ideal for simplifying work process and may just exacerbate things in the long run. The following sections detail our investigation into how well popular large language models can be prompted to consistently generate (partially) structured answers to questions based on contract clauses.

4 Models and Baseline Questions

4.1 Models

We employed OpenAI's *GPT-3.5-Turbo* (Ouyang et al., 2022) and *GPT-4* (OpenAI, 2023), Google's *PaLM2* (Anil et al., 2023) and Meta's *LlaMa2 13B* (Touvron et al., 2023a) Generative AI.

4.2 Baseline Questions

In our experimental setting, we draw upon a collection of previously annotated legal documents, annotated similarly to those described in (Roegiest et al., 2018), collected from EDGAR[9] and SEDAR[10] document repositories. These documents were originally annotated to train machine learning models to identify various legal clauses of interest to lawyers and other legal professionals (e.g., non-solicitation, environmental indemnity) and now we seek to answer high-level questions about these clauses. Our questions involve various combinations of legal reasoning, summarization, and extraction of data points in order to properly answer the question.

To test the effectiveness of our approaches, we used four legal questions, each requiring a different output format and answer options. A lawyer went through a subset of the annotated clauses for each question and provided the correct answer option or altered the set of answer options when a previously unforeseen potential answer was discovered (e.g., due to low prevalence). We provide a brief summary of the four questions used, their answer options, and the associated prevalence of each option (as appropriate) in Figure 2.

5 Structured Answer Generation

To generate structured answers, one might reasonably turn toward a more traditional solution by training a discriminative multi-class (or multi-label) classifier to produce clear answers to the questions presented in this work. Such solutions (e.g., SVMs, logistic regression) are well understood and highly optimized but come with a flaw, they require sufficient examples of each class to be effective (i.e.,

Q1) **Yes/No Selection**: The question "Is there a geographical restriction on solicitation?" answers if the parties to the agreement are restricted to a specified territory while soliciting business or services. We used a set of 200 *"non-solicitation"* clauses, which describe the provisions and restrictions for solicitation. There are 15 instances where there are geographical restrictions and 185 instances where there are no geographical restrictions. Options **O1** and **O2** in Figure 2 are the tested option variants for this question.

Q2) **Single Option Selection**: We used a set of 121 *"environmental indemnity"* clauses, which describe the provisions for security or protection from losses or damage caused by environmental contamination or disasters, to answer the question "Who indemnifies whom?". Only one of the following three options applies:

a) The landlord indemnifies the tenant,
b) The tenant indemnifies the landlord, and
c) The landlord and tenant indemnify each other.

There are 6, 71, and 39 instances of the above options, respectively, and 5 instances where the clause does not contain the answer to the question. Options **O3** and **O4** in Figure 2 are the tested option variants for this question.

Q3) **Multiple Options Selection**: The question "Can the agreement be terminated for convenience?" answers the conditions under which either party to the agreement is allowed to terminate the agreement without cause. We used a set of 225 *"termination for convenience"* clauses and a set of 6 options (**O5** in Figure 2):

a) 6 instances of "agreement may be terminated without any conditions or exceptions",
b) 208 instances of "agreement may be terminated with prior notice",
c) 5 instances of "agreement may be terminated after paying a termination fee",
d) 11 instances of "agreement may be terminated after a specified time period has elapsed",
e) 7 instances of "agreement may be terminated only by mutual consent of the parties", and
f) 5 instances of "agreement may not be terminated for convenience".

Q4) **Partially Structured Response Generation**: This question "What is the timeframe of the non-solicitation clause?", also based on the non-solicitation clause, determines the duration for which the non-solicitation clause applies. As this question produces a single response extracted or summarized from the clause, it is free-form and has no fixed set of options.

Figure 2: Questions used for testing the LLM models

low prevalence classes can be hard to overcome). For example, landlord indemnification is a relatively rare occurrence in our data and one for which data augmentation is not guaranteed to work. Indeed, we have attempted to address this in prior work (Chitta and Hudek, 2019) but the solution did not scale well for extremely low prevalence or nuanced differences between options. It has been our experience that such cases arise naturally in the legal domain where rare outcomes tend to be the most problematic and equally hard to identify at scale. Accordingly, models that require little to no training data (or other labelled) examples become compelling solutions to this problem and we spend the rest of this section discussing our experiments.

5.1 Zero-shot Semantic Similarity Matching

Prior to the rise of LLMs for generative tasks, a common use case was to perform some form of matching between questions and answers (Veeranna et al., 2016; Yin et al., 2019) based upon LLM embeddings of questions, potentially additional context, and the possible answers. As this is arguably a less labour intensive task than trying to find an ideal prompt for every question (or a one-size-fits-all prompt), we first turned to this approach in the hopes that it might allow end users to see value more quickly.

[9] `https://www.sec.gov/edgar`
[10] `https://www.sedarplus.ca/`

```
O1: a) Yes
    b) No

O2: a) There are geographical restrictions in the
       non-solicit clause.
    b) There are no geographical restrictions in the
       non-solicit clause.

O3: a) Landlord indemnifies Tenant.
    b) Tenant indemnifies Landlord.
    c) There is mutual indemnification.

O4: a) The landlord indemnifies the tenant.
    b) The tenant indemnifies the landlord.
    c) There is mutual indemnity between the landlord
       and the tenant.

O5: a) The agreement may be terminated without any
       conditions or exceptions.
    b) The agreement may be terminated with prior notice.
    c) The agreement may be terminated by either party but
       the terminating party has to pay a termination fee.
    d) The agreement may be terminated by either party
       after a specified time period has elapsed.
    e) The agreement may be terminated by mutual consent
       of the parties.
    f) The agreement may not be terminated for convenience.
```

Figure 3: Options used for testing the LLM models.

Options	PIL-LegalBERT	Ada
Q1: Is there a geographical restriction on solicitation?		
O1	41.2	8.0
O2	91.9	73.4
Q2: Who indemnifies whom?		
O3	32.2	5.5
O4	32.2	22.6
Q3: Can the agreement be terminated for convenience?		
O5	28.4	0.5

Table 1: Accuracy (in percentage) of the different embedding models with different answer options on the single option and multiple option questions.

Given the text of the clause T, and a set of answer options H, we use a sequence embedding model M (Selva Birunda and Kanniga Devi, 2021) to obtain the embeddings for the clause and the answer options and then predict the answer which has the highest similarity with the clause: $\tilde{h} = \arg\max_{h \in H} \cos\left(M\left(T\right), M\left(h\right)\right)$. We used two large language models to compare the performance of this method: (1) the LegalBERT model trained on the Pile-Of-Law dataset (Henderson et al., 2022)[11] and (2) the OpenAI Ada model (Neelakantan et al., 2022). We truncated the clauses to less than 512 and 8191 tokens in length, respectively, in order to adhere to model token limits.

5.1.1 Results

As seen in Table 1, **O1** is not a good option set for **Q1** due to the lack of context for any meaningful semantic matching but, in contrast,**O2** does much better because the options are clear fully-formed sentences. Both models suffer from the same issue by rarely predicting option (a) correctly, regardless of the option set, with the Ada model getting this right once and LegalBERT never predicting it correctly. The seemingly high accuracy is only due to the imbalanced distribution of the answers in the test dataset (185 instances of option (b) to 15 of option (a)). A similar situation holds for **Q2** with neither model being able to correctly predict option (a) and option (b) consistently.

The situation is worse for question **Q3** as without a tedious cut-off selection process (that may be untenable in the real world due to prevalence issues), similarity matching can only be used to easily predict the most similar option. With this in mind, even being lenient in our evaluation (i.e., does a model predict any correct option) neither model is able to perform well on this question. Overall, the LegalBERT model performs better than the Ada model, in all cases, because it has been trained on legal data but still performs far too poorly for end user applications. While more recent and complex systems, like Logiformer (Xu et al., 2022), may improve these results, such approaches are substantially more complicated than our prompt engineering technique and our preliminary exploration with them suggested additional fine-tuning would be needed.

5.2 Question Specific Prompts

Based upon preliminary manual investigations (Roegiest et al., 2023) into whether one could prompt LLMs to produce structured outputs, we turned to a more thorough and structured investigation of different LLMs and prompt styles. Although we tested our prompts on all four models, we focused on GPT-3.5-Turbo and optimized the prompts for it because of its reasonable costs, ease of incorporation into software (i.e., no infrastructure support), and general widespread adoption. The ideal would be to create bespoke prompts for every generative model but we did not believe that this approach would yield substantive improvements other than to indicate the delta between a tuned and untuned prompt. Essentially, if we know these prompts work consistently well on a single model and perform reasonably well on other similar models then we can have confidence that prompt templates are a viable solution irrespective of which model one chooses.

Our prompts (Figure 4) were constructed using learnings from our initial pilot exploration (Roegiest et al., 2023)[12] (across thousands of different

[11] https://huggingface.co/pile-of-law/legalbert-large-1.7M-2

[12] A prompt testing tool that can be used to run and test the prompts listed in this paper is available at https://github.com/zuvaai/gpt-tool.

```
P1: Read the following non-solicitation legal clause:
    {{Clause}}
    Pretend you are a party to the agreement in which the
    non-solicitation legal clause you have read exists in.
    You only know what you have read in this prompt.
    Is there a geographical restriction in the
    non-solicitation legal clause?
    If the clause does not specify, respond with: "Unable
    to determine". In your response, only include the
    single most correct option:
    {{Options}}
    In your response, only include the bucket names above.
    Do not provide an explanation or additional
    information.
```

```
P2: Read the following environmental indemnity legal clause:
    {{Clause}}
    Pretend you are a party to the agreement in which the
    environmental indemnity legal clause you have read exists
    in. You only know what you have read in this prompt.
    Who indemnifies whom?
    If the clause does not specify, respond with: "Unable
    to determine". In your response, only include the single
    most correct option:
    {{Options}}
    In your response, only include the bucket names above. Do
    not provide an explanation or additional information.
```

```
P3: Read the following termination for convenience legal clause:
    {{Clause}}
    Pretend you are a party to the agreement in which the termination for convenience legal clause you have read exists in.
    You only know what you have read in this prompt.
    Can the agreement be terminated for convenience according to the termination for convenience legal clause you have read?
    If the clause does not have any information about termination for convenience, respond with: "Unable to determine". In
    your response, only include the following most correct groups:
    {{Options}}
    In your response, only include the bucket names above. Do not provide an explanation or additional information.
```

```
P4: Read the following non-solicitation legal clause:
    {{Clause}}
    Pretend you are a party to the agreement in which the
    non-solicitation legal clause you have read exists in.
    You only know what you have read in this prompt.
    Extract the duration for which the non-solicitation
    clause is applicable. Do not extract any other
    information from the clause. If the clause does not
    contain this information, respond with
    "Unable to determine".
```

```
P5: Read the following  non-solicitation legal clause:

    {{Clause}}

    Pretend you are a party to the agreement in which the
    non-solicitation legal clause you have read exists in.
    You only know what you have read in this prompt.

    Extract the timeframe of the non-solicitation legal clause.
    Do not extract any other information from the clause.
    The response should be exact words from the text you have
    read. If the clause explicitly states the duration for
    which the non-solicitation clause applies, respond with
    this information extracted from the clause.
    If the clause does not explicitly state the duration for
    which the non-solicitation applies, and the
    non-solicitation applies for the whole duration of the
    agreement, respond with "term of the agreement".
    If the clause does not contain this information, respond
    with "Unable to determine".
```

Figure 4: Prompts used for testing the LLM models.

prompt, clause, and option combinations) which highlighted a strong need to embed the LLM role as one where they are party to the agreement (i.e., adopting a persona), provide escape hatches when no answer was appropriate (i.e., return "Unable to determine"), and limiting the potential for creative answering both in the prompt (i.e., "provide no justification") and in hyper-parameters (i.e., temperature set to 0). While these are not necessarily critical for success, we found that LLMs were generally more reliable and consistent in how they answered questions when these were factored into the prompt. Moreover, we never set a "system" message as there was no guarantee that a given model would support it or listen to it. Indeed, initial experiments using OpenAI models did not provide any strong indication that a "system" message would improve the outputs. We ensured clauses were shorter than $20,000$ characters in order to adhere to model token limits.

5.2.1 Results

For Q1, we started with the prompt **P1** shown in Figure 4. $\{\{Options\}\}$ is replaced by the options and $\{\{Clause\}\}$ is replaced by the text of the clause. The phrase "only include the single most correct option" aims to ensure that only **one** of the answer options is generated and our aforementioned guardrails (i.e., escape hatches and creative writing prevention) are used to ensure that the response from the API is able to be parsed, via regular expression, to obtain the structured answer to the question. All the models perform reasonably well with the **O1** option set (Figure 3) of just "yes" and "no," unlike the similarity matching approach. However, we find that with the more well-formed option set **O2**, both PaLM2 and Llama2 models improve substantially. The GPT-4 model, surprisingly, generates "Unable to determine" for many clauses with options **O2**, leading to a lower accuracy.

Prompt	Options	GPT-3.5 Turbo	GPT-4	PaLM2	LLaMA2-13
Q1: Is there a geographical restriction on solicitation?					
P1	O1	96.5	92.9	88.9	90.9
	O2	93.9	59.8	91.5	95.9
PT1	O2	77.4	62.2	91.4	91.9
Q2: Who indemnifies whom?					
P2	O3	66.1	94.2	79.3	47.9
	O4	67.8	95.0	84.3	44.6
PT1	O4	67.7	94.2	72.7	57.0
Q3: Can the agreement be terminated for convenience?					
P3	O5	96.0	56.4	79.6	30.2
PT2	O5	95.1	48.9	69.3	7.1

Table 2: Accuracy (in percentage) of the LLM models with the various combinations of prompts and options on the single option and multiple option questions.

Similar to **Q1**, **Q2** also needs only one option to be chosen and we use a similar prompt, **P2**, with options **O3** and **O4**. Options **O4** contain clear fully-formed sentences and are more effective than options **O3**, especially with the PaLM2 model. This is partly due to the fact that **O4** does not invite ad-

Prompt	Metric	GPT-3.5 Turbo	GPT-4	PaLM2	LLaMA2-13
Q4: What is the timeframe of the non-solicitation clause?					
P4	Rouge-l F1	0.397	0.422	0.215	0.079
	Exact match accuracy	23.6	25.1	1.5	0
	Semantic match accuracy	48.2	69.3	36.6	23.6
P5	Rouge-l F1	0.481	0.482	0.313	0.047
	Exact match accuracy	24.6	21.6	8.0	0
	Semantic match accuracy	64.8	86.9	51.3	8.0

Table 3: Performance of the LLM models with the different combinations of prompts and options on the partially structured response question.

ditional generation when compared to **O3**'s more "open-ended" phrasing as well as making it more clear what mutual indemnification means. Despite being tailored to GPT-3.5-Turbo, we see that GPT-4 and PaLM2 both answer this question much better than it. While it is not entirely clear why this happens, we suspect it may just be due to the complex nature of how indemnification, especially mutual indemnification, can be worded and that this might be captured less well by GPT-3.5-Turbo.

Q3 requires multiple option selection and so the prompt **P3** is styled to respond with the "most correct groups," and, like previous prompts, has the necessary guardrails to help constrain generation. As this is a more difficult style of question, we are more lenient and give partial credit if at least one of the correct options is present in the generated response. The results themselves are not all that revealing with GPT-3.5-Turbo being the most effective followed by the other very large models.

Finally, **Q4** requires partially structured free-text responses which can lead to increased creativity and hallucination by LLM models. Prompts for **Q4** seek to mitigate this issue by requiring models to "extract" only the relevant information, to not "extract" superfluous information in the prompt, and using our usual guardrails for generation. We evaluate the responses for this question using three metrics: (i) *Rouge-l F1-score* (Lin and Och, 2004) which measures the overlap between the longest co-occurring sequences in the generated response and the expected responses (i.e., higher is better); (ii) *exact match accuracy* which measures the percentage of clauses where the generated and expected responses match exactly; and (iii) *semantic match accuracy* which measures the percentage of clauses where a response contains all the pertinent information included in the expected response and is evaluated manually. *Semantic match accuracy* models the situation that the LLM response is correct but is not text extracted from the provided clause.

We found it more difficult to find an appropriate prompt to extract the relevant portion of the clause. Using the simple prompt **P4**, all models fail to perform well. The most common expected answer for the timeframe of non-solicitation was "during the term of the agreement" but all models were unable to produce this answer. We added additional instructions in prompt **P5**, to respond with the "term of the agreement" when applicable which resulted in substantial improvements to model efficacy.

The restriction to "not provide an explanation or additional information" is an attempt to mitigate a model's creativity but it is not consistently effective, and some amount of post-processing is required to obtain the structured response. For instance, the LLaMA2 model usually preceded the option selected with "Based on the clause you provided," and sometimes even generated garbled text. The PaLM2 model was the best at adhering to the prompt and generating only the option letter. The OpenAI models, in most cases, generated the text of the option along with the option letter.

In contrast with **Q4** despite the instructions attempting to avoid hallucinations, we found that they did occur occasionally with some of the most egregious examples coming from PaLM2 (e.g., saying a duration was 2 years when it was, in fact, 90 days). Due to the nature of how they were trained (i.e., to produce plausible English responses), all models required some amount of post-processing to remove a preamble that would make the response a valid sentence (e.g., OpenAI models had a preamble of "The duration for which the non-solicitation clause is applicable is", PaLM2 generated "The non-solicitation clause is applicable for").

We are not surprised that the Llama2 model performed particularly poorly on **Q4** based upon its prior performance, but are surprised that it generated many more unexpected responses than we would have anticipated. For example, it would sometimes respond with a question back to the user (e.g., "*Sure! I'd be happy to help you with that. Please go ahead and ask your question.*"). Some of Llama2's responses are surely attributable to it being a much smaller model relative to the others tested but may also stem from a much different set of training data. The details of its training data have not been publicly discussed in much detail (to the best of our knowledge) but it would appear that little of it resembled our prompts due to its poor performance on all but the simplest question (i.e., **Q1**). While we cannot make any claims about the training data of the other models, it appears that there may have been similar instances, either stylistically

```
PT1: Read the following {{Clause-name}} legal clause:
     {{Clause}}
     Pretend you are a party to the agreement in which the
     {{Clause-name}} legal clause you have read exists in.
     You only know what you have read in this prompt.
     Which of the following is true according to the
     {{Clause-name}} legal clause you have read?
     If the clause does not specify, respond with: "Unable
     to determine". In your response, only include the
     single most correct option:
     {{Options}}
     In your response, only include the bucket names above.
     Do not provide an explanation or additional
     information.

PT2: Read the following {{Clause-name}} legal clause:
     {{Clause}}
     Pretend you are a party to the agreement in which the
     {{Clause-name}} legal clause you have read exists in.
     You only know what you have read in this prompt.
     Which of the following is true according to the
     {{Clause-name}} legal clause you have read?
     If the clause does not specify, respond with: "Unable
     to determine". In your response, only include the
     following most correct groups:
     {{Options}}
     In your response, only include the bucket names above.
     Do not provide an explanation or additional
     information.
```

Figure 5: Prompt Templates for single option and multiple option questions.

(i.e., multiple choice) or thematically (i.e., legal), in their training data given their performance.

5.3 Reusable Prompt Templates

In the previous section, we saw promise in having specialized prompts for different questions but even then many elements were shared among them. Accordingly, we extend this approach to investigate the feasibility of "fill-in-the-blank" prompt templates that allow us to consolidate on fewer prompt possibilities. In examining our specialized prompts, we found that the key "changable" aspects of the prompts were: the name of the clause, the question being asked, and the answer options; everything else was largely equivalent or very nearly so. Based upon some analysis of our existing prompts, we created two generalized prompt templates, shown in Figure 5, that seek to satisfy single option and multiple option selection. The clause name and answer options need to be filled in by an end-user but we simplify the process by replacing bespoke questions with a generic one, "Which of the following is true according to the clause you have read?". The prompt template **PT1** asks the model to select the "single most correct option" and is meant for multiple choice questions. The prompt template **PT2**, on the other hand, asks for "the most correct groups" and is meant for questions for which more than a single option may be appropriate.

Based upon our building of these prompts and the results in Table 2, answer options can clearly play a non-trivial role when using the prompt templates as they need to contain sufficient information for the model to make a determination. Generic answer options, such as those in **O1**, obviously do not perform well but when the answer options are elaborate and contain sufficient context, the accuracy is only slightly worse than the accuracy of the question-specific prompts for most models. As before, the PaLM2 and LLaMA2 model perform worse than either OpenAI models but such an outcome is not unexpected given that these prompts were tailored to what worked for GPT-3.5-Turbo.

From these results and those of the previous section, we have strong evidence that creating general prompt templates to generate structured answers for single and multiple options questions is indeed possible and that model effectiveness is not seriously impacted by doing so. However, we have not had the same success for questions requiring partially structured responses, as there is high variability in the expected responses, which need multiple escape hatches and conditions to ensure only the correct information is produced.

6 Limitations and Future Work

In this work, we focused on optimizing prompts for GPT-3.5-Turbo for the sake of simplicity and cost. Moreover, as there are increasing numbers of models being made available for commercial use (Conover et al., 2023; Biderman et al., 2023; Almazrouei et al., 2023; Touvron et al., 2023b), we felt that overall GPT-3.5-Turbo provided a reasonable baseline due to it being an obvious "initial" starting point that one might use before jumping into fine-tuning an "open" model. The benefit to this was the somewhat surprising result from Tables 2 and 3 is that prompts optimized for one LLM can produce relatively competitive results (or exceed the base LLM) with the same prompt. Further exploration remains to determine how much benefit would be gained fine-tuning a smaller model, like Llama2, given that the much larger models are "by default" apparently much better at our desired tasks. Subsequent investigation into this is planned as it is far less cost efficient to fine-tune larger LLMs and more generally reducing model size has other social benefits (e.g., less carbon footprint).

We have also largely operated under the assumption that an end user has the appropriate clause easily available about which they can ask questions. As retrieval augmented generation has become a popular topic of research (Lewis et al., 2021), combining our approach with existing approach will invariably require examining how well these prompts and models deal with false positives. Our prompts do have escape mechanisms and guard rails to hopefully prevent obvious errors from occurring but we leave investigation of how errors propagate in end-to-end systems with our prompts to future work.

7 Conclusions

We have presented a structured answer generation task based on identifying the correct answer for a legal question given an associated clause from a document, detailed some issues with relying solely on natural language question answering, and explore solutions using unsupervised and generative methods. We have shown that the prompt-based generative methods exceed semantic similarity-based approaches and that despite question specific prompts performing better, that generalized prompts can be used with little decrease in overall effectiveness. Finally, partially structured answer generation is shown to be possible with bespoke prompts but generalized approaches do fare well due to the large amount of variance in the output formats that are required to accommodate the types of information desired.

References

Anthropic claude-2.

Ebtesam Almazrouei, Hamza Alobeidli, Abdulaziz Alshamsi, Alessandro Cappelli, Ruxandra Cojocaru, Merouane Debbah, Etienne Goffinet, Daniel Heslow, Julien Launay, Quentin Malartic, Badreddine Noune, Baptiste Pannier, and Guilherme Penedo. 2023. Falcon-40B: an open large language model with state-of-the-art performance.

Rohan Anil, Andrew M Dai, Orhan Firat, Melvin Johnson, Dmitry Lepikhin, Alexandre Passos, Siamak Shakeri, Emanuel Taropa, Paige Bailey, Zhifeng Chen, et al. 2023. Palm 2 technical report.

Stella Biderman, Hailey Schoelkopf, Quentin Anthony, Herbie Bradley, Kyle O'Brien, Eric Hallahan, Mohammad Aflah Khan, Shivanshu Purohit, USVSN Sai Prashanth, Edward Raff, Aviya Skowron, Lintang Sutawika, and Oskar van der Wal. 2023. Pythia: A suite for analyzing large language models across training and scaling.

Tom B. Brown, Benjamin Mann, Nick Ryder, Melanie Subbiah, Jared Kaplan, Prafulla Dhariwal, Arvind Neelakantan, Pranav Shyam, Girish Sastry, Amanda Askell, Sandhini Agarwal, Ariel Herbert-Voss, Gretchen Krueger, Tom Henighan, Rewon Child, Aditya Ramesh, Daniel M. Ziegler, Jeffrey Wu, Clemens Winter, Christopher Hesse, Mark Chen, Eric Sigler, Mateusz Litwin, Scott Gray, Benjamin Chess, Jack Clark, Christopher Berner, Sam McCandlish, Alec Radford, Ilya Sutskever, and Dario Amodei. 2020. Language models are few-shot learners.

Wei-Lin Chiang, Zhuohan Li, Zi Lin, Ying Sheng, Zhanghao Wu, Hao Zhang, Lianmin Zheng, Siyuan Zhuang, Yonghao Zhuang, Joseph E. Gonzalez, Ion Stoica, and Eric P. Xing. 2023. Vicuna: An open-source chatbot impressing GPT-4 with 90%* ChatGPT quality.

Radha Chitta and Alexander K. Hudek. 2019. A reliable and accurate multiple choice question answering system for due diligence. In *Proceedings of the International Conference on Artificial Intelligence and Law*, page 184–188.

Jonathan H Choi, Kristin E Hickman, Amy Monahan, and Daniel Schwarcz. 2023. ChatGPT goes to law school. *Social Science Research Network*.

Mike Conover, Matt Hayes, Ankit Mathur, Xiangrui Meng, Jianwei Xie, Jun Wan, Ali Ghodsi, Patrick Wendell, and Matei Zaharia. 2023. Hello dolly: Democratizing the magic of chatgpt with open models. `https://www.databricks.com/blog/2023/03/24/hello-dolly-democratizing-magic-chatgpt-open-models.html`.

Hoa Trang Dang, Jimmy Lin, and Daine Kelly. 2006. Overview of the trec 2006 question answering track. In *Proceedings of the Text Retrieval Conference*.

Tianyu Gao, Adam Fisch, and Danqi Chen. 2021. Making pre-trained language models better few-shot learners. In *Proceedings of the International Joint Conference on Natural Language Processing*, pages 3816–3830.

Peter Henderson, Mark S. Krass, Lucia Zheng, Neel Guha, Christopher D. Manning, Dan Jurafsky, and Daniel E. Ho. 2022. Pile of law: Learning responsible data filtering from the law and a 256gb open-source legal dataset.

Ziwei Ji, Nayeon Lee, Rita Frieske, Tiezheng Yu, Dan Su, Yan Xu, Etsuko Ishii, Ye Jin Bang, Andrea Madotto, and Pascale Fung. 2023. Survey of hallucination in natural language generation. *ACM Computing Surveys*, 55(12):1–38.

Daniel Martin Katz, Michael James Bommarito, Shang Gao, and Pablo Arredondo. 2023. Gpt-4 passes the bar exam. *Social Science Research Network*.

Aditya Kuppa, Nikon Rasumov-Rahe, and Marc Voses. 2023. Chain of reference prompting helps llm to think like a lawyer. In *Generative AI+ Law Workshop*.

Spyretta Leivaditi, Julien Rossi, and Evangelos Kanoulas. 2020. A benchmark for lease contract review. *CoRR*, abs/2010.10386.

Patrick Lewis, Ethan Perez, Aleksandra Piktus, Fabio Petroni, Vladimir Karpukhin, Naman Goyal, Heinrich Küttler, Mike Lewis, Wen tau Yih, Tim Rocktäschel, Sebastian Riedel, and Douwe Kiela. 2021. Retrieval-augmented generation for knowledge-intensive nlp tasks.

Chin-Yew Lin and Franz Josef Och. 2004. Automatic evaluation of machine translation quality using longest common subsequence and skip-bigram statistics. In *Proceedings of the Association for Computational Linguistics*, pages 605–612.

Pengfei Liu, Weizhe Yuan, Jinlan Fu, Zhengbao Jiang, Hiroaki Hayashi, and Graham Neubig. 2023. Pre-train, prompt, and predict: A systematic survey of prompting methods in natural language processing. *ACM Computing Surveys*, 55(9).

John J Nay, David Karamardian, Sarah B Lawsky, Wenting Tao, Meghana Bhat, Raghav Jain, Aaron Travis Lee, Jonathan H Choi, and Jungo Kasai. 2023. Large language models as tax attorneys: A case study in legal capabilities emergence. *arXiv preprint arXiv:2306.07075*.

Arvind Neelakantan, Tao Xu, Raul Puri, Alec Radford, Jesse Michael Han, Jerry Tworek, Qiming Yuan, Nikolas Tezak, Jong Wook Kim, Chris Hallacy, Johannes Heidecke, Pranav Shyam, Boris Power, Tyna Eloundou Nekoul, Girish Sastry, Gretchen Krueger, David Schnurr, Felipe Petroski Such, Kenny Hsu, Madeleine Thompson, Tabarak Khan, Toki Sherbakov, Joanne Jang, Peter Welinder, and Lilian Weng. 2022. Text and code embeddings by contrastive pre-training.

OpenAI. 2023. GPT-4 technical report.

Long Ouyang, Jeff Wu, Xu Jiang, Diogo Almeida, Carroll L. Wainwright, Pamela Mishkin, Chong Zhang, Sandhini Agarwal, Katarina Slama, Alex Ray, John Schulman, Jacob Hilton, Fraser Kelton, Luke Miller, Maddie Simens, Amanda Askell, Peter Welinder, Paul Christiano, Jan Leike, and Ryan Lowe. 2022. Training language models to follow instructions with human feedback.

Alec Radford, Karthik Narasimhan, Tim Salimans, Ilya Sutskever, et al. 2018. Improving language understanding by generative pre-training.

Laria Reynolds and Kyle McDonell. 2021. Prompt programming for large language models: Beyond the few-shot paradigm.

Adam Roegiest, Radha Chitta, Jonathan Donnelly, Maya Lash, Alexandra Vtyurina, and François Longtin. 2023. A search for prompts: Generating structured answers from contracts.

Adam Roegiest, Alexander K Hudek, and Anne McNulty. 2018. A dataset and an examination of identifying passages for due diligence. In *Proceedings of the international ACM SIGIR conference on research & development in information retrieval*, pages 465–474.

Victor Sanh, Albert Webson, Colin Raffel, Stephen H Bach, Lintang Sutawika, Zaid Alyafeai, Antoine Chaffin, Arnaud Stiegler, Teven Le Scao, Arun Raja, et al. 2021. Multitask prompted training enables zero-shot task generalization.

S Selva Birunda and R Kanniga Devi. 2021. A review on word embedding techniques for text classification. *Innovative Data Communication Technologies and Application: Proceedings of ICIDCA 2020*, pages 267–281.

Rohan Taori, Ishaan Gulrajani, Tianyi Zhang, Yann Dubois, Xuechen Li, Carlos Guestrin, Percy Liang, and Tatsunori B. Hashimoto. 2023. Stanford alpaca: An instruction-following llama model.

Hugo Touvron, Louis Martin, Kevin Stone, Peter Albert, Amjad Almahairi, Yasmine Babaei, Nikolay Bashlykov, Soumya Batra, Prajjwal Bhargava, Shruti Bhosale, Dan Bikel, Lukas Blecher, Cristian Canton Ferrer, Moya Chen, Guillem Cucurull, David Esiobu, Jude Fernandes, Jeremy Fu, Wenyin Fu, Brian Fuller, Cynthia Gao, Vedanuj Goswami, Naman Goyal, Anthony Hartshorn, Saghar Hosseini, Rui Hou, Hakan Inan, Marcin Kardas, Viktor Kerkez, Madian Khabsa, Isabel Kloumann, Artem Korenev, Punit Singh Koura, Marie-Anne Lachaux, Thibaut Lavril, Jenya Lee, Diana Liskovich, Yinghai Lu, Yuning Mao, Xavier Martinet, Todor Mihaylov, Pushkar Mishra, Igor Molybog, Yixin Nie, Andrew Poulton, Jeremy Reizenstein, Rashi Rungta, Kalyan Saladi, Alan Schelten, Ruan Silva, Eric Michael Smith, Ranjan Subramanian, Xiaoqing Ellen Tan, Binh Tang, Ross Taylor, Adina Williams, Jian Xiang Kuan, Puxin Xu, Zheng Yan, Iliyan Zarov, Yuchen Zhang, Angela Fan, Melanie Kambadur, Sharan Narang, Aurelien Rodriguez, Robert Stojnic, Sergey Edunov, and Thomas Scialom. 2023a. Llama 2: Open foundation and fine-tuned chat models.

Hugo Touvron, Louis Martin, Kevin Stone, Peter Albert, Amjad Almahairi, Yasmine Babaei, Nikolay Bashlykov, Soumya Batra, Prajjwal Bhargava, Shruti Bhosale, Dan Bikel, Lukas Blecher, Cristian Canton Ferrer, Moya Chen, Guillem Cucurull, David Esiobu, Jude Fernandes, Jeremy Fu, Wenyin Fu, Brian Fuller, Cynthia Gao, Vedanuj Goswami, Naman Goyal, Anthony Hartshorn, Saghar Hosseini, Rui Hou, Hakan Inan, Marcin Kardas, Viktor Kerkez, Madian Khabsa, Isabel Kloumann, Artem Korenev, Punit Singh Koura, Marie-Anne Lachaux, Thibaut Lavril, Jenya Lee, Diana Liskovich, Yinghai Lu, Yuning Mao, Xavier Martinet, Todor Mihaylov, Pushkar Mishra, Igor Molybog, Yixin Nie, Andrew Poulton, Jeremy Reizenstein, Rashi Rungta, Kalyan Saladi, Alan Schelten, Ruan Silva, Eric Michael Smith, Ranjan Subramanian, Xiaoqing Ellen Tan, Binh Tang, Ross Taylor, Adina Williams, Jian Xiang Kuan, Puxin Xu, Zheng Yan, Iliyan Zarov, Yuchen Zhang, Angela Fan, Melanie Kambadur, Sharan Narang, Aurelien Rodriguez, Robert Stojnic, Sergey Edunov, and Thomas Scialom. 2023b. LLaMA 2: Open foundation and fine-tuned chat models.

Dietrich Trautmann, Alina Petrova, and Frank Schilder. 2022. Legal prompt engineering for multilingual legal judgement prediction.

Karthik Valmeekam, Matthew Marquez, Sarath Sreedharan, and Subbarao Kambhampati. 2023. On the planning abilities of large language models – a critical investigation.

Sappadla Prateek Veeranna, Jinseok Nam, Eneldo Loza Mencıa, and Johannes Fürnkranz. 2016. Using semantic similarity for multi-label zero-shot classification of text documents. In *Proceeding of European Symposium on Artificial Neural Networks, Computational Intelligence and Machine Learning*, pages 423–428.

Yizhong Wang, Swaroop Mishra, Pegah Alipoormolabashi, Yeganeh Kordi, Amirreza Mirzaei, Anjana Arunkumar, Arjun Ashok, Arut Selvan Dhanasekaran, Atharva Naik, David Stap, et al. 2022. Benchmarking generalization via in-context instructions on 1,600+ language tasks.

Jules White, Quchen Fu, Sam Hays, Michael Sandborn, Carlos Olea, Henry Gilbert, Ashraf Elnashar, Jesse Spencer-Smith, and Douglas C. Schmidt. 2023. A prompt pattern catalog to enhance prompt engineering with chatgpt.

Fangzhi Xu, Jun Liu, Qika Lin, Yudai Pan, and Lingling Zhang. 2022. Logiformer: A two-branch graph transformer network for interpretable logical reasoning. In *Proceedings of the International ACM SIGIR Conference on Research and Development in Information Retrieval*, page 1055–1065.

Wenpeng Yin, Jamaal Hay, and Dan Roth. 2019. Benchmarking zero-shot text classification: Datasets, evaluation and entailment approach.

Tianyi Zhang, Faisal Ladhak, Esin Durmus, Percy Liang, Kathleen McKeown, and Tatsunori B Hashimoto. 2023. Benchmarking large language models for news summarization.

Yongchao Zhou, Andrei Ioan Muresanu, Ziwen Han, Keiran Paster, Silviu Pitis, Harris Chan, and Jimmy Ba. 2022. Large language models are human-level prompt engineers.

Legal Judgment Prediction: If You Are Going to Do It, Do It Right

Masha Medvedeva
eLaw Center for Law and Digital Technologies
& Department of Business Studies,
Faculty of Law,
Leiden University, the Netherlands
m.medvedeva@law.leidenuniv.nl

Pauline McBride
COHUBICOL,
Law, Science, Technology
and Society (LSTS),
Vrije Universiteit Brussel, Belgium
pauline.mcbride@vub.be

Abstract

The field of Legal Judgment Prediction (LJP) has witnessed significant growth in the past decade, with over 100 papers published in the past three years alone. Our comprehensive survey of over 150 papers reveals a stark reality: only ~7% of published papers are doing what they set out to do - predict court decisions. We delve into the reasons behind the flawed and unreliable nature of the remaining experiments, emphasising their limited utility in the legal domain. We examine the distinctions between predicting court decisions and the practices of legal professionals in their daily work. We explore how a lack of attention to the identity and needs of end-users has fostered the misconception that LJP is a near-solved challenge suitable for practical application, and contributed to the surge in academic research in the field. To address these issues, we examine three different dimensions of 'doing LJP right': using data appropriate for the task; tackling explainability; and adopting an application-centric approach to model reporting and evaluation. We formulate a practical checklist of recommendations, delineating the characteristics that are required if a judgment prediction system is to be a valuable addition to the legal field.

1 Introduction

The task of predicting court decisions has been a topic of great interest since at least the 60s (Lawlor, 1963; Mackaay and Robillard, 1974). It has gained traction in recent years due to policies promoting publishing case law around the world, and increased efficiency and popularity of machine learning.

Today there are more than 150 academic papers claiming to predict court decisions (a.k.a. Legal Judgment Prediction) using natural language processing (NLP) and machine learning, many reporting accuracies and F1-scores of over 90% (see, for instance, Sulea et al., 2017; Varga et al., 2021; Sert et al., 2022, among others).

The media has speculated about the advent of robojudges and automated lawyers for years (Griffin, 2016; Markou, 2020; Kelly, 2022). Many in the justice sector are persuaded that machine learning technologies might usefully be employed to predict the outcomes of cases (CEPEJ, 2018). Some judges believe these technologies could even make "very minor" decisions.[1]

Yet, these systems are not widely used. While there are a number of ethical considerations (Leins et al., 2020) including issues of bias in the data (Angwin et al., 2016) that could be the reason for the hesitancy, in this paper we will demonstrate that there may be a different root cause, namely that the setup of the experiments presented in the overwhelming majority of academic papers does not allow the systems to do what they claim to be doing - *predicting court decisions*.

2 Related work

The field of Legal Judgment Prediction (LJP) has rapidly expanded over the years, with over 150 papers published in the last 10 years. The majority of the papers that we reviewed use the *text* of historical decisions to make predictions on unseen data. Some do not use NLP, but rely on manually extracted variables to make the predictions (notably, Katz et al. (2017). We looked specifically at papers in English that conduct experiments on *court* decisions, rather than any other legal decisions (excluding, for instance Branting et al. (2021) focused on WIPO decisions).

Of all the countries whose court cases feature among the reviewed papers, China has the highest proportion overall (78 papers). China publishes millions of cases online, many of which are available as part of the CAIL2018 dataset (Xiao et al., 2018) with over 2 million cases. Bench-

[1] https://www.judiciary.uk/wp-content/uploads/2023/06/Law-Society-Scotland-Law-and-Tech-Conference-2023.pdf

Proceedings of the Natural Legal Language Processing Workshop 2023, pages 73–84
December 7, 2023

mark datasets attract many to develop new methods and improve the scores, with LexGLUE ECHR (Chalkidis et al., 2022) among the more prominent ones for the European Court of Human Rights (ECtHR). In fact, at least 27 papers we reviewed attempt to predict decisions of the ECtHR, with one providing access to a regularly updated website (`jurisays.com`) that predicts decisions in real-time.

A work that provides an even more ready-to-use tool is Galli et al. (2022). The paper includes a link to a website where one can input one's claims and receive a prediction for Italian and Bulgarian VAT cases.[2]

With so much published research, predicting court decisions (at least for some courts) may seem like a solved task, e.g. Sulea et al. (2017) achieves 99% accuracy for predicting decisions of French courts, Quemy and Wrembel (2022) achieves 98% accuracy for the judgments of the ECtHR.

3 Getting your 'facts' right

In this paper we focus on issues with the way that research in LJP is conducted today. The main issue, which concerns the experimental setup, was previously addressed in Pasquale and Cashwell (2018), (focusing on Aletras et al. (2016) paper), and later in Medvedeva et al. (2023) (reviewing a larger corpus of 27 papers). We are going to revisit this issue taking account of 171 papers in the field.

Presently, predictive systems predominantly rely on case facts extracted from judgments. Specifically, these machine learning systems are fed the text of the 'facts' section of the cases (and sometimes also the reasoning of the court) as inputs together with the corresponding decisions (e.g. violation/no violation of an article of the European Convention on Human Rights) as labels. The systems are trained to 'predict' decisions; they learn patterns within the input which correspond to particular labels. They are then evaluated on a test set (i.e. 'unseen' case facts that were not included in the training set). The 'facts' that comprise the test set, like those of the training set, are extracted from published final judgments. The labels used to evaluate the systems' performance on the test set can also be found in those judgments. While such systems might achieve high performance, they are never actually tested on 'real' data, that is data that is genuinely available to potential end-users before the judgment is reached or published. The actual user of these systems, let's say a lawyer looking to advise a client about the likely outcome of a court hearing, does not have access to the same formulation of the facts as is available and set out in the judgment. That formulation cannot exist until the judgment is made.

One might imagine that the 'facts' of the case set out in a judgment are the same as, equivalent to, or a reasonable proxy for the factual information available prior to the court's decision. However, this is incorrect. Facts very often *emerge* in the process of litigation. One side's account of the facts may (and typically will) be countered by the other side's account. Each side's account may be iteratively refined and expanded to respond to the other's. Factual evidence given by witnesses at a hearing may differ from earlier accounts given by those same witnesses. If, as is generally the case in lower courts, there is a dispute about the facts, the court will have to make a decision about the facts. In addition, courts are only concerned with those facts that are relevant for the decision in the case, taking account of the nature of the dispute or issue. That is, the courts are only concerned with those facts that relate to the legal rules which the court judges to be relevant. As a result the facts described in the judgment are often "highly selective summaries of the original case record, written by the decision-makers themselves and tailored for consistency with the decision." (Tippett et al., 2021). For all these reasons the 'facts' set out in the judgment may be very different - in substance and in form - from earlier accounts of the facts.

Some research confirms that the way in which the 'facts' of a case are formulated has a material effect on the performance of predictive systems (Tippett et al., 2021; Branting et al., 2020). Medvedeva et al. (2021) also experimented with the ECtHR data by comparing the results of training the model on the facts extracted from the final judgments (not available prior to decision-making) and training it on the facts as published by the court just after receiving the submission of the alleged victim of human right violation. Their work shows that models that perform well on the 'facts' extracted from final judgments do not perform nearly as well when trained on the 'real' data, available prior to the decisions. The best model (Hierarchical BERT) achieves an F1-score of 0.92 on final judgments and only 0.64 on facts available prior to the decision.

[2] `https://adele-tool.eu`

Systems trained and tested [3] on 'facts' extracted from judgments can only model that the facts described in a judgment correspond to a decision that *has already been made*; they do not in any way allow users to actually *predict* any judgments.

Although it is usual for LJP systems to rely on the 'facts' section of cases, some systems may use different information. For instance, Collenette et al. (2020) and Collenette et al. (2023) claim to predict decisions of the ECtHR by creating an Abstract Dialectical Frameworks decision tree based on factors the court considers when making decisions regarding the right to a fair trial. However, when used to 'predict' the outcome of new cases, the system depends on the user answering complex questions about 'base factors' (the leaf nodes of the decision tree) which can only be authoritatively decided by a judge. It depends, not on pre-existing information, but on interpretative decisions made by the user. The system is therefore unable to do the prediction without having part of what needs to be decided fed into it.

We limited our analysis to LJP papers published in the past 10 years (2014 until August 2023). Given the amount of papers published on the topic, our list might not contain all of the published research in the field, but we expect that we found most of the available papers. We relied on descriptions of the datasets presented in the papers in order to establish the data that the authors used for the experiments. We present the list of all reviewed papers, including information about their data and performance at `https://shorturl.at/pxKR3`. Out of 171 reviewed papers, we found only 12 ($\sim$7%) that use appropriate data for predicting decisions, with only 7 using text-based input. Additionally we found 3 papers that in principle might provide a way to predict future court decisions, but because their data is private and inaccessible, it is unclear whether all of the data used for the testing was available before the relevant judgment and therefore suitable for prediction of future outcomes. We discuss all 15 papers in section 5.

[3] In principle, one can *train* a machine learning system using various data sources, including the details within the final judgments or any information derived from them. Having additional, albeit imperfect data could potentially enhance the system's performance. However, it is imperative that *testing* is consistently performed using data accessible before the decision-making process takes place.

4 Prediction in law v. prediction in NLP

We hesitate to describe the activity of lawyers in advising about possible outcomes of cases as 'prediction'. Lawyers often qualify advice about outcomes by observing (correctly) that the law might change, that there may be room for different interpretations of the relevant law, that their client's account of the facts might not be accepted, that new issues (of fact and/or law) might arise in the course of the court proceedings. Lawyers will rarely offer a binary 'win or lose' prediction, a quantified confidence rating, or a prediction which is not hedged about with appropriate caveats (Vagts, 1978). This hesitation should not be mistaken for failure: the life of the law is its ability to adapt; the processes and procedures through which the facts of a case emerge - gradually and iteratively - are crucial for preserving the ability of the citizen to articulate their case (Waldron, 2011). Lawyers are both less and much more than fortune tellers. They have an active role to play in developing the law. Nevertheless their role in advising about the possible outcomes of cases *is* 'prediction' in the sense that they are concerned with *future* outcomes of cases. If lawyers want to know the outcome of an already decided case they can read it in the judgment.

Some few of the papers we reviewed use NLP to output a classification (e.g. violation/no violation) in response to a textual account of the facts which pre-dates the judgment. These systems are designed to predict a future outcome. However, most of the papers use NLP to output a classification in response to a textual account of facts extracted from an *existing* judgment. They classify facts in a judgment as associated with a specific verdict (i.e. a label), but the actual verdict can be found in the same judgment. There is therefore a mismatch between the usual framing of the task of LJP in NLP and a lawyer's understanding of 'prediction' of judgment. This mismatch might be understood as one of terminology. The machine learning community uses the word 'prediction' as a substitute for 'classification'; 'prediction' in this sense does not imply looking into the future. Lawyers, on the other hand, understand 'prediction' to entail prediction of some future event. For this reason Medvedeva et al. (2023) suggested researchers avoid the term 'prediction' and clearly differentiate between 'outcome identification, outcome-based judgement categorisation and outcome forecasting'. However, the mismatch is more deep-seated and significant than one of terminology. It concerns the nature of the task performed by LJP models and the utility of the models for the intended end-user. If these are to have real-world utility for lawyers, citizens or others (e.g. political scientists) who wish to anticipate the outcome of cases they must be able to offer *prediction of future judgments*. In other words, they must offer a prediction of what the judgment *will be*, not 'predict' what the judgment *was*.

Much current research relating to LJP pays little attention to who, precisely, might use these systems and for which use cases. The majority of papers simply state that these systems could be useful to 'legal professionals' without differentiating between, for example, judges, paralegals, prosecutors, defence lawyers, clerks of court. Each of these might have different reasons for using these systems, different obligations and professional responsibilities, and therefore different use cases. The possibility that citizens might use these systems is frequently overlooked. However, as a matter of practicality, if one is to build an LJP system which has utility for some class or classes of user, it is essential to consider why they might want to use the system and what data they might use as inputs to the system. Different users may have access to different kinds of information, in different formats and languages, from different sources, reflecting different versions of events, and at different stages before or during court proceedings. An LJP system built for a specific class of end-users needs to be trained and evaluated on the data that would be available to such users. Otherwise the results do not tell one anything about how the system would perform in a real-life scenario and the system may have little or no utility.

For example, a system built for prospective applicants to the ECtHR and intended for use before an application is submitted to the court would have to be trained and tested on data available to the applicant at that stage. Such data might include textual descriptions of the facts (and arguments) formulated by the applicant, or factual accounts extracted from earlier decisions in cases raised by the applicant in domestic courts. This data has limitations; the descriptions will only contain the version of events and arguments made on behalf of the applicant and (like the factual accounts extracted from the lower courts) would normally be in the language of the applicant's country of residence. This means that the system would have to be able to handle multiple languages or be designed for a specific country. On the other hand, let's say the system is built for a big law firm which wants to take account of the outcomes predicted by the system when advising clients. Again the system would have to be trained and tested on the kind of input data available to the user at the point of use of the system for the purposes of prediction. In the case of the law firm, this might consist of the firm's written submissions for hearings, with the system being evaluated against 'unseen' written submissions and the corresponding outcomes. Like Golumbia (2015) we believe that responsibility for judging should rest with humans, not with machines. Judges, should be independent, base their decisions on law, and should not defer to machines. We are therefore very much of the view, along with Bex and Prakken (2021), that these systems should not be used for decision making by judges or indeed as a means of allowing (or compelling) a judge to assess whether their proposed decision aligns with the predictions offered by such systems. If however, the system were to be developed for such purposes, solely from an experimental setup perspective, the data would have to reflect the data available to the judge *before* they issued their judgment. In all such cases the training data, test data and finally data used for predictions would have to be obtained and used in a way that respects copyright, confidentiality, data protection and relevant rules of court. Lawyers, judges and other legal professionals would have to ensure that use of such systems is in line with their professional obligations, codes of practice and legal and ethical norms. These considerations are relevant for the design of such systems and for the choice of input data whether for training, testing or prediction. Making clear who the end-user is, even if the system is not ready to be used, rather than doing research for the sake of research, paves the way for a more appropriate experimental setup.

5 Data

Unfortunately, while the text of a judgment is not appropriate data for making predictions for that judgment, it can be hard for researchers to find *good* data for LJP. In an ideal world researchers would use the same information as is available to the court and/or the parties, e.g. statements of victims or submissions by the parties. However, this data is not commonly available, with access to court records varying across jurisdictions. It may be restricted to physical (rather than online) access, to cases in higher courts, to certain kinds of case documents, or provided only for a fee (Naglič et al., 2013).

The papers that use appropriate data for future predictions consistently exhibit much poorer performance compared to those relying on flawed data. Among papers employing text-based input for training, only one achieves over 70% accuracy. Specifically, Medvedeva et al. (2020) attain 75% accuracy in predicting ECtHR decisions based on summaries from so-called communicated cases, prepared by the court, derived from applicant submissions, and published before the judgments are made. However, a study with a similar albeit smaller dataset subsequently reports a reduced accuracy rate of 65%-68% depending on the year of the test data (Medvedeva et al., 2021).

Note that these summaries are only available if and when the ECtHR accepts an application and only for a subset of cases. Consequently, depending on the end-user and their specific requirements, these summaries may still not suffice for making predictions. Since applicants do not have the case summary before they submit the applications to the court, it is suitable for prediction only once the legal proceedings begin. Then applicants may use the case summary as input to an LJP system to estimate their prospects of success, potentially opting for a settlement to avoid lengthy proceedings.

Using lower court decisions to predict higher court outcomes as explored by Waltl et al. (2017) and Jacob de Menezes-Neto and Clementino (2022) offers a way to use pre-judgment data, yet performance has been modest with the papers reporting F1-score of 57% and a Matthews Correlation Coefficient (MCC) of 0.37, respectively. Predicting court decisions is an inherently challenging task. The challenge is compounded by the fact that many countries and courts only publish a subset of their cases at each level, making it difficult to access sufficient data from both lower and higher courts.[4] It is crucial to acknowledge, however, that not all cases eligible for appeal to a higher court will actually pursue this course of action, introducing potential selection bias when training and evaluating the system.

Other papers that use text as input rely on various documents from different stages of legal proceedings. For example, Semo et al. (2022) uses plaintiff claims, McConnell et al. (2021) complaint documents, and Tippett et al. (2021) legal briefs. While these documents may be available before the decision is made, they typically represent the claims of one party, and therefore may not include all relevant information. The papers report accuracy scores of 67%, 61% and an MCC of 0.48, respectively.

The papers predicting decisions of the US Supreme Court (e.g. Sharma et al., 2015; Katz et al., 2017) often use a manually annotated SCDB dataset (Spaeth et al., 2014), containing 240 expert-annotated variables, rather than text from legal documents. Such data is rarely available for other courts, and would require significant manual effort to compile. These papers do not use textual input, yet both achieve 70% accuracy. Such data could potentially be supplemented with, for example, decisions of the lower court and/or expert opinions. For instance, Kaufman et al. (2017) use oral argument in combination with the annotated variables, therefore creating a system that can predict decisions once the court case started, reporting 74% accuracy. Chen and Eagel (2017) incorporate seemingly unrelated data like weather and news trends to improve the performance (up to 79% accuracy).

Similarly, published judgments, although unsuitable for directly predicting judgments, could serve as a source from which to extract factors or variables that are relevant to the outcomes of those cases. These factors, in turn, might be used for prediction. For instance, Hsieh et al. (2021) extract information about plaintiff and defendant, including their income and debt information, to make predictions about discretionary damages. However, it is not always obvious whether the factors are available in advance or will have to be established by the court. For example, França et al. (2020); dos Santos et al. (2020); Bagherian-Marandi et al. (2021) who also adopt this approach mention using client information, as well as extracting details from judgments. However, since their data is not published or available for examination the precise nature of the extracted features remains unclear. Bagherian-Marandi et al. (2021), for instance, has

[4] Some countries e.g. Brazil reportedly publish the majority of their case law (Jacob de Menezes-Neto and Clementino, 2022). Similarly, Danish Supreme Court cases are published together with underlying decisions of the lower courts, while the US Supreme Court publishes most case filings including parties' briefs.

the value of the claim as one of the features. This feature could relate either to the sum claimed in the initial submission (appropriate data) or the sum determined during the course of the proceedings, with the latter not being available prior to the judgment (inappropriate data). Therefore, the performance of these systems should be tested on data provided by the users rather than relying on extracted data. This approach ensures that the system's performance mirrors a real-world scenario.

Given the scarcity of papers conducting research on appropriate data and the relatively modest performance of many of those systems, it is evident that there is substantial room for investigation to establish the most effective approaches for LJP. We have offered examples of data that might be appropriate for LJP ('good' data). However further research is needed to establish what 'good' data is available to researchers in different jurisdictions, and, of this data, which may produce optimal results. Crucially however, and contrary to the approach adopted in the vast majority of papers, doing LJP 'right' depends on selecting and using data that predates the judgment.

6 Benchmark datasets

As we have discussed, the facts of the judgments that one is predicting are the wrong data for the LJP task. It follows that benchmark datasets, such as CAIL2018 (Xiao et al., 2018), LexGLUE ECHR A & B (Chalkidis et al., 2022) or ILDC CJPE (Malik et al., 2021) whose input data consists of facts extracted from judgments, are of little or no assistance for the task of prediction of future judgments. Models which predict a future judgment can only be benchmarked on a dataset containing textual representations of facts that are available before the judgment.

Endorsement by the NLP community of datasets such as CAIL2018, LexGLUE ECHR and ILDC CJPE as benchmarks for prediction of judgment has ramifications. Koch et al. (2021) note that "When they institutionalize benchmark datasets, task communities implicitly endorse these data as meaningful abstractions of a task or problem domain. The institutionalization of benchmarks influences the behavior of both researchers and end-users." CAIL2018, LexGLUE ECHR, ILDC CJPE and similar datasets implicitly signal to researchers, lawyers and policy makers that it is meaningful to carry out the task of prediction of judgment by using data extracted from cases in which the judgment is already available as the model input. They also implicitly signal that the performance scores of models tested on the datasets are meaningful indicators of performance in the real-world task of prediction of (future) judgment.

Do the 'predictions' output by models tested against such benchmarks have any real-world utility? We suggest they do not. Such 'predictions' involve labelling or categorising input data as correlated with a particular (already known) outcome (Medvedeva et al., 2023). These 'predictions' have no informational value for lawyers, their clients or others who wish to obtain a prediction of a future judgment (Bex and Prakken, 2021; Medvedeva et al., 2023). Moreover, to our knowledge there is no research indicating that any improvements of the results on such a dataset would translate to improved performance in a real-world context. In fact, we are only aware of research that has demonstrated the contrary (see Medvedeva et al. (2021).

To mitigate these issues, we propose that the ideal test set should - at a minimum - consist of data in which no information has been derived from the judgments that one is predicting. Instead, this data should be gathered from the parties involved in the case or from documents accessible before the decision-making process. Conducting an experiment in which data is gathered for cases that are still pending decisions, followed by a waiting period until the court issues its judgments for comparison, would be the most dependable method to safeguard against flawed test results. Although this approach may present increased difficulties due to its longitudinal nature, it would guarantee the reliability of the test results.

7 Addressing explainability

The real-world utility of LJP systems may also depend on their explainability. "[I]n Law the explanation is what matters" (Bench-Capon, 2021). When lawyers give advice about outcomes, they generally explain why an outcome or range of outcomes might be likely. They explain how the law may apply to the client's problem. Similarly, judges usually offer explanations which serve to justify their decisions with reference to the facts found to be established and the relevant law. This aspect of judicial practice relates to the public character of law and the ability of citizens to engage with the law (Waldron, 2008). Both lawyers and judges provide explanations which involve the exercise of legal reasoning (Branting, 2020). These explanations have a particular form. They link the facts of the case and the law to the conclusion; they are grounded in law. We also expect these explanations to meet a qualitative standard; we want them to accurately represent the law and to demonstrate sound reasoning.

Is it necessary that LJP systems issue explanations that are grounded in law? This may depend on how, by whom and for whose benefit these systems will be used. Despite our reservations, these systems might be used in place of judges, to make decisions rather than merely offering predictions. In that scenario, it would seem essential for such a system to be capable of providing an explanation of its output that is grounded in law (Završnik, 2020). Otherwise, how could one assess whether the output was justified according to legal standards, or how, and on what legal basis, litigants might challenge the output of the system? Similarly, if persons without legal representation use these systems to estimate their prospects of success in a court case, it would seem essential for the system to provide an explanation grounded in law. How else could such persons make sense of those outputs? If on the other hand lawyers use these systems as additional tools, it might be desirable but not essential for the system to provide explanations grounded in law. Lawyers should provide their own explanations of the outcome or outcomes they consider likely.

A range of approaches to explainability can be found in the LJP literature. For example, machine learning systems which frame LJP as a classification task may output an 'explanation' about which features the system treats as important. The system may output descriptions or visualisations of which words, sentences or paragraphs of the input data (usually the 'facts' of a case) contributed to the output predictions (Medvedeva et al., 2020; Malik et al., 2021). Alternatively, machine learning systems that treat LJP as a text generation task may generate text in the form of steps of reasoning (a chain of thought) or a legal syllogism together with a conclusion (a prediction) (Jiang and Yang, 2023). The 'reasoning' steps serve as the explanation. Hybrid systems which combine machine learning with symbolic reasoning approaches may output justifications of the predictions output by the system (Prakken and Ratsma, 2022). These justifications would not represent the 'reasoning steps' of the predictive model though they may provide an ex post explanation of the prediction.

The focus on explainability is welcome, and certain of these approaches may hold some promise. However, for most users and use cases, the explanations (if they are to be useful) must be grounded in law, relate to predictions of future judgments and evaluated for soundness by suitable methods. We are not aware of any LJP system that outputs 'explanations' that meet all three criteria. This explainability deficit is a significant limitation which is relevant for the evaluation of LJP models, for their real-world utility and for the potential benefits, harms and impacts associated with their use.

8 An ethical approach to model evaluation and reporting

We have suggested that current practice in relation to the evaluation of LJP models is frequently flawed, involving a race-to-the-top against benchmark datasets unsuited for the task of prediction of future judgments and a failure to consider intended users and use cases. If these issues are relevant for training and testing a system, they are also relevant for further evaluation and reporting. We favour an approach to evaluation which is "application-centric" (Hutchinson et al., 2022), that is, an approach which considers the fitness of the model for its real-world application context. An application-centric approach would necessarily entail a focus on the intended user and use case and highlight the unsuitability of LJP benchmark datasets comprising formulations of 'facts' only available at the point of judgment.

An application-centric approach takes account of direct benefits and harms to users and those affected by the outputs of the system (Hutchinson et al., 2022). Adoption of this approach to evaluation therefore requires a good understanding of the context in which a model is likely to be used, who will benefit or suffer adverse consequences as a result of such use and how those consequences are likely to arise. It requires a sufficient understanding of the way in which LJP systems might shape lawyers' advice and judges' determinations, ultimately affecting legal outcomes for citizens, and a recognition that these systems are "intended to inform decisions about matters central to human life or flourishing" (Mitchell et al., 2019). More concretely, it requires an appreciation that a citizen might suffer harm if, for example, a system suggests a claim will succeed when the claim is doomed to failure on legal grounds, or provides a judge with an overly harsh recommendation in relation to sentencing.

Crucially an application-centric approach takes into account the potential impact of "changes to the ecosystem itself" (Hutchinson et al., 2022). In the case of LJP systems this entails reflection on how the use of these systems may affect the ecosystems of law and legal practice. For example, if judges were to align their decisions with the outputs of LJP systems, this might lend credibility to the notion that machines can engage in legal reasoning, reduce the human element in decision-making, devalue legal reasoning and de-skill judges. Lawyers who use these systems might be "encourage[d] ... to base their litigation strategy on factors other than the legal merits of the case" (Diver et al., 2022). Law might stagnate; as Bench-Capon (2021) notes, the model producing the prediction can only be "trained on past decisions". There is a risk of confusing or conflating what LJP systems can do with the exercise of legal reasoning within a legal institutional framework which allows for "interpretation, contestation and argumentation" (Hildebrandt, 2019). The impacts are likely to be amplified if the systems are used for decision-making rather than decision-support. In that context, the inability of LJP systems to provide explanations grounded in law could have serious ramifications. Of course, the use of these systems might also produce benefits - the point is to reflect on the impact of the research and the technology on the application ecosystem.

We suggest that an application-centric approach is both necessary and appropriate where researchers maintain that the systems they develop have real-world utility. It encourages trust; instead of merely claiming real-world utility, researchers would demonstrate their attention to the context of application. It is "better aligned with the needs of decision-makers who consider whether to use a model in an application." (Hutchinson et al., 2022). Model cards, (Mitchell et al., 2019) which allow for reporting on the intended user, intended use case, the benefits, harms and social impacts, might be of use in this context. We encourage the use of such a reporting framework as a means of clearly and transparently communicating evaluations of models which look beyond accuracy metrics.

9 Discussion

Despite the perception of prolific research activity, the reality is that the LJP field has produced only a meagre 12 papers to date, covering 9 courts, and reporting performance scores between 56% and 79% accuracy. By diverting resources and attention towards systems that do not deliver on their promises, researchers and developers may be discouraged from pursuing more appropriate and impactful avenues. The atmosphere of competition, with numerous models claiming accuracy rates exceeding 90%, may hinder the publication of rigorous initial-stage research and incremental advancements in the field that produce much lower performance. Consequently, it impedes the overall progress of LJP research.

Such faulty research not only hampers scientific progress but also poses potential risks to individuals. For instance, a system such as ADELE, while conceived as an academic project, can be used to make predictions based on claims provided by users, even though it was not trained or evaluated on such data. Given the inflated scores of systems claiming to be predicting court decisions, there is a distinct possibility that these systems may eventually find their way onto the market and into courts.

We propose a number of recommendations to address the concerns outlined in this paper. We recommend that researchers building and reporting on systems that claim to do LJP identify the end-user, the application of the system and the stage in the legal process when the system would be used. Researchers should then evaluate whether the data they plan to use is available to the user at that stage of the proceedings or collect a new dataset. Depending on the purpose of the application one may choose to create a system that offers some form of explainability, whether in the sense of explaining how the model makes the prediction (for instance, for error analysis and correction) or, explanations that take the form of legal reasoning. When building such a system, even within academic research, one should keep in mind and report not only potential benefits, but also potential harms that might result from use of the system. We encourage developers to also consider the broader impact that the system may have on individuals, law, legal procedures and society as a whole. We summarise these recommendations in a schematic checklist available in Appendix A.

10 Conclusion

Our paper delves into the current landscape of Legal Judgment Prediction (LJP) research and its issues. Through examination of 171 papers, we find that only a small fraction of LJP papers which claim to predict court decisions achieve this objective. The majority falter by using the wrong data for the task at hand. Despite many papers reporting exceptionally high performance, it becomes evident that the task of LJP proves to be considerably more challenging when researchers use an appropriate experimental setup.

In addition, we scrutinise when and for whom LJP has real-world utility. We emphasise the importance of considering the end-user and the use case when developing the models. The prevalent reliance on readily available data and benchmark datasets is not in line with this focus. We advocate for a shift in approach to redirect the field away from a potentially futile trajectory, ultimately preventing the misallocation of resources on endeavors that lack practical utility within the legal domain.

Acknowledgements

The second author, Pauline McBride, is funded by the European Research Council (ERC) under the HORIZON2020 Excellence of Science programme ERC-2017-ADG No 788734

References

Nikolaos Aletras, Dimitrios Tsarapatsanis, Daniel Preoţiuc-Pietro, and Vasileios Lampos. 2016. Predicting judicial decisions of the European Court of Human Rights: A natural language processing perspective. *PeerJ Computer Science*, 2.

Julia Angwin, Jeff Larson, Surya Mattu, and Lauren Kirchner. 2016. Machine bias: there's software used across the country to predict future criminals. and it's biased against blacks. ProPublica 2016. Https://www.propublica.org/article/machine-bias-risk-assessments-in-criminal-sentencing.

Navid Bagherian-Marandi, Mehdi Ravanshadnia, and Mohammad-R Akbarzadeh-T. 2021. Two-layered fuzzy logic-based model for predicting court decisions in construction contract disputes. *Artificial intelligence and law*, pages 1–32.

Trevor Bench-Capon. 2021. The need for good old fashioned AI and law. *Jusletter-IT*, (fses):23–35.

Floris Bex and Henry Prakken. 2021. On the relevance of algorithmic decision predictors for judicial decision making. In *Proceedings of the Eighteenth International Conference on Artificial Intelligence and Law*, pages 175–179.

Karl Branting, Carlos Balhana, Craig Pfeifer, John S Aberdeen, and Bradford Brown. 2020. Judges are from Mars, pro se litigants are from Venus: Predicting decisions from lay text. In *JURIX*, pages 215–218.

L Karl Branting. 2020. Explanation in hybrid, two-stage models of legal prediction. In *The 3rd XAILA Workshop at JURIX*.

L Karl Branting, Craig Pfeifer, Bradford Brown, Lisa Ferro, John Aberdeen, Brandy Weiss, Mark Pfaff, and Bill Liao. 2021. Scalable and explainable legal prediction. *Artificial Intelligence and Law*, 29:213–238.

European Commission for the Efficiency of Justice CEPEJ. 2018. European ethical charter on the use of artificial intelligence in judicial systems and their environment. *European Ethical Charter on the Use of Artificial Intelligence in Judicial Systems and Their Environment*.

Ilias Chalkidis, Abhik Jana, Dirk Hartung, Michael Bommarito, Ion Androutsopoulos, Daniel Katz, and Nikolaos Aletras. 2022. LexGLUE: A benchmark dataset for legal language understanding in English. In *Proceedings of the 60th Annual Meeting of the Association for Computational Linguistics (Volume 1: Long Papers)*, pages 4310–4330, Dublin, Ireland. Association for Computational Linguistics.

Daniel L Chen and Jess Eagel. 2017. Can machine learning help predict the outcome of asylum adjudications? In *Proceedings of the 16th edition of the International Conference on Articial Intelligence and Law*, pages 237–240.

Joe Collenette, Katie Atkinson, and Trevor Bench-Capon. 2020. An explainable approach to deducing outcomes in European Court of Human Rights cases using ADFs. *Frontiers in Artificial Intelligence and Applications*, 326:21–32.

Joe Collenette, Katie Atkinson, and Trevor Bench-Capon. 2023. Explainable AI tools for legal reasoning about cases: A study on the European Court of Human Rights. *Artificial Intelligence*, 317:103861.

Laurence Diver, Pauline McBride, Masha Medvedeva, Arjun Bhubaneshwar Banerjee, Eva D'hondt, Tatiana Duarte Nicolau, Desara Dushi, Gianmarco Gori, Emilie Van Den Hoven, Paulus Meessen, et al. 2022. Typology of legal technologies. In *Cross-disciplinary Research in Computational Law (CRCL): Computational'Law'on Edge*.

Pedro TC dos Santos, Fernando Henrique, Venicius Garcia, Victor RS Ferreira, Antonino C dos Santos Neto, Johnatan C Souza, Caio Manfredini, João VF França, José MC Boaro, Geraldo Braz Junior, et al. 2020. Multiclass legal judgment outcome prediction for consumer lawsuits using XGBoost and TPE. In *2020 IEEE International Conference on Systems, Man, and Cybernetics (SMC)*, pages 881–886. IEEE.

João VF França, José MC Boaro, Pedro TC dos Santos, Fernando Henrique, Venicius Garcia, Caio Manfredini, Domingos AD Júnior, Francisco YC de Oliveira, Carlos EP Castro, Geraldo Braz Junior, et al. 2020. Legal judgment prediction in the context of energy market using gradient boosting. In *2020 IEEE International Conference on Systems, Man, and Cybernetics (SMC)*, pages 875–880. IEEE.

Federico Galli, Giulia Grundler, Alessia Fidelangeli, Andrea Galassi, Francesca Lagioia, Elena Palmieri, Federico Ruggeri, Giovanni Sartor, and Paolo Torroni. 2022. Predicting outcomes of Italian VAT decisions. In *Legal Knowledge and Information Systems*, pages 188–193. IOS Press.

David Golumbia. 2015. Judging like a machine. In *Postdigital aesthetics: art, computation and design*, pages 123–135. Springer.

Andrew Griffin. 2016. Robot judges could soon be helping out with court cases. Accessed: 11-08-2023.

Mireille Hildebrandt. 2019. Data-driven prediction of judgment. Law's new mode of existence?

Decheng Hsieh, Lieuhen Chen, and Taiping Sun. 2021. Legal judgment prediction based on machine learning: Predicting the discretionary damages of mental suffering in fatal car accident cases. *Applied Sciences*, 11(21):10361.

Ben Hutchinson, Negar Rostamzadeh, Christina Greer, Katherine Heller, and Vinodkumar Prabhakaran. 2022. Evaluation gaps in machine learning practice. In *Proceedings of the 2022 ACM Conference on Fairness, Accountability, and Transparency*, pages 1859–1876.

Elias Jacob de Menezes-Neto and Marco Bruno Miranda Clementino. 2022. Using deep learning to predict outcomes of legal appeals better than human experts: A study with data from Brazilian federal courts. *PloS one*, 17(7):e0272287.

Cong Jiang and Xiaolei Yang. 2023. Legal syllogism prompting: Teaching large language models for legal judgment prediction. In *Proceedings of the Nineteenth International Conference on Artificial Intelligence and Law*, pages 417–421.

Daniel Martin Katz, Michael J Bommarito II, and Josh Blackman. 2017. A general approach for predicting the behavior of the Supreme Court of the United States. *PloS one*, 12(4).

Aaron Kaufman, Peter Kraft, and Maya Sen. 2017. Machine learning, text data, and Supreme Court forecasting. *Project Report, Harvard University*.

Jemima Kelly. 2022. AI-driven justice may be better than none at all. Accessed: 11-08-2023.

Bernard Koch, Emily Denton, Alex Hanna, and Jacob G Foster. 2021. Reduced, reused and recycled: The life of a dataset in machine learning research. *arXiv preprint arXiv:2112.01716*.

Reed C Lawlor. 1963. What computers can do: Analysis and prediction of judicial decisions. *American Bar Association Journal*, pages 337–344.

Kobi Leins, Jey Han Lau, and Timothy Baldwin. 2020. Give me convenience and give her death: Who should decide what uses of NLP are appropriate, and on what basis? In *Proceedings of the 58th Annual Meeting of the Association for Computational Linguistics*, pages 2908–2913, Online. Association for Computational Linguistics.

Ejan Mackaay and Pierre Robillard. 1974. *Predicting judicial decisions: The nearest neighbour rule and visual representation of case patterns*, volume 3(3-4).

Vijit Malik, Rishabh Sanjay, Shubham Kumar Nigam, Kripa Ghosh, Shouvik Kumar Guha, Arnab Bhattacharya, and Ashutosh Modi. 2021. ILDC for CJPE: Indian legal documents corpus for court judgment prediction and explanation. *arXiv preprint arXiv:2105.13562*.

Christopher Markou. 2020. Are we ready for robot judges? Accessed: 11-08-2023.

Devin J McConnell, James Zhu, Sachin Pandya, and Derek Aguiar. 2021. Case-level prediction of motion outcomes in civil litigation. In *Proceedings of the Eighteenth International Conference on Artificial Intelligence and Law*, pages 99–108.

Masha Medvedeva, Ahmet Üstun, Xiao Xu, Michel Vols, and Martijn Wieling. 2021. Automatic judgement forecasting for pending applications of the European Court of Human Rights. In *Proceedings of the Fifth Workshop on Automated Semantic Analysis of Information in Legal Text (ASAIL 2021)*.

Masha Medvedeva, Martijn Wieling, and Michel Vols. 2023. Rethinking the field of automatic prediction of court decisions. *Artificial Intelligence and Law*, 31(1):195–212.

Masha Medvedeva, Xiao Xu, Martijn Wieling, and Michel Vols. 2020. JURI SAYS: Prediction system for the European Court of Human Rights. In *Legal Knowledge and Information Systems: JURIX 2020: The Thirty-third Annual Conference, Brno, Czech Republic, December 9-11, 2020*, volume 334, page 277. IOS Press.

Margaret Mitchell, Simone Wu, Andrew Zaldivar, Parker Barnes, Lucy Vasserman, Ben Hutchinson, Elena Spitzer, Inioluwa Deborah Raji, and Timnit Gebru. 2019. Model cards for model reporting. In *Proceedings of the conference on fairness, accountability, and transparency*, pages 220–229.

Vesna Naglič et al. 2013. National practices with regard to the accessibility of court documents.

Frank Pasquale and Glyn Cashwell. 2018. Prediction, persuasion, and the jurisprudence of behaviourism. *University of Toronto Law Journal*, 68(supplement 1):63–81.

Henry Prakken and Rosa Ratsma. 2022. A top-level model of case-based argumentation for explanation: formalisation and experiments. *Argument & Computation*, 13(2):159–194.

Alexandre Quemy and Robert Wrembel. 2022. ECHR-OD: On building an integrated open repository of legal documents for machine learning applications. *Information Systems*, 106:101822.

Gil Semo, Dor Bernsohn, Ben Hagag, Gila Hayat, and Joel Niklaus. 2022. ClassActionPrediction: A challenging benchmark for legal judgment prediction of class action cases in the US. In *Proceedings of the Natural Legal Language Processing Workshop 2022*, pages 31–46.

Mehmet Fatih Sert, Engin Yıldırım, and İrfan Haşlak. 2022. Using artificial intelligence to predict decisions of the turkish constitutional court. *Social Science Computer Review*, 40(6):1416–1435.

Ranti Dev Sharma, Sudhanshu Mittal, Samarth Tripathi, and Shrinivas Acharya. 2015. Using modern neural networks to predict the decisions of Supreme Court of the United States with state-of-the-art accuracy. In *International Conference on Neural Information Processing*, pages 475–483. Springer.

Harold Spaeth, Lee Epstein, Ted Ruger, Keith Whittington, Jeffrey Segal, and Andrew D Martin. 2014. Supreme Court database code book.

Octavia-Maria Sulea, Marcos Zampieri, Shervin Malmasi, Mihaela Vela, Liviu P Dinu, and Josef Van Genabith. 2017. Exploring the use of text classification in the legal domain. In *In Proceedings of the 2nd Workshop on Automated Semantic Analysis of Information in Legal Texts (ASAIL 2017)*.

Elizabeth C Tippett, Charlotte S Alexander, Karl Branting, Paul Morawski, Carlos Balhana, Craig Pfeifer, and Sam Bayer. 2021. Does lawyering matter? Predicting judicial decisions from legal briefs, and what that means for access to justice. *Tex. L. Rev.*, 100:1157.

Detlev F Vagts. 1978. Legal opinions in quantitative terms: The lawyer as haruspex or bookie. *Bus. Law.*, 34:421.

Dávid Varga, Zoltán Szoplák, Stanislav Krajci, Pavol Sokol, and Peter Gurský. 2021. Analysis and prediction of legal judgements in the Slovak criminal.

Jeremy Waldron. 2008. The concept and the rule of law. *Ga L Rev*, 43.

Jeremy Waldron. 2011. The rule of law and the importance of procedure. *Getting to the Rule of Law*, 3:4–5.

Bernhard Waltl, Georg Bonczek, Elena Scepankova, Jörg Landthaler, and Florian Matthes. 2017. Predicting the outcome of appeal decisions in Germany's tax law. In *International Conference on Electronic Participation*, pages 89–99. Springer.

Chaojun Xiao, Haoxi Zhong, Zhipeng Guo, Cunchao Tu, Zhiyuan Liu, Maosong Sun, Yansong Feng, Xianpei Han, Zhen Hu, Heng Wang, et al. 2018. CAIL2018: A large-scale legal dataset for judgment prediction. *arXiv preprint arXiv:1807.02478*.

Aleš Završnik. 2020. Criminal justice, artificial intelligence systems, and human rights. In *ERA forum*, volume 20, pages 567–583. Springer.

A Appendix A: Checklist for developing Legal Judgment Prediction systems

End-User:

☐ Clearly establish the end-user of the system.

System Application:

☐ Define the specific application and purpose of the system within the legal process.

☐ Determine the stage within the legal process where the system would be used (e.g. prior to going to court, during proceedings).

Data Evaluation:

☐ Assess whether the test set mirrors the data available to the user at the relevant stage of the legal proceeding according to the defined application.

Explainability:

☐ Evaluate whether the system needs to provide explanations for its predictions given the application and, if so, specify the nature of the explanations required.

Ethical considerations:

☐ Identify potential benefits or harms related to system performance, such as (incorrect) predictions affecting legal proceedings, individual's lives and legal protections.

☐ Consider potential broader repercussions of system design choices, including impacts on individuals, law, legal procedures, and society at large.

Beyond The Text: Analysis of Privacy Statements through Syntactic and Semantic Role Labeling

Yan Shvartzshnaider
York University, Toronto, Canada
yansh@yorku.ca

Ananth Balashankar*
New York University, New York, USA
ananth@nyu.edu

Thomas Wies
New York University, New York, USA
wies@cs.nyu.edu

Lakshminarayanan Subramanian
New York University, New York, USA
lakshmi@nyu.edu

Abstract

This paper formulates a new task of extracting privacy parameters from a privacy policy, through the lens of Contextual Integrity (CI), an established social theory framework for reasoning about privacy norms. Through extensive experiments, we further show that incorporating CI-based domain-specific knowledge into a BERT-based SRL model results in the highest precision and recall, achieving an F1 score of 84%. With our work, we would like to motivate new research in building NLP applications for the privacy domain.

1 Introduction

A privacy policy informs users about a company's information handling practices. However, privacy policies are lengthy documents, full of incomplete and vague statements that impose a significant cognitive burden on the reader to infer whether a given service respects their privacy (Bhatia et al., 2016a; Bhatia and Breaux, 2018; Reidenberg et al., 2015).

This challenge has inspired many recent works in applying natural language processing and machine learning techniques to automatically process privacy policies and retrieve the relevant information (Harkous et al., 2018; Ravichander et al., 2019). While these efforts help in identifying paragraphs in the privacy policy that mention sensitive information (Evans et al., 2017; Bhatia and Breaux, 2015), opt-out clauses (Sathyendra et al., 2016) or description of data collection practice (Sadeh et al., 2014), they focus on the policy as a whole rather than on the privacy implication of the individual privacy statements that it contains. In particular, they do not aim to identify relevant and often missing contextual information that is critical for unambiguously understanding the scope of individual statements. This paper focuses on a new NLP task that aids the analysis of privacy policies at this more fine-grained level.

To illustrate the problem, consider a typical example of an ambiguous privacy statement: "**Yahoo** *collects* **information about your transactions with us and with some of our business partners**, *including* **information about your use of financial products and services that we offer.**" At first glance, the statement may seem to provide all the relevant information about a first-party collection of transactional data. However, it in fact misses some crucial contextual information. To understand what is missing, we use the contextual integrity (CI) framework (Nissenbaum, 2009). CI defines privacy as an appropriate flow of information which is expressed in terms of five essential *CI parameters*: Sender, Recipient, Subject, Information Type, and Transmission Principle. The latter is a constraint on the information flow expressing the condition under which information is being transferred. The statement in our example specifies only 3 out of the 5 necessary parameters (highlighted in bold) – Subject, Recipient, and Information Type. This leaves the sender of the information and transmission principle to the reader's interpretation. In some cases, the relevant missing information appears in different places in the policy, for example, under different sections such as "When do we collect your information" or "Our partners". These, however, do not help in contextually positioning the above statement so that the reader can determine whether their expectations have been met.

In this paper, we show that existing NLP models and techniques can assist a human annotator in identifying relevant privacy parameters in the policy text. The proposed novel NLP task can support the following applications: automate comparative analysis of privacy policies using the theory of contextual integrity (Shvartzshnaider et al., 2019a; Sanfilippo et al., 2019); extraction and enforcement of prescribed CI-based policy from legal and co-

*currently at Google

Proceedings of the Natural Legal Language Processing Workshop 2023, pages 85–98
December 7, 2023 ©2023 Association for Computational Linguistics

operate document (Shvartzshnaider et al., 2019a; Sanfilippo et al., 2019), an enhanced auditing of existing privacy policies for correctness and consistency (Andow et al., 2019).

2 Contextual Integrity Primer

The theory of Contextual Integrity (CI) defines privacy as appropriate information flow in accordance with governing privacy norms. As mentioned in the introduction, CI provides a framework to capture and compare information flows against established norms. To perform an analysis of the privacy implications of a given information flow, CI requires identifying five essential parameters: actors (sender, receiver, subject), the type of information (attribute), and the condition or purpose of the information exchange (transmission principle). It is critical to state all five parameters to ensure a non-ambiguous privacy implication analysis. A misalignment of parameter values–i.e., an information flow that deviates from the established norm–constitutes a potential privacy violation.

For example, consider a medical context, an established norm states that a patient (sender) could share their (subject) medical information (information type) with their doctor (receiver) confidentially (transmission principle). An information flow (e.g., generated by an app or a system) that deviates from this norm (e.g., by changing the value of TP to public and/or sending the medical information to a different receiver) potentially violates the patient's privacy and requires further investigation. CI provides a heuristic to examine violating information flows in terms of how they contribute to values, functions, and purposes of a particular context (Nissenbaum, 2009).

CI and Privacy Policies By identifying the values of CI parameters in a privacy statement, we can reason about privacy implications in a way that more closely aligns with users' privacy expectations and societal norms.

This analysis can help in identifying potentially confusing or misleading statements, e.g., when one of the five parameters such as transmission principle or receiver is missing or ambiguous (Shvartzshnaider et al., 2019a). Furthermore, one can use the identified parameters to formalize the expressed informational norms and privacy rules in formal logic (Shvartzshnaider et al., 2019b; Datta et al., 2011). These formalisms can in turn be used to build systems that enforce the specified rules or automatically audit information flows to detect rule violations.

3 Related Work

Several recent efforts have focused on identifying important and relevant privacy statements using constituency parsing (Sathyendra et al., 2017, 2016; Evans et al., 2017), logistic regression (Ammar et al., 2012) and crowdsourcing (Wilson et al., 2016b) techniques. These works focus on other aspects of privacy policy analysis such as opt-out disclosure, right to information access, etc.

As we discuss in Section 4, our work explicitly looks to map the privacy statement to a fixed set of parameters. We also show that Question Answering (QA) models do not perform satisfactorily when applied to our task. Similar limitations of the reading comprehension models were observed by Ravichander et al. (2019), who composed the PRIVACYQA dataset, an annotated corpus consisting of 1750 questions about the contents of privacy policies such as "What data does this game collect?" and "Will my data be sold to advertisers?".

In prior work on automatic privacy statement analysis, Bhatia et al. (2016b) extracted privacy statements on information handling practices such as "collecting your e-mail address" or "sharing your location" using a typed dependency parser and crowdworker annotations. More relevant to our efforts, Bhatia and Breaux (2018) applied Semantic Roles theory to manually annotate five privacy statements and identify action verbs (action data) such as "collection", "retain", "use", "transfer" and associated semantic roles that capture who performs the action, how the action is carried out, etc.

Andow et al. (2019) developed PolicyLint to analyze privacy policy using sentence-level NLP techniques to capture statements in a four-element tuple (actor, action, data object, entity) to identify contradictory statements. Andow et al. (2020) used a simplified 3-tuple statement abstraction (actor, data object, entity), and identify incorrect and ambiguous statements. Trimananda et al. (2022) build on this effort to audit the traffic and privacy policies in Oculus VR systems. Per CI theory, both OVRseen and PoliCheck capture insufficient information to perform a privacy implication analysis, which requires five CI parameters. Nevertheless, we can use PolicyLint and PoliCheck libraries to help process privacy policies to generate statements that we can feed into our annotation pipeline.

Shvartzshnaider et al. (2019a) crowdsourced privacy policies annotation to compare policy versions, identifying missing contextual information and overloading of parameters that contribute to users' inability to understand the prescribed information practices. Our work automates the task of annotating privacy policies with the CI parameters.

4 Task Formulation

The CI parameter extraction task is as follows. Given a privacy statement $stmt$, apply a mapping function M to extract the CI parameters: sender, receiver (r), subject (s), attribute (att), transmission principle (tp):

$$M(stmt) = (s, r, sub, att, tp)$$

The main challenge behind the task is identifying the lexical items in the statement that correspond to the contextually relevant values to help downstream NLP tasks perform the privacy analysis. This is not a trivial task as privacy policies are not written with CI in mind. Often, policies are written by legal and policy teams whose primary concern is not readability. Many privacy statements are missing essential CI parameters and often comprise syntactically complex sentences (Bhatia and Breaux, 2018).

In the absence of an automatic way to extract CI parameters, researchers have employed crowdsourcing and manual annotation to perform the analysis (Shvartzshnaider et al., 2019a). However, these methods do not scale due to the high cost of annotation by experts and hence we propose an ML-based approach by training or mapping existing models trained on NLP tasks to extract CI parameters. Further, we expand on a growing body of research in human-in-the-loop ML-assisted validations (Section 5.3) to evaluate the precision and recall of the model annotations.

5 Methods

In this section, we describe our method to perform the CI parameter extraction task by incorporating the contextual semantics of CI parameters to modify two conventional NLP techniques: Syntactic Dependency Parser (DP) and BERT-based Semantic Role Labeling (SRL). We then describe how these individual techniques can be integrated into an end-to-end model to extract CI parameters from privacy policies. In addition, in our evaluation (Section 6), we also compare our method to three baseline models tailored to address the CI parameter extraction task: Question-Answering, BERT, and Hidden Markov Model.

5.1 Enhancing NLP tasks using CI

We focus on Syntactic DP and SRL-based approaches and describe how we have incorporated CI-based domain-specific knowledge.

5.1.1 CI-based Dependency parsing

Dependency parsing is the task of identifying syntactic roles or dependency types for each of the words in a sentence. This involves parsing a sentence and identifying the syntactic structure denoting the grammatical rules that govern a language. The parser (Honnibal and Johnson, 2015) uses a non-monotonic transition system that allows for a large number of parse trees for each intermediate state. This modified arc-eager transition system has been shown to repair earlier parsing mistakes. It allows for overwriting previous parsing decisions and achieves a higher accuracy as compared to the greedy parsing approaches. Not all the dependency types identified for the English language are relevant in our study. We use the DP outputs to identify the relevant CI parameters in the privacy statement.

To identify CI parameters at a single sentence level using local relationships, we run a typed dependency parser (DP) on the text of the policies. We accept paragraphs as input, split them into sentences, and parse each sentence using the Spacy I/O[1] dependency parser. The model (Honnibal and Montani, 2018) achieves near state-of-the-art performance on most NLP tasks[2]. Based on our analysis of DP outputs for a sample of statements, we identified the dependency types that mapped to specific CI parameters as shown in Table 1.

CI Parameter Type	Dependency types
Attribute	*dobj, parataxis, nsubj-pass*
Sender/Receiver	*nsubj*, pronouns
Transmission Principle	*xcomp, ccomp, advcl, oprd*
Subject	*poss, agent*

Table 1: Mapping of dependency types corresponding to CI parameters. To represent dependencies we use the Stanford Typed Dependency Manual (De Marneffe and Manning, 2011) notations.

[1] https://spacy.io

[2] https://spacy.io/usage/facts-figures

For example, for the following statement from the Google privacy policy, the DP parser will return the following dependency type tags (white nodes), which are mapped to the corresponding CI parameter (gray nodes):

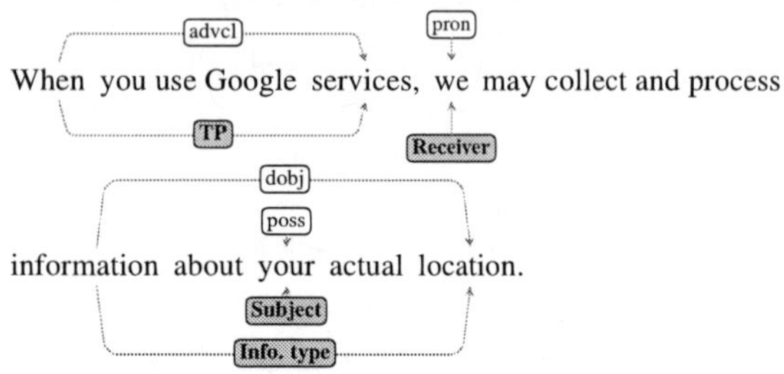

Note that, as is evident in Table 1, the dependency types cannot distinguish between the parameter of sender and receiver. For this, we defer to the task of SRL to identify based on the semantic meaning of the word.

CI-based Semantic Role Labeling Semantic Role Labeling (SRL) is the task of mapping words or phrases in a sentence to a semantic role such as that of an agent, goal, or result (Jurafsky and Martin, 2014). Often, in the classic natural language processing pipeline, this task is considered to have subsumed syntactic and parts-of-speech tasks within it (Tenney et al., 2019). For example, the task of distinguishing between a sender and a receiver can be done through SRL, but not through syntactic DP.

Similar to DP, we map the semantic roles to the relevant CI parameters. Table 2 shows the CI parameter mapping based on a verb's syntactic arguments. For example the verb "collect" has the following associated arguments (see PropBank corpus (Martha et al., 2005)): `ARG0`: agent, entity acquiring something, `ARG1`: thing acquired, `ARG2`: source, `ARG3`: more specific attribute of `ARG1` being collected, `ARG4`: benefactive.

To recover the predicate argument structure of a sentence we use an out-of-the-box AllenNLP implementation of the Bidirectional LSTM and SRL BERT models (Stanovsky et al., 2018; Shi and Lin, 2019). The first approach uses a bidirectional LSTM model for sequence tagging that allows for multiple overlapping tuples per sentence by extending deep BIO taggers for semantic role labeling, trained on the Open information extraction task. The second approach uses two sequence-to-sequence BERT models, one for predicate sense disambiguation, and another for argument identification and classification, with relevant parts of the sentence and predicate as part of the input, with a sequence of semantic role labels for outputs. For example, for the following statement, the BERT SRL model returns:

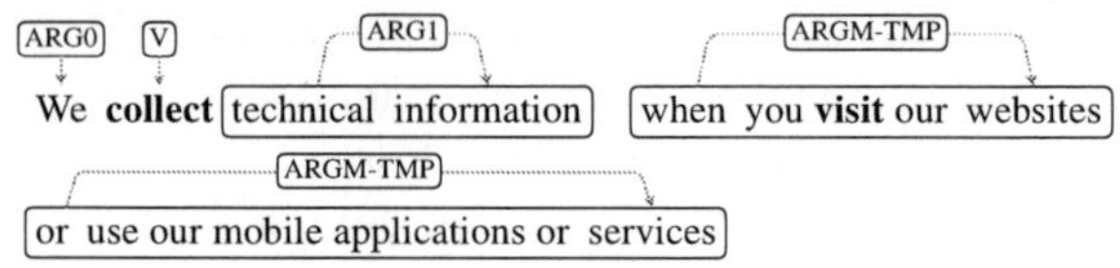

Example 1: SRL processed statement from a Walmart privacy policy

Based on the syntactic analysis of privacy policy statement sentences, we mapped the arguments onto the CI parameters. In the above example, `ARG0` is mapped to Recipient. `ARG1` is an Attribute, and `ARGM-TMP` is the TP. For each of the verbs, these mappings are slightly different, as shown in Table 2. This approach, although crude, covers a significant class of privacy policy statements that prescribe the flow of information.

	"Sending" action verbs	**"Receiving" action verbs**
Sender	*ARG2*	*ARG0*
Receiver	*ARG0*	*ARG2*
Attribute	*ARG1, C-ARG1*	
TP	*ARGM-TMP, ARGM-ADV, ARGM-MNR ARGM-PNC, ARGM-CAU*	

Table 2: Mapping semantic roles (notations) to specific CI parameters.

5.1.2 CI-related Semantic Frames

The SRL model returns verb-argument predicates for all the identified verbs in a sentence. Some of these verbs are not relevant to information exchange. For example, in the statement in Example 1, the verb "visits" does not convey semantically meaningful information regarding the exchange of technical information.

To reduce the number of false positives, we provide a list of verbs to the algorithm which highly correlates with information exchanges. The choice of verbs is based on a frequency analysis of verbs, along with filtering out verbs that are not related to information flows (as shown in Table 11 in the Appendix). It is helpful to think of this approach through the lens of the linguistic theory of Frame semantics (Fillmore et al., 1976), which posits that the specific meaning of words (frame elements) can be understood only as part of a particular context (semantic frames). In our approach, we would invoke CI-related semantic frames. Specifically, we look for SRL-predicates that are associated with any transfer of information (actual or perceived). This includes a list of verbs such as "sending", "sharing", "transmitting" and others that frequently appear in privacy policy text as identified by our POS analysis of the OPP-115 policies. In addition to invoking a general semantic frame, we differentiate between different roles of associated argument with each predicate. In particular, for predicates like "sending", "sharing", "transmitting" the ARG2 is typically associated with the agent role of a "sender", the ARG1 captures what was "sent" and ARG0 is associated with the receiving agent role. For verbs like "gather", "collect", "receive", "acquire" the roles are reversed: ARG0 is typically associated with a "sending" agent role, the ARG1 describes what is "Received", and ARG2 is associated with the "receiving" agent role. Grouping the verbs signifying a "sending" or a "receiving" action helps us map the corresponding arguments to the relevant CI parameters for Senders and Receivers. The mapping for TP and Attribute remains the same for all verbs. Finally, our SRL mapping does not include a semantic role mapping of the Subject parameter. We operate on the assumption that the CI subject parameter in most statements is the user.

5.1.3 Clues from CI to Improve SRL

We first gather the arguments from the SRL model and map them to CI parameters, as shown in Table 2. Identifying the arguments for all verbs in the privacy statement results in high recall numbers. Nevertheless, the precision suffers because not all of the verbs need to be invoked. To reduce the number of false positive mappings, we implement an Algorithm 1 which analyzes all the relevant SRL verbs to check whether any of them appear as part of the Transmission Principle (TP) relative to another verb. Specifically, after the arguments are mapped to CI parameters, we iterate through each verb in the sentence and remove it if it has already been mapped as part of a TP for another verb.

Algorithm 1

$Args \leftarrow$ *SRL(sentences)*
$Dict(Verb, CI_{params}) \leftarrow$ *MapToCI(Args)*
for all $verb_i \in Dict(Verb : CI_{params})$ **do**
  for all $verb_j \in Dict(Verb : CI_{params})$ **do**
    if $verb_i \in Dict[verb_j][TP]$ **then**
      $RemoveMappings(Dict(verb_i))$
    end if
  end for
end for

For example, in the following statement, the SRL model will pick up two predicates (verbs) and corresponding arguments:

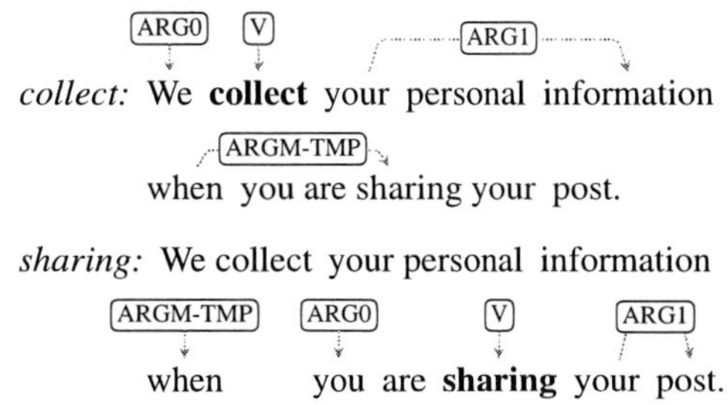

These arguments will be mapped to CI parameters, as described in the previous section. The verb "share" is redundant in this context since it is part of the TP of the verb "collect." Once we identify the *redundant* verb, we ignore all arguments associated with it, i.e., our algorithm does not consider these results. We do keep those parameters that overlap with the parameters produced by non-redundant verbs. For instance, in our example, we ignore the verb "share" and the associated with it arguments. Specifically, the [**ARG0:** you] and the [**ARG1:** your post] which otherwise will be mapped to a CI sender and attribute parameters, respectively.

5.2 Expert Annotation Task

We perform *m*odel-assisted annotation of close to a thousand privacy statements that discuss information exchanges across 50 policies (see Table 9 in the Appendix) from the OPP-115 Corpus (Wilson et al., 2016a).

5.2.1 Data processing

To extract relevant statements, we relied on existing OPP-115 corpus annotations of "data practices" in each of the segments of the policy. We limit our CI parameter extraction to labeled segments of the policy that discuss information exchanges such as segments labeled as "First Party Collection/Use", "Third party sharing/collection", and "Data Retention". We also cleaned that data to remove short parts of speech that are intrinsically captured by a syntactic parser.

The selected statements from the privacy policies were then presented to a human annotator, one of the authors who is an expert on CI. The expert then marked the valid results for each of the privacy statement sentences and CI parameters, which form the ground truth. A sentence was marked as a "valid" flow if it prescribed an information exchange of any kind. Otherwise, by default, all sentences are considered "invalid." Overall, the extraction phase resulted in a total of **2808** privacy statement sentences, out of which **994** were labeled as valid, containing **4048 CI parameters**. On average, a policy contains 18 valid statements, with outliers of 4 and 45 valid statements. Furthermore, our dataset contains: a) **4333** SRL labels (2846 true positives and 1487 false positives), **5974** DP labels (2484 true positives and 3490 false positives). Table 8 in the Appendix shows the annotation labels breakdown for each CI parameter.

Annotation reliability We assessed the reliability of the expert by co-coding with another author annotating 10 of the 50 policies to achieve a substantial to excellent agreement with Cohen's Kappa score range of 0.67-0.88 on the CI parameter annotations. Table 7 shows the corresponding breakdown of Cohen's Kappa score (McHugh, 2012) for each of the CI parameters.

Parameter	Cohen's Kappa Agreement score
Sender	0.88
Receiver	0.80
Attribute	0.63
Subject	0.73
TP	0.68

Table 3: The Cohen's Kappa agreement scores for CI parameters annotation.

5.3 ML-assisted expert validations

The outputs of the methods we have proposed in Section 5 may have an overlap with the ground truth. However, for CI parameters like the transmission principle, it is not clear if relying on an exact string match or a fuzzy match would consistently capture what makes any output a transmission principle. Hence, comparing the outputs with the expert annotations requires a careful analysis that goes beyond unigram/bigram/trigram match or fuzzy match of the two spans of text. Instead, we perform a validation of the outputs generated by the model, where the expert can confirm if the output matches the expectation and criteria for the five CI parameters[3]. Such a human-in-the-loop annotation process is necessary to check for any inconsistencies as shown in prior work for image annotations (Zurowietz et al., 2018; Marques and Barman, 2003), knowledge-oriented text tasks (Klie et al., 2018), clinical text annotations (South et al., 2012). The task involved comparing against ground-truth human annotations, and selecting among the model-based outputs, the ones that match the definition of a contextual integrity parameter. For example, although the model generated output "has an xx% match as per fuzzy match with the ground truth parameter:", it still does not capture the critical component that defines the transmission principle. Similarly, we see patterns for other CI parameters that are not easily definable in terms of rules that can scale with the number of models we compare against. This limitation is one that is highlighted in human-in-the-loop annotations and validations with domain expertise (Monarch, 2021), and improving the scaling of this process is left for future work.

5.4 Baseline Models

Question Answering As an exploratory experiment, we used an open domain QA model (AllenNLP library with the BiDAF model with GloVe embeddings[4]) to answer CI-related questions regarding each privacy statement. For example, to identify the marked CI parameters in the following privacy statement, we asked a variation of these questions: *"Who is transferring?"*, *"What is being transferred?"*, *"Who is the subject?"*, *"Who is the receiver/recipient?"*, *"Why, When, and How is the transfer facilitated?"*:

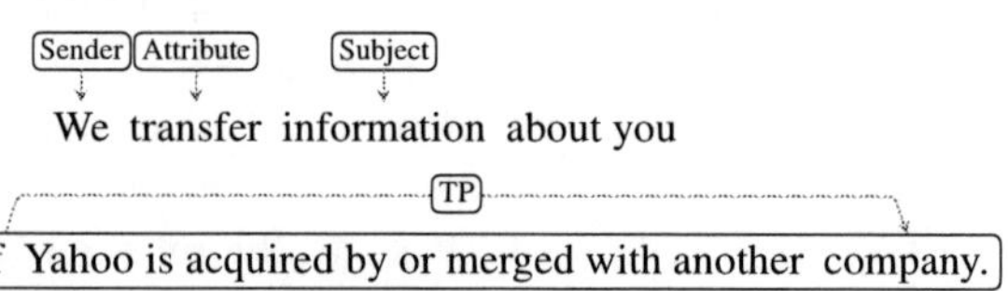

BERT We frame the CI parameter extraction task as a sequence-to-sequence transformation problem

[3]See Figure 3 in the Appendix of a screenshot of the choices that the annotation tool built for this purpose

[4]bidaf-model-2017.09.15-charpad.tar.gz

to fine-tune a Bidirectional Encoder Representations from Transformers (BERT) model (Devlin et al., 2018) on our dataset to map a sequence of words in privacy statements to a corresponding sequence of CI tags. The input sentence is tokenized as a sequence, and the output sequence is a per-token mapping between {None, Sender, Receiver, Attribute, TP and Subject} parameters. For training and testing, we transformed our dataset into the CoNLL2003 format and used the AllenNLP re-implementation of (Gardner et al., 2018) with the train-test split ratio as 80/20 and values of hyperparameters taken from (Gardner et al., 2017).

Hidden Markov Model As a baseline, we also formulate the CI parameter extraction as a part-of-speech (POS) tagging task and use a Hidden Markov Model (HMM) probabilistic model (Jurafsky and Martin, 2014) for annotating words in a sentence. Specifically, we train a trigram HMM by converting the dataset to CoNLL-2003 format (Sang and De Meulder, 2003) with CI parameters as the target labels and an 80/20 train-test split. By default, HMM relies on the Markov assumption that the probability of a particular state only depends on the preceding state. However, in order to enrich our HMM model, we consider the two previous states when predicting the current CI parameter, turning it into a trigram model. Further, we obtain the final transition probability distribution by linearly combining unigram, bigram, and trigram probability distributions:

$$P(t_i \mid t_{i-1}, t_{i-2}) = \lambda_1 P(t_i \mid t_{i-1}, t_{i-2}) + \lambda_2 P(t_i \mid t_{i-1}) + (1 - \lambda_1 - \lambda_2) P(t_i)$$

The parameters λ_1 and λ_2 are fine-tuned on the validation set with values 0.42 and 0.48 providing the best results. The Viterbi algorithm (Forney, 1973) is used in the decoding phase for the extended model.

6 Evaluation

We now compare the performance of the different models on the CI Annotation task using the dataset in Section 5.2 with some common baseline models repurposed for CI.

6.1 Baseline Performance

Table 4 shows the results of our expeditionary experiment. The overall F1 scores for the QA model indicate poor results for the extraction of all CI parameters. In our experiment, QA outputs multiple phrase predictions for each of the parameters. For precision, we calculate true positives as a fraction of all positives predicted for each parameter. For recall, we calculate the fraction of true positives to all correct parameters.

	Recall	**Precision**	**F1**
Attribute	0.21	0.15	0.17
Receiver	0.08	0.06	0.07
Sender	0.03	0.02	0.02
Subject	0.07	0.02	0.03
TP	0.21	0.16	0.18

Table 4: Precision, Recall, and overall F1 score for QA Comprehension model used for the CI parameter extraction task. The recall and precision values for a parameter are calculated by macro averaging over privacy statements.

This result aligns with previous uses of QA in the privacy domain (Ravichander et al., 2019), which observed that compared to a human annotator, using standard reading comprehension models for privacy policies returns unsatisfactory results. These experiences suggest that QA models require additional heuristics to filter the many false positives as a result of operating on a paragraph level and not on sentence-level statements.

Table 5 shows the results of training a trigram Hidden Markov Model and a fully-supervised BERT for the CI-parameter extraction task. Both models perform relatively poorly for our task, especially when it comes to the "Sender" parameter. HMM's overall F1 scores are slightly better for detecting other parameters, with the highest F1 score achieved for the TP parameter in both models.

	Recall		**Precision**		**F1**	
CI Param.	HMM	BERT	HMM	BERT	HMM	BERT
Attribute	0.67	0.61	0.57	0.51	0.62	0.55
Receiver	0.44	0.53	0.52	0.36	0.47	0.43
Sender	0.08	0.12	0.15	0.16	0.10	0.14
TP	0.80	0.75	0.68	0.55	0.74	0.64

Table 5: F1 Scores for fully-supervised HMM and fine-tuned BERT model. The recall and precision values are calculated on word level over the whole test set.

6.2 CI Improved Performance

Table 6 shows precision and recall for both DP (Spacy (Honnibal and Montani, 2018)) and SRL

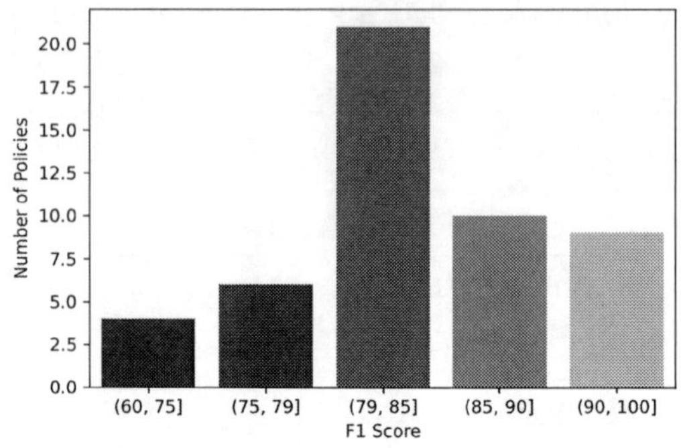

Figure 2: Histogram of F1 scores across privacy policies

models (AllenNLP BERT SRL (0.8.5) and (2.1.0)). Both DP and the two SRL models have high recall numbers. However, in DP the precision is lower, indicating that although DP identifies all the relevant instances, it also produces a large number of false positives. Overall, compared to DP, both SRL models have higher precision and recall. The AllenNLP (2.1.0) SRL-adapted structured BERT model (Shi and Lin, 2019), with comparable results[5] to robust models like RoBERTa (Liu et al., 2019) and T5 (Raffel et al., 2019) on CoNLL SRL datasets (Pradhan et al., 2013), produced better results compared to the earlier version (0.8.5) (Stanovsky et al., 2018). Furthermore, compared to DP, the SRL models have slightly higher recall numbers and much higher precision. We, however, note that SRL did not process 49 valid statements missing 159 valid CI parameters. In this case, the statements were ignored by our SRL algorithm because the semantic frame was not triggered as they contained verbs that our algorithm did not track. Some of these verbs are not always associated with information exchange, like "sell" and "rent".

6.2.1 Improved SRL

Table 6 shows the results for SRL after applying our algorithm incorporating domain-specific heuristics on both BERT SRL model versions. The precision results have improved across all the parameters, affecting recall only slightly. We note that our F1 metric is calculated on the phrase prediction level.

Performance across Policies: Figure 2 shows F1 score distributions for the annotated policies. The majority of policies (31) have F1 scores in the range of 80-89, which is consistent with the average F1 scores per parameter. Nine policies perform much better giving a high F1 value of more than 90, six policies are within the 75-80 range, and four policies in the 60-75 F1 range. Refer to Table 9 in the Appendix for the F1 scores for each policy.

[5]https://paperswithcode.com/sota/coreference-resolution-on-conll-2012

Model	CI Parameters	Recall	Precision	F1
DP	Attribute	0.68	0.43	0.53
	Subject	0.79	0.26	0.39
	TP	0.76	0.61	0.68
SRL (0.8.5)	Attribute	0.92	0.70	0.80
	Receiver	0.94	0.74	0.83
	Sender	0.95	0.63	0.75
	TP	0.89	0.69	0.78
SRL (2.1)	Attribute	0.88	0.71	0.79
	Receiver	0.88	0.75	0.81
	Sender	0.90	0.64	0.75
	TP	0.93	0.70	0.80
CI-SRL (0.8.5)	Attribute	0.90	0.75	0.82
	Receiver	0.88	0.79	0.83
	Sender	0.90	0.73	0.81
	TP	0.88	0.81	0.84
CI-SRL (2.1)	Attribute	0.88	0.78	0.83
	Receiver	0.87	0.81	0.84
	Sender	0.88	0.76	0.82
	TP	0.84	0.83	0.84

Table 6: F1 Scores for all the models: DP, SRL models and Improved SRL (CI-SRL). The recall and precision values for each parameter are calculated by macro averaging over privacy statements.

We analyzed the privacy statements for which our heuristic algorithm achieved low precision scores to understand the reasons behind the poor performance. Our SRL-based algorithm performed poorly on statements with semantically complex sentences. Semantically complex statements comprise multiple verb-predicates with related arguments that result in a large number of false positives. We also noticed a large number of false positives in long connected sentences that due to improper punctuation appear as a single sentence to our algorithm.

These cases are not only problematic for an NLP task but also require significant cognitive effort to analyze the privacy implications of the prescribed information flows. Rather than adapting our method to yield better results in these cases, we can use it to detect these complex sentences so that they can be restated more clearly.

7 Discussion

In this paper, we describe an NLP-based method to perform automatic CI annotation of privacy statements. This work has several implications for different stakeholders, some of which were discussed in (Shvartzshnaider et al., 2019a).

For consumers, who often find privacy policies too lengthy and complex to read, the CI annotation provides the ability to query the privacy policies for specific flows it prescribes. These can involve asking about mentions of specific "senders" and "recipients" in the privacy policies, the type of information being collected or shared, and listing the conditions and purposes. Beyond enumerating the prescribed CI parameters, the method enables contextual queries that reflect up to five CI parameters. For example, instead of asking about mentions of "location information," the query can include the senders, and recipients of interest, such as third parties, and contractors. The query can be further refined to include specific constraints under which location data is transferred, e.g., when the user is using the app.

The CI abstraction also allows for querying different privacy policies, potentially, from different sectors. Moreover, it can serve as a way to compare different versions of the same privacy policy to examine the new changes that were introduced in the latest version. We can identify which new flows were added or removed and, consequently, what data types, senders, recipients, subjects, and conditions were changed.

Finally, combining with existing crowdsourcing methodologies of learning users' privacy expectations (Apthorpe et al., 2018; Shvartzshnaider et al., 2016; Apthorpe et al., 2019), we can perform a large-scale analysis of what privacy policies align with users' expectations and existing societal norms.

For relevant agencies like the Federal Trade Commission, the CI-based analysis of privacy policies can serve as a robust auditing technique for prescribed data handling practices. Using the CI framework, the resulting information flows can be automatically compared with existing regulation (Apthorpe et al., 2019) and users' privacy expectations (Shvartzshnaider et al., 2016; Apthorpe et al., 2018). Furthermore, the analysis can help detect privacy statements with missing contextual information that results in ambiguous flows. Ultimately, we envision our work used as part of the overall evaluation framework for performing dynamic and static analysis of digital services, similar to (Sanfilippo et al., 2019). Specifically, the CI annotated policy fed into an automatic test suite for possible violation of privacy policy, regulation, or societal expectations.

7.1 Limitations

As discussed in Section 6, our methods result in high F1 scores (>80%) of annotations. Nevertheless, there are cases where our approach does not perform as well. Our evaluation of different models shows that a better SRL model coupled with domain knowledge heuristic improves results. Previous results (Shvartzshnaider et al., 2019a) showed that crowdworkers are able to identify CI parameters with high precision. Coupled with our approach, crowdworkers can filter the false positives and increase the precision further. Eliminating the need for validation of model outputs in the evaluation phase would also make it easy to evaluate better models in the future.

8 Conclusion

In this paper, we formulate the new CI parameter extraction NLP task for the analysis of privacy statements. We adapt several conventional NLP models (QA, HMM, BERT, DP and SRL) to perform the task and demonstrate that it cannot be solved trivially. In our evaluation of privacy statements of 50 real-world privacy policies, we show that a method combining clues from CI with syntactic DP coupled with type-specific SRL obtains the highest F1 score. We build on this insight to devise an algorithm that incorporates CI-based domain-specific knowledge to achieve higher precision and recall. The proposed algorithm post-processes ML outputs and increases automation of a tedious task that has so far been performed manually. Further improvements of this task, leveraging domain knowledge for complex scenarios will directly benefit downstream applications ranging from aiding the design and analysis of privacy policies to building systems that meet users' privacy expectations by construction.

References

Waleed Ammar, Shomir Wilson, Norman Sadeh, and Noah A Smith. 2012. Automatic categorization of privacy policies: A pilot study.

Benjamin Andow, Samin Yaseer Mahmud, Wenyu Wang, Justin Whitaker, William Enck, Bradley Reaves, Kapil Singh, and Tao Xie. 2019. Policylint: investigating internal privacy policy contradictions on google play. In *28th {USENIX} Security Symposium ({USENIX} Security 19)*, pages 585–602.

Benjamin Andow, Samin Yaseer Mahmud, Justin Whitaker, William Enck, Bradley Reaves, Kapil Singh, and Serge Egelman. 2020. Actions speak louder than words: Entity-Sensitive privacy policy and data flow analysis with PoliCheck. In *29th USENIX Security Symposium (USENIX Security 20)*, pages 985–1002. USENIX Association.

Noah Apthorpe, Yan Shvartzshnaider, Arunesh Mathur, Dillon Reisman, and Nick Feamster. 2018. Discovering smart home internet of things privacy norms using contextual integrity. *Proceedings of the ACM on Interactive, Mobile, Wearable and Ubiquitous Technologies*, 2(2):1–23.

Noah Apthorpe, Sarah Varghese, and Nick Feamster. 2019. Evaluating the contextual integrity of privacy regulation: Parents' iot toy privacy norms versus {COPPA}. In *28th USENIX Security Symposium (USENIX Security 19)*, pages 123–140.

Jaspreet Bhatia and Travis D Breaux. 2015. Towards an information type lexicon for privacy policies. In *Requirements Engineering and Law (RELAW), 2015 IEEE Eighth International Workshop on*, pages 19–24. IEEE.

Jaspreet Bhatia and Travis D Breaux. 2018. Semantic incompleteness in privacy policy goals. In *2018 IEEE 26th International Requirements Engineering Conference (RE)*, pages 159–169. IEEE.

Jaspreet Bhatia, Travis D Breaux, Joel R Reidenberg, and Thomas B Norton. 2016a. A theory of vagueness and privacy risk perception. In *2016 IEEE 24th International Requirements Engineering Conference (RE)*, pages 26–35. IEEE.

Jaspreet Bhatia, Travis D Breaux, and Florian Schaub. 2016b. Mining privacy goals from privacy policies using hybridized task recomposition. *ACM Transactions on Software Engineering and Methodology (TOSEM)*, 25(3):22.

Anupam Datta, Jeremiah Blocki, Nicolas Christin, Henry DeYoung, Deepak Garg, Limin Jia, Dilsun Kaynar, and Arunesh Sinha. 2011. Understanding and protecting privacy: Formal semantics and principled audit mechanisms. In *International Conference on Information Systems Security*, pages 1–27. Springer.

Marie-Catherine De Marneffe and Christopher D Manning. 2011. Stanford typed dependencies manual.

Jacob Devlin, Ming-Wei Chang, Kenton Lee, and Kristina Toutanova. 2018. BERT: pre-training of deep bidirectional transformers for language understanding. *CoRR*, abs/1810.04805.

Morgan C Evans, Jaspreet Bhatia, Sudarshan Wadkar, and Travis D Breaux. 2017. An evaluation of constituency-based hyponymy extraction from privacy policies. In *Requirements Engineering Conference (RE), 2017 IEEE 25th International*, pages 312–321. IEEE.

Charles J Fillmore et al. 1976. Frame semantics and the nature of language. In *Annals of the New York Academy of Sciences: Conference on the origin and development of language and speech*, volume 280, pages 20–32.

G David Forney. 1973. The viterbi algorithm. *Proceedings of the IEEE*, 61(3):268–278.

Matt Gardner, Joel Grus, Mark Neumann, Oyvind Tafjord, Pradeep Dasigi, Nelson Liu, Matthew Peters, Michael Schmitz, and Luke Zettlemoyer. 2018. Allennlp: A deep semantic natural language processing platform. *arXiv preprint arXiv:1803.07640*.

Matt Gardner, Joel Grus, Mark Neumann, Oyvind Tafjord, Pradeep Dasigi, Nelson HS Liu, Matthew Peters, Michael Schmitz, and Luke S Zettlemoyer. 2017. A deep semantic natural language processing platform. *arXiv preprint arXiv:1803.07640*.

Hamza Harkous, Kassem Fawaz, Rémi Lebret, Florian Schaub, Kang G Shin, and Karl Aberer. 2018. Polisis: Automated analysis and presentation of privacy policies using deep learning. In *27th {USENIX} Security Symposium ({USENIX} Security 18)*, pages 531–548.

Matthew Honnibal and Mark Johnson. 2015. An improved non-monotonic transition system for dependency parsing. In *Proceedings of the 2015 Conference on Empirical Methods in Natural Language Processing*, pages 1373–1378, Lisbon, Portugal. Association for Computational Linguistics.

Matthew Honnibal and Ines Montani. 2018. spacy 2: Natural language understanding with bloom embeddings, convolutional neural networks and incremental parsing. *To appear*.

Dan Jurafsky and James H Martin. 2014. *Speech and language processing*, volume 3. Pearson London.

Jan-Christoph Klie, Michael Bugert, Beto Boullosa, Richard Eckart de Castilho, and Iryna Gurevych. 2018. The inception platform: Machine-assisted and knowledge-oriented interactive annotation. In *Proceedings of the 27th International Conference on Computational Linguistics: System Demonstrations*, pages 5–9.

Yinhan Liu, Myle Ott, Naman Goyal, Jingfei Du, Mandar Joshi, Danqi Chen, Omer Levy, Mike Lewis, Luke Zettlemoyer, and Veselin Stoyanov. 2019.

Roberta: A robustly optimized bert pretraining approach. *arXiv preprint arXiv:1907.11692*.

Oge Marques and Nitish Barman. 2003. Semi-automatic semantic annotation of images using machine learning techniques. In *International semantic web conference*, pages 550–565. Springer.

Palmer Martha, Gildea Dan, and Kingsbury Paul. 2005. The proposition bank: a corpus annotated with semantic roles. *Computational Linguistics Journal*, 31(1).

Mary L McHugh. 2012. Interrater reliability: the kappa statistic. *Biochemia medica*, 22(3):276–282.

Robert Munro Monarch. 2021. *Human-in-the-Loop Machine Learning: Active learning and annotation for human-centered AI*. Simon and Schuster.

Helen Nissenbaum. 2009. *Privacy in context: Technology, policy, and the integrity of social life*. Stanford University Press.

Sameer Pradhan, Alessandro Moschitti, Nianwen Xue, Hwee Tou Ng, Anders Björkelund, Olga Uryupina, Yuchen Zhang, and Zhi Zhong. 2013. Towards robust linguistic analysis using OntoNotes. In *Proceedings of the Seventeenth Conference on Computational Natural Language Learning*, pages 143–152, Sofia, Bulgaria. Association for Computational Linguistics.

Colin Raffel, Noam Shazeer, Adam Roberts, Katherine Lee, Sharan Narang, Michael Matena, Yanqi Zhou, Wei Li, and Peter J. Liu. 2019. Exploring the limits of transfer learning with a unified text-to-text transformer. *CoRR*, abs/1910.10683.

Abhilasha Ravichander, Alan W Black, Shomir Wilson, Thomas Norton, and Norman Sadeh. 2019. Question answering for privacy policies: Combining computational and legal perspectives. In *Proceedings of the 2019 Conference on Empirical Methods in Natural Language Processing and the 9th International Joint Conference on Natural Language Processing (EMNLP-IJCNLP)*, pages 4949–4959, Hong Kong, China. Association for Computational Linguistics.

Joel R Reidenberg, Travis Breaux, Lorrie Faith Cranor, Brian French, Amanda Grannis, James T Graves, Fei Liu, Aleecia McDonald, Thomas B Norton, and Rohan Ramanath. 2015. Disagreeable privacy policies: Mismatches between meaning and users' understanding. *Berkeley Tech. LJ*, 30:39.

Norman Sadeh, Alessandro Acquisti, Travis D Breaux, Lorrie Faith Cranor, Aleecia M McDonald, Joel Reidenberg, Noah A Smith, Fei Liu, N Cameron Russell, Florian Schaub, et al. 2014. Towards usable privacy policies: Semi-automatically extracting data practices from websites' privacy policies. *Poster Proceedings, SOUPS*, pages 9–11.

Madelyn Sanfilippo, Yan Shvartzshnaider, Irwin Reyes, Helen Nissenbaum, and Serge Egelman. 2019. Disaster privacy/privacy disaster. *Journal of the Association for Information Science and Technology (JASIST)*.

Erik F Sang and Fien De Meulder. 2003. Introduction to the conll-2003 shared task: Language-independent named entity recognition. *arXiv preprint cs/0306050*.

Kanthashree Mysore Sathyendra, Florian Schaub, Shomir Wilson, and Norman Sadeh. 2016. Automatic extraction of opt-out choices from privacy policies. In *AAAI Fall Symposium on Privacy and Language Technologies*.

Kanthashree Mysore Sathyendra, Shomir Wilson, Florian Schaub, Sebastian Zimmeck, and Norman Sadeh. 2017. Identifying the provision of choices in privacy policy text. In *Proceedings of the 2017 Conference on Empirical Methods in Natural Language Processing*, pages 2764–2769.

Peng Shi and Jimmy Lin. 2019. Simple BERT models for relation extraction and semantic role labeling. *CoRR*, abs/1904.05255.

Yan Shvartzshnaider, Noah Apthorpe, Nick Feamster, and Helen Nissenbaum. 2019a. Going against the (appropriate) flow: A contextual integrity approach to privacy policy analysis. In *Proceedings of the AAAI Conference on Human Computation and Crowdsourcing*, volume 7, pages 162–170.

Yan Shvartzshnaider, Zvonimir Pavlinovic, Ananth Balashankar, Thomas Wies, Lakshminarayanan Subramanian, Helen Nissenbaum, and Prateek Mittal. 2019b. Vaccine: Using contextual integrity for data leakage detection. In *The World Wide Web Conference*, pages 1702–1712.

Yan Shvartzshnaider, Schrasing Tong, Thomas Wies, Paula Kift, Helen Nissenbaum, Lakshminarayanan Subramanian, and Prateek Mittal. 2016. Learning privacy expectations by crowdsourcing contextual informational norms. In *Fourth AAAI Conference on Human Computation and Crowdsourcing*.

Brett South, Shuying Shen, Jianwei Leng, Tyler Forbush, Scott DuVall, and Wendy Chapman. 2012. A prototype tool set to support machine-assisted annotation. In *BioNLP: Proceedings of the 2012 Workshop on Biomedical Natural Language Processing*, pages 130–139.

Gabriel Stanovsky, Julian Michael, Luke Zettlemoyer, and Ido Dagan. 2018. Supervised open information extraction. In *Proceedings of the 2018 Conference of the North American Chapter of the Association for Computational Linguistics: Human Language Technologies, Volume 1 (Long Papers)*, pages 885–895, New Orleans, Louisiana. Association for Computational Linguistics.

Ian Tenney, Dipanjan Das, and Ellie Pavlick. 2019. BERT rediscovers the classical NLP pipeline. In *Proceedings of the 57th Annual Meeting of the Association for Computational Linguistics*, pages 4593–4601, Florence, Italy. Association for Computational Linguistics.

Rahmadi Trimananda, Hieu Le, Hao Cui, Janice Tran Ho, Anastasia Shuba, and Athina Markopoulou. 2022. OVRseen: Auditing network traffic and privacy policies in oculus VR. In *31st USENIX Security Symposium (USENIX Security 22)*, Boston, MA. USENIX Association.

Shomir Wilson, Florian Schaub, Aswarth Abhilash Dara, Frederick Liu, Sushain Cherivirala, Pedro Giovanni Leon, Mads Schaarup Andersen, Sebastian Zimmeck, Kanthashree Mysore Sathyendra, N Cameron Russell, et al. 2016a. The creation and analysis of a website privacy policy corpus. In *Proceedings of the 54th Annual Meeting of the Association for Computational Linguistics (Volume 1: Long Papers)*, volume 1, pages 1330–1340.

Shomir Wilson, Florian Schaub, Rohan Ramanath, Norman Sadeh, Fei Liu, Noah A. Smith, and Frederick Liu. 2016b. Crowdsourcing annotations for websites' privacy policies: Can it really work? In *Proceedings of the 25th International Conference on World Wide Web*, WWW '16, pages 133–143, Republic and Canton of Geneva, Switzerland. International World Wide Web Conferences Steering Committee.

Martin Zurowietz, Daniel Langenkämper, Brett Hosking, Henry A Ruhl, and Tim W Nattkemper. 2018. Maia—a machine learning assisted image annotation method for environmental monitoring and exploration. *PloS one*, 13(11):e0207498.

Appendix

A Annotation reliability

We assessed the reliability of the expert by coding with another author annotating 10 of the 50 policies to achieve a substantial to excellent agreement with Cohen's Kappa score range of 0.67-0.88 on the CI parameter annotations. Table 7 shows the corresponding breakdown of Cohen's Kappa score (McHugh, 2012) for each of the CI parameters.

Parameter	Cohen's Kappa Agreement score
Sender	0.88
Receiver	0.80
Attribute	0.63
Subject	0.73
TP	0.68

Table 7: The Cohen's Kappa agreement scores for CI parameters annotation.

B Additional Tables

Parameter	No. of Labels
Sender	546
Subject	340
Attribute	1133
Receiver	928
TP	1101

Table 8: Annotated CI parameters labels

"Sending" action verbs	"Receiving" action verbs
share (1188)	acquire (27)
transfer (130)	learn (56)
exchange (7)	collect (1042)
show (49)	receive (376)
send (297)	use (346)
supply (59)	gather (78)
provide (1142)	include (629)
disclose(359)	contain (413)
submit (150)	ask (13@)
give (101)	accept (290)
deliver (109)	store (212)
mail (16)	require (504)
display (69)	save (30)
export (3)	record (118)
forward (22)	keep (77)
refer (60)	combine (51)
release (37)	get (21)
tell (44)	track (134)
pass (13)	

Table 11: Verbs used to trigger SRL semantic frames. The number in the brackets shows the frequency of appearance in the OPP-115 corpus.

Company	Recall	Precision	F1
Liquor	0.86	0.47	0.61
Lodgemfg	0.73	0.55	0.63
New Orleans Online	0.88	0.55	0.68
St. Louis fed	0.82	0.58	0.68
Google	0.79	0.67	0.73
UH	0.78	0.69	0.73
NBC Universal	0.80	0.67	0.73
Sheknows	0.87	0.67	0.75
Instagram	0.87	0.67	0.75
Gawker	0.87	0.67	0.76
Military	0.91	0.66	0.76
Citizen	0.87	0.68	0.76
Everydayhealth	0.84	0.72	0.77
FoxSports	0.94	0.66	0.78
CoffeeReview	0.88	0.70	0.78
Reference	0.95	0.67	0.79
Zacks	0.93	0.69	0.79
News Busters	0.87	0.73	0.79
DCCCD	0.81	0.78	0.80
PlayStation	0.88	0.73	0.80
ABCNews	0.88	0.74	0.80
Yahoo	0.81	0.80	0.80
High Gear Media	0.92	0.72	0.81
PBS	0.85	0.77	0.81
Fortune	0.93	0.72	0.81
Time inc	0.94	0.73	0.82
LatinPost	0.90	0.77	0.83
Lynda	0.90	0.78	0.84
IMDB	0.88	0.80	0.84
MSN	0.87	0.81	0.84
Reddit	0.89	0.80	0.84
Ted	0.97	0.77	0.86
NY Times	0.87	0.86	0.87
AOL	0.98	0.78	0.87
Geocaching	0.91	0.82	0.87
Amazon	0.90	0.84	0.87
TaylorSwift	0.96	0.81	0.88
USA	0.96	0.81	0.88
WashingtonPost	0.94	0.83	0.88
TheAtlantic	0.96	0.83	0.89
Dogbreedinfo	0.92	0.86	0.89
Austincc	0.93	0.85	0.89
Walmart	0.93	0.85	0.89
BankofAmerica	0.87	0.92	0.90
Fool	0.95	0.85	0.90
TicketMaster	0.91	0.89	0.90
SI	0.90	0.93	0.91
TheFreeDictionary	0.92	0.93	0.92
Earthkam	1.00	0.88	0.93
OpenSecrets	1.00	1.00	1.00

Table 9: F1 scores for all annotated policies

Model	CI Parameters	Recall	Precision	F1	TP	FP	FN
DP	Attribute	0.35	0.71	0.47	791	1490	322
	Subject	0.24	0.75	0.36	255	806	85
	TP	0.57	0.81	0.67	895	666	206
SRL (0.8.5)	Attribute	0.55	0.85	0.67	960	773	173
	Receiver	0.67	0.85	0.75	790	394	138
	Sender	0.55	0.86	0.67	470	381	76
	TP	0.62	0.74	0.67	814	498	287
SRL (2.1)	Attribute	0.64	0.66	0.74	952	626	181
	Receiver	0.70	0.85	0.74	787	335	141
	Sender	0.70	0.85	0.77	460	288	86
	TP	0.72	0.78	0.75	855	325	246
CI-SRL (0.8.5)	Attribute	0.60	0.83	0.7	939	617	194
	Receiver	0.72	0.81	0.76	754	298	174
	Sender	0.64	0.83	0.72	453	251	93
	TP	0.76	0.73	0.74	805	258	296
CI-SRL (2.1)	Attribute	0.69	0.81	0.75	923	416	210
	Receiver	0.78	0.80	0.79	743	212	185
	Sender	0.74	0.79	0.77	433	149	113
	TP	0.85	0.75	0.79	821	144	280

Table 10: F1 Scores for all the models: DP, SRL models and Improved SRL (CI-SRL). Here, the recall and precision values for each parameter is calculated using the total number of parameters, and not macro averaging over privacy statements as in Table 7. TP, FP and FN are the number of True Positive (TP) and False Positive (FP).

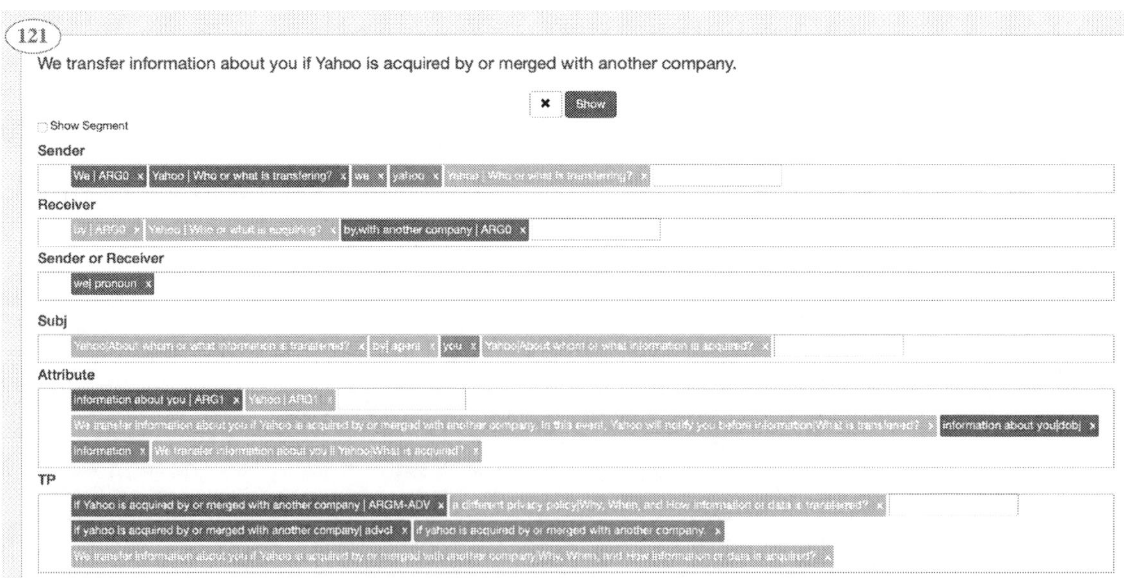

Figure 3: Annotation interface. The expert annotator marks which outputs matched the expectation and criteria for the five CI parameters.

Towards Mitigating Perceived Unfairness in Contracts from a Non-Legal Stakeholder's Perspective

Anmol Singhal, Preethu Rose Anish, Shirish Karande, and Smita Ghaisas
TCS Research, India
{anmol.singhal, preethu.rose, shirish.karande, smita.ghaisas}@tcs.com

Abstract

Commercial contracts are known to be a valuable source for deriving project-specific requirements. However, contract negotiations mainly occur among the legal counsel of the parties involved. The participation of non-legal stakeholders, including requirement analysts, engineers, and solution architects, whose primary responsibility lies in ensuring the seamless implementation of contractual terms, is often indirect and inadequate. Consequently, a significant number of sentences in contractual clauses, though legally accurate, can appear unfair from an implementation perspective to non-legal stakeholders. This perception poses a problem since requirements indicated in the clauses are obligatory and can involve punitive measures and penalties if not implemented as committed in the contract. Therefore, the identification of potentially unfair clauses in contracts becomes crucial. In this work, we conduct an empirical study to analyze the perspectives of different stakeholders regarding contractual fairness. We then investigate the ability of Pre-trained Language Models (PLMs) to identify unfairness in contractual sentences by comparing chain of thought prompting and semi-supervised fine-tuning approaches. Using BERT-based fine-tuning, we achieved an accuracy of 84% on a dataset consisting of proprietary contracts. It outperformed chain of thought prompting using Vicuna-13B by a margin of 9%.

1 Introduction

Contracts represent legally binding agreements among all participating stakeholders. Contract drafts typically undergo several iterations before they can be finalized, owing to their business criticality. The iterations involve extensive negotiations among legal professionals on accepting or rejecting parts of drafts put forth by other parties. This collaborative exchange of perspectives is critical in ensuring that all involved parties ultimately view the resulting contracts as acceptable.

Commercial contracts between enterprises are invaluable sources for deriving project-specific requirements (Sainani et al., 2020). The requirements indicated in the contractual clauses are obligatory. Therefore, it is important that they are perceived as practical and implementable by stakeholders responsible for meeting those commitments. However, these non-legal stakeholders, such as project managers, requirement analysts, engineers, solution architects, and delivery personnel, are not directly involved in contract negotiations. While in-house legal experts do consult various teams to understand the feasibility and scope of individual projects before drafting a contract, there is considerable room for oversight in the high-level discussions that take place (Tomlinson and Lewicki, 2015). The issue is further aggravated because the non-legal stakeholders share a limited understanding of Legalese, the specialized language used in contract writing. Consequently, many clauses can seem unfair to non-legal stakeholders despite being the results of iterative negotiations by legal experts. The perception of all involved stakeholders needs to be adequately captured during contract drafting for smooth governance (Karabulut et al., 2020).

In this work, we examine contracts from an angle of fairness, or lack thereof, from non-legal stakeholders' perspectives who must implement the obligatory requirements outlined within contracts. To achieve this goal, we conducted an empirical study involving legal and non-legal stakeholders who are often participants in contract negotiations and/or responsible for implementing the projects according to contract obligations. Our primary objective was to gain insights into their perceptions regarding fairness within contracts. Our analysis revealed multiple scenarios of unfairness that can occur within contract text. Some clauses are interpreted as 'clearly unfair' by both legal and non-legal stakeholders because they seem to be causing an obvious imbalance in parties' rights or obliga-

Proceedings of the Natural Legal Language Processing Workshop 2023, pages 99–112
December 7, 2023 ©2023 Association for Computational Linguistics

tions. Such clear unfairness is often encountered in clauses that address critical project management aspects, including unilateral termination, unilateral modification of terms, restrictions on indemnity claims, and jurisdictional matters. Our study also revealed that some clauses containing requirements may be considered 'potentially unfair' by non-legal stakeholders because of a risk of non-compliance arising due to the inclusion of ambiguous language. Such clauses can make certain parties vulnerable by significantly impacting the cost and effort associated with fulfilling the obligatory requirements. For instance, the sentence *The vendor should implement appropriate measures to ensure a level of security commensurate to the risk* vaguely specifies the measures required to implement the security controls. If the expectation regarding what constitutes 'appropriate' security controls differs between the vendor and the customer, the customer may perceive the vendor's enforcement of security controls as unfair and a breach of contract.

Based on the findings of the empirical study, we envisage building an automated assistant tailored to streamline the process of contract review by bringing in the perspectives of non-legal stakeholders. The assistant would: (1) identify contractual sentences likely to be perceived as unfair by non-legal stakeholders; (2) distinguish between clearly unfair and potentially unfair clauses; (3) recommend questions to be asked to the parties involved, thereby assisting in the resolution of the unfairness within the sentences. As a step towards building such a system, this paper presents our work on automating the classification of sentences as fair, potentially unfair, and clearly unfair. We investigate the ability of Pre-Trained Language Models (PLMs) to perform the classification by comparing Chain of Thought (CoT) prompting (Wei et al., 2023) and semi-supervised fine-tuning.

To date, prior work has primarily focused on detecting potentially unfair clauses within online Terms of Service (ToS) agreements, emphasizing fairness from a consumer-centric standpoint (Lippi et al., 2019). In comparison, our work delves into the intricate organizational dynamics and business context inherent with respect to commercial contracts. In our knowledge, this is the first work considering fairness in commercial contracts from the perspective of non-legal stakeholders. Furthermore, our research introduces a novel dimension by acknowledging ambiguity as a potential trigger for a perception of unfairness within contractual clauses—an aspect hitherto unexplored in the literature. Finally, making the perspectives of non-legal stakeholders available to legal teams while negotiating contracts is a first attempt, and building an automated assistant for this purpose contributes to both legal and non-legal stakeholders.

The primary contributions of this work can be summarized as follows: (1) We empirically analyze fairness in commercial contracts from the perspective of non-legal stakeholders; (2) We introduce a novel classification task tailored specifically for commercial contracts. This task categorizes sentences into three distinct classes: fair, potentially unfair, and clearly unfair; (3) We perform a set of experiments to examine the ability of PLMs on the novel classification task.

2 Related Work

2.1 Defining and Categorizing Fairness

Efforts to formulate a consistent definition of fairness have extended across various domains, including law, social science, and Machine Learning (ML). Fairness in a specific context may frequently vary and become a subject of contention among individuals or groups, depending upon the social and contextual elements at play (Selbst et al., 2019). Consequently, numerous formal and informal definitions of fairness have emerged within the body of literature (Verma and Rubin, 2018; Xiang and Raji, 2019; Pessach and Shmueli, 2022). Lippi et al. (2019) delineated fairness from a consumer's standpoint in online ToS agreements.

In the realm of contract negotiations, various parties and stakeholders involved are likely to have different and conflicting interests and perspectives (Poppo and Zhou, 2014). In such conditions, ensuring fairness becomes significant for all stakeholders involved (Kadefors, 2005). Unlike other domains, fairness in contract negotiations has broadly been categorized into procedural and distributive fairness from the perspective of stakeholders directly involved in negotiations (Welsh, 2003). In our research, we encapsulate the perception of fairness among non-legal stakeholders, individuals who are not directly engaged in contract negotiations but nonetheless constitute a substantial segment of the downstream implementation process.

2.2 Detecting Unfairness in Contracts

In recent years, efforts to automate the detection of unfair contractual clauses have gained momentum.

Micklitz et al. (2017) presented an empirical argument that it is possible to partly automate the process of abstract control of fairness of clauses in online consumer contracts. A notable work for detecting unfair clauses is CLAUDETTE (Lippi et al., 2019), a user-end tool that uses machine learning to identify and grade potentially unfair clauses in online ToS contracts. Lagioia et al. (2019) combined learning and reasoning tasks to enable CLAUDETTE to deal with rationales for improving its performance in detecting unfair clauses and to provide legal reasons why a clause is unfair. Ruggeri et al. (2021) proposed memory enhancement of Transformer models by expressing unstructured domain knowledge in natural language and evaluated their approach to unfairness detection in consumer contracts. (Ruggeri et al., 2022) used a memory attention network-based technique to explain unfairness in consumer contracts.

Our work differs from the abovementioned literature in the following aspects: (1) While previous literature focuses on the fairness of online service agreements from a consumer perspective, this work analyzes the fairness of commercial contracts from a non-legal stakeholders' lens. (2) Since we focus on commercial contracts, we highlight the multiple interpretations of fairness that emerge due to complex organizational structures and business processes. The existing literature does not focus on this context. (3) We uncover ambiguity as a potential factor for unfairness in commercial contracts, which, to the best of our knowledge, has not been done before.

3 Contract Fairness from a Non-Legal Stakeholder's Perspective

Our initial course of action was to empirically delineate the concept of unfairness in commercial contracts, particularly from a non-legal standpoint, and analyze if it differed from the viewpoint of legal stakeholders. Moreover, we sought to ascertain the extent of participation of non-legal stakeholders in contract negotiations.

3.1 Research Questions

The empirical study aimed at answering the following Research Questions (RQs):

RQ1: What scenarios constitute unfairness in contracts from a non-legal stakeholder's perspective?
RQ2: What is the impact of unfair contractual sentences on project implementation?
RQ3: How do the perceptions of unfairness among non-legal stakeholders differ from those of their legal counterparts?
RQ4: What is the extent of participation of non-legal stakeholders in contract negotiations?

3.2 Empirical Study Method

We conducted a questionnaire-based study involving 15 non-legal stakeholders to answer the abovementioned RQs. Henceforth, we refer to these stakeholders as study participants. We used social media platforms and connections within and outside a vendor organization to select the study participants. Our selection criteria included the following factors: (a) years of experience in dealing with project implementation activities on an industrial scale, (b) exposure to implementation and delivery in diverse geographies across the globe, and (c) familiarity with contracts or regulatory text. The participants who finally volunteered for the study, denoted as P1 to P15, hail from diverse organizational backgrounds with a global customer base. Their professional roles span across the spectrum of large-scale industrial project implementation, including directors, project managers, engineers, and requirement analysts. Subsequently, we shared the findings of the study with three legal professionals, denoted as P16 to P18, who currently serve as in-house legal counsel within their respective organizations and are actively involved in contract negotiations and compliance-related activities. We provide the details about each study participant in Appendix A.

To conduct the study, we circulated a questionnaire through e-mail, inviting study participants to provide their insights based on their experience. The questionnaire consisted of two sections. Section 1 enquired about participants' backgrounds and their familiarity with contractual obligations. Queries revolved around their professional roles, years of industry experience, and prior involvement in contract negotiations. Section 2 included questions concerning the impact and scenarios of unfairness in contract text. The participants were expected to write descriptive answers for each question. Additionally, we asked participants to furnish real-world examples of unfair contract clauses that illustrated their perspectives. The questionnaire is provided in Appendix B.

Two authors of this work consolidated the responses of the study participants. If the answers to any questions were unclear, the respective participants were approached again for clarification.

3.3 Outcomes of the Study

Answering RQ1: Each participant highlighted different scenarios of unfairness that may occur in contractual clauses. These scenarios can be grouped into four categories:

1) Imbalance in Rights or Obligations: Out of the 15 participants, 11 highlighted scenarios where there was a clear imbalance in the rights or obligations of the involved parties. For instance, 8 participants mentioned unfair cases where one party could be given unliteral rights to make decisions about the modification, termination, and jurisdiction of any agreement provisions. Five participants also explained that clauses that limited the liability of any party and imposed restrictions on claiming indemnity during the course of the project were unfair.

2) Ambiguous Language: 9 participants elucidated scenarios where the implementation boundaries were unclear, and there was a risk of non-compliance due to ambiguities in the contract. They believed that such ambiguous clauses should be perceived as unfair. For instance, P11 stated that ambiguous clauses where the imbalance between the obligations of two parties is implicitly present are potentially unfair. P8 mentioned that any clause including ambiguous language that can potentially cause conflicts between two parties and lead to loss of time and/or money should be considered unfair.

3) Project-specific Context: 6 participants elucidated context-specific scenarios concerning timelines, cost, and other delivery-related attributes that non-legal stakeholders may consider unfair. For instance, P13 explained that a supply chain management firm may incur significant losses while delivering perishable items if the contract does not establish appropriate timelines. P13 further stated that such timelines should be agreed upon in a contract only after consulting non-legal stakeholders with relevant expertise.

4) Human-Level Attributes: 4 participants also highlighted the importance of ensuring individual and group fairness for all stakeholders (Binns, 2019). For instance, P3 pointed out that no clause should be discriminatory or biased against any stakeholder based on social or demographic factors.

Based on these scenarios, we formulated the following definition:

A contractual sentence is fair if: (a) it does not cause a direct imbalance in parties' rights or obligations, (b) it does not include ambiguous language that causes a risk of non-compliance, (c) it includes project-specific details consistent with acceptable industry standards, and (d) it does not discriminate against any stakeholder based on social or demographic factors.

Answering RQ2: All the study participants from a non-legal background agreed that unfair sentences directly impacted the project lifecycle, including the phases of requirements elicitation, design, and implementation. Six of them also mentioned that a few sentences impacted overall project management and raised compliance-related issues, risking legal proceedings and financial losses for the parties.

Answering RQ3: The three participants having a legal background agreed with the identified scenarios and definition of fairness that emerged after analyzing the responses of non-legal stakeholders. However, they did not concur with the general perception of non-legal stakeholders regarding ambiguity being a factor that directly influences the fairness of contractual clauses. They explained that contracts deliberately infuse ambiguous language to ensure coverage and flexibility. While they agreed that certain ambiguities may introduce risk, they advised against over-specifying details within the contract document to remove ambiguities. Instead, they recommended that any ambiguous details in a contract that seemed potentially unfair to non-legal stakeholders should be clarified before implementation to avoid any confusion.

Answering RQ4: It was evident from participants' responses that non-legal stakeholders do not directly participate in contract negotiations. The legal stakeholders consult the heads/directors of different teams before agreeing with the terms and conditions imposed in the contract. However, these discussions are unstructured and on a high level. P12 and P14 further highlighted that reviewing contractual clauses becomes arduous for their teams due to a limited understanding of the complex language used in contracts. As a result, the general perception of people directly involved in implementation, such as requirement analysts, engineers, and project managers, is often left out.

4 Task Formulation

A key finding of our study was that the fairness perception of non-legal stakeholders might get overlooked during contract negotiations. Therefore, we decided to build an automated assistant that can leverage the reasoning capabilities of PLMs to

Unfairness Class	Definition	Example	Rationale for Unfairness
Potentially Unfair	This category includes all contractual sentences containing ambiguous language, which can potentially cause a risk of non-compliance.	Data Processor shall keep Personal Information sufficiently isolated from other data on the server in an appropriate manner to prevent it from being misused.	The example is potentially unfair because what constitutes sufficient isolation and appropriate manner is vague and could be interpreted in multiple ways. This ambiguity makes it difficult for the Data Processor to comply with the obligation and makes Personal Information susceptible to misuse.
Clearly Unfair	This category includes all clauses that deal with situations that lead to a direct imbalance in parties' rights or obligations.	Purchaser may modify the policies incorporated with this Order anytime, and Supplier will be obligated to implement such modifications.	The clause provides the Purchaser unilateral rights to modify the policies of the agreement without any prior notice to the Supplier.

Table 1: Description of Unfairness Classes

determine unfairness in contractual sentences from the perspective of non-legal stakeholders.

In order to build a contract negotiation assistant, we first analyzed if the unfairness scenarios highlighted by the empirical study participants could be detected automatically. While language models can be used to detect ambiguities (Lebanoff and Liu, 2018) and imbalances in rights and obligations (Lippi et al., 2019), the automated detection of project-specific details necessitates knowledge of contextual features such as organizational rules, accepted industry standards, and domain expertise. These aspects can differ across projects, and therefore, cannot be generalized to build a universal negotiation assistant. Therefore, we considered unfair project-specific details out of scope for automation. Furthermore, language models are presently incapable of reasoning about human-level attributes affecting fairness (Selbst et al., 2019). Consequently, we also did not include such attributes in our classification. We plan to analyze project-specific and human-level attributes affecting the fairness of contracts in future work.

With this background, we formulated three distinct classes for manually labeling our dataset from a non-legal stakeholder's perspective- fair, potentially unfair, and clearly unfair. Each of these classes can be explained as follows:

Fair: All contractual sentences that follow the definition of fairness mentioned in Section 3.3 are labeled as fair. Additionally, sentences containing ambiguous terms that do not directly impact implementation are marked fair. For instance, the clause *While visiting the Buyer's sites, Representatives of the Vendor shall conduct themselves in a businesslike manner* is vague because the term 'businesslike manner' can be interpreted by the Vendor in multiple ways. However, this clause is not unfair because it does not hold business criticality concerning the deliverables of the project.

Potentially Unfair: All sentences containing ambiguous language that can potentially cause a risk of non-compliance are labeled as potentially unfair. For instance, any clause dealing with Change Requests and Issue Management in the service industry is particularly susceptible to ambiguities. The accepted practice in the industry is that the vendor responsible for providing services charges extra to implement change requests. However, no extra charges can be levied by the vendor if the change request is raised due to an identified bug in the services provided. If vague terms such as 'appropriate' are used in clauses that contain requirements, the boundaries of the services remain ill-defined and may cause conflicts between the parties. Such conflicts can be avoided if ambiguous terms are clarified before implementation.

We note here that we do not expect the clarified details to be explicitly included in the contract drafts. As pointed out by legal stakeholders in the empirical study, contracts are written and will continue to be written in a language that is not over-specific and granular (Li, 2017). In this work, we focus on detecting potentially unfair sentences to clarify them between legal and non-legal stakeholders before the contracts are signed to mitigate any negative consequences.

Clearly Unfair: All sentences that cause a direct imbalance in parties' rights and obligations are labeled as clearly unfair. Lippi et al. (2019) identified scenarios that can lead to an imbalance in online ToS agreements. Based on the empirical study responses, we discovered that some of these scenarios also occur in commercial contracts. These include: (1) Jurisdiction-related restrictions; (2) Choice of law governing the contract; (3)

	#1	#2	#3	Total
Train before DA	401	165	34	600
Train after DA	401	165	179	745
Validation	164	58	18	240
Test	235	99	26	360

Table 2: Dataset Distribution[1]

Unilateral changes to the contract; (4) Unilateral Termination of the contract; (5) Indemnity-related concerns; (6) Arbitration.

Table 1 provides a description of the two unfair classes, along with examples and rationales.

5 Dataset Creation

5.1 Dataset Source

We used English proprietary contracts provided by a vendor organization to conduct our experiments. The dataset included 45 expired commercial contracts corresponding to nine business domains (healthcare, automotive, finance, banking, pharmaceuticals, telecom, utility, clothing-retail, and supermarket). These were digitized contracts present in HTML format. To extract text from these documents, we used HTML tags to identify the sections of each document and the contractual clauses contained within them. After identifying each contractual clause, we extracted individual sentences using a sentence tokenizer. We extracted 5940 contractual sentences from this dataset.

5.2 Labeling Process

We delegated the labeling to four non-legal stakeholders within a vendor organization (henceforth called annotators). Owing to the convoluted nature of contract text, the manual labeling of each sentence entails a substantial human effort. Therefore, we randomly selected 1200 sentences and instructed the annotators to assign one of the three identified classes to each sentence. The remaining sentences were kept unlabeled.

First, the annotators analyzed each contractual sentence and assigned a label denoting the appropriate class. As contracts contain vast paragraphs of text, while analyzing a particular sentence for fairness, the annotators checked whether the aspect that makes the sentence seem unfair was resolved in the preceding or succeeding text. If so, then the sentence was marked as fair.

Every sentence underwent independent annotation by two annotators. In instances of discrepancies between the annotators, the sentence was forwarded to a third annotator tasked with assigning the final label. The annotators dedicated ten working days to completing this task, expending an average of two hours daily. Additional details about the labeling process and inter-annotator agreement scores can be found in Appendix C. The dataset distribution after labeling is provided in Table 2. We performed a stratified 50:20:30 split to divide the dataset into train, validation, and test sets respectively. The stratified split was based on the distribution of target classes to ensure that all training, validation, and test sets have a proportionate number of sentences for each class. We also note here that the annotators did not observe any differences while labeling contracts belonging to different domains. Therefore, the proposed unfairness categories are domain-agnostic.

[1]#1 Fair; #2 Potentially Unfair; #3 Clearly Unfair; DA-Data Augmentation

6 Experiments

We performed the ternary classification using two methods- (1) Data Augmentation and Self-Training and (2) CoT Prompting.

6.1 Data Augmentation and Self-Training

We encountered a significant class imbalance in the dataset, as evident in Table 2. We had very few sentences that were labeled as clearly unfair. Therefore, we performed data augmentation of the training set to ensure a comparable number of sentences in each class (Singhal et al., 2022). We decided to harness the generative power of ChatGPT to generate sentences corresponding to the minority class. The few-shot prompt structure used for this task was as follows: (1) We specified the system behavior that sets the context for the task. (2) We described the relevant context required by ChatGPT to generate clearly unfair sentences. (3) We provided two examples of clearly unfair sentences based on the context provided. (4) We detailed the task to be performed by ChatGPT. (5) We specified the output format. The prompt used for data augmentation is provided in Appendix D. We got the generated sentences verified by two annotators to ensure consistency with the class definition. The training dataset distribution post-augmentation is given in Table 2.

After augmenting the training data, we decided to use self-training (Amini et al., 2022), a semi-supervised learning paradigm, to leverage the large corpus of unlabeled sentences present in the dataset. The unlabeled corpus consisted of 4740 sentences.

The self-training framework we incorporated

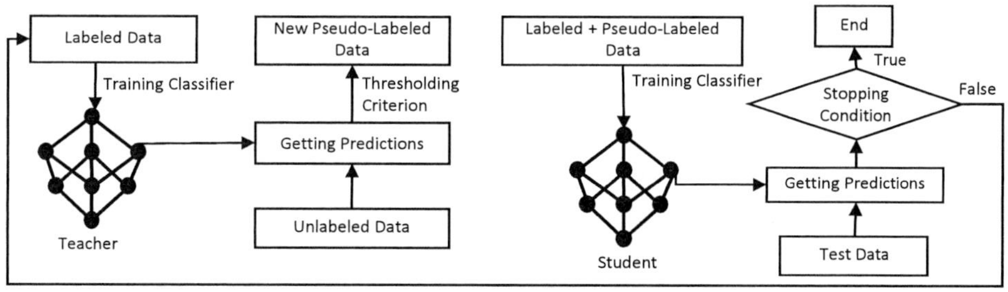

Figure 1: Self-Training Framework

consisted of 3 main steps: (1) We trained a language model for our ternary classification task using only the labeled training data, which we refer to as the Teacher model; (2) Using the Teacher, we obtained predictions on unlabeled data and filtered them based on a confidence threshold criterion. Next, we included the unlabeled sentences that passed the criterion in the training set and treated their predictions as pseudo-labels; (3) Using the augmented dataset of labeled and pseudo-labeled sentences, we trained a new model that we refer to as the Student. We followed these steps iteratively until we reached the stopping condition. In each subsequent iteration, the Student replaced the Teacher, and we assigned pseudo-labels to the remaining unlabeled data to train a new Student. The framework is depicted in Figure 1.

Our thresholding criterion inputs the confidence of the model predictions and the thresholds corresponding to each class. These thresholds act as hyperparameters, and we determined them after analyzing the model confidence after each iteration. Model confidence of an individual sentence refers to the probability corresponding to the predicted class of the sentence. If the confidence exceeds the given threshold, the criterion outputs 1, and the sentence is included for augmentation. In case the output is 0, the sentence is not included. The stopping criterion was when the accuracy did not improve on the test set after consecutive iterations of self-training. This criterion is standard practice in self-training (Amini et al., 2022).

6.2 Chain of Thought Prompting

Large Language Models (LLMs) have shown promising in-context learning capabilities and perform at par with fine-tuned language models on several downstream tasks (Liu et al., 2021). Therefore, in addition to self-training, we incorporated Chain of Thought (CoT) prompting (Wei et al., 2023) for LLMs as a multi-class classification technique. The prompting strategy is fundamentally anchored on the principle of giving the model' time to think'. This principle involves breaking down the overall task into a sequence of intermediate steps, subsequently enhancing the reasoning capabilities of LLMs beyond those offered by direct prompting.

We experimented with CoT in the few-shot setting. We also incorporated direct prompting as a baseline. The prompts used for performing the experiments are provided in Appendix E.

6.3 Experimental Setup

In the case of self-training, we used BERT (Devlin et al., 2018), a deep bi-directional Transformer-based architecture, to build our classifier. We used the open-source version of the pre-trained bert-base-cased model available on the Hugging-Face library. We used the PyTorch library (Paszke et al., 2019) to perform all our experiments. The details of all hyperparameters used for training the DL-based models are provided in Appendix F.

We used Vicuna (13B) (Chiang et al., 2023) and LLAMA-2 (13B) (Touvron et al., 2023) as base LLMs for our prompting experiments. We selected these LLMs because they are open-source and have shown a robust performance on multiple NLP benchmarks as compared to their close-sourced counterparts such as ChatGPT. Moreover, LLAMA-2 is available under a license which makes it free for commercial usage. We used the open-source Hugging face implementation for both of these LLMs. We set the temperature parameter 0 to obtain deterministic results. The maximum context length was set to 1024 tokens. All experiments were performed using an NVIDIA V100 GPU with 60 GB RAM and 32 GB GPU memory.

7 Results and Discussion

7.1 Classification Results

Table 3 shows the classwise F1 scores, macro F1 score, and the accuracy obtained on the ternary

Model	Technique	Fair F1	Potentially Unfair F1	Clearly Unfair F1	Macro F1	Accuracy
BERT	Vanilla	0.83	0.71	0.25	0.60	72.3%
	Data Augmentation	0.82	0.74	0.51	0.69	76.7%
	Data Augmentation + Self-Training	**0.85**	**0.79**	**0.58**	**0.74**	**84%**
Vicuna	Direct Prompt	0.83	0.61	0.45	0.63	63.2%
	CoT Prompt	0.84	0.73	0.57	0.71	75.4%
LLAMA-2	Direct Prompt	0.80	0.58	0.42	0.60	59.5%
	CoT Prompt	0.85	0.70	0.53	0.69	71%

Table 3: Results for Unfairness Detection

classification task using different techniques. The best-performing configuration was BERT with self-training and data augmentation, with an accuracy of 84% on the test set. As evident from the table, using self-training and data augmentation improved the performance of BERT by a margin of 12% as compared to its vanilla counterpart. While self-training alone improved the performance across all the classes, data augmentation especially boosted the f1 score across the clearly unfair class from 0.25 to 0.51. We provide the classwise and macro-level precision and recall scores obtained for all the experiments in Appendix G.

Self-Trained BERT outperformed few-shot CoT and direct prompting using both Vicuna and LLAMA-2. CoT prompting outperformed direct prompting for both Vicuna and LLAMA-2. CoT prompting using Vicuna performed with an accuracy of 75.4%. We observed that the difference in accuracies of CoT using Vicuna and Self-Trained BERT (approximately 9%) was mainly due to the drop across potentially unfair class. Vicuna erroneously classified many potentially unfair sentences as fair. This trend can be explained because Vicuna has not been specifically fine-tuned on this task, and therefore, misses out on ambiguities contributing to potential unfairness. Vicuna marginally outperformed LLAMA-2 on all prompting experiments. We believe these emerging results on prompting LLMs are promising as they remove the overhead of manual labeling and the unavailability of data for training.

7.2 Analysis

Progression of Self-Training: Figure 2 shows the change in model performance per iteration of self-training. As self-training progresses, the overall accuracy increased from 75.2% in iteration 1 (using only labeled data for training) to 84% in iteration 5 on the test set. Based on how self-training progresses, we can infer that an increase in the amount of pseudo-labeled data with each iteration leads to an increase in the training set's size, enabling the model to capture features across the three classes more efficiently.

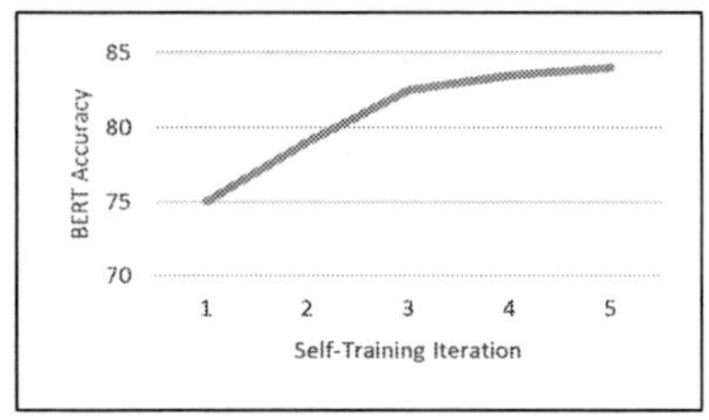

Figure 2: Self-Training Progression

Analyzing Model Predictions: We analyzed the model predictions obtained from the test data to determine any specific patterns in sentences misclassified by Self-Trained BERT. We found that approximately 40% of the misclassified sentences contained ambiguous terms but were followed by conditions that negate their ambiguity by establishing boundaries. For instance, the following sentence was misclassified- *The system shall frequently, but in any case, at least once in 2 weeks, prompt the user to update the login password.* In this sentence, though 'frequently' is a vague term, it is followed by the condition, 'once in 2 weeks', which sets a minimum criterion for the expected frequency of changing passwords. The presence of this minimum condition eliminates any ambiguity, and therefore, it should be classified as a fair sentence. However, our model wrongly classifies it as potentially unfair. This misclassification is because cases where terms such as 'frequently' are followed by disambiguating phrases such as conditions and criteria rarely occur in our dataset.

We also analyzed the reasoning generated by Vicuna for classification predictions using the CoT prompting experiments. We observed that the LLM followed the instructions and definitions in most cases. The model broke down the inference into the following steps: (a) It analyzed if the sentence is a right or obligation concerning any party. (b) It inferred if there was an imbalance in the right or obligation between parties. (c) It inferred if the sentence contained ambiguous terms. A shortcoming in the reasoning process was that the model could not correctly identify ambiguities relevant to project implementation. For instance, many sentences containing ambiguous terms such as 'frequently' and 'adequate' were marked fair. A similar trend was observed for LLAMA-2.

Mitigating the occurrence of misclassified sentences is critical to ensure the effectiveness of our envisioned negotiation assistant in the real world. Going forward, as future work, we plan to boost classification accuracy by incorporating human feedback into model training. A hybrid pipeline based on reinforcement learning with human feedback (RLHF) can further help LLMs discern details they tend to miss otherwise. In addition, augmenting CoT with other prompting techniques such as self-reflection also seems like a promising direction to improve results.

8 Conclusion

In this work, we analyzed and automatically detected unfairness in commercial contracts from the perspective of non-legal stakeholders. We conducted an empirical study to determine what constitutes unfairness according to non-legal stakeholders and how it differs from the perception of their legal counterparts. We discovered that non-legal stakeholders consider certain ambiguous sentences potentially unfair, even though they are legally accurate. Since these viewpoints are not directly highlighted during negotiations, we proposed building an automated negotiation assistant that can flag potentially unfair sentences according to non-legal stakeholders. As a step towards building such an assistant, we formulated a novel ternary classification task to detect unfairness in contracts. Our experiments using different PLMs and techniques revealed that self-trained BERT performed the classification with an accuracy of 84% on a proprietary contract dataset. It outperformed CoT prompting using Vicuna by a margin of 9%.

In the future, we plan to build an end-to-end assistant that can reason about unfairness in contracts from the perspective of non-legal stakeholders and recommend automatically generated questions to be asked during contract negotiations. Moreover, we plan to incorporate different hybrid and prompting-driven techniques to minimize misclassification. We also plan to analyze how project-specific attributes and human-level concerns can be incorporated into the assistant to generate more personalized questions for stakeholders.

Limitations

We note a few limitations of this work: 1) We cannot share the proprietary contracts used to conduct experiments with the outside world. The ownership of this data lies with the vendor organization collaborating with us. However, to enhance the reproducibility of our work, we have released the questionnaire used to conduct the empirical study and the annotation guidelines, prompts, and hyperparameters used to conduct the experiments. The ChatGPT-generated sentences are also part of the supplementary material. 2) Since we focus on commercial contracts, we cannot ascertain the generalizability of the empirical study findings to other legal documents. 3) Although we ensure the representativeness of our dataset by incorporating commercial contracts belonging to 9 different application domains, we cannot be certain that these contracts cover all possible unfairness scenarios. 4) This work focuses on contracts written in English. We do not consider contracts written in other languages. 5) We cannot use closed-source LLMs such as ChatGPT to conduct the experiments using proprietary data. We have reported results on open-source LLMs such as Vicuna and LLAMA-2 to mitigate this limitation.

Ethics Statement

We recognize and acknowledge the potential for misuse of our proposed contract negotiation assistant, including the possibility of adversarial exploitation to deliberately introduce unfairness into contractual clauses. Additionally, there exists a risk of unintended consequences due to inaccurate predictions when dealing with unseen data, which can have a ripple effect on contract negotiations. Consequently, we stress the importance of employing this assistant judiciously and primarily as a supplementary tool in contract negotiations. It should not be considered a substitute for the critical expertise legal professionals provide. Identifying unfairness within contractual sentences is intended to serve as an aid that can enhance the efficiency of experts' reviews, thereby reducing the time and effort expended in scrutinizing contract drafts. Ensuring that the assistant is aligned with ethical practices and is coupled with expert consultation to prevent unintended ramifications is crucial.

References

Massih-Reza Amini, Vasilii Feofanov, Loic Pauletto, Emilie Devijver, and Yury Maximov. 2022. Self-training: A survey.

Reuben Binns. 2019. On the apparent conflict between individual and group fairness.

Wei-Lin Chiang, Zhuohan Li, Zi Lin, Ying Sheng, Zhanghao Wu, Hao Zhang, Lianmin Zheng, Siyuan Zhuang, Yonghao Zhuang, Joseph E. Gonzalez, Ion Stoica, and Eric P. Xing. 2023. Vicuna: An open-source chatbot impressing gpt-4 with 90%* chatgpt quality.

Jacob Devlin, Ming-Wei Chang, Kenton Lee, and Kristina Toutanova. 2018. Bert: Pre-training of deep bidirectional transformers for language understanding.

Anna Kadefors. 2005. Fairness in interorganizational project relations: norms and strategies. *Construction Management and Economics*, 23(8):871–878.

Ahu Tuğba Karabulut, Mustafa Emre Civelek, Pınar Başar, Sabri Öz, and Ali Kucukcolak. 2020. The relationships among corporate governance principles and firm performance. *Accounting*.

Francesca Lagioia, Federico Ruggeri, Kasper Drazewski, Marco Lippi, Hans-Wolfgang Micklitz, Paolo Torroni, and Giovanni Sartor. 2019. Deep learning for detecting and explaining unfairness in consumer contracts.

Logan Lebanoff and Fei Liu. 2018. Automatic detection of vague words and sentences in privacy policies.

Shuangling Li. 2017. A corpus-based study of vague language in legislative texts: Strategic use of vague terms. *English for Specific Purposes*, 45:98–109.

Marco Lippi, Przemysław Pałka, Giuseppe Contissa, Francesca Lagioia, Hans-Wolfgang Micklitz, Giovanni Sartor, and Paolo Torroni. 2019. CLAUDETTE: an automated detector of potentially unfair clauses in online terms of service. *Artificial Intelligence and Law*, 27(2):117–139.

Pengfei Liu, Weizhe Yuan, Jinlan Fu, Zhengbao Jiang, Hiroaki Hayashi, and Graham Neubig. 2021. Pre-train, prompt, and predict: A systematic survey of prompting methods in natural language processing.

Hans-W. Micklitz, Przemysław Pałka, and Yannis Panagis. 2017. The Empire Strikes Back: Digital Control of Unfair Terms of Online Services. *Journal of Consumer Policy*, 40(3):367–388.

Adam Paszke, Sam Gross, Francisco Massa, Adam Lerer, James Bradbury, Gregory Chanan, Trevor Killeen, Zeming Lin, Natalia Gimelshein, Luca Antiga, Alban Desmaison, Andreas Kopf, Edward Yang, Zachary DeVito, Martin Raison, Alykhan Tejani, Sasank Chilamkurthy, Benoit Steiner, Lu Fang, Junjie Bai, and Soumith Chintala. 2019. Pytorch: An imperative style, high-performance deep learning library. In H. Wallach, H. Larochelle, A. Beygelzimer, F. d'Alché-Buc, E. Fox, and R. Garnett, editors, *Advances in Neural Information Processing Systems 32*, pages 8024–8035. Curran Associates, Inc.

Dana Pessach and Erez Shmueli. 2022. A review on fairness in machine learning. *ACM Comput. Surv.*, 55(3).

Laura Poppo and Kevin Zheng Zhou. 2014. Managing contracts for fairness in buyer–supplier exchanges. *Strategic Management Journal*, 35(10):1508–1527.

Federico Ruggeri, Francesca Lagioia, Marco Lippi, and Paolo Torroni. 2022. Detecting and explaining unfairness in consumer contracts through memory networks. *Artif. Intell. Law*, 30(1):59–92.

Federico Ruggeri, Marco Lippi, and Paolo Torroni. 2021. Membert: Injecting unstructured knowledge into bert.

Abhishek Sainani, Preethu Rose Anish, Vivek Joshi, and Smita Ghaisas. 2020. Extracting and classifying requirements from software engineering contracts. In *2020 IEEE 28th International Requirements Engineering Conference (RE)*, pages 147–157.

Andrew D. Selbst, Danah Boyd, Sorelle A. Friedler, Suresh Venkatasubramanian, and Janet Vertesi. 2019. Fairness and abstraction in sociotechnical systems. In *Proceedings of the Conference on Fairness, Accountability, and Transparency*, FAT* '19, page 59–68, New York, NY, USA. Association for Computing Machinery.

Anmol Singhal, Preethu Rose Anish, Pratik Sonar, and Smita S Ghaisas. 2022. Data is about detail - an empirical investigation for software systems with nlp at core. In *2022 IEEE/ACM 1st International Conference on AI Engineering – Software Engineering for AI (CAIN)*, pages 145–156.

Edward C Tomlinson and Roy J Lewicki. 2015. The negotiation of contractual agreements. *Journal of Strategic Contracting and Negotiation*, 1(1):85–98.

Hugo Touvron, Louis Martin, Kevin Stone, Peter Albert, Amjad Almahairi, Yasmine Babaei, Nikolay Bashlykov, Soumya Batra, Prajjwal Bhargava, Shruti Bhosale, Dan Bikel, Lukas Blecher, Cristian Canton Ferrer, Moya Chen, Guillem Cucurull, David Esiobu, Jude Fernandes, Jeremy Fu, Wenyin Fu, Brian Fuller, Cynthia Gao, Vedanuj Goswami, Naman Goyal, Anthony Hartshorn, Saghar Hosseini, Rui Hou, Hakan Inan, Marcin Kardas, Viktor Kerkez, Madian Khabsa, Isabel Kloumann, Artem Korenev, Punit Singh Koura, Marie-Anne Lachaux, Thibaut Lavril, Jenya Lee, Diana Liskovich, Yinghai Lu, Yuning Mao, Xavier Martinet, Todor Mihaylov, Pushkar Mishra, Igor Molybog, Yixin Nie, Andrew Poulton, Jeremy Reizenstein, Rashi Rungta, Kalyan Saladi, Alan Schelten, Ruan Silva, Eric Michael

Smith, Ranjan Subramanian, Xiaoqing Ellen Tan, Binh Tang, Ross Taylor, Adina Williams, Jian Xiang Kuan, Puxin Xu, Zheng Yan, Iliyan Zarov, Yuchen Zhang, Angela Fan, Melanie Kambadur, Sharan Narang, Aurelien Rodriguez, Robert Stojnic, Sergey Edunov, and Thomas Scialom. 2023. Llama 2: Open foundation and fine-tuned chat models.

Sahil Verma and Julia Rubin. 2018. Fairness definitions explained. In *2018 IEEE/ACM International Workshop on Software Fairness (FairWare)*, pages 1–7.

Jason Wei, Xuezhi Wang, Dale Schuurmans, Maarten Bosma, Brian Ichter, Fei Xia, Ed Chi, Quoc Le, and Denny Zhou. 2023. Chain-of-thought prompting elicits reasoning in large language models.

Nancy A Welsh. 2003. Perceptions of fairness in negotiation. *Marq. L. Rev.*, 87:753.

Alice Xiang and Inioluwa Deborah Raji. 2019. On the legal compatibility of fairness definitions.

A Participant Details

We approached 40 legal and non-legal stakeholders for conducting our empirical study, out of which 18 provided concrete responses. The participation in the study was voluntary and no compensation was provided. The details corresponding to these 18 stakeholders are provided in Table 4.

ID	Years of Experience	Current Designation / Role
P1	3	Requirement Analyst
P2	2	Requirement Analyst
P3	2	Software Engineer
P4	4	Software Engineer
P5	3	Software Engineer
P6	6	Solution Architect
P7	7	Solution Engineer
P8	10	Project Manager
P9	12	Project Manager
P10	9	Project Manager
P11	15	Senior Project Manager
P12	20	Business Director
P13	24	Delivery Head
P14	17	Director of Technology
P15	16	Director of Research
P16	8	Legal Counsel
P17	6	Legal Counsel
P18	6	Legal Counsel

Table 4: Details of Study Participants

B Questionnaire

The questionnaire used to conduct the empirical study consisted of two primary sections. The meticulous questionnaire design aimed to obtain a thorough understanding of fairness in contracts from our study participants.

The questions in Section 1 were as follows:

1. What is your current role/designation within your organization?
2. How many years of experience do you have in your current line of work?
3. Have you previously served in other roles? Please elaborate.
4. Do you have experience in processing or implementing contractual obligations?
5. Have you directly contributed to contract negotiations before?
6. If the answer to Q5 is yes, please specify your contribution.
7. If the answer to Q5 is no, please explain the process of contractual governance followed in your organization.

The questions in Section 2 were as follows:

1. What are the issues you face when you are tasked with implementing contractual obligations?
2. What constitutes unfairness in contractual clauses, according to you? Please specify all possible cases and provide examples to illustrate each of them.
3. How do unfair sentences impact overall project implementation/compliance?
4. Do you believe non-legal stakeholders' inputs should be considered during contract negotiations?

C Dataset Annotation Details

The annotators incorporated for the labeling task had more than five years of experience in implementing contractual obligations. Since the labeling task was part of their daily workload, they were not compensated for it separately. We ensured that the annotators did not have conflicting interests while labeling, which could affect their judgment regarding the unfairness of clauses. We familiarized them with the task by sharing ten sentences as a sample exercise. We reviewed the ten sentences shared with each annotator and addressed any doubts and issues that came up while labeling these sample sentences. Once the annotators were familiarized with the task, they labeled 600 sentences each.

The average inter-annotator agreement for assigning the binary labels, calculated using Cohen's kappa, was 0.64. All sentences where the two annotators differed in assigning the final label were forwarded to a third annotator.

Some key annotation guidelines provided to the annotators were as follows:

- The sentences that neither constitute rights nor obligations are fair.
- If the sentence applies equally to both parties, it is fair.
- Sentences with redacted information should be removed from the dataset.
- If the sentence applies to one party and is a right / obligation:
  - If any details related to an obligation are to be decided later, after consultation with the other party, the sentence is fair.
  - Any right subject to an ambiguous condition is potentially unfair.
  - Any right stated without any boundaries or conditions is potentially unfair.
  - A material obligation of a contract containing ambiguous language is potentially unfair.
  - Any right or obligation causing a clear imbalance between two parties is clearly unfair.

In case of labeling potentially unfair sentences, the annotators were further asked to check if the ambiguous language used in the sentence caused a risk of non-compliance. The sentence was labeled as fair if the ambiguous language did not affect any material obligation or right concerning any party.

D Data Augmentation Prompt

We used ChatGPT to generate sentences corresponding to the clearly unfair class in our dataset. We experimented with six prompts corresponding to the clear unfairness scenarios identified during the labeling exercise. We used the OpenAI API to interact with the model and used few-shot prompting to generate sentences that can be used for data augmentation. We generated approximately 25 sentences with each such prompt.

One of the prompts that we used to generate clearly unfair sentences was:

System Behavior: You are an assistant that generates contractual sentences based on the given context.

Context: A clause that allows one party to terminate the agreement unilaterally is clearly unfair.

Example 1: If Investor fails to cure the identified breach within thirty (30) days, Company may terminate this agreement without prior notice to Investor.
Example 2: Service Recipient may remove and replace any Supplier member, with or without cause, from providing the Services under this Agreement.

Task: Given the context and examples, generate 25 unique contractual sentences that are clearly unfair due to unilateral termination rights.

Output Format should be as follows: <List of Sentences>: [Sentence 1, Sentence 2, ...]

The other prompts used for data augmentation are provided as supplementary material to this work. We have also released the artificially generated sentences used for data augmentation as part of the package.

E Classification Prompts

We performed the ternary classification using two prompting strategies- Direct and Chain of Thought Prompting. We experimented with both strategies in the few-shot setting by providing two examples of potentially unfair and clearly unfair classes. The prompts used for both techniques are as follows:

Direct Prompt

System Behavior: You are an assistant who analyzes contractual sentences based on the given context.

Context: A contractual sentence that causes a clear imbalance in the rights or obligations between parties is clearly unfair. A sentence containing ambiguous language that causes non-compliance risk is potentially unfair. Otherwise, the sentence is fair.

Example 1: Service Recipient may remove and replace any Supplier member, with or without cause, from providing the Services under this Agreement.
Answer: Clearly Unfair

Example 2: Provider shall, upon request of Recipient, promptly enable Recipient to secure for itself, patent, trade secret, or any other proprietary rights.
Answer: Potentially Unfair

Task: Given the context and examples, classify the given contractual sentence as fair, potentially unfair, or clearly unfair.

Input Sentence: <input>

CoT Prompt

System Behavior: You are an assistant who analyzes contractual sentences based on the given context.

Context: A contractual sentence that causes a clear imbalance in the rights or obligations between parties is clearly unfair. A sentence containing ambiguous language that causes non-compliance risk is potentially unfair. Otherwise, the sentence is fair.

Example 1: Service Recipient may remove and replace any Supplier member, with or without cause, from providing the Services under this Agreement.
Answer: The given sentence gives termination and replacement rights to the Service Recipient. This right creates an imbalance between the Supplier and the Service Recipient because the Service Recipient can unilaterally make decisions for Supplier personnel. Therefore, the sentence is Clearly Unfair.

Example 2: Provider shall, upon request of Recipient, promptly enable Recipient to secure for itself, patent, trade secret, or any other proprietary rights.
Answer: The given sentence imposes an obligation on the Provider. However, the implementation boundaries are unclear because of the presence of vague terms such as promptly, thereby introducing a risk of non-compliance. Therefore, the sentence is potentially unfair.

Task: Given the context and examples, reason step by step and classify the given contractual sentence as fair, potentially unfair, or clearly unfair.

Input Sentence: <input>

F Hyperparameter Details

Initial results showed that BERT was prone to overfitting our train data. To overcome this issue, we used three strategies- (1) Early stopping based on the model accuracy on the test set; (2) L2 regularization with Adam optimizer; (3) Adding dropout to the final layer of BERT to introduce randomness in training. We used the grid-search method to obtain optimal hyperparameters for our model training. The hyperparameters used for self-training BERT are provided in Table 5.

Hyperparameters	**Values**
Batch Size	16
Learning Rate	[1e-6, 5e-6]
No. of epochs	12
No. of warmup steps	200
Weight decay	0.08
Dropout	[0.2, 0.45]
Max sequence length	256
Confidence Threshold Range	[0.6, 0.85]

Table 5: Hyperparameter Details

G Extended Results

Table 6 shows the classwise precision, recall, and F1 scores obtained for different experiments conducted in this work.

Model	Technique	Fair			Potentially Unfair			Clearly Unfair			Macro		
		P	R	F1	P	R	F1	P	R	F1	P	R	F1
BERT	Vanilla	0.82	0.83	0.83	0.74	0.68	0.71	0.24	0.26	0.25	0.60	0.59	0.60
	Data Augmentation	0.82	0.82	0.82	0.78	0.70	0.74	0.52	0.49	0.51	0.71	0.67	0.69
	Data Augmentation + Self-Training	**0.88**	0.84	**0.85**	**0.80**	**0.79**	**0.79**	**0.60**	0.56	**0.58**	**0.76**	**0.73**	**0.74**
Vicuna	Direct Prompt	0.81	0.84	0.83	0.62	0.60	0.61	0.47	0.43	0.45	0.63	0.62	0.63
	CoT Prompt	0.83	**0.86**	0.84	0.77	0.70	0.73	0.57	**0.57**	0.57	0.72	0.71	0.71
LLAMA-2	Direct Prompt	0.79	0.82	0.80	0.59	0.54	0.58	0.40	0.44	0.42	0.59	0.60	0.60
	CoT Prompt	0.86	0.85	0.85	0.73	0.68	0.70	0.56	0.50	0.53	0.72	0.68	0.69

Table 6: Precision and Recall Scores for Unfairness Detection

Connecting Symbolic Statutory Reasoning with Legal Information Extraction

Nils Holzenberger
Télécom Paris
Institut Polytechnique de Paris
nils.holzenberger@telecom-paris.fr

Benjamin Van Durme
Johns Hopkins University
vandurme@jhu.edu

Abstract

Statutory reasoning is the task of determining whether a given law – a part of a statute – applies to a given legal case. Previous work has shown that structured, logical representations of laws and cases can be leveraged to solve statutory reasoning, including on the StAtutory Reasoning Assessment dataset (SARA), but rely on costly human translation into structured representations. Here, we investigate a form of legal information extraction atop the SARA cases, illustrating how the task can be done with high performance. Further, we show how the performance of downstream symbolic reasoning directly correlates with the quality of the information extraction.

1 Introduction

Statutory reasoning is the task of reasoning about legal cases with legal statutes. It is generally contrasted with case-based reasoning, and is complementary to it in legal systems based on common law (Lawsky, 2017). The StAtutory Reasoning Assessment dataset (SARA) is a benchmark for statutory reasoning for US federal tax law (Holzenberger et al., 2020).

In some settings, laws and regulations can be encoded into first-order logic programs to reason about cases (El Hamdani et al., 2021; Merigoux et al., 2021a; Bench-Capon et al., 1987). In Holzenberger et al. (2020), SARA statutes and cases were manually translated into Prolog code, solving statutory reasoning in that context, in a process depicted in Figure 1. Here, we take the standpoint advocated by Merigoux et al. (2021a), and start with the premise that a structured form of the statutes is available, while cases are stated in natural language. In practice, many governments across the world use expert systems to compute taxes owed by taxpayers, maintained by a dedicated team of experts (Oskamp and Lauritsen, 2002; Merigoux et al., 2021b). In contrast, translating cases into a

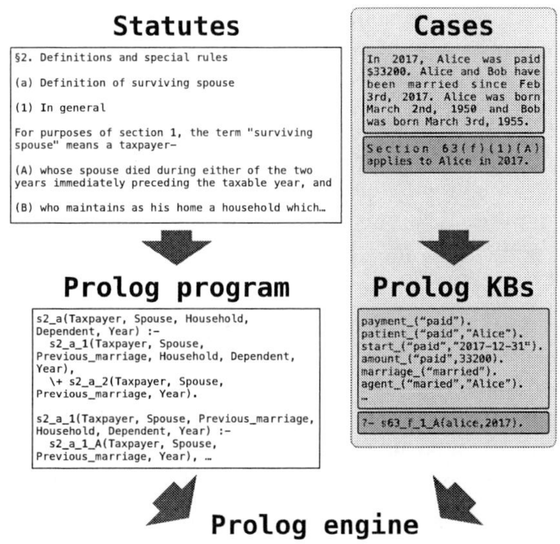

Figure 1: Statutory reasoning connects statutes and case descriptions. In previous work, both were manually translated into Prolog code to enable formal reasoning. Here, we illustrate the right portion of the figure: automated translation of cases into Prolog.

Knowledge Base (KB) requires a large amount of repetitive labor. Automating this translation task would be more scalable, and could take advantage of the high-quality expert system built on statutes.

In this work, we develop a form of Information Extraction (IE) for legal cases (Filtz et al., 2020), corresponding to the task highlighted on the right of Figure 1. We release a new version of the SARA dataset, with updated annotations for the Prolog KBs, and establish baseline results in extracting those KBs from case descriptions. This allows us to answer the following:

- What representation of Knowledge Base Elements (KBEs) in Prolog is appropriate for IE?
- How well can IE models perform on SARA?
- How does performance in IE translate to performance in statutory reasoning?

Proceedings of the Natural Legal Language Processing Workshop 2023, pages 113–131
December 7, 2023

We report improved scores on statutory reasoning, showing the benefit of a structured Prolog representation for statutes. We further show an intuitive correlation in IE performance with performance in statutory reasoning. This represents an exciting outcome for IE practitioners: the SARA dataset can provide a clearly motivated downstream task that is directly impacted by improved IE.

2 Related work

Statutory reasoning While the present work is mainly concerned with IE, it is done for the purpose of statutory reasoning (Holzenberger et al., 2020). This legal NLP task (Chalkidis et al., 2022; Zhong et al., 2020) is close to that of legal entailment (Rabelo et al., 2022) and case outcome prediction (Branting et al., 2021; Luo et al., 2017). Large Language Models (LLMs) have recently set state-of-the-art on statutory reasoning (Blair-Stanek et al., 2023; Guha et al., 2023).

Legal-domain IE IE has been done extensively on contracts, as a potentially high-impact application (Chalkidis et al., 2018; Glaser et al., 2018; Liepiņa et al., 2020). The goal is to automate routine legal tasks, such as legal contract analysis (Hendrycks et al., 2021) and contract management (Schneider et al., 2022). IE has also been attempted on regulatory texts: Chalkidis et al. (2019) released a dataset of legal documents produced by the EU annotated with a set of legal terms. There are datasets for classifying paragraphs in policies (Bartolini et al., 2004), extracting subject-object relationships (Alohaly et al., 2018), and identifying cross-references (Boella et al., 2019). Closer to this paper, IE has been applied to case law. Yao et al. (2022) introduce a dataset of Chinese court cases annotated with a custom event ontology. Navas-Loro and Santos (2018) offer a review of event extraction in the legal domain, both annotation schemas and computational models, as well as annotations of European Court of Justice cases. Filtz et al. (2020) provide a corpus of events based on the decisions of the European Court of Human Rights, and compare statistical and rule-based models for event extraction.

Semantic representations This paper is concerned with the extraction of events and their arguments by mapping the semantic content of language into a structured format (Sundheim, 1992). There are numerous formalisms for that purpose, and this section is limited to a few examples. Blackburn and Bos (2005) describe the role of first-order logic in representing the semantics of natural language. The book reviews fundamental issues in semantic representations, with the goal of making inferences. Abstract Meaning Representation (AMR) (Banarescu et al., 2013) represents the semantic content of sentences, without alignment to the syntax of the source text. Universal Conceptual Cognitive Annotation (Hershcovich et al., 2017) is aimed at more flexibility than AMR, especially cross-linguisticality, and its graphs feature more challenges for parsing than AMR graphs. Universal Decompositional Semantics (White et al., 2020) provides multiple layers of annotations, separating syntactic and semantic information, and decompositional semantics. There are semantic representations that aim to reflect the full content of language, such as Episodic Logic (Kim et al., 2021; Schubert et al., 2010). Closer to this work, the PropBank dataset (Palmer et al., 2005; O'Gorman et al., 2018) adds predicate-argument relations on top of the Penn Treebank parse trees (Marcus et al., 1993). This effort has been extended to more languages (Moeller et al., 2020; Anwar et al., 2016; Wu and Palmer, 2015). The structures considered here are represented using Neo-Davidsonian semantics (Castañeda, 1967; Davidson, 1967; Parsons, 1990). In particular, they only capture the content relevant for interpreting the SARA statutes. Previous work on semantic representations for the legal domain, including the tax-law domain, have made use of ad-hoc ontologies, depending on the application domain (Bench-Capon et al., 1987; Sherman, 1987; Merigoux et al., 2021a).

Task-oriented representations When performing semantic parsing for a specific task, it is possible to sacrifice expressivity for performance (Kollar et al., 2018). Zelle and Mooney (1996) introduce CHILL, a shift-reduce parser producing queries executable against the Geoquery database. With the same benchmark dataset, Zettlemoyer and Collins (2005) induce a grammar and a log-linear model to map questions to queries. Similarly, Berant et al. (2013) answer questions stated in natural language to a KB. They translate the question into a query that can be executed against the KB. Beltagy et al. (2014) use semantic parsing for the tasks of Recognizing Textual Entailment and Semantic Textual Similarity. Zhang et al. (2019) and Weir et al. (2020) generate SQL queries from natural language questions. Here too, compositionality can play a role (Pasupat and Liang, 2015). Campagna et al. (2019) focus on parsing language for virtual assistant commands. Goldwasser et al. (2011) introduce a method to train a semantic parser with self-supervision, using a model's own high-confidence predictions on the Geoquery dataset as training examples. Liang et al. (2011) offer an alternate approach, treating the semantic parse as a latent variable. We are not aware of any prior work on legal-domain task-oriented semantic parsing.

3 Annotation of SARA

In Holzenberger et al. (2020) and again in Holzenberger and Van Durme (2021), the semantics of each SARA case have been translated into a set of KBEs. These annotations, based on a custom ontology in Prolog, effectively make it possible to solve SARA with a Prolog program that reflects the semantics of the statutes. However, with IE in mind, the ontology has several design flaws. We will focus on two of them. First, the events are represented using strings and integers, without clear reference to the text of the case description. Second, the use of the ontology is somewhat inconsistent. We improve over this annotation scheme to enable the training of IE models.[1]

3.1 SARA semantics

The existing ontology relies on a set of predefined predicates, denoted using strings ending in "_". Those roughly 60 predicates are used to specify event and argument types. Instances of entities and events are referred to using strings and integers. For example, line 1 in Figure 2 expresses that `"gross income"` is an event of type `income_`.[2] Line 2 expresses that the event `"gross income"` occurred on January 1st, 2017. Line 3 expresses that the entity `"Alice"` is the `agent_` of the event `"gross income"`. Predicates that specify event types take a single argument, which is an instance of an event. Predicates that specify arguments take two arguments: the first one is the instance of an event, and the second one is an entity or, occasionally, an event. This follows Neo-Davidsonian semantics (Davidson, 1967).

Some case descriptions state facts that are repeated across multiple instances — see Appendix A for an example. Some cases explicitly state that a given part of the SARA statutes applies: "Alice's taxable income for the year 2017 is $22895." (case `s1_c_iii_neg`). These are expressed in terms of the corresponding Prolog predicates: `s63("Alice",2017,22895,_)`.

3.2 Design choices

Events and entities Our main improvement over Holzenberger and Van Durme (2021) is that we represent entities and events with a direct reference to the text of the case description. This is common practice in IE annotations (Walker et al., 2006). For that, entities and events are represented as structured `span` objects: `span(Value, Start_index, End_index)`.

`Start_index` and `End_index` are inclusive character indices into the case description, providing an anchor in the text for the entity or event. `Value` is a string or integer meant to be used internally by the Prolog program. For events and people, this is a string, which is often the same as the anchor, e.g. `"Alice"`. As much as possible, we use single words to represent events, as can be seen in the bottom left of Figure 4. For dates, `Value` is an integer representation of the date, as in lines 2 and 8 of Figure 2. `Value` can generally be parsed out of the anchor using rule-based heuristics (see Appendix B). For dollar amounts, `Value` is an integer (inferable from the anchor), as on line 4.

Ontology We enforce constraints on the ontology to make it more consistent, and thus improve the training of the IE system. Events that are considered instantaneous for the purposes of statutory reasoning are allowed to have a `start_` argument, but no `end_` argument.[3] See e.g. lines 17 and 21 in Figure 2, which are present in Holzenberger and Van Durme (2021), but absent in our annotation. Whenever the day of an event is not specified but only the year, we enforce that the value for `start_` is the first day of the specified year, and the last day for `end_` — see e.g. line 2.

Prolog program We adjust the Prolog program to the changes mentioned above. We implement functions to extract year, month and day from the integer representations of dates. When comparing

[1]The data can be found at `https://nlp.jhu.edu/law/sara_v3`.

[2]We use `Prolog` syntax highlighting, and occasionally omit final periods, which are normally part of Prolog syntax.

[3]Those are `birth_`, `death_`, `deduction_`, `income_`, `joint_return_` and `payment_`.

In 2017, Alice's gross income was $326332. Alice and Bob have been married since Feb 3rd, 2017, and have had the same principal place of abode since 2015. Alice was born March 2nd, 1950 and Bob was born March 3rd, 1955. Alice and Bob file separately in 2017. Bob has no gross income that year. Alice takes the standard deduction.

1	`income_("gross income")`	`income_(span("income", 23, 28))`
2	`start_("gross income", "2017-12-31")`	`start_(span("income", 23, 28), span(20170101, 3, 6))`
3	`agent_("gross income", "Alice")`	`agent_(span("income", 23, 28), span("Alice", 9, 13))`
4	`amount_("gross income", 326332)`	`amount_(span("income", 23, 28), span(326332, 35, 40))`
5	`marriage_("married")`	`marriage_(span("married", 67, 73))`
6	`agent_("married", "Alice")`	`agent_(span("married", 67, 73), span("Alice", 43, 47))`
7	`agent_("married", "Bob")`	`agent_(span("married", 67, 73), span("Bob", 53, 55))`
8	`start_("married", "2017-02-03")`	`start_(span("married", 67, 73), span(20170203, 81, 93))`
9	`residence_("principal place of abode")`	`residence_(span("abode", 137, 141))`
10	`agent_("principal place of abode", "Alice")`	`agent_(span("abode", 137, 141), span("Alice", 43, 47))`
11	`agent_("principal place of abode", "Bob")`	`agent_(span("abode", 137, 141), span("Bob", 53, 55))`
12	`patient_("principal place of abode", "the same principal place of abode")`	`patient_(span("abode", 137, 141), span("place", 128, 132))`
13	`start_("principal place of abode", "2015-01-01")`	`start_(span("abode", 137, 141), span(20150101, 149, 152))`
14	`birth_("Alice was born")`	`birth_(span("born", 165, 168))`
15	`agent_("Alice was born", "Alice")`	`agent_(span("born", 165, 168), span("Alice", 155, 159))`
16	`start_("Alice was born", "1950-03-02")`	`start_(span("born", 165, 168), span(19500302, 170, 184))`
17	`end_("Alice was born", "1950-03-02")`	[REMOVED]
18	`birth_("Bob was born")`	`birth_(span("born", 198, 201))`
19	`agent_("Bob was born", "Bob")`	`agent_(span("born", 198, 201), span("Bob", 190, 192))`
20	`start_("Bob was born", "1955-03-03")`	`start_(span("born", 198, 201), span(19550303, 203, 217))`
21	`end_("Bob was born", "1955-03-03")`	[REMOVED]

Figure 2: Case description and semantic annotation of `tax_case_5`. Left column: annotations from Holzenberger and Van Durme (2021). Right column: updated annotations. KBEs are aligned. The term [REMOVED] indicates content deprecated under the new standard introduced here.

events, we compare value, start and end indices. This enables distinguishing the events on lines 14 and 18 of Figure 2, even though the textual form of their anchor is identical. When comparing entities, we only compare values, enabling basic coreference, as between the `agent_` on lines 3 and 15.

Content of cases Further, we modified 4 cases. The conclusion of `s152_a_neg` was ambiguous, and possibly wrong, because Bob did indeed fulfill the criteria to be a dependent of Alice, as a qualifying child. We found that because of Prolog's closed-world assumption, Alice was triggering an exception, causing the Prolog solver to produce the expected (but incorrect) conclusion. We minimally edited the case to disambiguate it and produce the expected negative conclusion. We found cases `s152_b_1_pos` and `s152_b_1_neg` to be somewhat ambiguous, and added a single disambiguating sentence. Finally, throughout the world, Sunday is alternatively considered to be either the first or the last day of the week. This has an impact on cases involving section 3306. To avoid any ambiguities, in `3306_a_1_B_neg`, we changed March 19, 2017 to March 18; April 2, 2017 to April 1; and December 3, 2017 to December 2.

4 Model

Overview We frame the problem of IE as mapping the case description (a string) to a tree of depth 2 or less, like the one on Figure 3. Each node of the tree is a span in the case description, and each edge is labeled with an element from the ontology. The tree is built incrementally from the root: for each node, we predict its child nodes and the corresponding labelled edges. The example in Figure 3 is predicted in 3 steps, predicting (1) the nodes with full lines, (2) the top 3 nodes with dashed lines, and (3) the bottom 3 nodes with dashed lines. This section details the steps in this procedure, and line numbers refer to Algorithm 1, which describes how individual nodes and edges are predicted. Algorithm 2 describes how trees are predicted. To put this approach into context: we use a span-based parser, which incrementally segments the input text and types each segment (Das et al., 2014). We use the model described in Section 4.5 of Yarmohammadi et al. (2021), which has state-of-the-art performance for FrameNet parsing (Xia et al., 2021). We make one major change: we use a multi-layer perceptron instead of a BiLSTM. Appendix C describes how predicted KBEs are associated with probabilities.

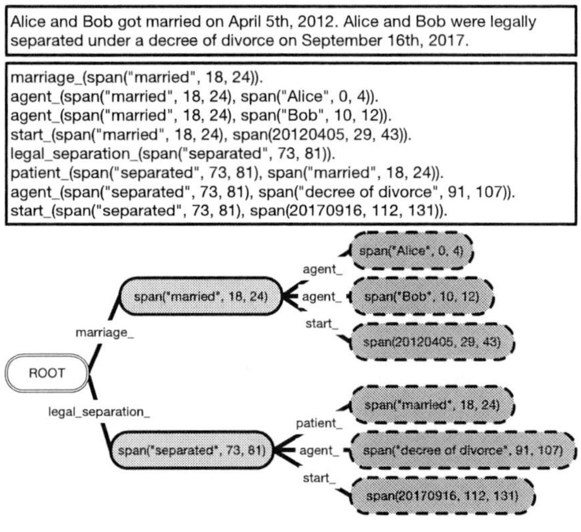

Figure 3: Inputs and outputs of the IE task for case s7703_a_2. Top frame: input case description. Bottom frame: output KB. Bottom: tree representation of the KB. Events are in orange with full line, and their arguments in purple with dashed line.

Features We use LLMs as pre-trained encoders (see Section 5.2). The case description is tokenized into $X = x_1, x_2, ..., x_n$ using the LLM's tokenizer. X is mapped to features $H = h_1, h_2, ..., h_n$ using the pre-trained encoder (line 2). Given the span of the parent node, we augment h_i with the distance between the span of the parent node and i. This distance is expressed in number of tokens, and represented using learned embeddings. If the parent node is the root of the tree, then we set the distance feature to the zero vector. We concatenate h_i and the distance feature p_i to obtain $f_i = [h_i, p_i]$ $(1 \leq i \leq n)$ where $[., .]$ denotes concatenation (line 3). Further, we compute x, the representation of the parent node, as the average of the tokens that represent the span of the parent node (line 4). If the parent node is the root, we set $x = v$ where v is a learnable vector embedding.

Finding nodes Given the parent node, we find its children as spans in the case description. We map each $g_i = [f_i, x]$ $(1 \leq i \leq n)$ to BIO logits with a multi-layer perceptron. We use a Conditional Random Field (Lafferty et al., 2001) with BIO tags to predict a set of spans $S = \{s_1, s_2, ..., s_m\}$. We denote this BIO tagger as $\mathcal{T}$ (line 5).

Predicting labels We now label the edges connecting each child node to the parent. Each span $s_j \in S$ has a start index s_j^{start} and an end index s_j^{end}.[4] On line 7, we map each span s_j to its representation $q_j = \frac{1}{s_j^{\text{end}} - s_j^{\text{start}} + 1} \sum_{k=s_j^{\text{start}}}^{s_j^{\text{end}}} f_k$ i.e. the average of the features in s_j.[5] We use a multi-layer perceptron $\mathcal{L}$ to map each $u_j = [q_j, x]$ $(1 \leq j \leq m)$ to label logits l_j (line 8).

Algorithm 1: Find the children of a given node and labels of edges. FINDCHILDREN(X, r)

Require: text X, root span r
Ensure: knowledge base elements K
1: $K \leftarrow \emptyset$
2: $H \leftarrow$ EMBED(X) *# embed text with pre-trained encoder* $\mathcal{E}$
3: $F \leftarrow$ AUGMENT(H, r) *# add distance features*
4: $x \leftarrow$ COMPUTESPANREPRESENTATION(H, r) *# compute contextualized representation of root span r*
5: $S \leftarrow$ BIOTAGGER(F, x) *# extract spans with BIO tagger* $\mathcal{T}$
6: **for** s in S **do**
7: $z \leftarrow$ COMPUTESPANREPRESENTATION(F, s) *# compute contextualized representation of span s*
8: $l \leftarrow$ PREDICTLABEL(z, x) *# predict label with classifier* $\mathcal{L}$
9: $K \leftarrow K \cup \{(l, r, s)\}$ *# add new KBE*
10: **end for**
11: **return** K

Algorithm 2: Predict the IE tree for a given case. PREDICTTREE(X)

Require: case description X
Ensure: tree T
1: $T \leftarrow \emptyset$
2: $Q \leftarrow$ [ROOT] *# queue of nodes to be processed*
3: **while** Q is not empty **do**
4: $q \leftarrow$ POP(Q) *# take first node*
5: $K \leftarrow$ FINDCHILDREN(X, q) *# find its children*
6: $T \leftarrow T \cup K$ *# add predicted relations to tree*
7: **if** q is ROOT **then**
8: **for** $l, r, s \in K$ **do**
9: $Q \leftarrow Q \cup \{s\}$ *# add children of the root to the queue, to predict one more level of children*
10: **end for**
11: **end if**
12: **end while**
13: **return** T

Training Our model consists of encoder $\mathcal{E}$, BIO tagger $\mathcal{T}$, label classifier $\mathcal{L}$, distance embeddings $\mathcal{D}$, and root representation v. We have gold spans for all nodes in the tree, that we use to generate gold sequences of BIO tags and to train $\mathcal{T}$. We

[4]At training time, S is the set of gold spans. At eval time, S is the set of spans predicted by the BIO tagger.

[5]For roughly 80% of gold spans, the span is a single token, so that $s_j^{\text{start}} = s_j^{\text{end}}$, and this amounts to selecting a single vector in the sequence $f_1, f_2, ..., f_n$.

use the loss

$$L_{\mathcal{T}} = -\frac{1}{|G|} \log p(G)$$

where G is the gold sequence of BIO tags, and $|G|$ its length in tokens. The labels of the edges are used to train $\mathcal{L}$, with the loss

$$L_{\mathcal{L}} = -\frac{1}{|U|} \sum_{(l,r,c) \in U} \log p(l|r, c)$$

where (l, r, c) is a triplet of (label, parent node, child node) from the training set U. Finally, $\mathcal{E}$, $\mathcal{D}$ and v are used to compute features input to $\mathcal{T}$ and $\mathcal{L}$. Information is passed from one module to the next in a differentiable way, making the entire model trainable end-to-end with the single loss function

$$L = \lambda L_{\mathcal{T}} + (1 - \lambda) L_{\mathcal{L}}$$

where $\lambda \in [0, 1]$ is a tradeoff hyperparameter.

5 Experiments

5.1 Data pre-processing

First, we run Prolog queries against each case to produce an exhaustive inventory of events and arguments. For example, the query `?- income_(X).` returns all events of type `income_`, and the query `?- agent_(X, Y).` returns all `X, Y` pairs such that entity `Y` is the agent of event `X`. We thus produce a set of cases containing only KBEs, to avoid the need to extract the rules shown in Appendix A. This dataset we refer to as the *full dataset*.

Some spans cannot be extracted using the IE framework described in Section 4. First, it cannot deal with overlapping spans. Out of 2 overlapping spans we keep the one that appears earliest in the case description. Second, some values cannot be inferred from their anchor. For example, some sentences describe repeating events, without explicitly mentioning all the dates of occurrence. This makes it impossible to extract those unmentioned dates. Appendix A describes one such event.

We produce the *partial dataset* by removing all unextractable spans and corresponding KBEs. Table 1 shows statistics on how many KBEs were removed in the process. The number of KBEs rejected can seem large in comparison to those kept. However, a fraction of the cases contains most rejected KBEs. Ranking the cases by number of KBEs rejected, the top 10% represent 96%, 98% and 71% of the rejected KBEs in train, dev and test, respectively. Figure 4 in Appendix G shows statistics on the partial dataset.

At training time, we use the partial dataset. At test time, we report IE scores against both the partial (Table 2) and full datasets (Table 4). To clarify the difference: the partial dataset contains only those KBEs from the full dataset that our framework is designed to handle. Both contain the same SARA cases. Note that this filtering only mildly affects the overall task of statutory reasoning, as can be seen in Table 3, TOPLINE: more than 90% of the cases in the partial dataset can still be solved by the Prolog program, despite missing KBEs.

	Train	Dev	Test
Kept	2830	664	1305
Rejected	3099	411	1719

Table 1: Number of KBEs kept and rejected, as described in Section 5.1.

The SARA dataset only provides a train/test split. For the purposes of early stopping and hyperparameter search, we split up the train set into a train and dev set, the same way that the train/test split was created in Holzenberger et al. (2020). We pair binary cases by the part of the statutes that they test: e.g. `s2_b_1_pos` and `s2_b_1_neg` are grouped together. We randomly select 20% of these groups for the dev set. We also randomly pick 20% of numerical cases to be used in the dev set. The result is a train set with 206 cases and a dev set with 50 cases.

5.2 Results

Information Extraction We use the AllenNLP codebase (Gardner et al., 2018) version 2.7.0 to code and train models.[6] We use stochastic gradient descent with early stopping on the dev set.

Performance of a given model is measured as its F1 score, averaged across cases. We count a KBE predicted by the model as correct if it appears exactly in the gold KB. The model receives no credit for a slightly inaccurate span or label.

We use Optuna (Akiba et al., 2019) to search for the best set of hyperparameters. Appendix F reports the range of hyperparameters explored and best hyperparameters found. We measure performance for a given set of hyperparameters as the

[6]Code for experiments can be found at `https://github.com/SgfdDttt/sara-ie`.

mean F1 score across 3 different runs, with 3 different random seeds. This is to mitigate variability from random initializations.

In Table 2, we report precision, recall and F1 scores, for dev and test sets, on the partial dataset. We report results on the full dataset in Table 4 in Appendix D. We compare 5 different pre-trained encoders (used to map X to H in Section 4):

- LEGALBERT: the legal-domain encoder of Holzenberger et al. (2020), trained on a subset of the `case.law` corpus (caselaw), starting from `bert-base-cased`,
- LEGALBERT': an alternative trained by Zheng et al. (2021) on more data,
- BERT: BERT-base-cased (Devlin et al., 2019), which has the same architecture and training objective as both LEGALBERTs, but was trained on general-domain English,
- ROBERTA: RoBERTa-base (Liu et al., 2019) which was shown to achieve higher performance than BERT on downstream tasks, and
- T5: T5-base (Raffel et al., 2020), which was shown to achieve higher performance than RoBERTa on downstream tasks. We only use the encoder of T5-base in our experiments, discarding the decoder.

Error analysis We compare model outputs on 3 binary cases and 3 numerical cases picked at random from the test set.[7] We report the detail of the error analysis in Appendix E. From this sample, it seems that models are generally able to correctly detect all event anchors, and to further type them correctly in at least 90% of cases. Predicting arguments correctly is still a challenge, and an important one: a single missing argument can throw off the Prolog program, especially in computing tax amounts. For example, missing the `amount_` argument to an `income_` event is practically as bad as not detecting the `income_` event in the first place. When arguments are predicted, their value tends to be correct, and in any case of the right type (strings *versus* integers). For example, models rarely mistake the `agent_` of an event: they either predict it correctly, or miss it entirely. In addition, the more events there are, the harder it is to get all arguments right. To summarize, models mainly struggle with arguments. They both (1) miss arguments entirely, having generally higher precision than recall, and (2) occasionally predict additional arguments, such as predicting two `amount_` arguments by tagging all integers preceded by a "$" sign.

Statutory reasoning We further measure how useful model outputs are for statutory reasoning, and report results in Table 3. We feed the KB produced with IE to the Prolog program. We add any statements about statutes of the form `s63("Alice",2017,22895,_)` to the KB, as described in Section 3.1. In addition to the five models above, we report results on (1) TOPLINE, which is the partial KB used to train models, and (2) EMPTY, which corresponds to a model that predicts no KBEs. Since we evaluated each model by running training and test with 5 different random seeds, we pick the model with the highest dev F1 score to produce the KB used for this evaluation on statutory reasoning.

5.3 Discussion

Focusing on the IE scores, LEGALBERT performs best out of all encoders, and T5 performs worst, with large performance gaps between encoders. For T5, only the encoder was used, and presumably, more training data is needed to retrain it as a standalone encoder. Legal-domain pre-training clearly yields performance improvements. As can be seen by comparing LEGALBERT and LEGALBERT', for the SARA dataset, more data does not automatically translate to better performance.

As noted in the caption of Table 3, results from Holzenberger et al. (2020), Holzenberger and Van Durme (2021) and Blair-Stanek et al. (2023) are not directly comparable to ours. Holzenberger et al. (2020) and Blair-Stanek et al. (2023) apply NLP models directly to the text of the cases and statutes, without using any Prolog code. Holzenberger and Van Durme (2021) rely on a set of lightweight semantic annotations of the statutes and cases to develop a neuro-symbolic model for statutory reasoning; they also exclude Prolog code. Contrary to prior work mentioned in this paragraph, we use a human-curated Prolog representation of the statutes.

Holzenberger et al. (2020) report that majority baselines achieve 50% entailment, and 20% numerical accuracies on the test set. Performance of

[7] In binary cases, the outcome to be predicted is either "Yes" or "No". In numerical cases, the outcome is an integer, representing a dollar amount of taxes owed.

Model	Dev Precision	Recall	F1	Test Precision	Recall	F1
LEGALBERT	**88.7** $\pm$ 0.6	**88.6** $\pm$ 0.6	**88.1** $\pm$ 0.3	**88.1** $\pm$ 0.2	**91.0** $\pm$ 0.5	**87.0** $\pm$ 0.3
LEGALBERT'	87.4 $\pm$ 1.0	83.2 $\pm$ 1.4	84.4 $\pm$ 0.8	85.4 $\pm$ 0.9	84.6 $\pm$ 1.4	82.7 $\pm$ 0.9
BERT	85.9 $\pm$ 2.1	75.1 $\pm$ 2.5	78.7 $\pm$ 1.6	85.2 $\pm$ 2.3	77.0 $\pm$ 2.3	77.4 $\pm$ 1.8
ROBERTA	84.5 $\pm$ 0.6	80.8 $\pm$ 1.5	81.9 $\pm$ 0.9	86.4 $\pm$ 0.7	83.9 $\pm$ 1.6	82.0 $\pm$ 1.0
T5	73.2 $\pm$ 0.6	56.2 $\pm$ 2.4	62.1 $\pm$ 1.5	71.6 $\pm$ 1.1	59.0 $\pm$ 1.3	61.4 $\pm$ 1.0

Table 2: Performance metrics on the IE task measured on the partial dataset. Scores are computed across 5 runs with different random seeds. We format statistics as *average* $\pm$ *standard error*. Best scores are **bolded**.

Model	Entailment Train	Dev	Test	Numerical Train	Dev	Test
Holzenberger et al. (2020)	-	-	55 $\pm$ 8.3	-	-	25 $\pm$ 17.1
Holzenberger and Van Durme (2021)	-	-	59 $\pm$ 8.2	-	-	45 $\pm$ 19.7
Blair-Stanek et al. (2023)	-	-	71 $\pm$ 7.6	-	-	-
TOPLINE	93.7 $\pm$ 3.4	97.1 $\pm$ 5.0	97 $\pm$ 2.8	98.4 $\pm$ 2.6	93.8 $\pm$ 11.0	90 $\pm$ 11.9
EMPTY	69.7 $\pm$ 6.4	67.6 $\pm$ 13.8	71 $\pm$ 7.6	26.6 $\pm$ 9.3	18.8 $\pm$ 17.7	25 $\pm$ 17.2
LEGALBERT	**88.7** $\pm$ 4.4	88.2 $\pm$ 9.5	**89** $\pm$ 5.2	**73.4** $\pm$ 9.3	**56.2** $\pm$ 22.5	**60** $\pm$ 19.4
LEGALBERT'	86.6 $\pm$ 4.7	**91.2** $\pm$ 8.4	86 $\pm$ 5.8	68.8 $\pm$ 9.7	50.0 $\pm$ 22.6	**60** $\pm$ 19.4
BERT	79.6 $\pm$ 5.6	73.5 $\pm$ 13.0	81 $\pm$ 6.5	46.9 $\pm$ 10.5	37.5 $\pm$ 21.9	45 $\pm$ 19.7
ROBERTA	79.6 $\pm$ 5.6	79.4 $\pm$ 11.9	79 $\pm$ 6.8	50.0 $\pm$ 10.5	43.8 $\pm$ 22.5	40 $\pm$ 19.4
T5	78.2 $\pm$ 5.8	73.5 $\pm$ 13.0	76 $\pm$ 7.1	31.2 $\pm$ 9.7	25.0 $\pm$ 19.6	25 $\pm$ 17.2

Table 3: Statutory reasoning accuracies (in %) with 90% confidence interval, obtained by applying the Prolog solver to the predicted KBs. Accuracies are measured using the metrics described in Holzenberger et al. (2020); numerical predictions need not match the ground truth exactly to be correct. Best scores within the IE-based approaches are **bolded**. The top three lines are not directly comparable, and are provided for reference.

EMPTY on statutory reasoning is higher than that. First, with the EMPTY KBs containing no facts, it is generally hard to prove anything at all, so that negative cases tend to succeed thanks to Prolog's negation as failure. Second, since statements about statutes are added automatically to the KB, cases that rely on them have a chance to succeed.

There is overall strong Pearson correlation between F1 and statutory reasoning scores: on the test set, 80% for entailment accuracy, and 88% for numerical accuracy. This shows that, for the SARA dataset, improvements in IE translate to improvements in statutory reasoning. This suggests that IE is important for statutory reasoning, and encourages progress on this task. IE models tend to perform better than EMPTY on statutory reasoning, so that even imperfect IE is useful for statutory reasoning. Still, there is room for improvement, both for IE and for statutory reasoning.

Here, the choice of ontology limits the information that the IE model can effectively extract from the SARA cases. In particular, the current ontology expresses time with two relations, `start_` and `end_`. In contrast, natural language can express time in many different ways, which can occasionally be hard to parse into a structured form (Filtz et al., 2020). SARA cases may contain the information that an event is ongoing, or happening at a certain point in time, without explicitly referring to a start or end time. Event calculus (Kowalski and Sergot, 1986; Miller and Shanahan, 2002) could be used to represent a wider spectrum of time expressions, reducing the amount of rejected KBEs. It would also make it possible for the logical representation to align more closely to the language of the case description. This would yield a better inductive bias for the IE models while not sacrificing expressivity. More generally, progress on IE could be made by picking a more expressive, more general ontology, such that the translation between language and logical form would be more straightforward. But this would require re-writing the Prolog solver, to accommodate the new ontology, and to encode relevant commonsense knowledge.

Finally, the use of explicit KBEs introduces interpretability and auditability in the model's output, since it becomes clear what facts are used to perform statutory reasoning. This is generally absent from the direct application of LLMs to statutory reasoning, even if this can be mitigated with prompt engineering (Blair-Stanek et al., 2023).

6 Conclusion

We improve the SARA ontology and re-annotate cases for their semantics. Compared to the previous iteration of the SARA dataset, the KBEs and overall structure are now richer and more complete. We also take a step towards more consistent annotations, and more extractable KBEs. We adapt state-of-the-art IE models to extract KBEs from case descriptions. With empirical results on the SARA dataset, we find that good performance with a strict metric can be reached on this small dataset, and that performance in IE translates directly into performance in statutory reasoning.

We see three main directions for future work. First, as stated in Section 5.1, the current ontology is not flexible enough to both (1) allow for KBEs closely aligned to the case description, and (2) express complex relationships, in particular time relationships. This is one major limitation that could be addressed, and would likely require overhauling the expert system representing the statutes. Second, we have so far assumed that the statutes were parsed into a logical form ahead of time. A meaningful step would be to augment the approach presented here with the automated extraction of the logical form of statutes, effectively performing semantic parsing. Finally, cases in SARA are not representative of the full scope and diversity of legal cases. Real-world legal cases are generally much longer, the language is denser, and the phrasing is more diverse. We see the choice of an ontology and the annotation of data as two crucial challenges.

7 Limitations

In this paper, we performed experiments on the SARA dataset, a semi-synthetic dataset for US federal tax law. The conclusions drawn about legal-domain IE and about statutory reasoning should take care to understand that this dataset is not representative of the full scope of legal data.

Acknowledgments

This work has been supported by the U.S. National Science Foundation under grant No. 2204926. Any opinions, findings, and conclusions or recommendations expressed in this article are those of the authors and do not necessarily reflect the views of the National Science Foundation.

References

Takuya Akiba, Shotaro Sano, Toshihiko Yanase, Takeru Ohta, and Masanori Koyama. 2019. Optuna: A next-generation hyperparameter optimization framework. In *Proceedings of the 25th ACM SIGKDD International Conference on Knowledge Discovery & Data Mining, KDD 2019, Anchorage, AK, USA, August 4-8, 2019*, pages 2623–2631. ACM.

Manar Alohaly, Hassan Takabi, and Eduardo Blanco. 2018. A deep learning approach for extracting attributes of ABAC policies. In *Proceedings of the 23nd ACM on Symposium on Access Control Models and Technologies, SACMAT 2018, Indianapolis, IN, USA, June 13-15, 2018*, pages 137–148. ACM.

Maaz Anwar, Riyaz Ahmad Bhat, Dipti Misra Sharma, Ashwini Vaidya, Martha Palmer, and Tafseer Ahmed Khan. 2016. A proposition bank of urdu. In *Proceedings of the Tenth International Conference on Language Resources and Evaluation LREC 2016, Portorož, Slovenia, May 23-28, 2016*. European Language Resources Association (ELRA).

Laura Banarescu, Claire Bonial, Shu Cai, Madalina Georgescu, Kira Griffitt, Ulf Hermjakob, Kevin Knight, Philipp Koehn, Martha Palmer, and Nathan Schneider. 2013. Abstract meaning representation for sembanking. In *Proceedings of the 7th Linguistic Annotation Workshop and Interoperability with Discourse, LAW-ID@ACL 2013, August 8-9, 2013, Sofia, Bulgaria*, pages 178–186. The Association for Computer Linguistics.

Roberto Bartolini, Alessandro Lenci, Simonetta Montemagni, Vito Pirrelli, and Claudia Soria. 2004. Semantic mark-up of italian legal texts through nlp-based techniques. In *Proceedings of the Fourth International Conference on Language Resources and Evaluation, LREC 2004, May 26-28, 2004, Lisbon, Portugal*. European Language Resources Association.

Islam Beltagy, Stephen Roller, Gemma Boleda, Katrin Erk, and Raymond J. Mooney. 2014. Utexas: Natural language semantics using distributional semantics and probabilistic logic. In *Proceedings of the 8th International Workshop on Semantic Evaluation, SemEval@COLING 2014, Dublin, Ireland, August 23-24, 2014*, pages 796–801. The Association for Computer Linguistics.

Trevor J. M. Bench-Capon, G. O. Robinson, Tom Routen, and Marek J. Sergot. 1987. Logic programming for large scale applications in law: A formalisation of supplementary benefit legislation. In *Proceedings of the First International Conference on Artificial Intelligence and Law, ICAIL '87, Boston, MA, USA, May 27-29, 1987*, pages 190–198. ACM.

Jonathan Berant, Andrew Chou, Roy Frostig, and Percy Liang. 2013. Semantic parsing on freebase from question-answer pairs. In *Proceedings of the 2013 Conference on Empirical Methods in Natural*

Language Processing, EMNLP 2013, 18-21 October 2013, Grand Hyatt Seattle, Seattle, Washington, USA, A meeting of SIGDAT, a Special Interest Group of the ACL, pages 1533–1544. ACL.

Patrick Blackburn and Johan Bos. 2005. *Representation and Inference for Natural Language - a First Course in Computational Semantics*. CSLI Studies in Computational Linguistics. CSLI Publications.

Andrew Blair-Stanek, Nils Holzenberger, and Benjamin Van Durme. 2023. Can GPT-3 perform statutory reasoning? *CoRR*, abs/2302.06100.

Guido Boella, Luigi Di Caro, and Valentina Leone. 2019. Semi-automatic knowledge population in a legal document management system. *Artif. Intell. Law*, 27(2):227–251.

Luther Karl Branting, Craig Pfeifer, Bradford Brown, Lisa Ferro, John S. Aberdeen, Brandy Weiss, Mark Pfaff, and Bill Liao. 2021. Scalable and explainable legal prediction. *Artif. Intell. Law*, 29(2):213–238.

Giovanni Campagna, Silei Xu, Mehrad Moradshahi, Richard Socher, and Monica S. Lam. 2019. Genie: a generator of natural language semantic parsers for virtual assistant commands. In *Proceedings of the 40th ACM SIGPLAN Conference on Programming Language Design and Implementation, PLDI 2019, Phoenix, AZ, USA, June 22-26, 2019*, pages 394–410. ACM.

caselaw. 2019. Caselaw access project.

Hector Neri Castañeda. 1967. Comment on D. Davidson's "The logical forms of action sentences". *The Logic of Decision and Action*.

Ilias Chalkidis, Ion Androutsopoulos, and Achilleas Michos. 2018. Obligation and prohibition extraction using hierarchical rnns. In *Proceedings of the 56th Annual Meeting of the Association for Computational Linguistics, ACL 2018, Melbourne, Australia, July 15-20, 2018, Volume 2: Short Papers*, pages 254–259. Association for Computational Linguistics.

Ilias Chalkidis, Manos Fergadiotis, Prodromos Malakasiotis, and Ion Androutsopoulos. 2019. Large-scale multi-label text classification on EU legislation. In *Proceedings of the 57th Conference of the Association for Computational Linguistics, ACL 2019, Florence, Italy, July 28- August 2, 2019, Volume 1: Long Papers*, pages 6314–6322. Association for Computational Linguistics.

Ilias Chalkidis, Abhik Jana, Dirk Hartung, Michael J. Bommarito II, Ion Androutsopoulos, Daniel Martin Katz, and Nikolaos Aletras. 2022. Lexglue: A benchmark dataset for legal language understanding in english. In *Proceedings of the 60th Annual Meeting of the Association for Computational Linguistics (Volume 1: Long Papers), ACL 2022, Dublin, Ireland, May 22-27, 2022*, pages 4310–4330. Association for Computational Linguistics.

Dipanjan Das, Desai Chen, André F. T. Martins, Nathan Schneider, and Noah A. Smith. 2014. Frame-semantic parsing. *Comput. Linguistics*, 40(1):9–56.

Donald Davidson. 1967. The logical forms of action sentences. *The Logic of Decision and Action*.

Jacob Devlin, Ming-Wei Chang, Kenton Lee, and Kristina Toutanova. 2019. BERT: pre-training of deep bidirectional transformers for language understanding. In *Proceedings of the 2019 Conference of the North American Chapter of the Association for Computational Linguistics: Human Language Technologies, NAACL-HLT 2019, Minneapolis, MN, USA, June 2-7, 2019, Volume 1 (Long and Short Papers)*, pages 4171–4186. Association for Computational Linguistics.

Rajaa El Hamdani, Majd Mustapha, David Restrepo Amariles, Aurore Clément Troussel, Sébastien Meeùs, and Katsiaryna Krasnashchok. 2021. A combined rule-based and machine learning approach for automated GDPR compliance checking. In *ICAIL '21: Eighteenth International Conference for Artificial Intelligence and Law, São Paulo Brazil, June 21 - 25, 2021*, pages 40–49. ACM.

Erwin Filtz, María Navas-Loro, Cristiana Santos, Axel Pollercs, and Sabrina Kirrane. 2020. Events matter: Extraction of events from court decisions. In *Legal Knowledge and Information Systems - JURIX 2020: The Thirty-third Annual Conference, Brno, Czech Republic, December 9-11, 2020*, volume 334 of *Frontiers in Artificial Intelligence and Applications*, pages 33–42. IOS Press.

Matt Gardner, Joel Grus, Mark Neumann, Oyvind Tafjord, Pradeep Dasigi, Nelson F. Liu, Matthew E. Peters, Michael Schmitz, and Luke Zettlemoyer. 2018. Allennlp: A deep semantic natural language processing platform. *CoRR*, abs/1803.07640.

Ingo Glaser, Bernhard Waltl, and Florian Matthes. 2018. Named entity recognition, extraction, and linking in german legal contracts. In *IRIS: Internationales Rechtsinformatik Symposium*, pages 325–334.

Dan Goldwasser, Roi Reichart, James Clarke, and Dan Roth. 2011. Confidence driven unsupervised semantic parsing. In *The 49th Annual Meeting of the Association for Computational Linguistics: Human Language Technologies, Proceedings of the Conference, 19-24 June, 2011, Portland, Oregon, USA*, pages 1486–1495. The Association for Computer Linguistics.

Neel Guha, Julian Nyarko, Daniel E. Ho, Christopher Ré, Adam Chilton, Aditya Narayana, Alex Chohlas-Wood, Austin Peters, Brandon Waldon, Daniel N. Rockmore, Diego Zambrano, Dmitry Talisman, Enam Hoque, Faiz Surani, Frank Fagan, Galit Sarfaty, Gregory M. Dickinson, Haggai Porat, Jason Hegland, Jessica Wu, Joe Nudell, Joel

Niklaus, John J. Nay, Jonathan H. Choi, Kevin Tobia, Margaret Hagan, Megan Ma, Michael A. Livermore, Nikon Rasumov-Rahe, Nils Holzenberger, Noam Kolt, Peter Henderson, Sean Rehaag, Sharad Goel, Shang Gao, Spencer Williams, Sunny Gandhi, Tom Zur, Varun Iyer, and Zehua Li. 2023. Legalbench: A collaboratively built benchmark for measuring legal reasoning in large language models. *CoRR*, abs/2308.11462.

Dan Hendrycks, Collin Burns, Anya Chen, and Spencer Ball. 2021. CUAD: an expert-annotated NLP dataset for legal contract review. In *Proceedings of the Neural Information Processing Systems Track on Datasets and Benchmarks 1, NeurIPS Datasets and Benchmarks 2021, December 2021, virtual*.

Daniel Hershcovich, Omri Abend, and Ari Rappoport. 2017. A transition-based directed acyclic graph parser for UCCA. In *Proceedings of the 55th Annual Meeting of the Association for Computational Linguistics (Volume 1: Long Papers)*, pages 1127–1138, Vancouver, Canada. Association for Computational Linguistics.

Nils Holzenberger, Andrew Blair-Stanek, and Benjamin Van Durme. 2020. A dataset for statutory reasoning in tax law entailment and question answering. In *Proceedings of the Natural Legal Language Processing Workshop 2020 co-located with the 26th ACM SIGKDD International Conference on Knowledge Discovery & Data Mining (KDD 2020), Virtual Workshop, August 24, 2020*, volume 2645 of *CEUR Workshop Proceedings*, pages 31–38. CEUR-WS.org.

Nils Holzenberger and Benjamin Van Durme. 2021. Factoring statutory reasoning as language understanding challenges. In *Proceedings of the 59th Annual Meeting of the Association for Computational Linguistics and the 11th International Joint Conference on Natural Language Processing, ACL/IJCNLP 2021, (Volume 1: Long Papers), Virtual Event, August 1-6, 2021*, pages 2742–2758. Association for Computational Linguistics.

Gene Kim, Mandar Juvekar, and Lenhart Schubert. 2021. Monotonic inference for underspecified episodic logic. In *Proceedings of the 1st and 2nd Workshops on Natural Logic Meets Machine Learning (NALOMA)*, pages 26–40, Groningen, the Netherlands (online). Association for Computational Linguistics.

Thomas Kollar, Danielle Berry, Lauren Stuart, Karolina Owczarzak, Tagyoung Chung, Lambert Mathias, Michael Kayser, Bradford Snow, and Spyros Matsoukas. 2018. The alexa meaning representation language. In *Proceedings of the 2018 Conference of the North American Chapter of the Association for Computational Linguistics: Human Language Technologies, NAACL-HLT 2018, New Orleans, Louisiana, USA, June 1-6, 2018, Volume 3 (Industry Papers)*, pages 177–184. Association for Computational Linguistics.

Robert A. Kowalski and Marek J. Sergot. 1986. A logic-based calculus of events. *New Gener. Comput.*, 4(1):67–95.

John D. Lafferty, Andrew McCallum, and Fernando C. N. Pereira. 2001. Conditional random fields: Probabilistic models for segmenting and labeling sequence data. In *Proceedings of the Eighteenth International Conference on Machine Learning (ICML 2001), Williams College, Williamstown, MA, USA, June 28 - July 1, 2001*, pages 282–289. Morgan Kaufmann.

Sarah B Lawsky. 2017. A logic for statutes. *Fla. Tax Rev.*, 21:60.

Percy Liang, Michael I. Jordan, and Dan Klein. 2011. Learning dependency-based compositional semantics. In *The 49th Annual Meeting of the Association for Computational Linguistics: Human Language Technologies, Proceedings of the Conference, 19-24 June, 2011, Portland, Oregon, USA*, pages 590–599. The Association for Computer Linguistics.

Rūta Liepiņa, Federico Ruggeri, Francesca Lagioia, Marco Lippi, Kasper Drazewski, and Paolo Torroni. 2020. Explaining potentially unfair clauses to the consumer with the CLAUDETTE tool. In *Proceedings of the Natural Legal Language Processing Workshop 2020 co-located with the 26th ACM SIGKDD International Conference on Knowledge Discovery & Data Mining (KDD 2020), Virtual Workshop, August 24, 2020*, volume 2645 of *CEUR Workshop Proceedings*, pages 61–64. CEUR-WS.org.

Yinhan Liu, Myle Ott, Naman Goyal, Jingfei Du, Mandar Joshi, Danqi Chen, Omer Levy, Mike Lewis, Luke Zettlemoyer, and Veselin Stoyanov. 2019. Roberta: A robustly optimized BERT pretraining approach. *CoRR*, abs/1907.11692.

Bingfeng Luo, Yansong Feng, Jianbo Xu, Xiang Zhang, and Dongyan Zhao. 2017. Learning to predict charges for criminal cases with legal basis. In *Proceedings of the 2017 Conference on Empirical Methods in Natural Language Processing, EMNLP 2017, Copenhagen, Denmark, September 9-11, 2017*, pages 2727–2736. Association for Computational Linguistics.

Mitchell P. Marcus, Beatrice Santorini, and Mary Ann Marcinkiewicz. 1993. Building a large annotated corpus of english: The penn treebank. *Comput. Linguistics*, 19(2):313–330.

Denis Merigoux, Nicolas Chataing, and Jonathan Protzenko. 2021a. Catala: a programming language for the law. *Proc. ACM Program. Lang.*, 5(ICFP):1–29.

Denis Merigoux, Raphaël Monat, and Jonathan Protzenko. 2021b. A modern compiler for the french tax code. In *CC '21: 30th ACM SIGPLAN International Conference on Compiler Construction, Virtual Event, Republic of Korea, March 2-3, 2021*, pages 71–82. ACM.

Rob Miller and Murray Shanahan. 2002. Some alternative formulations of the event calculus. In *Computational Logic: Logic Programming and Beyond, Essays in Honour of Robert A. Kowalski, Part II*, volume 2408 of *Lecture Notes in Computer Science*, pages 452–490. Springer.

Sarah Moeller, Irina Wagner, Martha Palmer, Kathryn Conger, and Skatje Myers. 2020. The Russian PropBank. In *Proceedings of the 12th Language Resources and Evaluation Conference*, pages 5995–6002, Marseille, France. European Language Resources Association.

María Navas-Loro and Cristiana Santos. 2018. Events in the legal domain: first impressions. In *Proceedings of the 2nd Workshop on Technologies for Regulatory Compliance co-located with the 31st International Conference on Legal Knowledge and Information Systems (JURIX 2018), Groningen, The Netherlands, December 12, 2018*, volume 2309 of *CEUR Workshop Proceedings*, pages 45–57. CEUR-WS.org.

Tim O'Gorman, Sameer Pradhan, Martha Palmer, Julia Bonn, Kathryn Conger, and James Gung. 2018. The new propbank: Aligning propbank with AMR through POS unification. In *Proceedings of the Eleventh International Conference on Language Resources and Evaluation, LREC 2018, Miyazaki, Japan, May 7-12, 2018*. European Language Resources Association (ELRA).

Anja Oskamp and Marc Lauritsen. 2002. AI in law practice? so far, not much. *Artif. Intell. Law*, 10(4):227–236.

Martha Palmer, Daniel Gildea, and Paul Kingsbury. 2005. The Proposition Bank: An Annotated Corpus of Semantic Roles. *Computational Linguistics*, 31(1):71–106.

Terence Parsons. 1990. *Events in the Semantics of English*, volume 334. MIT press Cambridge, MA.

Panupong Pasupat and Percy Liang. 2015. Compositional semantic parsing on semi-structured tables. In *Proceedings of the 53rd Annual Meeting of the Association for Computational Linguistics and the 7th International Joint Conference on Natural Language Processing of the Asian Federation of Natural Language Processing, ACL 2015, July 26-31, 2015, Beijing, China, Volume 1: Long Papers*, pages 1470–1480. The Association for Computer Linguistics.

Juliano Rabelo, Randy Goebel, Mi-Young Kim, Yoshinobu Kano, Masaharu Yoshioka, and Ken Satoh. 2022. Overview and discussion of the competition on legal information extraction/entailment (COLIEE) 2021. *Rev. Socionetwork Strateg.*, 16(1):111–133.

Colin Raffel, Noam Shazeer, Adam Roberts, Katherine Lee, Sharan Narang, Michael Matena, Yanqi Zhou, Wei Li, and Peter J. Liu. 2020. Exploring the limits of transfer learning with a unified text-to-text transformer. *Journal of Machine Learning Research*, 21(140):1–67.

Julián Moreno Schneider, Georg Rehm, Elena Montiel-Ponsoda, Víctor Rodríguez-Doncel, Patricia Martín-Chozas, María Navas-Loro, Martin Kaltenböck, Artem Revenko, Sotirios Karampatakis, Christian Sageder, Jorge Gracia, Filippo Maganza, Ilan Kernerman, Dorielle Lonke, Andis Lagzdins, Julia Bosque-Gil, Pieter Verhoeven, Elsa Gomez Diaz, and Pascual Boil Ballesteros. 2022. Lynx: A knowledge-based AI service platform for content processing, enrichment and analysis for the legal domain. *Inf. Syst.*, 106:101966.

Lenhart K. Schubert, Benjamin David Van Durme, and Marzieh Bazrafshan. 2010. Entailment inference in a natural logic-like general reasoner. In *Commonsense Knowledge, Papers from the 2010 AAAI Fall Symposium, Arlington, Virginia, USA, November 11-13, 2010*, volume FS-10-02 of *AAAI Technical Report*. AAAI.

David M. Sherman. 1987. A prolog model of the income tax act of canada. In *Proceedings of the First International Conference on Artificial Intelligence and Law, ICAIL '87, Boston, MA, USA, May 27-29, 1987*, pages 127–136. ACM.

Beth Sundheim. 1992. Overview of the fourth message understanding evaluation and conference. In *Proceedings of the 4th Conference on Message Understanding, MUC 1992, McLean, Virginia, USA, June 16-18, 1992*, pages 3–21. ACL.

Christopher Walker, Stephanie Strassel, Julie Medero, and Kazuaki Maeda. 2006. ACE 2005 multilingual training corpus (LDC2006T06). *Philadelphia: Linguistic Data Consortium.*

Nathaniel Weir, Prasetya Utama, Alex Galakatos, Andrew Crotty, Amir Ilkhechi, Shekar Ramaswamy, Rohin Bhushan, Nadja Geisler, Benjamin Hättasch, Steffen Eger, Ugur Çetintemel, and Carsten Binnig. 2020. Dbpal: A fully pluggable NL2SQL training pipeline. In *Proceedings of the 2020 International Conference on Management of Data, SIGMOD Conference 2020, online conference [Portland, OR, USA], June 14-19, 2020*, pages 2347–2361. ACM.

Aaron Steven White, Elias Stengel-Eskin, Siddharth Vashishtha, Venkata Subrahmanyan Govindarajan, Dee Ann Reisinger, Tim Vieira, Keisuke Sakaguchi, Sheng Zhang, Francis Ferraro, Rachel Rudinger, Kyle Rawlins, and Benjamin Van Durme. 2020. The universal decompositional semantics dataset and decomp toolkit. In *Proceedings of The 12th Language Resources and Evaluation Conference, LREC 2020, Marseille, France, May 11-16, 2020*, pages 5698–5707. European Language Resources Association.

Shumin Wu and Martha Palmer. 2015. Improving Chinese-English PropBank alignment. In *Proceedings of the Ninth Workshop on Syntax, Semantics and Structure in Statistical Translation*, pages 74–82, Denver, Colorado, USA. Association for Computational Linguistics.

Patrick Xia, Guanghui Qin, Siddharth Vashishtha, Yunmo Chen, Tongfei Chen, Chandler May, Craig Harman, Kyle Rawlins, Aaron Steven White, and Benjamin Van Durme. 2021. LOME: Large ontology multilingual extraction. In *Proceedings of the 16th Conference of the European Chapter of the Association for Computational Linguistics: System Demonstrations*, pages 149–159, Online. Association for Computational Linguistics.

Feng Yao, Chaojun Xiao, Xiaozhi Wang, Zhiyuan Liu, Lei Hou, Cunchao Tu, Juanzi Li, Yun Liu, Weixing Shen, and Maosong Sun. 2022. LEVEN: A large-scale chinese legal event detection dataset. In *Findings of the Association for Computational Linguistics: ACL 2022, Dublin, Ireland, May 22-27, 2022*, pages 183–201. Association for Computational Linguistics.

Mahsa Yarmohammadi, Shijie Wu, Marc Marone, Haoran Xu, Seth Ebner, Guanghui Qin, Yunmo Chen, Jialiang Guo, Craig Harman, Kenton Murray, Aaron Steven White, Mark Dredze, and Benjamin Van Durme. 2021. Everything is all it takes: A multipronged strategy for zero-shot cross-lingual information extraction. In *Proceedings of the 2021 Conference on Empirical Methods in Natural Language Processing, EMNLP 2021, Virtual Event / Punta Cana, Dominican Republic, 7-11 November, 2021*, pages 1950–1967. Association for Computational Linguistics.

John M. Zelle and Raymond J. Mooney. 1996. Learning to parse database queries using inductive logic programming. In *Proceedings of the Thirteenth National Conference on Artificial Intelligence and Eighth Innovative Applications of Artificial Intelligence Conference, AAAI 96, IAAI 96, Portland, Oregon, USA, August 4-8, 1996, Volume 2*, pages 1050–1055. AAAI Press / The MIT Press.

Luke S. Zettlemoyer and Michael Collins. 2005. Learning to map sentences to logical form: Structured classification with probabilistic categorial grammars. In *UAI '05, Proceedings of the 21st Conference in Uncertainty in Artificial Intelligence, Edinburgh, Scotland, July 26-29, 2005*, pages 658–666. AUAI Press.

Rui Zhang, Tao Yu, Heyang Er, Sungrok Shim, Eric Xue, Xi Victoria Lin, Tianze Shi, Caiming Xiong, Richard Socher, and Dragomir R. Radev. 2019. Editing-based SQL query generation for cross-domain context-dependent questions. In *Proceedings of the 2019 Conference on Empirical Methods in Natural Language Processing and the 9th International Joint Conference on Natural Language Processing, EMNLP-IJCNLP 2019, Hong Kong, China, November 3-7, 2019*, pages 5337–5348. Association for Computational Linguistics.

Lucia Zheng, Neel Guha, Brandon R. Anderson, Peter Henderson, and Daniel E. Ho. 2021. When does pretraining help?: assessing self-supervised learning for law and the casehold dataset of 53, 000+ legal holdings. In *ICAIL '21: Eighteenth International Conference for Artificial Intelligence and Law, São Paulo Brazil, June 21 - 25, 2021*, pages 159–168. ACM.

Haoxi Zhong, Chaojun Xiao, Cunchao Tu, Tianyang Zhang, Zhiyuan Liu, and Maosong Sun. 2020. How does NLP benefit legal system: A summary of legal artificial intelligence. In *Proceedings of the 58th Annual Meeting of the Association for Computational Linguistics, ACL 2020, Online, July 5-10, 2020*, pages 5218–5230. Association for Computational Linguistics.

A Repeated events

The sentence "Bob earned $300000 every year from 2015 to 2019." (case `s2_b_3_B_pos`) is represented in Prolog as:

```
bob_income(Year, Event, Start_day,
           End_day) :-
    between(2015, 2019, Year),
    atom_concat("earned ", Year, Event),
    first_day_year(Year, Start_day),
    last_day_year(Year, End_day).

income_(span(Event, 286, 291)) :-
    bob_income(_, Event, _, _).

agent_(span(Event, 286, 291),
       span("Bob", 282, 284)) :-
    bob_income(_, Event, _, _).

amount_(span(Event, 286, 291),
        span(300000, 294, 299)) :-
    bob_income(_, Event, _, _).

start_(span(Event, 286, 291),
       span(Start_day, 317, 320)) :-
    bob_income(_, Event, Start_day, _).
```

This makes it possible to generate 4 different `payment_` events and their arguments:

```
income_(span("earned 2015", 286, 291)).
agent_(span("earned 2015", 286, 291),
       span("Bob", 282, 284)).
amount_(span("earned 2015", 286, 291),
        span(300000, 294, 299)).
start_(span("earned 2015", 286, 291),
       span(20150101, 317, 320)).

income_(span("earned 2016", 286, 291)).
agent_(span("earned 2016", 286, 291),
       span("Bob", 282, 284)).
amount_(span("earned 2016", 286, 291),
        span(300000, 294, 299)).
start_(span("earned 2016", 286, 291),
       span(20160101, 317, 320)).

income_(span("earned 2017", 286, 291)).
agent_(span("earned 2017", 286, 291),
```

```
        span("Bob", 282, 284)).
amount_(span("earned 2017", 286, 291),
         span(300000, 294, 299)).
start_(span("earned 2017", 286, 291),
        span(20170101, 317, 320)).

income_(span("earned 2018", 286, 291)).
agent_(span("earned 2018", 286, 291),
        span("Bob", 282, 284)).
amount_(span("earned 2018", 286, 291),
         span(300000, 294, 299)).
start_(span("earned 2018", 286, 291),
        span(20180101, 317, 320)).

income_(span("earned 2019", 286, 291)).
agent_(span("earned 2019", 286, 291),
        span("Bob", 282, 284)).
amount_(span("earned 2019", 286, 291),
         span(300000, 294, 299)).
start_(span("earned 2019", 286, 291),
        span(20190101, 317, 320)).
```

With the model of Section 4, it is not possible to generate a date in 2016, so that it cannot generate the fact:

```
start_(span("earned 2016", 286, 291),
        span(20160101, 317, 320))
```

B Dates in IE

B.1 Encoding

In order to facilitate handling time in Prolog, we represent a date as a base-10 integer of the form YYYYMMDD. For example, August 23rd, 2017 is represented as 20170823. In that, we follow Sherman (1987). This makes it straightforward to order two dates, to extract the day from date `d` as `d%100`, the month as `(d/100)%100`, and so on. It is also possible to compute the day of the week, or the index of the week in the current year. In practice, whenever the full date is stated in the case text, that is the anchor for the date. For instance, "Alice and Bob got married on August 24th, 1970" contains a clear anchor for the date 19700824. Sometimes, days are not mentioned explicitly: "In 2020, Alice earned $33200." Decomposing this sentence into events, we get

```
income_(span("earned", 15, 20)).
agent_(span("earned", 15, 20),
        span("Alice", 9, 13)).
amount_(span("earned", 15, 20),
         span(33200, 23, 27)).
start_(span("earned", 15, 20),
        span(D, S, E)).
```

By default, here, we set `D=20200101`. Any date that is the argument of a `start_` relation, and where only the year is specified, defaults to the first day of that year. Similarly, any date that is the argument of an `end_` relation and where only the year is specified, defaults to the last day of that year. This is enforced at annotation time. It is thus sufficient to find the string "2020" as the argument to the `start_` relation to get it right. `S` and `E` are set to the start and end of "2020": `S=3` and `E=6`.

B.2 Decoding

At decoding time, we look for arguments to `start_` and `end_` relations, and do our best to convert them to dates. The model of Section 4 returns spans. First, we get the surface form of that span, i.e. the string that was selected by the IE model. Next, we use the `datetime` package from Python and its `strptime` function to parse the string. We try an ordered list of possible regular expressions for dates, going from most specific ("August 24th, 1970") to least specific ("2020"). If one of them works, we will have a value at least for the year, and in the best case, values for year, month and day. From there, we can deduce missing values for month and day, following the convention with `start_` and `end_` mentioned above. If none of the regular expressions work, we look for a 4-digit integer as close as possible to the span, and use that as the year. Failing that, we set the year to 0. In our error analysis in Appendix E, we have found that dates were generally either extracted correctly, or not extracted at all, which suggests that the above heuristic is not a limiting factor in the performance.

C Probabilities of Knowledge Base Elements

As depicted in Figure 3, the tree can be represented as a set of pairs and triplets. Here, we will use the language of KBEs, which are either pairs (l, r) or triplets (l, r, c). Pairs (l, r) contain an event predicate l and a span r. Triplets (l, r, c) contain an argument predicate l, a span r, and a span c. Our model parameterizes their probability as follows.

For a pair, $p(l, r) = p(l|r)p(r)$. The probability of the span $p(r)$ is computed as the probability assigned to r by the BIO tagger $\mathcal{T}$ (line 6 of Algorithm 1). This is computed by summing the probabilities of all BIO sequences that allow r as a span. The probability $p(l|r)$ is assigned to event predicate l by the label classifier $\mathcal{L}$ (line 8). It is the probability that r is labeled with l.

For a triplet, $p(l, r, c) = p(l|r, c)p(c|r)p(r)$. The probability of the span $p(r)$ is given by the BIO tagger, as above. The probability of the second span $p(c|r)$ is given by the BIO tagger when conditioned on r. Here too, $p(c|r)$ is computed by summing the probabilities of all BIO sequences that allow c as a span. Finally, the probability of the argument predicate $p(l|r, c)$ is given by the classifier.

D Additional results

In Table 4, the target KB is the set of KBEs contained in the original SARA cases. We report precision, recall and F1 scores, for dev and test sets. Consequently,

- recall scores are systematically lower in Table 4 as compared to Table 2, and
- precision scores are identical.[8]

E Error analysis

We compare model outputs on 3 binary cases and 3 numerical cases picked at random from the test set. We only mention the errors made by the models. Table 5 shows the answers produced by the Prolog program and the KB on those 6 cases.

TAX_CASE_78. This case has 6 events. LEGALBERT misses one argument of the first out of two `residence_` events, and overpredicts a second `start_` date. LEGALBERT mispredicts the `patient_` of the second `residence_` event, but nonetheless makes a sensible prediction. Together with LEGALBERT', BERT and T5, LEGALBERT correctly detects a `payment_` event, even though that event had been discarded as part of pre-processing, as described in Section 5.1. For the first `residence_` event, LEGALBERT' mispredicts Bob as the `agent_` instead of Charlie, predicts 2 `start_` dates, and 2 `patient_` arguments. For the second `residence_` event, LEGALBERT' predicts 2 `agent_` and 2 `patient_` arguments, one too many in each case. BERT, ROBERTA and T5 make similar predictions, getting all the event anchors right, but missing about half the arguments per event.

TAX_CASE_34. This case contains a single `income_` event. All 5 models perfectly predict the gold KB.

[8]Precision is higher in Table 4 for dev precision for LEGALBERT. This difference comes from one out of the five runs, where AllenNLP returned precisions of 88.6 and 88.7. This is unexpected, and can presumably be ascribed to an artefact in rounding in Python. The remaining four runs have identical precision, and this single discrepancy led to different means, 88.74 and 88.76.

TAX_CASE_28. This case contains 3 events. LEGALBERT misses a token when predicting the `amount_` argument of the `payment_` event: it predicts "53" instead of "53200". LEGALBERT' perfectly predicts all 3 events and their arguments. BERT misses the `purpose_` of `service_`, and predicts 2 `amount_` arguments for the same `income_` event, confusing `amount_` of `payment_` event and that of `income_` event. ROBERTA predicts the `income_` event and its arguments, but then additionally predicts 3 arguments: an extra `agent_` (also Alice, but a different mention), `start_` (some other date in the case), and `amount_` (the `amount_` of the `income_` event). ROBERTA misses the `purpose_` of the `service_` event. Like BERT , ROBERTA predicts two `amount_` arguments for the `income_` event. T5 correctly predicts all 3 events, but misses half the arguments of the `payment_` event, and misses the `agent_` of the `income_` event.

s68_A_2_POS. This case contains a single `income_` event. All models perfectly predict the gold KB, except for T5 missing the `agent_` argument, and BERT predicting that 2 different "Alice" spans are both `agent_` arguments of the `income_` event.

s3306_C_10_B_NEG. This case contains 4 events. LEGALBERT predicts 2 `start_` dates to the `medical_patient_` event. LEGALBERT' fails to classify a hospital as a hospital, instead classifying it as an educational institution. It incorrectly infers `start_` and `end_` dates to the `service_` event. BERT correctly classifies a hospital as a hospital, but misses an argument of that event. It fails to predict that Alice is a patient at this hospital, as well as what hospital someone is a patient at, and incorrectly infers `start_` and `end_` arguments to the `payment_` event, like LEGALBERT'. ROBERTA misses the `agent_` of the `hospital_` event, and predicts 2 `start_` dates to `medical_patient_`. T5 correctly classifies the hospital, and otherwise misses or hallucinates one or two arguments per event. For example, it detects the fact that someone is a patient at a hospital, but fails to predict the `agent_` of that relation, and predicts two `start_` dates.

s152_A_NEG. This case contains a single event: a `brother_` relationship between Alice and Bob. LEGALBERT, LEGALBERT' and ROBERTA correctly predict the KB. BERT and T5 miss the `patient_` of the relationship.

Model	Dev Precision	Recall	F1	Test Precision	Recall	F1
LEGALBERT	**88.8** $\pm$ 0.6	**83.1** $\pm$ 0.6	**83.6** $\pm$ 0.3	**88.1** $\pm$ 0.2	**79.0** $\pm$ 0.3	**77.5** $\pm$ 0.3
LEGALBERT'	87.4 $\pm$ 1.0	78.3 $\pm$ 1.3	80.2 $\pm$ 0.8	85.4 $\pm$ 0.9	75.4 $\pm$ 0.8	74.4 $\pm$ 0.6
BERT	85.9 $\pm$ 2.1	71.2 $\pm$ 2.4	75.0 $\pm$ 1.5	85.2 $\pm$ 2.3	69.4 $\pm$ 1.7	70.0 $\pm$ 1.4
ROBERTA	84.5 $\pm$ 0.6	76.2 $\pm$ 1.4	77.6 $\pm$ 0.8	86.4 $\pm$ 0.7	74.2 $\pm$ 1.1	73.4 $\pm$ 0.8
T5	73.2 $\pm$ 0.6	52.8 $\pm$ 2.1	58.8 $\pm$ 1.4	71.6 $\pm$ 1.1	52.8 $\pm$ 0.8	55.1 $\pm$ 0.8

Table 4: Performance metrics on the IE task measured on the full dataset. Scores are computed across 5 runs with different random seeds. We format statistics as *average* $\pm$ *standard error*. Best scores are **bolded**.

	tax_case_78	tax_case_34	tax_case_28	s68_a_2_pos	s3306_c_10_B_neg	s152_a_neg
LEGALBERT	$15213	$2684	$344428	Yes	No	No
LEGALBERT'	$15213	$2684	$344848	Yes	No	No
BERT	*$0*	$2684	$365916	Yes	No	No
ROBERTA	*$0*	$2684	$365916	Yes	No	No
T5	*$0*	$2684	*$0*	Yes	No	No
EMPTY	*$0*	$0	*$0*	Yes	No	No
TOPLINE	$15213	$2684	$344848	Yes	No	No
Correct answer	$14470	$2684	$344848	Yes	No	No

Table 5: Answers obtained with the Prolog program and the KBs extracted with different encoders. The cases are those analyzed in Appendix E. Incorrect answers are in *red italics*.

F Hyperparameters

In Section 5.2, we use Optuna (Akiba et al., 2019) to find good hyperparameters for each pre-trained encoder, running 100 experiments per encoder. In Table 6, we report the range searched over for each hyperparameter. If there is a single value under "value range", it means this hyperparameter was set and not searched over with Optuna. Each experiment consists of 3 training runs with 3 different random seeds, using the average micro F1 score on the validation set.

We also report the hyperparameters of the best performing models, in Tables 7, 8, 9, 10, and 11. For each number, we report up to 5 significant digits.

G Data statistics

Figure 4 reports statistics on the dataset used for IE, as well as some examples.

Part of model	Hyperparameter	Value range
Encoder $\mathcal{E}$	Transformer model encoding the case description X	{bert-base-cased, roberta-base, t5-base, zlucia/custom-legalbert, jhu-clsp/LegalBert}
Distance embeddings $\mathcal{D}$	Size of the embeddings encoding the distance of each token to the event anchor	{8, 16, 32, 64,128, 256, 512}
Label classifier $\mathcal{L}$	Feature dropout in between the layers of the MLP	[0, 0.8]
	Number of units per layer	{32, 64, 128, 256, 512, 1024, 2048}
	Number of layers	{1, 2, 3, 4}
BIO tagger $\mathcal{T}$	Feature dropout in between the layers of the MLP	Always equal to the dropout of $\mathcal{L}$
	Number of units	{32, 64, 128, 256, 512, 1024, 2048}
	Number of layers	{1, 2, 3, 4}
Trainer	Batch size	{8, 16, 32, 64, 128, 256}
	Learning rate	[1e-6, 1e-3]
	Learning rate scheduler	reduce_on_plateau — this scheduler halves the learning rate when the validation score stops improving
	Optimizer	huggingface_adamw
	Maximum number of epochs to train for	200
	Patience	20
	Gradient clipping	1.0
Loss function	Loss trade-off — see λ in Section 4	[0, 1]

Table 6: Hyperparameter ranges in the hyperparameter search.

Part of model	Hyperparameter	Value
Encoder $\mathcal{E}$	Transformer model	jhu-clsp/LegalBert
Distance embeddings $\mathcal{D}$	Size	8
Label classifier $\mathcal{L}$	Feature dropout	$7.6067 \cdot 10^{-2}$
	Number of units	2048
	Number of layers	3
BIO tagger $\mathcal{T}$	Feature dropout	-
	Number of units	1024
	Number of layers	3
Trainer	Batch size	8
	Learning rate	$6.1891 \cdot 10^{-5}$
Loss function	Loss trade-off	$7.5288 \cdot 10^{-1}$

Table 7: Hyperparameters of best LEGALBERT model.

Part of model	Hyperparameter	Value
Encoder $\mathcal{E}$	Transformer model	zlucia/custom-legalbert
Distance embeddings $\mathcal{D}$	Size	8
Label classifier $\mathcal{L}$	Feature dropout	$4.7806 \cdot 10^{-1}$
	Number of units	2048
	Number of layers	1
BIO tagger $\mathcal{T}$	Feature dropout	-
	Number of units	2048
	Number of layers	3
Trainer	Batch size	8
	Learning rate	$3.8743 \cdot 10^{-5}$
Loss function	Loss trade-off	$9.3341 \cdot 10^{-1}$

Table 8: Hyperparameters of best LEGALBERT' model.

Part of model	Hyperparameter	Value
Encoder $\mathcal{E}$	Transformer model	`bert-base-cased`
Distance embeddings $\mathcal{D}$	Size	8
Label classifier $\mathcal{L}$	Feature dropout Number of units Number of layers	$1.5865 \cdot 10^{-1}$ 64 1
BIO tagger $\mathcal{T}$	Feature dropout Number of units Number of layers	- 256 4
Trainer	Batch size Learning rate	16 $7.7282 \cdot 10^{-5}$
Loss function	Loss trade-off	$4.4946 \cdot 10^{-1}$

Table 9: Hyperparameters of best BERT model.

Part of model	Hyperparameter	Value
Encoder $\mathcal{E}$	Transformer model	`roberta-base`
Distance embeddings $\mathcal{D}$	Size	8
Label classifier $\mathcal{L}$	Feature dropout Number of units Number of layers	$3.8621 \cdot 10^{-1}$ 2048 2
BIO tagger $\mathcal{T}$	Feature dropout Number of units Number of layers	- 2048 2
Trainer	Batch size Learning rate	32 $1.1132 \cdot 10^{-4}$
Loss function	Loss trade-off	$6.6690 \cdot 10^{-1}$

Table 10: Hyperparameters of best RoBERTa model.

Part of model	Hyperparameter	Value
Encoder $\mathcal{E}$	Transformer model	`t5-base`
Distance embeddings $\mathcal{D}$	Size	8
Label classifier $\mathcal{L}$	Feature dropout Number of units Number of layers	$3.7523 \cdot 10^{-1}$ 64 1
BIO tagger $\mathcal{T}$	Feature dropout Number of units Number of layers	- 1024 1
Trainer	Batch size Learning rate	32 $5.6507 \cdot 10^{-4}$
Loss function	Loss trade-off	$5.0650 \cdot 10^{-1}$

Table 11: Hyperparameters of best T5 model.

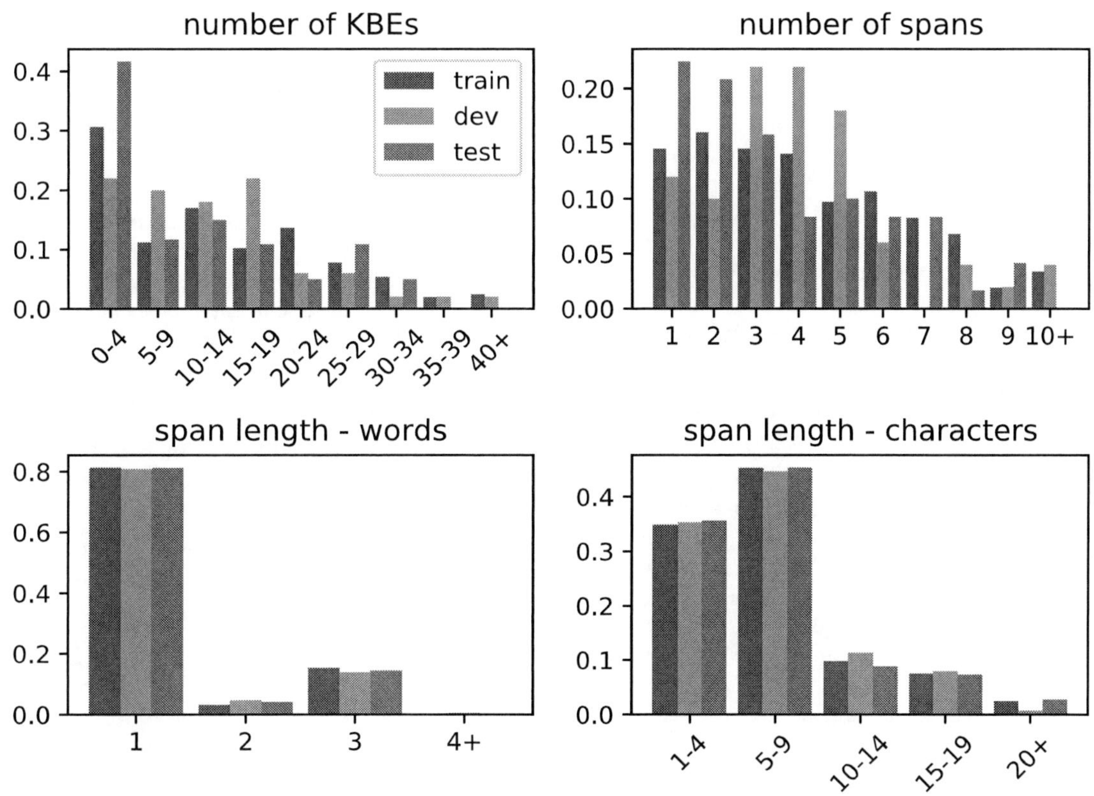

Examples of spans of length 1, 2 and 3: "Alice", "Bob", "marriage", "joint return", "Feb 3rd, 1992" and "decree of divorce".

Figure 4: Statistics of the data used for IE (partial dataset). Number of KBEs and spans are per case. The large number of 3-word spans is due to many date expressions being 3-word phrases.

Retrieval-based Evaluation for LLMs: A Case Study in Korean Legal QA

Cheol Ryu **Seolhwa Lee** **Subeen Pang** **Chanyeol Choi**
Linq Labs
{cheol.ryu,seolhwa.lee,subeen.pang,jacob.choi}@getlinq.com

Hojun Choi **Myeonggee Min**
Law&Good
{hojun.choi,mgmin}@lawandgood.com

Jy-yong Sohn*
Yonsei University
jysohn1108@yonsei.ac.kr

Abstract

While large language models (LLMs) have demonstrated significant capabilities in text generation, their utilization in areas requiring domain-specific expertise, such as law, must be approached cautiously. This caution is warranted due to the inherent challenges associated with LLM-generated texts, including the potential presence of factual errors. Motivated by this issue, we propose Eval-RAG, a new evaluation method for LLM-generated texts. Unlike existing methods, Eval-RAG evaluates the validity of generated texts based on the related document that are collected by the retriever. In other words, Eval-RAG adopts the idea of retrieval augmented generation (RAG) for the purpose of evaluation. Our experimental results on Korean Legal Question-Answering (QA) tasks show that conventional LLM-based evaluation methods can be better aligned with Lawyers' evaluations, by combining with Eval-RAG. In addition, our qualitative analysis show that Eval-RAG successfully finds the factual errors in LLM-generated texts, while existing evaluation methods cannot.

1 Introduction

Recent advances of large language models (LLMs) are remarkable, in various natural language generative tasks such as translation or summarization. However, LLMs are prone to generating hallucinated text (Ji et al., 2023), i.e., the texts generated by LLMs are sometimes having factual errors, which implies the unreliability of the LLM-generated text. Consequently, it is necessary to develop a proper system of evaluating LLM-generated text, for using LLMs in real-world applications.

Various methods are proposed for evaluating natural language generation (NLG) (Papineni et al., 2002; Lin, 2004; Zhang et al., 2020). However, it is known that such classical evaluation methods have room for improvement compared with the human evaluation, especially for evaluating question answering (QA) tasks (Liu et al., 2023).

* Corresponding author

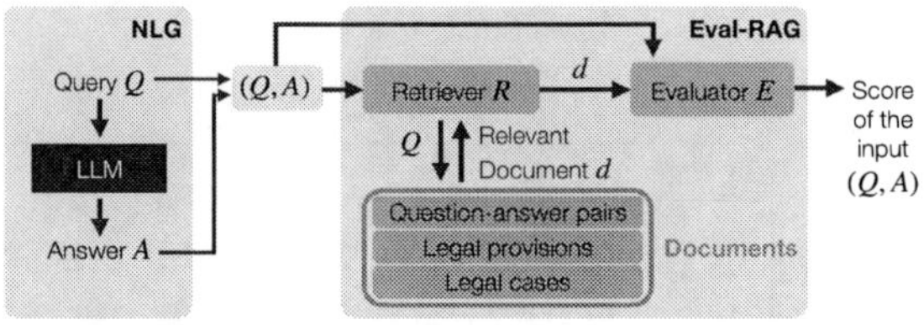

Figure 1: The proposed Eval-RAG method for Legal QA task. Suppose an LLM generates answer A for the query Q. Eval-RAG is a framework for evaluating the quality of the answer, using retriever R and evaluator E. First, R retrieves the document d relevant to the query Q. Second, E evaluates the score of (Q, A) based on the contents of the retrieved document d.

To address this issue of classical methods, recent approaches considered evaluating LLM-generated texts by another LLM (Chan et al., 2023; Liu et al., 2023; Wang et al., 2023b). Although the LLM-based evaluation methods outperforms classical methods, they are suffering from innate issues of LLMs, such as the lack of training data on specialized domains and the inability to reflect recent data.

Main Contributions In this paper, we propose Eval-RAG, a retrieval-based method evaluating LLM-generated texts. Eval-RAG first retrieves the document relevant to the generation task, and then evaluates the texts based on the relevant document. This method can be considered as applying retrieval-augmented generation (RAG) concept on the existing LLM-based evaluation systems. Our experimental results on Korean legal QA tasks show that Eval-RAG outperforms existing evaluation methods, in terms of higher correlation with the human evaluation. Our qualitative analysis also shows that Eval-RAG overcomes the limitation of existing LLM-based evaluation methods which cannot judge the hallucination of LLMs.

Proceedings of the Natural Legal Language Processing Workshop 2023, pages 132–137
December 7, 2023 ©2023 Association for Computational Linguistics

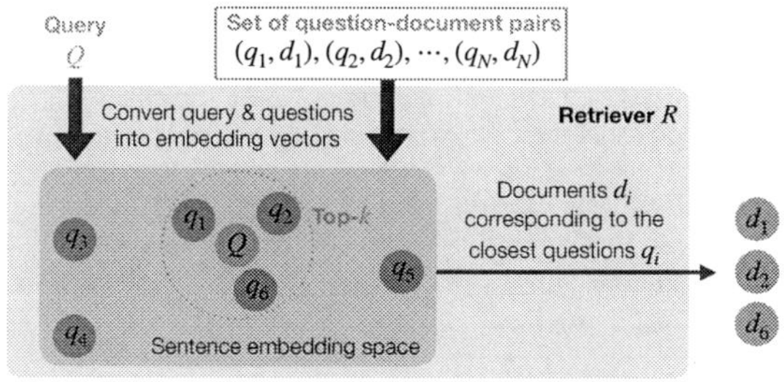

Figure 2: The pipeline of retriever.

2 Method

Here we introduce the proposed Eval-RAG framework depicted in Fig. 1, which has two main components: the retriever R and the evaluator E. Once an LLM generates answer A for the query Q, Eval-RAG evaluates whether answer A is proper or not for the query Q. First, the retriever R finds legal documents d that are relevant to the query Q. Second, the evaluator E evaluates the validity of answer based on the related document d.

Retriever Fig. 2 illustrates how retriever R retrieves the documents d related with the query Q. This process contains three steps: data collection, sentence embedding, and query processing. In Step 1, we collect three different types of publicly available legal documents: (1) legal question-answer pairs, (2) legal provisions and (3) legal cases (precedents). Since our focus is given to QA tasks, we convert these documents into (question, document containing the answer) format, denoted by (q, d), in the following manner. Given the legal question-answer (q, a) pairs, we extract related document d from the answer a. For other documents d (legal provisions and legal cases), we use LLMs to generate relevant questions q. Table 1 shows the examples of question-document pair (q, d) for each data source, which are translated from the Korean using *DeepL*[1]. In Step 2, the question-document pairs $\{(q_i, d_i)\}_{i=1}^{N}$ collected in step 1 are stored in a vector database (Johnson et al., 2019) by using a sentence embedding model, which converts a sentence q into an n-dimensional vector. In Step 3, given query Q and the set of questions $\{q_i\}_{i=1}^{N}$ collected in step 2, the retriever R first finds the question q_i that is most similar to Q (in the sentence embedding space) and returns the relevant document d_i.

[1]http://deepl.com/

Evaluator The quality of answer A to a given query Q is evaluated based on the relevant document d, as shown in Fig. 1. Recall that existing LLM-based evaluators (Chan et al., 2023; Liu et al., 2023; Wang et al., 2023b) ask LLMs for the evaluation, where the prompts include Q and A, along with the evaluation criteria and methods for evaluation. The evaluator proposed by us is built on top of these methods, by adding the relevant document d (delivered from retriever R) in the prompt. This allows E to evaluate based on the relevant documents. Note that our method (evaluating LLMs based on related documents) is motivated by the RAG methods (which generates texts with the aid of retrieved documents), and thus we call our evaluation method as Eval-RAG. Table 2 provides an example of how an associated document d is added to the prompt of the existing method called *FairEval* (Wang et al., 2023b). It is worth noting that Eval-RAG can be combined with any existing LLM-based evaluation methods.

3 Experiments

We tested the performances of Eval-RAG and baselines for Korean legal QA tasks, specifically focused on the questions related to divorce.

Experimental Setup The divorce-related QA pairs used for the retriever are collected from *Korea Legal Aid Corporation*[2], while the legal provisions and cases mentioned in the QA pairs are gathered from *Korea Legislation Research Institute*[3]. The number of QA pairs, provisions, and cases used in the experiment were 287, 84, and 240, respectively. we used GPT-4 to generate relevant questions for each provision and case. The query set ($n = 100$) used in the experiment was selected from actual client consultation cases at the law firm *Law&Good*[4]. For each query, we prepared three types of answers: an actual answer from a legal professional (*Lawyer*), an answer generated by assigning the role of a lawyer to ChatGPT (*gpt*), and an answer generated with the inclusion of relevant documents (*rag*). We used OpenAI's 'text-embedding-ada-002' sentence embedding model to store questions in vector database.

[2]https://www.klac.or.kr

[3]https://www.klri.re.kr

[4]https://www.lawandgood.com

q: Does divorce evidence have an expiration date?
a: Yes, there is an expiration date for divorce evidence. Article 841 of the Civil Act of Republic of Korea stipulates that divorce evidence is valid for six months from the date the spouse becomes aware of the evidence and two years from the date of the grounds for filing.
d: Article 841 of the Civil Act (Extinction of Right to Apply for Divorce due to Unchastity) The spouse may not file for a divorce when the spouse has given a prior consent or an ex post facto forgiveness, or when six months have passed since the date the spouse becomes aware of the event or two years have passed since the date of the event.

q: I want to know what I can or should do with the items etc. that I gave to and received from the was-to-be-spouse as engagement gifts in case of a disengagement.
provision: Article 806 of the Civil Code (Termination of Engagement and Right to Claim Damages) Upon termination of an engagement, either party may claim compensation for damages from the negligent other party.
d: Article 806 of the Civil Act (Dissolution of Matrimonial Engagement and Claims for Damages) Upon the termination of an engagement, a party may claim compensation for damages from the negligent other party.

q: I would like to raise a claim for division of property on divorce upon the severance pay of the other party/spouse as well. Is this possible?
case: Case No. 2013MU2250 (Main Issues and Holdings) Whether the future retirement benefits are subject to the division of property on divorce when one of the divorcees is still employed at the time of divorce and has not yet retired(affirmative) and the scope of such division.
d: Case No. 2013MU2250 (Summary of Decision) Because it is required to work for a certain period of time to receive retirement benefits, as far as the cooperation of the spouse is recognized to have contributed to such work, the retirement benefits may be subject to a division of property.

Table 1: Examples of (question, relevant document) pair, denoted by (q, d), for three types of data sources: (1) legal question-answer pair (q, a), (2) legal provision, and (3) legal case.

You are a helpful and precise assistant for checking the quality of the answer. Please evaluate the answer based on stated relevant law of South Korea.
[Question]{question}
[The Start of Assistant 1's Answer] {answer_1} [The End of Assistant 1's Answer]
[The Start of Assistant 2's Answer] {answer_2} [The End of Assistant 2's Answer]
[The Start of Relevant Law of South Korea]{document}[The End of Relevant Law of South Korea]

Table 2: The prompt of Eval-RAG based on FairEval (Wang et al., 2023b). Black sentences are originally designed by FairEval, while blue sentences are designed by Eval-RAG.

Methods & Performance Metrics We compare the performances of different methods: (1) the latest LLM-based evaluators, ChatEval (Chan et al., 2023) and FairEval (Wang et al., 2023b), (2) these latest evaluators combined with Eval-RAG, and (3) the human grading evaluated by the lawyers, where all scores are scaled with minimum score 1 and the maximum score 10. Due to the limit of the available prompt length of the evaluator, the retriever returns only one relevant document of the question closest to the query. The human grading for the three types of answers for each query is considered as the benchmark, and we measured the correlation between this benchmark and each method, using *Pearson*, *Spearman*, and *Kendall* correlation coefficients.

Result Table 3 compares different evaluation methods, in terms of the correlation between the score of each method and the human grading. One can confirm that existing evaluators (FairEval and ChatEval) can be improved when combined with Eval-RAG, for both GPT-3.5 and GPT-4.

Table 4 provides qualitative comparison of evaluation methods, for a specific query Q. The table on the top shows query Q, the answer A generated by GPT and RAG (denoted by (gpt) and (rag)), and the related document d. The bottom table compares the evaluation of (gpt) and (rag) for different evaluation methods: Lawyer (human evaluation), ChatEval and ChatEval combined with Eval-RAG.

Here, (gpt) and (rag) have opposing views on the divorce-related capital gains tax. Note that the document d and the lawyer's evaluation indicate that (rag) is correct and (gpt) is incorrect.

Table 3: Correlation between the score of each evaluation method and the human grading. FairEval-RAG means FairEval combined with Eval-RAG.

Evaluator	Pearson	Spearman	Kendall
FairEval (GPT-3.5)	0.0432	0.0515	0.0457
FairEval-RAG (GPT-3.5)	0.1156	0.1264	0.1108
FairEval (GPT-4)	0.4972	0.4999	0.4299
FairEval-RAG (GPT-4)	**0.5923**	**0.5841**	**0.4991**
ChatEval (GPT-3.5)	0.1091	0.0896	0.0768
ChatEval-RAG (GPT-3.5)	0.0905	0.0816	0.0735
ChatEval (GPT-4)	0.4467	0.4541	0.4115
ChatEval-RAG (GPT-4)	**0.5103**	**0.5129**	**0.4618**

However, ChatEval's evaluation, based on LLM's knowledge, fails to recognize that (gpt) is incorrect. In contrast, Eval-RAG, referencing the necessary document d for evaluation, assesses (rag) as the more appropriate answer. This observation is consistent across both the GPT-3.5 and GPT-4 models. More specifically, only the evaluation of ChatEval-RAG (GPT-4) accurately states that (gpt) is incorrect based on document d.

4 Related Work

QA and LLM Question answering (QA) is a task of providing answers to a given question, which is explored in last decades (Rogers et al., 2023; Zhu et al., 2021; Bolotova et al., 2022). Recently, there are studies on QA for specific domains such as law (Ravichander et al., 2019; Wang et al., 2023a; Louis et al., 2023), and studies on long-form question answering (LFQA) which involves searching external documents relevant to a given query, and then generating paragraph-length answers (Krishna et al., 2021; Wang et al., 2022; Xu et al., 2023). The area of QA is greatly advanced using large language models (LLMs) (OpenAI, 2023). However, LLMs have several limitations, such as the generation of hallucinated text (Ji et al., 2023). One way of overcoming the limitations of LLMs is to us the Retrieval Augmented Generation (RAG) method, which integrates the retrieval module (which retrieves information from some data source) and the text generation module (which generates texts based on the retrieved information) in a unified framework (Lewis et al., 2020). RAG methods have recently demonstrated strong performance in QA (Mialon et al., 2023; Lazaridou et al., 2022; Khattab et al., 2023).

NLG Metrics Various types of metrics were developed to measure the quality of natural language generation (NLG). Bilingual Evaluation Understudy (BLEU) (Papineni et al., 2002) is a widely used metric for evaluating machine translation systems. It measures the similarity between the machine-generated output and the reference translation based on n-gram precision. Recall-Oriented Understudy for Gisting Evaluation (ROUGE) (Lin, 2004) is a family of metrics for evaluating text summarization systems. ROUGE measures the similarity between the machine-generated summary and the reference summary based on n-gram overlap and sentence-level overlap. BLEU (Papineni et al., 2002) and ROUGE (Lin, 2004) are also used for QA evaluation, but are not suitable because they are designed as translations and summaries, respectively. BERTScore (Zhang et al., 2020) is a evaluation metric for similarity between two sentences, by using pre-trained BERT models. BERTScore is shown to outperform other metrics in QA tasks. However, BERTscore is not reliable when the texts contain domain-specific knowledge due to the limitations of BERT model (Chalkidis et al., 2020).

LLM evaluation Recently, evaluating generated texts using LLMs is proposed (Fu et al., 2023; Liu et al., 2023; Wang et al., 2023b; Chan et al., 2023). G-Eval (Liu et al., 2023) proposes probability-weighting schemes to calibrate the evaluation score from LLM. FairEval (Wang et al., 2023b) proposes a new evaluation methodology, motivated by the observation that the evaluation results can vary depending on the order of inputs in the prompt. ChatEval (Chan et al., 2023) proposes a novel approach where multiple agents engage in a discussion to evaluate the generated text. Our paper is built on top of these LLM-based evaluations, and outperforms these baselines by using retrieval-based-evaluation.

5 Conclusion

In this paper, we proposed Eval-RAG, a new method of evaluating LLM-generated texts, with the aid of retrieved documents that are related with the target task. Our experiments on Korean Legal QA tasks show that existing LLM-based evaluations can be better aligned with ground-truth human evaluation, when combined with Eval-RAG.

6 Ethical considerations

The example we tested the performance might include sensitive case information of clients. However, it is essential to emphasize that this ethical concern is alleviated, as the samples in question have been withheld from public disclosure.

Q: We would like to know whether the transfer of real estate ownership from one party to the other through a division of property on divorce is subject to the capital gains tax.
(gpt): The transfer of real estate ownership from one party to the other in a divorce constitutes a transfer of property for valuable consideration. Capital gains tax is a tax incurred under the Income Tax Act when properties such as real estate, etc. are transferred. However, the transfer of real estate resulting from the division of property in divorce may be exempted from capital gains tax under Article 9 of the Income Tax Act.
(rag): According to the Supreme Court precedent Case No. 2002DU6422, the division of property constitutes a partition of the article jointly owned and the legal principles on a partition of the article jointly owned shall be applied. The partition of the article jointly owned is understood to be a change in the form of ownership by concentrating the co-owned share which was exercised in proportion to the co-owned share in the article jointly owned into an ownership of a specific part of the article and making it subsist only on that specific part of the article. For this reason, the division of property in a divorce is deemed to be a transfer of property for valuable consideration and thereby is not subject to capital gains tax.
d: Case No. 96NU14401 (Summary of Decision) A division of property in a divorce by agreement to liquidate the de facto marital property is substantially a partition of the article jointly owned in light of its legal nature, the object and scope of such division. Therefore, legal principles on a partition of the article jointly owned shall be apply mutatis mutandis, and the transfer of property by the result of such division is not a transfer of property for valuable consideration which is subject to capital gains tax.

Lawyer : The score of $(gpt) = 4$, the score of $(rag) = 8$
ChatEval (GPT-3.5) : After carefully reviewing the responses of both AI assistants, I found that (gpt) provided a more accurate and detailed answer. (gpt) correctly stated that transferring ownership of a property during divorce proceedings is considered a transfer of assets and may be subject to transfer income tax. Moreover, (gpt) provided the specific conditions that must be met for the transfer to be exempt from transfer income tax. **In contrast,** (rag) **incorrectly stated** that transferring ownership of a property during divorce proceedings is not considered a transfer of assets and therefore not subject to transfer income tax. Therefore, the score of $(gpt) = 8$, The score of $(rag) = 5$.
ChatEval-RAG (GPT-3.5) : Based on the stated relevant law of South Korea, (rag)'s answer is more accurate and relevant to the question. The law clearly states that the division of property in divorce is not considered a transfer of ownership and therefore not subject to transfer income tax. (rag) correctly cites a relevant court case to support this. (gpt)'s answer is also helpful, but it does not provide as much detail on the specific law and court case. Therefore, the score of $(gpt) = 7$, the score of $(rag) = 9$.
ChatEval (GPT-4) : (gpt) provided a detailed and accurate response, explaining the conditions under which the transfer of property due to divorce can be exempt from transfer income tax. This is in line with the Transfer Income Tax Law in South Korea. (rag), while citing a specific case, seems to have misunderstood the nature of property division in a divorce and its tax implications. Therefore, the score of $(gpt) = 9$, the score of $(rag) = 6$.
ChatEval-RAG (GPT-4) : Based on the stated relevant law of South Korea, Case 2002DU6422, the division of property during a divorce does not constitute a paid transfer of assets. (rag) correctly pointed this out and provided an accurate interpretation of the law. On the other hand, (gpt) **incorrectly stated** that the division of property during a divorce constitutes a paid transfer of assets and could be subject to capital gains tax. However, (gpt) did provide detailed information about the conditions for exemption from capital gains tax, which could be useful information for the user. The score of $(gpt) = 6$, the score of $(rag) = 9$.

Table 4: **(Top):** An example query Q, the answers generated by GPT and RAG, and related document d. **(Bottom):** Evaluation of generated texts by Lawyer, ChatEval (Chan et al., 2023) and ChatEval-RAG, a short-hand notation for combining ChatEval with Eval-RAG. The evaluation with Eval-RAG aligns better with the evaluation of Lawyer.

References

Valeriia Bolotova, Vladislav Blinov, Falk Scholer, W. Bruce Croft, and Mark Sanderson. 2022. A non-factoid question-answering taxonomy. In *Proceedings of the 45th International ACM SIGIR Conference on Research and Development in Information Retrieval*, page 1196–1207. Association for Computing Machinery.

Ilias Chalkidis, Manos Fergadiotis, Prodromos Malakasiotis, Nikolaos Aletras, and Ion Androutsopoulos. 2020. LEGAL-BERT: The muppets straight out of law school. In *Findings of the Association for Computational Linguistics: EMNLP 2020*, pages 2898–2904. Association for Computational Linguistics.

Chi-Min Chan, Weize Chen, Yusheng Su, Jianxuan Yu, Wei Xue, Shanghang Zhang, Jie Fu, and Zhiyuan Liu. 2023. Chateval: Towards better llm-based evaluators through multi-agent debate.

Jinlan Fu, See-Kiong Ng, Zhengbao Jiang, and Pengfei Liu. 2023. GPTScore: Evaluate as you desire.

Ziwei Ji, Nayeon Lee, Rita Frieske, Tiezheng Yu, Dan Su, Yan Xu, Etsuko Ishii, Ye Jin Bang, Andrea Madotto, and Pascale Fung. 2023. Survey of hallucination in natural language generation. *ACM Comput. Surv.*, 55(12).

Jeff Johnson, Matthijs Douze, and Hervé Jégou. 2019. Billion-scale similarity search with GPUs. *IEEE Transactions on Big Data*, 7(3):535–547.

Omar Khattab, Keshav Santhanam, Xiang Lisa Li, David Hall, Percy Liang, Christopher Potts, and Matei Zaharia. 2023. Demonstrate-search-predict: Composing retrieval and language models for knowledge-intensive NLP.

Kalpesh Krishna, Aurko Roy, and Mohit Iyyer. 2021. Hurdles to progress in long-form question answering.

Angeliki Lazaridou, Elena Gribovskaya, Wojciech Stokowiec, and Nikolai Grigorev. 2022. Internet-augmented language models through few-shot prompting for open-domain question answering.

Patrick Lewis, Ethan Perez, Aleksandra Piktus, Fabio Petroni, Vladimir Karpukhin, Naman Goyal, Heinrich Küttler, Mike Lewis, Wen-tau Yih, Tim Rocktäschel, Sebastian Riedel, and Douwe Kiela. 2020. Retrieval-augmented generation for knowledge-intensive NLP tasks. In *Advances in Neural Information Processing Systems*, volume 33, pages 9459–9474. Curran Associates, Inc.

Chin-Yew Lin. 2004. ROUGE: A package for automatic evaluation of summaries. In *Text Summarization Branches Out*, pages 74–81, Barcelona, Spain. Association for Computational Linguistics.

Yang Liu, Dan Iter, Yichong Xu, Shuohang Wang, Ruochen Xu, and Chenguang Zhu. 2023. G-eval: NLG evaluation using GPT-4 with better human alignment.

Antoine Louis, Gijs van Dijck, and Gerasimos Spanakis. 2023. Interpretable long-form legal question answering with retrieval-augmented large language models.

Grégoire Mialon, Roberto Dessì, Maria Lomeli, Christoforos Nalmpantis, Ram Pasunuru, Roberta Raileanu, Baptiste Rozière, Timo Schick, Jane Dwivedi-Yu, Asli Celikyilmaz, Edouard Grave, Yann LeCun, and Thomas Scialom. 2023. Augmented language models: a survey.

OpenAI. 2023. GPT-4 technical report.

Kishore Papineni, Salim Roukos, Todd Ward, and Wei-Jing Zhu. 2002. BLEU: A method for automatic evaluation of machine translation. In *Proceedings of the 40th Annual Meeting on Association for Computational Linguistics*, page 311–318. Association for Computational Linguistics.

Abhilasha Ravichander, Alan W Black, Shomir Wilson, Thomas Norton, and Norman Sadeh. 2019. Question answering for privacy policies: Combining computational and legal perspectives. In *Proceedings of the 2019 Conference on Empirical Methods in Natural Language Processing and the 9th International Joint Conference on Natural Language Processing (EMNLP-IJCNLP)*, pages 4947–4958. Association for Computational Linguistics.

Anna Rogers, Matt Gardner, and Isabelle Augenstein. 2023. QA dataset explosion: A taxonomy of NLP resources for question answering and reading comprehension. *ACM Comput. Surv.*, 55(10).

Peiyi Wang, Lei Li, Liang Chen, Zefan Cai, Dawei Zhu, Binghuai Lin, Yunbo Cao, Qi Liu, Tianyu Liu, and Zhifang Sui. 2023a. Large language models are not fair evaluators.

Peiyi Wang, Lei Li, Liang Chen, Dawei Zhu, Binghuai Lin, Yunbo Cao, Qi Liu, Tianyu Liu, and Zhifang Sui. 2023b. Large language models are not fair evaluators.

Shufan Wang, Fangyuan Xu, Laure Thompson, Eunsol Choi, and Mohit Iyyer. 2022. Modeling exemplification in long-form question answering via retrieval. In *Proceedings of the 2022 Conference of the North American Chapter of the Association for Computational Linguistics: Human Language Technologies*, pages 2079–2092. Association for Computational Linguistics.

Fangyuan Xu, Yixiao Song, Mohit Iyyer, and Eunsol Choi. 2023. A critical evaluation of evaluations for long-form question answering.

Tianyi Zhang, Varsha Kishore, Felix Wu, Kilian Q. Weinberger, and Yoav Artzi. 2020. BERTScore: Evaluating text generation with BERT.

Fengbin Zhu, Wenqiang Lei, Chao Wang, Jianming Zheng, Soujanya Poria, and Tat-Seng Chua. 2021. Retrieving and reading: A comprehensive survey on open-domain question answering.

Legal NLP Meets MiCAR: Advancing the Analysis of Crypto White Papers

Carolina Camassa
Bank of Italy
carolina.camassa@bancaditalia.it

Abstract

In the rapidly evolving field of crypto assets, white papers are essential documents for investor guidance, and are now subject to unprecedented content requirements under the European Union's Markets in Crypto-Assets Regulation (MiCAR). Natural Language Processing (NLP) can serve as a powerful tool for both analyzing these documents and assisting in regulatory compliance. This paper delivers two contributions to the topic. First, we survey existing applications of textual analysis to unregulated crypto asset white papers, uncovering a research gap that could be bridged with interdisciplinary collaboration. We then conduct an analysis of the changes introduced by MiCAR, highlighting the opportunities and challenges of integrating NLP within the new regulatory framework. The findings set the stage for further research, with the potential to benefit regulators, crypto asset issuers, and investors.

1 Introduction

White papers are the cornerstone of information disclosure for Initial Coin Offerings (ICOs), a modern fundraising method that sells tokens to a diverse group of investors (Fisch, 2019). These fundraisings represent an alternative method for entrepreneurial finance, with similarities to IPOs, venture capital, and presale crowdfunding (Howell et al., 2020).

When a new ICO is announced, it is usually accompanied by the *white paper*, a text document that contains information for the investors and bears some similarities, at least in intent, with an IPO prospectus. However, unlike their regulated counterparts, white papers have so far operated in a largely unregulated landscape.

Thanks to this regulatory vacuum, the type of content varies widely, but it usually includes (Bourveau et al., 2022; Zhang et al., 2019) a description of the service offered and its value proposition, the composition of the project team, financial details about the offer, and explanations of the technologies underlying the project. Due to their public accessibility and richness in data, white papers have been a frequent subject of studies aimed at extracting market insights through textual analysis (Fisch (2019); Thewissen et al. (2022); Florysiak and Schandlbauer (2022) among others).

The current ICO market is characterized by a pronounced level of *information asymmetry* between crypto issuers and investors (Bourveau et al., 2022; Chen, 2019). These circumstances, easily explained by the lack of regulation, led to investigation into the prevalence of fraud and scams among ICOs (Liebau and Schueffel, 2019; Karimov and Wójcik, 2021). It is not uncommon for white papers to be a vehicle for misinformation, sometimes resorting to imprecise claims and exaggerated language (Momtaz, 2021) to lure investors.

1.1 Introduction to the MiCA Regulation

In this context of fragmented or absent regulation of the crypto assets market, the European Union has been making an effort to unify regulation in its member states on this aspect. The vehicle for this unification is the *Regulation on Markets in Crypto Assets* (abbreviated as MiCAR). The text of the regulation was published on the Official Journal of the European Union on June 9th, 2023 (150, 2023) [1], and the norms will become fully applicable by December 30th, 2024. Its entry into force will provide clarity and protection for European citizens, but it will also require considerable effort on the part of issuers (Florysiak, 2022).

The MiCAR aims to regulate crypto asset public offerings—commonly known as ICOs—the admission of those crypto assets to trading on platforms, and additional related services to customers.

One key focus is the standardization of white paper content; the regulation mandates the inclusion of specific elements, such as details about the token of-

[1] OJ L 150, 9.6.2023, p. 40–205

Proceedings of the Natural Legal Language Processing Workshop 2023, pages 138–148
December 7, 2023 ©2023 Association for Computational Linguistics

fering, the associated risks, and team composition, with an emphasis on textual clarity and readability.

These new rules are engineered not just to to enable European citizens to make informed investment decisions, but also to assist national authorities in monitoring crypto asset offerings.

1.2 Motivation and main contributions

The goal of this study is to overview current Natural Language Processing applications to the analysis of crypto asset white papers, and identify how new applications can assist stakeholders in adapting to the upcoming MiCA regulation.
Given that much of the existing research comes from economics and finance, this work aims to bridge the domain gap, enabling future Computer Science (CS) researchers to leverage all relevant work on the topic. It also provides a starting point for researchers and practitioners in the legal NLP domain to adapt existing methods to this new topic.
The organization of this work is as follows:

- A survey of NLP applications to crypto asset white papers and Initial Public Offering (IPO) prospectuses is provided in Section 2.
- Section 3 goes into detail on how the new MiCA regulation will impact the structure and content of white papers.
- Finally, Section 4 highlights the challenges and opportunities of harnessing NLP techniques to aid all stakeholders involved in the MiCAR compliance process.

2 Related work: NLP in ICO White Papers and IPO Prospectuses

2.1 NLP and ICO white papers

A survey of the field shows that most existing studies on crypto asset white papers are published in economics and finance venues, with little overlap with CS research.

A recurring research goal is using information extracted from the content of white papers to make predictions about the likelihood of success of an ICO. In this context, the type of signal extracted can vary widely, as do the predictive models used. Some studies on the topic relies exclusively on manual text analysis (Bourveau et al., 2022; Thewissen et al., 2023; Fisch, 2019); this review focuses instead on those studies that incorporate at least one NLP method, setting dictionary-based approaches as the minimum threshold for inclusion[2].
Figure 1 shows a taxonomy of the studies grouped according to the variables of interest and the type

[2]Excluded work typically relies on page length (Samieifar and Baur, 2021; Bourveau et al., 2018) or readability metrics such as the Gunning-Fog index or the Flesch Reading Ease score (Zhang et al., 2019).

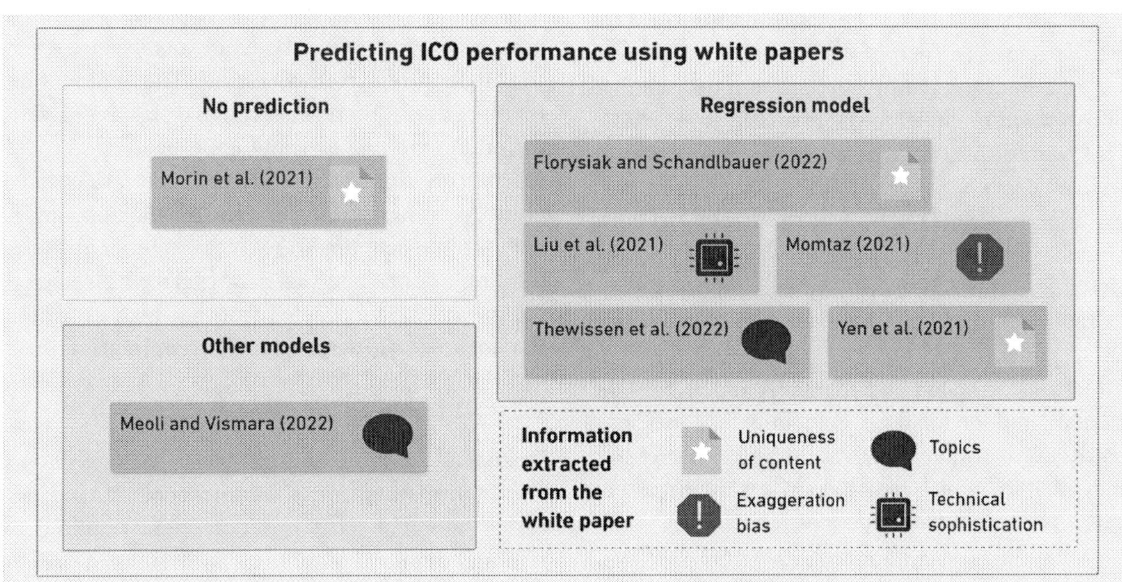

Figure 1: A shared research objective in existing studies that apply NLP to crypto asset white papers is predicting the degree of success of an ICO. The figure shows the experiments surveyed in section 2.1, grouped according to the type of prediction model used and the variables extracted from the text.

Study	Dataset size	Sentiment analysis	Topic modeling	Document similarity	NER
Florysiak and Schandlbauer (2022)	2,665			✓	✓
Liu et al. (2021)	1,629	✓	✓		
Meoli and Vismara (2022)	451	✓	✓		✓
Momtaz (2021)	495	✓			
Morin et al. (2021)	3,299			✓	
Thewissen et al. (2022)	5,210	✓	✓		✓
Yen et al. (2021)	1,064			✓	

Table 1: Overview of existing literature applying NLP techniques to crypto asset white papers, along with the dataset size and the techniques used. Most works come from the economics and finance domains.

of model, and Table 1 lists the dataset size and NLP tasks for each.

Momtaz (2021) uses a dictionary-based feature extraction method first proposed by Hu and Liu (2004) to capture the *exaggeration bias* in white papers. Momtaz argues that, in the absence of regulation, issuers of crypto asset tokens may have an incentive to positively exaggerate the quality of their venture to attract investors. The analysis confirms that there is a pervasive positive bias in the content of white papers, and that ICOs with this characteristic raise more funds in less time.

A common strategy is to use variations of the Latent Dirichlet Allocation (LDA) algorithm (Blei et al., 2003) to extract topic information from the white papers. The output of the model can be used, for example, to quantify the amount of technical information included in the text (Liu et al., 2021). This variable shows that crypto assets with high *technology indexes* are more likely to have positive long-run performances of the associated ICOs. Thewissen et al. (2022) use SENTLDA (Bao and Datta, 2014), a sentence-level version of LDA, to extract 30 topics from an extensive collection of white papers. The topics generated by the algorithm are evaluated and manually labeled by the authors, and the topic assignment is then used as a regression variable. The results of the regression show that the topics contained in a white paper can partially explain the success of ICOs.

Given the large amount of new ICOs published each year, some research has focused on looking for similarities among published white papers. Using a term-frequency approach initially developed for IPO prospectuses by Hanley and Hoberg (2010), Florysiak and Schandlbauer (2022) and Yen et al. (2021) assess the informational value of these documents. Here, a white paper is considered more informative if it introduces new or additional information not found in similar papers. The outcomes indicate a correlation between high informational content, or uniqueness, and success metrics such as fundraising and post-ICO market values. Separately, Morin et al. (2021) investigate text similarity across white papers using three metrics: TF-IDF, cosine similarity, and pairwise similarity. Their findings reveal that 19% of ICO white papers exhibit high similarity to previously published ones. Finally, Meoli and Vismara (2022) combine sentiment analysis, NER, topic modeling, sentiment analysis and document structure analysis to extract useful features from the text. The features are then used to train a set of binary classifiers, with different machine learning approaches, to predict whether an ICO was successful or not. The best machine learning model outperforms the benchmark, a traditional econometric forecasting model. A feature importance analysis confirms the relevance of the information extracted from the text, especially the document structure and the sentiment score.

2.2 NLP and IPO prospectuses

Textual analysis methods have also been used to extract information from the contents of IPO prospectuses. A prospectus is a document required by national financial regulatory authorities to present an investment offering—such as stocks, bonds, and mutual funds—to the public, or to obtain admission to trading on a regulated market. It contains all the details of the financial offer and must inform in-

Part	Description
A	Information about the offeror or the person seeking admission to trading
B	Information about the issuer, if different from the offeror or person seeking admission to trading
C	Information about the operator of the trading platform
D	Information about the crypto asset project
E	Information about the offer to the public of crypto assets or their admission to trading
F	Information about the crypto assets
G	Information on the rights and obligations attached to the crypto assets
H	Information on the underlying technology
I	Information on the risks

Table 2: Content requirement categories for crypto assets "other than"—one of the three types of assets regulated by MiCAR.

vestors of the risks involved with investing. These features make the documents partially similar, at least in intent, to crypto asset white papers.

Tao et al. (2018) train a custom embedding model using the WORD2VEC algorithm (Mikolov et al., 2013), to find and analyze sentences in the text that represent "forward looking statements" (FLS). These statements are meant to provide useful information about the company's future performance. Li et al. (2018) apply a keyword-based approach to the same task.

Sharpe and Decker (2022) perform sentiment analysis to look for the effect of text sentiment on the probability of an IPO being withdrawn.

Finally, Hanley and Hoberg (2010) devise a method—previously mentioned in 2.1—to separate the information content of a prospectus into *standard* and *informative* components. The components are derived from term frequency data and they are used to quantify how much of the content is also found in documents published in the same time period—or in the same industry—and how much of it is unique to a specific document.

2.3 Conclusions from the survey

While there seems to be a healthy amount of research interest in the topic, most of the existing literature covers a very limited array of NLP techniques and tasks. As an hypothesis, this might be a result of the lack of intersection between this particular domain of economics and finance research and CS research.

More advanced NLP methodologies have successfully been applied in various regulatory and legal settings. The following section contains examples of such works and argues for the transferability of these computational approaches to the analysis and regulation of future crypto asset white papers.

3 How MiCA changes the regulatory landscape

The MiCA regulation is broad and covers three categories of crypto assets: *asset-referenced tokens*, *e-money tokens*, and *crypto assets other than*[3]. The latter category also includes *utility tokens*, a specific type of crypto asset that has no financial purposes and is only intended to provide access to a good or a service supplied by its issuer. Some types of crypto assets, such as *Non-Fungible Tokens* (NFTs), are not covered by the regulation.

For each crypto asset category , the regulation contains norms regarding the content and issuance of the white paper, the conduct of business, in addition to organizational and financial requirements.

In alignment with the objective of the study, the rest of the work will focus only on the norms for white paper content, and in particular those valid for the crypto "other than" category. While the requirements vary across the three asset categories, the differences are marginal in the scope of the analysis. Another reason supporting this choice is the fact that the "other than" category has the largest set of requirements for white papers—see Appendix A.

[3]For brevity; the full definition in the text is "crypto assets other than asset-referenced tokens or e-money tokens".

Minimum content requirements. Each whitepaper must satisfy a comprehensive list of minimum content requirements[4] that are organized around macro-areas, listed in Table 2 in the case of "other than" crypto assets. A comparison with the other two categories is provided in Appendix A.

Table 3 shows some examples of these requirements, accompanied by related excerpts taken from existing (pre-regulation) white papers.

Other requirements In addition to minimum content requirements, other MiCAR norms impact white paper content and could have implications for future NLP applications on the topic.

- **Future value of the assets:** issuers of crypto assets are forbidden[5] from making claims about the future value of the asset in the white paper, aside from clarifying that the token might lose its value partially or in full [6]. These kinds of forward-looking statements have previously been analysed in IPO prospectuses—see Section 2.2.

- **Document language:** according to the regulation[7], *"the white paper shall be drawn up in an official language of the home Member State, or in a language customary in the sphere of international finance"*. Using a language other than English could pose some challenges that are examined in Section 4.

- **Document template:** the MiCA regulation states[8] that the white paper must adhere to the template and form established by the European Securities and Markets Authority (ESMA) and the European Banking Authority (EBA). As of October 2023, no template has been published yet, although consultations on technical requirements are in progress.

4 NLP in the MiCAR Landscape: Opportunities and Challenges

4.1 What NLP can do: exploring possibilities.

Even if there is currently a gap in NLP research applied to the topic of crypto white papers, other legal domains have benefited from collaboration with CS researchers (Zhong et al., 2020).

Tasks involving the interpretation and analysis of legal texts have been a popular subject for the legal NLP community. Current research mostly relies on pre-trained Transformer-based (Vaswani et al., 2017) models, with rising interest in the use of Large Language Models (LLMs) (Guha et al., 2023; Yu et al., 2023).

The rest of the section explores some avenues for applying existing NLP techniques to the MiCA regulatory framework.

Predicting the outcome of compliance checks. Given a text passage from a white paper and a MiCAR requirement, it would be beneficial to have a model capable of correctly and automatically check if the passage complies with the regulation. There have been attempts to solve this problem for different regulatory domains. For example, Zufall et al. (2020) attempt to automate the decision of whether an online post is subject to the European Union's Legal Framework against the Expression of Hatred. As part of their approach to classify hate speech from a legal standpoint, they trained GBERT (Chan et al., 2020) as a multi-class classifier on a manually annotated hate speech dataset. The model showed poor performance, suggesting that the task might be too complex for the model's capabilities. The task could be similarly challenging in the case of MiCAR, making it a good candidate for further research.

Matching passages with requirements. If automating compliance checks proves too difficult—or even undesirable—another useful application could be simply to identify which regulation norms are relevant to each text passage.

In a similar task, Ravichander et al. (2019) collects a set of annotated questions about the contents of privacy policies, in which the model must determine if the text passage contains an answer to the provided question, and classify the question-passage pair as Relevant or Irrelevant.

Abualhaija et al. (2022) use language models from the BERT family (Devlin et al., 2019), finetuned on the task of Question Answering, to assist requirements engineers in finding text passages relevant to their analysis of compliance requirements.

Question answering and information retrieval. Letting users ask questions about the content of a white paper—be it a potential investor trying to understand the project, or a regulator looking for a specific paragraph—is one of the most obvious and

[4] As outlined in Annexes I, II, and III of the regulation.
[5] Articles *6.4, 6.5a, 19.3, 19.4a.*
[6] Does not apply to *e-money tokens.*
[7] Articles *6.9, 19.8,* and *51.8.*
[8] Articles *6.10-6.12*

potentially useful applications of NLP to this topic. Given the length and complexity of the regulation, stakeholders could also benefit from an efficient way to retrieve norms from the MiCAR text.
QA and IR systems in the legal and regulatory domain pose some specific challenges compared to traditional question answering (Abdallah et al., 2023). Among others, they usually require highly specialized datasets curated by legal experts, and there is less room for error since an imprecise or factually wrong answer could negatively impact a legal decision.

To mitigate the data problem, the authors of LEGALBENCH (Guha et al., 2023) collect over 150 annotated datasets in the legal domain, including QA tasks. Since regulated white papers will be publicly available, the research community could contribute to this effort in the future with a QA dataset inspired by the MiCA regulation.

LLMs for reasoning and summarization. As demonstrated in LEGALBENCH (Guha et al., 2023), Large Language Models can now achieve good performance on some challenging legal reasoning tasks in a zero-shot setting. While supervised approaches may still outperform these models, there is a clear advantage in using LLMs as they don't require labeled datasets. Selecting the appropriate instruction and few-shot examples for the prompt can further improve performance (Yu et al., 2023; Trautmann et al., 2022).

Aside from reasoning, another promising application of LLMs is summarization. The emergence of training methods that use human preference data (Stiennon et al., 2020) has led to models that can produce high-quality summaries of text, including those in the legal domain (Pont et al., 2023), without domain-specific training. In the MiCAR context, both the regulation text and the white papers are long and often dense, making summarization a useful tool for regulators and investors interested in quickly analyzing their contents.

Named Entity Recognition. Some of the MiCAR requirements entail entity extraction, from the traditional kind (e.g., the list of persons involved in managing the project) to more domain-specific types of entities such as Legal Norm and Organization. Named entities are also useful for document organization and search. However, NER algorithms are particularly sensible to domain shifts: When general-purpose NER algorithms are used in texts from a narrow domain, there is often a performance degradation. To work around this limitation, Au et al. (2022) and Smădu et al. (2022) train entity recognition algorithms on annotated legal datasets in different languages. Given that crypto asset white papers are also financial

Part	Disclosure item	White paper sample
E	E5: the total number of crypto assets to be offered to the public or admitted to trading.	A total of 200 million tokens is put into circulation through a private sale and a public ICO.
	E14: Information about technical requirements that the purchaser is required to fulfil to hold the crypto assets.	To engage with the ████ protocol, individuals must first download ████ App.
H	H1: The consensus mechanism, where applicable.	The IBFT PoA is the default consensus mechanism on ████ Blockchain.
	H5: Information on the audit outcome of the technology used, if such an audit was conducted.	Two separate security assessments were conducted over a period of several months and conducted by the audit firms ████ and ████.
I	I4: A description of the risks associated with project implementation.	(...), no security measures can provide absolute protection against unauthorized access and data breaches.

Table 3: Examples of the minimum content requirements from MiCAR, accompanied by redacted excerpts taken from existing, unregulated, white papers. The first column shows the requirement category. All categories and their descriptions are listed in Table 2.

documents, NER models trained on data from the financial domain might also be an option (Salinas Alvarado et al., 2015; Francis et al., 2019).

4.2 Challenges

NLP can simplify the understanding of crypto asset white papers, aid regulators in MiCAR compliance, and reduce the effort required for issuers to generate compliant documents. It can also benefit investors by enabling them to make more informed decisions, if they are given the tools to better assimilate the contents of white papers.

However, there are also potential obstacles due to the narrow scope of application and the complexity of the subject matter.

Adapting to the legal and regulatory domain. As previously mentioned, performance degradation can occur when using general-purpose language models on narrow domains. This is not limited to entity recognition, but also impacts other tasks. One way of diminishing this effect could be making use of the models released by the legal NLP research community, such as LEGAL-BERT (Chalkidis et al., 2020) and POLBERT, a subsequent model trained on the Pile of Law (Henderson* et al., 2022) dataset.

Since white papers contain terms and language specific to the financial domain, models like FINBERT (Araci, 2019) and FINGPT (Yang et al., 2023) could also be appropriate. However, the world of crypto assets brings even more lexical issues with its acronyms and neologisms[9].

Domain shift between white papers and regulation. In the past, the issuers of crypto asset white papers have used very different language compared to the legal jargon found in regulatory texts. This difference might make it harder to find semantic similarities between white paper passages and the relevant regulation articles—one of the possible applications mentioned in Section 4.1.

Keymanesh et al. (2021) encounter a similar issue in developing a QA system that answers citizen queries about privacy policies, and they partially overcome it by using paraphrasing techniques for query expansion.

Language. The regulation allows using either the local language of the state the crypto asset will be issued in, or a language commonly used in finance. Although we can expect most papers to be in English, the usage of other languages might introduce difficulties, especially in combination with the aforementioned domain shift. There is ongoing research (Niklaus et al., 2023; Chalkidis et al., 2023) that aims to make available language models and NLP datasets that support multiple languages in the legal domain.

Document structure and length. In the largest study encountered (Thewissen et al., 2022), with a sample of 5210 white papers, the median document length is 30 pages, and the maximum is 167. As the number of required disclosure items rises with the introduction of MiCAR, we might see these numbers increasing.

Handling long documents in NLP presents unique challenges. Both traditional sequence models and transformer-based models struggle, with most BERT-based models having a maximum sequence length of 512 tokens. Even among recent LLMs, few exceed the limit of 4,096 tokens[10]. To get around this problem, Mamakas et al. (2022) modify LONGFORMER (Beltagy et al., 2020) and LEGAL-BERT (Chalkidis et al., 2020) to handle texts up to 8,192 tokens.

Until the regulation templates for white papers are released, it cannot be determined whether they will be required to adhere to a provided document structure. For documents that are not presegmented, Aumiller et al. (2021) propose a segmentation system for legal documents that uses topic modeling to split a given text into semantically coherent spans for downstream applications.

4.3 Implications for stakeholders

Regulators. NLP could help regulators by partially automating compliance checks, reducing the administrative burden on competent authorities. It can also improve the speed and accuracy of oversight with ad-hoc tools for domain experts, enabling them to respond more rapidly to market changes and potential infringements.

Issuers of crypto assets. For issuers, NLP-based tools can assist in drafting white papers that are compliant with MiCAR guidelines from the start. This can reduce the time and costs associated with legal consultations and revisions, making it easier to enter and operate within the European market.

[9]The Cryptopedia glossary from Gemini contains over 1000 terms unique to the crypto community.

[10]A limit which includes both input and output tokens.

Potential investors. From an investor's perspective, NLP-generated analyses of white papers can provide a more transparent and easily interpretable data source, democratizing access to investment information about the crypto asset market.

5 Conclusions

Crypto asset white papers are valuable data sources for NLP practitioners due to their public availability and rich informational content. The entry into force of the MiCAR opens new avenues for NLP applications to assist various stakeholders, including regulators, issuers, and potential investors, in navigating compliance and regulatory oversight.

Our survey of existing literature on the textual analysis of white papers revealed an active but siloed field that could benefit significantly from interdisciplinary collaboration between computer science, finance, and legal experts. Existing work in the legal NLP field could serve as a foundation for developing algorithms and models tailored to this new regulatory landscape.

Researchers have a clear opportunity to contribute to this emerging area, with the potential not only to streamline regulatory processes but also to create a more transparent and accountable crypto asset ecosystem.

Limitations

The work inevitably contains some speculative elements, given that, while the MiCAR text is public, no regulated white papers are available yet, and no regulatory workflows are yet finalized or known. The new white papers will be expected to follow a template designed by the ESMA, which has not been released yet. Therefore, the analysis of possible NLP applications, opportunities, and challenges is partially grounded in the structures and contents of existing, unregulated white papers, and it may not be entirely applicable to regulated ones.

Acknowledgments

The author would like to thank Marco Benedetti and Andrea Gentili for their valuable feedback. Special thanks are also extended to Claudia Biancotti, Daniele Natalizi, and Mattia Suardi for their insights into clarifying various aspects of the MiCAR regulation.

References

OJ L 150. 2023. Regulation (eu) 2023/1114 of the european parliament and of the council of 31 may 2023 on markets in crypto-assets. *Official Journal of the European Union*, 150:40–205.

Abdelrahman Abdallah, Bhawna Piryani, and Adam Jatowt. 2023. Exploring the state of the art in legal qa systems. *arXiv preprint arXiv:2304.06623*.

Sallam Abualhaija, Chetan Arora, Amin Sleimi, and Lionel C. Briand. 2022. Automated question answering for improved understanding of compliance requirements: A multi-document study. In *2022 IEEE 30th International Requirements Engineering Conference (RE)*. IEEE.

Dogu Araci. 2019. Finbert: Financial sentiment analysis with pre-trained language models. *arXiv preprint arXiv:1908.10063*.

Ting Wai Terence Au, Vasileios Lampos, and Ingemar Cox. 2022. E-NER — an annotated named entity recognition corpus of legal text. In *Proceedings of the Natural Legal Language Processing Workshop 2022*, pages 246–255, Abu Dhabi, United Arab Emirates (Hybrid). Association for Computational Linguistics.

Dennis Aumiller, Satya Almasian, Sebastian Lackner, and Michael Gertz. 2021. Structural text segmentation of legal documents. In *Proceedings of the Eighteenth International Conference on Artificial Intelligence and Law*, pages 2–11.

Yang Bao and Anindya Datta. 2014. Simultaneously discovering and quantifying risk types from textual risk disclosures. *Management Science*, 60(6):1371–1391.

Iz Beltagy, Matthew E Peters, and Arman Cohan. 2020. Longformer: The long-document transformer. *arXiv preprint arXiv:2004.05150*.

David M Blei, Andrew Y Ng, and Michael I Jordan. 2003. Latent dirichlet allocation. *Journal of machine Learning research*, 3(Jan):993–1022.

Thomas Bourveau, Emmanuel T De George, Atif Ellahie, and Daniele Macciocchi. 2018. Initial coin offerings: Early evidence on the role of disclosure in the unregulated crypto market. *Available at SSRN*, 3193392.

Thomas Bourveau, Emmanuel T De George, Atif Ellahie, and Daniele Macciocchi. 2022. The role of disclosure and information intermediaries in an unregulated capital market: Evidence from initial coin offerings. *Journal of Accounting Research*, 60(1):129–167.

Ilias Chalkidis, Manos Fergadiotis, Prodromos Malakasiotis, Nikolaos Aletras, and Ion Androutsopoulos. 2020. LEGAL-BERT: The muppets straight out of law school. In *Findings of the Association for Computational Linguistics: EMNLP 2020*, pages 2898–2904, Online. Association for Computational Linguistics.

Ilias Chalkidis, Nicolas Garneau, Catalina Goanta, Daniel Katz, and Anders Søgaard. 2023. LeXFiles and LegalLAMA: Facilitating English multinational legal language model development. In *Proceedings of the 61st Annual Meeting of the Association for Computational Linguistics (Volume 1: Long Papers)*, pages 15513–15535, Toronto, Canada. Association for Computational Linguistics.

Branden Chan, Stefan Schweter, and Timo Möller. 2020. German's next language model. In *Proceedings of the 28th International Conference on Computational Linguistics*, pages 6788–6796, Barcelona, Spain (Online). International Committee on Computational Linguistics.

Kun Chen. 2019. Information asymmetry in initial coin offerings (icos): Investigating the effects of multiple channel signals. *Electronic Commerce Research and Applications*, 36:100858.

Jacob Devlin, Ming-Wei Chang, Kenton Lee, and Kristina Toutanova. 2019. BERT: pre-training of deep bidirectional transformers for language understanding. In *Proceedings of the 2019 Conference of the North American Chapter of the Association for Computational Linguistics: Human Language Technologies, NAACL-HLT 2019, Minneapolis, MN, USA, June 2-7, 2019, Volume 1 (Long and Short Papers)*, pages 4171–4186. Association for Computational Linguistics.

Christian Fisch. 2019. Initial coin offerings (ICOs) to finance new ventures. *Journal of Business Venturing*, 34(1):1–22.

David Florysiak. 2022. Utility tokens, markets in crypto assets regulation (micar), and the costs of being public. *Markets in Crypto Assets Regulation (MiCAR), and the Costs of Being Public (December 7, 2022)*.

David Florysiak and Alexander Schandlbauer. 2022. Experts or charlatans? ICO analysts and white paper informativeness. *Journal of Banking & Finance*, 139(C).

Sumam Francis, Jordy Van Landeghem, and Marie-Francine Moens. 2019. Transfer learning for named entity recognition in financial and biomedical documents. *Information*, 10(8):248.

Neel Guha, Julian Nyarko, Daniel E. Ho, Christopher Ré, Adam Chilton, Aditya Narayana, Alex Chohlas-Wood, Austin Peters, Brandon Waldon, Daniel N. Rockmore, Diego Zambrano, Dmitry Talisman, Enam Hoque, Faiz Surani, Frank Fagan, Galit Sarfaty, Gregory M. Dickinson, Haggai Porat, Jason Hegland, Jessica Wu, Joe Nudell, Joel Niklaus, John Nay, Jonathan H. Choi, Kevin Tobia, Margaret Hagan, Megan Ma, Michael Livermore, Nikon Rasumov-Rahe, Nils Holzenberger, Noam Kolt, Peter Henderson, Sean Rehaag, Sharad Goel, Shang Gao, Spencer Williams, Sunny Gandhi, Tom Zur, Varun Iyer, and Zehua Li. 2023. Legalbench: A collaboratively built benchmark for measuring legal reasoning in large language models.

Kathleen Weiss Hanley and Gerard Hoberg. 2010. The information content of ipo prospectuses. *The Review of Financial Studies*, 23(7):2821–2864.

Peter Henderson*, Mark S. Krass*, Lucia Zheng, Neel Guha, Christopher D. Manning, Dan Jurafsky, and Daniel E. Ho. 2022. Pile of law: Learning responsible data filtering from the law and a 256gb open-source legal dataset.

Sabrina T Howell, Marina Niessner, and David Yermack. 2020. Initial coin offerings: Financing growth with cryptocurrency token sales. *The Review of Financial Studies*, 33(9):3925–3974.

Minqing Hu and Bing Liu. 2004. Mining opinion features in customer reviews. In *AAAI*, volume 4, pages 755–760.

Bedil Karimov and Piotr Wójcik. 2021. Identification of scams in initial coin offerings with machine learning. *Frontiers in Artificial Intelligence*, 4:718450.

Moniba Keymanesh, Micha Elsner, and Srinivasan Parthasarathy. 2021. Privacy policy question answering assistant: A query-guided extractive summarization approach. *arXiv preprint arXiv:2109.14638*.

Yiming Li, Baogang Wei, Yonghuai Liu, Liang Yao, Hui Chen, Jifang Yu, and Wenhao Zhu. 2018. Incorporating knowledge into neural network for text representation. *Expert Systems with Applications*, 96:103–114.

Daniel Liebau and Patrick Schueffel. 2019. Cryptocurrencies and icos: Are they scams? an empirical study. *An Empirical Study (January 23, 2019)*.

Yukun Liu, Jinfei Sheng, and Wanyi Wang. 2021. Technology and cryptocurrency valuation: Evidence from machine learning. In *Technology and Cryptocurrency Valuation: Evidence from Machine Learning: Liu, Yukun ajdnSheng, Jinfei ajd Wang, Wanyi*. SSRN.

Dimitris Mamakas, Petros Tsotsi, Ion Androutsopoulos, and Ilias Chalkidis. 2022. Processing long legal documents with pre-trained transformers: Modding LegalBERT and longformer. In *Proceedings of the Natural Legal Language Processing Workshop 2022*, pages 130–142, Abu Dhabi, United Arab Emirates (Hybrid). Association for Computational Linguistics.

Michele Meoli and Silvio Vismara. 2022. Machine-learning forecasting of successful icos. *Journal of Economics and Business*, 121:106071.

Tomas Mikolov, Ilya Sutskever, Kai Chen, Greg S Corrado, and Jeff Dean. 2013. Distributed representations of words and phrases and their compositionality. *Advances in neural information processing systems*, 26.

Paul P Momtaz. 2021. Entrepreneurial finance and moral hazard: evidence from token offerings. *Journal of Business Venturing*, 36(5):106001.

Andrew Morin, Marie Vasek, and Tyler Moore. 2021. Detecting text reuse in cryptocurrency whitepapers. In *2021 IEEE International Conference on Blockchain and Cryptocurrency (ICBC)*, pages 1–5. IEEE.

Joel Niklaus, Veton Matoshi, Matthias Stürmer, Ilias Chalkidis, and Daniel E. Ho. 2023. Multilegalpile: A 689gb multilingual legal corpus.

Thiago Dal Pont, Federico Galli, Andrea Loreggia, Giuseppe Pisano, Riccardo Rovatti, and Giovanni Sartor. 2023. Legal summarisation through llms: The prodigit project. *arXiv preprint arXiv:2308.04416*.

Abhilasha Ravichander, Alan W Black, Shomir Wilson, Thomas Norton, and Norman Sadeh. 2019. Question answering for privacy policies: Combining computational and legal perspectives. In *Proceedings of the 2019 Conference on Empirical Methods in Natural Language Processing and the 9th International Joint Conference on Natural Language Processing (EMNLP-IJCNLP)*, pages 4947–4958, Hong Kong, China. Association for Computational Linguistics.

Julio Cesar Salinas Alvarado, Karin Verspoor, and Timothy Baldwin. 2015. Domain adaption of named entity recognition to support credit risk assessment. In *Proceedings of the Australasian Language Technology Association Workshop 2015*, pages 84–90, Parramatta, Australia.

Shadi Samieifar and Dirk G Baur. 2021. Read me if you can! an analysis of ico white papers. *Finance Research Letters*, 38:101427.

Jared Sharpe and Keith Decker. 2022. Prospectus language and IPO performance. In *Proceedings of the Fourth Workshop on Financial Technology and Natural Language Processing (FinNLP)*, pages 154–162, Abu Dhabi, United Arab Emirates (Hybrid). Association for Computational Linguistics.

Răzvan-Alexandru Smădu, Ion-Robert Dinică, Andrei-Marius Avram, Dumitru-Clementin Cercel, Florin Pop, and Mihaela-Claudia Cercel. 2022. Legal named entity recognition with multi-task domain adaptation. In *Proceedings of the Natural Legal Language Processing Workshop 2022*, pages 305–321, Abu Dhabi, United Arab Emirates (Hybrid). Association for Computational Linguistics.

Nisan Stiennon, Long Ouyang, Jeffrey Wu, Daniel Ziegler, Ryan Lowe, Chelsea Voss, Alec Radford, Dario Amodei, and Paul F Christiano. 2020. Learning to summarize with human feedback. *Advances in Neural Information Processing Systems*, 33:3008–3021.

Jie Tao, Amit V Deokar, and Ashutosh Deshmukh. 2018. Analysing forward-looking statements in initial public offering prospectuses: a text analytics approach. *Journal of Business Analytics*, 1(1):54–70.

James Thewissen, Prabal Shrestha, Wouter Torsin, and Anna M Pastwa. 2022. Unpacking the black box of ico white papers: A topic modeling approach. *Journal of Corporate Finance*, 75:102225.

Jennifer Thewissen, James Thewissen, Wouter Torsin, and Özgür Arslan-Ayaydin. 2023. Linguistic errors and investment decisions: the case of ico white papers. *The European Journal of Finance*, 29(7):826–868.

Dietrich Trautmann, Alina Petrova, and Frank Schilder. 2022. Legal prompt engineering for multilingual legal judgement prediction. *arXiv preprint arXiv:2212.02199*.

Ashish Vaswani, Noam Shazeer, Niki Parmar, Jakob Uszkoreit, Llion Jones, Aidan N Gomez, Łukasz Kaiser, and Illia Polosukhin. 2017. Attention is all you need. *Advances in neural information processing systems*, 30.

Hongyang Yang, Xiao-Yang Liu, and Christina Dan Wang. 2023. Fingpt: Open-source financial large language models.

Ju-Chun Yen, Tawei Wang, and Yu-Hung Chen. 2021. Different is better: how unique initial coin offering language in white papers enhances success. *Accounting & Finance*, 61(4):5309–5340.

Fangyi Yu, Lee Quartey, and Frank Schilder. 2023. Exploring the effectiveness of prompt engineering for legal reasoning tasks. In *Findings of the Association for Computational Linguistics: ACL 2023*, pages 13582–13596, Toronto, Canada. Association for Computational Linguistics.

Shuyu Zhang, Walter Aerts, Liping Lu, and Huifeng Pan. 2019. Readability of token whitepaper and ico first-day return. *Economics Letters*, 180:58–61.

Haoxi Zhong, Chaojun Xiao, Cunchao Tu, Tianyang Zhang, Zhiyuan Liu, and Maosong Sun. 2020. How does NLP benefit legal system: A summary of legal artificial intelligence. In *Proceedings of the 58th Annual Meeting of the Association for Computational Linguistics*, pages 5218–5230, Online. Association for Computational Linguistics.

Frederike Zufall, Marius Hamacher, Katharina Kloppenborg, and Torsten Zesch. 2020. A legal approach to hate speech: Operationalizing the eu's legal framework against the expression of hatred as an nlp task.

A MiCAR Content Requirements Categories

A.1 Categories for Crypto Assets "other than"

Found in Annex I of the regulation.

- **Part A:** Information about the offeror or the person seeking admission to trading
- **Part B:** Information about the issuer, if different from the offeror or person seeking admission to trading
- **Part C:** Information about the operator of the trading platform in cases where it draws up the crypto asset white paper
- **Part D:** Information about the crypto asset project
- **Part E:** Information about the offer to the public of crypto assets or their admission to trading
- **Part F:** Information about the crypto assets
- **Part G:** Information on the rights and obligations attached to the crypto assets
- **Part H:** Information on the underlying technology
- **Part I:** Information on the risks

	Part A	Part B	Part C	Part D	Part E	Part F	Part G	Part H	Part I
Crypto "other than"	10	8	9	6	19	2	10	5	5

Table 4: Category count for each Part in the content requirements, for crypto assets "other than".

A.2 Categories for Asset-Referenced Tokens and E-money Tokens

Found in Annexes II and III of the regulation.

- **Part A:** Information about the issuer of the token
- **Part B:** Information about the token
- **Part C:** Information about the offer to the public of the token or its admission to trading
- **Part D:** Information on the rights and obligations attached to the token
- **Part E:** Information on the underlying technology
- **Part F:** Information on the risks
- **Part G:** Information on the reserve of assets

	Part A	Part B	Part C	Part D	Part E	Part F	Part G
Asset-referenced Tokens	12	5	15	17	5	6	5
E-money tokens	13	3	4	8	6	3	-

Table 5: Category count for each Part in the content requirements, for asset-referenced and e-money tokens.

Low-Resource Deontic Modality Classification in EU Legislation

Kristina Minkova **Shashank M Chakravarthy** **Gijs van Dijck**
Brightlands Institute for Smart Society & Maastricht Law and Tech Lab
Maastricht University, the Netherlands

Abstract

In law, it is important to distinguish between obligations, permissions, prohibitions, rights, and powers. These categories are called deontic modalities. This paper evaluates the performance of two deontic modality classification models, LEGAL-BERT and a Fusion model, in a low-resource setting. To create a generalized dataset for multi-class classification, we extracted random provisions from European Union (EU) legislation. By fine-tuning previously researched and published models, we evaluate their performance on our dataset against fusion models designed for low-resource text classification. We incorporate focal loss as an alternative for cross-entropy to tackle issues of class imbalance. The experiments indicate that the fusion model performs better for both balanced and imbalanced data with a macro F1-score of 0.61 for imbalanced data, 0.62 for balanced data, and 0.55 with focal loss for imbalanced data. When focusing on accuracy, our experiments indicate that the fusion model performs better with scores of 0.91 for imbalanced data, 0.78 for balanced data, and 0.90 for imbalanced data with focal loss.

1 Introduction

Obligations, permissions, prohibitions, rights, and/or powers are deontic modalities that commonly appear in legal documents. Precise identification of deontic modalities within legal texts holds importance for understanding and determining legal positions, responsibilities, and legal actions. It can contribute to automated compliance checking (Amor and Dimyadi, 2021; Dimyadi and Amor, 2013; Hashmi et al., 2018; Abdelmoneim, 2012), norm identification (Aires et al., 2017, 2019), and generation and analysis of legal policies and argumentation. Deontic modality classification (DMC) allows machines to efficiently interpret regulatory texts and easily adapt to changes in legislation (Abdelmoneim, 2012; Dias, 2022). Thus, by pursuing the objectives of this research, we aim to address the limitations of traditional human or rule-based approaches and manual processing by leveraging neural networks for DMC.

DMC is a Natural Language Processing (NLP) task, in which, given a text with *N* normative statements S=($s_1, s_2, s_3, ..., s_n$), a classifier is trained to label deontic modalities in each statement (Sun et al., 2023). Limited datasets are available for DMC. Waltl et al. (2017) constructed a dataset based on the German tenancy law containing 913 sentences in German. The Data Protection Regulation Compliance (DAPRECO) (Robaldo et al., 2020) dataset contains GDPR data represented in LegalRuleML (Athan et al., 2013). DAPRECO contains around 966 instances with 271 obligations, 76 permissions, and 619 constitutive rules. Rather than using or constructing a dataset that focuses on a particular legal topic or domain (e.g., GDPR, tenant law), we aimed to enhance the generalizability of the results by randomly extracting 200 provisions from EU regulations.

Prior DMC research that relied on machine learning is commonly based on annotated datasets with little or no information about the annotation process and the agreement scores. As far as agreement scores are reported, scores of between .74 and .82 are reported, which is higher than observed by Braun (2023), who, after examining 29 publications on legal datasets, found average agreement scores of .76 (Cohen's kappa), .675 (Fleiss' kappa), and .677 (Krippendorff's alpha), with the highest Krippendorff's alpha value not exceeding .78. Our research relies on an annotated dataset that resulted from multiple revision rounds by the annotators and an arbiter. We believe this approach yielded high-quality annotations, but with a limited number of annotated provisions. This is why we test fusion models, which are designed for low resource settings.

With this research on DMC, we aim to answer

Proceedings of the Natural Legal Language Processing Workshop 2023, pages 149–158
December 7, 2023

the following questions -

1. Does a fusion model outperform a BERT-based model? (RQ1)

2. Which strategy (imbalanced dataset, balanced dataset, focal loss) provides the best results for the BERT-based and the fusion model? (RQ2)

To answer these questions, we explore a model of contrasting design - a pretrained language model on EUR-Lex data called LEGAL-BERT - and a fusion model that is smaller, not pre-trained, and designed specifically for low-resource text classification. The models are experimented on a manually curated multi-class sentence level classification data, with the help of three annotators, preserving different interpretations of the law and the genuine disagreement regarding the deontic class.

We report on the experiment setup, the various results, highlight the future opportunities for improving the models in order to give more insight on the challenges associated with low-resource DMC in EU legislation, and report the limitations of the proposed models.

2 Related Work

DMC has traditionally relied on rule-based approaches, resulting in a labor-intensive process prone to human biases (Wyner and Peters, 2011). Various studies have been conducted that have adopted machine-learning approaches to automatically detect deontic clauses. Sun et al. (2023) proposed a new method for BERT fine-tuning termed as DeonticBERT, classifying obligations, permissions, prohibitions, and other sentences from German tenancy law and Chinese social security policies, reported F1 scores of .89 (DeonticBERT) and .94 (BiLSTM). Liga and Palmirani (2022) found scores of .82 (obligations), .55 (permissions), .89 (constitutive rules) for the classification of obligations, permissions, and constitutive rules in 707 GDPR provisions by performing transfer learning based on BERT by leveraging the symbolic information of LegalXML formats. Bakker et al. (2022), focusing on Dutch legislation, came to .52 and .74 accuracy scores, by describing a method, by using rule-based and transformed based approach, to extract structured representations in the FLINT language. Waltl et al. (2019) and Glaser et al. (2018) evaluated a rule-based & machine learning approach, reporting an average of F1 scores of .83 when for German tenancy law, among other things, classifying duties, permissions, and prohibitions. Joshi et al. (2021) found .90 precision and recall scores, with BERT, for the classification of obligations, permissions, and prohibitions in contractual provisions. Shaghaghian et al. (2020), also focusing on contracts, achieved F1 scores of .92 for the classification of obligations by exploring various language, whereas Chalkidis et al. (2018) found F1 scores of .90 and .84 for obligations and prohibitions, respectively, in contractual provisions by utilising hierarchical BiLSTM. Dragoni et al. (2018), remarkably, reported precision scores of between .96 and 1.00 by combining various Natural Language Processing techniques towards extraction of obligations, permissions, and prohibitions in two Australian laws. Various other studies may be included that focus on classifying legal rules, including O'Neill et al. (2017), Waltl et al. (2017), Peters and Wyner (2016), Gao and Singh (2014), Francesconi (2010), de Maat et al. (2010), Francesconi and Passerini (2007), and Biagioli et al. (2005). A more complete and detailed overview will be available at van Dijck et al. (in preparation).

Our study adds to previous studies by comparing different approaches, including fusion-models for low resource settings, using focal loss to address class imbalance, performing multi-class classification based on randomly selected statutory provisions from EU regulations, and building and testing models for annotators separately due to genuine disagreement amongst the annotators.

3 Methods

The architecture and parameters of both LEGAL-BERT and the fusion model were optimized according to their performance on the data from one of the three annotators. Focal loss was used to address significant class imbalance by providing more weight to difficult-to-classify examples and less weight to examples in the majority class(es). Furthermore, the final fine-tuned versions of both models were trained separately on the three different datasets (one per annotator) for multi-class classification, where the full provisions were split into separate sentences or clauses for simplicity and where the possible labels were 'Obligation','Permission', 'Power', 'Prohibition', 'Right' or 'None' (i.e., non-annotated text).

3.1 Data Collection and Annotation

To cater to diverse domains within EU legislation in English without utilizing any translation services, we constructed a dataset by extracting 200 provisions from EU law[1]. To extract these 200 unique diverse provisions, an extractor was used by first querying the SPARQL endpoint provided by EU publications office[2] for regulations that are in force and not repealed. The random selection of articles of EU regulations was expected to enhance the generalizability of the results, at least with respect to EU legislation. On obtaining the provisions, three annotators annotated text as 'Obligation', 'Permission', 'Power', 'Prohibition', 'Right', or no annotation. The annotators were law students with different nationalities who also had received basic training in NLP. They engaged more than three months in over ten practice rounds to familiarize themselves with the annotation guidelines. Subsequently, the annotators labeled the same provisions and had the possibility to revise annotations after receiving feedback on where they disagreed. An arbiter corrected the annotations not made in accordance with the annotation guidelines. The agreement scores increased at each step. The annotation process and inter-rater and intra-rater agreement scores are reported elsewhere (van Dijck et al., in preparation). The annotation guidelines will be made available at `https://doi.org/10.34894/ZJJ`.

The possibility of genuine disagreement is the reason why we trained models for the three annotators separately. The first annotator, A1, made 567 annotations, 445 of which were obligations, 83 permissions, 17 prohibitions, 13 rights, and 9 power sentences. A2 annotated 561 sentences - 436 obligations, 77 permissions, 16 prohibitions, 16 rights, and 16 power sentences. A3 labeled 566 sentences - 436 obligations, 79 permissions, 16 prohibitions, 15 rights, and 20 power sentences. There were also 225 non-annotations, which were shuffled and split equally into three separate sets and added to the datasets of each annotator in order to learn the models to distinguish deontic and non-deontic sentences. Normal data distribution and neutral skewness (skewness between -0.05 and 0.05) were preferred as they generally lower the misclassification rate and bias of classifiers (Trafimow et al., 2018; Larasati et al., 2019; Liu et al., 2019). Since the datasets were highly skewed towards the 'Obligation' class (> 2 right-skewness), we undersampled (randomly) the obligations so that each dataset contained less than 100 instances of obligations, thus, reducing the skewness to around 1. The resulting balanced datasets were stored separately in order to investigate the impact of the class imbalance on the classifiers. The class distribution of each dataset is provided in Table 1.

Class	A1	A2	A3
None	75	75	75
Obligation	444 **(88)**	435 **(79)**	435 **(82)**
Permission	83	77	79
Power	9	16	20
Prohibition	17	16	16
Right	13	16	15
Skewness	2.18 **(0.99)**	2.11 **(0.95)**	2.05 **(0.93)**
Total	641 **(285)**	635 **(279)**	640 **(287)**

Table 1: Class distribution of the data per annotator (the number of instances after the sample reduction is given in parentheses)

The three datasets annotated by each of the annotators (A1, A2, A3) are referred to as A1, A2 and A3 respectively in further sections of the paper.

3.2 Classification Models

LEGAL-BERT. LEGAL-BERT (Chalkidis et al., 2020) is a variation of the BERT model (Devlin et al., 2018), having the same architecture as BERT but pre-trained from scratch on large corpora of legal texts in order to learn the domain-specific vocabulary and deeper semantics. The pre-training data includes EU and UK legislation, European Court of Justice (ECJ/CJEU) cases, European Court of Human Rights (ECtHR) cases, US court cases, and US contracts (Chalkidis et al., 2020). This in-domain knowledge of LEGAL-BERT has shown to earn significant performance gains over the fine-tuned BERT model, especially for more complex tasks such as multi-label classification (Chalkidis et al., 2020). Furthermore, Liga and Palmirani (2022) conducted experiments on deontic rule classification considering obligation, permission, constitutive and non-rule samples, which showed that, even on class-unbalanced and limited data (n = 831), the weight average accuracy of 81% produced by LEGAL-BERT outperforms a BERT

[1] `https://eur-lex.europa.eu/homepage.html` visited on September 20, 2023

[2] `http://publications.europa.eu/webapi/rdf/sparql` visited on September 20, 2023

model. We use EURLEX-BERT-BASE (uncased), trained on EUR-Lex data, for testing on our dataset.

According to Devlin et al. (2018), BERT models can be fine-tuned for downstream tasks by adding a dropout layer with a ratio of 0.1 and a classification layer of size 768. Chalkidis et al. (2020), on the other hand, suggested increasing the ratio to 0.2 for LEGAL-BERT, whereas Liga and Palmirani (2022) added two linear layers on top of the pretrained model, each activated using `ReLu` and having a dropout of 0.2, and a final output layer, activated with a `softmax` function. These three fine-tuning strategies were evaluated and compared based their performance on the data from annotator A1.

In terms of hyper-parameters, our initial experiments using the values (learning rate of 1e-5 and drop-out rate of 0.2) suggested by Chalkidis et al. (2020) indicated that there is overfitting. A batch size of 32 was unsuitable for our GPU resources and the model continued to underfit at 4 epochs. Thus, we optimized our model for learning rate $\in \{4e-6, 6e-6, 8e-6, 1e-5, 2e-5\}$, batch size $\in \{4, 8, 16\}$, and epochs $\in \{5, 6\}$. The LEGAL-BERT model was trained using Cross-Entropy (CE) loss and Adam optimizer. Given the class imbalance of the data (Lin et al., 2017), Focal loss (FL) with $\gamma \in \{0, 5\}$ with step increments of 1 was also investigated (Cao et al., 2022).

Fusion model. We investigated the fusion model architecture proposed by Maheen et al. (2022), which aims to utilize the strengths of CNN and (Bi)LSTM architectures - the spatial invariance of CNNs and the long-term dependencies capturing of RNNs, while minimizing the effect of their respective weaknesses – the limited global context and vanishing gradient. CNN layers slide a fixed-size window of length (n) over the word embeddings to extract local features, which are subsequently fed into the (Bi)LSTM layers to learn the sequential dependence of the words. The baseline model had the following structure:

CNN + Attention layer + BiLSTM + CNN

Fine-tuning efforts involved testing different fusion chain configurations by adding/removing layers and/or replacing BiLSTM with LSTM layers and searching over different layer sizes, as recommended by Maheen et al. (2022) and presented in Table 2. This was implemented by using `RandomSearch` from the `keras-tuner` library on 10 trials.

Layer	Minimal value	Maximum value	Step size
`CNN_1`	16	96	16
`CNN_1 dropout`	0.1	0.5	0.1
`Attention layer`	16	128	16
`(Bi)LSTM`	32	256	32
`(Bi)LSTM dropout`	0.1	0.5	0.1
`CNN_2`	32	256	32
`CNN_2 dropout`	0.1	0.5	0.1
`CNN_3`	32	256	32
`CNN_3 dropout`	0.1	0.5	0.1

Table 2: Layer sizes of the fusion chain

The investigated fusion variants were as follows:
1. CNN + A + BiLSTM
2. CNN + A + BiLSTM + CNN
3. CNN + A + BiLSTM + CNN + CNN
4. CNN + A + BiLSTM + CNN + BiLSTM
5. CNN + A + LSTM
6. CNN + A + LSTM + CNN
7. CNN + A + LSTM + CNN + CNN
8. CNN + A + LSTM + CNN + LSTM

where *A* stands for attention vector.

The fusion models were trained using Sparse Categorical Loss and Adam optimizer with a learning rate in the range of 2e-5 to 1e-3, following a step size of 2e-5 over 20 epochs, as suggested by Maheen et al. (2022). Preliminary tests showed that in our case the fusion performs best with smaller batch sizes (than the proposed 50), thus, we used a batch size of 4. Similar to LEGAL-BERT, we also experimented with focal loss in the fusion models. Early stopping was employed as a regularization technique with patience of 4 epochs.

4 Results

4.1 LEGAL-BERT

The best fine-tuning strategy for LEGAL-BERT was first identified. LEGAL-BERT was trained on all three available datasets (A1, A2, and A3) and its variations (imbalanced, balanced, and focal loss for imbalanced data) with the available fine-tuning strategies (namely Devlin et al. (2018)/ Chalkidis et al. (2020)/ Liga and Palmirani (2022)).

Table 3 shows that the strategy of Devlin et al. (2018) performed best across all scenarios (imbalanced, balanced, focal loss for imbalanced data) for the A1 dataset, whereas regularization of Chalkidis et al. (2020) and the additional neural layers of Liga and Palmirani (2022) had a negative impact. However, the latter two approaches benefited from using focal loss (2% increase in accuracy).

For A2 and A3, although the models yielded high accuracy, the results surpassed their respective training performance, indicating a possible prob-

Annotator	Imbalanced data	Balanced data	Focal loss
A1	**0.902**/ 0.870/ 0.850	**0.783**/ 0.675/ 0.518	**0.902**/ 0.891/ 0.876
A2*	**0.780**/ 0.759/ 0.770	0.789/ **0.800**/ 0.656	0.832/ 0.759/ **0.843**
A3*	0.865/ 0.859/ **0.891**	**0.767**/ **0.767**/ 0.522	0.818/ **0.891**/ 0.807

Table 3: Accuracy results for the datasets of different annotators according to the LEGAL-BERT fine-tuning architecture of Devlin et al. (2018)/ Chalkidis et al. (2020)/ Liga and Palmirani (2022) (highest results for each annotator are in bold); * Models trained on datasets from this annotator yield a test accuracy higher than their training accuracy

Epochs	Batch size	Lr = 4e-6	Lr = 6e-6	Lr = 8e-6	Lr = 1e-5	Lr = 2e-5
5	4	0.876	0.860	0.876	0.881	**0.902**
	8	0.876	0.876	0.876	0.870	0.850
	16	0.813	0.834	0.850	0.845	0.870
6	4	0.813	0.850	0.803	0.881	0.876
	8	0.839	0.881	0.865	0.870	0.865
	16	0.575	0.767	0.860	0.865	0.860

Table 4: Test accuracy results of the baseline LEGAL-BERT, dropout = 0.1, for different hyperparameters

lem in the training process. Even after balancing, the data had a moderate skewness of 0.9-1%, which might have caused the easily classifiable examples in the data to be allocated to the test set during the train/test split. Therefore, the performance of the LEGAL-BERT finetuned according to Devlin et al. (2018) and trained on data from A1 is considered further and evaluated.

The results of the experiments with various hyperparameters, for A1 dataset, is shown in Table 4.

Focal loss. The accuracy obtained with LEGAL-BERT could have been caused by the highly skewed dataset (i.e., a high number of instances with 'obligation' class, as seen in Table 1). To cater to this imbalanced data, the fine-tuning strategy was further investigated by replacing the 'Cross Entropy' loss function with 'Focal loss' for imbalanced A1 data. For focal loss, a gamma value of 2 was chosen. The accuracy of the model trained on the imbalanced data from A1 remained the same (0.9) and decreased with other gamma values (Table 5).

	LEGAL-BERT	FUSION
$\gamma = 0$	0.902	0.896
$\gamma = 1$	0.870	0.876
$\gamma = 2$	**0.902**	0.870
$\gamma = 3$	0.876	0.876
$\gamma = 4$	0.891	0.865
$\gamma = 5$	0.870	**0.891**

Table 5: Performance (accuracy) of LEGAL-BERT and CNN + attention + BiLSTM + CNN trained on the data from A1 with *Focal Loss* depending on the different γ values; FL is equivalent to CE for $\gamma = 0$

Class imbalance. With the A1 dataset, LEGAL-BERT performed with an average macro F1-score of 0.44 for all variations of data (imbalanced, balanced, focal loss with imbalanced data) (Table 6).

In Table 6, it can be observed that balancing the classes (manually) significantly lowered the precision of the LEGAL-BERT model (30% decrease) when recognizing the 'obligation' class. It seemingly drew the attention of the model towards the permissions and the non-deontic sentences and minimizes the false positives of these classes (around 10% higher recall than the imbalanced data). Focal loss increased the F1-score on the 'Permission' class by 6% but decreased for the 'None' class.

Furthermore, Table 6 shows that the 'Power', 'Prohibition', and 'Right' classes were completely unrecognized by the model. Even though focal loss is intended to dynamically scale the loss function in favor of minority classes, samples below 20 proved insufficient for learning the specific patterns and expressions for each label. The striking difference of 30%-40% between the macro and weighted average accuracy also indicates that the class imbalance had a considerable impact on the models' performance.

4.2 Fusion Model

Considering the architecture difference between LEGAL-BERT and fusion model, we start by identifying which fusion model architecture provided a high accuracy. According to the results in Table 7, although the performance difference between architectures was minor, the models that had the structure CNN + A + BiLSTM, with or without a second CNN layer, produced the highest accuracy -

	Precision	Recall	F1-score	Support
None	0.95/ 0.92/ 0.90	0.90/ 1.00/ 0.90	0.92/ 0.96/ 0.90	20/ 23/ 20
Obligation	0.91/ 0.61/ 0.92	0.99/ 0.94/ 0.98	0.95/ 0.74/ 0.95	141/ 18/ 141
Permission	0.80/ 0.83/ 0.82	0.80/ 0.93/ 0.90	0.80/ 0.88/ 0.86	20/ 27/20
Power	0./ 0./ 0.	0./ 0./ 0.	0./ 0./ 0.	2/ 2/2
Prohibition	0./ 0./ 0.	0./ 0./ 0.	0./ 0./ 0.	6/ 7/ 6
Right	0./ 0./ 0.	0./ 0./ 0.	0./ 0./ 0.	4/ 6/ 4
Accuracy			0.90/ 0.78/ 0.90	193/ 83/ 193
Macro avg	0.44/ 0.39/ 0.44	0.45/ 0.48/ 0.46	**0.45/ 0.43/ 0.45**	193/ 83/ 193
Weighted avg	0.85/ 0.66/ 0.85	0.90/ 0.78/ 0.90	0.87/ 0.71/ 0.87	193/ 83/ 193

Table 6: Classification report of the best-performing LEGAL-BERT models (dropout = 0.1) trained on the A1 dataset **(imbalanced/ balanced/ focal loss)**

89.6%.

Fusion architecture	Test accuracy
CNN + A + BiLSTM	**0.896**
CNN + A + BiLSTM + CNN	**0.896**
CNN + A + BiLSTM + CNN + CNN	0.886
CNN + A + BiLSTM + CNN + BiLSTM	0.876
CNN + A + LSTM	0.886
CNN + A + LSTM + CNN	0.886
CNN + A + LSTM + CNN + CNN	0.886
CNN + A + LSTM + CNN + LSTM	0.876

Table 7: Performance of different fusion architectures

Annotator	Imbalanced data	Balanced data	Focal loss
A1	0.896/ **0.904**	0.678/ **0.826**	0.880/ **0.886**
A2	0.829/ **0.896**	0.764/ **0.809**	0.808/ **0.896**
A3	**0.881**/ 0.871	0.756/ **0.814**	0.850/ **0.871**

Table 8: Evaluation results (accuracy) for the datasets of different annotators for 'CNN + A + BiLSTM' / 'CNN + A + BiLSTM + CNN' (highest results for each annotator are in bold)

The specific layer sizes and dropout ratios determined by the RandomSearch were: CNN_1 size = 48 (dropout = 0.1), attention layer size = 80, BiLSTM_1 size = 256 (dropout = 0.2), CNN_2 size = 224 (dropout = 0.3) and learning rate = 9.4e-4. These parameters were used in the subsequent analysis. Although the two fusion architectures performed similarly, extracting deeper features with an additional CNN layer proved to be beneficial, except for the imbalanced data of A3 (Table 8). There is no significant difference for the annotators, except for the fact that models trained on data from A1 overall achieved the highest accuracy results. Balancing the obligations class on average caused around a 10% decrease, whereas focal loss resulted in an approximately 1.4% decrease across datasets and model architectures.

Focal loss. Table 5 reveals that focal loss did not benefit the fusion model. However, using $\gamma = 5$, the prediction accuracy was only 0.05 lower than the benchmark. Focal loss did not make any significant difference in the overall classification performance but it did eliminate the model's responsiveness to the 'Right' label as seen in Table 9.

Class imbalance. Table 9 provides more insight into the classification metrics per label for A1. In general, the majority classes - 'None', 'Obligation', and 'Permission', were correctly classified by the models, trained on the imbalanced (with or without focal loss) and the balanced data from A1. On the other hand, due to their insufficient sample quantity, power statements were completely mislabeled.

In contrast to LEGAL-BERT, which was able to recognize only half of the labels, the fusion model performed much better achieving an average macro F1-score of 0.6 across A1 dataset variations. For smaller classes like 'Prohibition' and 'Right', the fusion model achieved 0.67 and 0.33 F1-scores respectively with the imbalanced data. The balancing of the obligations class yielded an improvement in the precision and recall of the classes 'None' and 'Prohibition' (10% increase), yet it proved detrimental for the remaining classes.

4.3 Error Analysis

The LEGAL-BERT and fusion model showed considerable overlap in the statements that were misclassified: 12/15 of the misclassified statements by the fusion model were also misclassified by the LEGAL-BERT-based model, whereas 12/19 of the misclassified statements by LEGAL-BERT overlapped with the misclassifications by the fusion model. Table 10 shows how the predicted labels differed for the imbalanced dataset.

Some misclassifications could, particularly in the fusion model, be considered genuine disagreement. For instance, the statement 'the electronic complaint form to be submitted to the odr platform shall be accessible to (...)' (predicted label

	Precision	Recall	F1-score	Support
None	0.76/ 0.91/ 0.80	0.84/ 0.95/ 0.84	0.80/ 0.93/ 0.82	19/ 22/ 19
Obligation	0.95/ 0.97/ 0.93	0.95/ 0.88/ 0.96	0.95/ 0.92/ 0.95	133/ 32/ 133
Permission	0.84/ 0.67/ 0.84	0.96/ 0.95/ 0.93	0.90/ 0.78/ 0.88	28/ 19/ 28
Power	0./ 0. / 0.	0./ 0./ 0.	0./ 0./ 0.	2/ 3/ 2
Prohibition	0.80/ 1.00/ 0.80	0.57/ 0.67/ 0.57	0.67/ 0.80/ 0.67	7/ 3/ 7
Right	0.50/ 0.50/ 0.	0.25/ 0.20/ 0.	0.33/ 0.29/ 0.	4/ 5/ 4
Accuracy			0.91/ 0.83/ 0.90	193/ 84/ 193
Macro avg	0.64/ 0.67/ 0.56	0.60/ 0.61/ 0.55	**0.61/ 0.62/ 0.55**	193/ 84/
Weighted avg	0.89/ 0.82/ 0.87	0.91/ 0.83/ 0.90	0.90/ 0.82/ 0.89	193/ 84/ 193

Table 9: Classification report of the CNN + A + BiLSTM + CNN trained on the data from annotator A1 **(imbalanced/ balanced/ focal loss)**

(fusion) = obligation, true label = right) may be considered a right (entitlement), yet it can also be interpreted as an obligation if it is read as 'shall be *made* accessible'. Sometimes, misclassifications were observed in statements with important terms in the legislative provisions that the model might not have been trained on. For instance, the combination 'only may' in 'only activities linked to the closure of the programme may be carried out between January and September' indicates an obligation (true label) whereas the predicted label by the fusion model was a permission, which would have been correct if the sentence would not have contained the word 'only'. This type of misclassification can perhaps be fixed with additional, more diverse training data. Other misclassifications did not have obvious explanations. For instance, the sentence 'list of parts or equipment which may pose a serious risk to (...) is set out in annex x to this regulation' (predicted label (fusion/LEGAL-BERT) = obligation/permission, true label = none) clearly does not contain an obligation.

Fusion		*LEGAL-BERT*	
Predicted label	*True label*	*Predicted label*	*True label*
None	Obligation	None	Prohibition
None	Prohibition	Obligation	None
Obligation	None	Obligation	Permission
Obligation	None	Obligation	Permission
Obligation	None	Obligation	Permission
Obligation	Right	Obligation	Permission
Obligation	Right	Obligation	Prohibition
Obligation	Right	Obligation	Prohibition
Obligation	Right	Obligation	Prohibition
Obligation	Prohibition	Obligation	Prohibition
Permission	Obligation	Obligation	Prohibition
Permission	None	Obligation	Right
Permission	Power	Obligation	Right
Permission	Power	Obligation	Right
Prohibition	Permission	Obligation	Right
		Permission	None
		Permission	Obligation
		Permission	Power
		Permission	Power

Table 10: Misclassfications

5 Discussion

RQ1: Does a fusion model outperform a BERT-based model? When evaluating with macro F1-scores, it is seen that the fusion model outperforms LEGAL-BERT significantly. The similar results for the three annotators indicate that the models tested were adaptive to differences in input. Overall, the findings suggest that fusion models might be a suitable approach for testing DMC in a low-resource setting.

RQ2: Which strategy (imbalanced dataset, balanced dataset, focal loss) provides the best results for the BERT-based and the fusion model? LEGAL-BERT performed with a macro F1-score of 0.45 for imbalanced data (with obligations having higher instances), 0.43 on balanced data, and 0.45 with focal loss as loss function for imbalanced data. In comparison, the fusion model performed with a macro F1-score of 0.61 for imbalanced data, 0.62 with balanced data, and 0.55 with focal loss as loss function for imbalanced data.

As the data was skewed towards the 'Obligation' class, evaluating with macro F1-score highlights the performance of the model per available class. The fusion model performed better with an increase of 10-20% with macro F1-scores across variations of the dataset when compared to LEGAL-BERT. LEGAL-BERT saw a decrease in performance when the data was more balanced, whereas the fusion model performed consistently well across dataset variations.

It should be noted that the fusion model did not require any pre-training on large text corpora. Moreover, the fusion model exhibited a lower discrepancy between the macro and weighted average accuracy, indicating its higher resilience to class imbalance and thus making it more suitable for low-resource settings. Solely evaluating with accuracy can misrepresent the true performance of a model.

6 Conclusion and Future Work

Previous research has tested models that were trained on large corpus or fine-tuned on datasets of a single domain with data resources ranging from 500 to 1000 instances to perform DMC. With the annotation process being time-consuming, we relied on a carefully annotated dataset of 200 legislative provisions of EU regulations that were randomly sampled and that consequently covered a variety of legal topics. Legal text can be interpreted in multiple ways, and instead of curating a single dataset based on Inter-Rater Reliability (IRR) scores, we trained multiple models for each annotator to understand the variation in model behavior.

We tested previously researched BERT-based models with low resources and evaluated them against a fusion model designed for low-resource text classification. LEGAL-BERT model and other variations through fine-tuning under performed for imbalanced data and further dropped in performance with balanced data despite the large corpora of EU Legislative text utilized for pre-training. On the other hand, a fusion model ('CNN + A + BiLSTM + CNN' variation) designed for low-resource text classification performed consistently well with both balanced and imbalanced data without the need for any pre-training on large corpora of text.

Future activities may focus on the challenging task of creating representative datasets that include more powers, prohibitions, and rights while maintaining a sufficient number of obligations and permissions. Future research may also include exploring and testing approaches that handle differences in annotations between annotators as a result of genuine disagreement (as opposed to disagreements due to mistakes). In this respect, we plan to explore the ensemble approach for models trained on each annotator to take into consideration the disagreements between annotators.

7 Ethical Implications and Limitations

The random sampling benefited the generalizability of the results yet resulted in class imbalance, as the dataset contained many obligations but few powers, prohibitions, and rights.

No ethical concerns were identified. The models were trained on publicly available data (EU legislation) and no personal information (names) of the annotators was included in any model training.

Acknowledgments. We would like to thank the anonymous reviewers for their helpful comments.

Reproducibility. The data and code will be made available at `https://doi.org/10.34894/HQ8LIH`, the annotation guidelines at `https://doi.org/10.34894/ZJJ`.

Author Contributions. Research design, SMC&KM; Data collection, GvD; Analysis, KM; writing—original draft preparation, KM&SMC&GvD; writing—review and editing, SMC&GvD&KM; supervision, SMC&GD; funding acquisition, GvD. All authors have read and agreed to the published version of the manuscript.

Funding. This research was funded by the European Union H2020 Research and Innovation Program under Grant Agreement No. 101006828—Flying Forward 2020.

References

Dareen Abdelmoneim. 2012. Semantic deontic modeling and text classification for supporting automated environmental compliance checking in construction.

João Paulo Aires, Roger Granada, Juarez Monteiro, Rodrigo Barros, and Felipe Meneguzzi. 2019. Classification of Contractual Conflicts via Learning of Semantic Representations. pages 1764–1766.

João Paulo Aires, Daniele Evelin Viana Pinheiro, Vera Lúcia Antunes De Lima, and Felipe Meneguzzi. 2017. Norm conflict identification in contracts. *Artificial Intelligence and Law*, 25(4):397–428.

Robert Amor and Johannes Dimyadi. 2021. The promise of automated compliance checking. *Developments in the built environment*, 5:100039.

Tara Athan, Harold Boley, Guido Governatori, Monica Palmirani, Adrian Paschke, and Adam Wyner. 2013. Oasis legalruleml. In *proceedings of the fourteenth international conference on artificial intelligence and law*, pages 3–12.

Roos Bakker, Romy A.N. van Drie, Maaike de Boer, Robert van Doesburg, and Tom van Engers. 2022). Semantic role labelling for dutch law texts. Proceedings of the Thirteenth Language Resources and Evaluation Conference, pages 448–457. European Language Resources Association.

C. Biagioli, E. Francesconi, A. Passerini, S. Montemagni, and C. Soria. 2005. Automatic semantics extraction in law documents. page 133–140. Association for Computing Machinery.

Daniel Braun. 2023. I beg to differ: how disagreement is handled in the annotation of legal machine learning data sets. *Artificial Intelligence and Law*.

Lu Cao, Xinyue Liu, and Hong Shen. 2022. *Adaptable focal loss for imbalanced text classification*.

Ilias Chalkidis, Ion Androutsopoulos, and Achilleas Michos. 2018. Obligation and Prohibition Extraction Using Hierarchical RNNs. *Proceedings of the 56th Annual Meeting of the Association for Computational Linguistics (Volume 2: Short Papers)*.

Ilias Chalkidis, Manos Fergadiotis, Prodromos Malakasiotis, Nikolaos Aletras, and Ion Androutsopoulos. 2020. LEGAL-BERT: The Muppets straight out of Law School.

Emile de Maat, Kai Krabben, and Radboud Winkels. 2010. Machine learning versus knowledge based classification of legal texts. In *Proceedings of the 2010 conference on Legal Knowledge and Information Systems: JURIX 2010: The Twenty-Third Annual Conference*, page 87–96. IOS Press.

Jacob Devlin, Ming-Wei Chang, Kenton Lee, and Kristina Toutanova. 2018. BERT: Pre-training of Deep Bidirectional Transformers for Language Understanding.

João Dias. 2022. State of the Art in Artificial Intelligence applied to the Legal Domain.

Johannes Dimyadi and Robert Amor. 2013. Automated Building Code Compliance Checking - Where is it at? *ResearchGate*.

Mauro Dragoni, Serena Villata, Williams Rizzi, and Guido Governatori. 2018. Combining natural language processing approaches for rule extraction from legal documents. In *AI Approaches to the Complexity of Legal Systems*, pages 287–300. Springer International Publishing.

E. Francesconi and A. Passerini. 2007. Automatic classification of provisions in legislative texts. *Artificial Intelligence and Law*, 15(1):1–17.

Enrico Francesconi. 2010. Legal rules learning based on a semantic model for legislation. In *Proceedings of the LREC 2010 Workshop on the Semantic Processing of Legal Texts (SPLeT-2010)*.

Xibin Gao and Munindar P. Singh. 2014. Extracting normative relationships from business contracts. page 101–108. International Foundation for Autonomous Agents and Multiagent Systems.

Ingo Glaser, Elena Scepankova, and Florian Matthes. 2018. Classifying semantic types of legal sentences: Portability of machine learning models. In *Jurix*, Frontiers in Artificial Intelligence and Applications., pages 61–70.

Mustafa Hashmi, Pompeu Casanovas, and Louis De Koker. 2018. Legal Compliance Through Design: Preliminary Results of a Literature Survey. *ResearchGate*.

Vivek Joshi, Preethu Rose Anish, and Smita Ghaisas. 2021. Domain adaptation for an automated classification of deontic modalities in software engineering contracts. page 1275–1280. Association for Computing Machinery.

Aisyah Larasati, Apif M. Hajji, and Anik Dwiastuti. 2019. The relationship between data skewness and accuracy of Artificial Neural Network predictive model. *IOP conference series*, 523(1):012070.

Davide Liga and Monica Palmirani. 2022. *Transfer Learning for Deontic Rule Classification: The Case Study of the GDPR*.

Tsung-Yi Lin, Priya Goyal, Ross Girshick, Kaiming He, and Piotr Dollár. 2017. Focal loss for dense object detection. In *2017 IEEE International Conference on Computer Vision (ICCV)*, pages 2999–3007.

Tianyu Liu, Wenhui Fan, and Cheng Wu. 2019. A hybrid machine learning approach to cerebral stroke prediction based on imbalanced medical dataset. *Artificial Intelligence in Medicine*, 101:101723.

Syed Mustavi Maheen, Moshiur Rahman Faisal, Md. Rafakat Rahman Karim, and Md. Shahriar. 2022. Alternative non-BERT model choices for the textual classification in low-resource languages and environments.

James O'Neill, Paul Buitelaar, Cecile Robin, and Leona O' Brien. 2017. Classifying sentential modality in legal language: a use case in financial regulations, acts and directives. page 159–168. Association for Computing Machinery.

Wim Peters and Adam Wyner. 2016. Legal text interpretation: Identifying hohfeldian relations from text. Proceedings of the Tenth International Conference on Language Resources and Evaluation (LREC'16), pages 379–384. European Language Resources Association (ELRA).

Livio Robaldo, Cesare Bartolini, Monica Palmirani, Arianna Rossi, Michele Martoni, and Gabriele Lenzini. 2020. Formalizing gdpr provisions in reified i/o logic: the dapreco knowledge base. *Journal of Logic, Language and Information*, 29:401–449.

S. Shaghaghian, L. Y. Feng, B. Jafarpour, and N. Pogrebnyakov. 2020. Customizing contextualized language models for legal document reviews. In *2020 IEEE International Conference on Big Data (Big Data)*, pages 2139–2148.

Jingyun Sun, Shaobin Huang, and Chi Wei. 2023. A BERT-based deontic logic learner. *Information Processing & Management*, 60(4):103374.

David Trafimow, Tonghui Wang, and Cong Wang. 2018. From a sampling precision perspective, skewness is a friend and not an enemy! *Educational and Psychological Measurement*, 79(1):129–150.

Gijs van Dijck, Carlos Aguilera, and Shashank M Chakravarthy. in preparation. (Dis)agreement and the annotation of EU legislative provisions.

Bernhard Waltl, Georg Bonczek, Elena Scepankova, and Florian Matthes. 2019. Semantic types of legal norms in german laws: classification and analysis using local linear explanations. *Artificial Intelligence and Law*, 27(1):43–71.

Bernhard Waltl, Johannes Muhr, Ingo Glaser, Georg Bonczek, Elena Scepankova, and Florian Matthes. 2017. Classifying legal norms with active machine learning. In *JURIX*, pages 11–20.

Adam Wyner and Wim Peters. 2011. On rule extraction from regulations. *International Conference on Legal Knowledge and Information Systems*, pages 113–122.

Automatic Anonymization of Swiss Federal Supreme Court Rulings

Joel Niklaus[1,2,3 *] **Robin Mamié**[4 *]

Matthias Stürmer[1,2] **Daniel Brunner**[4] **Marcel Gygli**[2]

[1]University of Bern [2]Bern University of Applied Sciences
[3]Stanford University [4]Swiss Federal Supreme Court

Abstract

Releasing court decisions to the public relies on proper anonymization to protect all involved parties, where necessary. The Swiss Federal Supreme Court relies on an existing system that combines different traditional computational methods with human experts. In this work, we enhance the existing anonymization software using a large dataset annotated with entities to be anonymized. We compared BERT-based models with models pre-trained on in-domain data. Our results show that using in-domain data to pre-train the models further improves the F1-score by more than 5% compared to existing models. Our work demonstrates that combining existing anonymization methods, such as regular expressions, with machine learning can further reduce manual labor and enhance automatic suggestions.

1 Introduction

The Swiss Federal Supreme Court (SFSC) is the highest judicial authority in Switzerland. It is the final arbiter in legal disputes and ensures the uniform application of federal law throughout the country. It consists of several divisions specialized in different areas of law, including civil, criminal, administrative, and social security matters (Glaser et al., 2021). In a year, the SFSC roughly handles 7K cases and publishes its rulings. In this process, personal information must be anonymized from the rulings in order to protect involved parties. In the traditional setting, court rulings are anonymized by skilled experts. This task is highly complex, as the removal/anonymization of a word is dependent on the context it is written in. For example, *Zuerich* needs to be removed if it is part of the name of the legal entity "Zurich Insurance Group", but not if it is a reference to the city. At the SFSC, experts are already supported in their work through an application called *Anom2* (see Figure 1). *Anom2* provides access to various methods and algorithms for finding and replacing text entities (e.g., with regular expressions. The aim of this work is to enhance the capabilities of *Anom2* with Machine Learning capabilities that provide the user with more suggestions that need to be anonymized. Our results show that this approach allows users to find more elements that require anonymization.

* Equal contribution.

2 Related Work

For identifying elements that might require anonymization, a process called Named Entity Recognition (NER) is employed. Traditionally, NER recognizes and categorizes text parts according to a set of semantic categories like *Location (LOC)*, *Organization (ORG)*, or *Person (PER)* (Benikova et al., 2014). As these classes are not enough for the anonymization of court cases (Leitner et al., 2020) suggested expanding this list to seven coarse and 19 fine-grained classes, including entities such as *Judge (RR)*, or *Lawyer (AN)*. Using this dataset (Darji et al., 2023) fine-tuned GermanBERT (Chan et al., 2020), clearly outperforming a BiLSTM-CRF+ model. Similar approaches have been applied and tested in other languages, such as Romanian (Pais et al., 2021), Greek (Angelidis et al., 2018), Portuguese (Luz de Araujo et al., 2018), and multilingually (de Gibert et al., 2022; Niklaus et al., 2023a).

Domain-specific pretraining has flourished in the legal domain recently. Chalkidis et al. (2020) pretrained LegalBERT on EU and UK legislation, ECHR and US cases, and US contracts. Zheng et al. (2021) pretrained CaseHoldBERT on US case law, while Henderson et al. (2022) trained PoL-BERT on the 256 GB Pile of Law corpus. Niklaus and Giofré (2022) pretrained Longformer (Beltagy et al., 2020) models using the Replaced

Proceedings of the Natural Legal Language Processing Workshop 2023, pages 159–165
December 7, 2023 ©2023 Association for Computational Linguistics

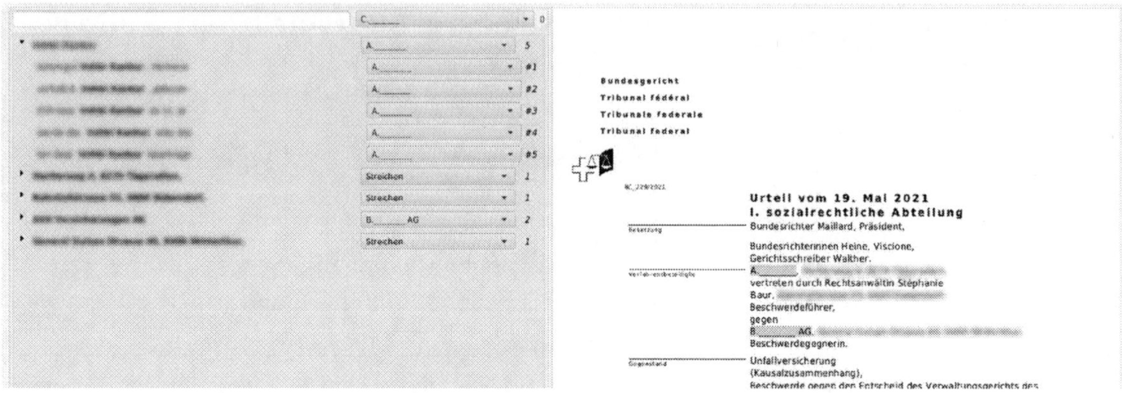

Figure 1: Main window of *Anom2*. Anonymizations are configured on the left, and the anonymized court ruling appears on the right. The system highlights completed anonymizations in gold and the current setting in yellow.

Token Detection (RTD) task on the Pile of Law. Hua et al. (2022) used RTD to pretrain Reformer (Kitaev et al., 2020) models on 6 GB of US case law. Finally, Niklaus et al. (2023b) released a large multilingual legal corpus and trained various legal models. We continue pretraining the German, French, and Italian models for 800K and 300K steps more for base and large models, respectively. Rasiah et al. (2023) pretrain models on Swiss legal data, termed Legal-Swiss-RoBERTa.

Document anonymization has a long tradition in the medical domain, where personal data need to be removed from documents. Initially, this task was handled using methods such as semantic lexicons (Ruch et al., 2000) or regular expressions to replace text occurrences. Recently, this has been expanded to include BERT-style models as well (Mao and Liu, 2019). In the legal domain, Glaser et al. (2021) worked on 1400 anonymized German rulings. Using already anonymized rulings, they trained different Recurrent Neural Networks (RNN) using BERT embeddings. Using this approach, they achieved a maximum of 68.9% precision and 79.1% recall rates. Garat and Wonsever (2022) performed similar work on 80K documents from Uruguayan courts. Our work specifically tackles court decisions by the SFSC. We compare the generic cased mBERT model (Devlin et al., 2019a) with models pre-trained on in-domain data (such as Legal-Swiss-RoBERTa-base (Rasiah et al., 2023)). We also investigate monolingual model performance in the three languages of the SFSC rulings: German, French, and Italian.

Much prior work used SFSC cases as data for their research because of wide availability in three languages, giving good coverage of the most important Swiss case law. Niklaus et al. (2021, 2022) introduced and studied judgment prediction on SFSC rulings. Brugger et al. (2023) investigated and improved multilingual sentence boundary detection in the legal domain using SFSC decisions. Christen et al. (2023) studied negation scope resolution and Nyffenegger et al. (2023) investigated how easily LLMs can re-identify persons occurring in anonymized SFSC decisions. Rasiah et al. (2023) created a large benchmark of ten text classification tasks, two text generation tasks, an information retrieval, and a citation extraction task.

3 Dataset

We used 119156 rulings (77262 German, 40099 French, 6795 Italian) Supreme court decisions and split them into sentences using Spacy (Honnibal et al., 2020). We prepared the decisions for NER based on the manual labels from the paralegals who performed manual anonymizations. The histograms in Figure 2 illustrate the distribution of four key measures, namely, Number of Tokens, Anonymized Tokens, Entities, and Anonymized Entities, in three languages: German (de), French (fr), and Italian (it). Different color schemes for each language enhance the visual interpretability of the plots. Measures concerning tokens and entities exhibit a long-tailed distribution, signifying a concentration of instances at the lower end of the value spectrum. Specifically, the distribution of Number of Tokens and Number of Entities is examined within a 10 to 100,000 range, capturing their broad spread. In contrast, anonymized tokens and entities are evaluated within a 1 to 10,000 range, reflecting their constrained distribution.

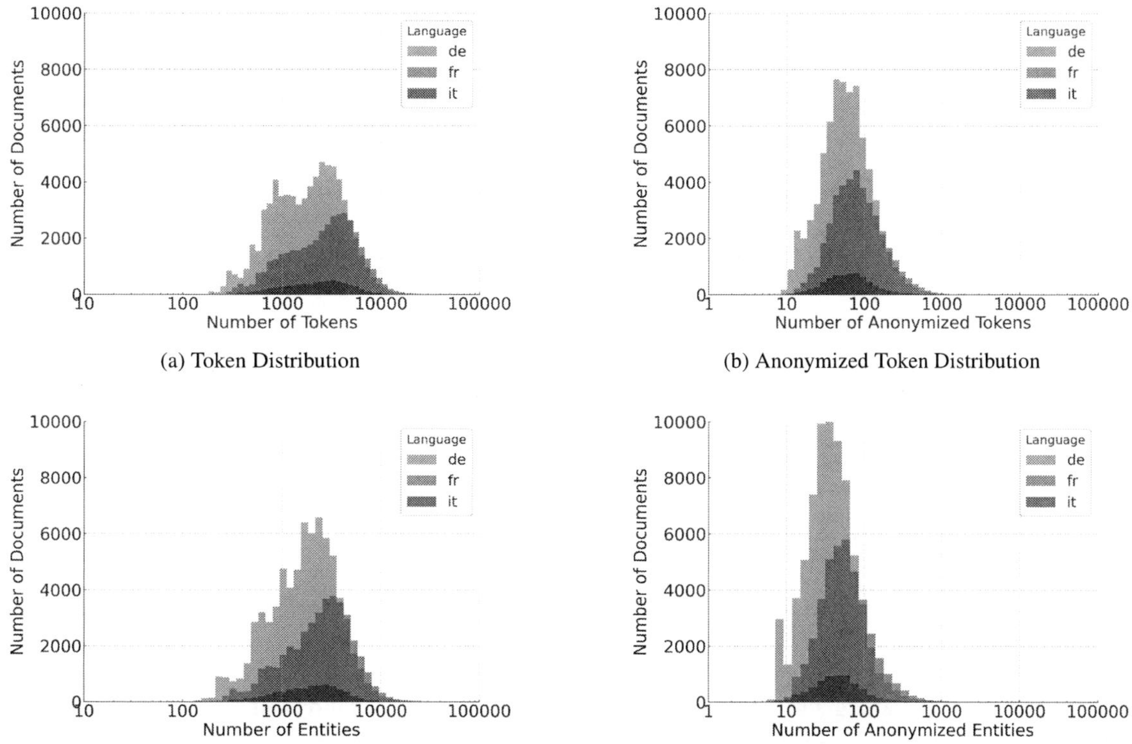

(a) Token Distribution

(b) Anonymized Token Distribution

(c) Entity Distribution

(d) Anonymized Entity Distribution

Figure 2: Histograms illustrating the distribution of (anonymized) tokens and entities across the three languages.

4 Legal Pretraining

To improve the SFSC anonymization system, we pretrained legal-specific models on diverse legal text in German, French, and Italian.

(a) We warm-start (initialize) our models from the original XLM-R checkpoints (base or large) of Conneau and Lample (2019). Model recycling is a standard process followed by many (Wei et al., 2021; Ouyang et al., 2022) to benefit from starting from an available "well-trained" PLM, rather from scratch (random). XLM-R was trained on 2.5 TB of cleaned CommonCrawl data in 100 languages.

(b) We train a new tokenizer of 32K BPEs on the training subsets to better cover legal language. However, we reuse the original XLM-R embeddings for all lexically overlapping tokens (Pfeiffer et al., 2021), i.e., we warm-start word embeddings for tokens that already exist in the original XLM-R vocabulary, and use random ones for the rest.

(c) We continue pretraining our monolingual models on our pretraining corpus with batches of 512 samples for an additional 1M/500K steps for the base/large model. We do initial warm-up steps for the first 5% of the total training steps with a linearly increasing learning rate up to $1e{-}4$, and then follow a cosine decay scheduling, following recent trends. For half of the warm-up phase (2.5%), the Transformer encoder is frozen, and only the embeddings, shared between input and output (MLM), are updated. We also use an increased 20/30% masking rate for base/large models respectively, where also 100% of the predictions are based on masked tokens, compared to Devlin et al. (2019b)[1], based on the findings of Wettig et al. (2023).

(d) We consider mixed cased models, i.e., both upper- and lowercase letters covered, similar to recently developed large PLMs (Conneau and Lample, 2019; Raffel et al., 2020; Brown et al., 2020).

(e) This leaves us with two models for each language (base and large). Additionally, we consider the multilingual legal models pretrained by Niklaus et al. (2023b) and the Swiss legal models pretrained by Rasiah et al. (2023).

5 Anonymization System

The SFSC employs an anonymization system, *Anom2*, to assist paralegals in anonymizing rul-

[1] Devlin et al. (2019b) – and much follow-up work – used a 15% masking ratio, and a recipe of 80/10/10% of predictions made across masked/randomly-replaced/original tokens.

Table 1: Evaluation Results. Best results per setup are in **bold**.

Model	Normal			Uniformizing		
	Precision	Recall	F1-Score	Precision	Recall	F1-Score
Multilingual Models						
bert-base-multilingual-cased	90.72	83.76	87.10	85.85	**94.95**	**90.17**
Legal-XLM-RoBERTa-base	**94.84**	81.98	87.94	**89.93**	86.85	88.36
Legal-Swiss-RoBERTa-base	92.26	**92.57**	**92.42**	83.13	94.85	88.60
Monolingual Models						
bert-base-german-cased	95.14	80.00	86.92	**91.49**	**85.86**	**88.58**
Legal-German-RoBERTa-base	**95.40**	**80.09**	**87.07**	89.20	84.97	87.03
dbmdz/bert-base-french-europeana-cased	**95.86**	81.84	88.30	**88.92**	89.14	**89.03**
Legal-French-RoBERTa-base	95.45	**83.48**	**89.06**	88.77	**89.17**	88.97
dbmdz/bert-base-italian-cased	93.49	80.21	86.35	76.71	83.85	80.12
Legal-Italian-RoBERTa-base	**94.16**	**80.59**	**86.85**	**84.03**	**84.06**	**84.05**

ings for public access. The main UI is shown in Figure 1. Upon loading a ruling, the application auto-identifies terms requiring anonymization and lists them on the left, along with replacement text. The search function allows direct term marking for anonymization. *Anom2* uses different algorithms for the search for text that needs to be anonymized:

Conventional is based on a statistical analysis of the loaded ruling. Using *polyglot*[2] an initial set of named entities is detected. Using the specific knowledge of the format, the rubrum is dynamically detected, allowing for the labelling of important names and addresses.

BERT performs the recognition of entities to be anonymized using a BERT (Devlin et al., 2019a) model fine-tuned for NER. Entity recognition is performed on the sentence level, as the rulings are often too long for the model. This approach could lead to inconsistencies in recognition, as a term identified in one sentence might not be identified in another. This is solved in post-processing, where any identified term is automatically anonymized in the whole document.

Legal-Swiss-RoBERTa-base works analogously to the BERT method, but uses a fine-tuned *Legal-Swiss-RoBERTa-base* (Rasiah et al., 2023) model.

6 Experimental Setup

We used the following hyperparameters for all evaluated models: batch size of 64, learning rate of 5e-5, and weight decay of 0.01. We employed the seqeval metric for evaluation. We set the maximum sequence length to 192 tokens, which we determined to be the optimal trade-off between average sentence size and training time for computational efficiency. We used early stopping based on the F1-score of the validation set, which constitutes 10% of the entire dataset, following an 80-10-10 split for the training, validation, and test sets, respectively. Training ceases once the F1-score on the validation set starts to decline. Due to resource constraints (we only had two Tesla T4 GPUs) we could only run one random seed per model.

We define and configure two special parameters:

1) *TruncationStrideRatio*: We set this parameter to 0.5. When a sentence exceeds 192 tokens, we truncate it using a specific overlap strategy. The overlap consists of half of the previous snippet and half of the next snippet.

2) *NonAnonymizedSentencesRatioToAnonymizedSentences*: We set the ratio at 1.5, including only 150% of sentences without anonymization examples compared to those with examples. This minimizes data redundancy and maximizes utility.

7 Results

Table 1 presents a comprehensive evaluation of various BERT and RoBERTa-based models on two different conditions: Normal and Uniformizing. For the Normal condition, in the multilingual setting, Legal-XLM-RoBERTa-base exhibits the highest Precision at 94.84%, while Legal-Swiss-RoBERTa-base demonstrates superior Recall and F1-Score values, achieving 92.57% and 92.42% respectively. With Uniformizing, we describe the process of forcing the model to replace all occurrences of a detected term across the whole docu-

[2]See: https://polyglot.readthedocs.io

ment. This approach leads to better Recall, but reduces Precision. In the Uniformized case, again Legal-XLM-RoBERTa-base shows highest Precision, while mBERT achieves highest Recall and F1-Score. The improved Recall and F1-Score in the Normal condition show that pre-training on legal data can improve the performance of models. We observe similar behavior for the monolingual models. All models pre-trained on legal data achieve a higher F1-Score than generic monolingual models.

8 Discussion

We pretrained models on Swiss legal data and performed a detailed comparison of legal and generic models, both multilingually and monolingually in the ruling anonymization task. Our experiments indicate that pretraining on legal data improves the performance of models significantly compared to generic multi- or monolingual models.

To reduce errors in sentence splitting, we suggest future work to use legal specific sentence splitters (Brugger et al., 2023). Due to computational constraints we only experimented with base size encoder models. Future work may expand this by also testing larger models.

Acknowledgements

We greatly appreciate Google's generous support of TPUs v3-8 machines for pretraining the models. This work has been partially supported by the Swiss National Research Programme "Digital Transformation" (NRP-77) grant number 187477.

References

I. Angelidis, Ilias Chalkidis, and M. Koubarakis. 2018. Named Entity Recognition, Linking and Generation for Greek Legislation. In *JURIX*.

Iz Beltagy, Matthew E Peters, and Arman Cohan. 2020. Longformer: The long-document transformer. *arXiv preprint arXiv:2004.05150*.

Darina Benikova, Chris Biemann, and Marc Reznicek. 2014. NoSta-D Named Entity Annotation for German: Guidelines and Dataset. In *Proceedings of the Ninth International Conference on Language Resources and Evaluation (LREC'14)*, pages 2524–2531, Reykjavik, Iceland. European Language Resources Association (ELRA).

Tom Brown, Benjamin Mann, Nick Ryder, Melanie Subbiah, Jared D Kaplan, Prafulla Dhariwal, Arvind Neelakantan, Pranav Shyam, Girish Sastry, Amanda Askell, Sandhini Agarwal, Ariel Herbert-Voss, Gretchen Krueger, Tom Henighan, Rewon Child, Aditya Ramesh, Daniel Ziegler, Jeffrey Wu, Clemens Winter, Chris Hesse, Mark Chen, Eric Sigler, Mateusz Litwin, Scott Gray, Benjamin Chess, Jack Clark, Christopher Berner, Sam McCandlish, Alec Radford, Ilya Sutskever, and Dario Amodei. 2020. Language models are few-shot learners. In *Advances in Neural Information Processing Systems*, volume 33, pages 1877–1901. Curran Associates, Inc.

Tobias Brugger, Matthias Stürmer, and Joel Niklaus. 2023. MultiLegalSBD: A Multilingual Legal Sentence Boundary Detection Dataset. ArXiv:2305.01211 [cs].

Ilias Chalkidis, Manos Fergadiotis, Prodromos Malakasiotis, Nikolaos Aletras, and Ion Androutsopoulos. 2020. LEGAL-BERT: The Muppets straight out of Law School. In *Findings of the Association for Computational Linguistics: EMNLP 2020*, pages 2898–2904.

Branden Chan, Stefan Schweter, and Timo Möller. 2020. German's Next Language Model. *arXiv:2010.10906 [cs]*. ArXiv: 2010.10906.

Ramona Christen, Anastassia Shaitarova, Matthias Stürmer, and Joel Niklaus. 2023. Resolving Legalese: A Multilingual Exploration of Negation Scope Resolution in Legal Documents.

Alexis Conneau and Guillaume Lample. 2019. Cross-lingual Language Model Pretraining. In *Advances in Neural Information Processing Systems*, volume 32. Curran Associates, Inc.

Harshil Darji, Jelena Mitrović, and Michael Granitzer. 2023. German BERT Model for Legal Named Entity Recognition:. In *Proceedings of the 15th International Conference on Agents and Artificial Intelligence*, pages 723–728, Lisbon, Portugal. SCITEPRESS - Science and Technology Publications.

Ona de Gibert, A García-Pablos, Montse Cuadros, and Maite Melero. 2022. Spanish datasets for sensitive entity detection in the legal domain. In *Proceedings of the Thirteenth International Conference on Language Resources and Evaluation (LREC'22), Marseille, France, june. European Language Resource Association (ELRA).* Dataset URL: https://tinyurl.com/mv65cp66.

Jacob Devlin, Ming-Wei Chang, Kenton Lee, and Kristina Toutanova. 2019a. BERT: Pre-training of Deep Bidirectional Transformers for Language Understanding. In *Proceedings of the 2019 Conference of the North American Chapter of the Association for Computational Linguistics: Human Language Technologies, Volume 1 (Long and Short Papers)*, pages 4171–4186, Minneapolis, Minnesota. Association for Computational Linguistics.

Jacob Devlin, Ming-Wei Chang, Kenton Lee, and Kristina Toutanova. 2019b. BERT: Pre-training of deep bidirectional transformers for language understanding. In *Proceedings of the 2019 Conference of the North American Chapter of the Association for Computational Linguistics: Human Language Technologies, Volume 1 (Long and Short Papers)*, pages 4171–4186, Minneapolis, Minnesota. Association for Computational Linguistics.

Diego Garat and Dina Wonsever. 2022. Automatic Curation of Court Documents: Anonymizing Personal Data. *Information*, 13(1):27.

Ingo Glaser, Tom Schamberger, and Florian Matthes. 2021. Anonymization of german legal court rulings. In *Proceedings of the Eighteenth International Conference on Artificial Intelligence and Law*, pages 205–209, São Paulo Brazil. ACM.

Peter Henderson, Mark S. Krass, Lucia Zheng, Neel Guha, Christopher D. Manning, Dan Jurafsky, and Daniel E. Ho. 2022. Pile of Law: Learning Responsible Data Filtering from the Law and a 256GB Open-Source Legal Dataset. ArXiv:2207.00220 [cs].

Matthew Honnibal, Ines Montani, Sofie Van Landeghem, and Adriane Boyd. 2020. spaCy: Industrial-strength Natural Language Processing in Python.

Wenyue Hua, Yuchen Zhang, Zhe Chen, Josie Li, and Melanie Weber. 2022. LegalRelectra: Mixed-domain Language Modeling for Long-range Legal Text Comprehension. ArXiv:2212.08204 [cs].

Nikita Kitaev, Łukasz Kaiser, and Anselm Levskaya. 2020. Reformer: The Efficient Transformer. *arXiv:2001.04451 [cs, stat]*. ArXiv: 2001.04451.

Elena Leitner, Georg Rehm, and Julián Moreno-Schneider. 2020. A Dataset of German Legal Documents for Named Entity Recognition. *arXiv:2003.13016 [cs]*. ArXiv: 2003.13016.

Pedro Henrique Luz de Araujo, Teófilo E. de Campos, Renato R. R. de Oliveira, Matheus Stauffer, Samuel Couto, and Paulo Bermejo. 2018. LeNER-Br: A Dataset for Named Entity Recognition in Brazilian Legal Text. In *Computational Processing of the Portuguese Language*, Lecture Notes in Computer Science, pages 313–323, Cham. Springer International Publishing.

Jihang Mao and Wanli Liu. 2019. Hadoken: a BERT-CRF Model for Medical Document Anonymization. In *Proceedings of the Iberian Languages Evaluation Forum co-located with 35th Conference of the Spanish Society for Natural Language Processing, IberLEF@SEPLN 2019, Bilbao, Spain, September 24th, 2019*, volume 2421 of *CEUR Workshop Proceedings*, pages 720–726. CEUR-WS.org.

Joel Niklaus, Ilias Chalkidis, and Matthias Stürmer. 2021. Swiss-Judgment-Prediction: A Multilingual Legal Judgment Prediction Benchmark. In *Proceedings of the Natural Legal Language Processing Workshop 2021*, pages 19–35, Punta Cana, Dominican Republic. Association for Computational Linguistics.

Joel Niklaus and Daniele Giofré. 2022. BudgetLongformer: Can we Cheaply Pretrain a SotA Legal Language Model From Scratch? ArXiv:2211.17135 [cs].

Joel Niklaus, Veton Matoshi, Pooja Rani, Andrea Galassi, Matthias Stürmer, and Ilias Chalkidis. 2023a. Lextreme: A multi-lingual and multi-task benchmark for the legal domain.

Joel Niklaus, Veton Matoshi, Matthias Stürmer, Ilias Chalkidis, and Daniel E. Ho. 2023b. MultiLegalPile: A 689GB Multilingual Legal Corpus. ArXiv:2306.02069 [cs].

Joel Niklaus, Matthias Stürmer, and Ilias Chalkidis. 2022. An Empirical Study on Cross-X Transfer for Legal Judgment Prediction. In *Proceedings of the 2nd Conference of the Asia-Pacific Chapter of the Association for Computational Linguistics and the 12th International Joint Conference on Natural Language Processing (Volume 1: Long Papers)*, pages 32–46, Online only. Association for Computational Linguistics.

Alex Nyffenegger, Matthias Stürmer, and Joel Niklaus. 2023. Anonymity at Risk? Assessing Re-Identification Capabilities of Large Language Models. ArXiv:2308.11103 [cs].

Long Ouyang, Jeff Wu, Xu Jiang, Diogo Almeida, Carroll L. Wainwright, Pamela Mishkin, Chong Zhang, Sandhini Agarwal, Katarina Slama, Alex Ray, John Schulman, Jacob Hilton, Fraser Kelton, Luke Miller, Maddie Simens, Amanda Askell, Peter Welinder, Paul Christiano, Jan Leike, and Ryan Lowe. 2022. Training language models to follow instructions with human feedback.

Vasile Pais, Maria Mitrofan, Carol Luca Gasan, Vlad Coneschi, and Alexandru Ianov. 2021. Named Entity Recognition in the Romanian Legal Domain. In *Proceedings of the Natural Legal Language Processing Workshop 2021*, pages 9–18, Punta Cana, Dominican Republic. Association for Computational Linguistics.

Jonas Pfeiffer, Ivan Vulić, Iryna Gurevych, and Sebastian Ruder. 2021. UNKs everywhere: Adapting multilingual language models to new scripts. In *Proceedings of the 2021 Conference on Empirical Methods in Natural Language Processing*, pages 10186–10203, Online and Punta Cana, Dominican Republic. Association for Computational Linguistics.

Colin Raffel, Noam Shazeer, Adam Roberts, Katherine Lee, Sharan Narang, Michael Matena, Yanqi Zhou, Wei Li, and Peter J. Liu. 2020. Exploring the Limits of Transfer Learning with a Unified Text-to-Text Transformer. *Journal of Machine Learning Research*, 21(140):1–67.

Vishvaksenan Rasiah, Ronja Stern, Veton Matoshi, Matthias Stürmer, Ilias Chalkidis, Daniel E. Ho, and Joel Niklaus. 2023. SCALE: Scaling up the Complexity for Advanced Language Model Evaluation. ArXiv:2306.09237 [cs].

P. Ruch, R. H. Baud, A. M. Rassinoux, P. Bouillon, and G. Robert. 2000. Medical document anonymization with a semantic lexicon. *Proceedings. AMIA Symposium*, pages 729–733.

Jason Wei, Maarten Bosma, Vincent Y. Zhao, Kelvin Guu, Adams Wei Yu, Brian Lester, Nan Du, Andrew M. Dai, and Quoc V. Le. 2021. Finetuned language models are zero-shot learners. *CoRR*, abs/2109.01652.

Alexander Wettig, Tianyu Gao, Zexuan Zhong, and Danqi Chen. 2023. Should you mask 15% in masked language modeling? In *Proceedings of the 17th Conference of the European Chapter of the Association for Computational Linguistics*, pages 2985–3000, Dubrovnik, Croatia. Association for Computational Linguistics.

Lucia Zheng, Neel Guha, Brandon R. Anderson, Peter Henderson, and Daniel E. Ho. 2021. When Does Pretraining Help? Assessing Self-Supervised Learning for Law and the CaseHOLD Dataset. *arXiv:2104.08671 [cs]*. ArXiv: 2104.08671 version: 3.

Exploration of Open Large Language Models for eDiscovery

Sumit Pai[1*], Sounak Lahiri[1*], Ujjwal Kumar[1*], Krishanu Das Baksi[1], Elijah Soba[2], Michael Suesserman[2], Nirmala Pudota[1], Jonathan Foster[2], Edward Bowen[2], Sanmitra Bhattacharya[2]
[1]Deloitte & Touche Assurance & Enterprise Risk Services India Private Limited, India
[2]Deloitte & Touche LLP, United States
{sumpai, sanmbhattacharya}@deloitte.com

Abstract

The rapid advancement of Generative Artificial Intelligence (AI), particularly Large Language Models (LLMs), has led to their widespread adoption for various natural language processing (NLP) tasks. One crucial domain ripe for innovation is the Technology-Assisted Review (TAR) process in Electronic discovery (eDiscovery). Traditionally, TAR involves manual review and classification of documents for relevance over large document collections for litigations and investigations. This process is aided by machine learning and NLP tools which require extensive training and fine-tuning. In this paper, we explore the application of LLMs to TAR, specifically for predictive coding. We experiment with out-of-the-box prompting and fine-tuning of LLMs using parameter-efficient techniques. We conduct experiments using open LLMs and compare them to commercially-licensed ones. Our experiments demonstrate that open LLMs lag behind commercially-licensed models in relevance classification using out-of-the-box prompting. However, topic-specific instruction tuning of open LLMs not only improve their effectiveness but can often outperform their commercially-licensed counterparts in performance evaluations. Additionally, we conduct a user study to gauge the preferences of our eDiscovery Subject Matter Specialists (SMS) regarding human-authored versus model-generated reasoning. We demonstrate that instruction-tuned open LLMs can generate high quality reasonings that are comparable to commercial LLMs.

1 Introduction

Electronic discovery (eDiscovery) (Oard et al., 2013) refers to the process of identifying, collecting, and preserving electronic documents and data for the purpose of legal proceedings, investigations, or regulatory compliance. During legal procedures, including litigation proceedings and corporate mergers and acquisitions, the court often issues a *production request*. The request mandates the parties involved to produce documents pertinent to the case. A large team of legal practitioners meticulously examines millions of digital records to identify the ones that are relevant to the production request. This step is a crucial phase of the eDiscovery process, commonly referred to as responsiveness determination. During this early step, legal practitioners often employ Artificial Intelligence (AI)-based tools to help them identify and prioritize the documents for review. This essential component of the eDiscovery process is referred to as Technology-Assisted Review (TAR) (Cormack and Grossman, 2014).

Another related domain focused on management and extraction of relevant information from electronic documents for legal purposes is Legal Information Retrieval (LIR). However, the important distinctions between eDiscovery and the general domain of LIR (Ganguly et al., 2023) are in their purpose, and nature of documents under consideration. eDiscovery is related to request for production of documents and data that are often in the form of email correspondences, text messages, articles, and financial declarations. In contrast, LIR is related to finding legal information in response to specific queries from legal databases, case law repositories, legislative archives, and other legal resources. The language used in the documents for these two tasks differ with the latter being richer in legal terminology. In this paper, our primary focus is on documents pertinent to eDiscovery.

Traditional approaches to TAR have focused on Boolean querying (Blair and Maron, 1985; Baron et al., 2007), information retrieval (Oard et al., 2013) and active learning methodologies (Cormack and Grossman, 2016; McDonald et al., 2018). In recent years, the use of supervised learning on labeled documents, referred to as *predictive cod-*

[*]These authors contributed equally to this work

ing (Brown, 2015; Yang et al., 2021), has gained more popularity within TAR workflows. Predictive coding often employs binary text classification based on textual, syntactic, semantic, and other data-driven features. Motivated by the application of LLMs in zero-shot and few-shot learning in various domains, including recommender systems and document annotation (Hou et al., 2023; Törnberg, 2023; Dai et al., 2022; Ahmed and Devanbu, 2022), we propose a novel approach to predictive coding using LLMs. Furthermore, we go beyond the predictive capabilities of LLMs, and leverage them to provide reasonings for the predictions. This capability can assist human reviewers in making more informed decisions. The use of LLMs for predictive coding and reasoning represents a paradigm shift in a domain burdened by the ever-increasing volume of documents and escalating review costs (Yang et al., 2021).

In this paper, we utilize open LLMs, notably Large Language Model Meta AI v2 (LLaMA2 - 13B and 70B versions) (Touvron et al., 2023) and Falcon-7B[1], as well as the commercially licensed Generative Pre-trained Transformer (GPT)-3.5-turbo model[2], for both predictive coding and reasoning. We explore various methods to use these LLMs effectively, including zero-shot prompting, fine-tuning for instruction following (i.e., instruction tuning), and reasoning generation. Additionally, we conduct a user study involving eDiscovery Subject Matter Specialists (SMSs) to evaluate the quality of reasoning generated by these models, and those authored by a legal SMS. The publicly available Enron email dataset (Grossman et al., 2011) is used in our experiments. This dataset comprises of a large corpus of emails and attachments that had to be reviewed for their responsiveness to production requests. We present experimental results of the various LLM-based predictive coding approaches on this dataset.

The paper presents related research in Section 2, describes the datasets used in Section 3, outlines the experimental approaches in Section 4, and reports the results of classification models as well as user preferences for generated reasonings in Section 5.

[1]https://falconllm.tii.ae/

[2]https://platform.openai.com/docs/models/gpt-3-5

2 Related Work

The application of AI in eDiscovery for the purposes of document prioritization, reasoning, and decision-making are not a recent development (Araszkiewicz et al., 2022; Ashley and Bridewell, 2010; Conrad, 2010). Notably, the Text Retrieval Conference (TREC) had consistently featured a dedicated Legal track from 2006 to 2011 (Baron et al., 2006; Tomlinson et al., 2007; Oard et al., 2008; Hedin et al., 2009; Cormack et al., 2010; Grossman et al., 2011), where eDiscovery was given prime importance, with emphasis on retrieval and ranking-based approaches. Several shared tasks related to eDiscovery, including TAR and privilege review, were organized to stimulate and advance research in this specialized domain.

Typical TAR solutions can be decomposed into retrieval-based (Oard et al., 2013) and classification-based approaches (Barnett et al., 2009) (Lewis, 2010). Both of these approaches are instrumental in facilitating the prioritization of documents for subsequent review processes. Alongside these methods, active learning strategies (Cormack and Grossman, 2016; McDonald et al., 2018) have been extensively explored to boost the operational efficiency of these models. These strategies incorporate relevance feedback provided by human reviewers to enhance model performance. However, it's imperative to acknowledge that certain feedback-based processes can be inherently slow, expensive and inconsistent. In this paper, we primarily focus on the classification-based approach, also referred to as predictive coding, which has gained prominence in recent years.

Conventional TAR approaches are often perceived as black box systems, making it challenging to trust their decisions. The generation of reasoning and explanation for TAR models has received limited attention. Previous approaches (Chhatwal et al., 2018; Villata et al., 2020) focused on training models to identify snippets (at sentence level) within documents that are classified as either responsive or non-responsive. However, these approaches necessitate training on annotated data, which is both time-consuming and resource-intensive.

In this work, we focus on leveraging the capabilities of generative LLMs for both classification and reasoning. These architectures, rooted in the Transformer framework (Vaswani et al., 2017), are characterized by their auto-regressive decoders. Typically, these models are trained on vast and diverse corpora of textual data, demonstrating remarkable proficiency in comprehending natural language instructions across diverse domains. These LLMs are able to generate coherent natural language responses when provided with appropriate prompts (Liu et al., 2023). They can interpret the topics specified in the prompts and execute them effectively. In this study, we experiment with some open LLMs, such as LLaMA2 (13B and 70B versions) and Falcon-7B, as well as commercially licensed models like GPT-3.5-turbo.

3 Dataset

In this section, we describe the dataset used for our experiments. We used the Electronic Discovery Reference Model (EDRM) Enron Email Data Set Version 2, which is the post-processed version employed in the TREC 2011 Legal eDiscovery track (Grossman et al., 2011). This dataset serves as a rich resource for exploring various facets of eDiscovery, particularly in the context of email communication.

3.1 Source and Composition

The EDRM Enron Email Data Set Version 2 originates from the Enron Corporation, once a leading energy company in the United States that collapsed in 2001 due to accounting malpractices. The dataset was used in the TREC Legal eDiscovery track from 2009 to 2011. The post-processed dataset is meticulously organized into 159 directories, each capturing the email communication records of individuals associated with the company, offering a distinct insight into corporate communication.

3.2 Formats

The dataset is divided into two primary categories:

- **Emails**: This subset comprises a substantial portion of the dataset, with a total of 455,449 email messages. Each email has a distinct document ID and is stored as plain text with the naming convention `doc_id.txt`. These emails are central to our analyses and experiments.

- **Attachments**: In addition to the emails, the dataset contains 230,143 attachment files. Each attachments is linked to a specific email message and follows the naming format `doc_id.number.txt`, where `number` indicates its sequential order.

Attachments are treated as separate documents.

3.3 Experimental Focus

Following the specifications of the Learning Task of the TREC 2011 Legal Track, we focused on three available topics, numbered 401, 402, and 403. Detailed description of each topic is provided in Appendix A.1. The task organizers offered a choice to use either emails, attachments, or both. Evaluations of the submitted runs for this shared task encompassed these three options. In our experiments, we concentrate on analyzing emails from each of the aforementioned topics. For simplicity and consistency, attachments were intentionally excluded due to their potentially large size and varied formats, such as spreadsheets, presentations, and webpages.

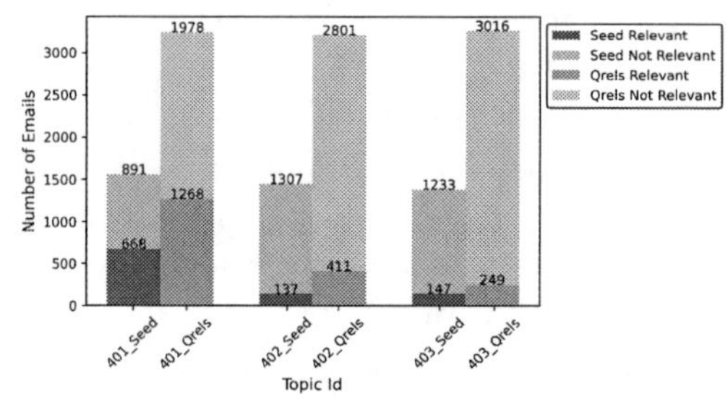

Figure 1: Distribution of emails across the seed dataset and qrels. The color-coded stacked bars show the number of relevant and non-relevant emails for each topic.

3.4 Training and Testing Data

For our experiments, we used two primary components from the Learning Task of the TREC 2011 Legal Track:

- **Seeds**: The seed data was used to fine-tune the LLMs to adapt to the eDiscovery domain, especially in the context of Enron's email communications.

- **Qrels**: The query relevance judgments (qrels) served as our test set. This dataset allowed us to evaluate the effectiveness of the LLMs in identifying relevant documents within the Enron Dataset for the given topics.

Figure 1 shows the distribution of emails across the three topics used in our study. The seed data and qrels for each topic are highly imbalanced with a majority of documents being non-relevant.

We focused on topics from the 2011 TREC Legal track, rather than prior years (i.e. 2009 and 2010 TREC Legal tracks), for two main reasons. Firstly, each topic from this year featured a relatively larger number of labeled documents in both the seed and qrel sets, and showcased a diverse range of label distributions. For instance, Topic 401 displayed a fairly balanced distribution between relevant and non-relevant documents, whereas other topics exhibited significant imbalances. Secondly, the dataset from this year provided a sufficient number of topic statements to effectively evaluate the capability and generalizability of our approach when applied to predictive coding.

4 Methodology

In this study, we primarily focus on examining several generative models from the decoder-only auto-regressive family, a subset of the broader category of LLMs. These models have gained significant attention and adoption following the introduction of ChatGPT[3]. Legal departments and law firms have expressed interest in utilizing these models to enhance their document review processes, achieving both scalability and cost-efficiency. We explore four models: Falcon (7B version), LLaMA2 (both 13B and 70B versions), and GPT (3.5 turbo version). Our experimentation involves two distinct methodologies: out-of-the-box (OOB) prompting approach and fine-tuning of open LLMs, with a special emphasis on Falcon 7B and LLaMA2 13B, which have been shown to outperform other open LLMs of similar size across various benchmarks[4]. We detail these methodologies in the subsequent sections.

4.1 Prompt Engineering

A common method to interact with a decoder-based auto-regressive LLMs is through *prompts*. A prompt is a natural language instruction that combines topic specifications, contextual information, and input parameters for executing the specified tasks. The LLM interprets the task described in the prompt and generates corresponding responses. Prompting greatly improves the usability of decoder-only models, allowing users without technical knowledge to effectively interact with them using just natural language. Without the knowledge of the technical intricacies, such as coding or statistical methodologies, one can easily interact with these models using this zero-shot approach. The art of crafting effective prompts has paved the way for a new area of research known as *prompt engineering*. Prompt engineering (Liu et al., 2023) is an iterative process which entails the creation, evaluation, and refinement of prompts, all aimed at enhancing performance outcomes for the targeted topic.

In this paper, we present a systematic approach towards prompt engineering grounded on performance evaluation on a sample set of qrels. We started with an initial prompt for each topic, and iteratively refined it to derive a final optimized prompt. To ensure that the prompt template, topic statement, and email content all fit within the context length limitations of the LLMs used in this study, we truncated each emails to its first 300 tokens (emails from our dataset have a median word count of < 50). To evaluate the effectiveness of incremental updates to the prompts, we computed macro F1 score on a randomly chosen subset of 50 emails from the qrels for each topic, and then compared the results through each iteration. The prompt which gave us optimal performance on this smaller prompt-evaluation subset was then applied on the entire set of qrels (test set) for a comprehensive evaluation. In the early stages of prompt engineering, our primary emphasis was on classification metrics. However, after achieving optimal performance, we shifted our focus to producing high-quality reasoning, achieved by providing the model with explicit guidance through the prompt.

4.2 Instruction Tuning

Instruction tuning is the process of fine-tuning LLMs to follow instructions for targeted tasks (Wei et al., 2021). The process necessitates the use of an instruction dataset, comprised of instruction-output pairs that function as the training data. Within the scope of the predictive coding application, our primary objective is to evaluate the relevance of emails in relation to topic statements (typically characterized as production requests). To facilitate this, instructions or prompts are crafted in simple English by describing the topic of relevance determination, and providing the email and topic statement, and finally providing the expected output in plain text

[3]https://chat.openai.com/

[4]https://huggingface.co/spaces/HuggingFaceH4/open_llm_leaderboard

– either 'Yes' or 'No' – based on the email's relevance to the given topic. To fine-tune the models, we create the prompt and its corresponding output using the seed set from our dataset. The evaluation is conducted on the qrels.

LLMs can be instruction tuned through various methods. While a typical approach involves full fine-tuning, it often comes with significant infrastructure requirements. As an alternate, parameter-efficient techniques like Low Rank Adaptation (LoRA) (Hu et al., 2021) and Quantized LoRA (qLoRA) (Dettmers et al., 2023) offer a way to fine-tune on relatively modest infrastructure, while maintaining performance that's comparable to full fine-tuning (Liu et al., 2022). This can be further augmented by aligning the model with human preferences using Reinforcement learning with Human Feedback (RLHF). However, RLHF demands a vast collection of manually curated preference data. In this paper, our primary delve into the exploration of LoRA and qLoRA. Their minimal infrastructure requirements and cost-effectiveness make these techniques especially fitting for our research objectives.

LoRA is a fine-tuning methodology that decomposes the model's weight matrix into a low-rank approximation. This approximation is subsequently trained on topic-specific data, capturing nuanced, topic-specific intricacies while the original weights are kept frozen. As a result, this approach introduces fewer trainable parameters, requiring significantly less compute power. It also requires a lower volume of training data compared to more extensive fine-tuning approaches.

Upon the completion of the learning process, the resultant LoRA adapter weights can be merged with the original LLM weights. This produces an updated set of weights for subsequent inference. LoRA adapters can either be integrated across the model weight layers or be selectively applied to specific layers, offering flexibility in adaptation. This choice dictates the number of trainable parameters utilized during the learning process. We conducted a hyperparameter search on various LoRA parameters, to identify the optimal combination of these values for each topic statement.

qLoRA is a fine-tuning technique designed to reduce the Graphics Processing Unit (GPU) memory requirements of a model by employing weight quantization. In essence, this method involves converting the base model's wide range of weight values into a more compact range through min-max scaling. As a result, the transformed weights require less memory for storage. To illustrate this, consider the storage of integers ranging from -128 to 127, which requires 8 bits of storage. However, by mapping these values to a narrower range, like -16 to 15, only 4 bits are needed. This reduction in bit width effectively decreases the memory footprint by a factor of 2. When applied across the model's weight matrix, this quantization leads to significant memory savings. As an example, if the initial model occupies 50GB of memory, the quantized model only needs 25GB of GPU memory. Importantly, the original weights can be restored by implementing an inverse scaling operation, albeit with a marginal loss of information.

4.3 Explanation Generation

One notable advantage of using LLMs over traditional text classification-based models is their ability to generate explanations. By providing appropriate prompts, these models can generate coherent reasoning to explain model predictions. Smaller LLMs, such as LLaMA2-13B, typically exhibit limited proficiency in reasoning through OOB prompting, especially when compared to their larger counterparts like LLaMA2-70B (Wei et al., 2022). These smaller models are often less verbose and tend to repetitively reiterate the topic statement.

Nonetheless, there's potential to improve the reasoning capabilities of these models through instruction tuning. Such improvement demands access to annotated reasoning data, which is not readily available for the Enron emails dataset. In this dataset, our seed set is restricted to binary labels (yes/no) of relevance. To address this limitation, we utilize the LLaMa2-70B model with OOB prompting to generate reasoning on the seed set. Subsequently, the generated reasoning (on correctly predicted labels) serves as the foundation for instruction tuning of the LLaMA2-13B model for improved explanation generation.

4.4 User Study

We conducted a user study to evaluate the quality of reasoning that different models generated concerning the relevance of emails to given topic statements. For this assessment, we curated a set of 20 distinct predictions by randomly sampling from the qrels. We focused solely on cases where every model made accurate predictions. We created a questionnaire that was distributed to five eDiscovery SMSs who has knowledge in the domain of legal document review.

The primary objective of this study was to gauge human preferences for reasoning generated by different models. Each annotator was presented with a question comprising the email text, the topic statement, the actual label, and five separate reasoning outputs generated by five different techniques. A snapshot of this survey is shown in Appendix A.2.

Of the five techniques used, one reasoning instance was crafted by a SMS from our eDiscovery team (not involved in the subsequent survey). The other four were generated using the following methods: LLaMA2-13B OOB, LLaMA2-70B OOB, LLaMA2-13B fine-tuned, and GPT-3.5 OOB. To reduce biases, these reasoning outputs were presented to annotators in a random sequence. Annotators were then asked to rate each reasoning on a scale of 1 to 5, where 5 denoted the top preference and 1 the lowest. Annotators were urged to avoid assigning tied scores whenever possible, aiming to derive a clear ranking indicative of preference.

Interestingly, the 13B fine-tuned model occasionally generated outputs similar to those of the 70B OOB model. This overlap was expected since the 70B OOB model was used to create the ground truth data for the 13B model. Consequently, occasional ties in the reasoning scores were anticipated. After gathering the preference data, we analysed the results and ranked the models based on the preferences of the SMSs.

5 Results

In this section, we present the results of applying LLMs to the predictive coding process. The training and evaluation were conducted on the seed data and qrels for topics 401, 402, and 403 from the TREC 2011 Legal track. Model performance was evaluated on the qrels using standard classification metrics, such as precision, recall, and macro F1 scores.

5.1 Prompt Engineering

Table 1 shows the initial prompt, which through several iterations of performance improvements on a sample set of qrels, was refined to derive the final prompt. For the sake of brevity, we focus exclusively on results for the LLaMA2-13B model. In the final prompt, several elements collectively contribute to achieving the improved outcome: the strategic emphasis on distinct terms such as "email", "topic", and "relevant", the consistent use of these terms throughout the prompt, a clear demarcation between inputs and their surrounding context, precise specification of the desired output structure, and intentional guidance provided to the model for task execution.

The results of OOB prompting for Falcon-7B, LLaMA2-13B, LLaMA2-70B, and GPT-3.5 are presented in the top third of Table 2. The results clearly show that GPT-3.5 outperforms other open LLMs when used through OOB prompting (even with the more effective model-specific prompt engineering).

We make an interesting observation that a chosen prompt for one model might not produce favorable results when used with other models. As a result, we crafted prompts tailored to each model. The underlying rationale behind these varied outcomes are still a subject of ongoing research and fall outside the scope of this paper.

In terms of GPU memory requirements, we were able to conduct OOB inference on two 40GB A100 GPUs for both Falcon-7B and LLaMA2-13B. However, for the LLaMA2-70B model, a more substantial hardware configuration with eight 40GB A100 GPUs was required.

5.2 Instruction Tuning

We limited our model selection for instruction tuning to those compatible with two 40GB A100 GPUs. Consequently, the instruction tuning process was solely performed on the Falcon-7B and LLaMa2-13B models. Due to the significant cost of instruction tuning for GPT-3.5, we opted not to include it in this study. The instruction tuning process followed the methodologies outlined in Section 4.2, and the improved results achieved after extensive hyperparameter tuning (described in Appendix A.3) are detailed in the last four rows of Table 2.

In order to instruction tune our models, we used the improved prompt described in the preceding subsection. This fine-tuning process utilized the seed set and was subsequently evaluated against the qrels. As shown in Table 2, for both LLaMA2-13B and Falcon-7b models, the LoRA instruction tuned models outperform their OOB counterparts in determining relevancy. This is quite significant for topic 401 as the seed set was sufficiently balanced. For Falcon, we saw an improvement from an F1 score of 0.39 to 0.79, while for LLaMA2-13B this

You are a subject matter expert reviewing a document to evaluate if it is related to a topic. Respond with Yes if the document is directly or indirectly related to the topic or No if not related. On a new line, give a reason. *Topic: topic_statement* *Email: email_text* (a)	*As a subject matter expert, youQr task is to read the following email and determine from its contents whether it is related to the provided topic.* *Email: """email_text"""* *Topic: """topic_statement"""* *Task: Decide whether the email is related to the topic or not. Provide a simple 'yes' or 'no' answer. Additionally, give a reason to support your answer, by summarizing parts of email that helped you make this decision.* *Answer and Reason:* (b)

Table 1: The initial prompt (a) and the final improved prompt (b) were iteratively developed for the LLaMA2-13B model. An evaluation was conducted using a random sample of 50 questions spanning the three topics. The initial prompt yielded a macro average F1 score of 0.29, whereas the improved prompt achieved a significantly improved F1 score of 0.51. Improved prompt (b) exhibits a deliberate emphasis on specific terms, such as "email", "topic", and "related", which are consistently employed throughout the prompt. Notably, the email and topic statements are distinctly delineated by the use of triple quotes. Additionally, a structured output format is outlined. The model is directed to provide its reasoning by "summarizing parts of the emails". This iterative refinement process represents a systematic and methodical approach to enhance the prompt, resulting in improved performance for classification and reasoning.

		401			402			403		
Type	**Model**	**F1**	**Precision**	**Recall**	**F1**	**Precision**	**Recall**	**F1**	**Precision**	**Recall**
OOB	Falcon 7B	0.39	0.51	0.50	0.33	0.48	0.46	0.28	0.47	0.42
	LLaMa v2 13B	0.56	0.56	0.56	0.54	0.55	0.59	0.47	0.52	0.56
	LLaMa v2 70B	0.58	0.71	0.66	0.63	0.69	0.61	0.66	0.66	0.65
	GPT 3.5	0.61	0.76	0.62	**0.66**	**0.82**	0.62	0.66	0.64	0.68
LoRA	Falcon 7B	0.79	0.79	0.80	0.60	0.59	0.60	0.60	0.59	0.66
	LLaMa v2 13B	**0.85**	**0.84**	**0.86**	0.59	0.59	**0.66**	**0.68**	**0.68**	0.67
qLoRA	Falcon 7B	0.74	0.79	0.78	0.60	0.76	0.58	0.53	0.58	**0.77**
	LLaMa v2 13B	0.69	0.71	0.69	0.62	0.61	**0.66**	0.63	0.61	0.69

Table 2: Comparison of LLM Performance Metrics on TREC 2011 Topics 401, 402, and 403 for the assessment of emails relevance to topic statements. The uppermost four rows pertain to Out-of-Box (OOB) prompting, the subsequent two rows are dedicated to LoRA-based fine-tuned models, and the final two rows concern qLoRA fine-tuned models.

jumped from 0.56 to 0.85. Both these models, surpassed GPT-3.5-turbo OOB results on this topic statement. These results empirically highlight the advantages of LoRA instruction tuning. Similarly, for qLoRA finetuned models, we see a performance improvement compared to OOB prompting across all the topics. However, this is not as significant as LoRA finetuned models.

5.3 Quality of reasoning

The summary of the user study for evaluating the quality of reasoning can be found in Fig 3. The figure shows the mean score obtained by different techniques that were used for reasoning generation. Notably, of the five reasoning techniques assessed, the rationale generated by the LLaMA2-70B OOB model was the one preferred by the SMSs of our eDiscovery team, achieving a mean preference score of 3.58 with a standard error of 0.12. On the other hand, the reasoning produced by the LLaMA2-13B OOB model was the least favored, as reflected by its mean score of 2.08 and a standard error of 0.14. Furthermore, the reasoning generated by the LLaMA2-70B OOB and LLaMA2-13B fine-tuned models were preferred over SMS generated reasoning, which had a mean score of 3.01 and standard error of 0.15.

It is interesting to observe that the reasoning capability of the LLaMA2-13B model significantly improved after fine-tuning, as supported by the

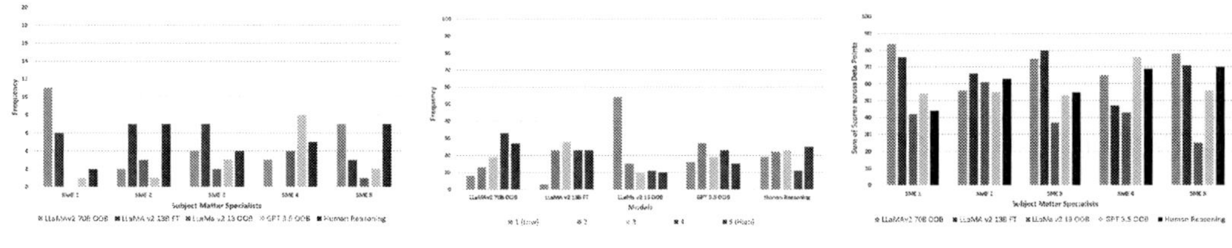

(a) (b) (c)

Figure 2: Frequency distribution of reasoning preference scores ascribed to various techniques by the 5 Subject Matter Specialists (SMSs) engaged in the survey. A total of 20 email samples were presented to each SMSs, along with their relevance to a topic (401). They were provided with five distinct rationales, generated by five distinct techniques, in support of the email's topical relevance. SMSs were instructed to score the reasonings on a scale of 1-5, wherein 5 signified the highest preference and 1 indicated the lowest preference. 2(a) shows the number of times a reasoning generation technique is ranked at the first position by SMSs. 2(b) shows the sum of scores received by each technique on the 20 questions for each SMSs. 2(c) shows the distribution of scores received by each model across the SMSs and questions.

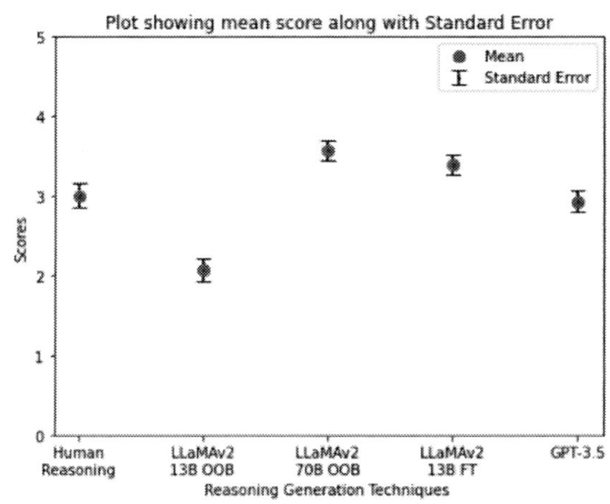

Figure 3: Mean and standard error of reasoning preference scores for each model as rated by SMSs

SMS preferences. This improvement is reflected in a mean score of 3.4 and a standard error of 0.12, further corroborating our initial hypothesis that fine-tuning contributes to improved performance. Surprisingly, the average preference score for GPT-3.5 was notably lower, coming in at 2.94 with a standard error of 0.13.

Detailed results of the survey are shown in Figure 2. Figure 2(a) provides insights into the frequency with which a technique was ranked highest by a SMS. Figure 2(b) shows the cumulative scores accrued by various techniques during when assessed by different SMSs. Figure 2(c) displays the distribution of scores that individual models received from the entire pool of SMSs and questions. Notably, of all the techniques reviewed, the LLaMA2-13B OOB model consistently registered a low score in a majority of evaluations conducted by the SMSs.

6 Conclusion

This study is among of the first works to assess the efficacy of generative LLMs in the eDiscovery document review process. We compare the classification performance of various open and commercially-licensed LLMs, and demonstrate that although OOB performance of open LLMs are worse compared to GPT-3.5, these models can be finetuned to achieve comparable results to GPT-3.5. Moreover, we conduct a user study and show that the SMSs favored AI-generated reasoning over human reasoning, underscoring the viability of these approaches in eDiscovery.

In terms of scalability, we suggest that there is no inherent need to deploy large models such as GPT-3.5 or LLaMa2-70B for production purposes. The LLaMA2-13B model, which fits on just two 40GB A100 GPUs, can be fine-tuned to yield similar classification performance and reasoning that rivals human reasoning – as supported by our user study. This approach offers significant savings in infrastructure costs associated with model deployment.

7 Future Work

In future, we aim to extend the scope of this work by including all the TREC topics from 2009 to 2011. Additionally, we intend to enhance our framework by including attachments, allowing for a deeper analysis. We also plan to undertake the prioritization task, wherein we focus on computing ranking metrics such as F1@k, precision@k, recall@k, where k represents the number of documents reviewed. This will allow us to conduct a thorough examination of model performance across the Enron emails corpus and in turn help us identify the specific 'k' at which recall surpasses certain court-mandated thresholds.

Furthermore, we plan to conduct a large-scale user study, involving a broader cohort of annotators and an expanded array of survey questions. We also plan to assess the degree of inter-annotator agreement within this extended study, employing established metrics such as Cohens Kappa (Smeeton, 1985) or Krippendorf Alpha (Gwet, 2011) to quantify the level of consensus among annotators.

References

Toufique Ahmed and Premkumar Devanbu. 2022. Few-shot training llms for project-specific code-summarization. In *Proceedings of the 37th IEEE/ACM International Conference on Automated Software Engineering*, pages 1–5.

Michał Araszkiewicz, Trevor Bench-Capon, Enrico Francesconi, Marc Lauritsen, and Antonino Rotolo. 2022. Thirty years of artificial intelligence and law: overviews. *Artificial Intelligence and Law*, 30(4):593–610.

Kevin D Ashley and Will Bridewell. 2010. Emerging ai & law approaches to automating analysis and retrieval of electronically stored information in discovery proceedings. *Artificial Intelligence and Law*, 18:311–320.

Thomas Barnett, Svetlana Godjevac, Jean-Michel Renders, Caroline Privault, John Schneider, and Robert Wickstrom. 2009. Machine learning classification for document review. In *DESI III: The ICAIL Workshop on Globaal E-Discovery/E-Disclosure*. Citeseer Princeton, NJ, USA.

Jason R Baron, R Braman, K Withers, T Allman, M Daley, and G Paul. 2007. The sedona conference® best practices commentary on the use of search and information retrieval methods in e-discovery. In *The Sedona conference journal*, volume 8.

Jason R Baron, David D Lewis, and Douglas W Oard. 2006. Trec 2006 legal track overview. In *TREC*. Citeseer.

David C Blair and Melvin E Maron. 1985. An evaluation of retrieval effectiveness for a full-text document-retrieval system. *Communications of the ACM*, 28(3):289–299.

Shannon Brown. 2015. Peeking inside the black box: A preliminary survey of technology assisted review (tar) and predictive coding algorithms for ediscovery. *Suffolk J. Trial & App. Advoc.*, 21:221.

Rishi Chhatwal, Peter Gronvall, Nathaniel Huber-Fliflet, Robert Keeling, Jianping Zhang, and Haozhen Zhao. 2018. Explainable text classification in legal document review a case study of explainable predictive coding. In *2018 IEEE international conference on big data (Big Data)*, pages 1905–1911. IEEE.

Jack G Conrad. 2010. E-discovery revisited: the need for artificial intelligence beyond information retrieval. *Artificial Intelligence and Law*, 18(4):321–345.

Gordon V Cormack and Maura R Grossman. 2014. Evaluation of machine-learning protocols for technology-assisted review in electronic discovery. In *Proceedings of the 37th international ACM SIGIR conference on Research & development in information retrieval*, pages 153–162.

Gordon V Cormack and Maura R Grossman. 2016. Scalability of continuous active learning for reliable high-recall text classification. In *Proceedings of the 25th ACM international on conference on information and knowledge management*, pages 1039–1048.

Gordon V Cormack, Maura R Grossman, Bruce Hedin, and Douglas W Oard. 2010. Overview of the trec 2010 legal track. In *TREC*.

Zhuyun Dai, Vincent Y Zhao, Ji Ma, Yi Luan, Jianmo Ni, Jing Lu, Anton Bakalov, Kelvin Guu, Keith B Hall, and Ming-Wei Chang. 2022. Promptagator: Few-shot dense retrieval from 8 examples. *arXiv preprint arXiv:2209.11755*.

Tim Dettmers, Artidoro Pagnoni, Ari Holtzman, and Luke Zettlemoyer. 2023. Qlora: Efficient finetuning of quantized llms.

Debasis Ganguly, Jack G Conrad, Kripabandhu Ghosh, Saptarshi Ghosh, Pawan Goyal, Paheli Bhattacharya, Shubham Kumar Nigam, and Shounak Paul. 2023. Legal ir and nlp: the history, challenges, and state-of-the-art. In *European Conference on Information Retrieval*, pages 331–340. Springer.

Maura R. Grossman, Gordon V. Cormack, Bruce Hedin, and Douglas W. Oard. 2011. Overview of the TREC 2011 legal track. In *Proceedings of The Twentieth Text REtrieval Conference, TREC 2011, Gaithersburg, Maryland, USA, November 15-18, 2011*, volume 500-296 of *NIST Special Publication*. National Institute of Standards and Technology (NIST).

Kilem L Gwet. 2011. On the krippendorff's alpha coefficient. *Manuscript submitted for publication. Retrieved October*, 2(2011):2011.

Bruce Hedin, Stephen Tomlinson, Jason R Baron, and Douglas W Oard. 2009. Overview of the trec 2009 legal track. In *TREC*.

Yupeng Hou, Junjie Zhang, Zihan Lin, Hongyu Lu, Ruobing Xie, Julian McAuley, and Wayne Xin Zhao. 2023. Large language models are zero-shot rankers for recommender systems. *arXiv preprint arXiv:2305.08845*.

Edward J. Hu, Yelong Shen, Phillip Wallis, Zeyuan Allen-Zhu, Yuanzhi Li, Shean Wang, Lu Wang, and Weizhu Chen. 2021. Lora: Low-rank adaptation of large language models.

David D Lewis. 2010. Afterword: data, knowledge, and e-discovery. *Artificial Intelligence and Law*, 18(4):481–486.

Haokun Liu, Derek Tam, Mohammed Muqeeth, Jay Mohta, Tenghao Huang, Mohit Bansal, and Colin Raffel. 2022. Few-shot parameter-efficient fine-tuning is better and cheaper than in-context learning.

Pengfei Liu, Weizhe Yuan, Jinlan Fu, Zhengbao Jiang, Hiroaki Hayashi, and Graham Neubig. 2023. Pre-train, prompt, and predict: A systematic survey of prompting methods in natural language processing. *ACM Computing Surveys*, 55(9):1–35.

Graham McDonald, Craig Macdonald, and Iadh Ounis. 2018. Active learning strategies for technology assisted sensitivity review. In *European Conference on Information Retrieval*, pages 439–453. Springer.

Douglas W Oard, Björn Hedin, Stephen Tomlinson, and Jason R Baron. 2008. Overview of the trec 2008 legal track. In *TREC*, pages 500–277.

Douglas W Oard, William Webber, et al. 2013. Information retrieval for e-discovery. *Foundations and Trends® in Information Retrieval*, 7(2–3):99–237.

Nigel C. Smeeton. 1985. Early history of the kappa statistic. *Biometrics*, 41(3):795–795.

Stephen Tomlinson, Douglas W Oard, Jason R Baron, and Paul Thompson. 2007. Overview of the trec 2007 legal track. In *TREC*.

Petter Törnberg. 2023. Chatgpt-4 outperforms experts and crowd workers in annotating political twitter messages with zero-shot learning. *arXiv preprint arXiv:2304.06588*.

Hugo Touvron, Louis Martin, Kevin Stone, Peter Albert, Amjad Almahairi, Yasmine Babaei, Nikolay Bashlykov, Soumya Batra, Prajjwal Bhargava, Shruti Bhosale, Dan Bikel, Lukas Blecher, Cristian Canton Ferrer, Moya Chen, Guillem Cucurull, David Esiobu, Jude Fernandes, Jeremy Fu, Wenyin Fu, Brian Fuller, Cynthia Gao, Vedanuj Goswami, Naman Goyal, Anthony Hartshorn, Saghar Hosseini, Rui Hou, Hakan Inan, Marcin Kardas, Viktor Kerkez, Madian Khabsa, Isabel Kloumann, Artem Korenev, Punit Singh Koura, Marie-Anne Lachaux, Thibaut Lavril, Jenya Lee, Diana Liskovich, Yinghai Lu, Yuning Mao, Xavier Martinet, Todor Mihaylov, Pushkar Mishra, Igor Molybog, Yixin Nie, Andrew Poulton, Jeremy Reizenstein, Rashi Rungta, Kalyan Saladi, Alan Schelten, Ruan Silva, Eric Michael Smith, Ranjan Subramanian, Xiaoqing Ellen Tan, Binh Tang, Ross Taylor, Adina Williams, Jian Xiang Kuan, Puxin Xu, Zheng Yan, Iliyan Zarov, Yuchen Zhang, Angela Fan, Melanie Kambadur, Sharan Narang, Aurelien Rodriguez, Robert Stojnic, Sergey Edunov, and Thomas Scialom. 2023. Llama 2: Open foundation and fine-tuned chat models.

Ashish Vaswani, Noam Shazeer, Niki Parmar, Jakob Uszkoreit, Llion Jones, Aidan N Gomez,Łukasz Kaiser, and Illia Polosukhin. 2017. Attention is all you need. *Advances in neural information processing systems*, 30.

S Villata et al. 2020. Sentence embeddings and high-speed similarity search for fast computer assisted annotation of legal documents. In *Legal Knowledge and Information Systems: JURIX 2020: The Thirty-third Annual Conference, Brno, Czech Republic, December 9-11, 2020*, volume 334, page 164. IOS Press.

Jason Wei, Maarten Bosma, Vincent Y Zhao, Kelvin Guu, Adams Wei Yu, Brian Lester, Nan Du, Andrew M Dai, and Quoc V Le. 2021. Finetuned language models are zero-shot learners. *arXiv preprint arXiv:2109.01652*.

Jason Wei, Xuezhi Wang, Dale Schuurmans, Maarten Bosma, Fei Xia, Ed Chi, Quoc V Le, Denny Zhou, et al. 2022. Chain-of-thought prompting elicits reasoning in large language models. *Advances in Neural Information Processing Systems*, 35:24824–24837.

Eugene Yang, David D. Lewis, and Ophir Frieder. 2021. On minimizing cost in legal document review workflows. In *Proceedings of the 21st ACM Symposium on Document Engineering*. ACM.

A Appendix

A.1 Topic Statements

The three topics, numbered 401, 402, and 403, used in the TREC 2011 Legal Track learning task are described below:

A.1.1 Topic 401

All documents or communications that describe, discuss, refer to, report on, or relate to the design, development, operation, or marketing of enrononline, or any other online service offered, provided, or used by the Company (or any of its subsidiaries, predecessors, or successors-in-interest), for the purchase, sale, trading, or exchange of financial or other instruments or products, including but not limited to, derivative instruments, commodities, futures, and swaps.

A.1.2 Topic 402

All documents or communications that describe, discuss, refer to, report on, or relate to whether the purchase, sale, trading, or exchange of over-the-counter derivatives, or any other actual or contemplated financial instruments or products, is, was, would be, or will be legal or illegal, or permitted or prohibited, under any existing or proposed rule(s), regulation(s), law(s), standard(s), or other proscription(s), whether domestic or foreign.

A.1.3 Topic 403

All documents or communications that describe, discuss, refer to, report on, or relate to the environmental impact of any activity or activities undertaken by the Company, including but not limited to, any measures taken to conform to, comply with, avoid, circumvent, or influence any existing or proposed rule(s), regulation(s), law(s), standard(s), or other proscription(s), such as those governing environmental emissions, spills, pollution, noise, and/or animal habitats.

A.2 User Survey

Figure 4 shows the snapshot of the survey spreadsheet provided to the SMSs. The first part contains the instructions and the topic statement. These panes were frozen while the annotator could scroll through the rest of the data. Each row consisted of an email content, followed by the relevancy to the topic statement, and the five reasonings which the annotators had to rate. The reasonings were randomly shuffled to prevent annotator bias.

A.3 Hyperparameter Ranges

We conducted an extensive hyperparameter search to tune model parameters for instruction tuning. We primarily tuned LoRA parameters such as rank (r), scaling factor (alpha), target modules (the layers where the adapters are inserted), learning rate, and number of epochs. For the rank parameter, we considered values of 4, 8, 16, and 32. The scaling factor was checked for values of 16 and 32. For adapter placement, we examined insertion into one or more of the following layers: query-key-value, attention output, upsampling, or downsampling. The learning rate was varied across three orders of magnitude: 1e-3, 1e-4, and 1e-5. Similarly, the number of epochs was chosen from the range of 1 to 4. To ensure a detailed exploration of the hyperparameter space, we randomly sampled 16 distinct combinations from these ranges for each model. All the qLoRA experiments were done in 4 bit precision with same hyperparameter ranges as described above.

Our Ask	For the Topic statement given below, we have selected 10 responsive and 10 non responsive emails. With each of the emails, we have provided reasonings generated by 5 different models (not in any order). You need to score each of these reasoning on a discrete scale of 1 to 5, where 1 is the lowest preference and 5 is the highest preference. Try to avoid ties unless really required.										
Topic Statement	Discussion regarding design, development, operation, or marketing of enrononline, or any other online service offered, provided, or used by enron (or any of its subsidiaries, predecessors, or successors-in-interest), for the purchase, sale, trading, or exchange of financial or other instruments or products, including but not limited to, derivative instruments, commodities, futures, and swaps.										
NOTE	The reasoning generated by some models may be incomplete. Rate these answers as well - on the same scale (1-5).										
	Reasonings						Preference based on a scale of 1(low)-5(high)				
email_text	actual_label	Reasoning 1	Reasoning 2	Reasoning 3	Reasoning 4	Reasoning 5	Reasoning 1	Reasoning 2	Reasoning 3	Reasoning 4	Reasoning 5
Subject: RE: We will only be able to get Kiodex the customers EOL trades as per the agreement. If the customer so desire they can ask us to send their non-EOl trades to Kiodex for processing, but that is outside the Kiodex/ENW agreement.	Relevant	the email is related to the topic because it mentions "kiodex" and "eol trades," which suggests that the email is discussing the trading of financial instruments, specifically those related to commodities and futures. the email also mentions "non-eol trades," which suggests that the email is discussing the trading of financial instruments outside of the enrononline platform.	the email mentions kiodex, which is an online service offered by enron for the trading and processing of financial instruments. it also discusses the agreement between kiodex and enw (presumably enron) regarding the submission of trades. therefore, the email is related to the topic.	the email is related to the topic because it mentions kiodex, which is a platform for trading environmental commodities, and discusses the agreement between kiodex and enron regarding the processing of trades. the email also mentions eol trades, which are trades that are executed outside of kiodex, but can be sent to kiodex for processing if the customer desires.	yes, the email is related to the topic. the email is about the design, development, operation, or marketing of enrononline, which is an online service offered by enron for the purchase, sale, trading, or exchange of financial or other instruments or products, including but not limited to, derivative instruments, commodities, futures, and swaps. the email discusses the agreement between enron and	this short email has no mention of enron, but (presumably) eol is an acronym for enrononline (enw is also presumably short for some enron entity, the counterparty to kiodex in their agreement). the term "trades" indicates a financial transaction likely of the kind made on enrononline. therefore the email is a discussion of the operation of enrononline.					
Subject: EnronOnline and NYMEX Vin, Glad we could hook up yesterday. The gist of what we are interested in is providing EnronOnline's liquidity to local NYMEX traders. I would like to explore the concept of NYMEX's clearing corp or another clearer standing in the middle between Enron and these locals. EnronOnline's architecture provides for a Master user, such as a Clearing Corp, to set up as many sub-users (local traders) as it wants. Each sub-user has trading rights as designated and controlled by the master. We would envision the Clearing Corp. handling it credit arrangements with the locals, and negotiating its relationship with Enron. I know this is pretty simple stuff, but every long journey starts with a small step. Please let me your interest in pursuing this sort of arrangement or a variant thereof. Thanks, Andy Zipper Vice President Enron Corp.	Relevant	the email discusses the concept of providing enrononline's liquidity to local nymex traders and the possibility of using a clearing corp. to facilitate this process. the email also mentions enrononline's architecture and its ability to set up sub-users with trading rights designated by the master user. these elements directly relate to the design, development, operation, and marketing	the email discusses the concept of providing enrononline's liquidity to local nymex traders and exploring the idea of a clearing corporation standing in the middle between enron and the locals. it also mentions the architecture of enrononline and the role of a clearing corp in handling credit arrangements and negotiating relationships. these topics are directly related to the design, development, and operation of enrononline and its online service for trading financial instruments.	the email discusses the possibility of providing enrononline's liquidity to local nymex traders, which falls under the topic of design, development, operation, or marketing of enrononline or any other online service offered by enron. the email also mentions enrononline's architecture and its ability to set up sub-users, which further supports the idea that the email is related to the	enrononline appears in the subject line of this email along with nymex, a prominent exchange. the body of the email contains many references to enrononline in the context of a discussion of a potential interaction with nymex clearing. it is a discussion of the design, development and potential operation of enrononline.	yes, the email is related to the topic. the email is about the design, development, operation, or marketing of enrononline, which is an online service offered by enron for the purchase, sale, trading, or exchange of financial or other instruments or products, including but not limited to, derivative instruments, commodities, futures, and swaps. the email discusses the concept of providing enron					

Figure 4: Snapshot of the survey spreadsheet.

Retrieval-Augmented Chain-of-Thought in Semi-structured Domains

Vaibhav Mavi
New York University
vm2241@nyu.edu

Abulhair Saparov
New York University
as17582@nyu.edu

Chen Zhao
New York University
cz1285@nyu.edu

Abstract

Applying existing question answering (QA) systems to specialized domains like law and finance presents challenges that necessitate domain expertise. Although large language models (LLMs) have shown impressive language comprehension and in-context learning capabilities, their inability to handle very long inputs/contexts is well known. Tasks specific to these domains need significant background knowledge, leading to contexts that can often exceed the maximum length that existing LLMs can process. This study explores leveraging the semi-structured nature of legal and financial data to efficiently retrieve relevant context, enabling the use of LLMs for domain-specialized QA. The resulting system outperforms contemporary models and also provides useful explanations for the answers, encouraging the integration of LLMs into legal and financial NLP systems for future research.

1 Introduction

Building NLP systems for answering questions in the legal and financial domains could save time and resources, ensure compliance, and enhance the overall accuracy and effectiveness of legal and financial operations (Nay et al., 2023; Yang et al., 2023). Applying QA systems to such domains poses unique challenges. These domains feature complex jargon, nuanced phrasing, and contextual dependencies that require specialized knowledge and expertise (Katz et al., 2023; Wu et al., 2023a). A system tailored to these domains should be able to efficiently process and analyze large volumes of legal, financial, or regulatory documents, extracting relevant insights and answering targeted queries.

Large language models (LLMs) have shown impressive performance on several NLP tasks (Zhao et al., 2023). de Padua et al. (2023) show that LLMs trained on large amounts of data are able to obtain the necessary domain knowledge through in-context learning (ICL) (Brown et al., 2020). However, a major limitation of LLMs is the limit on the input size. There are many attempts to address this limitation (Press et al., 2022; Haviv et al., 2022; Zhu et al., 2023) and multiple transformer models are able to handle longer contexts (OpenAI, 2023; Rozière et al., 2023; Dai et al., 2019; Sun et al., 2023b). However, (Liu et al., 2023) show that model performance on certain parts of the input decreases with input size. Further, the cost and latency of LLMs increases with the input size.

The context required for legal and financial questions is often large and may not fit within the token limit, requiring more efficient retrieval. Financial and legal documents are often semi-structured. For example, Figure 1 shows a section from the US Internal Revenue Code. The text is organized into subsections, paragraphs and bullet points, which we leverage for better information retrieval. Further, financial reports often contain quantities in tabular format. We exploit these structures in a prompting approach that incorporates retrieval to workaround the context token limit.

We evaluate the proposed method on two datasets: FinQA (Chen et al., 2021) and SARA (Holzenberger et al., 2020). These datasets feature complex questions which require multiple steps of reasoning and arithmetic computations, which is challenging for language systems. We adopt chain-of-thought (CoT) prompting (Wei et al., 2023) for generating the answers since it is well suited for performing reasoning in a step-by-step manner. A chain of thought is a coherent sequence of reasoning steps that lead to the correct answer in a step-by-step manner. Providing examples of question-answer pairs along with their CoTs prepended to the test question causes GPT-3 to likewise output a CoT along with the answer for the test question, and improve its overall reasoning accuracy. CoT prompting is especially useful for complex tasks which require multiple steps of reasoning over the given input.

Proceedings of the Natural Legal Language Processing Workshop 2023, pages 178–191

§7703. Determination of marital status	s7703
(a) General rule	s7703(a)
(1) the determination of whether an individual is married shall be made as of the close of his taxable year ...	s7703(a)(1)
(2) an individual legally separated from his spouse under a decree of divorce or of separate maintenance ...	s7703(a)(2)
(b) Certain married individuals living apart	s7703(b)
For purposes of those provisions of this title which refer to this subsection, if-	s7703(b)
(1) an individual who is married (within the meaning of subsection (a)) and who files a separate return ...	s7703(b)(1)
(2) such individual furnishes over one-half of the cost of maintaining such household during the year, and	s7703(b)(2)
(3) during the last 6 months of the taxable year, such individual's spouse is not a member of such household,	s7703(b)(3)
such individual shall not be considered as married.	s7704(b)

Figure 1: An example of a statute from US Internal Revenue Code (left) and the subsection name assigned to each sentence after parsing as described in section 4.1.1 (right).

The results demonstrate that this simple and efficient approach outperforms state-of-the-art models in these domains. Training LLMs on financial and legal data may not be feasible as they may contain sensitive information. The use of ICL circumvents the problem and avoids expensive and tedious process of data collection and training. This makes the proposed approach a practical solution in scenarios where labeled data is limited or expensive to obtain. Additionally, CoT prompting offers the advantage of generating explanations and facilitating interpretability in critical domains where it is a key obstacle for the adoption of AI systems (Danilevsky et al., 2020). However, a major drawback of the approach is that it is task-specific. In particular, the retrieval relies on the structure within in the data and needs to be adapted to data from different sources[1].

We hope our work fosters research on coupling LLMs with retrieval in domains such as finance and law, where the ability to extract insights and answer questions about vast amounts of domain-specific data has many practical applications.

2 Related work

Previous work has proposed training specialized LLMs for financial and legal domains (Wu et al., 2023a; Huang et al., 2023; Nguyen, 2023; Yang et al., 2023). However, doing so requires a large amount of data, compute and cost.

Sun et al. (2023a) evaluate GPT-2 on FinQA (Chen et al., 2021). Blair-Stanek et al. (2023) evaluate GPT-3 with different prompting techniques on SARA where the context includes all the sections from the statutes. Since the input size of GPT-3 is limited, the prompts only included a subset of sections, which may not contain the required information. Further, fewer in-context examples were used for CoT as compared to few-shot learning. Li et al. (2023) and Wu et al. 2023b observe better performance with more in-context examples.

Nay et al. (2023) test various GPT models with ICL to answer multiple choice questions over tax laws. A retriever augmented setting is tested where a dense passage retriver, GTR (Ni et al., 2021), retrieves the top 4 relevant sections to the questions. Since entire sections are passed to the LLMs, the text has to be truncated.

This study extends past work by complementing LLMs with a retriever that extracts the relevant text from within the statutes, allowing for larger contexts and more in-context examples in the prompt.

3 Data

We use two datasets containing questions that involve multi-step logical and arithmetic reasoning from the legal and financial domains respectively.

3.1 SARA

StAtutory Reasoning Assessment dataset (SARA) (Holzenberger et al., 2020) is designed to evaluate statutory reasoning over a set of sections extracted from the US Internal Revenue Code (IRC). For each of the subsections contained in the selected sections, there are two hand-written case scenarios. Correctly solving these cases requires multiple steps of arithmetic as well as logical reasoning. For instance, some cases require computing the amount of tax owed according to a given section, only if the section applies to the given case. Thus, this dataset serves as a challenging task for an AI system, requiring domain expertise and reasoning abilities.

3.2 FinQA

FinQA (Chen et al., 2021) is a financial QA dataset. It comprises of 8,281 examples where each question is accompanied by a financial report, containing text as well as a table. The report contains the necessary information to correctly answer the question. FinQA poses many challenges for a QA system. The questions require retrieval, arithmetic and logical reasoning simultaneously over tables

[1]The code for this work is publicly available at `github.com/vaibhavg152/Retrieval-Augmented-Chain-of-Thought-in-Semi-structured-Domains`

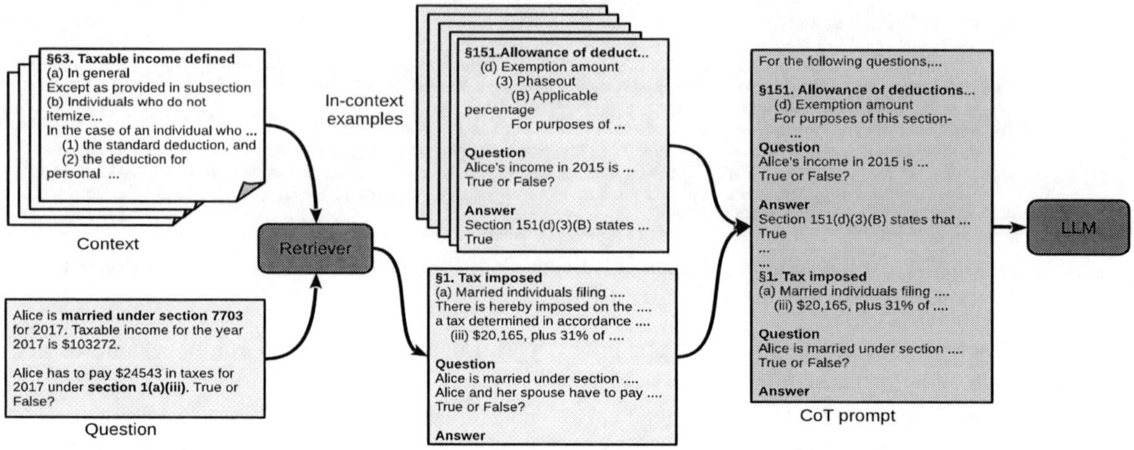

Figure 2: An overview of the proposed system on a sample input from SARA. The retriever extracts the relevant information from the context and combines it with the question. In-context examples are appended with the retrieval output to construct a prompt which is used for querying LLMs to generate an answer along the chain-of-thought.

and text. The questions also require an understanding of financial jargon. Finally, multiple reasoning steps are required to derive the answer.

4 Methodology

Figure 2 shows an overview of our proposed approach, which consists of two main components: retrieval and answering. The retrieval step involves filtering paragraphs from text and rows from tables that are relevant to the question. The retrieved information is then passed to the answering model.

4.1 Retrieval

Retrieval is essential for fully leveraging ICL and CoT reasoning abilities of LLMs. It can help to prevent the required context from exceeding the token limit, while also allowing the prompt to include enough in-context examples along with their CoT explanations. It can also help to reduce the time and cost of inference.

We propose to leverage the structure present in the data to retrieve the relevant context from the legal statutes and financial reports. This structure is specific to the data source and the retriever needs to be designed accordingly. In our analysis, we explore datasets with two different sources: SARA, where a template-based algorithm can be used for effective retrieval; and FinQA, where a more sophisticated pre-trained retrieval model is required.

4.1.1 SARA

As shown in Figure 1, the statutes in SARA are organized in a hierarchical structure with sections, sub-sections, paragraphs, and bullets. This hierarchical structure offers valuable information for efficient and accurate retrieval.

Figure 3 in the Appendix shows an example of a question from SARA. The questions contain references to the specific sub-sections they pertain to. Firstly, a simple regular expression-based extractor scans the question text to identify the relevant section name.

Next, a rule-based statute parser extracts the mentioned sub-section. The parser reads each sentence in the given statutes and assigns it to the most specific sub-section to which the sentence belongs. Figure 1 shows an example of a parsed statute section. We explore three retrieval strategies:

1. `mentioned-only`: The retriever returns all the sentences that are assigned to sub-sections containing the queried sub-section as a prefix. For Figure 1, a query for sub-section $7703(a)(1)$ will result in sentences assigned to $s7703$, $s7703(a)$ and $s7703(a)(1)$.
2. `entire-section`: Retriever returns the entire sub-section. In Figure 1, a query for sub-section $7703(a)(1)$ will result in sentences assigned to $s7703, s7703(a), s7703(a)(1)$, as well as $s7703(a)(2)$.
3. `references`: Retriever returns sub-sections mentioned in the question along with those that are referenced in these retrieved subsections[2].

4.1.2 FinQA

The absence of a hierarchical structure in FinQA reports makes it impractical to adopt a rule-based approach for retrieval. Chen et al. (2021) convert the tables into text and then use BERT for retrieving relevant sentences from the report.

[2]It is intuitive to consider an approach that recursively retrieves text from sections mentioned in the sections retrieved in the previous step. However, this recursive approach proves to be impractical as it generates excessively large contexts.

However, using templates to convert tables into text leads to very long contexts. These templates can also introduce grammatical and logical errors, leading to a loss in the performance of the answering module. Thus, we use a tabular format during the answering step in order to exploit the structure (see Figure 5 in Appendix).

We also evaluate the system with gold retrieved sentences (GPT3-Gold, LLaMA2-70B-Gold).

4.2 Answering

In this study, we test GPT-3 (`text-davinci-003`) (Brown et al., 2020) and LLaMA-2 (Touvron et al., 2023) to answer the queries. We experiment with different prompting techniques, namely *zero-shot*, *few-shot* and *chain-of-thought* prompting. CoT prompting has been shown to improve the ICL abilities of sufficiently large LLMs (Zhao et al., 2023) and is especially useful for tasks that require multiple steps of reasoning.

In the zero-shot setting, the model is given the retrieved context and the question and is expected to output just the answer without any explanation.

In the few-shot setting, we further include in-context examples of question-answer pairs (8 examples for SARA and 12 examples for FinQA[3]).

In the CoT setting, we use the same in-context examples as used for the few-shot setting but each example also includes a CoT explanation. These explanations are manually written for each example. The model is expected to generate the answer along with the CoT explanations for the test cases.

For all questions in a dataset, we use the same prompt containing the same in-context examples which are selected using prompt tuning as described in Appendix section A.1.

Figures 4 and 5 in the Appendix show the CoT prompts used for SARA and FinQA respectively.

5 Experimental setup

5.1 Evaluation

For SARA, the task is formulated as an entailment task and is evaluated as a binary classification task.

For FinQA, Chen et al. (2021) propose **program accuracy** where the model is expected to generate a 'program' along with the answer. A program is a sequence of mathematical operations that leads to the final answer. The evaluation thus compares the output program with the gold standard program and checks if the two evaluate to the same answer.

We also measure the **answer accuracy** by ignoring errors only in units, prefix, suffix, precision digits or rounding errors.

Model name	Accuracy
Majority baseline [11]	50.0 ± 8.22
Feed-forward [11]	54.0 ± 8.20
Legal-BERT [11]	49.0 ± 8.22
BERT [12]	59.0 ± 8.09
GPT-3 (0-shot) [3]	71.0 ± 7.46
GPT-3 (CoT) [3]	57.0 ± 8.14
GPT-3 (dynamic) [3]	60.0 ± 8.06
GPT-3 + Ret	**81.6 ± 4.22**
LLaMA2-7B + Ret	53.5 ± 5.43
LLaMA2-7B_chat + Ret	54.4 ± 5.43
LLaMA2-13B + Ret	57.5 ± 5.39
LLaMA2-13B_chat + Ret	66.7 ± 5.13
LLaMA2-70B + Ret	71.1 ± 4.94

Table 1: Comparison of proposed system's performance on SARA with the existing baselines. The top section shows non-LLM based methods. The middle section shows the evaluation results from Blair-Stanek et al. (2023). The bottom section shows the results of our proposed system with 'Ret' representing the proposed retrieval. Results are shown with the 90% confidence interval.

5.2 Comparison with existing methods

Tables 1 and 2 show results on SARA and FinQA respectively[4]. Descriptions of the baselines are provided in Appendix Section B.

On SARA, both GPT-3 and LLaMA2-70B surpass the existing methods by a significant margin. We also observe the expected trend of the performance improving with the increase in the model size, with GPT-3 (175B) performing significantly better with LLaMA-2 models (Kaplan et al., 2020)[5].

On the other hand, the performance on FinQA with GPT-3 is comparable with baselines in terms of program accuracy but lags behind in answer accuracy. We believe this behavior is due to arithmetic errors made by LLMs (Qian et al., 2023), resulting in cases with correct programs but incorrect answers. Our approach with LLaMA2-13B/70B and GPT-3 outperforms general crowd workers

[3]Tabular data in FinQA leads to shorter retrieved context and allows more examples per prompt.

[4]For testing on FinQA, we randomly sample 200 examples from the public test set due to the high cost of LLM queries.

[5]Although Touvron et al. (2023) report similar performance of LLaMA-2 to GPT-3 on benchmark datasets, the task addressed here is domain-specific and requires more complex mathematical and logical reasoning than the benchmarks they use for evaluation.

Model	Program acc	Answer acc
Longformer [2]	21.90 ± 2.01	20.48 ± 1.96
ELASTIC [35]	57.54 ± 2.40	62.16 ± 2.36
DyRRen [17]	61.29 ± 2.37	63.30 ± 2.34
TabT5 [1]	**68.00 ± 2.27**	**70.79 ± 2.21**
APOLLO [28]	65.60 ± 2.31	67.99 ± 2.27
FinQANet-BERT [6]	58.86 ± 2.39	61.24 ± 2.37
GPT-3-BERT	**68.00 ± 5.43**	52.50 ± 5.81
LLaMA2-7B-BERT	25.50 ± 5.07	16.50 ± 4.32
LLaMA2-7B_chat-BERT	34.50 ± 5.53	14.50 ± 4.10
LLaMA2-13B-BERT	52.50 ± 5.81	33.00 ± 5.47
LLaMA2-13B_chat-BERT	50.50 ± 5.82	26.50 ± 5.13
LLaMA2-70B-BERT	60.50 ± 5.69	51.00 ± 5.81
Human non-expert [6]	48.17 ± 2.43	50.68 ± 2.43
Human expert [6]	87.49 ± 1.61	91.16 ± 1.38
FinQANet-Gold [6]	68.76 ± 2.25	**70.00 ± 2.23**
GPT-3-Gold	**72.50 ± 5.19**	56.50 ± 5.77
LLaMA2-70B-Gold	63.00 ± 5.62	54.50 ± 5.79

Table 2: Comparison with state of the art and baselines methods on FinQA. Results are presented with a 90% confidence interval.

Retrieval strategy	Accuracy
`entire-section`	52.50 ± 12.99
`references`	75.00 ± 11.26
`mentioned-only`	**77.50 ± 10.86**

Table 3: Comparison of the three retrieval strategies used with GPT-3 on SARA validation set.

who lack domain expertise in finance, whereas it falls short compared to financial experts.

The bottom section of Table 2 highlights the effectiveness of GPT-3 over FinQANet (Chen et al., 2021) when provided with the gold retrieved results. However, LLaMA-2 shows sub-par performance.

5.3 Ablation studies

Comparison of prompting techniques: Table 4 in the Appendix shows the evaluation results for zero-shot, few-shot and CoT prompting. CoT prompting leads to significantly better results across all models.

Comparing retrieval strategies: As outlined in section 4, we test three different retrieval strategies for SARA. Table 3 reveals that `mentioned-only` and `references` perform significantly better than `entire-section`. The questions in SARA are designed in a way where additional context apart from the mentioned sub-sections is not required. The difference in accuracy indicates the benefit of more targeted retrieval for model performance, since over-retrieval may dilute the signal provided by more directly relevant context.

Case analysis We perform manual qualitative inspection of the generated CoT explanations and report the analysis in Appendix section D.2.

6 Discussion

This study aims to utilize LLMs for challenging domain-specific QA tasks by using ICL along with retrieval techniques that leverage the semi-structured nature of financial and legal data. The proposed approach is simple and performs well compared to existing systems. It exploits ICL which avoids the costly and time-consuming processes of data collection and training. Since the proposed system produces a chain-of-thought with each output, it is easily interpretable and errors can be identified and rectified by human supervision (Danilevsky et al., 2020).

We hope this work will encourage researchers to delve deeper into the analysis and development of LLM-integrated NLP systems and retrieval-augmented LLMs.

7 Limitations

The retrieval algorithms in our study are specifically tailored to each dataset. Despite good reasoning abilities, the evaluation reveals that arithmetic errors are common. Further, inference with LLMs can be costly with latency higher than traditional approaches, making it sub-optimal for handling large volumes of data efficiently.

These limitations point to interesting future directions such as using arithmetic tools as plugins (Schick et al., 2023) for better performance and more generalizable retrieval algorithms. Further, several domain-specific LLMs can be tested (Huang et al., 2023; Yang et al., 2023; Wu et al., 2023a).

8 Acknowledgements

We sincerely thank the anonymous reviewers for their valuable feedback. For the experiments with LLaMA2, we thank the NYU IT High Performance Computing resources, services, and staff expertise.

References

Ewa Andrejczuk, Julian Martin Eisenschlos, Francesco Piccinno, Syrine Krichene, and Yasemin Altun. 2022. Table-to-text generation and pre-training with tabt5.

Iz Beltagy, Matthew E. Peters, and Arman Cohan. 2020. Longformer: The long-document transformer.

Andrew Blair-Stanek, Nils Holzenberger, and Benjamin Van Durme. 2023. Can gpt-3 perform statutory reasoning?

Tom Brown, Benjamin Mann, Nick Ryder, Melanie Subbiah, Jared D Kaplan, Prafulla Dhariwal, Arvind Neelakantan, Pranav Shyam, Girish Sastry, Amanda Askell, Sandhini Agarwal, Ariel Herbert-Voss, Gretchen Krueger, Tom Henighan, Rewon Child, Aditya Ramesh, Daniel Ziegler, Jeffrey Wu, Clemens Winter, Chris Hesse, Mark Chen, Eric Sigler, Mateusz Litwin, Scott Gray, Benjamin Chess, Jack Clark, Christopher Berner, Sam McCandlish, Alec Radford, Ilya Sutskever, and Dario Amodei. 2020. Language models are few-shot learners. In *Advances in Neural Information Processing Systems*, volume 33, pages 1877–1901. Curran Associates, Inc.

Ilias Chalkidis, Manos Fergadiotis, Prodromos Malakasiotis, Nikolaos Aletras, and Ion Androutsopoulos. 2020. LEGAL-BERT: The muppets straight out of law school. In *Findings of the Association for Computational Linguistics: EMNLP 2020*, pages 2898–2904, Online. Association for Computational Linguistics.

Zhiyu Chen, Wenhu Chen, Charese Smiley, Sameena Shah, Iana Borova, Dylan Langdon, Reema Moussa, Matt Beane, Ting-Hao Huang, Bryan Routledge, and William Yang Wang. 2021. FinQA: A dataset of numerical reasoning over financial data. In *Proceedings of the 2021 Conference on Empirical Methods in Natural Language Processing*, pages 3697–3711, Online and Punta Cana, Dominican Republic. Association for Computational Linguistics.

Zihang Dai, Zhilin Yang, Yiming Yang, Jaime Carbonell, Quoc Le, and Ruslan Salakhutdinov. 2019. Transformer-XL: Attentive language models beyond a fixed-length context. In *Proceedings of the 57th Annual Meeting of the Association for Computational Linguistics*, pages 2978–2988, Florence, Italy. Association for Computational Linguistics.

Marina Danilevsky, Kun Qian, Ranit Aharonov, Yannis Katsis, Ban Kawas, and Prithviraj Sen. 2020. A survey of the state of explainable AI for natural language processing. In *Proceedings of the 1st Conference of the Asia-Pacific Chapter of the Association for Computational Linguistics and the 10th International Joint Conference on Natural Language Processing*, pages 447–459, Suzhou, China. Association for Computational Linguistics.

Raul Salles de Padua, Imran Qureshi, and Mustafa U. Karakaplan. 2023. Gpt-3 models are few-shot financial reasoners.

Adi Haviv, Ori Ram, Ofir Press, Peter Izsak, and Omer Levy. 2022. Transformer language models without positional encodings still learn positional information. In *Findings of the Association for Computational Linguistics: EMNLP 2022*, pages 1382–1390, Abu Dhabi, United Arab Emirates. Association for Computational Linguistics.

Nils Holzenberger, Andrew Blair-Stanek, and Benjamin Van Durme. 2020. A dataset for statutory reasoning in tax law entailment and question answering.

Nils Holzenberger and Benjamin Van Durme. 2021. Factoring statutory reasoning as language understanding challenges. In *Proceedings of the 59th Annual Meeting of the Association for Computational Linguistics and the 11th International Joint Conference on Natural Language Processing (Volume 1: Long Papers)*, pages 2742–2758, Online. Association for Computational Linguistics.

Quzhe Huang, Mingxu Tao, Zhenwei An, Chen Zhang, Cong Jiang, Zhibin Chen, Zirui Wu, and Yansong Feng. 2023. Lawyer llama technical report.

Jared Kaplan, Sam McCandlish, Tom Henighan, Tom B. Brown, Benjamin Chess, Rewon Child, Scott Gray, Alec Radford, Jeffrey Wu, and Dario Amodei. 2020. Scaling laws for neural language models.

Daniel Martin Katz, Dirk Hartung, Lauritz Gerlach, Abhik Jana, and Michael J. Bommarito II au2. 2023. Natural language processing in the legal domain.

Mukai Li, Shansan Gong, Jiangtao Feng, Yiheng Xu, Jun Zhang, Zhiyong Wu, and Lingpeng Kong. 2023. In-context learning with many demonstration examples.

Xiao Li, Yin Zhu, Sichen Liu, Jiangzhou Ju, Yuzhong Qu, and Gong Cheng. 2022. Dyrren: A dynamic retriever-reranker-generator model for numerical reasoning over tabular and textual data.

Nelson F. Liu, Kevin Lin, John Hewitt, Ashwin Paranjape, Michele Bevilacqua, Fabio Petroni, and Percy Liang. 2023. Lost in the middle: How language models use long contexts.

John J. Nay, David Karamardian, Sarah B. Lawsky, Wenting Tao, Meghana Bhat, Raghav Jain, Aaron Travis Lee, Jonathan H. Choi, and Jungo Kasai. 2023. Large language models as tax attorneys: A case study in legal capabilities emergence.

Ha-Thanh Nguyen. 2023. A brief report on lawgpt 1.0: A virtual legal assistant based on gpt-3.

Jianmo Ni, Chen Qu, Jing Lu, Zhuyun Dai, Gustavo Hernández Ábrego, Ji Ma, Vincent Y. Zhao, Yi Luan, Keith B. Hall, Ming-Wei Chang, and Yinfei Yang. 2021. Large dual encoders are generalizable retrievers.

Rodrigo Nogueira and Kyunghyun Cho. 2020. Passage re-ranking with bert.

OpenAI. 2023. Gpt-4 technical report. *ArXiv*, abs/2303.08774.

Ofir Press, Noah A. Smith, and Mike Lewis. 2022. Train short, test long: Attention with linear biases enables input length extrapolation.

Jing Qian, Hong Wang, Zekun Li, Shiyang Li, and Xifeng Yan. 2023. Limitations of language models in arithmetic and symbolic induction. In *Proceedings of the 61st Annual Meeting of the Association for Computational Linguistics (Volume 1: Long Papers)*, pages 9285–9298, Toronto, Canada. Association for Computational Linguistics.

Baptiste Rozière, Jonas Gehring, Fabian Gloeckle, Sten Sootla, Itai Gat, Xiaoqing Ellen Tan, Yossi Adi, Jingyu Liu, Tal Remez, Jérémy Rapin, Artyom Kozhevnikov, Ivan Evtimov, Joanna Bitton, Manish Bhatt, Cristian Canton Ferrer, Aaron Grattafiori, Wenhan Xiong, Alexandre Défossez, Jade Copet, Faisal Azhar, Hugo Touvron, Louis Martin, Nicolas Usunier, Thomas Scialom, and Gabriel Synnaeve. 2023. Code llama: Open foundation models for code.

Timo Schick, Jane Dwivedi-Yu, Roberto Dessì, Roberta Raileanu, Maria Lomeli, Luke Zettlemoyer, Nicola Cancedda, and Thomas Scialom. 2023. Toolformer: Language models can teach themselves to use tools.

Jiashuo Sun, Hang Zhang, Chen Lin, Yeyun Gong, Jian Guo, and Nan Duan. 2023a. Apollo: An optimized training approach for long-form numerical reasoning.

Yutao Sun, Li Dong, Barun Patra, Shuming Ma, Shaohan Huang, Alon Benhaim, Vishrav Chaudhary, Xia Song, and Furu Wei. 2023b. A length-extrapolatable transformer. In *Proceedings of the 61st Annual Meeting of the Association for Computational Linguistics (Volume 1: Long Papers)*, pages 14590–14604, Toronto, Canada. Association for Computational Linguistics.

Hugo Touvron, Louis Martin, Kevin Stone, Peter Albert, Amjad Almahairi, Yasmine Babaei, Nikolay Bashlykov, Soumya Batra, Prajjwal Bhargava, Shruti Bhosale, Dan Bikel, Lukas Blecher, Cristian Canton Ferrer, Moya Chen, Guillem Cucurull, David Esiobu, Jude Fernandes, Jeremy Fu, Wenyin Fu, Brian Fuller, Cynthia Gao, Vedanuj Goswami, Naman Goyal, Anthony Hartshorn, Saghar Hosseini, Rui Hou, Hakan Inan, Marcin Kardas, Viktor Kerkez, Madian Khabsa, Isabel Kloumann, Artem Korenev, Punit Singh Koura, Marie-Anne Lachaux, Thibaut Lavril, Jenya Lee, Diana Liskovich, Yinghai Lu, Yuning Mao, Xavier Martinet, Todor Mihaylov, Pushkar Mishra, Igor Molybog, Yixin Nie, Andrew Poulton, Jeremy Reizenstein, Rashi Rungta, Kalyan Saladi, Alan Schelten, Ruan Silva, Eric Michael Smith, Ranjan Subramanian, Xiaoqing Ellen Tan, Binh Tang, Ross Taylor, Adina Williams, Jian Xiang Kuan, Puxin Xu, Zheng Yan, Iliyan Zarov, Yuchen Zhang, Angela Fan, Melanie Kambadur, Sharan Narang, Aurelien Rodriguez, Robert Stojnic, Sergey Edunov, and Thomas Scialom. 2023. Llama 2: Open foundation and fine-tuned chat models.

Jason Wei, Xuezhi Wang, Dale Schuurmans, Maarten Bosma, Brian Ichter, Fei Xia, Ed Chi, Quoc Le, and Denny Zhou. 2023. Chain-of-thought prompting elicits reasoning in large language models.

Shijie Wu, Ozan Irsoy, Steven Lu, Vadim Dabravolski, Mark Dredze, Sebastian Gehrmann, Prabhanjan Kambadur, David Rosenberg, and Gideon Mann. 2023a. Bloomberggpt: A large language model for finance.

Zhiyong Wu, Yaoxiang Wang, Jiacheng Ye, and Lingpeng Kong. 2023b. Self-adaptive in-context learning: An information compression perspective for in-context example selection and ordering.

Hongyang Yang, Xiao-Yang Liu, and Christina Dan Wang. 2023. Fingpt: Open-source financial large language models.

Jiaxin Zhang and Yashar Moshfeghi. 2022. Elastic: Numerical reasoning with adaptive symbolic compiler.

Wayne Xin Zhao, Kun Zhou, Junyi Li, Tianyi Tang, Xiaolei Wang, Yupeng Hou, Yingqian Min, Beichen Zhang, Junjie Zhang, Zican Dong, Yifan Du, Chen Yang, Yushuo Chen, Zhipeng Chen, Jinhao Jiang, Ruiyang Ren, Yifan Li, Xinyu Tang, Zikang Liu, Peiyu Liu, Jian-Yun Nie, and Ji-Rong Wen. 2023. A survey of large language models.

Dawei Zhu, Nan Yang, Liang Wang, Yifan Song, Wenhao Wu, Furu Wei, and Sujian Li. 2023. Pose: Efficient context window extension of llms via positional skip-wise training.

A Appendix

A.1 Prompt tuning

We iteratively refine the prompt using the validation sets of 40 samples for each dataset, with the aim of finding a prompt that encompasses a diverse range of cases while avoiding an overabundance of trivial or similar examples.

B Baselines

On SARA, we evaluate our system against the following baselines:

- **Majority baseline:** A trivial baseline that predicts the majority class for all the samples.
- **Feed-forward:** The feed-forward networks evaluated by Holzenberger et al. (2020).
- **Legal-BERT:** A BERT model trained specifically on legal domain (Chalkidis et al., 2020) and adapted for SARA by Holzenberger et al. (2020).
- **BERT:** A BERT model adopted for SARA by Holzenberger and Van Durme (2021)
- **GPT-3 (0-shot):** GPT-3 evaluated with a 0-shot prompt and without retrieval (Blair-Stanek et al., 2023).

- **GPT-3 (CoT):** GPT-3 evaluated with a CoT prompt and without retrieval (Blair-Stanek et al., 2023).

- **GPT-3 (dynamic):** GPT-3 evaluated with a dynamic few-shot prompt and without retrieval(Blair-Stanek et al., 2023). The prompt includes different in-context examples for different questions.

On FinQA, we compare our system with the following baselines in Table 2:

- **Pre-trained Longformer:** Longformer (Beltagy et al., 2020) is a model designed to take long input documents in one step. The model can be seen as a representative of one-step approaches.

- **FinQANet:** (Chen et al., 2021) use an LSTM decoder with attention for implementing the program generator and different models of BERT for retrieval.

- **ELASTIC:** (Zhang and Moshfeghi, 2022) use an adaptive symbolic compiler to generate the program.

- **DyRRen:** (Li et al., 2022) employ dynamic reranking of retrieved facts in every step.

- **TabT5:** (Andrejczuk et al., 2022) use a T5 model pre-trained on the Wikipedia tables.

- **APOLLO:** (Sun et al., 2023a) The retriever is based on the sequence-pair classification following (Nogueira and Cho, 2020). The program generator leverages a BERT encoder and an LSTM decoder with attention mechanism along with consistency-based reinforcement learning.

Text
Alice and Bob got married on April 5th, 2012.
Bob died September 16th, 2017.

Question
Section 7703(a)(1) applies to Alice for the year 2012.
Answer
Entailment

Figure 3: A case in SARA for section 7703.

Model	Zero-shot	Few-shot	CoT
LLaMA2-7B	50.4 ± 5.4	58.8 ± 5.3	53.5 ± 5.4
LLaMA2-7B_chat	42.1 ± 5.3	51.8 ± 5.4	54.4 ± 5.4
LLaMA2-13B	43.9 ± 5.4	53.1 ± 5.4	57.5 ± 5.4
LLaMA2-13B_chat	60.1 ± 5.3	53.9 ± 5.4	66.7 ± 5.1
LLaMA2-70B	49.6 ± 5.4	67.5 ± 5.1	71.1 ± 4.9
GPT-3	64.9 ± 5.2	74.6 ± 4.7	81.6 ± 4.2

Table 4: Comparison of different prompting techniques used on SARA. The prompts used are as described in section 4.2 and shown in Appendix section E. Note that the results shown here are from our proposed retrieval-augmented method, and not the same as the baselines shown in Table 1, which come from Blair-Stanek et al. (2023).

	Correct CoT	Incorrect CoT
Correct ans	23	8
Incorrect ans	3	6

Table 5: Results of the manual analysis performed on the validation set using GPT-3.

C Data examples

Figure 3 shows a question from SARA.

D Ablation studies

D.1 Zero-shot, few-shot and CoT prompting

Table 4 shows the performance of different models with different prompting techniques.

D.2 Case analysis

SARA We conducted a manual analysis of the model's output on the validation set. Table 5 presents the results of this analysis on SARA, indicating the number of examples where both the answer and the chain-of-thought reasoning provided by the model were correct, both were incorrect and cases where one of them was incorrect. We found that in 58.5% of the examples, the model accurately predicted both the output and the reasoning. For the remaining cases, we categorized the errors into four distinct categories, shown in Table 6.

Reasoning Error type	# of cases
Arithmetic errors	8
Logical errors	6
Context too long	2
Retrieval error	1

Table 6: Error analysis on the validation set of SARA.

Error type	# of cases
Arithmetic error	3
Logical error	2
Annotation error	2
Retrieval error	3

Table 7: Error analysis of the incorrect examples on 40 samples from FinQA.

FinQA On the constructed validation set comprising 40 samples, we observe that 30 samples have correct answers as well as corresponding programs. For the remaining 10 samples, we manually classify the errors into different categories, as shown in Table 7.

E Prompts

Figures 4 and 5 show the prompts used for SARA and FinQA respectively.

For the following questions, answer true or false based on the given context. For example:

§151. Allowance of deductions for personal exemptions
(d) Exemption amount
For purposes of this section-
(3) Phaseout
(B) Applicable percentage
For purposes of subparagraph (A), the term "applicable percentage" means 2 percentage points for each $2,500 (or fraction thereof) by which the taxpayer's adjusted gross income for the taxable year exceeds the applicable amount in effect under section 68(b). In the case of a married individual filing a separate return, the preceding sentence shall be applied by substituting "$1,250" for "$2,500". In no event shall the applicable percentage exceed 100 percent.

Question
Alice's income in 2015 is $276932. Alice is not married. The applicable amount according to section 68(b) is $250000.
Under section 151(d)(3)(B), the applicable percentage for Alice for 2015 is equal to 22. True or False?

Answer
Section 151(d)(3)(B) states that the applicable percentage means 2 percentage points for each $2,500 (or fraction thereof) by which the adjusted gross income exceeds the applicable amount in effect under section 68(b). The question states that the applicable amount according to section 68(b) is $250000 and Alice's income is $276932 for the year 2015. Therefore, the amount by which the income exceeds the applicable amount according to section 68(b) is 276932-250000 = 26932. There are 26932/2500 = 10.78 multiples of 2500 in 26932. 2 percentage points for each multiple of $2,500 is 2*10.78 = 21.56 which rounds to 22. Thus, the applicable percentage is equal to 22 and the hypothesis is correct.
True

§152. Dependent defined
(c) Qualifying child
For purposes of this section-
(1) In general
The term "qualifying child" means, with respect to any taxpayer for any taxable year, an individual-
(B) who has the same principal place of abode as the taxpayer for more than one-half of such taxable year,

Question
Alice has a son, Bob. From September 1st, 2015 to November 3rd, 2019, Alice and Bob lived in the same home.
Section 152(c)(1)(B) applies to Bob with Alice as the taxpayer for the year 2016. True or False?

Answer
Section 152(c)(1)(B) only applies to someone who has the same principal place of abode as the taxpayer for more than one-half of the taxable year. The question states that Bob is Alice's son who lived in the same house from September 1st, 2015 to November 3rd 2019. The whole of 2016 falls within September 1st, 2015 to November 3rd 2019. Therefore, Bob had the same principal place of abode as Alice for more than one-half of 2016. Thus, section 152(c)(1)(B) applies to Bob with Alice as the taxpayer for the year 2016.
True

§3306. Definitions
(a) Employer
(3) Domestic service
In the case of domestic service in a private home, local college club, or local chapter of a college fraternity or sorority, the term "employer" means, with respect to any calendar year, any person who during the calendar year or the preceding calendar year paid wages in cash of $1,000 or more for such service.

Question
Alice has paid $3200 in cash to Bob for agricultural labor done from Feb 1st, 2017 to Sep 2nd, 2017. Bob has paid $4200 in cash to Alice for domestic service in his home, done from Apr 1st, 2017 to Sep 2nd, 2018.
Section 3306(a)(3) applies to Bob for the year 2018. True or False?

Answer
Section 3306(a)(3) states that in case of domestic service in a private home, the term "employer" means any person who during the preceding calendar year paid wages in cash of $1,000 or more for such service. The question states that Bob has paid $4200 in cash to Alice for domestic service in his home, done from Apr 1st, 2017 to Sep 2nd, 2018. 4200 is greater than 1000 and 2017 is the preceding year of 2018. Thus, section 3306(a)(3) applies to Bob for the year 2018.
True

§63. Taxable income defined
(f) Aged or blind additional amounts
(1) Additional amounts for the aged
The taxpayer shall be entitled to an additional amount of $600-
(A) for himself if he has attained age 65 before the close of his taxable year, and

Question
In 2017, Alice was paid $33200. Alice and Bob have been married since Feb 3rd, 2017. Alice was born March 2nd, 1950 and Bob was born March 3rd, 1955.
Section 63(f)(1)(A) applies to Alice in 2017. True or False?

Answer
Section 63(f)(1)(A) applies to a person only if he has attained age 65 before the close of his taxable year. Alice was born March 2nd, 1950. Alice turned 65 on March 2nd, 2015. March 2nd, 2015 is before the close of the taxable year 2017. Thus, section 63(f)(1)(A) applies to Alice in 2017.
True

§151. Allowance of deductions for personal exemptions

(d) Exemption amount

For purposes of this section-

(3) Phaseout

(B) Applicable percentage

For purposes of subparagraph (A), the term "applicable percentage" means 2 percentage points for each $2,500 (or fraction thereof) by which the taxpayer's adjusted gross income for the taxable year exceeds the applicable amount in effect under section 68(b). In the case of a married individual filing a separate return, the preceding sentence shall be applied by substituting "$1,250" for "$2,500". In no event shall the applicable percentage exceed 100 percent.

Question

Alice's income in 2015 is $395276. The applicable amount according to section 68(b) is $250000.
Under section 151(d)(3)(B), the applicable percentage for Alice for 2015 is equal to 118. True or False?

Answer

Section 151(d)(3)(B) states that in no event shall the applicable percentage exceed 100. 118 exceeds 100. Therefore, the applicable percentage cannot be equal to 118 and the hypothesis is incorrect.
False

§152. Dependent defined

(c) Qualifying child

For purposes of this section-

(1) In general

The term "qualifying child" means, with respect to any taxpayer for any taxable year, an individual-

(B) who has the same principal place of abode as the taxpayer for more than one-half of such taxable year,

Question

Alice has a son, Bob. From September 1st, 2015 to November 3rd, 2019, Alice and Bob lived in the same home.
Section 152(c)(1)(B) applies to Bob with Alice as the taxpayer for the year 2015. True or False?

Answer

Section 152(c)(1)(B) states that the qualifying child has the same principal place of abode as the taxpayer for more than one-half of such a taxable year. The question states that Bob is Alice's son who lived in the same house from September 1st, 2015 to November 3rd 2019. November 3rd 2019 is after the end of 2015. The time between September 1st,2015 and the end of 2015 is 4 months. Half a year is 6 months. 4 is less than 6. Therefore, Bob had the same principal place of abode as Alice for less than one-half of 2015. Thus, section 152(c)(1)(B) does not apply to Bob with Alice as the taxpayer for the year 2015.
False

§3306. Definitions

(b) Wages

For purposes of this chapter, the term "wages" means all remuneration for employment, including the cash value of all remuneration (including benefits) paid in any medium other than cash; except that such term shall not include-

(15) any payment made by an employer to a survivor or the estate of a former employee after the calendar year in which such employee died;

Question

Alice employed Bob for agricultural labor from Feb 1st, 2011 to November 19th, 2019. On November 25th, Bob died from a heart attack. On December 20th, 2019, Alice paid Charlie, Bob's surviving spouse, Bob's outstanding wages of $1200.
Section 3306(b)(15) applies to the payment that Alice made to Charlie in 2019. True or False?

Answer

Section 3306(b)(15) applies only after the calendar year in which the employee died. The question states that Alice employed Bob for agricultural labor from Feb 1st, 2011 to November 19th, 2019. Bob died on November 25th and on December 20th, Alice paid Charlie. Thus, the payment is made in the same calendar year in which Bob died. Thus, section 3306(b)(15) does not apply to the payment that Alice made to Charlie in 2019.
False

§1. Tax imposed

(b) Heads of households

There is hereby imposed on the taxable income of every head of a household (as defined in section 2(b)) a tax determined in accordance with the following:

(i) 15% of taxable income if the taxable income is not over $29,600;

Question

Alice is a head of household for the year 2017. Alice's taxable income for the year 2017 is $1172980.
Alice has to pay $442985 in taxes for the year 2017 under section 1(b)(i). True or False?

Answer

Section 1(b)(i) applies only if the taxable income is not over $29,600. The question states that Alice's taxable income for the year 2017 is $1172980. 1172980 is greater than 29600. Therefore section 1(b)(i) does not apply to Alice in 2017 and the amount of taxes to be paid by Alice is unknown.
False

§151. Allowance of deductions for personal exemptions

(a) Allowance of deductions

In the case of an individual, the exemptions provided by this section shall be allowed as deductions in computing taxable income.

Question

Alice's income in 2015 is $100000. She gets one exemption of $2000 for the year 2015 under section 151(c). Alice is not married.
Alice's total exemption for 2015 under section 151(a) is equal to $6000. True or False?

Answer

Figure 4: Chain-of-thought prompt for SARA for a sample. The complete prompt contains 8 in-context examples with CoT explanations followed by the question that the model is supposed to answer. The in-context examples and explanations remain the same for all questions in the dataset. The text highlighted in yellow are the CoT explanations that we hand-crafted, while the test question is shown in blue.

The balance as of December 31 2009 of $540 is 604. The balance as of December 31 2010 of $540 is $2063.

Question

What was the percentage change in warranty reserve between 2009 and 2010?

Answer

The change in reserve between 2009 and 2010 is equal to 2063 - 604. The percentage change is equal to 100 times the previous result divided by 604.

Program: subtract(2063, 604), divide(#0, 604)
Final answer: 242%

In fiscal 2018, net cash used for financing activities of $755.1 million consisted primarily of cash dividends paid to stockholders of $440.9 million and purchases of common stock of $195.1 million and net repayments of debt of $120.1 million.

Question

In 2018 what was the percent of the net cash used for financing activities used for the purpose of purchases of common stock?

Answer

The net cash used for financing activities was 755.1 million and the cash dividends paid for the purchases of common stock was 195.1 million. Therefore, the percent of the net cash used for financing activities used for the purpose of purchases of common stock is 100 times 195.1 divided by 755.1.

Program: divide(195.1, 755.1)
Final answer: 25.84%

The capital purchase obligations of payments due in total is 12068 million. The capital purchase obligations of payments due by a period of less than 1 year is 9689 million. The capital purchase obligations of payments due by a period of 1-3 years is 2266 million. The capital purchase obligations of payments due by a period of 3-5 years is 113 million. The capital purchase obligations of payments due by a period of more than 5 years is 2014 million. The total of all the payments due is $65947 million. The total of payments due by a period of less than 1 year is $14265 million. The total of payments due by a period of 1-3 years is $10432 million. The total of payments due by a period of 3-5 years is $10067 million. The total of payments due by a period of more than 5 years is $31183 million.

Question

What percentage of total contractual obligations do capital purchase obligations make up as of December 30, 2017?

Answer

Total of contractual obligations payments due is $65947 million. Total of capital purchase obligations is $12068 million. The percentage that $12068 million is of $65497 million is equal to 100*(12068/65947).

Program: divide(12068, 65947)
Final answer: 18%

The impact on net income for the year that ended on December 31, 2006 is $-3680 thousand. The impact on net income for the year that ended on December 31, 2005 is $-1016 thousand. The impact on net income for the year that ended on December 31, 2004 is $-403 thousand.

Question
What was the difference, in thousands, in impact on the net income due to compensation expense for stock options and restricted stock between 2004 and 2005?

Answer
The impact on the net income for the year 2004 was $-403 thousand and the impact on the net income for the year 2005 is $-1016 thousand. The difference, in thousands, is equal to 1016-403.

Program: subtract(1016, 403)
Final answer: 613

The following is a reconciliation of basic shares to diluted shares: The diluted weighted-average shares for the year that ended on December 31, 2014 is 172.8 million. The diluted weighted-average shares for the year that ended on December 31, 2013 is 158.7 million. The diluted weighted-average shares for the year that ended on December 31, 2012 is 145.8 million.

Question
What was the average, in millions, of weighted-average diluted shares from 2012-2014?

Answer
The average of weighted-average diluted shares from 2012-2014 in millions, is equal to the average of 172.8, 158.7 and 145.8 which is equal to (172.8 + 158.7 + 145.8)/3.

Program: add(172.8, 158.7), add(#0, 145.8), divide(#1, const_3)
Final answer: 158.8

The future minimum lease payments under noncancellable operating leases for office space in effect at December 31, 2008 are $8.8 million in 2009, $6.6 million in 2010, $3.0 million in 2011 , $1.8 million in 2012 and $1.1 million in 2013.

Question
What was the average future minimum lease payments under noncancellable operating leases for office space from 2009 to 2013 in millions.

Answer
The average of the future minimum lease payments under noncancellable operating leases for office space from 2009 to 2013 in millions, is the average of 8.8, 6.6, 3.0, 1.8 and 1.1 which is equal to (8.8+6.6+3.0+1.8+1.1)/5.

Program: add(8.8, 6.6), add(#0, 3.0), add(#1, 1.8), add(#2, 1.1), divide(#3, const_5)
Final answer: 4.26

The amount per share for the payment date of 2018 is $1.90 and the total amount is $262 million. On November 2, 2018, the board declared a cash dividend of $0.50 per share that was paid on January 25, 2019 to the stockholders of record on December 31, 2018, for an aggregate amount of $68 million.

Question
Considering the year 2018, what is the percentage of the cash dividend paid per share concerning the total amount paid per share?

Answer
The cash dividend that was paid to the stockholders of record for 2018 was $0.50 per share. The total amount paid for 2018 is $1.90 per share. The percentage that $0.50 is of $1.90 is equal to 100*(0.50/1.90).

Program: divide(0.50, 1.90)
Final answer: 26.31%

The additional collateral or termination payments for a one-notch downgrade, as of December 2014 is $1072 million. The additional collateral or termination payments for a one-notch downgrade, as of December 2013 is $911 million. The additional collateral or termination payments for a two-notch downgrade, as of December 2014 is $2815 million. The additional collateral or termination payments for a two-notch downgrade, as of December 2013 is $2989 million.

Question
What is the difference in the required additional collateral or termination payments for a two-notch downgrade and additional collateral or termination payments for a one-notch downgrade in millions in 2014?

Answer
The required additional collateral or termination payments for a two-notch downgrade in 2014 is $2815 million and for a one-notch downgrade in 2014 is $1072 million. The difference in millions is 2815-1072.

Program: subtract(2815, 1072)
Final answer: 1743

The proved undeveloped reserves as of December 31, 2012 of U.S. is $407. The proved undeveloped reserves as of December 31, 2012 of Canada is $433. The total proved undeveloped reserves as of December 31, 2012 is $840. Devon Energy Corporation and subsidiaries notes to consolidated financial statements 2013 (continued) proved undeveloped reserves. The following table presents the changes in Devon 2019s total proved undeveloped reserves during 2012 (in mmboe). On December 31, 2012, Devon had 840 mmboe of proved undeveloped reserves. This represents a 7 percent increase as compared to 2011 and represents 28 percent of its total proved reserves.

Question
What is the approximate total amount of proved reserves?

Answer
On December 31, 2012, Devon had 840 mmboe of proved undeveloped reserves which represents 28 percent of its total proved reserves. Therefore, the total proved reserves are 840 divided by 28% which is equal to 840*100/28.

Program: divide(const_100, 28), multiply(#0, 840)
Final answer: 2998.8

The interest payments in 2010, 2009 and 2008 totaled $189 million, $201 million and $228 million, respectively.

Question
What would 2011 interest payments be based on the rate of change in 2009 to 2010?

Answer
The rate of change of interest payments from 2009 to 2010 is equal to 189 divided by 201. Using the same rate of change, the interest payment of 2011 would be equal to 189 times 189 divided by 201.

Program: divide(189, 201), multiply(189, #0)
Final answer: 177.7

The revenue of the year that ended on December 31, 2015 is $7426 million. The revenue of the year that ended on December 31, 2014 is $7834 million. The revenue of the year that ended on December 31, 2013 is $7789 million. The trustees of the plan have certain rights to request that our U.K. working capital increased by $77 million from $809 million on December 31, 2014 to $886 million on December 31, 2015.

Question
What is the working capital turnover in 2015?

Answer
The working capital turnover is calculated by dividing the company's net annual sales by its average working capital. The working capital was $809 million in 2014 and $886 in 2015. Therefore, the average working capital is equal to (809 + 886)/2. The revenue of the year 2015 us $7426. Therefore, the working capital turnover is equal to $7426 million divided by (809 + 886)/2.

Program: add(809, 886), divide(#0, const_2), divide(7426, #1)
Final answer: 8.8

The jpmorgan chase on December 31, 2013 is $100.00. The jpmorgan chase on December 31, 2014 is $109.88. The jpmorgan chase on December 31, 2015 is $119.07. The jpmorgan chase on December 31, 2016 is $160.23 ; the jpmorgan chase on December 31, 2017 is $203.07. The jpmorgan chase on December 31, 2018 is $189.57. The kbw bank index on December 31, 2013 is 100.00. The kbw bank index on December 31, 2014 is $109.36. The kbw bank index on December 31, 2015 is $109.90. The kbw bank index on December 31, 2016 is $141.23. The kbw bank index on December 31, 2017 is $167.49. The kbw bank index on December 31, 2018 is $137.82.

Question
Did jpmorgan chase outperform the kbw bank index?

Answer
The jpmorgan chase index increased from $100.00 in 2013 to $189.57 in 2018, while the kbw bank index increased from $100.00 in 2013 to $137.82 in 2018. jpmorgan chase outperformed the kbw bank if 189.57 is greater than 137.82.

Program: greater(189.57, 137.82)
Final answer: yes

The following table reconciles cash provided by operating activities (gaap measure) to free cash flow (non-gaap measure) : millions of dollars 2008 2007 2006 .

millions of dollars | 2008 | 2007 | 2006 ||
cash provided by operating activities | $ 4070 | $ 3277 | $ 2880 ||
cash used in investing activities | -2764 (2764) | -2426 (2426) | -2042 (2042) ||
free cash flow | $ 825 | $ 487 | $ 516 ||

we plan to continue implementation of total safety culture (tsc) throughout our operations .

Question
What was the percent of the cash provided by operating activities?

Program:

Figure 5: Chain-of-thought prompt for FinQA for a sample. The complete prompt contains 12 in-context examples with CoT explanations followed by the question that the model is supposed to answer. The in-context examples and explanations remain the same for all questions in the dataset. The text highlighted in yellow are the CoT explanations that we hand-crafted, while the test question is shown in blue.

Joint Learning for Legal Text Retrieval and Textual Entailment: Leveraging the Relationship between *Relevancy* and *Affirmation*

Hai-Long Nguyen[1], **Thi-Hai-Yen Vuong**[1], **Ha-Thanh Nguyen**[2] and **Xuan-Hieu Phan**[1]
[1] *VNU University of Engineering and Technology*, Hanoi
[2] *National Institute of Informatics*, Tokyo, Japan
{long.nh, yenvth, hieupx}@vnu.edu.vn
nguyenhathanh@nii.ac.jp

Abstract

In legal text processing and reasoning, one normally performs information retrieval to find relevant documents of an input question, and then performs textual entailment to answer the question. The former is about *relevancy* where as the latter is about *affirmation* (or *conclusion*). While relevancy and affirmation are two different concepts, there is obviously a connection between them. That is why performing retrieval and textual entailment sequentially and independently may not make the most of this mutually supportive relationship. This paper, therefore, propose a multi–task learning model for these two tasks to improve their performance. Technically, in the COLIEE dataset, we use the information of Task 4 (conclusions) to improve the performance of Task 3 (searching for legal provisions related to the question). Our empirical findings indicate that this supportive relationship truly exists. This important insight sheds light on how leveraging relationship between tasks can significantly enhance the effectiveness of our multi-task learning approach for legal text processing.

1 Introduction

In legal text processing and reasoning, legal document retrieval and textual entailment are two important tasks. Given an input legal question, the former helps to narrow down and locates a subset of most relevant documents while the latter attempts to give a yes/no answer to the question by analyzing those relevant documents. Legal document retrieval and textual entailment have several challenges, such as intricate legal language structures (Nguyen et al., 2022b), scarcity of annotated legal data (Nguyen et al., 2022a; Yoshioka et al., 2021), rich vocabulary with multiple meanings (Nguyen et al., 2021), and high dependency and the interrelationship between legal statutes (Vuong et al., 2022).

In this paper, we focus on these two tasks within the context of the Competition on Legal Information Extraction/Entailment (COLIEE) (Rabelo et al., 2021b, 2022). In COLIEE, the retrieval task (a.k.a Task 3) involves the retrieval of relevant statutes from a database of Japanese civil code statutes regarding an input yes/no legal question. The textual entailment task (a.k.a Task 4) aims to confirm the entailment of a yes/no answer based on the anlsysis of the retrieved civil code statutes. Traditionally, these two tasks have been addressed independently as two separate steps without considering their interdependence. This formulation approach should ignore a mutually supportive relationship between them.

In this work, our main idea is that the joint and simultaneous learning and inference of these two tasks can make the most of the mutual relationship between *relevancy* and *affirmation*. In some cases, truly relevant statutes that confirm an input question may not relevant in terms of having common vocabulary in traditional information retrieval. Our hypothesis is that this joint and "bi–directional" learning will make more accurate decisions in each task. Especially, legal entailment information (Task 4) can help to improve the performance of the retrieval task (Task 3).

Technically, we propose a multi–task learning framework that integrate and learn Task 3 and Task 4 simultaneously. This should allow the exploitation of shared features and relevant information that may be ignored in the independent and separate training of these tasks. Our method aims to leverage the strengths of the mentioned techniques to deal with the challenges of legal text processing as well as make use of the relationship between *relevancy* and *affirmation* to improve the performance of legal text retrieval and entailment tasks.

The remaining of the paper is organized as follows. Section 2 mentions related work. Section 3 addresses the problem. Section 4 presents our multi–task learning method. The experiments, results, and anlsysis are described in Section 5. Finally, Section 6 draws our conclusions.

Proceedings of the Natural Legal Language Processing Workshop 2023, pages 192–201
December 7, 2023

2 Related Work

Various methods have been proposed to tackle legal text retrieval and textual entailment in the COLIEE competition. Researchers have identified BM25 as a useful baseline for statute retrieval, and several studies have focused on combining lexical and neural ranking models (Rosa et al., 2021; Askari et al., 2021). With the COLIEE 2020 dataset, Vuong et al. observed an equivalence between the Entailment relation and the relation between the topic sentence and other sentences in a passage. Consequently, the research team employed a weak-labeling method to generate additional data and trained a supporting model. Using this supporting model as a pre-trained model helped the research team achieve the highest performance in tasks 1 and 2 of COLIEE 2020 (Vuong et al., 2023). A Graph-Augmented Dense Statue Retriever (G-DSR) which leverages legislation's structural aspects using a graph neural network surpassed robust retrieval benchmarks when evaluated on a real-world SAR dataset expertly annotated by professionals (Louis et al., 2023). For improving the retrieval performance in task 1 of COLIEE 2021, Abolghasemi et al. used multi–task learning which combined document–level representation learning and ranking objective (Abolghasemi et al., 2022).

For Legal Textual Entailment, approaches involve IR-based systems, BERT ensemble methods, and transformer-based techniques combined with textual similarity (Kim et al., 2019; Rabelo et al., 2021a). Yoshioka et al. employed an systematic method for creating training data for syntatic structure understanding (Yoshioka et al., 2021). Multi–task learning has been employed to overcome data scarcity in the domain, addressing tasks such as translation, summarization, multi–label classification, and legal case retrieval and entailment (Elnaggar et al., 2018).

3 Problem Statement

3.1 Legal Document Retrieval

Legal document retrieval refers to the task of finding relevant legal documents given a query, which could be a legal question or a legal statement. In this work, the set of legal documents that need to be retrieved is the statute law. Let $D = d_1, d_2, ..., d_n$ be a collection of legal documents. Given a query q (i.e., a legal question or statement), this task is to retrieve a subset documents $D_q \subset D$ such that these documents are semantically related to q, that is, they could be used to answer or explain q. The problem can be described using a relevance evaluation function 1. This problem is particularly challenging due to the complexity of legal documents and the vast amount of available legal materials (Ruhl et al., 2017; Katz et al., 2020).

$$f(query, d_i) = \mathbf{R} \tag{1}$$

where $\mathbf{R}$ having two values, 0 and 1, corresponding to relevance (YES_R) and non-relevance (NO_R) respectively.

3.2 Legal Textual Entailment

Legal textual entailment involves the identification of entailment relationship between a set of relevant articles and a given query. Two types of relationship is pre–defined including "*documents entail the query*" and "*documents entail the negative form of the query*". In other words, the goal of this task is to answer the question: *arcording to the relevant documents, whether the query is true or false?*.

Specifically, let q be the input query and D_q be a set of relevant articles of q. The goal is to determine which form of entailment holds: $Entail(D_q, q)$ or $Entail(D_q, \textbf{not}\ q)$. The problem can be described using expression 1.

$$g(q, D_q) = \mathbf{E} \tag{2}$$

where $\mathbf{E}$ having two values including:

- $Entail(q, D_q)$ denotes YES_T, corresponding to the content of the document set D_q proving the query q to be true.
- $Entail(-q, D_q)$ is denoted as NO_T, corresponding to the content of the document set D_q proving the negation of the query q to be true.

The entailment relationship identification is a complicated task due to several reasons. First, recent NLP deep learning models are mostly based on the semantic similarity between sentences or documents. This approach is not suitable because this task requires the logical analysis and reasoning based on the actual content of the query and documents. Second, the document length is significantly long and the combination of multiple relevant documents in lexical–level can create a large document which exceeds the input limit of normal NLP deep learning model. Therefore, building a model which can efficiently determines the entailment relationship is challenging and requires logical reasoning that is beyond semantic similarity.

3.3 Legal Outcome-based Retrieval (*LOR*) Problem

When additional navigational information is added at the output stage, the conventional Retrieval problem typically transforms into an Outcome-based Retrieval problem. Addressing the Outcome-based Retrieval problem often yields significantly improved results compared to solely tackling the conventional Retrieval problem, as the additional navigational information could profoundly influences the model's outcome. In this section, we present a methodology to transition the Legal Retrieval problem discussed in Section 3.1 into a Legal Outcome-based Retrieval *(LOR)* problem, with the expectation that addressing the LOR problem will enhance the results of the Retrieval problem.

3.3.1 Decomposing the Textual Entailment Relationship

The essence of the relationship $g(query, D_q)$ signifies that the correctness of the query will be determined based on the synthesized content of all relevant documents $D_q = d_{i_1}, d_{i_2}, ..., d_{i_n}$. However, the task of combining legal texts poses a considerable challenge due to the extensive length of each legal document, which surpasses the capabilities of current mid-level language models. Furthermore, determining the correctness of the query necessitates a logical combination of the content from all relevant legal documents.

Therefore, in this research, we propose simplifying the original entailment relationship using smaller sub-relationships. Specifically, the decomposition process is represented by expression (3).

$$g(q, [a_1, a_2, ..., a_n]) = \mathbf{E}$$
$$\Leftrightarrow \begin{cases} g(q, a_1) & = \mathbf{E} \\ g(q, a_2) & = \mathbf{E} \\ ... & \\ g(q, a_n) & = \mathbf{E} \end{cases} \tag{3}$$

In this study, we propose *IIA* (Insufficient Information to Answer) label when legal texts cannot definitively answer the query as either yes or no. Therefore, in addition to $\mathbf{E}$ - the Textual Entailment Relationship having two values, YES_T and NO_T, it also includes *IIA*.

The textual-entailment relationships decomposition as described above may lead to cases where the relationships $g(query, a_i)$ become inaccurate in certain situations. The first scenario occurs when, within the set of related legal documents $[d_{i_1}, d_{i_2}, ..., d_{i_n}]$, only a small subset of documents contain content that can answer the query, while the remaining, although related, do not provide usable content to answer the query. Decomposing the relationship according to expression (3) in this case can result in changing the relationship between the query and related but insufficiently informative documents from *IIA* to YES_T or NO_T. The second scenario arises when any two documents, although containing content related to the query, have content that conditionally negates each other in specific cases. Therefore, simplifying the relationship according to expression 3 can lead to a reversal of the actual relationship between the query and each document. Examples of two mentioned scenarios are provided in the Figure 1.

The two scenarios mentioned occur rarely, and their impact on our research approach is insignificant. In our preliminary analysis of the 782 legal articles in the corpus, there are 34 instances that fall into the scenario 2, determined by using key terms indicative of conditional negation within legal language With the scenario 1, the queries that involve more than two related legal documents account for about 21.39% in the dataset. Despite the presence of these scenarios, they have a limited impact on the training phase and the overall effectiveness of our method.

3.3.2 The Transformation of Legal Retrieval into Legal Outcome-based Retrieval

The utilization of outcome-based retrieval often yields better results than conventional retrieval due to the added navigational information, resulting in more focused and targeted searches. Therefore, in this study, we propose the use of Decomposed Textual Entailment information to enhance the performance of the Retrieval phase in finding relevant legal documents.

Through the decomposition of the Entailment relationship, each pair $(query, a_i)$ are not only associated with the Relevant relationship ($\mathbf{R}$) denoted by two labels, YES_R and NO_R, but also with the Textual Entailment relationship ($\mathbf{E}$) featuring three labels, namely YES_T, NO_T, and *IIA*. Based on the observation that legal experts tend to seek legal documents with relevant content to support

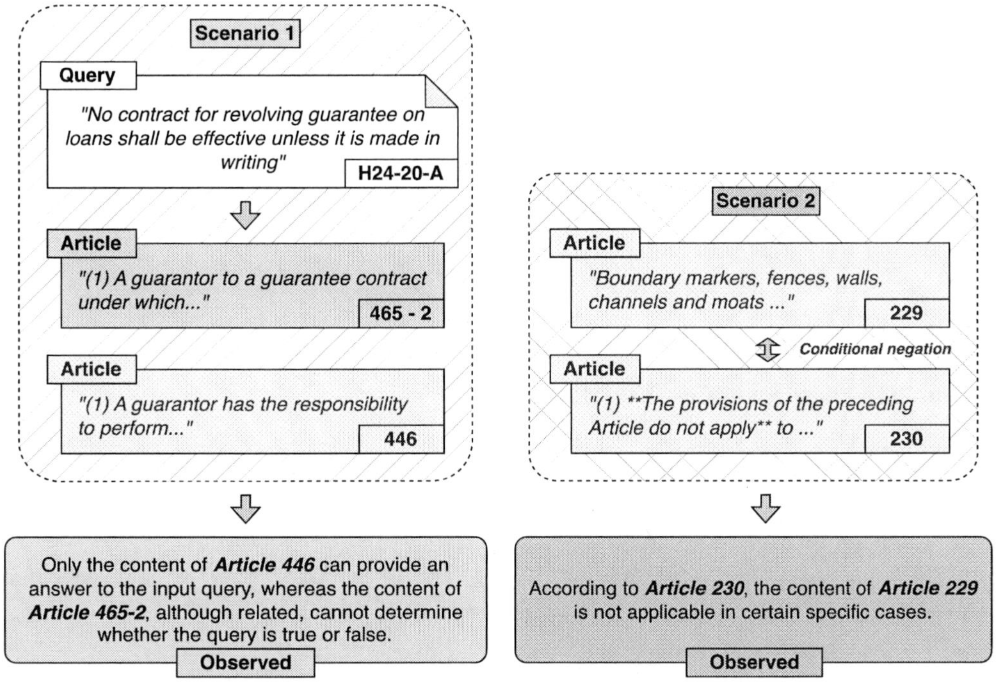

Figure 1: Two scenarios that affect the Textual Entailment Decomposition

their stance on whether a statement/query is true or false, we assume that the correctness of a query plays a crucial role in determining whether a legal document is related to that query or not. With this assumption, the Multi-Task Learning model that combines two streams of information, $\mathbf{R}$ and $\mathbf{E}$ is proposed. Specifically, the Decomposed Textual Entailment relationship is introduced as one of the two outputs of the model, alongside the Relevant relationship. The aim is that the Entailment information will impact the back-propagation process during training phase, allowing the model to learn more effectively and achieve better optimization. The architecture of the proposed Multi-Task model which is present in Figure 2 is based on the BERT architecture, with the addition of two Classification layers that output two corresponding labels for Retrieval and Entailment.

4 Legal Document Retrieval and Textual Entailment with Multi–Task Model

4.1 Pre–ranking Phase by BM25 Model

Due to the large number of documents in the corpus, directly using deep learning models here would consume a significant amount of resources and be inefficient. Therefore, the pre-ranking step is essential to quickly filter candidates from the corpus that are lexically relevant to the query. This speeds up both the training and inference phases without significant information loss. The BM25 model is chosen for its statistical-based approach, fast runtime, and effectiveness in retrieval tasks. Furthermore, the correlation score computed by the BM25 model can also be utilized to integrate with the output of the multi-task model, thereby compensating for the recall aspect of the retrieval system. With a set of document $D = \{d_1, d_2, ..., d_m\}$ and a query q which contains n terms $q = [t_1^q, t_2^q, ..., t_n^q]$, the relevant score between the query q and document d_j computed by BM25 (Equation 6) is the mutiplication of TF score (Equation 5) and IDF score (Equation 4).

$$IDF(t_i^q) = \ln\left(1 + \frac{m - f(t_i^q) + 0.5}{f(t_i^q) + 0.5}\right) \quad (4)$$

$$TF(t_i^q, d_j) = \frac{g(t_i^q, d_j) * (k1 + 1)}{g(t_i^q, d_j) + k1 * [1 - b + b * R(d_j)]} \quad (5)$$

$$score_{q,d_j} = \sum_{i=1}^{n} IDF(t_i^q) * TF(t_i^q, d_j) \quad (6)$$

where:

- $f(t)$ represents the number of documents in D containing the token t.
- $g(t, d)$ represents the frequency of token t occurring in document d.
- $k1$ is a parameter that determine the term frequency saturation which ensures that words

with high occurrence frequencies do not significantly influence the final score.

- b implies the impact of the document length on the final score.

- $R(d) = \frac{lenOf(d)}{averageLen}$ is the ratio between the length of document d and the average length of all documents in D.

4.2 Re–ranking Phase by Multi–Task Model

In the second phase of the retrieval system, the multi-task model is utilized to calculate correlation scores based on the semantics of the query and the legal documents. Specifically, the model adopts a pre-trained model for encoding the semantic of the input sequence and contains two corresponding outputs for the retrieval and textual-entailment tasks. Through this architectural design, the model parameters will be updated based on the information from both loss functions: one originating from the retrieval task and the other from the textual entailment task. In other words, instead of solely basing on their contents for determining whether the query and the related document are relevant, the model will learn how to integrate the information about the correctness of the query and vice versa, determining the correctness of the query based on the content provided in the document. Figure 2 illustrates the detailed architecture of the multi-task model used in the re-ranking phase.

In this architecture, both the query and the legal text are simultaneously input into the model. The output vector representing the special token [CLS] is used as a semantic representation for the query-text pair. Subsequently, this representation vector is passed through two separated linear layers corresponding to each task (retrieval task and textual-entailment task). The retrieval head of the model consists of two nodes representing the outcomes of YES_R or NO_R. Meanwhile, the textual-entailment output of the model comprises three nodes corresponding to the three labels: YES_T, NO_T and *IIA*.

The output calculation formula for each task is described by Equation 7. Supposed that the input sequence is $T = [t_1, t_2, ..., t_n]$. The language model, denoted as the *LM* function, embeds the semantic information of the input sequence into a d-dimensional vector.

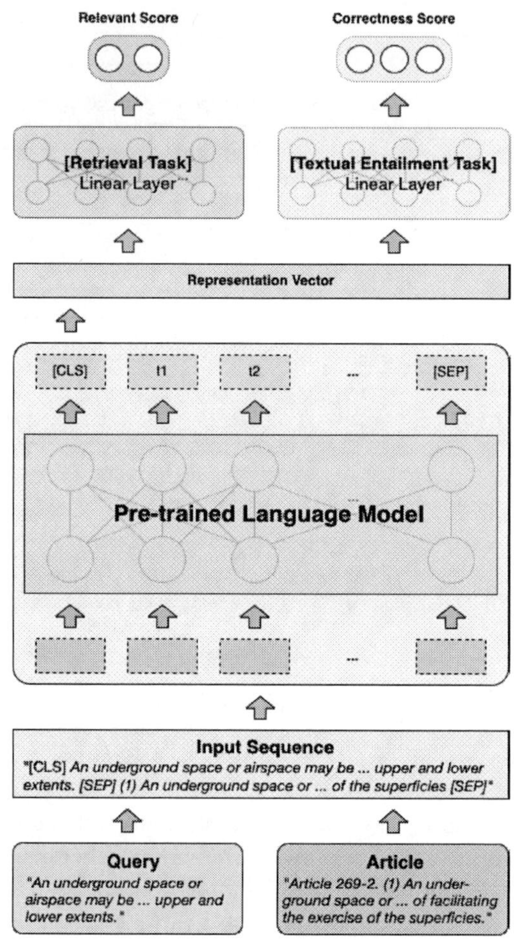

Figure 2: Bert-based multi-task model architecture

$$\begin{aligned} \mathbf{V}_{CLS} &= LM([t_1, t_2, ..., t_n]) \\ \mathbf{H}_{retrieval} &= softmax(\mathbf{V}_{CLS} * \mathbf{W}_R) \\ \mathbf{H}_{entail} &= softmax(\mathbf{V}_{CLS} * \mathbf{W}_T) \end{aligned} \quad (7)$$

where:

- $\mathbf{V}_{CLS} \in \mathcal{R}^d$ is the representation vector of special [CLS] token with d is the hidden dimension of the language model.

- $\mathbf{W}_R \in \mathcal{R}^{d\mathrm{x}2}$, $\mathbf{W}_T \in \mathcal{R}^{d\mathrm{x}3}$ are the matrix weights of retrieval head and textual-entailment head, respectively.

- $\mathbf{H}_{retrieval} \in \mathcal{R}^2$ is a vector containing the probabilities of two labels: relevant and irrelevant, for the retrieval task.

- $\mathbf{H}_{entail} \in \mathcal{R}^3$ is a vector containing the probabilities of three labels: irrelevant, entails, and does not entail, for the textual entailment task.

Due to the model having two output heads, there will be two loss functions: one for the retrieval head and one for the textual entailment head. Both loss functions utilize the Cross Entropy formula; however, due to the data imbalance in the retrieval task, the loss function for the retrieval head will be weighted for each label. Equation 8 and 9 represent the loss function for the retrieval head and the textual entailment head, respectively.

$$\mathcal{L}_{re} = -\sum_{c=0}^{1} w_c \log \frac{\exp(pr_c)}{\sum_{i=1}^{c}\exp(pr_i)} yr_c \quad (8)$$

$$\mathcal{L}_{en} = -\sum_{c=0}^{2} \log \frac{\exp(pe_c)}{\sum_{i=1}^{c}\exp(pe_i)} ye_c \quad (9)$$

where:

- $w \in \mathcal{R}^2$ is the weight of each label in retrieval task.
- $pr \in \mathcal{R}^2$, $pe \in \mathcal{R}^3$ are the vector containing the probability for each class of retrieval task and entailment task, respectively.
- $yr \in \mathcal{R}^2$, $ye \in \mathcal{R}^3$ are the one-hot label vector of retrieval task and entailment task, respectively.

Two loss functions $\mathcal{L}_{re}$ and $\mathcal{L}_{en}$ are combined through an addition operation. The equal weighting of the combination reflects the equal importance of the two tasks in model training procedure. The final loss used in training phase is present in Equation 10.

$$\mathcal{L} = \mathcal{L}_{re} + \mathcal{L}_{en} \quad (10)$$

5 Experiments and Results

5.1 COLIEE Dataset

We use two datasets for our evaluation, COLIEE 2022[1] and COLIEE 2023[2], with $F2$ as the main metric (Rabelo et al., 2022). The statue law corpus in both datasets is sourced from the Japanese Civil Code, encompassing a collection of 782 legal provisions. Table 1 provides an overview of basic statistics on the statue law corpus. The statistical analysis shows that the corpus contains a maximum of 655 words for English and 755 words for Japanese. These figures exceed the maximum input length supported by BERT-based models, which may lead to the loss of semantic information when truncating the text during model input.

[1]https://sites.ualberta.ca/~rabelo/COLIEE2022/
[2]https://sites.ualberta.ca/~rabelo/COLIEE2023/

Table 1: Statute Law Corpus Statistic

Statue Law Corpus		
#word per legal article		
	en	jp
Min	1	6
Max	655	755
Average	71.83	93.34

Table 2: Data Statistics

		COLIEE 2022		**COLIEE 2023**	
		Train	**Test**	**Train**	**Test**
# query case		887	109	996	101
# word per query					
Min	en	6	13	6	11
	jp	10	18	10	15
Max	en	149	91	149	87
	jp	202	125	202	109
Average	en	39	42	39	42
	jp	51	52	51	54
# relevant article per query					
Max		6	5	6	2
Average		1.28	1.20	1.28	1.29

The COLIEE 2022 dataset comprises 996 labeled instances, while the COLIEE 2023 dataset consists of 996 labeled instances as well. The dataset includes both English and Japanese versions, where Japanese is the original language of the dataset, and the English dataset is a translation version from Japanese through a translation process. Table 2 provides basic statistics on the COLIEE 2022 and 2023 datasets for both the Japanese and English versions. Based on the table, the maximum number of words in a civil law provision is 655 (for the English version) and 755 (for the Japanese version). This poses challenges for the re-ranking phase with BERT-based models, as their maximum input length is limited to 512 tokens.

5.2 Pre–ranking by BM25 Model

BM25 is employed as the first retrieval phase to extract highly relevant legal documents based on textual similarity. The pre-ranking phase aims to maintain a high recall score with an appropriate number of candidate documents within a reasonable time frame. We experiment with multiple thresholds of 30, 100, 200, and 500 and with English version of the dataset.Table 3 exhibits the statistics of the experimented top-k thresholds and their corresponding recall scores.

Top-k threshold selection balances time and recall score. A low top-k decreases recall scores but reduces retrieval time while a high top-k increases

Table 3: Recall score of corresponding top-k

Top-k candidates	Recall score			
	COLIEE 2022		COLIEE 2023	
	Train	Test	Train	Test
30	0.7590	0.9359	0.7784	0.8465
100	0.8394	0.9482	0.8513	0.9208
200	0.8829	0.9706	0.8926	0.9604
500	0.9441	0.9862	0.9487	0.9801

recall scores at the expense of longer retrieval time. As per Table 3, a top-k value of *30* is used to generate training data for re-ranking model, which helps mitigate data imbalance and reduce training time. For the inference process, a top-k value of *500* optimizes the recall score and minimizes the removal of relevant legal documents in the re-ranking phase.

5.3 Implementation Details

The multi-task model in Section 4.2 is used for filtering candidate documents obtained from the pre-ranking phase. While the pre-ranking phase prioritizes processing time and recall score, the re-ranking phase aims to improve the precision score.

To train this multi-task model, the candidate documents from the BM25 model are pairwise combined with the query, forming document-query sample pairs. Each pair has two labels: a retrieval label (either YES_R or NO_R) and a textual entailment label (YES_T, NO_T, or *IIA*).

The dataset consists of English and Japanese versions, with the English version being machine-translated from the original Japanese. To compare the performance of the model on both versions, the pre-trained *Multilingual BERT* parameters are used to initialize the model's backbone.

In addition, the pre-trained parameters of the *monot5-base-msmarco* (Nogueira et al., 2020) model are utilized, since the task belongs to the retrieval domain. However, as this pre-trained model is entirely in English, the multi-task model with the T5 backbone is only experimented on the English dataset of the COLIEE competition.

To maintain generalization and simplicity in deployment, the SGD optimizer (Mikolov et al., 2011) is used (Keskar and Socher, 2017). Two versions of the model corresponding to each language are trained for a total of 20 epochs.

5.4 Results on Retrieval Tasks with The COLIEE Dataset

With the parameter settings as described in the previous section, the multi-task model based on the pre-trained *Multilingual BERT* and *Mono-T5-base* was experimented with and evaluated on the COLIEE datasets of 2022 and 2023 using the F2-measure. In addition, to compare the effectiveness of the proposed multi-task approach in improving retrieval performance, a single-task models were also experimented. The investigated models include: single-task model using pre-trained Multilingual BERT, multi-task model using pre-trained *Multilingual BERT* - both architectures were tested with English and Japanese datasets. The pre-trained *Mono-T5-base* parameters were also used for evaluating, but only with the English dataset.

Finally, an ensemble process was used to optimize the strengths of the individual models and improve retrieval performance on the private test set. The ensemble method involved combining the relevant score of the BM25 model and the six aforementioned models. Two ensemble strategies were implemented: weighted ensemble and voting ensemble. In the weighted ensemble strategy, the final relevant score will be determined by calculating the weighted sum of each individual model whose weights will be determined through a grid search process on the validation set. Equation 11 represents the formula for combining the retrieval results of all six experimented models.

$$\begin{gathered} \textit{relevant\_score} = \sum_{i=1}^{n} w_i * s_i \\ s.t: \sum_{i=1}^{n} w_i = 1 \end{gathered} \tag{11}$$

where:

- n is the total number of models that are ensembled.
- w_i represents the weight of model i.
- s_i represents the relevant score calculated by model i.

In the voting strategy, each model's prediction is treated as a vote. All the votes are counted and the final decision is made based on the majority. If the majority of models predict relevance, the pair of question-legal document is deemed relevant; otherwise, it is considered as non-relevant.

Table 4 and Table 5 respectively present the best results achieved by participating teams in the COLIEE competition of 2022 and 2023, along with the results of the proposed models in this study. The

Table 4: F2-measure of all models and other teams (Kim et al., 2022) evaluated on COLIEE 2022 dataset

Model	F2	P	R
HUKB (Yoshioka et al., 2022)	0.820	**0.818**	0.841
OVGU (Wehnert et al., 2022)	0.779	0.778	0.805
JNLP (Bui et al., 2022)	0.770	0.687	0.838
UA	0.764	0.807	0.764
LLNTU	0.642	0.674	0.639
(1) Single BERT JP	0.786	0.667	**0.897**
(2) Single BERT EN	0.776	0.658	0.879
(3) Single MonoT5 EN	0.783	0.706	0.845
(4) Multi-Task BERT JP	0.827	0.755	**0.897**
(5) Multi-Task BERT EN	0.781	0.716	0.833
(6) MultiTask MonoT5 EN	0.799	0.723	0.871
(7) Voting Ensemble	0.815	0.768	0.856
(8) Weighted Ensemble	**0.829**	0.792	0.865

Table 5: F2-measure of all models and other teams evaluated on COLIEE 2023 dataset

Model	F2	P	R
CAPTAIN	0.757	**0.726**	0.792
JNLP	0.745	0.645	**0.822**
NOWJ	0.727	0.682	0.767
HUKB	0.673	0.628	0.708
LLNTU	0.654	0.733	0.644
UA	0.564	0.621	0.564
(1) Single BERT JP	0.707	0.600	0.807
(2) Single BERT EN	0.579	0.566	0.614
(3) Single MonoT5 EN	0.689	0.627	0.762
(4) Multi-Task BERT JP	0.731	0.670	0.782
(5) Multi-Task BERT EN	0.688	0.623	0.777
(6) MultiTask MonoT5 EN	0.695	0.598	0.797
(7) Voting Ensemble	0.727	0.682	0.767
(8) Weighted Ensemble	**0.773**	0.723	**0.822**

result tables clearly shows that the models trained on the Japanese dataset consistently outperform the models trained on the English dataset. As previously analyzed, the English dataset undergoes translation process, resulting in significant loss of important information. This loss adversely affects the retrieval effectiveness of the models, leading to a significant decrease in performance.

The multi-task model achieves higher F2 scores than single models on the COLIEE 2022 and 2023 datasets. For 2022 dataset, *(4) Multi-Task BERT JP* outperforms *(1) Single-BERT JP* by 4.1%, *(5) Multi-Task BERT EN* by 0.5%, and *(6) Multi-Task MonoT5 EN* by 1.6%. In 2023, *(4) Multi-Task BERT JP* has a higher F2 score by 2.4%, *(5) Multi-Task BERT EN* by 10.9%, and *Multi-Task MonoT5 EN* by 0.6%.

Furthermore, the multi–task model achieves remarkable results when compared to other teams in the competition. Specifically, on the COLIEE 2022 dataset, the *(4) Multi-Task BERT JP* model achieves an F2 score of 0.827, surpassing the highest-scoring team, HUKB2, with an F2 score of 0.820. As for the COLIEE 2023 dataset, the *Multi-Task BERT JP* model achieves an F2 score of 0.731, surpassing the third-place team, HUKB1, with an F2 score of 0.673.

Two ensemble methods, voting ensemble and weighted ensemble, were used to combine retrieval score from six single models (1 to 6). The voting ensemble increased the average precision score but harmed the average recall score, decreasing the overall F2 score. The weighted ensemble achieved F2 scores surpassing the top-performing team on both COLIEE 2022 and 2023 datasets without using large language models. On the 2022 dataset, the F2 score was 0.829, surpassing the top team by 0.9%. On the 2023 dataset, the F2 score was 0.773, surpassing the top team by 1.6%. This shows the effectiveness of the weighted ensemble method in utilizing the strengths of individual models and the importance of ensemble methods for improving retrieval results.

6 Conclusions

In this study, we proposed a multi-task learning framework for legal document retrieval and textual entailment within the COLIEE dataset, introducing Legal Outcome-based Retrieval (LOR) to enhance traditional legal retrieval. The approach decomposes textual entailment relationships and transforms retrieval into an outcome-based problem, leveraging the relationship between relevancy and affirmation. The experimental results highlight the effectiveness of multi-task learning and reveal potential future research directions, such as expanding to other legal domains, languages, and utilizing advanced deep learning models to improve legal document retrieval and textual entailment tasks.

Limitations

Although integrating information from the entailment task significantly improves the effectiveness of retrieval, the results of the entailment task itself are not yet highly accurate. This can be attributed to several possible reasons. The first reason is that determining the correctness of a query is a non-trivial task that requires incorporating the semantics of all relevant documents to reach a final conclusion. However, the proposed model only utilizes the semantic of a single (query, document) pair to perform this task. Second, in this study, the correctness of the query is determined by a rule stating that if any of the (query, document) pairs have the label as *correct*, the query will be considered *correct*. However, this approach is logically incorrect in many cases where one (query, document) pair is labeled as *correct* while another (query, document) pair is labeled as 'incorrect'. In the future, research on integrating the semantics of all relevant legal documents to determine the correctness of a query will need to be carefully considered and pursued.

Acknowledgements

This work was supported by the AIP challenge funding related with JST, AIP Trilateral AI Research, Grant Number JPMJCR20G4.

Hai-Long Nguyen was funded by the Master, PhD Scholarship Programme of Vingroup Innovation Foundation (VINIF), code VINIF.2022.ThS.050.

References

Amin Abolghasemi, Suzan Verberne, and Leif Azzopardi. 2022. Improving bert-based query-by-document retrieval with multi-task optimization. In *European Conference on Information Retrieval*, pages 3–12. Springer.

AA Askari, SV Verberne, O Alonso, S Marchesin, M Najork, and G Silvello. 2021. Combining lexical and neural retrieval with longformer-based summarization for effective case law retrieva. In *Proceedings of the second international conference on design of experimental search & information REtrieval systems*, pages 162–170. CEUR.

MQ Bui, C Nguyen, DT Do, NK Le, DH Nguyen, and TTT Nguyen. 2022. Using deep learning approaches for tackling legal's challenges (coliee 2022). In *Sixteenth International Workshop on Juris-informatics (JURISIN)*.

Ahmed Elnaggar, Christoph Gebendorfer, Ingo Glaser, and Florian Matthes. 2018. Multi-task deep learning for legal document translation, summarization and multi-label classification. In *Proceedings of the 2018 Artificial Intelligence and Cloud Computing Conference*, pages 9–15.

Daniel Martin Katz, Corinna Coupette, Janis Beckedorf, and Dirk Hartung. 2020. Complex societies and the growth of the law. *Scientific reports*, 10(1):18737.

Nitish Shirish Keskar and Richard Socher. 2017. Improving generalization performance by switching from adam to sgd. *arXiv preprint arXiv:1712.07628*.

Mi-Young Kim, Juliano Rabelo, and Randy Goebel. 2019. Statute law information retrieval and entailment. In *Proceedings of the Seventeenth International Conference on Artificial Intelligence and Law*, pages 283–289.

Mi-Young Kim, Juliano Rabelo, Randy Goebel, Masaharu Yoshioka, Yoshinobu Kano, and Ken Satoh. 2022. Coliee 2022 summary: Methods for legal document retrieval and entailment. In *JSAI International Symposium on Artificial Intelligence*, pages 51–67. Springer.

Antoine Louis, Gijs van Dijck, and Gerasimos Spanakis. 2023. Finding the law: Enhancing statutory article retrieval via graph neural networks. In *Proceedings of the 17th Conference of the European Chapter of the Association for Computational Linguistics*, pages 2761–2776, Dubrovnik, Croatia. Association for Computational Linguistics.

Tomas Mikolov, Stefan Kombrink, Anoop Deoras, Lukar Burget, and Jan Cernocky. 2011. Rnnlm-recurrent neural network language modeling toolkit. In *Proc. of the 2011 ASRU Workshop*, pages 196–201.

Ha-Thanh Nguyen, Minh-Phuong Nguyen, Thi-Hai-Yen Vuong, Minh-Quan Bui, Minh-Chau Nguyen, Tran-Binh Dang, Vu Tran, Le-Minh Nguyen, and Ken Satoh. 2022a. Transformer-based approaches for legal text processing: Jnlp team-coliee 2021. *The Review of Socionetwork Strategies*, 16(1):135–155.

Ha-Thanh Nguyen, Manh-Kien Phi, Xuan-Bach Ngo, Vu Tran, Le-Minh Nguyen, and Minh-Phuong Tu. 2022b. Attentive deep neural networks for legal document retrieval. *Artificial Intelligence and Law*, pages 1–30.

Ha-Thanh Nguyen, Vu Tran, Phuong Minh Nguyen, Thi-Hai-Yen Vuong, Quan Minh Bui, Chau Minh Nguyen, Binh Tran Dang, Minh Le Nguyen, and Ken Satoh. 2021. Paralaw nets–cross-lingual sentence-level pretraining for legal text processing. *arXiv preprint arXiv:2106.13403*.

Rodrigo Nogueira, Zhiying Jiang, Ronak Pradeep, and Jimmy Lin. 2020. Document ranking with a pretrained sequence-to-sequence model. In *Findings of the Association for Computational Linguistics: EMNLP 2020*, pages 708–718, Online. Association for Computational Linguistics.

Juliano Rabelo, Randy Goebel, Mi-Young Kim, Yoshinobu Kano, Masaharu Yoshioka, and Ken Satoh. 2022. Overview and discussion of the competition on legal information extraction/entailment (coliee) 2021. *The Review of Socionetwork Strategies*, 16(1):111–133.

Juliano Rabelo, Mi-Young Kim, and Randy Goebel. 2021a. The application of text entailment techniques in coliee 2020. In *New Frontiers in Artificial Intelligence: JSAI-isAI 2020 Workshops, JURISIN, LENLS 2020 Workshops, Virtual Event, November 15–17,*

2020, Revised Selected Papers 12, pages 240–253. Springer.

Juliano Rabelo, Mi-Young Kim, Randy Goebel, Masaharu Yoshioka, Yoshinobu Kano, and Ken Satoh. 2021b. Coliee 2020: methods for legal document retrieval and entailment. In *New Frontiers in Artificial Intelligence: JSAI-isAI 2020 Workshops, JURISIN, LENLS 2020 Workshops, Virtual Event, November 15–17, 2020, Revised Selected Papers 12*, pages 196–210. Springer.

Guilherme Moraes Rosa, Ruan Chaves Rodrigues, Roberto Lotufo, and Rodrigo Nogueira. 2021. Yes, bm25 is a strong baseline for legal case retrieval. *arXiv preprint arXiv:2105.05686*.

JB Ruhl, Daniel Martin Katz, and Michael J Bommarito. 2017. Harnessing legal complexity. *Science*, 355(6332):1377–1378.

Yen Thi-Hai Vuong, Quan Minh Bui, Ha-Thanh Nguyen, Thi-Thu-Trang Nguyen, Vu Tran, Xuan-Hieu Phan, Ken Satoh, and Le-Minh Nguyen. 2022. Sm-bert-cr: a deep learning approach for case law retrieval with supporting model. *Artificial Intelligence and Law*, pages 1–28.

Yen Thi-Hai Vuong, Quan Minh Bui, Ha-Thanh Nguyen, Thi-Thu-Trang Nguyen, Vu Tran, Xuan-Hieu Phan, Ken Satoh, and Le-Minh Nguyen. 2023. Sm-bert-cr: a deep learning approach for case law retrieval with supporting model. *Artificial Intelligence and Law*, 31(3):601–628.

Sabine Wehnert, Libin Kutty, and Ernesto William De Luca. 2022. Using textbook knowledge for statute retrieval and entailment classification. In *JSAI International Symposium on Artificial Intelligence*, pages 125–137. Springer.

Masaharu Yoshioka, Yasuhiro Aoki, and Youta Suzuki. 2021. Bert-based ensemble methods with data augmentation for legal textual entailment in coliee statute law task. In *Proceedings of the eighteenth international conference on artificial intelligence and law*, pages 278–284.

Masaharu Yoshioka, Youta Suzuki, and Yasuhiro Aoki. 2022. Hukb at the coliee 2022 statute law task. In *JSAI International Symposium on Artificial Intelligence*, pages 109–124. Springer.

Super-SCOTUS: A multi-sourced dataset for the Supreme Court of the US

Biaoyan Fang[◇*] **Trevor Cohn**[◇†] **Timothy Baldwin**[◇,♠] **Lea Frermann**[◇]
[◇]The University of Melbourne, Australia
[♠]MBZUAI
{biaoyan,tcohn,tbaldwin,lfrermann}@unimelb.edu.au

Abstract

Given the complexity of the judiciary in the US Supreme Court, various procedures, along with various resources, contribute to the court system. However, most research focuses on a limited set of resources, e.g., court opinions or oral arguments, for analyzing a specific perspective in court, e.g., partisanship or voting. To gain a fuller understanding of these perspectives in the legal system of the US Supreme Court, a more comprehensive dataset, connecting different sources in different phases of the court procedure, is needed. To address this gap, we present a multi-sourced dataset for the Supreme Court, comprising court resources from different procedural phases, connecting language documents with extensive metadata. We showcase its utility through a case study on how different court documents reveal the decision direction (conservative vs. liberal) of the cases. We analyze performance differences across three protected attributes, indicating that different court resources encode different biases, and reinforcing that considering various resources provides a fuller picture of the court procedures. We further discuss how our dataset can contribute to future research directions.[1]

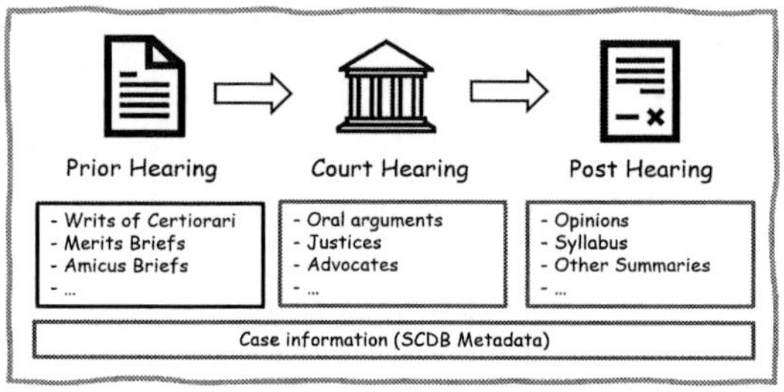

Figure 1: The jurisdiction procedure of the Supreme Court. Data resources highlighted in blue are included in Super-SCOTUS, our multi-sourced dataset.

1 Introduction

With the increasing attention to legal text processing, recent research has proposed various legal corpora, covering different sources, e.g., court documents (Zheng et al., 2021; Chalkidis et al., 2022a; Niklaus et al., 2021; Henderson et al., 2022; Locke and Zuccon, 2018) or legal contracts (Tuggener et al., 2020; Hendrycks et al., 2021; Lippi et al., 2019), and tackling legal analysis with a diverse set of tasks, e.g., text classification (Chalkidis et al., 2022a,b), juridical output prediction (Zhong et al., 2018; Cui et al., 2022) and case summarization (Ye et al., 2018; Shukla et al., 2022).

In the Supreme Court of the US (SCOTUS), several procedures contribute to the court results and reasoning process (Stern and Gressman, 1950). As illustrated in Figure 1, for instance, a *writ of certiorari* is needed for the petition of the appeal to the SCOTUS. *Merits briefs* in which petitioners and respondents lay out their arguments to the Court, are required before the oral arguments take place, which in turn can clarify or elaborate on points made in the briefs. Justices further discuss and decide the case, and afterwards issue *Opinions* which explain the reasoning behind the final judgment. We present a comprehensive data set of SCOTUS proceedings and meta data to enable holistic language analysis of the court.

Various SCOTUS resources have been gathered from different phases of the ruling procedure and formulated in diverse tasks in order to analyze different perspectives of the court, e.g., voting (Ruger et al., 2004; Katz et al., 2017; Dietrich et al., 2019), partisanship (Bergam et al., 2022) and topic prediction (Chalkidis et al., 2022a,b). However, each work comprises only a limited set of resources with a specific focus on one particular court perspective.

In light of this observation, we take a step forward and create a multi-sourced SCOTUS dataset,

*Now at CSIRO Data61.
†Now at Google DeepMind.
[1]Dataset and code are made available at https://github.com/biaoyanf/Super-SCOTUS.

Proceedings of the Natural Legal Language Processing Workshop 2023, pages 202–214
December 7, 2023 ©2023 Association for Computational Linguistics

i,e., Super-SCOTUS (Section 3). Figure 1 illustrates the scope and structure of our dataset. We focus on the phases of the court hearing and post hearing, augmented with relevant metadata on the cases and justices.[2] Our corpus connects publicly-available resources including oral arguments and various post-hearing annotations and summaries, including Opinions and case summaries.

To showcase the utility of our data set, we present a case study in Section 4 where we ask *how do different court documents reflect the direction of the final court decision (as conservative or liberal).* We predict the decision direction from input documents from the phases of the court hearing (Oral arguments) and post-hearing (Syllabus). We consider three sensitive case attributes, derived from the meta data of our corpus, to analyse group disparity of our classifiers with respect to (1) Issue Area, (2) Vote Distribution, and (3) Winning Side. We observe that, compared to oral arguments, case direction is easier to decode from the syllabus. The group disparity across three protected attributes indicates that different court materials might encode different biases, suggesting the necessity of considering various resources for the full analysis of the Supreme Court. We finally point out potential directions and use cases for future work (Section 5).

In summary, our contributions are (1) a publicly available multi-sourced SCOTUS dataset, comprising various court information from different procedure phases. (2) a case study, addressing the research question of *how do the court materials reflect the case direction*, overall and wrt. discrepancy for three protected attributes (3) a summary of the different layers of legal texts in the Supreme Court and a discussion for future research directions building on our dataset.

2 Related Work

The judiciary in court, as the base of the legal system, has been one of the key focuses in the legal domain (Martin and Quinn, 2002; Epstein et al., 2010; Devins and Baum, 2017; Zheng et al., 2021; Fang et al., 2023a). For the analysis of SCOTUS, although various corpora exist, each corpus consists of a limited fraction of the court resources and analyzes a specific perspective of the court, e.g., topic prediction on court opinions (Chalkidis et al., 2022a,b).

The LexGLUE corpus (Chalkidis et al., 2022a) is a benchmark dataset for legal language understanding and formulates the SCOTUS resource as a topic classification task. Specifically, the SCOTUS partition includes the opinion of the case,[3] and annotates the opinions with the issue area (topic), obtained from the Supreme Court Database (SCDB) (Spaeth et al., 2021), described in Section 3. Furthermore, Chalkidis et al. (2022b) considered the same SCOTUS task but with a focus on the fairness of classification models. They investigated various debiasing methods in the context of the legal domain. However, their fairness study of SCOTUS was limited to only one resource: opinion text.

To enrich the utilization of conversational data, expanding from Danescu-Niculescu-Mizil et al. (2012), Convokit (Chang et al., 2020) contains the transcripts of oral arguments of SCOTUS cases between 1955 to 2019.[4] This partition is also included as one of the sources in our Super-SCOTUS dataset (Section 3).

The SC-stance dataset (Bergam et al., 2022) combines the SCOTUS case questions annotated by the Oyez website and the corresponding SCOTUS opinion from a Kaggle dataset (Fiddler, 2022) to predict the political stands in court. They derived and labeled the political stands of the questions and opinions based on the winning side of cases from SCDB, i,e., favoring petitioners or respondents.

Henderson et al. (2022) proposed a large legal corpus, called Pile of Law, with approx. 256G (growing) legal and administrative text which concentrates on the US legal system, with the aim to provide a comprehensive corpus for legal text without containing toxic or private content. This corpus also includes SCOTUS opinions and the transcripts of oral arguments.

Bauer et al. (2023) annotated a dataset of approx. 436K US court opinions, including Supreme and Federal Courts, with key passages and summaries. However, their dataset is not publicly available.

As we discussed, current research only focuses on a limited partition of the SCOTUS resources. A more comprehensive dataset that covers various court resources is needed in order to understand how various court materials from different phases contribute to and reflect the Supreme Court. To address this gap, we provide a publicly-available multi-sourced SCOTUS dataset, connecting vari-

[2]We do not cover documents prior to hearing as these are not typically released to the public.

[3]Obtained from https://www.courtlistener.com/

[4]Obtained from https://www.oyez.org/

ous resources in different phases of the court procedure and enriching the dataset with additional annotations from the post-hearing phase.

3 The Super-SCOTUS Dataset

As shown in Figure 1, the court system comprises several stages. Since most pre-hearing documents are not publicly available, our dataset includes the resources from the court hearing and post-hearing, listed in Section 3.1. We detail our dataset construction in Section 3.2.

3.1 Dataset Sources

Supreme Court DataBase (SCDB)[5] This database (Spaeth et al., 2021) is recognized as the definitive source for analysis of the SCOTUS. It provides comprehensive structural metadata in over 50 categories such as justice votes, issue areas, and decision directions, for all SCOTUS cases between 1791 and 2021. Each case is labeled with a unique case ID.

Oral Arguments[6] We consider the oral arguments in the courtroom from Convokit (Chang et al., 2020), containing the transcripts of SCOTUS oral arguments among justices, advocates and amicus curiae for cases from 1955 to 2019. Each utterance is annotated with the speaker and the speaking time. Case IDs of the transcripts are also provided and aligned with the SCDB. It is worth noting that one case could have multiple conversations as cases can be re-argued at a later time.

Post-hearing Documents Justia[7] provides the following post-hearing data from 1791 to present: (1) **Syllabus**, a preliminary section of a court ruling that outlines the core facts and issues of the case, and the path that the case has been taken to the court, and (2) **Opinion**, set out the Court's judgment decision and its reasoning. The opinion might also include a *Concurrence* by judges who agree with the majority opinion but publish their own reasoning; and a *Dissent*, which provides the reasoning of justices who voted against the majority. Additionally, Justia provides (3) **Primary Holding**, a high-level summary of the case ruling, and (4) **Justia Summary**, a lay-friendly summary of the opinion. Primary holding and justice summary

	# cases covered
ConvoKit arguments	6,733
SCDB Metedata	6,721
Wikipedia Summary	1,191
Justia Syllabus	6,604
Justia Opinion	6,647
Justia Primary Holding	999
Justia Summary	602
Oyez Facts of the Case	2,945
Oyez Questions	2,946
Oyez Conclusions	2,944
Year Range	1955-2019
Justices	35

Table 1: Super-SCOTUS dataset statistics.

are additional case summaries, created by licensed attorneys from the platform with the aim to readability. This contrasts with the syllabus which was created by the court's reporter, and serves the primary purpose of official documentation.

Case Facts, Questions, and Conclusions For each SCOTUS case since 1789, Oyez[8] provides (1) **Facts of the Case**, summarizing the background of the case and the ruling from the lower court, (2) **Key Questions** addressed in the case, and (3) the **Conclusions**, i.e., answers to the key questions, also serving as a high-level summary of the voting reasoning. All information is collated by the editorial team of Justia.

Wikipedia Summary[9] Wikipedia provides a one-sentence summary of a set of notable Supreme Court cases from 1789 up to the present.

Justice Information We manually collect metadata for all justices from Wikipedia, Oyez, and the SCOTUS website,[10] with 10 attributes: year of birth; state of birth; gender; nominating president; nominating party; year of joining the court; chief justice (binary); year becoming chief justice; self-reported affiliated party; and ideal point (conservative or liberal) from Martin-Quinn score (MQ score; (Martin and Quinn, 2002)).

3.2 Dataset Creation

We crawled the data from the listed resources and automatically linked them at the case level. The overall statistics and coverage of SCOTUS cases

[5]http://scdb.wustl.edu/. A full list of SCDB attributes is provided in Appendix B.

[6]https://convokit.cornell.edu/documentation/supreme.html

[7]https://supreme.justia.com/

[8]https://www.oyez.org/

[9]https://en.wikipedia.org/wiki/Lists_of_United_States_Supreme_Court_cases, categorized by Chief Justice.

[10]https://www.supremecourt.gov/about/members_text.aspx

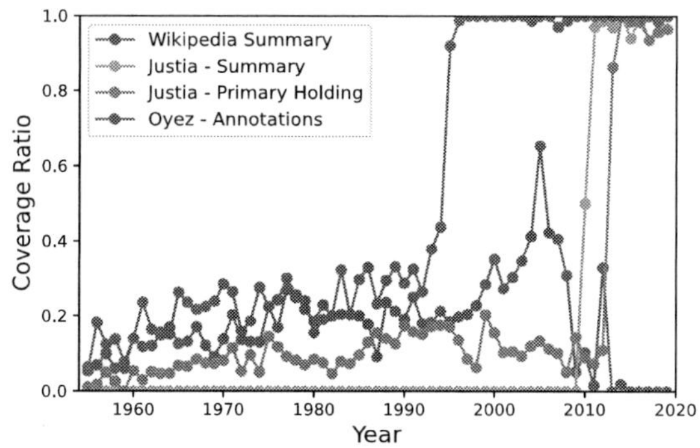

Figure 2: Case coverage of annotations. We show the annotations from Oyez (i.e., Facts of the Case, Question, and Conclusions) as "Oyez - Annotations" as the temporal coverages of those annotations are almost identical.

are shown in Table 1.[11] We used the Oral Arguments from ConvoKit as the base source, and augmented it with the other resources. In other words, Supreme Court cases that are not in the Convokit dataset are not included.

We linked the oral arguments with the SCDB based on the unique SCOTUS docket IDs. To parse the data from Justia, we separated the syllabus and opinion identifying the boundary of the two sections with a rule-based method. We separated the sections of Opinions, Concurrence, and Dissent based on the HTML tags provided by the website.[12] We automatically connected the Justica resources to the SCBD using case citations and discarded the Justia resources that are not explicitly matched by the citations. We linked cases in Oyez using the URLs in the oral argument data from Convokit. We utilized the case titles to match the data from the Wikipedia summary and the SCOTUS cases.

As shown in Table 1, the summaries from Justia, Oyez, and Wikipedia do not cover the SCOTUS cases comprehensively as they are not part of the official court-released documents. Annotations from Oyez and Justia are most complete for cases since 1995 and 2013, respectively (Figure 2). Wikipedia summaries exist only for notable cases, so no temporal pattern is observed.

[11]Detailed statistics of all resources are shown in Appendix A.

[12]Note that only 1109 (out of 6733) cases contain section separation tags. Sections could be also embedded in one whole document, i.e., no explicit HTML tags. We do not make separations for those cases.

Total Cases		5,205	
Oral Arguments	- avg. sentences	462	
	- avg. words	10,866	
Syllabus	- avg. sentences	33	
	- avg. words	837	
Decision Direction	- Conservative	2,617	(50.3%)
	- Liberal	2,588	(49.7%)

Table 2: Statistics of the Decision Direction Prediction dataset, derived from Super-SCOTUS.

4 Decision Direction Prediction from Diverse Sources

As described in Section 2, most NLP research focuses on only a single type of document (predominantly Opinion documents (Zheng et al., 2021)) and typically a single task, e.g., the classification of the overall case topic (Chalkidis et al., 2022a,b). Here, we (a) propose a novel task of *decision direction prediction* which encodes information about case topic, justices' voting, and political leaning; and (b) consider this task across documents from the 'Court Hearing' and the 'Post Hearing' phase. Finally, we leverage the rich meta-data of Super-SCOTUS to study biases in the respective sources.

To demonstrate the utility of Super-SCOTUS, we study how different court materials reflect the *decision direction* of a case. Decision direction is coded as a binary variable as *Conservative* or *Liberal* by legal experts for the SCDB. Both the case outcome and the issue area (case topic) are taken into account during this labeling. For instance, in the issue area of criminal procedure, a Liberal label could indicate that the case outcome is 'pro civil liberties' or 'pro-underdog', and vice versa for Conservative. For cases related to economy, a Liberal label could indicate 'pro administrative action.[13]

4.1 Method

Data We consider two types of Super-SCOTUS documents, namely the Oral Arguments from the court hearing phase (OA), and the Syllabus from post-hearing (SL), and predict case decision direction. We remove cases which (i) do not have labels for voting result, decision direction, and issue area; (ii) were discussed in more than one oral argument session; (iii) lack the syllabus or opinion; or (iv) include companion cases, where multiple cases are jointly discussed. The statistics of the result-

[13]For full guidelines, see `http://scdb.wustl.edu/documentation.php?var=decisionDirection`.

ing dataset is shown in Table 2. Following previous work (Chalkidis et al., 2022a,b), the dataset is chronologically split into training (4133 cases, 1955-2002), development (536 cases, 2003-2010), and test (536 cases, 2011-2019) sets.

Protected attributes To further understand the model performance under different court documents, we investigate group disparities based on three groups which represent important perspectives of the cases: (1) **Issue Area**, indicating the general topic of the case (e.g., civil rights); (2) **Winning Side**, binary, whether the voting result favored the petitioner or respondent; and (3) **Vote Distribution**, the percentage of justices that vote with the majority categorized into five equal-width bins, indicating level of justice agreement.[14]

Models We include the following models: (1) BERT[15] (Devlin et al., 2019), pretrained on large generic domain corpus and served as a benchmark transformer-based model for various tasks, and (2) Legal-BERT[16] (Chalkidis et al., 2020), a domain-specific language model pretrained on English legal text, including court cases and legislation. We include the non-neural models Logistic Regression (LR) and Linear Support Vector Machine (SVM) with uni-gram TF-IDF features. We also report majority and random baselines.

For the non-neural baselines, we use grid search for the regularization parameter C with L2 penalty. For transformer-based methods, due to the input limitation, we consider either the first ($*$-first) or the last ($*$-last) 510 tokens of a particular document type, as the model input. We finetune models for 50 epochs with a batch size of 8, and a learning rate of 1e-5. We select the models with the best macro F1 on the development set.

4.2 Main Results

To study how different court materials reflect the case decision direction, we test how reliably decision direction can be predicted by various models based on different input documents. Table 3 shows that all models outperform the random and majority baseline, and that models based on the syllabus (bottom) are more reliable than oral argument-based prediction (center). This is unsurprising

Input	Model	μ-F1	m-F1
-	Random	50.1	50.0
	Majority	52.1	32.4
Oral Argument	LR	52.4	50.1
	SVM	52.1	49.2
	BERT - first	**56.3**	**56.3**
	BERT - last	52.1	51.1
	Legal BERT - first	54.3	54.0
	Legal BERT - last	47.2	47.0
Syllabus	LR	57.1	57.1
	SVM	57.3	57.3
	BERT - first	53.7	53.7
	BERT - last	**66.2**	**65.9**
	Legal BERT - first	53.2	51.7
	Legal BERT - last	64.4	63.6

Table 3: Test results on decision direction prediction tasks with different inputs, i.e. oral arguments and syllabus. "μ-F1" and "m-F1" denote micro-F1 and macro-F1, respecitvely.

given that the syllabus is written after the court decision and explicitly states the case decision outcome, while oral arguments precede the decision and reflect justices' leanings implicitly at most as justices should not have made up their mind or aim to appear objective (Black et al., 2011; Dietrich et al., 2019). Holding the input type fixed, BERT outperforms Legal-BERT on our task. One possible reason is that the syllabus and oral arguments mostly contain generic words rather than legal vocabulary. Models trained on oral arguments perform better when using the first 510 tokens, which encode the case background and introduction. Models trained on the syllabus perform better when using the last 510 tokens, where the case decision is stated in terms, e.g., *affirmed* or *reversed* (but importantly *not* in terms of the ideological direction we are predicting here). We overall observe a relatively modest improvement of all models over the baseline, indicating the challenging nature of the task in particular for oral arguments-based models.

4.3 Group Disparity Analysis

Perhaps more interestingly than raw performance, we are now in a position to investigate different biases exhibited by models trained on different court documents. To this end, we analyze model performance for different *groups* of cases. We consider only the best (bolded) models from Table 3 based on the syllabus (BERT-last) and oral arguments (BERT-first). Following Chalkidis et al. (2022b), we first consider our three protected groups (Section 4.1) in isolation (Single Attribute) and subse-

[14]We do not use vote count as not all cases are voted by all 9 justices.

[15]https://huggingface.co/bert-base-uncased

[16]https://huggingface.co/nlpaueb/legal-bert-base-uncased

Group	m-F1(↑)		train(%)(↑)	KL(↓)
	OA	SL		
Issue Area				
Criminal	55.9	68.7	**980 (24%)**	0.03
Economic	54.0	54.5	766 (19%)	0.02
Civil Rights	51.1	**77.4**	701 (17%)	**0.00**
Judicial Power	57.1	63.2	516 (12%)	0.02
1st Amendment	**68.3**	65.3	341 (8%)	0.05
Winning Side				
Petitioner	55.2	**68.1**	**2630 (64%)**	**0.00**
Respondent	**58.2**	60.8	1503 (36%)	**0.00**
Vote Distribution (% majority)				
50% - 60%	48.9	78.5	694 (17%)	0.01
60% - 70%	**64.4**	**80.9**	760 (18%)	0.05
70% - 80%	49.3	69.6	590 (14%)	0.02
80% - 90%	56.4	64.6	466 (11%)	**0.00**
90% - 100%	59.2	52.5	**1585 (38%)**	0.01

Table 4: Left: Group disparity results (mF1) across attribute groups with syllabus input for the best BERT models trained on Oral Arguments (OA) and on Syllabus (SL). Right: Representation Inequality ("train(%)") and Temporal Concept Drift ("KL"). The best (least harmful) values are highlighted in **bold**.

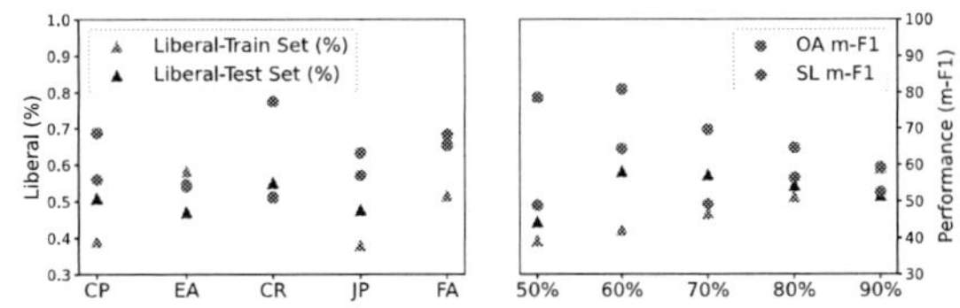

(a) Issue Area (b) Vote Distribution

Figure 3: Percentage of Liberal decisions in the train (grey) and test set (black) vs. Model Performance based on OA (blue) and SL (red) on the test set. "CP", "EA", "CR", "JP", and "FA" denote "Criminal Procedure", "Economic Activity", "Civil Rights", "Judicial Power" and "First Amendment", respectively. "$k\%$" denotes Vote Distribution in $k\%$ - $(k+10)\%$, where $k \in [50, 60, 70, 80, 90]$.

quently their intersections (Cross-Attribute).

Single Attribute Disparity Table 4 (left) displays the macro-F1 score achieved for different partitions of cases, i.e., by Issue Area (top), Winning Side (center), and Vote Distribution (bottom). Overall, performance in different groups varies, especially in the groups of Issue Area and Vote Distribution with mF1 varying by >10 points. Interestingly, for Vote Distribution the Syllabus-based model performs better when the voting pattern is more disparate, i.e., when the percentage of majority voting is close to 50%.

Additionally, although the SL-based model generally performs better than the OA-based model, there are select subgroups for which oral arguments may provide more signals on decision direction, e.g., 1st Amendment under Issue Area cases and high vote agreement (90%-100%) under Vote Distribution, indicating the difference of bias entailed in different court documents.

To rule out that performance disparity is caused by idiosyncrasies of our data set, we consider two more general factors (Chalkidis et al., 2022b): (1) representation inequality, as number of training instances per group, and (2) Temporal Concept Drift as measured by the KL-divergence of per group label distribution between the training and test sets.

Table 4 (column #train(%)) shows the group representation in the training data, and reveals that performance does not correlate with representation. For instance, the largest Issue Area of "Criminal Law" does not achieve best performance. Turning to temporal concept drift (column KL), we observe low drift throughout. Drift does not predict group disparities either. For instance, for Issue Area the best performing labels from Syllabus and the Oral Arguments-based model have the highest and lowest KL, respectively.

Finally, we inspect if the label distribution correlates with group-specific model performance, focussing on the multi-class variables Issue Area and Vote Distribution. We show the label distributions of decision direction under different attribute groups, unpacking the KL-divergence in the train (grey) and test (black) sets, and compare them with the model performance in Figure 3. We do not observe severe label imbalance in the train and test sets across different attribute groups (little variance in the grey and black lines in Figure 3 (a) and (b)). We do not observe a significant correlation between Syllabus performance (SL, red) and label distribution (grey and black) under Pearson R ($p > 0.1$) across groups. The same holds for the relation of Oral Argument input (OA, blue) to label distribution.

Cross-Attribute Disparity Attributes are not necessarily independent of each other (Chalkidis et al., 2022b). To further unpack how different groups interact, we inspect performance discrepancies in groups that intersect on two of our attributes. In particular we intersect Issue Area with Winning

Side (Table 5 and 6, top) and Vote Distributions (Table 5 and 6, bottom). We do so for the OA-based model in Table 5 and the SL-based model in Table 6.

Table 5 (top) reveals for the OA-based model that, although models predicted 'Respondent Winners' with higher Macro-F1 in the overall analysis (Table 4), the picture is less clear in the intersection with Issue Area, where 'Petitioner Winners' are predicted with higher Macro-F1 for three out of five cases (CP, EA and most strikingly FA). Moving to the SL-based model (Table 6, top), we see that 'Petitioner Winners' are predicted with higher Macro-F1 than 'Respondent Winners' across issue areas, in agreement with the overall results in Table 4, suggesting the prevalent bias of Winning Side in the SL-based model. One possible reason is the explicit statement of the case outcome, which makes it easier for the SL-based model to learn the case direction signals. Further investigation, e.g., removing the voting result from the last few sentences in Syllabus (Malik et al., 2021), would be worthy to explore to understand the impact.

In Table 5, the performance varies in the cross-attributes of the Issue Area and Vote Distribution, indicating the complexity of identifying case direction across attributes from Oral Arguments. For our SL-based model in Table 6 (bottom), we observe that attributes in Issue Area that showed overall high performance, consistently achieve better performance across different Vote Distributions. Aligned with the overall results in Table 4, we also observe poor performance under unanimous cases throughout issue areas. One possible reason is that unanimous cases generally include important cases and historically those critical cases do not reflect much political leaning (Devins and Baum, 2017), one factor that would affect the case direction.

Overall, we show that models with different court documents as input (Oral Arguments vs. Syllabus) exhibit different performance discrepancies for different attribute groups. This is certainly due to the different nature in style and content of the documents. Our corpus and framework allow to systematically analyse downstream performance biases implied by different inputs – a mandatory prerequisite for any predictive models in high-stakes applications like the legal domain.

	Group A: Issue Area				
Group B:	CP	EA	CR	JP	FA
Petitioner	**52.4**	**59.2**	46.4	54.1	**79.2**
Respondent	40.3	42.6	**59.0**	**59.6**	45.1
50% - 60%	52.4	**60.6**	47.5	26.7	–
60% - 70%	**72.0**	45.0	**64.9**	**75.0**	–
70% - 80%	44.0	52.1	24.5	–	**73.3**
80% - 90%	49.7	49.7	–	–	–
90% - 100%	44.6	55.4	60.0	53.9	66.7

Table 5: MacroF1 results in cross-attribute influence on the BERT model with **Oral Arguments** input, intersecting Issue Area with either Winning Side (top) or Vote Distribution (bottom). **Best** and worst performing group per Issue Area are highlighted.

5 Conclusion and Future Vision

We presented a publicly-available multi-sourced dataset for the analysis of the US Supreme Court, namely the Super-SCOTUS dataset. Specifically, we focus on various resources from the phases of the court hearing and post hearing, connecting court-released data, both text documents (Opinions, Syllabus) and structured data (voting outcomes, issue areas), and enriching it with various summaries from different legal platforms, including key questions/conclusions of the court from Oyez and landmark case summaries from Wikipedia.

Our dataset supports a variety novel of NLP tasks (Section 5.1), where the empirical experiments in this paper only scratched the surface. To demonstrate the utility of Super-SCOTUS, we propose the challenging novel task of Decision Direction prediction, where labels encode the ideological direction most aligned with the case outcome (Liberal vs Conservative). We presented a case study using different court materials as input, namely Oral Arguments and Syllabus, and analyzed performance discrepancies of the best resulting models regarding three attribute groups. We observed that model performance varies with different inputs. The group disparity analysis further shows the performance difference across attributes, indicating that different biases exist in models trained on different court documents and suggesting the importance of considering various sources in the analysis of the court.

5.1 Future Vision

With the rich resources incorporated in our Super-SCOTUS corpus, we now have the opportunity to further enhance and expand the legal research in

	Group A: Issue Area				
Group B:	CP	EA	CR	JP	FA
Petitioner	**67.5**	**54.6**	**80.6**	**66.8**	**74.9**
Respondent	49.3	54.3	69.3	49.5	33.3
50% - 60%	**96.3**	44.8	81.5	**80.4**	–
60% - 70%	75.6	**71.8**	**100.0**	75.0	–
70% - 80%	66.4	55.6	**100.0**	–	**66.7**
80% - 90%	68.9	49.7	–	–	–
90% - 100%	45.2	52.1	61.0	43.3	56.4

Table 6: Same as Table 5, but with **Syllabus** based model input.

various tasks.

Court Decision Direction Prediction Our case study on decision prediction (Section 4) shows that different court documents—Oral Arguments versus Syllabus—entail different biases towards the prediction task. This analysis can be further expanded to other documents, e.g., Justia summary and Oyez conclusions, in order to gain a fuller understanding of court materials. The specific task of decision direction prediction would not be the end goal itself, but rather serve as vehicle to explore the biases and information encoded in those different documents, and how they impact downstream task performance. Furthermore, one might explore the impact of selecting certain information from those documents, or *summarizing* them automatically, would impact model performance.

Court Judgment Prediction We acknowledge the ethical concerns of legal judgement prediction, and do not recommend the task as benchmark task. That said, our data set allows to systematically study the extent to which justices' decisions are encoded in various court documents – most interestingly both during the court hearing (e.g., in Oral Arguments (Dietrich et al., 2019; Epstein et al., 2010; Epstein and Weinshall, 2021)) and post hearing. Related research casts the Court Judgment Prediction task based on documents from the post-hearing phase (Cui et al., 2022; Sim et al., 2015, 2016; Zhong et al., 2018) or purely on case characteristic (Ruger et al., 2004; Katz et al., 2017) and analyzes the results separately.

Ideology and Partisanship Most research develops the analysis of ideology and partisanship based on justices' voting (Martin and Quinn, 2002, 2007; Bailey and Maltzman, 2011; Bailey, 2013; Devins and Baum, 2017), assuming judicial preferences could be represented by their voting. It is also well-established that politicians choose words carefully in order to convey specific messages (Entman, 1993; Lakoff, 2010; Robinson et al., 2017). Building on our dataset, we now can investigate how the court documents, e.g., speeches from justices, advocates, or amicus curiae, reveal their partisan affiliations, and in how far their words align with their voting results (Bergam et al., 2022; Fang et al., 2023b).

Court Summarization Given the substantial length of most official legal documents and their high degree of expert language that is barely understandable to lay people, recent research has been focusing on extracting or summarizing key information from legal text (Ye et al., 2018; Wu et al., 2020; Shukla et al., 2022; Deroy et al., 2023; Bhattacharya et al., 2019; Shukla et al., 2022; Bauer et al., 2023).

Super-SCOTUS is a multi-reference summarization data set. It combines full-length court documents with various levels of summarization, aligned by case IDs. One promising and under-explored direction is to extract key contents from written Opinions and to generate the Syllabus. Additionally, the annotation of case questions, stating the key question addressed in the case, could be viewed as an 'extreme summary' of the case. Generating the key questions given the syllabus, opinion, and/or transcripts of oral arguments would be both challenging and a practically highly useful NLP application to increase accessibility of SCOTUS data to the general public. One natural related task would be how to answer those key questions, i.e., to generate the Conclusions in our data set, addressing the questions with judgment output and reasoning, given the facts of the case and other additional documents.

Model Speaker's Behaviors Increasing attention has been paid to understand the conversational behavior in the courtroom, e.g., association with voting (Epstein et al., 2010; Bergam et al., 2022; Epstein and Weinshall, 2021; Dietrich et al., 2019) and social dynamic in speakers' responses (Danescu-Niculescu-Mizil et al., 2012; Fang et al., 2023a). Particular for justices, with the rich metadata in our Super-SCOTUS annotations and various types of text from justices, we could further unlock research in analyzing court behaviors from different parties, e.g., to what extent the spoken text in the courtroom reveals the attributes of speakers, what linguist signals in spoken text those attribute groups encode, and furthermore how those signals correlate to their written documents.

Fairness and Bias In the context of the legal domain, one of the principal values is equality and non-discrimination (Xenidis and Senden, 2019). Although the definition of equality in law is completely the same, this also applies to the development of legal AI systems (Barfield, 2020; Chalkidis et al., 2022b; Wachter et al., 2020; Zhong et al., 2020). Particulary, Chalkidis et al. (2022b) benchmarked the evaluation of fairness in legal classification tasks over four jurisdictions, including SCOTUS with a task of issue area prediction along with two attribute groups (Respondent Type and Decision Direction). However, their analysis only focused on one specific court document, i.e., Opinions. With the availability of rich metadata (over 50 structural labels) and various text documents in phases of court hearing and post hearing, our Super-SCOTUS corpus provides an opportunity to systematically and comprehensively evaluate model fairness and debiasing methods in the classification tasks of SCOTUS.

Furthermore, attempts have also been made in summarizing or generating key content from written legal documents (Ye et al., 2018; Wu et al., 2020; Shukla et al., 2022; Bhattacharya et al., 2019). However, most research only focuses on the generation performance but not through the lens of fairness. Our multi-sourced dataset includes diverse layers of summaries connected with comprehensive metadata of the SCOTUS cases. This provides a unique opportunity to evaluate the fairness and bias of generation summarization models in the context of the legal domain and further benefit the development of fair legal systems.

Our creation of Super-SCOTUS takes a step further in this direction by giving the accessibility of comparing external resources with various SCOTUS-related materials, for instance, investigating partisanship alignment in the congressional records and various Supreme Court documents.

Ethics Statement

Social Impact We created a multi-sourced dataset which comprises diverse perspectives on the court hearing and post-hearing procedures, including both text and rich meta data. We presented a case study to showcase the potentials of our data set and discussed opportunities for future work. As a single, comprehensive resource Super-SCOTUS facilitates research in the legal domain from various perspectives (Section 5.1).

Acknowledging the importance of ethics in the legal domain (Tsarapatsanis and Aletras, 2021), we follow Chalkidis et al. (2022b) in arguing that the development of legal technology should not only rely on the performance of the majority group, and add that it additionally should not rely on only a single document source. Our data set allows to study these questions, e.g., by identifying the confounders in court documents that lead to unfair or unreliable behavior.

Personal Information Super-SCOTUS contains personal information, e.g., about the petitioners and respondents (from the SCDB data base). Given that all cases are (reasonably) high profile by definition of being considered at the SCOTUS, and the data was obtained from public repositories we did not redact this information. We encourage researchers to consider the potential impacts of personal information in their research. The usage of the data has to be in compliance with US law.

Additionally, we manually added gender and nominated party of SCOTUS justices as additional meta data, again sourced from public databases (Wikipedia). Given the impact of Supreme Court justices on the US legal system, we collect this data to provide more comprehensive context for the analysis of the US Supreme Court as in the whole system, but not at the individual level. We make no attempt to target any justices, nor encourage it.

Credit Attribution / Licensing The Convokit dataset is distributed under the MIT license. The usae of official data by the Supreme Court (SCDB) must comply with US law. Annotations from Justia are provided as open access contributed pro-bono by licensed attorneys.[17] Data from Oyez is under Creative Commons Attribution-NonCommercial 4.0 International License.[18] Annotations from Wikipedia are available under the Creative Commons Attribution-ShareAlike License 4.0.[19] We release the Super-SCOTUS dataset under a CC-BY-NC-SA-4.0 license.[20]

[17] https://law.justia.com/annotations/

[18] https://creativecommons.org/licenses/by-nc/4.0/

[19] https://en.wikipedia.org/wiki/Wikipedia:Text_of_the_Creative_Commons_Attribution-ShareAlike_4.0_International_License

[20] https://creativecommons.org/licenses/by-nc-sa/4.0/

References

Michael A Bailey. 2013. Is today's court the most conservative in sixty years? challenges and opportunities in measuring judicial preferences. *The Journal of Politics*, 75(3):821–834.

Michael A Bailey and Forrest Maltzman. 2011. *The constrained court: Law, politics, and the decisions justices make*. Princeton University Press.

Woodrow Barfield. 2020. *The Cambridge Handbook of the Law of Algorithms*. Cambridge University Press.

Emmanuel Bauer, Dominik Stammbach, Nianlong Gu, and Elliott Ash. 2023. Legal extractive summarization of us court opinions. *arXiv preprint arXiv:2305.08428*.

Noah Bergam, Emily Allaway, and Kathleen Mckeown. 2022. Legal and political stance detection of SCOTUS language. In *Proceedings of the Natural Legal Language Processing Workshop 2022*, pages 265–275, Abu Dhabi, United Arab Emirates (Hybrid). Association for Computational Linguistics.

Paheli Bhattacharya, Kaustubh Hiware, Subham Rajgaria, Nilay Pochhi, Kripabandhu Ghosh, and Saptarshi Ghosh. 2019. A comparative study of summarization algorithms applied to legal case judgments. In *Advances in Information Retrieval: 41st European Conference on IR Research, ECIR 2019, Cologne, Germany, April 14–18, 2019, Proceedings, Part I 41*, pages 413–428. Springer.

Ryan C Black, Sarah A Treul, Timothy R Johnson, and Jerry Goldman. 2011. Emotions, oral arguments, and supreme court decision making. *The Journal of Politics*, 73(2):572–581.

Ilias Chalkidis, Manos Fergadiotis, Prodromos Malakasiotis, Nikolaos Aletras, and Ion Androutsopoulos. 2020. LEGAL-BERT: The muppets straight out of law school. In *Findings of the Association for Computational Linguistics: EMNLP 2020*, pages 2898–2904, Online. Association for Computational Linguistics.

Ilias Chalkidis, Abhik Jana, Dirk Hartung, Michael Bommarito, Ion Androutsopoulos, Daniel Katz, and Nikolaos Aletras. 2022a. LexGLUE: A benchmark dataset for legal language understanding in English. In *Proceedings of the 60th Annual Meeting of the Association for Computational Linguistics (Volume 1: Long Papers)*, pages 4310–4330, Dublin, Ireland. Association for Computational Linguistics.

Ilias Chalkidis, Tommaso Pasini, Sheng Zhang, Letizia Tomada, Sebastian Schwemer, and Anders Søgaard. 2022b. FairLex: A multilingual benchmark for evaluating fairness in legal text processing. In *Proceedings of the 60th Annual Meeting of the Association for Computational Linguistics (Volume 1: Long Papers)*, pages 4389–4406, Dublin, Ireland. Association for Computational Linguistics.

Jonathan P. Chang, Caleb Chiam, Liye Fu, Andrew Wang, Justine Zhang, and Cristian Danescu-Niculescu-Mizil. 2020. ConvoKit: A toolkit for the analysis of conversations. In *Proceedings of the 21th Annual Meeting of the Special Interest Group on Discourse and Dialogue*, pages 57–60, 1st virtual meeting. Association for Computational Linguistics.

Junyun Cui, Xiaoyu Shen, Feiping Nie, Zheng Wang, Jinglong Wang, and Yulong Chen. 2022. A survey on legal judgment prediction: Datasets, metrics, models and challenges. *arXiv preprint arXiv:2204.04859*.

Cristian Danescu-Niculescu-Mizil, Lillian Lee, Bo Pang, and Jon Kleinberg. 2012. Echoes of power: Language effects and power differences in social interaction. In *Proceedings of the 21st international conference on World Wide Web*, pages 699–708.

Aniket Deroy, Kripabandhu Ghosh, and Saptarshi Ghosh. 2023. How ready are pre-trained abstractive models and llms for legal case judgement summarization? *arXiv preprint arXiv:2306.01248*.

Neal Devins and Lawrence Baum. 2017. Split definitive: How party polarization turned the Supreme Court into a partisan court. *The Supreme Court Review*, 2016(1):301–365.

Jacob Devlin, Ming-Wei Chang, Kenton Lee, and Kristina Toutanova. 2019. BERT: Pre-training of deep bidirectional transformers for language understanding. In *Proceedings of the 2019 Conference of the North American Chapter of the Association for Computational Linguistics: Human Language Technologies, Volume 1 (Long and Short Papers)*, pages 4171–4186, Minneapolis, Minnesota. Association for Computational Linguistics.

Bryce J Dietrich, Ryan D Enos, and Maya Sen. 2019. Emotional arousal predicts voting on the us supreme court. *Political Analysis*, 27(2):237–243.

Robert M Entman. 1993. Framing: Toward clarification of a fractured paradigm. *Journal of communication*, 43(4):51–58.

Lee Epstein, William M Landes, and Richard A Posner. 2010. Inferring the winning party in the Supreme Court from the pattern of questioning at oral argument. *The Journal of Legal Studies*, 39(2):433–467.

Lee Epstein and Keren Weinshall. 2021. *The Strategic Analysis of Judicial Behavior: A Comparative Perspective*. Cambridge University Press.

Biaoyan Fang, Trevor Cohn, Timothy Baldwin, and Lea Frermann. 2023a. It's not only What You Say, It's also Who It's Said to: Counterfactual Analysis of Interactive Behavior in the Courtroom. In *Proceedings of The 13th International Joint Conference on Natural Language Processing and the 3rd Conference of the Asia-Pacific Chapter of the Association for Computational Linguistics*, Nusa Dua, Bali. Association for Computational Linguistics.

Biaoyan Fang, Trevor Cohn, Timothy Baldwin, and Lea Frermann. 2023b. More than Votes? Voting and Language based Partisanship in the US Supreme Court. In *Findings of the 2023 Conference on Empirical Methods in Natural Language Processing*, Singapore. Association for Computational Linguistics.

Garrett Fiddler. 2022. SCOTUS Opinions. Full text and metadata of all opinions written by SCOTUS justices through 2020.

Peter Henderson, Mark Krass, Lucia Zheng, Neel Guha, Christopher D Manning, Dan Jurafsky, and Daniel Ho. 2022. Pile of law: Learning responsible data filtering from the law and a 256gb open-source legal dataset. In *Advances in Neural Information Processing Systems*, volume 35, pages 29217–29234. Curran Associates, Inc.

Dan Hendrycks, Collin Burns, Anya Chen, and Spencer Ball. 2021. CUAD: An expert-annotated nlp dataset for legal contract review. *NeurIPS*.

Daniel Martin Katz, Michael J Bommarito, and Josh Blackman. 2017. A general approach for predicting the behavior of the supreme court of the united states. *PloS one*, 12(4):e0174698.

George Lakoff. 2010. *Moral politics: How liberals and conservatives think.* University of Chicago Press.

Marco Lippi, Przemysław Pałka, Giuseppe Contissa, Francesca Lagioia, Hans-Wolfgang Micklitz, Giovanni Sartor, and Paolo Torroni. 2019. Claudette: an automated detector of potentially unfair clauses in online terms of service. *Artificial Intelligence and Law*, 27:117–139.

Daniel Locke and Guido Zuccon. 2018. A test collection for evaluating legal case law search. In *The 41st International ACM SIGIR Conference on Research & Development in Information Retrieval*, SIGIR '18, page 1261–1264, New York, NY, USA. Association for Computing Machinery.

Vijit Malik, Rishabh Sanjay, Shubham Kumar Nigam, Kripabandhu Ghosh, Shouvik Kumar Guha, Arnab Bhattacharya, and Ashutosh Modi. 2021. ILDC for CJPE: Indian legal documents corpus for court judgment prediction and explanation. In *Proceedings of the 59th Annual Meeting of the Association for Computational Linguistics and the 11th International Joint Conference on Natural Language Processing (Volume 1: Long Papers)*, pages 4046–4062, Online. Association for Computational Linguistics.

Andrew D Martin and Kevin M Quinn. 2002. Dynamic ideal point estimation via Markov chain Monte Carlo for the US Supreme Court, 1953–1999. *Political analysis*, 10(2):134–153.

Andrew D Martin and Kevin M Quinn. 2007. Assessing preference change on the US Supreme Court. *The journal of law, economics, & organization*, 23(2):365–385.

Joel Niklaus, Ilias Chalkidis, and Matthias Stürmer. 2021. Swiss-judgment-prediction: A multilingual legal judgment prediction benchmark. In *Proceedings of the Natural Legal Language Processing Workshop 2021*, pages 19–35, Punta Cana, Dominican Republic. Association for Computational Linguistics.

Michael D Robinson, Ryan L Boyd, Adam K Fetterman, and Michelle R Persich. 2017. The mind versus the body in political (and nonpolitical) discourse: Linguistic evidence for an ideological signature in US politics. *Journal of Language and Social Psychology*, 36(4):438–461.

Theodore W Ruger, Pauline T Kim, Andrew D Martin, and Kevin M Quinn. 2004. The supreme court forecasting project: Legal and political science approaches to predicting supreme court decision making. *Columbia law review*, pages 1150–1210.

Abhay Shukla, Paheli Bhattacharya, Soham Poddar, Rajdeep Mukherjee, Kripabandhu Ghosh, Pawan Goyal, and Saptarshi Ghosh. 2022. Legal case document summarization: Extractive and abstractive methods and their evaluation. In *Proceedings of the 2nd Conference of the Asia-Pacific Chapter of the Association for Computational Linguistics and the 12th International Joint Conference on Natural Language Processing (Volume 1: Long Papers)*, pages 1048–1064, Online only. Association for Computational Linguistics.

Yanchuan Sim, Bryan Routledge, and Noah Smith. 2015. The utility of text: the case of amicus briefs and the supreme court. In *Proceedings of the AAAI Conference on Artificial Intelligence*, volume 29.

Yanchuan Sim, Bryan Routledge, and Noah A. Smith. 2016. Friends with motives: Using text to infer influence on SCOTUS. In *Proceedings of the 2016 Conference on Empirical Methods in Natural Language Processing*, pages 1724–1733, Austin, Texas. Association for Computational Linguistics.

Harold Spaeth, Lee Epstein, Ted Ruger, Jeffrey Segal, Andrew D. Martin, and Sara Benesh. 2021. Supreme court database, version 2021 release 01. Washington University Law.

Robert L Stern and Eugene Gressman. 1950. *Supreme Court practice: jurisdiction, procedure, arguing and briefing techniques, forms, statutes, rules for practice in the Supreme Court of the United States.* Bureau of national affairs.

Dimitrios Tsarapatsanis and Nikolaos Aletras. 2021. On the ethical limits of natural language processing on legal text. In *Findings of the Association for Computational Linguistics: ACL-IJCNLP 2021*, pages 3590–3599, Online. Association for Computational Linguistics.

Don Tuggener, Pius von Däniken, Thomas Peetz, and Mark Cieliebak. 2020. LEDGAR: A large-scale multi-label corpus for text classification of legal provisions in contracts. In *Proceedings of the Twelfth*

Language Resources and Evaluation Conference, pages 1235–1241, Marseille, France. European Language Resources Association.

Sandra Wachter, Brent Mittelstadt, and Chris Russell. 2020. Bias preservation in machine learning: the legality of fairness metrics under eu non-discrimination law. *W. Va. L. Rev.*, 123:735.

Yiquan Wu, Kun Kuang, Yating Zhang, Xiaozhong Liu, Changlong Sun, Jun Xiao, Yueting Zhuang, Luo Si, and Fei Wu. 2020. De-biased court's view generation with causality. In *Proceedings of the 2020 Conference on Empirical Methods in Natural Language Processing (EMNLP)*, pages 763–780, Online. Association for Computational Linguistics.

Raphaële Xenidis and Linda Senden. 2019. Eu non-discrimination law in the era of artificial intelligence: Mapping the challenges of algorithmic discrimination. *Raphaële Xenidis and Linda Senden, 'EU non-discrimination law in the era of artificial intelligence: Mapping the challenges of algorithmic discrimination'in Ulf Bernitz et al (eds), General Principles of EU law and the EU Digital Order (Kluwer Law International, 2020)*, pages 151–182.

Hai Ye, Xin Jiang, Zhunchen Luo, and Wenhan Chao. 2018. Interpretable charge predictions for criminal cases: Learning to generate court views from fact descriptions. In *Proceedings of the 2018 Conference of the North American Chapter of the Association for Computational Linguistics: Human Language Technologies, Volume 1 (Long Papers)*, pages 1854–1864, New Orleans, Louisiana. Association for Computational Linguistics.

Lucia Zheng, Neel Guha, Brandon R. Anderson, Peter Henderson, and Daniel E. Ho. 2021. When does pretraining help? assessing self-supervised learning for law and the casehold dataset of 53,000+ legal holdings. In *Proceedings of the Eighteenth International Conference on Artificial Intelligence and Law*, ICAIL '21, page 159–168, New York, NY, USA. Association for Computing Machinery.

Haoxi Zhong, Zhipeng Guo, Cunchao Tu, Chaojun Xiao, Zhiyuan Liu, and Maosong Sun. 2018. Legal judgment prediction via topological learning. In *Proceedings of the 2018 Conference on Empirical Methods in Natural Language Processing*, pages 3540–3549, Brussels, Belgium. Association for Computational Linguistics.

Haoxi Zhong, Chaojun Xiao, Cunchao Tu, Tianyang Zhang, Zhiyuan Liu, and Maosong Sun. 2020. How does NLP benefit legal system: A summary of legal artificial intelligence. In *Proceedings of the 58th Annual Meeting of the Association for Computational Linguistics*, pages 5218–5230, Online. Association for Computational Linguistics.

A Detailed Dataset Statistic

Table 7 provides a detailed statistic of the Super-SCOTUS corpus.

B A Full list of SCDB Attributes

Table 8 provides a full list of SCDB attributes.

	# cases covered		Number
ConvoKit arguments	6,733	- avg. sentences - avg. words	512 12,191
SCDB Metedata	6,721	- # attributes	53
Wikipedia Summary	1,191	- avg. sentences - avg. words	1 71
Justia Syllabus	6,604	- avg. sentences - avg. words	32 791
Justia Opinion	6,647	- avg. sentences - avg. words	340 9,276
Justia Primary Holding	999	- avg. sentences - avg. words	1 37
Justia Summary	602	- avg. sentences - avg. words	12 305
Oyez Facts of the Case	2,945	- avg. sentences - avg. words	8 199
Oyez Questions	2,946	- avg. sentences - avg. words	1 36
Oyez Conclusions	2,944	- avg. sentences - avg. words	7 211

Table 7: Detailed statistics of Super-SCOTUS.

0	adminAction	1	adminActionState	2	authorityDecision1
3	authorityDecision2	4	caseDisposition	5	caseDispositionUnusual
6	caseId	7	caseIssuesId	8	caseName
9	caseOrigin	10	caseOriginState	11	caseSource
12	caseSourceState	13	certReason	14	chief
15	dateArgument	16	dateDecision	17	dateRearg
18	decisionDirection	19	decisionDirectionDissent	20	decisionType
21	declarationUncon	22	docket	23	docketId
24	issue	25	issueArea	26	jurisdiction
27	lawMinor	28	lawSupp	29	lawType
30	lcDisagreement	31	lcDisposition	32	lcDispositionDirection
33	ledCite	34	lexisCite	35	majOpinAssigner
36	majOpinWriter	37	majVotes	38	minVotes
39	naturalCourt	40	partyWinning	41	petitioner
42	petitionerState	43	precedentAlteration	44	respondent
45	respondentState	46	sctCite	47	splitVote
48	term	49	threeJudgeFdc	50	usCite
51	voteId	52	voteUnclear		

Table 8: A list of SCDB attributes (Spaeth et al., 2021).

Transferring Legal Natural Language Inference Model from a US State to Another: What Makes It So Hard?

Alice Saebom Kwak[1], **Gaetano Vincent Forte**[2], **Derek E. Bambauer**[2], **Mihai Surdeanu**[3]

[1]Department of Linguistics, The University of Arizona
[2]James E. Rogers College of Law, The University of Arizona
[3]Department of Computer Science, The University of Arizona
{alicekwak, fortegv, derekbambauer, msurdeanu}@arizona.edu

Abstract

This study investigates whether a legal natural language inference (NLI) model trained on the data from one US state can be transferred to another state. We fine-tuned a pre-trained model on the task of evaluating the validity of legal will statements, once with the dataset containing the Tennessee wills and once with the dataset containing the Idaho wills. Each model's performance on the in-domain setting and the out-of-domain setting are compared to see if the models can across the states. We found that the model trained on one US state can be mostly transferred to another state. However, it is clear that the model's performance drops in the out-of-domain setting. The F1 scores of the Tennessee model and the Idaho model are 96.41 and 92.03 when predicting the data from the same state, but they drop to 66.32 and 81.60 when predicting the data from another state. Subsequent error analysis revealed that there are two major sources of errors. First, the model fails to recognize equivalent laws across states when there are stylistic differences between laws. Second, difference in statutory section numbering system between the states makes it difficult for the model to locate laws relevant to the cases being predicted on. This analysis provides insights on how the future NLI system can be improved. Also, our findings offer empirical support to legal experts advocating the standardization of legal documents.

1 Introduction

This study investigates whether a legal natural language inference model trained on the data from one US state can be transferred to different US states. Natural Language Inference (NLI) is a textual reasoning task determining whether a premise entails, contradicts, or is neutral to a hypothesis. Kwak et al. (2022) suggests that the validity assessment of legal documents (e.g, wills) can be framed into a NLI task. It adapts the traditional NLI approach to fit in the legal domain. Unlike the general setting where a model gets two inputs (i.e., premise and hypothesis), the legal NLI model requires three inputs: a legal document of which validity would be assessed, a condition (a circumstance relevant to the validity assessment of the legal document), and a law. This is an intriguing adaptation, but it also introduces the potential of overfitting on the law texts.

Developing legal NLI models that can evaluate the validity of legal documents provides much benefit to legal professionals and anyone involved in writing such legal documents. Assessing the legal documents' validity through legal NLI models can reduce the time and resource required for review. It can also increase the validity of legal documents by preventing any errors at creation time. In addition, legal NLI models can serve as foundations for downstream tasks such as legal document review automation, electronic will system, and smart contract.

As US states have different legal systems, there is no guarantee that a legal NLI model trained on one state would work in another state. However, training a model with data from all US states is a time and labor intensive task. Further, it is often the case that we have access to data from only a few states. Given these practical difficulties, transferring a model trained on one US state to other states is a great alternative to training a model on every state from scratch. To this end, we explore whether a legal NLI model trained on one US state is transferable to another state. We also conduct error analysis to identify any pitfalls in transferring a model trained on one state to another.

We focus on a specific task in this study to evaluate a validity of a legal will statement. We chose to focus on this task for two reasons. First, probate code is one of the fields where US states are divided into two groups: states which have adopted Uniform Probate Code (UPC) in full vs. states which

Proceedings of the Natural Legal Language Processing Workshop 2023, pages 215–222
December 7, 2023 ©2023 Association for Computational Linguistics

have not adopted the full UPC. This clear division makes a good testing case for our study. We tested if a model trained on the data from a state belonging to the former group (i.e., Idaho) works for the data from a state belonging to the latter group (i.e., Tennessee), and vice versa. Another reason is that this task is highly practical. Wills are important legal documents that allow people to maintain control over their assets. Unlike most legal documents, wills are commonly written by/for people without legal training. However, will execution/probate is not always straightforward, and there is a risk that mistakes in will writing or execution procedure invalidate parts of the will. Developing a model that can evaluate the validity of a will statements can help preventing such mistakes. In addition, as previously mentioned, the model can serve as a foundation for developing electronic will system. Given all the benefits that the model could provide, we decided to conduct our study on this task.

The main contribution of our study is as follows:

- We investigate domain transfer between two US states for a language model fine-tuned for legal NLI. We found out that such a legal NLI model trained on one state can be mostly transferred to another state. However, it is clear that the model's performance drops in the cross-state setting. The F1 scores of the Tennessee model and the Idaho model are 96.41 and 92.03 when predicting the data from the same state, but they drop to 66.32 and 81.60 when predicting the data from another state (i.e., Tennessee model predict Idaho data and vice versa).
- We conducted an error analysis on the model's cross-state predictions and identified two sources of error. We found out that stylistic differences between state laws (e.g., terms, formats, capitalization) and differences in statutory section numbering formats can be obstacles to transferring a model trained on one state to another.

2 Related Works

2.1 NLI in the legal domain

NLI in the legal domain is gaining attention in the recent years. Koreeda and Manning (2021) presents a dataset for document level natural language inference for contracts. Bruno and Roth (2022) introduces LawngNLI constructed from US legal opinions. It is a long-premise benchmark for in-domain generalization from short to long contexts and for implication-based retrieval. Mathur et al. (2022) presents a new document-level natural language inference model using optimal evidence selection. The study also proposes a new dataset called CaseHoldNLI on the task of legal judicial reasoning, which is used for the model testing. Kwak et al. (2022) introduces a legal NLI dataset for the validity assessment of legal will statements. Despite this increased interest in legal NLI tasks, there is no prior work that attempted cross-domain transfer in the legal NLI.

2.2 Domain transfer in legal natural language processing

There are several studies that have investigated domain transfer for legal natural language processing tasks. Salaka et al. (2018) proposes a transfer learning approach to build an automatic sentiment annotator for legal domain using the manually annotated data on movie reviews. Chalkidis et al. (2021) introduces a multi-lingual and multi-label legal document classification dataset for zero-shot cross-lingual transfer. Bannihatti Kumar et al. (2022) investigates the cross-domain transferability of text generation models for legal text. Niklaus et al. (2022) explores transfer learning techniques on Legal Judgment Prediction in various settings, including cross-lingual transfer, cross-domain transfer, cross-regional transfer, and cross-jurisdiction transfer. T.y.s.s et al. (2023) investigates domain adaptation from Legal Judgment Prediction on European court of Human Rights cases into an article-aware classification task.

Existing works mostly focus on either cross-domain (Salaka et al. 2018; Bannihatti Kumar et al. 2022; T.y.s.s et al. 2023) or cross-lingual (Chalkidis et al. 2021) transfer. Our study, on the other hand, explores the possibility of cross-jurisdiction transfer for the legal NLI task between the US states. Niklaus et al. (2022) explores the possibility of cross-jurisdiction transfer, but it is between different countries (from Indian to Swiss cases), not between the states within the same country. Also, as previously stated, there was no prior attempt made for exploring domain transfer in the legal NLI. Our study aims to fill in this gap.

Types of inputs	Example	Label
Statement	I, [Person-1], residing in the County of Cassia, State of Idaho, being of full legal age and being of sound and disposing mind and not acting under duress, menace, fraud, or undue influence of any person whomsoever, do make, publish and declare this my Last Will and Testament and expressly revoke all other and former Wills and Codicils to Wills made by me.	
Condition	The testator was over 18 years old and of sound mind when executing this will.	**support**
Law	15-2-501. WHO MAY MAKE A WILL. Any emancipated minor or any person eighteen (18) or more years of age who is of sound mind may make a will. A married woman may dispose of her property, whether separate or community, in the same manner as any other person subject to the restrictions imposed by this code.	

Table 1: The legal NLI datasets used in this study contain three inputs: statement, condition, and law. Statement is a sentence or a short paragraph excerpted from a legal will. Condition is a circumstance related to the evaluation of a will statement's validity. For example, testator's age or mental capacity at the time of will execution is a condition relevant to the evaluation of validity of the will execution. Law is a state provision on which the validity of a legal will statement is evaluated. The inputs are classified as either "support", "refute", or "unrelated", depending on whether the condition and the law support, refute or are unrelated with the given will statement.

3 Methods

To figure out if a legal NLI model trained on a single US state can be transferred to other states, we compared a model's performance on the in-domain data (i.e., the data which is from the same state as the model is trained on) and its performance on the out-of-domain data (i.e., the data which is from a state other than the one the model is trained on). We fine-tuned a pre-trained model on a task of evaluating the validity of legal will statements, once with the dataset containing the Tennessee wills and once with the dataset containing the Idaho wills.

The format of the datasets is distinct from the traditional NLI datasets in that it contains three types of inputs (statement, condition, and law) rather than two (premise and hypothesis). *Statement* is a sentence or a short paragraph excerpted from a legal will. Its legal validity is assessed based on the other two input types. *Condition* is a circumstance relevant to the evaluation of validity of a will statement. Lastly, *Law* is a state provision that the will statement's validity is assessed on. These inputs are labeled as either *support*, *refute*, or *unrelated*, depending on whether the condition and the law support, refute, or are unrelated to the will statement given. The table 1 shows the datasets are formatted with an example for each input type. For further details on the datasets, see the section 3.1. The model we fine-tuned with our dataset is roberta-large-mnli (Liu et al., 2019). For the implementation of the fine-tuning, see the section 3.2.

We used the fine-tuned models to predict both the in-domain testing data (i.e., Tennessee model predicts Tennessee data and Idaho model predicts Idaho data) and the out-of-domain data (i.e., Tennessee model predicts Idaho data and Idaho model predicts Tennessee data). To better understand the models' behaviors, we generated confusion matrices with the models' predictions and conducted error analysis by using Local interpretable model-agnostic explanations (LIME; Ribeiro et al. 2016).

3.1 Datasets

We use two datasets in our study: a dataset containing legal wills from Tennessee (Kwak et al., 2022) and a dataset containing legal wills from Idaho. The Tennessee dataset was introduced in Kwak et al. (2022). The dataset contains 23 wills from Tennessee, splitted into 1,014 data points. Each data point consists of a legal will statement (usually a sentence excerpted from a will) accompanied with hypothetical conditions at the time of will execution and/or probate and state laws relevant (or irrelevant) to the evaluation of the legal will statement's validity. The dataset is annotated with three

Model - Data	Precision	Recall	F1	Accuracy
TN - TN (in-domain)	96.67	96.25	96.41	96.86
ID - ID (in-domain)	91.06	93.34	92.03	93.82
TN - ID (out-of-domain)	80.59	62.62	66.32	76.23
ID - TN (out-of-domain)	80.70	83.42	81.60	82.94

Table 2: This table shows the performances of the Tennessee (TN) model and the Idaho (ID) model in two test settings: in-domain and out-of-domain. In-domain means that the model predicted on the testing partition from the same state, while out-of-domain means that the model predicted on the data from a different state. Both models show decent performance on the in-domain test setting. The F1 scores (weighted average) for Tennessee model and Idaho model in the in-domain setting are 96.41 and 92.03, respectively. Both models' F1 scores (weighted average) are considerably lower in the out-of-domain setting, but Tennessee model suffer more dramatically (Tennessee model: 66.32, Idaho model: 81.60)

labels: support, refute, and unrelated. ("support": condition & law supports the will statement; "refute": condition & law refutes the will statement, "unrelated": the law is unrelated to the validity assessment of the given legal will statement.) See table 1 for the further details on the format of the dataset.

We created a new dataset containing legal wills from Idaho, following the format of the dataset introduced in Kwak et al. (2022). We collected 14 Idaho wills from the U.S. Wills and Probates datasets in Ancestry.[1] The collected wills were manually anonymized by replacing any personal information into special tokens (e.g., names into [Person-n] and addresses into [Address-n]) and so on), as suggested by Suntwal et al. (2019). The wills were splitted into 1,039 statements. We added hypothetical conditions and state laws relevant (or irrelevant) to the evaluation of the statement's validity, as Kwak et al. (2022) did. The dataset was also annotated with three labels: support, refute, and unrelated. The annotation was done by two annotators: one law student and one non-law graduate student. They were given a clear annotation guideline. They also had ample discussions during the annotation process to ensure the consistency of the dataset. The kappa agreement score between the two annotators is 0.89. The dataset creation and annotation process was supervised and reviewed by a law professor.

3.2 Model fine-tuning

We fine-tuned a transformer model with the two datasets introduced above. We chose to fine-tune roberta-large-mnli (Liu et al., 2019) as it was shown to be the best performing model in the given task setting by Kwak et al. (2022). We went through two separate fine-tuning processes: once with the Tennessee dataset to get a model working on Tennessee legal wills ("Tennessee model" from now on) and once with the Idaho dataset to get a model working on Idaho legal wills ("Idaho model" from now on). The two fine-tuning processes were done independently of each other, meaning that the result of these fine-tuning processes was two separate models (Tennessee model and Idaho model) each learned Tennessee data and Idaho data respectively, not one model that learned both. The fine-tuning was done on PyTorch 1.11.0 with Cuda 11.3 using the HuggingFace Trainer class, and hyperparameters were tuned on the development partition.

3.3 Error Analysis

We generated confusion matrices with the models' predictions in the cross-state setting (i.e., Tennessee model predicting Idaho data and Idaho model predicting Tennessee data). With the generated matrices, we identified the most salient error types. NLP experts and law experts in our team worked together to analyze the potential causes for these error types. We employed Local interpretable model-agnostic explanations (LIME; Ribeiro et al. 2016) to analyze the errors. LIME provides human interpretable explanations on individual predictions of any machine learning classifiers (or models) by highlighting the words that had impact on the model's prediction. With the LIME explanations, we were able to find potential causes for the major error types.

4 Results

Table 2 shows the performances of Tennessee model and Idaho model in two different settings: in-domain (predicting the testing partitions from

[1] Court documents such as probated wills are in the public domain in the US.

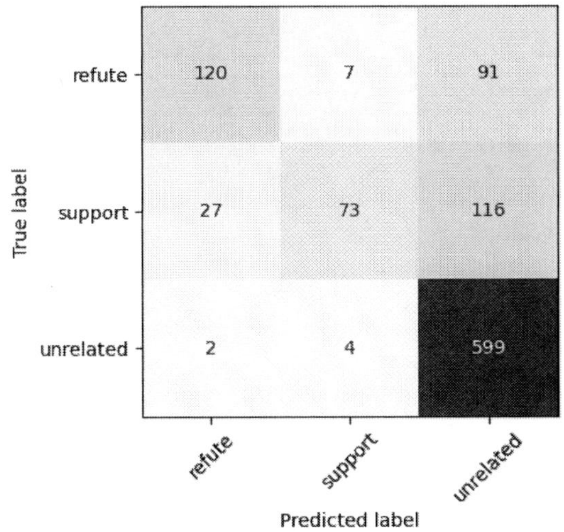

Figure 1: A confusion matrix generated with the Tennessee model's predictions on Idaho data. It is noticeable that the majority of the model's errors (207/247) is from incorrectly predicting support (116/247) or refute cases (91/247) as unrelated cases.

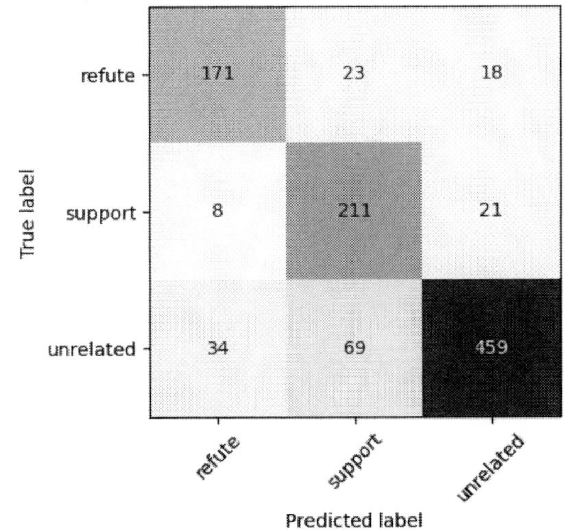

Figure 2: A confusion matrix generated with the Idaho model's predictions on Tennessee data. It is worth noting that more than half of the model's errors (103/173) is from incorrectly predicting unrelated cases as support (69/173) or refute cases (34/173).

the same state) and out-of-domain (predicting the data from a different state). Both Tennessee model and Idaho model show decent performance in the in-domain setting, as suggested by high F1 scores (Tennessee model: 96.41, Idaho model: 92.03). However, in the out-of-domain setting, the performance of both models drops considerably. Both models' F1 scores are considerably lower in the out-of-domain setting, but Tennessee model suffers more dramatically (Tennessee model: 66.32, Idaho model: 81.60).

To figure out the cause of the performance drop, we generated confusion matrices with both models' predictions in the out-of-domain setting. Figure 1 shows the confusion matrix generated with Tennessee models' predictions on Idaho data. It is noticeable that the majority of the model's errors (207/247) is from incorrectly predicting support (116/247) or refute cases (91/247) as unrelated cases. Figure 2 presents the confusion matrix generated with Idaho models' predictions on Tennessee data. This time, more than half of the errors (103/173) originated from incorrectly predicting unrelated cases as support (69/173) or refute cases (34/173).

5 Error Analysis

We identified two major error types by observing the confusion matrices. The first is that the Tennessee model wrongly predicts support or refute cases as unrelated when predicting Idaho data (207/247). The second is that the Idaho model wrongly predicts unrelated cases as support or refute cases (103/173). We focus on analyzing these two error types in this section.

5.1 Failure to Recognize Relevant Laws

The major issue found from the Tennessee model's performance in the out-of-domain setting is that it fails to identify relevant laws from Idaho state code. The model confuses support or refute cases with unrelated cases, meaning that it does not recognize the laws that are relevant to will execution or probate. There are two potential causes for this error. First, it can be that the Idaho dataset contains many laws that are not in the Tennessee dataset. Second, it can be that the stylistic differences in law (e.g., terms, formats, capitalization) made it difficult for the model to recognize similar laws. To find out what portion of errors are attributable to the differences in the state codes, we compared the laws contained in the Tennessee dataset to the ones contained in the Idaho dataset.[2]

As a result of the comparison, we found that only 79 out of 207 errors are attributable to the

[2]As the model would have learned only the laws that are contained in the dataset, we restricted the range of comparison only to the laws that are contained in the datasets used for the model training. Therefore, our analysis on the difference of Tennessee and Idaho statutes may not hold outside the context of this study.

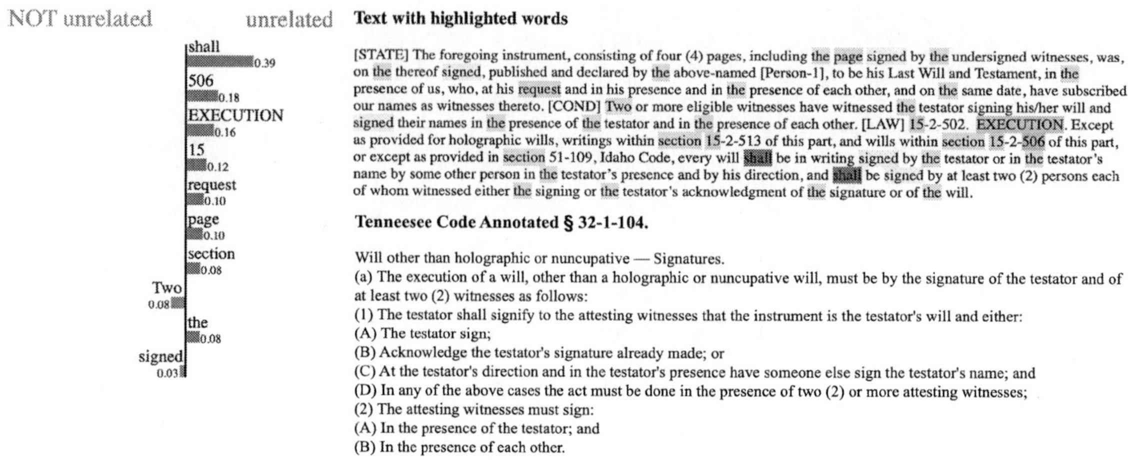

Figure 3: The chart on the left and the figure on the upper right present the LIME explanation on a case where Tennessee model failed to recognize the law relevant to the will execution (Idaho Statute 15-2-502) and made wrong prediction on the Idaho data(a "support" case as an "unrelated" case). The explanation shows that the model made prediction based on terms and numbers (e.g., 506, 15, request, section) that are not present in the equivalent law in Tennessee (Tennessee Code Annotated, 32-1-104; presented in the lower right side).

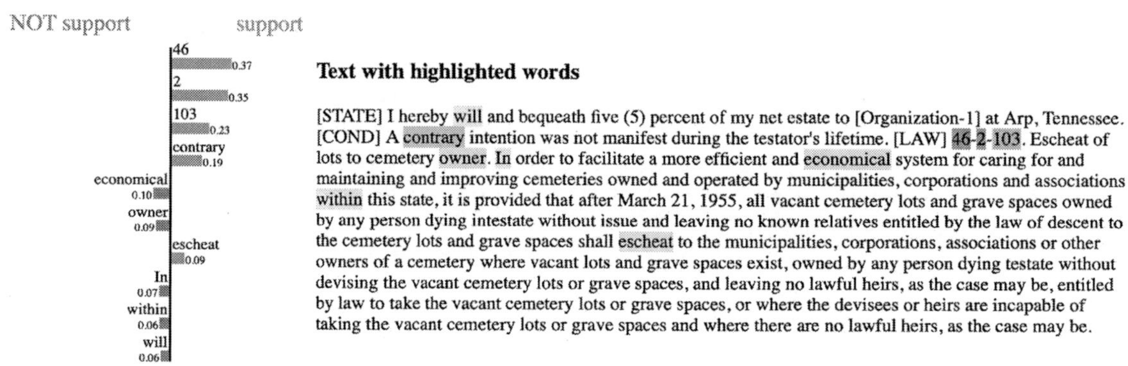

Figure 4: The figure presents the LIME explanation on a case where Idaho model makes wrong prediction on the Tennessee data based on the statutory section number. The model predicted an "unrelated" case as a "support" case, based on the statutory section number (i.e., 46, 2, 103).

differences between the laws contained in the Tennessee dataset and the ones contained in the Idaho dataset. These error cases contained Idaho statutes of which equivalence could not be found from the statutes in the Tennessee dataset. One such example is Idaho Statute 15-3-914 ("DISPOSITION OF UNCLAIMED ASSETS"). This law states that the personal representative shall distribute the share of any missing heir, devisee or claimant to their trustee, and if no trustee has been appointed for them, the personal representative shall file the report of abandoned property required by section 14-517. However, the equivalence of such statute cannot be found from the Tennessee dataset. Therefore, it is not surprising that Tennessee model failed to recognize this statute as a relevant one.

However, the rest of the errors (128/207) are not attributable to the differences in the state codes as the provisions contained in these cases have the equivalence in the Tennessee state code.[3] In these cases, it is likely that the model failed to see the connections between the similar provisions due to the stylistic differences in law. For example, Tennessee model failed to identify the Idaho provision pertaining to will execution (Idaho Statute 15-2-502), even though there is a similar provision in Tennessee (Tennessee Code Annotated 32-1-104). The model made incorrect predictions on every data

[3]The criterion we used to determine the equivalence of two laws is whether one law can replace the other in evaluating the will statements' validity without altering the result.

point containing this law (39 errors in total) and dictated it as unrelated despite the law's relevance to the will execution. Figure 3 presents a LIME explanation for one of such cases. The explanation shows that the model relied on terms/numbers that are not present in the equivalent law in Tennessee (Tennessee Code Annotated 32-1-104), such as *section*, *506*, and *15*. This shows that the model failed to see the connection between the two laws, even though the model was already trained on the Tennessee law (Tennessee Code Annotated 32-1-104).

It is also worth noting that the model relied on the word *EXECUTION*, which is highly relevant to the given will statement, when dictating the law as "unrelated". The model (i.e., roberta-large-mnli) is case-sensitive, so it distinguishes between the word in lower case (*execution*) and the word in upper case (*EXECUTION*). In Tennessee state code, it is very uncommon that a word is fully capitalized. However, in Idaho state code, all titles are presented in full capitalization (e.g., Idaho Statute 15-2-502. EXECUTION). As the model did not see the word in full capitalization during the training, the model fails to recognize the relevance of the word to the given will statement. This illustrates how a minor format difference, such as capitalization, can interfere with the model's performance.

5.2 Difference in Statutory Section Numbering System

The Idaho model makes incorrect predictions on cases that should be labeled as "unrelated" in the out-of-domain setting (103/173). The LIME explanations revealed that the model primarily relies on statutory section numbers when making these wrong predictions. Figure 4 shows one such case. The model depended on *46*, *2*, and *103* when predicting the case as "support."

This error is attributable to the difference in statutory section numbering system. While majority of the Idaho laws (which are mostly unrelated to will execution and/or probate) use Title-Chapter+Section numbering (e.g., Title: 14, Chapter: 1, Section: 1 = 14-101), a small portion of laws (e.g., Uniform Probate Code) use Title-Chapter-Section numbering (e.g., Title: 15, Chapter: 2, Section: 502 = 15-2-502). Most of the laws in the dataset that have Title-Chapter-Section numbering are relevant to the will execution and/or probate.[4] The Idaho model uses this numbering format difference to distinguish between laws relevant to will execution and/or probate and those that are not. However, this pattern does not exist in Tennessee data as all Tennessee laws have the same numbering format (i.e., Title-Chapter-Section). As Tennessee laws use the same numbering format as the Uniform Probate Code, the Idaho model would have predicted a large portion of "unrelated" cases in Tennessee data as "support" or "refute" based on the statutory section number format. This shows how a seemingly unrelated factor, such as statutory section numbering format, can have an impact on the model's performance.

6 Conclusion

This study found that legal natural language inference model trained on the data from one US state can be transferred to another state, but the performance deteriorates considerably. The F1 scores of the Tennessee model and the Idaho model are 96.41 and 92.03 when predicting the data from the same state, but they drop to 66.32 and 81.60 when predicting the data from another state (i.e., Tennessee model predict Idaho data and vice versa).

Our error analysis found two major causes for the performance drop. First, we found that the model struggles with identifying the equivalent laws across states when there are stylistic differences (e.g., terms, formats, capitalization, and etc.) between laws. We also found that difference in statutory section numbering system between the states makes it harder for the model to locate laws relevant to the cases that they are predicting on.

This analysis gives hints for the design of the future legal NLI systems. For instance, it is expected that including a knowledge base with equivalent laws between states would enhance the model's performance on predicting the cross-state data. The knowledge base should help with the normalization of statutory section numbers across the states. Normalization of the law text formats (e.g., capitalization) would also improve the model's performance on the data from across the states.

The analysis also provides empirical support to legal experts for the argument that legal documents such as wills should be standardized. As illustrated by our analysis, differences in legal documents' texts or formats between the states can easily interfere with the model's performance.

[4] Uniform Commercial Code (UCC) laws in Idaho Statute also have Title-Chapter-Section numbering, but the number of UCC laws included in our dataset is very few (8 out of 1039 data points.

Standardization of legal documents would facilitate the development of legal NLI system that can work across the states. Our open-access dataset and source code are publicly available at: `https://github.com/ml4ai/nli4wills-corpus`

Acknowledgements

We thank the reviewers for their thoughtful comments and suggestions. This work was partially supported by the National Science Foundation (NSF) under grant #2217215, and by University of Arizona's Provost Investment Fund. Mihai Surdeanu declares a financial interest in lum.ai. This interest has been properly disclosed to the University of Arizona Institutional Review Committee and is managed in accordance with its conflict of interest policies.

References

Vinayshekhar Bannihatti Kumar, Kasturi Bhattacharjee, and Rashmi Gangadharaiah. 2022. Towards cross-domain transferability of text generation models for legal text. In *Proceedings of the Natural Legal Language Processing Workshop 2022*, pages 111–118, Abu Dhabi, United Arab Emirates (Hybrid). Association for Computational Linguistics.

William Bruno and Dan Roth. 2022. LawngNLI: A long-premise benchmark for in-domain generalization from short to long contexts and for implication-based retrieval. In *Findings of the Association for Computational Linguistics: EMNLP 2022*, pages 5019–5043, Abu Dhabi, United Arab Emirates. Association for Computational Linguistics.

Ilias Chalkidis, Manos Fergadiotis, and Ion Androutsopoulos. 2021. MultiEURLEX - a multi-lingual and multi-label legal document classification dataset for zero-shot cross-lingual transfer. In *Proceedings of the 2021 Conference on Empirical Methods in Natural Language Processing*, pages 6974–6996, Online and Punta Cana, Dominican Republic. Association for Computational Linguistics.

Yuta Koreeda and Christopher Manning. 2021. ContractNLI: A dataset for document-level natural language inference for contracts. In *Findings of the Association for Computational Linguistics: EMNLP 2021*, pages 1907–1919, Punta Cana, Dominican Republic. Association for Computational Linguistics.

Alice Kwak, Jacob Israelsen, Clayton Morrison, Derek Bambauer, and Mihai Surdeanu. 2022. Validity assessment of legal will statements as natural language inference. In *Findings of the Association for Computational Linguistics: EMNLP 2022*, pages 6047–6056, Abu Dhabi, United Arab Emirates. Association for Computational Linguistics.

Yinhan Liu, Myle Ott, Naman Goyal, Jingfei Du, Mandar Joshi, Danqi Chen, Omer Levy, Mike Lewis, Luke Zettlemoyer, and Veselin Stoyanov. 2019. Roberta: A robustly optimized bert pretraining approach. *arXiv preprint arXiv:1907.11692*.

Puneet Mathur, Gautam Kunapuli, Riyaz Bhat, Manish Shrivastava, Dinesh Manocha, and Maneesh Singh. 2022. DocInfer: Document-level natural language inference using optimal evidence selection. In *Proceedings of the 2022 Conference on Empirical Methods in Natural Language Processing*, pages 809–824, Abu Dhabi, United Arab Emirates. Association for Computational Linguistics.

Joel Niklaus, Matthias Stürmer, and Ilias Chalkidis. 2022. An empirical study on cross-X transfer for legal judgment prediction. In *Proceedings of the 2nd Conference of the Asia-Pacific Chapter of the Association for Computational Linguistics and the 12th International Joint Conference on Natural Language Processing (Volume 1: Long Papers)*, pages 32–46, Online only. Association for Computational Linguistics.

Marco Túlio Ribeiro, Sameer Singh, and Carlos Guestrin. 2016. "why should I trust you?": Explaining the predictions of any classifier. *CoRR*, abs/1602.04938.

Viraj Salaka, Menuka Warushavithana, Nisansa de Silva, Amal Shehan Perera, Gathika Ratnayaka, and Thejan Rupasinghe. 2018. Fast approach to build an automatic sentiment annotator for legal domain using transfer learning. In *Proceedings of the 9th Workshop on Computational Approaches to Subjectivity, Sentiment and Social Media Analysis*, pages 260–265, Brussels, Belgium. Association for Computational Linguistics.

Sandeep Suntwal, Mithun Paul, Rebecca Sharp, and Mihai Surdeanu. 2019. On the importance of delexicalization for fact verification. In *Proceedings of the 2019 Conference on Empirical Methods in Natural Language Processing and the 9th International Joint Conference on Natural Language Processing (EMNLP-IJCNLP)*, pages 3413–3418, Hong Kong, China. Association for Computational Linguistics.

Santosh T.y.s.s, Oana Ichim, and Matthias Grabmair. 2023. Zero-shot transfer of article-aware legal outcome classification for European court of human rights cases. In *Findings of the Association for Computational Linguistics: EACL 2023*, pages 605–617, Dubrovnik, Croatia. Association for Computational Linguistics.

Large Language Models are legal but they are not: Making the case for a powerful LegalLLM

Thanmay Jayakumar, Fauzan Farooqui*, **Luqman Farooqui***
Visvesvaraya National Institute of Technology, Nagpur, India
{thanmayjayakumar, fauzanfarooqui7, luqmanfarooqui99}@gmail.com

Abstract

Realizing the recent advances in Natural Language Processing (NLP) to the legal sector poses challenging problems such as extremely long sequence lengths, specialized vocabulary that is usually only understood by legal professionals, and high amounts of data imbalance. The recent surge of Large Language Models (LLM) has begun to provide new opportunities to apply NLP in the legal domain due to their ability to handle lengthy, complex sequences. Moreover, the emergence of domain-specific LLMs has displayed extremely promising results on various tasks. In this study, we aim to quantify how general LLMs perform in comparison to legal-domain models (be it an LLM or otherwise). Specifically, we compare the zero-shot performance of three general-purpose LLMs (ChatGPT-3.5, LLaMA-2-70b, and Falcon-180b) on the LEDGAR subset of the LexGLUE benchmark for contract provision classification. Although the LLMs were not explicitly trained on legal data, we observe that they are still able to classify the theme correctly in most cases. However, we find that their mic-F1/mac-F1 performance is upto 19.2/26.8% lesser than smaller models fine-tuned on the legal domain, thus underscoring the need for more powerful legal-domain LLMs.

1 Introduction

Legal professionals typically deal with large amounts of textual information on a daily basis to make well-informed decisions in their practice. This can become very tedious and demanding due to the overwhelming amount of data they must manage and the meticulous attention to detail necessary to maintain the required precision in their work. Thanks to the rise of LLMs, many tasks such as sentiment analysis, named entity recognition, information retrieval, etc. can now be handled by neural models. Though this holds true for the legal domain as well (Sun, 2023), they aren't used to make direct decisions. Nevertheless, these automated systems that produce legal predictions and generations, are predominantly useful as advisory tools for legal practitioners that can augment their decision-making process.

Transformers (Vaswani et al., 2017) have become the *de facto* method for many text classification and multiple choice question answering tasks. BERT (Devlin et al., 2019), a transformer-encoder, and its derived models like RoBERTa (Liu et al., 2019) are commonly employed in legal NLP tasks. Pre-training such models on legal corpora can help a model adapt to a specific domain by fine-tuning it with domain-specific data. LegalBERT (Chalkidis et al., 2020) is one such BERT model that was trained on legal-oriented data. CaseLaw-BERT (Zheng et al., 2021), PoL-BERT (Henderson et al., 2022), and LexLM (Chalkidis et al., 2023) are a few more BERT-based variants pre-trained for the legal domain. Although they show remarkable performance on various legal tasks in comparison with general-purpose BERT models, one limit of these models is that BERT's input size can only incorporate a maximum of 512 tokens. For short sequences this may seem enough, but in the case of long documents which is commonly found in the legal domain, where input texts can go over 5000 tokens (and requiring *even* more in few-shot settings), it can be a severe drawback as a lot of important information will get truncated.

Due to this limit, BERT-based models aren't employed as-is in long-document tasks. Typically, methods like hierarchical attention are utilized where the long document is split into segments of max length (512 in the case of BERT models) and these segments are independently encoded. These segment embeddings are then aggregated with stacked transformers to get the overall encoding of the entire document. Similarly, recurrent

*These authors contributed equally

Proceedings of the Natural Legal Language Processing Workshop 2023, pages 223–229
December 7, 2023 ©2023 Association for Computational Linguistics

transformers (Dai et al., 2019; Yang et al., 2019; Ding et al., 2021) were proposed to process long documents by encoding its representation from individual segments in a recurrent fashion. Sparse attention is another method that has been proposed to tackle long sequence inputs (Ainslie et al., 2020; Zaheer et al., 2020). Longformer (Beltagy et al., 2020) uses a combination of local and global attention mechanisms to save on computational complexity and enables the processing of up to 4096 tokens. A number of other works (Dai et al., 2022; Mamakas et al., 2022) show that transformer-based architectures that can capture longer text boast major benefits, even more so when augmented with strategies like sparse-attention and hierarchical networks. This again underlines an important direction for verbose legal datasets. Our contributions can be summarized as follows:

- We conduct experiments to compare and analyze the zero-shot performance of three general LLMs to start-of-the-art in-domain models on the LEDGAR subset of LexGLUE (Chalkidis et al., 2022). We analyze our results and provide insights for further research.
- We provide an overview of the most recent LLM research, the benchmarks and datasets developed for legal NLP, the challenges faced when applying them to legal tasks, and popular approaches that try to solve them. We believe this to be a useful primer for anyone looking to get a bird's eye view of the field.

2 Related Work

In this section, we outline the relevant research on LLMs, efforts using them for legal domain tasks, and finally the benchmarks and datasets.

2.1 Large Language Models

OpenAI GPT: GPT (Generative Pre-trained Transformer) (Radford et al., 2019; Brown et al., 2020) and the popular ChatGPT variant developed by OpenAI are a family of transformer-decoder pre-trained with a vast amount of text data to perform generative and language modeling tasks and allows a reasonable context length sufficient to carry out long-document processing. For instance, GPT 3.5 allows a maximum of 4096 tokens, and GPT 4 allows a stunning maximum of 32,768, ideal for data consisting of long sequences.

Google PaLM: PaLM (Pathways Language Model) (Chowdhery et al., 2022; Anil et al., 2023) is an LLM having 540 billion parameters that was trained on the Pathways architecture. Although PaLM was initially trained to handle sequence lengths of up to 2048 tokens, it was increased to 8096 in the 340 billion parameter PaLM 2 for a longer comprehension of the input.

Meta LLaMA: LLaMA (Large Language Model Meta AI) (Touvron et al., 2023) is a collection of foundation language models ranging from 7 billion to 70 billion parameters. It was pre-trained natively on 2048 input tokens, but recent research has shown that the context length of LLMs can be extended efficiently with minimal training steps (Peng et al., 2023) and they have released two variations of LLaMA boasting a context length of 64k and 128k respectively.

TII Falcon[1]: As of the time of writing, this work by Technology Innovation Institute (TII) is not yet published but the model has been released by them. It boasts of being the largest open-source model to date of writing having 180 billion parameters, and also the highest ranking model on the Huggingface Leaderboard. It includes models with 180B, 40B, 7.5B, and 1.3B parameters, trained on TII's RefinedWeb dataset (Penedo et al., 2023).

2.2 LLMs on the legal domain

LexGPT: (Lee, 2023) finetune GPT-J models on the Pile of Law dataset (Henderson et al., 2022) and experiment with generative models for legal classification tasks. They observe that fine-tuning such out-of-the-box GPTs do not beat the state-of-the-art and in fact, provides low performance compared to discriminative models. This insightfully shows the need to bridge the gap between powerful LLMs for the legal domain.

PolicyGPT: This work (Tang et al., 2023) demonstrates how LLMs in zero-shot settings can perform remarkably well in text classification of privacy policies on several baseline LLMs. This points out how a LegalLLM may hold promise in enhancing performance on other general tasks.

Zero-and-Few-shot GPT: (Chalkidis, 2023)

[1] https://falconllm.tii.ae/falcon.html

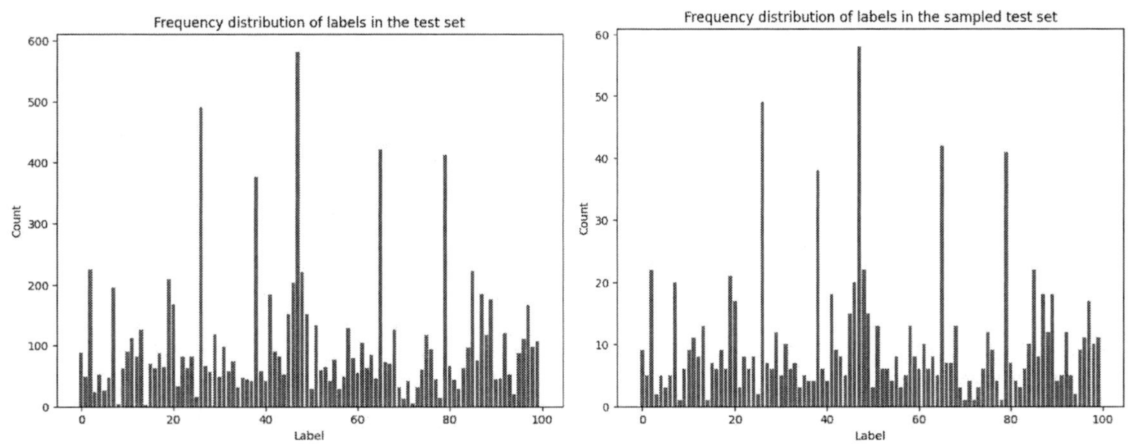

Figure 1: The frequency distributions of the 100 LEDGAR labels in the original LEDGAR test set from LexGLUE (left); and in our sampled test set of 1000 examples (right)

conduct experiments most similar to ours. This study evaluates the performance of ChatGPT on the LexGLUE benchmark in both zero-shot and few-shot settings (for the latter, examples were given in the instruction prompt, which seems to benefit the model when the number of examples and labels are around the same). They find that ChatGPT performs very well, but severely lacks in performance compared to smaller models trained on in-domain datasets.

Resonating these findings, the work of (Savelka, 2023) investigates how an LLM (a GPT model) performs on a semantic annotation task in the zero-shot setting, without being fine-tuned on in-domain datasets. The LLM is primed with a short sentence description of each annotation label and is tasked with labeling a short span of text. They observe that while the LLM performs surprisingly well given the zero-shot setting, its performance was still far off from the model that was trained on the in-domain data. In summary, both these studies highlight the potential fine-tuned LLMs can bring to the legal domain.

2.3 Datasets and Benchmarks

LexGLUE: (Chalkidis et al., 2022) present a unified evaluation framework to benchmark models. The datasets and tasks were curated from other sources of data considering various factors into account such as availability, size, difficulty, etc. They present scores of various Pre-trained Language Models (PLMs) on their benchmark. While doing so, they point out interesting results that suggest that PLMs fine-tuned on legal datasets and tasks do perform better, albeit PLMs fine-tuned on only one sub-domain don't improve on performance on the same sub-domain. Put together, their observations point out the need for a general LegalLLM (powerful enough to outperform other models on all criteria of the benchmark).

LegalBench: (Guha et al., 2023) This benchmark comprises 162 tasks representing six distinct forms of legal reasoning and outlines an empirical evaluation of 20 LLMs. They demonstrate how LegalBench supports easing communication between legal professionals and LLM developers by using the IRAC framework in the case of American law. They observe that LLMs typically perform better on classification tasks than application-based ones. They also find that for some tasks, in-context examples are not required, or only marginally improve performance. They thus conclude that the task performance in LLMs is mostly driven by the task description used in the prompt.

Pile of Law: (Henderson et al., 2022) The surge in LLM development emphasizes the need for responsible practices in filtering out biased, explicit, copyrighted, and confidential content during pre-training. Present methodologies are ad hoc and do not account for context. This paper outlines a method for filtering in the legal domain that handles the trade-offs. Thus, Pile of Law, a growing 256GB dataset of open-source English legal and administrative data was introduced to aid in legal tasks. It allows for the understanding of government-established content filtering guidelines and illustrates various ways to learn responsible data filtering from the law.

MultiLegalPile: (Chalkidis et al., 2021) The MultiLegalPile is a 689 GB substantial dataset that spans 24 EU languages across 17 jurisdictions. It addresses the scarce availability of multilingual pre-training data in specific domains such as law, encompassing diverse legal data sources with varying licenses. With further pre-training of XLM-R models (Conneau et al., 2019), the study attains new SotA results on LEXTREME (Niklaus et al., 2023). The transformation of the XLM-R base model into a Longformer yields a fresh SotA in four LEXTREME datasets. In certain languages, monolingual models substantially outperform the XLM-R base model, achieving language-specific SotA in five languages. In LexGLUE, English models secure SotA in five of seven tasks.

3 Experimental Setup and Results

In this section, we describe our experimental approach, along with specifics of our evaluations.

3.1 Dataset and Metrics

We use the LEDGAR subset of the LexGLUE benchmark for our experiments due to its readiness to work on LLMs (for example, the other datasets do not have the label names; only the label indices are provided). Given a provision contract, the model is expected to classify the contract from 100 given labels of EDGAR themes. As mentioned, there is a high imbalance of data in datasets containing legal corpora. In particular, refer to Figure 1 for the label distribution in the LEDGAR subset of the LexGLUE benchmark. This could result in difficulties such as biased models, poor generalization, and classification scores due to data imbalance. To overcome these difficulties and enhance model evaluations, typically the F1-score is reported for such models instead of accuracy. The macro-F1 score is an even better metric in the case of data imbalance compared to micro-F1, and it is due to this reason that the macro-F1 scores are typically lower than the micro-F1 on legal tasks.

As for the sequence lengths, (Chalkidis, 2023) report the average token length of the instruction-following examples in all the LexGLUE subsets - the highest being 3.6k tokens. This restricts the capability of LLM performance due to truncation as noted earlier, and this is also highlighted in the study - few-shot settings could not be evaluated for datasets having averaged token length of more than 2k for a single example, and in many cases, the prompts were already truncated up to 4k tokens (the maximum limit of ChatGPT). The average token length of the LEDGAR subset is 0.6k.

3.2 Setup

For our experiments, we use the LEDGAR subset of the LexGLUE dataset. As baselines, we take three LLMs - ChatGPT (GPT-3.5), LLaMA-2 (70b), and Falcon (180b). As the models are very large, we use Huggingface Chat for LLaMA and Falcon. Due to this constraint, we only evaluated on a subset of 1,000 examples. However, we made sure that the subset had a label frequency distribution close to the original dataset 1 so that the evaluations may be generalized as much as possible.

We use zero-shot prompting to evaluate the above-mentioned LLMs, building on their benefit as explained earlier by other works (Tang et al., 2023; Guha et al., 2023). However, in the custom instructions (in ChatGPT) and system instructions (in Huggingface) we entered the list of EDGAR theme classes that the model should choose from. In the same fashion, to ensure that the model does not generate anything out of the list, we explicitly mentioned this as an instruction. The exact instructions that we use are provided in the appendix.

Model	**mic. F1**	**mac. F1**	**# params.**
Falcon-Chat	70.9	60.7	180b
ChatGPT	70.6	58.7	175b
LLaMA-Chat	70.4	59.6	70b
LexGPT	*83.9*	*74.0*	6b
LegalBERT	**88.2**	**83.0**	0.11b

Table 1: Comparison of general LLMs (first three models, tested on a zero-shot setting) to models fine-tuned on legal-domain datasets (last two). The current Legal-LLM is LexGPT, but the much smaller LegalBERT shows state-of-the-art performance on LEDGAR.

3.3 Results and Discussion

For our experiments, we use three baseline general-purpose chat variants - ChatGPT-3.5, Falcon-180b, and LLaMA-2-70b - and present the results in Table 1. General-purpose LLMs perform less well than smaller in-domain models. The best general LLM, Falcon-Chat, performs 19.2% mic-F1 and 26.8% mac-F1 lower than the best in-domain model, LegalBERT, which itself is much smaller than the LexGPT, the LegalLLM. Our findings echo that of (Chalkidis, 2023).

Notably, for class labels with only one example in our sampled test set, the three chat-variants surprisingly show the same results: they fail to predict them correctly excepting the *Qualification* label (the others being *Assigns, Books, Powers, and Sanctions*. Similarly, *Indemnity* is always misclassified as *Indemnifications* (three examples in total). Further, labels that are semantically similar are difficult for the models to handle since they frequently mislabel such contract provision themes. For example, (*Taxes*, *Tax Withholdings* and *Withholdings*) is almost always labeled as *Tax Withholdings* by all the models. (*Jurisdictions, Submission To Jurisdiction, Consent To Jurisdiction*) is almost always labeled as *Submission To Jurisdiction* in the case of ChatGPT and *Jurisdiction* in the case of Falcon and LLaMA. As for (*Applicable Laws, Governing Laws, Compliance With Laws*), we observe that *Governing Laws* was easiest to predict with an average accuracy of 90%, and *Compliance With Laws* with 80%, but *Applicable Laws* performs very poorly with 0% accuracy for LLaMA and Falcon and 20% for ChatGPT - predicting only one from a total of 5 samples correctly. However, in the case of (*Payments, Fees, Interests* the models seem to predict them correctly in about 60% of the cases, with *Payments* appearing at least once for *Fees* and *Interests*. On average, only 95 of the 100 classes in the reference labels are present in the predictions.

3.4 Subjective Analysis

Our findings highlight that the perceived advantages LLMs have over BERT-based models (such as the sheer amount of large parameters, extended context length, and the amount of pre-training knowledge), cannot substitute for the obvious edge in-domain data gives to the much smaller models. Even when the LLM is trained so (LexGPT), it couldn't perform as well as the discriminative model (LegalBERT). This could be expected as the latter is more naturally suited for the benchmark's classification tasks than generative models which are prone to issues like hallucination. Our label-wise findings seem to support this too.

However, the current legal benchmarks are limited to NLU tasks. In general, it would be ideal to have a powerful LegalLLM that can perform both generative and discriminative tasks. Our findings show that there is a unique challenge in the legal domain: if we have to build a better LegalLLM, we need to find better methods to take advantage of the in-domain legal data for LLMs as simply fine-tuning it isn't enough. As the authors of LexGPT mention, reinforcement learning from human feedback could be extremely helpful in improving LexGPT, providing ways for the first LegalLLM to produce state-of-the-art results.

However, if we limit the application of legal models to NLU tasks, our findings turn optimistic. The results show that the LLMs' ability to process large context may not be necessary for classification - we hypothesize this could be because verbose legal text could turn out to have very similar semantic content, so the additional context may not be useful. This hypothesis could be echoed by findings from (Shaikh et al., 2020), who show that a careful selection of a handful of textual features in a verbose dataset is strong enough to help statistical models achieve high accuracies for binary classification.

This in fact should be good news, as it means legal practitioners can avoid having to use or train unnecessarily large or expensive models (both carbon-wise and cost-wise). Much smaller in-domain models like LegalBERT are nevertheless superior and should be used for practical applications, as also suggested by (Chalkidis, 2023)

4 Conclusion

In this work, we examine three general-purpose LLMs' zero-shot performance on a multi-class contract provision classification task using the LEDGAR dataset of LexGLUE. Our study shows that these LLMs, even though aren't explicitly trained in legal data, can still demonstrate respectable theme classification performance. The results highlight the need for better LegalLLMs adapted to the specifics of the legal industry, which has been underexplored compared to other domains. In light of this, we also present a review of related datasets and models, which we hope will help get an overview of the field.

References

Joshua Ainslie, Santiago Ontanon, Chris Alberti, Vaclav Cvicek, Zachary Fisher, Philip Pham, Anirudh Ravula, Sumit Sanghai, Qifan Wang, and Li Yang. 2020. ETC: Encoding long and structured inputs in transformers. In *Proceedings of the 2020 Conference on Empirical Methods in Natural Language Processing (EMNLP)*, pages 268–284, Online. Association for Computational Linguistics.

Rohan Anil, Andrew M Dai, Orhan Firat, Melvin Johnson, Dmitry Lepikhin, Alexandre Passos, Siamak Shakeri, Emanuel Taropa, Paige Bailey, Zhifeng Chen, et al. 2023. Palm 2 technical report. *arXiv preprint arXiv:2305.10403*.

Iz Beltagy, Matthew E Peters, and Arman Cohan. 2020. Longformer: The long-document transformer. *arXiv preprint arXiv:2004.05150*.

Tom Brown, Benjamin Mann, Nick Ryder, Melanie Subbiah, Jared D Kaplan, Prafulla Dhariwal, Arvind Neelakantan, Pranav Shyam, Girish Sastry, Amanda Askell, et al. 2020. Language models are few-shot learners. *Advances in neural information processing systems*, 33:1877–1901.

Ilias Chalkidis. 2023. Chatgpt may pass the bar exam soon, but has a long way to go for the lexglue benchmark. *arXiv preprint arXiv:2304.12202*.

Ilias Chalkidis, Manos Fergadiotis, and Ion Androutsopoulos. 2021. MultiEURLEX - a multi-lingual and multi-label legal document classification dataset for zero-shot cross-lingual transfer. In *Proceedings of the 2021 Conference on Empirical Methods in Natural Language Processing*, pages 6974–6996, Online and Punta Cana, Dominican Republic. Association for Computational Linguistics.

Ilias Chalkidis, Manos Fergadiotis, Prodromos Malakasiotis, Nikolaos Aletras, and Ion Androutsopoulos. 2020. LEGAL-BERT: The muppets straight out of law school. In *Findings of the Association for Computational Linguistics: EMNLP 2020*, pages 2898–2904, Online. Association for Computational Linguistics.

Ilias Chalkidis, Nicolas Garneau, Catalina Goanta, Daniel Katz, and Anders Søgaard. 2023. LeXFiles and LegalLAMA: Facilitating English multinational legal language model development. In *Proceedings of the 61st Annual Meeting of the Association for Computational Linguistics (Volume 1: Long Papers)*, pages 15513–15535, Toronto, Canada. Association for Computational Linguistics.

Ilias Chalkidis, Abhik Jana, Dirk Hartung, Michael Bommarito, Ion Androutsopoulos, Daniel Katz, and Nikolaos Aletras. 2022. LexGLUE: A benchmark dataset for legal language understanding in English. In *Proceedings of the 60th Annual Meeting of the Association for Computational Linguistics (Volume 1: Long Papers)*, pages 4310–4330, Dublin, Ireland. Association for Computational Linguistics.

Aakanksha Chowdhery, Sharan Narang, Jacob Devlin, Maarten Bosma, Gaurav Mishra, Adam Roberts, Paul Barham, Hyung Won Chung, Charles Sutton, Sebastian Gehrmann, et al. 2022. Palm: Scaling language modeling with pathways. *arXiv preprint arXiv:2204.02311*.

Alexis Conneau, Kartikay Khandelwal, Naman Goyal, Vishrav Chaudhary, Guillaume Wenzek, Francisco Guzmán, Edouard Grave, Myle Ott, Luke Zettlemoyer, and Veselin Stoyanov. 2019. Unsupervised cross-lingual representation learning at scale. *arXiv preprint arXiv:1911.02116*.

Xiang Dai, Ilias Chalkidis, Sune Darkner, and Desmond Elliott. 2022. Revisiting transformer-based models for long document classification. In *Findings of the Association for Computational Linguistics: EMNLP 2022*, pages 7212–7230, Abu Dhabi, United Arab Emirates. Association for Computational Linguistics.

Zihang Dai, Zhilin Yang, Yiming Yang, Jaime Carbonell, Quoc Le, and Ruslan Salakhutdinov. 2019. Transformer-XL: Attentive language models beyond a fixed-length context. In *Proceedings of the 57th Annual Meeting of the Association for Computational Linguistics*, pages 2978–2988, Florence, Italy. Association for Computational Linguistics.

Jacob Devlin, Ming-Wei Chang, Kenton Lee, and Kristina Toutanova. 2019. BERT: Pre-training of deep bidirectional transformers for language understanding. In *Proceedings of the 2019 Conference of the North American Chapter of the Association for Computational Linguistics: Human Language Technologies, Volume 1 (Long and Short Papers)*, pages 4171–4186, Minneapolis, Minnesota. Association for Computational Linguistics.

SiYu Ding, Junyuan Shang, Shuohuan Wang, Yu Sun, Hao Tian, Hua Wu, and Haifeng Wang. 2021. ERNIE-Doc: A retrospective long-document modeling transformer. In *Proceedings of the 59th Annual Meeting of the Association for Computational Linguistics and the 11th International Joint Conference on Natural Language Processing (Volume 1: Long Papers)*, pages 2914–2927, Online. Association for Computational Linguistics.

Neel Guha, Julian Nyarko, Daniel E Ho, Christopher Ré, Adam Chilton, Aditya Narayana, Alex Chohlas-Wood, Austin Peters, Brandon Waldon, Daniel N Rockmore, et al. 2023. Legalbench: A collaboratively built benchmark for measuring legal reasoning in large language models. *arXiv preprint arXiv:2308.11462*.

Peter Henderson, Mark Krass, Lucia Zheng, Neel Guha, Christopher D Manning, Dan Jurafsky, and Daniel Ho. 2022. Pile of law: Learning responsible data filtering from the law and a 256gb open-source legal dataset. *Advances in Neural Information Processing Systems*, 35:29217–29234.

Jieh-Sheng Lee. 2023. Lexgpt 0.1: pre-trained gpt-j models with pile of law. *arXiv preprint arXiv:2306.05431*.

Yinhan Liu, Myle Ott, Naman Goyal, Jingfei Du, Mandar Joshi, Danqi Chen, Omer Levy, Mike Lewis, Luke Zettlemoyer, and Veselin Stoyanov. 2019. Roberta: A robustly optimized bert pretraining approach. *arXiv preprint arXiv:1907.11692*.

Dimitris Mamakas, Petros Tsotsi, Ion Androutsopoulos, and Ilias Chalkidis. 2022. Processing long legal documents with pre-trained transformers: Modding LegalBERT and longformer. In *Proceedings of the Natural Legal Language Processing Workshop 2022*, pages 130–142, Abu Dhabi, United Arab Emirates (Hybrid). Association for Computational Linguistics.

Joel Niklaus, Veton Matoshi, Pooja Rani, Andrea Galassi, Matthias Stürmer, and Ilias Chalkidis. 2023. Lextreme: A multi-lingual and multi-task benchmark for the legal domain. *arXiv preprint arXiv:2301.13126*.

Guilherme Penedo, Quentin Malartic, Daniel Hesslow, Ruxandra Cojocaru, Alessandro Cappelli, Hamza Alobeidli, Baptiste Pannier, Ebtesam Almazrouei, and Julien Launay. 2023. The refinedweb dataset for falcon llm: outperforming curated corpora with web data, and web data only. *arXiv preprint arXiv:2306.01116*.

Bowen Peng, Jeffrey Quesnelle, Honglu Fan, and Enrico Shippole. 2023. Yarn: Efficient context window extension of large language models. *arXiv preprint arXiv:2309.00071*.

Alec Radford, Jeff Wu, Rewon Child, David Luan, Dario Amodei, and Ilya Sutskever. 2019. Language models are unsupervised multitask learners.

Jaromir Savelka. 2023. Unlocking practical applications in legal domain: Evaluation of gpt for zero-shot semantic annotation of legal texts. *arXiv preprint arXiv:2305.04417*.

Rafe Athar Shaikh, Tirath Prasad Sahu, and Veena Anand. 2020. Predicting outcomes of legal cases based on legal factors using classifiers. *Procedia Computer Science*, 167:2393–2402.

Zhongxiang Sun. 2023. A short survey of viewing large language models in legal aspect. *arXiv preprint arXiv:2303.09136*.

Chenhao Tang, Zhengliang Liu, Chong Ma, Zihao Wu, Yiwei Li, Wei Liu, Dajiang Zhu, Quanzheng Li, Xiang Li, Tianming Liu, et al. 2023. Policygpt: Automated analysis of privacy policies with large language models. *arXiv preprint arXiv:2309.10238*.

Hugo Touvron, Thibaut Lavril, Gautier Izacard, Xavier Martinet, Marie-Anne Lachaux, Timothée Lacroix, Baptiste Rozière, Naman Goyal, Eric Hambro, Faisal Azhar, et al. 2023. Llama: Open and efficient foundation language models. *arXiv preprint arXiv:2302.13971*.

Ashish Vaswani, Noam Shazeer, Niki Parmar, Jakob Uszkoreit, Llion Jones, Aidan N Gomez, Łukasz Kaiser, and Illia Polosukhin. 2017. Attention is all you need. *Advances in neural information processing systems*, 30.

Zhilin Yang, Zihang Dai, Yiming Yang, Jaime Carbonell, Russ R Salakhutdinov, and Quoc V Le. 2019. Xlnet: Generalized autoregressive pretraining for language understanding. *Advances in neural information processing systems*, 32.

Manzil Zaheer, Guru Guruganesh, Kumar Avinava Dubey, Joshua Ainslie, Chris Alberti, Santiago Ontanon, Philip Pham, Anirudh Ravula, Qifan Wang, Li Yang, et al. 2020. Big bird: Transformers for longer sequences. *Advances in neural information processing systems*, 33:17283–17297.

Lucia Zheng, Neel Guha, Brandon R Anderson, Peter Henderson, and Daniel E Ho. 2021. When does pretraining help? assessing self-supervised learning for law and the casehold dataset of 53,000+ legal holdings. In *Proceedings of the eighteenth international conference on artificial intelligence and law*, pages 159–168.

A Custom Prompt

For reproducibility, we present the prompts that we use for all our experiments. The following is the entry to the Custom Instructions setting of ChatGPT. For HuggingChat, we simply provide both the instructions to the Custom System Prompt box.

What would you like ChatGPT to know about you to provide better responses? *I want you to be an EDGAR contract provision classifier. Given a contract provision, you should correctly identify the EDGAR theme. Do not give any explanations.*

How would you like ChatGPT to respond? *One answer from the following list: [{{paste the list here}}]. Do not give an option that is not in the list.*

On the Potential and Limitations of Few-Shot In-Context Learning to Generate Metamorphic Specifications for Tax Preparation Software

Dananjay Srinivas[*1] **Rohan Das**[*1] **Saeid Tizpaz-Niari**[2]
Ashutosh Trivedi[1] **Maria Leonor Pacheco**[1]
[1] University of Colorado Boulder [2]University of Texas El Paso
[1]{first.last}@colorado.edu [2]saeid@utep.edu

Abstract

Due to the ever-increasing complexity of income tax laws in the United States, the number of US taxpayers filing their taxes using tax preparation software (henceforth, tax software) continues to increase. According to the U.S. Internal Revenue Service (IRS), in FY22, nearly 50% of taxpayers filed their individual income taxes using tax software. Given the legal consequences of incorrectly filing taxes for the taxpayer, ensuring the correctness of tax software is of paramount importance. *Metamorphic testing* has emerged as a leading solution to test and debug legal-critical tax software due to the absence of correctness requirements and trustworthy datasets. The key idea behind metamorphic testing is to express the properties of a system in terms of the relationship between one input and its slightly metamorphosed twinned input. Extracting metamorphic properties from IRS tax publications is a tedious and time-consuming process. As a response, this paper formulates the task of generating metamorphic specifications as a *translation task* between properties extracted from tax documents—expressed in natural language—to a contrastive first-order logic form. We perform a systematic analysis on the potential and limitations of *in-context* learning with *Large Language Models* (LLMs) for this task, and outline a research agenda towards automating the generation of metamorphic specifications for tax preparation software.

1 Introduction

Recent surveys estimate that between 40 to 50% of taxpayers in the United States use tax preparation software to file their taxes (Farrington, 2023). Given the pervasive use of these systems and the penalties associated with filing taxes incorrectly (IRS, 2023), making sure that tax preparation software is free of bugs is of paramount importance. However, there are considerable challenges that make the application of standard software testing approaches infeasible in this domain. Among these, the absence of correctness requirements and the lack of publicly available benchmarks (due to obvious privacy concerns) are primary obstacles to automatic testing and debugging of such systems.

To address these challenges, Tizpaz-Niari et al. (2023) introduced a testing framework for U.S. tax preparation software guided by *metamorphic relations*. The authors define metamorphic relations as relations between two similar individuals who differ in key characteristics that put them in different tax income buckets. This way, they are able to evaluate the outcome of an individual taxpayer in comparison with individuals who are deemed similar to them. With the help of tax preparation experts, they were able to manually derive a comprehensive set of critical correctness properties of tax preparation outcomes expressed in first-order logic, and develop a search strategy to automatically generate test cases for an open-source tax preparation software. While their approach was successful, deriving formal metamorphic specifications is a time-consuming process that requires significant domain expertise. Moreover, any changes to the tax code would require continuous efforts to make sure that specifications remain up to date.

In this paper, we set out to explore whether recent advances in Large Language Models (LLMs) (Brown et al., 2020; Touvron et al., 2023a; Taori et al., 2023; Wang et al., 2023) can help reduce the manual effort required to derive metamorphic specifications for this domain. While supervised learning without sizeable training datasets is infeasible, recent findings show that LLMs can perform surprisingly well in few-shot scenarios for a wide variety of language tasks, including traditional NLP tasks like translation and question-answering (Brown et al., 2020), vision-language tasks (Monajatipoor et al., 2023), and socio-linguistic tasks like morality framing (Roy et al., 2022).

*Equal Contribution

Proceedings of the Natural Legal Language Processing Workshop 2023, pages 230–243
December 7, 2023

To perform our study, we first define the extraction of metamorphic specifications for tax preparation software as a *language to first-order logic translation* task. To do this, we curate a dataset of 33 high-quality natural language properties derived from tax documents* and their corresponding formal logic representation Tizpaz-Niari et al. (2023). As curating these high-quality examples is expensive, we formulate the problem as a few-shot learning task and experiment with various *in-context learning* strategies to obtain a formal representation for each property. In-context learning is a task-adaptation technique that does not update the parameters of the LLM, but rather primes the model response by providing a sequence of demonstrations (Brown et al., 2020). Recent work has shown that in-context learning can lead to better out-of-domain performance than few-shot fine-tuning (Awadalla et al., 2022; Si et al., 2023).

We perform a comprehensive analysis of our results and show that using few-shot in-context learning, the model makes between 1-2 mistakes per property on average when generating predicates, variables and operators. While this is encouraging for a model that has barely seen any in-domain, tasks-specific data, there is a lot of room for improvement before these specifications are usable for automated testing. This work represents a first step towards the automated generation of metamorphic specifications for tax preparation software. In Sec. 5 we outline a research agenda for this purpose.

2 Related Work

Converting natural language utterances to logic forms has a long history in the Natural Language Processing community. Semantic parsing is a long-standing NLP task that looks at this problem (Kamath and Das, 2019). Most of the work in this space has been either tailored to going from natural language to linguistically-motivated meaning representations (Palmer et al., 2010; Banarescu et al., 2013), or to executable programs like SQL queries (Sun et al., 2018) and robotic commands (Dukes, 2014). The solutions employed for these domains are not readily applicable to our case. On the one hand, datasets for linguistically motivated meaning representations usually deal with simple general utterances, and their structured forms are very distinct from the structured forms needed for automated software verification. On the other hand, executable domains like SQL have the advantage that there are large-scale, readily available repositories of in-domain data, which is not the case for low-resource, closed domains like tax preparation software.

More recently, there has been increased interest in exploring NLP techniques to derive formal specifications from technical documentation. For example, Pacheco et al. (2022) look at the task of extracting finite-state machines from network protocol RFCs, Zhang et al. (2020) extract LTL correctness specifications from prose policies for IoT apps, and Chen et al. (2019) look at sentences in a developer guide to extend the finite-state machines for a small set of payment services. In all of these cases, authors are either able to leverage off-the-shelf parsers or employ supervised methods over a curated in-domain dataset.

3 Task Description

Metamorphic testing is a well-studied strategy in the systems community (Chen et al., 2020). It was developed to circumvent the absence of oracles (i.e., black box modules that decide whether the output of the system is correct for a given input). The main idea behind metamorphic testing is that correctness can be established by contrasting multiple input-output behaviors (Segura et al., 2016). The running example is search-engine validation; while it might be impossible to know the expected items that should be returned for any search query q, if we have a more restrictive query q', we know that the number of retrieved items for q should be greater than the number of retrieved items for q'. This allows for developing strategies to test whether systems satisfy the metamorphic relations.

To formulate our task, we build on the definition of metamorphic specifications for tax-preparation software proposed by Tizpaz-Niari et al. (2023). We have a fixed set P of metamorphic properties written in natural language, expressing aspects of the U.S. Individual Income Tax Returns that relate to disability, credits, and deductions. For each property $p \in P$, we want to synthesize a specification s in first-order logic that captures the metamorphic property. Fig. 1 shows an example of the input and expected output. In Appendix A, we detail the syntax and semantics of metamorphic specifications used for the tax preparation software, as well as the

*These documents include Form 1040 (U.S. Individual Income Tax Return), Publication 596 (Earned Income Tax Credit), Schedule 8812 (Qualifying Children and Other Dependents), and Form 8863 (Education Credits).

Input: Property	Output: Specification
An individual with the married filing jointly (MFJ) status with a disabled spouse must receive similar or higher tax benefits compared to a similar individual but without the disabled spouse.	$\forall \mathbf{x}(\mathbf{x}.sts = MFJ) \implies \forall \mathbf{y}((\mathbf{x} \equiv_{s\_blind} \mathbf{y}) \wedge (\mathbf{x}.s\_blind \wedge \neg \mathbf{y}.s\_blind)) \implies \mathcal{F}(\mathbf{x}) \geq \mathcal{F}(\mathbf{y})$

Table 1: An example of input and expected output. Here, the quantification is over the domain of taxpaying individuals, the relation $\equiv_{pred}$ relates equal individuals except for predicate $pred$, and the function $\mathcal{F}$ characterizes the tax return for an individual.

full list of formal specifications for metamorphic relations used for demonstration and testing.

4 Experimental Evaluation

In this section, we evaluate the performance of LLMs on the natural language to metamorphic specifications translations. We first outline the evaluation dimensions that we consider, then we describe our experimental setup and results.

4.1 Evaluation Dimensions

In order to investigate LLMs' abilities to convert natural language properties into metamorphic specifications, we evaluate different dimensions to identify how the number of examples that the model gets to observe, the prompting strategies used, the LLM implementation used, as well as the characteristics of the task affect model performance.

Number of examples for few-shot learning: We look at the effect that the number of demonstrations has on model performance. Since we are working with an extremely reduced dataset, we limit the maximum number of examples that the model sees to two.

In-context learning strategies: We seek to study if decomposed prompting (Khot et al., 2023) is effective in translating natural language into formal metamorphic specifications. To do this, we compare the performance between an end-to-end **(E2E)** prompting strategy and different decomposed strategies. To do this, we break down the task of generating metamorphic relations into two sub-tasks: (1) Generating the relevant logical predicates, and (2) Generating the specification in first-order logic. We experiment with two decomposed strategies; the first one **(Implicit)** allows the model to access the context used to generate the predicates by prompting each task subsequently, while the second one **(Explicit)** decouples the predicate and FOL generation entirely, allowing each module to completely focus on its sub-task. Example prompts for all strategies are provided in App. B.

LLM implementation: We evaluate all three learning strategies on GPT-3.5. However, since we do not have access to the GPT-3.5 weights, we are reliant on APIs provided by OpenAI. In the interest of transparency and reproducibility, we also try out the Explicit strategy on Alpaca (Taori et al., 2023), an open-source instruction-tuned model built over LLaMA 2 (Touvron et al., 2023b).

Example difficulty: Different properties can be captured by varying numbers of predicates. In our evaluation, we compare the model performance against the number of predicates required to capture a metamorphic property. We stipulate that the difficulty of capturing a metamorphic expression increases as the number of predicates increases.

Error types: We qualitatively evaluate the different types of errors that the model makes. We qualify different errors by looking at specific cases where the model generated incorrect predicates, operators, or variables.

4.2 Results

Experimental Setup: For GPT-3.5, we prompt via the ChatCompletion API provided by OpenAI. We use the default API settings as outlined in their documentation. For Alpaca, we use the fine-tuned weights from the LoRa-adapted (Hu et al., 2021) Alpaca 7B model, and run inference to generate responses for our prompts.

Performance Metrics and Annotation: Standard generation metrics like BLEU, ROGUE, ChrF and BLEURT rely either on word and character matching (Papineni et al., 2002; Lin, 2004; Popović, 2015), or semantic embedding similarity (Sellam et al., 2020). Metrics that rely on lexical matching are ill-suited to evaluate the generation of first-order-logic propositions, as the operators, predicate names and variables used can vary significantly while maintaining semantic consistency (e.g., the operation $x \equiv_S y$ and the predicate $EqualExcept(x, y, S)$ express the same relationship). Similarly, embedding-based metrics that have been trained on large textual repositories do not account for valid substitutions in logic that lack similarity in natural language (e.g., $\mathcal{F}(x)$ and $TaxReturn(x)$ can be used to denote the same predicate). For this reason, we resort to human evaluation and define a quality score ranging from 1 to 5 based on the following rubric:

Rating	Explanation
5	The generated predicates or FOL match the ground truth.
4	The generated identities have the correct semantic sense, but incorrect format.
3	There is 1 mistake in the set of predicates, variables, operators
2	There are 2 mistakes in the set of predicates, variables, operators
1	The generated identities are completely incorrect.

Table 2: Rubric for Performance Quality

Using this rubric, the first two authors of this paper annotated the generated texts with their qualitative judgments. A total of 33 examples were evaluated (see Appendix A), and average results are reported in Tables 3 and 4.

Predicate and FOL quality based on prompting style and number of examples: In Table 3, we look at the effect that examples have on different styles of prompting. We found that on average, **GPT Explicit** decomposed prompting performed best among all strategies when demonstrations were provided. Additionally, we find higher variation in results for **GPT E2E**, suggesting that decomposed prompting might lead to slightly more consistent results. As expected, demonstrating with a higher number of examples helps the model generate better translations. Nevertheless, the average quality for all strategies sits solidly in the middle of the rubric (about 1-2 errors per example), shedding light on the limitations of few-shot in-context learning as-is for this task. **Alpaca Explicit** produces nearly identical results to **GPT Explicit** in the zero-shot scenario. However, performance does not improve when Alpaca is provided with two examples instead of just one, unlike **GPT Explicit**. The Alpaca implementation tested is significantly smaller (7B vs. 175B for GPT 3.5). We hypothesize that Alpaca 7B likely needs access to more context to be able to improve its performance for this task. We leave an in-depth exploration of the capabilities of smaller LLMs for future work.

Effect of predicate complexity on translation: In this evaluation, we fix the number of examples the model sees to two. We then evaluate how different numbers of predicates affect the quality of translations. Results can be seen in Tab. 4. For all strategies, there is a clear drop in performance for harder examples. This is consistent with our hypothesis that more complex propositions are more difficult to translate. Similarly to the previous analysis, we find that performance on decomposed prompting performs better than E2E prompting. Given the overhead of manual evaluation, we limited this test to GPT-3.5.

In Appendix C, we provide generation examples for each score in the annotation rubric.

4.3 Qualitative Analysis of Errors

In this section, we qualitatively evaluate different errors after qualifying them on the basis of correctness with regard to 1) Predicates; 2) Variables; and 3) Operators. We observe that while the model is somewhat robust in translating natural language into logic, it encounters problems when trying to express identities in metamorphic forms.

Errors observed in predicates: The most common error that we observed in the translations was due to a lack of consideration for predicates that are expected in metamorphic templates; such as $EqualExcept(x, y, S)$. where x and y are entities that are similar except through the set of predicates defined in S.

Errors observed in variables: We see that models often declare variables or omit variables without much structure. Due to the stochastic nature of LLM predictions, it often reuses (or is primed to reuse) the same variables it has declared for different predicates; automatically invalidating the metamorphic translation.

Errors observed in operators: Models often imitate the same operators that were provided in the prompts. For instance, when we provided a prompt that used $\geq$; the prompt generated the prediction using the same operator to describe the opposite kind of relationship. Similarly, the model frequently uses commonly occurring pairs of logic notation like ($\forall$ and $\exists$).

Summarizing qualitative analysis: Our qualitative study revealed that while LLMs hold the potential to perform well on metamorphic translation tasks, we also observe simple errors caused due to stochastic dependencies. More training data or post-hoc filtering may benefit this approach from generating erroneous responses.

5 Findings, Limitations and Future Work

Our experiments show that while LLMs are able to make some headway in the task of metamorphic translation, more work needs to be done to

n-shot	GPT E2E		GPT Implicit		GPT Explicit		Alpaca Explicit	
	Pred.	FOL	Pred.	FOL	Pred.	FOL	Pred.	FOL
0	1.77 (0.99)	1.19 (0.49)	1.15 (0.46)	1.03 (0.19)	1.00 (0.00)	1.03 (0.19)	1.00 (0.00)	1.00 (0.00)
1	3.29 (1.38)	2.25 (1.48)	3.46 (1.39)	1.27 (0.60)	4.03 (1.02)	2.77 (1.28)	1.61 (1.09)	1.74 (2.02)
2	3.96 (1.15)	2.85 (1.70)	3.65 (1.09)	1.42 (0.95)	4.27 (0.87)	3.16 (1.23)	1.63 (1.08)	1.71 (1.16)

Table 3: Average (S.D.) quality scores for Predicate and FOL generation by in-context learning strategy.

Strategy	# Predicates < 4		$4 \leq$ # Predicates < 6		# Predicates ≥ 6	
	Pred.	FOL	Pred.	FOL	Pred.	FOL
GPT E2E	3.83 (1.60)	3.16 (2.04)	4.07 (0.95)	3.31 (1.54)	3.88 (1.25)	1.88 (1.46)
GPT Implicit	3.50 (1.22)	1.83 (1.60)	3.66 (0.88)	1.50 (0.79)	3.75 (1.39)	1.00 (0.00)
GPT Explicit	4.20 (1.03)	3.50 (0.97)	4.58 (0.67)	3.58 (1.08)	3.88 (0.83)	2.13 (1.25)

Table 4: Average (S.D.) quality scores for Predicate and FOL generation for each in-context learning strategy, grouped by difficulty level in terms of the number of ground truth predicates in the statement.

improve performance in order to build safeguards for tax preparation software. Below, we list three key directions for future work.

Task-oriented prompt learning: It is clear that few-shot in-context learning is not enough to fully automate the generation of metamorphic specifications for tax preparation software. Recent work has shown that learning prompts that are tailored specifically to the task at hand can help improve in-context learning performance (Chung et al., 2022; Han et al., 2022; Zhang et al., 2023). Going forward, we would like to explore strategies to dynamically adapt prompting strategies to maximize performance and minimize common mistakes.

Leveraging additional data sources: While we do not have access to a comprehensive dataset containing metamorphic specifications, there are several external resources that we could indirectly exploit to design weakly-supervised methods and representation learning strategies for the task at hand. For example, we could exploit unlabeled tax-centric documents, out-of-domain language-to-logic datasets, and LLMs trained over code and other structured representations. There is a body of work on task-adaptive pre-training (Gururangan et al., 2020), domain adaptation (Daumé III, 2007), and code-based LLMs for semantic parsing (Shin and Van Durme, 2022) that we could exploit to either complement or replace vanilla in-context learning.

Closing the loop: While we explored the task of generating metamorphic specifications by translating from properties in natural language to contrastive first-order logic forms, this task alone is not sufficient to fully automate the verification of tax preparation software. To close the loop, two tasks remain: (1) Automatically extracting properties from free-form tax documents, and (2) Taking potentially noisy specifications and generating executable tests. While closing the loop is an ambitious task, we hypothesize that these additional steps could help inform the translation process, potentially improving performance. For example, if we could automatically extract more properties - even if noisy- from raw documents, we could easily expand the training examples without additional manual cost. Moreover, connecting the extracted specifications with symbolic, executable modules, could serve as a form of indirect feedback to inform the translation module.

6 Acknowledgements

Tizpaz-Niari and Trivedi were partially supported by the NSF under grants CCF-2317206 and CCF-2317207. This work utilized the Alpine high-performance computing resource at the University of Colorado Boulder. Alpine is jointly funded by the University of Colorado Boulder, the University of Colorado Anschutz, Colorado State University, and the NSF (award 2201538).

References

Anas Awadalla, Mitchell Wortsman, Gabriel Ilharco, Sewon Min, Ian Magnusson, Hannaneh Hajishirzi, and Ludwig Schmidt. 2022. Exploring the landscape of distributional robustness for question answering models. In *Findings of the Association for Computational Linguistics: EMNLP 2022*, pages 5971–5987,

Abu Dhabi, United Arab Emirates. Association for Computational Linguistics.

Laura Banarescu, Claire Bonial, Shu Cai, Madalina Georgescu, Kira Griffitt, Ulf Hermjakob, Kevin Knight, Philipp Koehn, Martha Palmer, and Nathan Schneider. 2013. Abstract Meaning Representation for sembanking. In *Proceedings of the 7th Linguistic Annotation Workshop and Interoperability with Discourse*, pages 178–186, Sofia, Bulgaria. Association for Computational Linguistics.

Tom Brown, Benjamin Mann, Nick Ryder, Melanie Subbiah, Jared D Kaplan, Prafulla Dhariwal, Arvind Neelakantan, Pranav Shyam, Girish Sastry, Amanda Askell, Sandhini Agarwal, Ariel Herbert-Voss, Gretchen Krueger, Tom Henighan, Rewon Child, Aditya Ramesh, Daniel Ziegler, Jeffrey Wu, Clemens Winter, Chris Hesse, Mark Chen, Eric Sigler, Mateusz Litwin, Scott Gray, Benjamin Chess, Jack Clark, Christopher Berner, Sam McCandlish, Alec Radford, Ilya Sutskever, and Dario Amodei. 2020. Language models are few-shot learners. In *Advances in Neural Information Processing Systems*, volume 33, pages 1877–1901. Curran Associates, Inc.

T. Y. Chen, S. C. Cheung, and S. M. Yiu. 2020. Metamorphic testing: A new approach for generating next test cases.

Yi Chen, Luyi Xing, Yue Qin, Xiaojing Liao, XiaoFeng Wang, Kai Chen, and Wei Zou. 2019. Devils in the guidance: Predicting logic vulnerabilities in payment syndication services through automated documentation analysis. In *28th USENIX Security Symposium (USENIX Security 19)*, pages 747–764, Santa Clara, CA. USENIX Association.

Hyung Won Chung, Le Hou, Shayne Longpre, Barret Zoph, Yi Tay, William Fedus, Yunxuan Li, Xuezhi Wang, Mostafa Dehghani, Siddhartha Brahma, Albert Webson, Shixiang Shane Gu, Zhuyun Dai, Mirac Suzgun, Xinyun Chen, Aakanksha Chowdhery, Alex Castro-Ros, Marie Pellat, Kevin Robinson, Dasha Valter, Sharan Narang, Gaurav Mishra, Adams Yu, Vincent Zhao, Yanping Huang, Andrew Dai, Hongkun Yu, Slav Petrov, Ed H. Chi, Jeff Dean, Jacob Devlin, Adam Roberts, Denny Zhou, Quoc V. Le, and Jason Wei. 2022. Scaling instruction-finetuned language models.

Hal Daumé III. 2007. Frustratingly easy domain adaptation. In *Proceedings of the 45th Annual Meeting of the Association of Computational Linguistics*, pages 256–263, Prague, Czech Republic. Association for Computational Linguistics.

Kais Dukes. 2014. SemEval-2014 task 6: Supervised semantic parsing of robotic spatial commands. In *Proceedings of the 8th International Workshop on Semantic Evaluation (SemEval 2014)*, pages 45–53, Dublin, Ireland. Association for Computational Linguistics.

Robert Farrington. 2023. How much americans pay to file their taxes. *The College Investor*.

Suchin Gururangan, Ana Marasović, Swabha Swayamdipta, Kyle Lo, Iz Beltagy, Doug Downey, and Noah A. Smith. 2020. Don't stop pretraining: Adapt language models to domains and tasks. In *Proceedings of the 58th Annual Meeting of the Association for Computational Linguistics*, pages 8342–8360, Online. Association for Computational Linguistics.

Seungju Han, Beomsu Kim, Jin Yong Yoo, Seokjun Seo, Sangbum Kim, Enkhbayar Erdenee, and Buru Chang. 2022. Meet your favorite character: Open-domain chatbot mimicking fictional characters with only a few utterances. In *Proceedings of the 2022 Conference of the North American Chapter of the Association for Computational Linguistics: Human Language Technologies*, pages 5114–5132, Seattle, United States. Association for Computational Linguistics.

J. Edward Hu, Yelong Shen, Phillip Wallis, Zeyuan Allen-Zhu, Yuanzhi Li, Shean Wang, and Weizhu Chen. 2021. Lora: Low-rank adaptation of large language models. *ArXiv*, abs/2106.09685.

IRS. 2023. Penalties. *Internal Revenue Services Website*.

Aishwarya Kamath and Rajarshi Das. 2019. A survey on semantic parsing. In *Automated Knowledge Base Construction (AKBC)*.

Tushar Khot, Harsh Trivedi, Matthew Finlayson, Yao Fu, Kyle Richardson, Peter Clark, and Ashish Sabharwal. 2023. Decomposed prompting: A modular approach for solving complex tasks. In *The Eleventh International Conference on Learning Representations*.

Chin-Yew Lin. 2004. ROUGE: A package for automatic evaluation of summaries. In *Text Summarization Branches Out*, pages 74–81, Barcelona, Spain. Association for Computational Linguistics.

Masoud Monajatipoor, Liunian Harold Li, Mozhdeh Rouhsedaghat, Lin Yang, and Kai-Wei Chang. 2023. MetaVL: Transferring in-context learning ability from language models to vision-language models. In *Proceedings of the 61st Annual Meeting of the Association for Computational Linguistics (Volume 2: Short Papers)*, pages 495–508, Toronto, Canada. Association for Computational Linguistics.

Maria Leonor Pacheco, Max von Hippel, Ben Weintraub, Dan Goldwasser, and Cristina Nita-Rotaru. 2022. Automated attack synthesis by extracting finite state machines from protocol specification documents. In *43rd IEEE Symposium on Security and Privacy, SP 2022, San Francisco, CA, USA, May 22-26, 2022*, pages 51–68. IEEE.

Martha Palmer, Daniel Gildea, and Nianwen Xue. 2010. *Semantic Roles*, pages 1–19. Springer International Publishing, Cham.

Kishore Papineni, Salim Roukos, Todd Ward, and Wei-Jing Zhu. 2002. Bleu: a method for automatic evaluation of machine translation. In *Proceedings of the 40th Annual Meeting of the Association for Computational Linguistics*, pages 311–318, Philadelphia, Pennsylvania, USA. Association for Computational Linguistics.

Maja Popović. 2015. chrF: character n-gram F-score for automatic MT evaluation. In *Proceedings of the Tenth Workshop on Statistical Machine Translation*, pages 392–395, Lisbon, Portugal. Association for Computational Linguistics.

Shamik Roy, Nishanth Sridhar Nakshatri, and Dan Goldwasser. 2022. Towards few-shot identification of morality frames using in-context learning. In *Proceedings of the Fifth Workshop on Natural Language Processing and Computational Social Science (NLP+CSS)*, pages 183–196, Abu Dhabi, UAE. Association for Computational Linguistics.

Sergio Segura, Gordon Fraser, Ana B. Sanchez, and Antonio Ruiz-Cortés. 2016. A survey on metamorphic testing. *IEEE Transactions on Software Engineering*, 42(9):805–824.

Thibault Sellam, Dipanjan Das, and Ankur Parikh. 2020. BLEURT: Learning robust metrics for text generation. In *Proceedings of the 58th Annual Meeting of the Association for Computational Linguistics*, pages 7881–7892, Online. Association for Computational Linguistics.

Richard Shin and Benjamin Van Durme. 2022. Few-shot semantic parsing with language models trained on code. In *Proceedings of the 2022 Conference of the North American Chapter of the Association for Computational Linguistics: Human Language Technologies*, pages 5417–5425, Seattle, United States. Association for Computational Linguistics.

Chenglei Si, Zhe Gan, Zhengyuan Yang, Shuohang Wang, Jianfeng Wang, Jordan Lee Boyd-Graber, and Lijuan Wang. 2023. Prompting GPT-3 to be reliable. In *The Eleventh International Conference on Learning Representations*.

Yibo Sun, Duyu Tang, Nan Duan, Jianshu Ji, Guihong Cao, Xiaocheng Feng, Bing Qin, Ting Liu, and Ming Zhou. 2018. Semantic parsing with syntax- and table-aware SQL generation. In *Proceedings of the 56th Annual Meeting of the Association for Computational Linguistics (Volume 1: Long Papers)*, pages 361–372, Melbourne, Australia. Association for Computational Linguistics.

Rohan Taori, Ishaan Gulrajani, Tianyi Zhang, Yann Dubois, Xuechen Li, Carlos Guestrin, Percy Liang, and Tatsunori B. Hashimoto. 2023. Stanford alpaca: An instruction-following llama model. https://github.com/tatsu-lab/stanford_alpaca.

Saeid Tizpaz-Niari, Verya Monjezi, Morgan Wagner, Shiva Darian, Krystia Reed, and Ashutosh Trivedi. 2023. Metamorphic testing and debugging of tax preparation software. In *45th IEEE/ACM International Conference on Software Engineering: Software Engineering in Society, SEIS@ICSE 2023, Melbourne, Australia, May 14-20, 2023*, pages 138–149. IEEE.

Hugo Touvron, Thibaut Lavril, Gautier Izacard, Xavier Martinet, Marie-Anne Lachaux, Timothée Lacroix, Baptiste Rozière, Naman Goyal, Eric Hambro, Faisal Azhar, Aurelien Rodriguez, Armand Joulin, Edouard Grave, and Guillaume Lample. 2023a. Llama: Open and efficient foundation language models.

Hugo Touvron, Louis Martin, Kevin R. Stone, Peter Albert, Amjad Almahairi, Yasmine Babaei, Nikolay Bashlykov, Soumya Batra, Prajjwal Bhargava, Shruti Bhosale, Daniel M. Bikel, Lukas Blecher, Cristian Cantón Ferrer, Moya Chen, Guillem Cucurull, David Esiobu, Jude Fernandes, Jeremy Fu, Wenyin Fu, Brian Fuller, Cynthia Gao, Vedanuj Goswami, Naman Goyal, Anthony S. Hartshorn, Saghar Hosseini, Rui Hou, Hakan Inan, Marcin Kardas, Viktor Kerkez, Madian Khabsa, Isabel M. Kloumann, A. V. Korenev, Punit Singh Koura, Marie-Anne Lachaux, Thibaut Lavril, Jenya Lee, Diana Liskovich, Yinghai Lu, Yuning Mao, Xavier Martinet, Todor Mihaylov, Pushkar Mishra, Igor Molybog, Yixin Nie, Andrew Poulton, Jeremy Reizenstein, Rashi Rungta, Kalyan Saladi, Alan Schelten, Ruan Silva, Eric Michael Smith, R. Subramanian, Xia Tan, Binh Tang, Ross Taylor, Adina Williams, Jian Xiang Kuan, Puxin Xu, Zhengxu Yan, Iliyan Zarov, Yuchen Zhang, Angela Fan, Melanie Kambadur, Sharan Narang, Aurelien Rodriguez, Robert Stojnic, Sergey Edunov, and Thomas Scialom. 2023b. Llama 2: Open foundation and fine-tuned chat models. *ArXiv*, abs/2307.09288.

Yizhong Wang, Yeganeh Kordi, Swaroop Mishra, Alisa Liu, Noah A. Smith, Daniel Khashabi, and Hannaneh Hajishirzi. 2023. Self-instruct: Aligning language models with self-generated instructions. In *Proceedings of the 61st Annual Meeting of the Association for Computational Linguistics (Volume 1: Long Papers)*, pages 13484–13508, Toronto, Canada. Association for Computational Linguistics.

Hengyuan Zhang, Dawei Li, Yanran Li, Chenming Shang, Chufan Shi, and Yong Jiang. 2023. Assisting language learners: Automated trans-lingual definition generation via contrastive prompt learning. In *Proceedings of the 18th Workshop on Innovative Use of NLP for Building Educational Applications (BEA 2023)*, pages 260–274, Toronto, Canada. Association for Computational Linguistics.

Shiyu Zhang, Juan Zhai, Lei Bu, Mingsong Chen, Linzhang Wang, and Xuandong Li. 2020. Automated generation of ltl specifications for smart home iot using natural language. In *2020 Design, Automation & Test in Europe Conference & Exhibition (DATE)*, pages 622–625.

A Metamorphic Relations.

Syntax and Semantics. We review the syntax and semantics of first-order logic for metamorphic specification in the context of tax preparation software. Let $X = \{X_1, X_2, \ldots, X_n\}$ is the set of variables corresponding to various fields about an individual in the tax return form and $\mathcal{F} : \mathcal{D}_1 \times \mathcal{D}_2 \times \cdots \times \mathcal{D}_n \to \mathbb{R}_{\geq 0}$ is the *federal tax return* computed by the software, where $\mathcal{D}_i$ is the domain of variable X_i. We write $\mathcal{D}$ for $\mathcal{D}_1 \times \mathcal{D}_2 \times \cdots \times \mathcal{D}_n$. These variables correspond to intuitive labels such as `age` (numerical variable), `blind` (Boolean variable), and `sts` (filing status with values such as MFJ, married filing jointly, and MFS, married filing separately). For an individual $\mathbf{x} \in \mathcal{D}$, we write $\mathbf{x}(i)$ for the value of i-th variable, or $\mathbf{x}.\mathtt{lab}$ for the value of variable `lab`. Let $\mathcal{L}$ be the set of all labels.

For labels $L \subseteq \mathcal{L}$ and inputs $\mathbf{x} \in \mathcal{D}$ and $\mathbf{y} \in \mathcal{D}$, we say that $\mathbf{y}$ is a metamorphose of $\mathbf{x}$ with the exceptions of labels L, and we write $\mathbf{x} \equiv_L \mathbf{y}$ if $\forall \ell \notin L$ we have that $\mathbf{x}.\ell = \mathbf{y}.\ell$. A metamorphic relation is a first-order logic formula with variables in X, constants from domains in $\mathcal{D}$, relation $\equiv_L$, comparisons $\{<, \leq, =, \geq, >\}$ over numeric variables, predicate $\neg$ (negation) for Boolean valued labels, real-valued function for federal tax return $\mathcal{F} : \mathcal{D} \to \mathbb{R}$, Boolean connectives $\wedge, \vee, \neg, \implies, \iff$, and quantifiers $\exists x.\phi(x)$ and $\forall x.\phi(x)$ with natural interpretations. We assume that the formulas are given in the prenex normal form, i.e. a block of quantifiers followed by a quantifier free formula.

Selected Specifications. Following (Tizpaz-Niari et al., 2023), we consider aspects of Individual Income Tax Return that relate to disability, credits, and deductions. Specifically, we focus on on fields related to the standard deductions for senior and disable individuals; the Earned Income Tax Credit (EITC), a refundable tax credits for lower income households; the Child Tax Credit (CTC), a non-refundable credit to reduce the taxes owed based on the number of qualifying children under the age of 17; the Educational Tax Credit (ETC) that helps students with the cost of higher education by lowering their owed taxes or increasing their refund; and the Itemized Deduction (ID), an option for taxpayers with significant tax deductible expenses.

We use scenarios and examples described in the policies above to synthesize metamorphic relations. Table 5 shows 33 metamorphic relations in 6 domains for the tax year 2020. For properties #9 to #12, we assume $MAGI$ (modified adjusted gross income) is equivalent to AGI. Next, we provide a brief explanation of some of these properties.

1. A senior (over age of 65) must receive similar or better tax benefits when compared to a person without the seniority who is similar in every other aspect (due to higher standard deductions for seniors).

2. A blind individual must receive similar or better tax benefits when compared to a person without the disability who is similar in every other aspect (due to higher standard deductions for blind individuals).

3. An individual with the married filing jointly (MFJ) status with a senior spouse must receive similar or higher tax benefits compared to a similar individual but without the senior spouse.

4. An individual with the married filing jointly (MFJ) status with a disabled spouse must receive similar or higher tax benefits compared to a similar individual but without the disabled spouse.

5. An individual who files with the head of household (HoH) status should receive similar or higher tax return benefits compared to a similar individual who files with the single status.

6. An individual who files the tax with the qualified widow (QW) status should receive similar or higher tax return benefits compared to a similar individual who files the tax with single status.

7. An individual who files the tax with the qualified widow (QW) status should receive similar or higher tax return benefits compared to a similar individual who files with the head of household (HoH) status.

8. An individual with the married filing separately (MFS) status who claims EITC credits should receive the same tax return compared to a similar individual (with the same status) who does not claim EITC credits.

9. An individual with the married filing jointly (MFJ) status with AGI over $56,844$ who claims EITC credits should receive the same tax return compared to a similar individual

(with the same status) who does not claim EITC credits.

10. An individual with the married filing jointly (MFJ) status with AGI less than or equal $56,844$ who claims EITC credits should receive a higher tax returns compared to a similar individual who has AGI greater than $56,844$.

11. Among two qualified individuals with EITC, one with higher EITC claims receives higher or equal tax return benefits.

12. An individual who has the investment income less than \$3,650, computed as the sum of lines 2a, 2b, 3a, and 7 in Form 1040, should receive a higher tax returns compared to a similar individual with the investment income greater than \$3,650.

13. An individual with single status with AGI less than or equal to $15,820$ who is 25 years old or older should receive a higher tax returns compared to a similar individual who is younger than 25 years old.

14. An individual with head of household status with AGI less than or equal to $15,820$ who is 25 years old or older should receive a higher tax returns compared to a similar individual who is younger than 25 years old.

15. An individual with head of household status with AGI less than or equal to $41,757$ and with one qualified children who is younger than 25 years old should receive a similar return compared to a similar individual who is 25 years or older (the age test is not relevant when having at least one qualified children).

16. An individual with qualifying widow status with AGI less than or equal to $15,820$ who is 25 years old or older without any qualified children should receive a higher tax returns compared to a similar individual who is younger than 25 years old.

17. An individual with Qualifying Widow status with AGI less than or equal to $41,757$ and with one qualified children who is younger than 25 years old should receive a similar return compared to a similar individual who is 25 years or older.

18. A married filing jointly status with AGI less than or equal to $21,710$ who is 25 years old or older without any qualified children should receive a higher tax returns compared to a similar individual who is younger than 25 years old.

19. An individual with Qualifying Widow status with AGI less than or equal to $47,646$ and with one qualified children who is younger than 25 years old should receive a similar return compared to a similar individual who is 25 years or older.

20. An individual who is qualified for EITC credit with no qualified children should receive a similar or lower tax returns compared to a similar individual with one qualified children.

21. An individual who is qualified for EITC credit with one or less qualified children should receive a similar or lower tax returns compared to a similar individual with two qualified children.

22. An individual who is qualified for EITC credit with two or less qualified children should receive a similar or lower tax returns compared to a similar individual with three qualified children.

23. An individual who is qualified for EITC credit with three or less qualified children should receive a similar tax returns compared to a similar individual with more than three qualified children.

24. Among two qualified married filing jointly (MFJ) individuals, one with higher child tax credits receives higher or equal tax return benefits.

25. This 4-property requires a comparison between four "similar" individuals since there is a relation between two variables of interests: AGI and the number of qualified children/others to claim a CTC. An individual with more qualified dependents must receive higher or similar tax return benefits than an individual with fewer dependents after adjusting for the effects of income levels on the calculations of both the final return and the amounts of CTC claims. Expressing this property requires holding the income of two individuals

the same per each qualified number of children/others.

26. An individual with the married filing separately (MFS) status who claims CTC credits should receive similar tax benefits compared to a similar individual with MFS status who does not claim CTC.

27. An individual with the married filing jointly (MFJ) status with AGI over $180k$ who claims ETC should receive similar tax benefits compared to a similar individual who does not claim ETC.

28. An individual with the married filing jointly (MFJ) status with AGI below $160k$ who claims ETC received higher or similar tax return benefits compared to a similar individual who does not claim ETC or claims a lower amount of ETC credit.

29. This 4-property requires a comparison between four "similar" individuals as the rule changes for individuals with AGI below 160k and between 160k and 180k. By holding AGI constant between two individuals with AGI below 160k (varying the ETC claims) and two individuals with AGI between 160k and 180k (varying the ETC claims with the same rate), the property requires that individuals with lower income (below $160k$) receive higher or similar tax returns.

30. An individual who files with medical/dental expenses (MDE) below 7.5% of their AGI and itemizes their deductions receives the same return as a similar individual with no MDE claims.

31. An individual who files with a standard deduction who claims itemized deduction (Line 12) should receive similar tax returns compared to a similar individual who does not claim itemized deduction.

32. An individual who files with itemized deductions below the standard deductions receive a lower or similar tax return benefits compared to a similar individual who files with the standard deductions.

33. An individual who files with itemized deductions above the standard deductions receive a higher or similar tax return benefits compared to a similar individual who claims standard deductions.

Table 5: Metamorphic properties for five domains in the US tax (2020) policies. $\mathcal{F}$ is federal tax return where negative values mean the individual owns payment to the IRS, sts is filing status, s_lab is spouse's field lab, MFJ: married filing jointly, MFS is married filing separately, S is single filing, HoH is head of household filing, QW is qualifying widow filing, AGI is adjusted gross income, $L27$ is line 27 of IRS 1040 for Earned Income Tax Credit (EITC), QC is the number of qualified children, OD is the number of other dependents, CTC is child tax credits, $L19$ is line 19 of IRS 1040 for Child Tax Credit (CTC), $L29$ is line 29 of IRS 1040 for Education Tax Credit (ETC), MDE is medical/dental expenses reported in line 1 of schedule A, iz is to use itemized deductions (ID) vs. standard deductions, and $L12$ is total itemized deductions (ID) from schedule A.

Id	Domain	Metamorphic Property
1	Disability	$\forall \mathbf{x}, \mathbf{y}((\mathbf{x} \equiv_{age} \mathbf{y}) \land (\mathbf{x}.age \geq 65) \land (\mathbf{y}.age < 65)) \implies \mathcal{F}(\mathbf{x}) \geq \mathcal{F}(\mathbf{y})$
2	Disability	$\forall \mathbf{x}, \mathbf{y}((\mathbf{x} \equiv_{blind} \mathbf{y}) \land (\mathbf{x}.blind \land \neg \mathbf{y}.blind)) \implies \mathcal{F}(\mathbf{x}) \geq \mathcal{F}(\mathbf{y})$
3	Disability	$\forall \mathbf{x}(\mathbf{x}.sts = MFJ) \implies \forall \mathbf{y}((\mathbf{x} \equiv_{s\_age} \mathbf{y}) \land (\mathbf{x}.s\_age \geq 65) \land (\mathbf{y}.s\_age < 65)) \implies \mathcal{F}(\mathbf{x}) \geq \mathcal{F}(\mathbf{y})$
4	Disability	$\forall \mathbf{x}(\mathbf{x}.sts = MFJ) \implies \forall \mathbf{y}((\mathbf{x} \equiv_{s\_blind} \mathbf{y}) \land (\mathbf{x}.s\_blind \land \neg \mathbf{y}.s\_blind)) \implies \mathcal{F}(\mathbf{x}) \geq \mathcal{F}(\mathbf{y})$
5	Status	$\forall \mathbf{x}, \mathbf{y}((\mathbf{x} \equiv_{sts} \mathbf{y}) \land (\mathbf{x}.sts = HoH) \land (\mathbf{y}.sts = S)) \implies \mathcal{F}(\mathbf{x}) \geq \mathcal{F}(\mathbf{y})$
6	Status	$\forall \mathbf{x}, \mathbf{y}((\mathbf{x} \equiv_{sts} \mathbf{y}) \land (\mathbf{x}.sts = QW) \land (\mathbf{y}.sts = S)) \implies \mathcal{F}(\mathbf{x}) \geq \mathcal{F}(\mathbf{y})$
7	Status	$\forall \mathbf{x}, \mathbf{y}((\mathbf{x} \equiv_{sts} \mathbf{y}) \land (\mathbf{x}.sts = QW) \land (\mathbf{y}.sts = HoH)) \implies \mathcal{F}(\mathbf{x}) \geq \mathcal{F}(\mathbf{y})$
8	EITC	$\forall \mathbf{x}(\mathbf{x}.sts = MFS) \implies \forall \mathbf{y}(\mathbf{x} \equiv_{L27} \mathbf{y} \land \mathbf{x}.L27 > 0.0 \land \mathbf{y}.L27 = 0.0) \implies \mathcal{F}(\mathbf{x}) = \mathcal{F}(\mathbf{y})$
9	EITC	$\forall \mathbf{x}(\mathbf{x}.sts = MFJ) \land (\mathbf{x}.AGI > 56,844) \implies \forall \mathbf{y}(\mathbf{x} \equiv_{L27} \mathbf{y} \land \mathbf{x}.L27 > 0.0 \land \mathbf{y}.L27 = 0.0) \implies \mathcal{F}(\mathbf{x}) = \mathcal{F}(\mathbf{y})$
10	EITC	$\forall \mathbf{x}((\mathbf{x}.sts = MFJ) \land (\mathbf{x}.L27 > 0.0)) \implies \forall \mathbf{y}(\mathbf{x} \equiv_{AGI} \mathbf{y} \land \mathbf{x}.AGI \leq 56,844 \land \mathbf{y}.AGI > 56,844) \implies \mathcal{F}(\mathbf{x}) \geq \mathcal{F}(\mathbf{y})$
11	EITC	$\forall \mathbf{x}(\mathbf{x}.sts = MFJ) \land (\mathbf{x}.AGI \leq 56,844) \implies \forall \mathbf{y}((\mathbf{x} \equiv_{L27} \mathbf{y}) \land \mathbf{x}.L27 \geq \mathbf{y}.L27) \implies \mathcal{F}(\mathbf{x}) \geq \mathcal{F}(\mathbf{y})$
12	EITC	$\forall \mathbf{x}(\mathbf{x}.L27 > 0.0) \forall \mathbf{y}(\mathbf{x} \equiv_{\{L2a,L2b,3b,7\}} \mathbf{y} \land \mathbf{x}.L2a + \mathbf{x}.L2b + \mathbf{x}.L3b + \mathbf{x}.L7 > 3,650) \land \mathbf{y}.L2a + \mathbf{y}.L2b + \mathbf{y}.L3b + \mathbf{y}.L7 \leq 3,650) \implies \mathcal{F}(\mathbf{x}) \leq \mathcal{F}(\mathbf{y})$
13	EITC	$\forall \mathbf{x}(\mathbf{x}.sts = S) \land (\mathbf{x}.AGI \leq 15,820) \land (\mathbf{x}.L27 > 0.0) \implies \forall \mathbf{y}((\mathbf{x} \equiv_{Age} \mathbf{y}) \land (\mathbf{x}.Age < 25) \land (\mathbf{y}.Age \geq 25)) \implies \mathcal{F}(\mathbf{x}) < \mathcal{F}(\mathbf{y})$
14	EITC	$\forall \mathbf{x}(\mathbf{x}.sts = HoH) \land (\mathbf{x}.AGI \leq 15,820) \land (\mathbf{x}.L27 > 0.0) \land (\mathbf{x}.QC = 0) \implies \forall \mathbf{y}((\mathbf{x} \equiv_{Age} \mathbf{y}) \land (\mathbf{x}.Age < 25) \land (\mathbf{y}.Age \geq 25)) \implies \mathcal{F}(\mathbf{x}) < \mathcal{F}(\mathbf{y})$
15	EITC	$\forall \mathbf{x}(\mathbf{x}.sts = HoH) \land (\mathbf{x}.AGI \leq 41,756) \land (\mathbf{x}.L27 > 0.0) \land (\mathbf{x}.QC = 1) \implies \forall \mathbf{y}((\mathbf{x} \equiv_{Age} \mathbf{y}) \land (\mathbf{x}.Age < 25) \land (\mathbf{y}.Age \geq 25)) \implies \mathcal{F}(\mathbf{x}) = \mathcal{F}(\mathbf{y})$
16	EITC	$\forall \mathbf{x}(\mathbf{x}.sts = QW) \land (\mathbf{x}.AGI \leq 15,820) \land (\mathbf{x}.L27 > 0.0) \land (\mathbf{x}.QC = 0) \implies \forall \mathbf{y}((\mathbf{x} \equiv_{Age} \mathbf{y}) \land (\mathbf{x}.Age < 25) \land (\mathbf{y}.Age \geq 25)) \implies \mathcal{F}(\mathbf{x}) < \mathcal{F}(\mathbf{y})$
17	EITC	$\forall \mathbf{x}(\mathbf{x}.sts = QW) \land (\mathbf{x}.AGI \leq 41,756) \land (\mathbf{x}.L27 > 0.0) \land (\mathbf{x}.QC = 1) \implies \forall \mathbf{y}((\mathbf{x} \equiv_{Age} \mathbf{y}) \land (\mathbf{x}.Age < 25) \land (\mathbf{y}.Age \geq 25)) \implies \mathcal{F}(\mathbf{x}) = \mathcal{F}(\mathbf{y})$
18	EITC	$\forall \mathbf{x}(\mathbf{x}.sts = MFJ) \land (\mathbf{x}.AGI \leq 21,710) \land (\mathbf{x}.L27 > 0.0) \land (\mathbf{x}.QC = 0) \implies \forall \mathbf{y}((\mathbf{x} \equiv_{Age} \mathbf{y}) \land (\mathbf{x}.Age < 25) \land (\mathbf{y}.Age \geq 25)) \implies \mathcal{F}(\mathbf{x}) < \mathcal{F}(\mathbf{y})$
19	EITC	$\forall \mathbf{x}(\mathbf{x}.sts = MFJ) \land (\mathbf{x}.AGI \leq 47,646) \land (\mathbf{x}.L27 > 0.0) \land (\mathbf{x}.QC = 1) \implies \forall \mathbf{y}((\mathbf{x} \equiv_{Age} \mathbf{y}) \land (\mathbf{x}.Age < 25) \land (\mathbf{y}.Age \geq 25)) \implies \mathcal{F}(\mathbf{x}) = \mathcal{F}(\mathbf{y})$
20	EITC	$\forall \mathbf{x}(\mathbf{x}.L27 > 0.0) \land (\mathbf{x}.QC = 0) \implies \forall \mathbf{y}((\mathbf{x} \equiv_{QC} \mathbf{y}) \land (\mathbf{y}.QC = 1) \implies \mathcal{F}(\mathbf{x}) \leq \mathcal{F}(\mathbf{y})$

Continuation of Previous Table.

Id	Domain	Metamorphic Property
21	EITC	$\forall \mathbf{x}(\mathbf{x}.L27{>}0.0)\wedge(\mathbf{x}.QC{\leq}1) \implies \forall \mathbf{y}((\mathbf{x}{\equiv_{QC}}\mathbf{y})\wedge(\mathbf{y}.QC{=}2) \implies \mathcal{F}(\mathbf{x}){\leq}\mathcal{F}(\mathbf{y})$
22	EITC	$\forall \mathbf{x}(\mathbf{x}.L27{>}0.0)\wedge(\mathbf{x}.QC{\leq}2) \implies \forall \mathbf{y}((\mathbf{x}{\equiv_{QC}}\mathbf{y})\wedge(\mathbf{y}.QC{=}3) \implies \mathcal{F}(\mathbf{x}){\leq}\mathcal{F}(\mathbf{y})$
23	EITC	$\forall \mathbf{x}(\mathbf{x}.L27{>}0.0)\wedge(\mathbf{x}.QC{=}3) \implies \forall \mathbf{y}((\mathbf{x}{\equiv_{QC}}\mathbf{y})\wedge(\mathbf{y}.QC{>}3) \implies \mathcal{F}(\mathbf{x}){=}\mathcal{F}(\mathbf{y})$
24	CTC	$\forall \mathbf{x}(\mathbf{x}.sts{=}MFS)\wedge(\mathbf{x}.AGI{\leq}200k) \implies$ $\forall \mathbf{y}((\mathbf{x}{\equiv_{L19}}\mathbf{y})\wedge(\mathbf{x}.L19{\geq}\mathbf{y}.L19)) \implies \mathcal{F}(\mathbf{x}){\geq}\mathcal{F}(\mathbf{y}))$
25	CTC	$\forall \mathbf{x},\mathbf{x}'(\mathbf{x}.sts{=}\mathbf{x}'.sts{=}MFJ)\wedge(\mathbf{x}.AGI{<}400k)\wedge(\mathbf{x}'.AGI{\geq}400k)\wedge\lceil \mathbf{x}'.AGI{-}400k\rceil_{1k}{*}$ $0.05{<}\mathbf{x}'.QC * 2k + \mathbf{x}.OD * 0.5k \implies \forall \mathbf{y},\mathbf{y}'(\mathbf{x}{\equiv_{\{QC,OD\}}}\mathbf{y})\wedge(\mathbf{x}'{\equiv_{\{QC,OD\}}}\mathbf{y}') \wedge$ $(0{\leq}\mathbf{y}.QC{=}\mathbf{y}'.QC{\leq}\mathbf{x}.QC{=}\mathbf{x}'.QC \leq 10) \wedge (0{\leq}\mathbf{y}.OD{=}\mathbf{y}'.OD \leq \mathbf{x}.OD{=}\mathbf{x}'.OD \leq$ $10) \implies (\mathcal{F}(\mathbf{x}) - \mathcal{F}(y)) \geq (\mathcal{F}(x') - \mathcal{F}(y'))$
26	ETC	$\forall \mathbf{x}(\mathbf{x}.sts = MFS) \implies \forall \mathbf{y}(\mathbf{x}{\equiv_{L29}}\mathbf{y} \wedge \mathbf{x}.L29 > 0.0 \wedge \mathbf{y}.L29 = 0.0) \implies$ $\mathcal{F}(\mathbf{x}){=}\mathcal{F}(\mathbf{y})$
27	ETC	$\forall \mathbf{x}(\mathbf{x}.sts{=}MFJ) \wedge (\mathbf{x}.AGI{\geq}180k) \implies \forall \mathbf{y}(\mathbf{x}{\equiv_{L29}}\mathbf{y} \wedge \mathbf{x}.L29{>}0.0 \wedge$ $\mathbf{y}.L29{=}0.0) \implies \mathcal{F}(\mathbf{x}){=}\mathcal{F}(\mathbf{y})$
28	ETC	$\forall \mathbf{x}(\mathbf{x}.sts{=}MFJ) \wedge (\mathbf{x}.AGI{\leq}160k) \implies \forall \mathbf{y}(\mathbf{x}{\equiv_{L29}}\mathbf{y} \wedge$ $\mathbf{x}.L29{\geq}\mathbf{y}.L29) \implies \mathcal{F}(\mathbf{x}){\geq}\mathcal{F}(\mathbf{y})$
29	ETC	$\forall \mathbf{x},\mathbf{x}'(\mathbf{x}.sts{=}\mathbf{x}'.sts{=}MFJ) \wedge (\mathbf{x}.AGI{\leq}160k) \wedge (160k{<}\mathbf{x}'.AGI{<}180k) \implies$ $\forall \mathbf{y},\mathbf{y}'((\mathbf{x} \equiv_{L29} \mathbf{y}) \wedge (\mathbf{x}' \equiv_{L29} \mathbf{y}') \wedge (\mathbf{x}.L29 = \mathbf{x}'.L29 \geq \mathbf{y}.L29 =$ $\mathbf{y}'.L29)) \implies (\mathcal{F}(\mathbf{x}) - \mathcal{F}(y)) \geq (\mathcal{F}(x') - \mathcal{F}(y'))$
30	ID	$\forall \mathbf{x},\mathbf{y}(\mathbf{x}{\equiv_{MDE}}\mathbf{y}) \wedge (\mathbf{x}.MDE{\leq}\mathbf{x}.AGI * 7.5\%) \wedge (\mathbf{y}.MDE{=}0.0) \implies \mathcal{F}(\mathbf{x}){=}\mathcal{F}(\mathbf{y})$
31	ID	$\forall \mathbf{x}(\neg \mathbf{x}.iz) \implies \forall \mathbf{y}(\mathbf{x}{\equiv_{MDE}}\mathbf{y} \wedge \mathbf{x}.MDE{>}0.0 \wedge \mathbf{y}.MDE{=}0.0) \implies \mathcal{F}(\mathbf{x}){=}\mathcal{F}(\mathbf{y})$
32	ID	$\forall \mathbf{x}(\mathbf{x}.sts{=}MFJ) \implies$ $\forall \mathbf{y}((\mathbf{x}{\equiv_{iz,L12}}\mathbf{y})\wedge(\mathbf{x}.iz{\wedge}\neg\mathbf{y}.iz)\wedge(\mathbf{x}.L12{\leq}24.8k{\wedge}\mathbf{y}.L12{=}0.0)) \implies \mathcal{F}(\mathbf{x}){\leq}\mathcal{F}(\mathbf{y})$
33	ID	$\forall \mathbf{x}(\mathbf{x}.sts{=}MFJ) \implies$ $\forall \mathbf{y}((\mathbf{x}{\equiv_{iz,L12}}\mathbf{y})\wedge(\mathbf{x}.iz{\wedge}\neg\mathbf{y}.iz)\wedge(\mathbf{x}.L12{>}24.8k{\wedge}\mathbf{y}.L12{=}0.0)) \implies \mathcal{F}(\mathbf{x}){\geq}\mathcal{F}(\mathbf{y})$

B Prompt Examples

Figure 1: Example of an End2End prompt, that looks at generating predicates and FOL in the same prompt. This is an example for nshot = 1; the example was omitted and another added for 0-shot and 2-shot respectively.

```
For the following statement.

"A senior (over age of 65) must receive similar or better tax benefits when compared to a person without the
seniority who is similar in every other aspect (due to higher standard deductions for seniors)."

In this case, the first order predicates are:

Senior(x) : x is an individual who is senior.

Tax(t, x): t is the tax paid by individual x

EqualExcept(x, z, S): where x and z are equal individuals except differing only by the predicates in set S.

Using these predicates, you can generate the following rules in first order logic.

∀x∀y(Senior(x)  ∧ EqualExcept(x,y,{Senior}) → Tax(t,x) ≤ Tax(t,y)

In the following statement

"An individual with the married filing jointly (MFJ) status with a senior spouse must receive  similar or
higher tax benefits compared to a similar individual but without the senior spouse."

In this statement, what would the predicates look like?

Generation Format: you SHOULD ALWAYS generate your answer in the following format

{your generated predicates}

{your generated first order logic statement}

DO NOT generate any other text.
```

Figure 2: Example of a prompt to generate predicates. The prompt is the same for explicit and implicit setups. This is an example for nshot = 1; the example was omitted and another added for 0-shot and 2-shot respectively.

```
For the following statement.

"A senior (over age of 65) must receive similar or better tax benefits when compared to a
person without the seniority who is similar in every other aspect (due to higher standard
deductions for seniors)."

The first order predicates for this statement would look like:
Senior(x) : x is an individual who is senior.
Tax(t, x): t is the tax paid by individual x
EqualExcept(x, z, S): where x and z are equal individuals except differing only by the
predicates in set S.

For the following statement.
"An individual with the married filing jointly (MFJ) status with a senior spouse must receive
similar or higher tax benefits compared to a similar individual but without the senior
spouse."

In this statement, what would the predicates look like?
Generation Format: you SHOULD ALWAYS generate the predicates in the following format
{your generated predicates}
DO NOT generate any other text.
```

Figure 3: Example of a prompt to generate FOL, given that predicates were already generated. This setup is only used in explicit cases (as predicates are provided through context in implicit cases). This is an example for nshot = 1; the example was omitted and another added for 0-shot and 2-shot respectively.

```
Take a look at the following statement.
"A senior (over age of 65) must receive similar or better tax benefits when compared to a person without the seniority who is
similar in every other aspect (due to higher standard deductions for seniors)."

The first order predicates for this statement would look like:
Senior(x) : x is an individual who is senior.
Tax(t, x): t is the tax paid by individual x
EqualExcept(x, z, S): where x and z are equal individuals except differing only by the predicates in set S.

These predicates can be used to generate the following first order logic.
∀x∀y(Senior(x)  ∧ EqualExcept(x,y,{Senior}) → Tax(t,x) ≤ Tax(t,y)
For the following statement.

"An individual with the married filing jointly (MFJ) status with a senior spouse must receive similar or higher tax benefits
compared to a similar individual but without the senior spouse."

The first order predicates for this statement would look like:
Senior(x): x is an individual who is senior.
MarriedFilingJointly(x): x has the married filing jointly status.
Tax(t, x): t is the tax paid by individual x.
Spouse(x, y): x is the spouse of y.
EqualExcept(x, z, S): where x and z are equal individuals except differing only by the predicates in set S.
Using these predicates, represent the statement in first order logic.
Generation Format: you SHOULD ALWAYS generate the first order logic in the following format
{your generated first order logic statement}
DO NOT generate any other text.
```

C Example Generations for Annotation Rubric

Metamorphic Statement	Generated Predicates	Generated First Order Logic	Explanation	Score
An individual with the married filing jointly (MFJ) status with AGI over $56,844 who claims EITC credits should receive the same tax return compared to a similar individual (with the same status) who does not claim EITC credits.	MFJ(x): x is an individual with the married filing jointly status. AGI(y, x): y is the adjusted gross income of individual x. ClaimEITC(x): x claims EITC credits. TaxReturn(t, x): t is the tax return of individual x. EqualExcept(x, z, S): where x and z are equal individuals except differing only by the predicates in set S.	$\forall x \forall y (MFJ(x) \land AGI(y,x) > 56844 \land ClaimEITC(x) \land EqualExcept(x,y,ClaimEITC) \implies TaxReturn(t,x) = TaxReturn(t,y)$	The model correctly predicts that AGI criteria is applicable to both individuals in question, and only differs on EITC status.	5
An individual with single status with AGI less than or equal to $15,820 who is 25 years old or older should receive a higher tax returns compared to a similar individual who is younger than 25 years old.	Single(x): x is an individual with single status. AGI(x, a): x has adjusted gross income of a. Younger(x, y): x is younger than y years old. TaxReturns(r, x): x receives r in tax returns.	$\forall x \forall y (Single(x) \land AGI(x, a) \leq 15820 \land Older(x, 25) \land Younger(y, 25) \land EqualExcept(x,y,AGI) \implies TaxReturns(r, x) > TaxReturns(r, y)$	All the predicates have been generated correctly. However, the predicate "EqualExcept" should only apply to age of the individual and not the AGI. This makes some semantic sense, but is incorrect (not usable).	4
An individual who files the tax with the qualified widow (QW) status should receive similar or higher tax return benefits compared to a similar individual who files the tax with single status.	QW(x): x is an individual who files the tax with the qualified widow status. Single(x): x is an individual who files the tax with single status. TaxReturn(t, x): t is the tax return received by individual x. SimilarOrHigher(x, y): individual x receives similar or higher tax return benefits compared to individual y.	$\forall x \forall y (QW(x) \land EqualExcept(x,y,QW) \implies SimilarOrHigher(x,y)$	The system makes a mistake in predicates - it does not use the "Single" status to make a judgement on tax return status.	3
An individual with the married filing jointly (MFJ) status with a disabled spouse must receive similar or higher tax benefits compared to a similar individual but without the disabled spouse.	MFJ(x): x is an individual with the married filing jointly status. Disabled(y): y is an individual who is disabled. Tax(t, x): t is the tax paid by individual x. SimilarOrHigher(x, z, S): where x and z are similar individuals except for the predicates in set S.	$\forall x \forall y (MFJ(x) \land Disabled(y) \land SimilarOrHigher(x, y, Disabled) \implies Tax(t, x) \leq Tax(t, y)$	Here, the system misses the predicate "Spouse(x)". In addition to this, the greater than operator is flipped (or there is a mistake in the "Tax(t, x)" predicate as well).	2
An individual with the married filing jointly (MFJ) status with a senior spouse must receive similar or higher tax benefits compared to a similar individual but without the senior spouse.	MFJ(x): x is an individual with the married filing jointly status. SeniorSpouse(y): y is a senior spouse of an individual. Tax(t, x): t is the tax paid by individual x. EqualExcept(x, z, S): where x and z are equal individuals except differing only by the predicates in set S.	$\forall x \forall y (MFJ(x) \land SeniorSpouse(y) \land EqualExcept(x, y, MFJ, SeniorSpouse) \implies Tax(t, x) \leq Tax(t, y)$	Here, the SeniorSpouse is incorrectly applied to individual y. Additionally, the predicate EqualExcept takes more than one predicate (and is redundant). Lastly, the $\leq$ is flipped (or the "Tax" predicate is incorrect).	1

Table 6: In this table, we show examples of our qualitative score rubric. A rating of 5 usually means that the generated logic can be used for metamorphic testing. All these examples were sourced from 2-shot examples in the explicit setup.

AsyLex: A Dataset for Legal Language Processing of Refugee Claims

Claire Barale[1] **Mark Klaisoongnoen**[2] **Pasquale Minervini**[1]
Michael Rovatsos[1] **Nehal Bhuta**[3]
[1]School of Informatics, The University of Edinburgh
[2]EPCC, The University of Edinburgh [3]School of Law, The University of Edinburgh
claire.barale@ed.ac.uk

Abstract

Advancements in natural language processing (NLP) and language models have demonstrated immense potential in the legal domain, enabling automated analysis and comprehension of legal texts. However, developing robust models in Legal NLP is significantly challenged by the scarcity of resources. This paper presents AsyLex, the first dataset specifically designed for Refugee Law applications to address this gap. The dataset introduces 59,112 documents on refugee status determination in Canada from 1996 to 2022, providing researchers and practitioners with essential material for training and evaluating NLP models for legal research and case review. Case review is defined as entity extraction and outcome prediction tasks. The dataset includes 19,115 gold-standard human-labeled annotations for 20 legally relevant entity types curated with the help of legal experts and 1,682 gold-standard labeled documents for the case outcome. Furthermore, we supply the corresponding trained entity extraction models and the resulting labeled entities generated through the inference process on AsyLex. Four supplementary features are obtained through rule-based extraction. We demonstrate the usefulness of our dataset on the legal judgment prediction task to predict the binary outcome and test a set of baselines using the text of the documents and our annotations. We observe that models pretrained on similar legal documents reach better scores, suggesting that acquiring more datasets for specialized domains such as law is crucial. The dataset is available at https://huggingface.co/datasets/clairebarale/AsyLex.

1 Introduction

While large language models (LLMs) have gained significant attention in NLP, many real-world applications have yet to leverage their capabilities fully. One of the main challenges lies in the fact that these models heavily rely on training or fine-tuning models with specific datasets to effectively transfer their capabilities to real-world and specialized applications. However, collecting such datasets is often time-consuming and expensive, primarily due to the need for human annotation. This challenge becomes even more pronounced in specialized domains where human annotators require domain expertise. Collecting thousands of annotations is a barrier to developing advanced NLP tools that support researchers and practitioners in the legal domain.

	Main text	Case cover	Case outcome
Documents	59,112	45,882	32,627
Sentences	4,946,438	-	53,977
Paragraphs	1,781,240	-	-
Labels	16	8	3
Labeled (human)	16,628	2,487	1,682
Labeled (rule-based)	-	57,408	-
Labeled (inferred)	6,154,226	123,802	30,944

Table 1: Overview of AsyLex

Refugee Law is a specific area of law that currently lacks publicly available datasets and benchmarks to evaluate NLP applications and compare their performance with standard baselines. Lawyers specializing in Refugee Law devote a significant amount of time to reviewing past cases to prepare for new ones. This process of legal research and case review is not only time-consuming but also expensive. Given the limited resources and funding available in Refugee Law, where a majority of claimants rely on legal aid, it becomes even more critical to find ways to free up time and speed up the case review process.

The availability of a comprehensive dataset in Refugee Law would have significant benefits. It would enable lawyers to efficiently search and analyze relevant cases, extract valuable insights, and apply them to new cases. By streamlining the case review process, lawyers could save time, reduce

Proceedings of the Natural Legal Language Processing Workshop 2023, pages 244–257
December 7, 2023

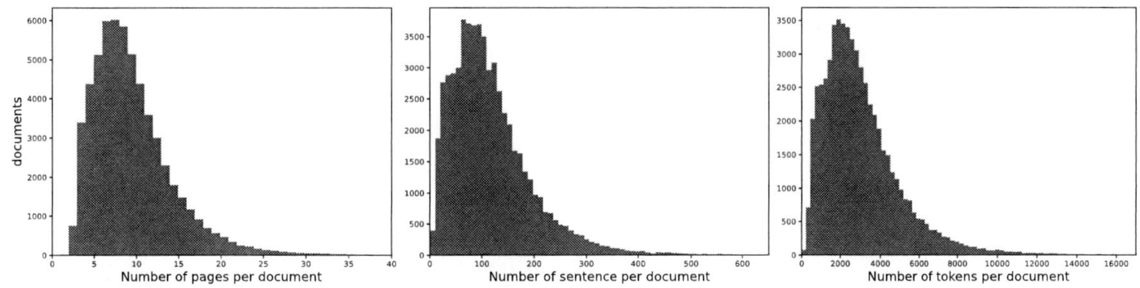

Figure 1: Distribution of text input length, measured in pages, sentences, and tokens

costs, and ultimately provide more efficient legal assistance to those seeking refugee protection. The absence of a Refugee Law dataset affects lawyers and claimants, as Refugee Status Determination (RSD) plays a pivotal role in determining refugee protection. Refugee protection decisions directly impact the lives of the approximately 4.6 million asylum seekers worldwide as of mid-2022[1]. To provide a concrete example, 48,014 new claims and 10,055 appeals were filed[2] in Canada alone in 2021. Processing times of refugee claims range from a few months to several years.

This variation in processing times exacerbates the uncertainty and instability experienced by asylum seekers. By enhancing access to data, we aim to promote fairness, effectiveness, and improved outcomes for individuals seeking refuge globally. Automating aspects of case review and providing high-quality data can facilitate better access to legal counseling and support for claimants.

Our dataset is particularly valuable because we collected a total of 76,523 gold annotations (both from human labeling and rule-based) and trained specific information extraction models to gain insights and structure the dataset (section 3) to facilitate two tasks: (1) entity extraction for legal search and (2) legal judgment prediction. Both tasks, according to lawyers we consulted, have the potential to help draft new claims for refugee protection. We experiment with judgment prediction on different baseline masked language models to showcase the dataset's potential (section 4).

AsyLex contributes directly to applying NLP in high-stakes legal domains and as a novel research asset to the NLP research community. Specifically, our contributions are as follows:

1. We provide the anonymized raw text of the decision documents by case, by paragraphs, and by sentences;
2. We implement a state-of-the-art methodology for annotating our dataset, with a primary emphasis on speed and replicability for other datasets;
3. We provide documents labeled with their decision outcome for the task of legal judgment prediction;
4. We provide the set of extracted sentences that directly indicates the determination of each case with gold-standard annotations on the outcome;
5. We provide gold-labeled data for relevant legal entity types for entity extraction; and
6. We use state-of-the-art Transformer-based models for text classification to accurately predict the outcome of cases and evaluate the presented data.

In addition to the data, the code of the experiments is public and can be found at: `https://github.com/clairebarale/AsyLex`.

2 Related Work

Legal NLP Legal NLP is an active and promising field of research. Legal information is predominantly conveyed through text, with crucial details typically documented in written form. In principle, this makes the law an ideal domain for leveraging natural language processing techniques. However, applying NLP in the legal domain brings about notable challenges. These challenges arise from the distinct structure, specialized vocabulary, contextual nuances, importance of legal citations, and high stakes in legal applications. A wide range of tasks and functionalities have been explored in

[1]United Nations High Commissioner for Refugees report: `https://www.unhcr.org/global-trends-report-2022`

[2]`https://irb.gc.ca/en/statistics/Pages/index.aspx`

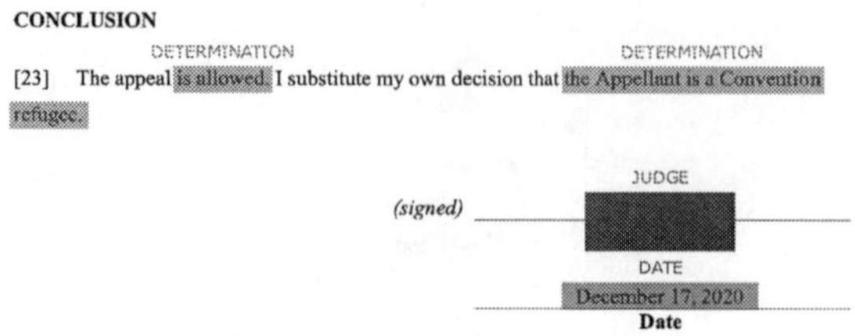

Figure 2: Example of the end of a case document containing the determination sentence, the name of the judge, and the date of the decision

legal NLP (Zhong et al., 2018), such as legal summarization (Elaraby and Litman, 2022; Aumiller et al., 2022), legal information extraction and retrieval (Bommarito II et al., 2021; Brüninghaus and Ashley, 2001; Chalkidis et al., 2021), legal question answering, automatic text generation, text classification (Chalkidis et al., 2022b, 2019c), legal judgment prediction (Katz et al., 2017; Branting et al., 2019, 2018; Chalkidis et al., 2019a) or multi-task benchmarks (Chalkidis et al., 2022a).

With this dataset, we target two tasks for **Case Review**: **(i) Entity Extraction** and **(ii) Legal Judgment Prediction**. Legal judgment prediction is a common task in legal AI. Work has been conducted on legal datasets gathering decisions from the Supreme Court of the United States (Katz et al., 2017; Martin et al., 2004; Ruger et al., 2004a; Undavia et al., 2018) or the European Court of human rights (Medvedeva et al., 2020; Kaur and Bozic, 2019). Similar studies have been conducted on asylum decision data sets (Chen and Eagel, 2017; Dunn et al., 2017; Rehaag, 2012). However, most of these works rely on statistical data rather than text documents. One reason is the lack of specialized language resources and datasets available in law. We recognize this gap and aim to address it by providing a new dataset of legal texts, thereby contributing to legal NLP research. Legal information extraction and classification are difficult tasks because approaches are mostly supervised and, therefore, require precisely labeled datasets.

Legal NLP Datasets While large language models have recently made natural language tasks more accessible, their utilization in the legal domain has been relatively limited. One of the reasons behind this is the need to adapt these models to legal applications (Gururangan et al., 2020). These are typically trained on general corpora and may not fully capture the intricacies of legal text, as shown by previous studies (Barale et al., 2023). In our information extraction pipeline, we observed that LegalBERT outperformed RoBERTa in accuracy, highlighting the significance of fine-tuning models specifically for legal tasks.

A range of datasets for legal NLP tasks in English exists in Tax Law (Holzenberger et al., 2020), European Legislation and the European Court of Human Rights (Chalkidis et al., 2019b,a), Corporate and Contract Law (Hendrycks et al., 2021; Tuggener et al., 2020), Supreme Court cases and US court cases (Ruger et al., 2004b; Zheng et al., 2021). LeXFiles is the most comprehensive to date (Chalkidis et al., 2023). However, no such dataset is available for refugee decisions. To further investigate how well large language models perform on specialized tasks and to ensure advances also benefit the field of Refugee Law, we curated the first-ever dataset of refugee status determination cases in English. This dataset will serve as a valuable resource to train and evaluate models tailored to the unique challenges and requirements of Refugee Law.

3 AsyLex: a Case Review Dataset

Case Review Our dataset focuses on facilitating the legal application of case review. Case review includes similar past case retrieval and case analysis and is an essential part of legal research. Lawyers face the challenge of dealing with an overwhelming number of cases under significant time constraints. Additionally, they require valuable insights to guide them in identifying critical elements for new application drafting. The anticipated benefit of our research is to expedite the legal case review process while offering supplementary insights to enhance efficiency.

The dataset contains labeled data suited for two NLP tasks: **(1) Entity extraction** and **(2) Legal Judgment Prediction**. For the first task of interest, we offer a total of 19,115 human-labeled annotated samples, data spanning across 22 categories, an additional 57,408 annotations using rule-based extraction on the *case cover*, along with 6,278,028 silver-standard labeled samples inferred through a named-entity recognition model presented in details in Barale et al. (2023). For the *case cover*, which constitutes the first page of each case and contains meta-data about each document, we annotated 346 documents. Details of the number of labeled samples per category are shown in Table 3 for the *case cover* and in Table 4 for the full body

	Case #123259 – *Initial* Case Cover *shown in Annex*	Case #100049
extracted_dates	'april 04 , 2019', '2020', 'december 17, 2020', 'december 15, 2020'	'august 14, 2013', 'august 15, 2013', '2013'
loc_hearing	['toronto', 'on']	['ottawa', 'ontario', 'montreal', 'quebec']
tribunal	['refugee appeal division']	['immigration appeal division']
public_private_hearing	-	-
in_chamber_virtual	-	['videoconference']
judge	-	dana kean
date_decision	-	-
text_case_cover	immigration and refugee board...	immigration and refugee board...

Table 2: Example of two case documents' *Case Cover* and the additional structured information provided in AsyLex

Label	gold	inferred
extracted_dates	1,219	45,884
loc_hearing	871	43,715
tribunal	278	34,203
public_private_hearing	307	-
in_chamber_virtual	7,224	-
judge_name	18,691	-
date_decision	31,186	-
person	119	-

Table 3: Entities Annotations on the *Case Cover*

Label	gold	inferred
CLAIMANT_EVENT	3,730	-
CLAIMANT_INFO	687	209,623
GPE	1,545	1,027,918
NORP	206	206,927
ORG	1,041	748,612
PROCEDURE	1,788	617,659
CREDIBILITY	1,020	464,504
DETERMINATION	342	116,489
DOC_EVIDENCE	1,878	861,357
EXPLANATION	1,274	362,973
DATE	1,474	975,625
LAW	874	317,277
LAW_CASE	211	125,497
LAW_REPORT	47	30,892
LEGAL_GROUND	158	88,873
PERSON	353	-

Table 4: Entities Annotations on the *Main Text*

text of the documents.

For the second task of interest, we provide a comprehensive collection of data for legal judgment prediction, which comprises a test set with 1,682 gold-standard classified documents and a train set with 30,944 classified documents. In addition, we provide the raw text of the document cases in full text and split it into sentences, each presented with their corresponding case number (decisionID).

3.1 Dataset Assembly Pipeline

Dataset Source We retrieved 59,112 historic decision documents (dated 1996 to 2022, as shown in Figure 4) from the online services of the Canadian Legal Information Institute (CanLII) to curate a collection of federal refugee cases. The documents are initially collected both in PDF and HTML and are all available online. Our automated retrieval process is more efficient and error-resistant than manual retrieval, covers all available cases to date, and is superior to human-based manual retrieval in terms of error proneness and processing time. We obtain two sets: (1) a set of *Case Covers* that consists of semi-structured data and displays meta-information (Appendix A) and (2) a *Main Text* set that contains the body of each case, in full text.

Anonymization When retrieved, the data had already undergone a partial anonymization process to protect sensitive information such as names and locations. However, certain cases still contained identifiable details. To reinforce privacy protection, we took additional steps to anonymize all documents using *Microsoft Presidio* tool[3] and a sequence-labeling task. This involved utilizing our trained NER model to identify personal names (labeled as PERSON) and replacing them with the placeholder X. Our fine-tuned RoBERTa transformer achieved an F1 score of 85.71% on this label.

Choice of Categories The labels have been defined and decided upon with the help of experienced refugee lawyers. We chose labels that represent characteristics reflective of similarity among different cases to facilitate future legal searches. While each case exhibits individual characteristics, legal practitioners typically search for similarities based on elements such as the constitution of the panel, the country of origin and the characteristics of the claimant, the year the claim was made in relation to a particular geopolitical situation, the legal procedures involved, the grounds for the decision, relevant legislation, as well as other cases or reports that are cited.

[3]https://github.com/microsoft/presidio

Flagged Phrase	# of Occurrences
male	5493
canadian citizen	4508
female appellant	4126
woman	2844
roma	2758
female claimant	2329
male appellant	2209
male claimant	1912
female	1688
minor appellant	1655
minor appellants	1257
community	1227
canadian citizens	1018
citizen of china	917
homosexual	833
women	827
lesbian	811
associate appellant	782
citizen of haiti	709
man	677

Table 5: The 20 most frequently flagged phrases with the label CLAIMANT_INFO, using LegalBERT fine-tuned on our dataset (best run evaluated with F1 score is reported here).

Collecting gold-standard annotations Recognizing the importance of collecting annotations of high quality in the domain of Refugee Law, we first collect manually labeled annotations, as explained in Barale et al. (2023). After consulting with refugee lawyers to determine appropriate annotation guidelines, we annotated the data ourselves. We chose to annotate the text split by sentences, as we have found that annotating by paragraph takes more time for the annotator.

For the **human annotation** task, we used state-of-the-art semi-automatic annotation tools: the `Prodigy` annotation tool[4] was used under an academic research license in order to speed up and improve the manual labeling work in terms of consistency and accuracy of annotations. To collect annotated samples on traditional NER labels (`DATE`, `ORG`, `GPE`, `PERSON`, `NORP`, `LAW`), we use suggestions from general purpose pretrained embeddings. For the rest of the labels (`CLAIMANT_INFO`, `CLAIMANT_EVENT`, `PROCEDURE`, `DOC_EVIDENCE`, `EXPLANATION`, `DETERMINATION`, `CREDIBILITY`) and with the aim of improving consistency of annotation, we created a terminology base with the help of lawyers based on `word2vec` (Mikolov et al., 2013). At annotation time, patterns are matched with sentences considered for annotation; the human annotator only corrects them, creating a gold-annotated set of sentences and considerably speeding up the labeling task.

Second, recognizing the different kinds of target information, we also performed a complementary **rule-based extraction and labeling** for the following categories of interest: the name of the judge, the date of the decision, and whether the hearing was in-person, virtual, private, or public. This mostly consisted of searching the text for keywords that we had predefined in advance in our terminology base. For `judge_name` and `date_decision` in the *Case Cover*, we rely on cross-checking information between the names and dates extracted from the first page and the name and date present at the very end of each case in a format presented in Figure 2. Similarly, we determine the outcome of 1,682 cases by keyword search on keywords that are present at the end of a case in some documents to indicate the final decision, *positive* of *negative*. We then manually review the assigned label and this allows us to determine the final outcome with a high degree of certainty and low ambiguity.

Generating Silver-standard Annotated Data To gather more labeled cases, we used a transformer-based text classification model to generate silver-standard labels that indicate the outcome of each case. We first used our NER model to extract the sentences pertaining to the decision outcomes, which were flagged with the label `DETERMINATION`. The extracted sentences contain on average 5.01 tokens. We then trained a classifier on gold-labeled sentences with positive or negative outcomes which for future research are destined to be used as a test set. Because of the imbalance of the available data we oversample our set of gold-standard labels on the extracted sentences labeled *granted*. Since there may be multiple extracted sentences per case, we employed a majority vote mechanism to determine the outcome of each case. Sentences that could not be confidently classified as positive or negative (i.e. those which returned a weight between 0.4 and 0.6) were categorized as *Uncertain* and account for 19.09% of the analyzed sentences. The results using different pretraining are presented in Table 6 with a best-achieved accuracy of 99.34%. We further comment on those results in section 4. In total, we classify 52,234 sentences into three categories: granted (1), rejected (0), and uncertain (2). Thereby we obtain the deci-

[4]`Prodigy`: `https://prodi.gy/docs`

DETERMINATION Extracted Sentences							
	BERT	**RoBERTa**	**DeBERTa**	**LegalBERT**	**CaseHOLD**	**PoL**	**LexLM**
Accuracy	**99.34**	99.15	98.94	98.73	99.15	98.52	88.98
Macro F1	**98.82**	98.43	98.02	97.67	98.43	97.30	82.59
Weighted F1	**99.36**	99.15	98.94	98.73	99.15	98.53	89.74

Table 6: Results of the sentence classification task, on the best-achieved run, after oversampling (Appendix C)

Label	Precision	Recall	F1
CLAIMANT_EVENT	66.29	64.80	65.54
CLAIMANT_INFO	88.64	88.64	88.64
CREDIBILITY	80.43	77.08	78.72
DATE	85.19	93.88	89.32
DETERMINATION	72.41	67.74	70.00
DOC_EVIDENCE	82.95	86.90	84.88
EXPLANATION	81.43	61.29	69.94
GPE	96.24	98.90	97.55
LAW	51.61	60.38	55.65
LAW_CASE	62.50	71.43	66.67
NORP	90.00	85.71	87.80
ORG	89.00	90.82	89.90
PROCEDURE	69.51	65.52	67.46
LEGAL_GROUND	60.00	42.86	50.00

Table 7: Evaluation metrics for the LegalBERT-based fine-tuned entity extraction model

sion outcome for a total of 30,944 case documents (to use as the training split) of which 21.68% are positive decisions as detailed in Table 8.

Similarly, we infer from our previously trained entity extraction model, on the remaining sentences extracted from each document. This allows us to collect silver-standard annotations for the whole dataset of the *main text*. For inference, we use our best-performing trained NER model, which relies on LegalBERT and for which the achieved performance numbers on each concerned category can be found in Table 7 (Chalkidis et al., 2020; Barale et al., 2023).

Outcome \ Split	Test (Gold)	Train (Inferred)
Granted	311	6,709
Rejected	1,371	18,264
Uncertain	-	5,971
Total	**1,682**	**30,944**

Table 8: Outcome distribution of the cases

3.2 Dataset Description and Statistics

From the *Case Covers* entity extraction, we are able to detect the tribunal in 23,022 documents. 92.19% of the decision in this sample are appeal decisions rendered by the Refugee Appeal Division, and the rest (7.80%) is rendered by the Refugee Protection Division in the first instance (flagged with `tribunal`). In terms of location of the hearings (`loc_hearing`), the most commonly found is Toronto with 55.31% of the documents analyzed, second is Montreal with 21.54%, followed by Vancouver with 13.57%, Ottawa with 5.09%, Calgary with 2.57%, Edmonton 1.18%, Winnipeg 0.48%, Halifax 0.25% (figures on 28,127 documents for which the hearing location was detected). We find that 981 documents indicate that the hearing was held by video conference (`in_chamber_virtual`, a field that was mostly added since 2020 during the covid-19 pandemic), the rest defaults to in-chambers hearing. We flagged only 3 private hearings on the whole dataset (`public_private_hearing`).

From the *main text*, we choose to detail two of the extracted categories of entities: GPE and CLAIMANT_INFO which are respectively described in Figure 3 and Table 5. We believe the latter is a valuable foundation for further document classification and analysis of potential biases across cases. The former category extracts mentions of locations and in particular countries. This can refer to country of origin or country of transit. It is also to note that there can be multiple occurrences of one or several countries per case.

4 Experiments: Text Classification for Outcome Prediction

This task serves multiple purposes. Firstly, it is of interest to lawyers and the claimant as they seek to measure the probability of winning the case. Additionally, they aim to understand the grounds on which cases can be won and identify the key factors that require attention to enhance the chances

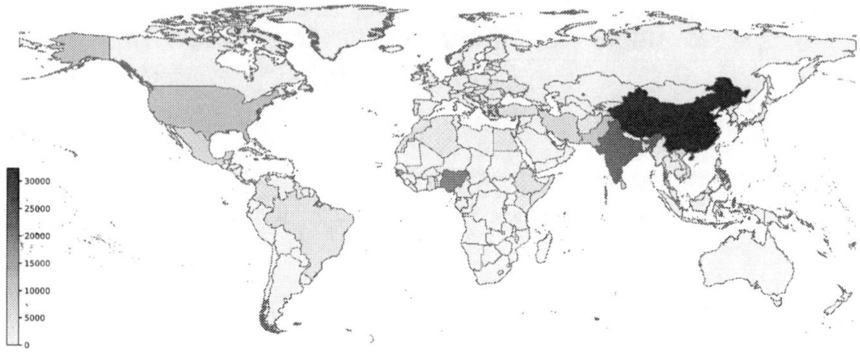

Figure 3: Occurrences of countries on the whole dataset text

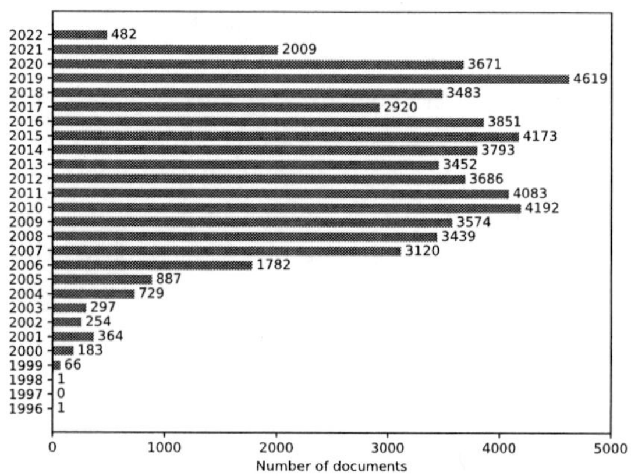

Figure 4: Distribution of the documents over the years by the date of the decision

of success. For judges, engaging in this task offers the potential to analyze their decisions, leading to potential improvements and increased consistency. Furthermore, researchers can utilize this task to assess the fairness of Refugee Status Determination (RSD) decisions and uncover potential biases.

Task: Judgment Prediction The task consists of predicting whether the decision outcome was positive (refugee status granted) or negative (the claim was rejected).

Data The task is performed on two sets of data: the entities extracted from the *case cover* and on the sentences flagged as `determination` by our entity extraction model as described in section 3.1. After cleaning the dataset of *case covers*, we obtained a total of 25,232 documents, 6,985 of which are cases with a positive outcome, i.e. 27.68% of our dataset of *case covers*. After splitting 80-20%, we obtain a train set of 20,186 documents and a test set of 5,046 documents (Appendix D).

We concatenate the entities to form one string per document, separating each type of entity with a separation token. An input string example: *"2010 april 28 2010[SEP]toronto ontario[SEP]in chambers[SEP]april 28 2010"*.

Metrics and Evaluation We evaluate the accuracy, macro F1, and weighted F1 to take into account the initial imbalance in the classes of our dataset, where a majority of cases have a negative decision outcome. The macro average F1 score treats the two classes equally regardless of the number of examples in the set, while the weighted F1 score considers the number of examples in each class, accounting for the class distribution. We present our evaluation on a test set of unseen sequences. For the *Case Cover* entities classifier, we compare to a majority baseline, a trivial baseline that predicts the majority class ("rejected") for all the samples.

Baseline and Models Used We fine-tune our binary classifier on different baseline models with a language modeling objective, both pretrained on general-purpose data (BERT, RoBERTa, and DeBERTa-V3 (Devlin et al., 2019; Liu et al., 2019; He et al., 2023)) and on legal documents (Legal-BERT, CaseHOLD (Chalkidis et al., 2020; Zheng et al., 2021), Pile of Law (Henderson et al., 2022) and LexLM (Chalkidis et al., 2023)). We exclusively employ BERT-based architectures for several reasons. Firstly, BERT's masked language modeling objective aligns well with our language understanding goals. Secondly, BERT's fine-tuning capabilities allow us to fully leverage our dataset, making it particularly suitable for our benchmark task. Additionally, we utilize BERT as a baseline due to its proven robustness. Prior research has

Case Cover Entities								
	Majority	BERT	RoBERTa	DeBERTa	LegalBERT	CaseHOLD	PoL	LexLM
Accuracy	72.36	72.49	74.45	**74.79**	74.57	74.61	74.36	73.96
Macro F1	42.00	66.20	64.26	66.02	65.97	**67.78**	67.53	65.79
Weighted F1	60.77	72.80	72.77	73.91	73.82	**74.39**	74.18	73.26

Table 9: Results of the legal judgment prediction task on the best-achieved run. *Majority* is the majority baseline

demonstrated that BERT-based architectures excel in contextual understanding compared to autoregressive language models. We leave a detailed comparison to future work.

RoBERTa and DeBERTav3 are built upon a larger corpus (160GB) compared to BERT's 16 GB corpus. Pile of Law's corpus is the largest with 256GB, followed by LexLM with 175GB. DeBERTav3 holds fewer parameters (86M) than RoBERTa and improves upon it by using a disentangled attention mechanism. CaseHOLD consists of 37GB of American case law while LegalBERT has the smallest corpus with 12 GB. LegalBERT (US and EU), Pile of Law (US, Canada, EU) CaseHOLD and LexLM (US, Canada, EU, UK, India) are the corpora that include human rights and asylum texts which is the closest domain match to AsyLex.

Experimental Set Up We fine-tune the pretrained language models on AsyLex. We perform a hyperparameter search using the Optuna library[5]. The details of the hyperparameter used for each implementation can be found in Appendix E.

Experimental Results The results of the two experiments conducted on the task of Legal Judgment Prediction are presented in Table 6 and 9. They demonstrate the improved performance of models pretrained on legal documents and relevant legal domains, compared to general-purpose models.

Firstly, one must note that the task of determination sentences judgment prediction is much easier than the prediction task on the dataset of *case covers entities*. On the determination sentences classification task, BERT reaches the best level of accuracy with 99.34%, the second best being achieved by the RoBERTa and CaseHOLD models. On the concatenated entities classification, DeBERTa achieves the best accuracy, very closely with Pile of Law, LegalBERT, and CaseHOLD. As the classes are imbalanced, it is worth noting that the best macro F1 score is in fact achieved by CaseHOLD with 67.78%. Similarly, in the first experiment, BERT achieved the best macro F1 score with 99.82%. All models exhibit closely comparable scores (within one percent), suggesting that the difference in performance between them is not significant. LexLM is the only model showing a significantly lower score. One conjecture is that the English legal pretraining corpus's magnitude exacerbates the model's difficulty in retrieving legal information.

As expected, the classifier directly fined-tune on determination sentences achieves superior performance across all evaluation metrics. However, the classifier trained on entities extracted from the case also demonstrates promising results. This highlights the possibilities for leveraging extracted entities in subsequent studies.

These findings collectively demonstrate the significant advantages of utilizing pretrained models specifically designed for legal documents, with a close match in the legal domain, in the context of Judgment Prediction and therefore the importance of gathering data for legal NLP. The superiority of CaseHOLD and Pile of Law showcases the potential of domain-specific language models to enhance the performance of legal NLP tasks.

5 Conclusion

We introduce a high-quality dataset of annotated refugee claims to streamline case review procedures and contribute to the overall effectiveness of legal practitioners' workflows. Furthermore, we explore the performance of generic models in specialized domains, particularly in the context of Refugee Law. This dataset aims to not only enable advancements in legal NLP but also specifically address the scarcity of resources in Refugee Law. By providing researchers and practitioners access to high-quality labeled data, we hope to foster further research and innovation in this crucial area, ultimately facilitating the development of intelligent legal systems with applications in Refugee Law and beyond.

[5]https://github.com/optuna/optuna

Limitations

In this section, we enumerate the limitations and shortcomings of our work:

- The need to train Transformer-based architectures to perform inference on a large dataset is a limitation as the process typically requires parallelization efforts across GPUs and CPUs to finish within acceptable time frames of multiple hours to several days.
- The manual annotation process for entity extraction and text classification is a weakness: while it results in gold-standard annotations, it is very time-consuming. One of the proposed solutions of this work is to use human labeling in combination with rule-based extraction. However, in future work, it would be interesting to look at methods of indirect supervision and automated annotation generation.
- The dataset contains text in English only and is therefore destined for further research on English-speaking jurisdictions only.

Ethics Statement

Firstly, the proposed dataset contains sensitive personal data. The documents were already available online with partial anonymization. We perform further anonymization of all cases. Second, the task of outcome prediction presented in this paper is not intended to be used for automating the final decision. It is presented in this paper to provide a baseline for future work, with the goal of further analyzing the decision-making process, possible biases, and inconsistencies in the features leading to a decision outcome.

AsyLex is intented to be used for research purposes only.

References

Dennis Aumiller, Ashish Chouhan, and Michael Gertz. 2022. EUR-lex-sum: A multi- and cross-lingual dataset for long-form summarization in the legal domain. In *Proceedings of the 2022 Conference on Empirical Methods in Natural Language Processing*, pages 7626–7639, Abu Dhabi, United Arab Emirates. Association for Computational Linguistics.

Claire Barale, Michael Rovatsos, and Nehal Bhuta. 2023. Automated refugee case analysis: A NLP pipeline for supporting legal practitioners. In *Findings of the Association for Computational Linguistics: ACL 2023*, pages 2992–3005, Toronto, Canada. Association for Computational Linguistics.

Michael J Bommarito II, Daniel Martin Katz, and Eric M Detterman. 2021. Lexnlp: Natural language processing and information extraction for legal and regulatory texts. In *Research Handbook on Big Data Law*, pages 216–227. Edward Elgar Publishing.

K. Branting, B. Weiss, B. Brown, C. Pfeifer, A. Chakraborty, L. Ferro, M. Pfaff, and A. Yeh. 2019. Semi-Supervised Methods for Explainable Legal Prediction. In *Proceedings of the Seventeenth International Conference on Artificial Intelligence and Law*, pages 22–31, Montreal QC Canada. ACM.

L Karl Branting, Alexander Yeh, Brandy Weiss, Elizabeth Merkhofer, and Bradford Brown. 2018. Inducing predictive models for decision support in administrative adjudication. In *AI Approaches to the Complexity of Legal Systems: AICOL International Workshops 2015-2017: AICOL-VI@ JURIX 2015, AICOL-VII@ EKAW 2016, AICOL-VIII@ JURIX 2016, AICOL-IX@ ICAIL 2017, and AICOL-X@ JURIX 2017, Revised Selected Papers 6*, pages 465–477. Springer.

Stefanie Brüninghaus and Kevin D Ashley. 2001. Improving the representation of legal case texts with information extraction methods. In *Proceedings of the 8th international conference on Artificial Intelligence and Law*, pages 42–51.

Ilias Chalkidis, Ion Androutsopoulos, and Nikolaos Aletras. 2019a. Neural legal judgment prediction in English. In *Proceedings of the 57th Annual Meeting of the Association for Computational Linguistics*, pages 4317–4323, Florence, Italy. Association for Computational Linguistics.

Ilias Chalkidis, Emmanouil Fergadiotis, Prodromos Malakasiotis, Nikolaos Aletras, and Ion Androutsopoulos. 2019b. Extreme multi-label legal text classification: A case study in EU legislation. In *Proceedings of the Natural Legal Language Processing Workshop 2019*, pages 78–87, Minneapolis, Minnesota. Association for Computational Linguistics.

Ilias Chalkidis, Emmanouil Fergadiotis, Prodromos Malakasiotis, and Ion Androutsopoulos. 2019c. Large-scale multi-label text classification on EU legislation. In *Proceedings of the 57th Annual Meeting of the Association for Computational Linguistics*, pages 6314–6322, Florence, Italy. Association for Computational Linguistics.

Ilias Chalkidis, Manos Fergadiotis, Prodromos Malakasiotis, Nikolaos Aletras, and Ion Androutsopoulos. 2020. LEGAL-BERT: The muppets straight out of law school. In *Findings of the Association for Computational Linguistics: EMNLP 2020*, pages 2898–2904, Online. Association for Computational Linguistics.

Ilias Chalkidis, Manos Fergadiotis, Dimitrios Tsarapatsanis, Nikolaos Aletras, Ion Androutsopoulos, and Prodromos Malakasiotis. 2021. Paragraph-level rationale extraction through regularization: A case study on European court of human rights cases. In *Proceedings of the 2021 Conference of the North American Chapter of the Association for Computational Linguistics: Human Language Technologies*, pages 226–241, Online. Association for Computational Linguistics.

Ilias Chalkidis, Nicolas Garneau, Catalina Goanta, Daniel Katz, and Anders Søgaard. 2023. LeXFiles and LegalLAMA: Facilitating English multinational legal language model development. In *Proceedings of the 61st Annual Meeting of the Association for Computational Linguistics (Volume 1: Long Papers)*, pages 15513–15535, Toronto, Canada. Association for Computational Linguistics.

Ilias Chalkidis, Abhik Jana, Dirk Hartung, Michael Bommarito, Ion Androutsopoulos, Daniel Katz, and Nikolaos Aletras. 2022a. LexGLUE: A benchmark dataset for legal language understanding in English. In *Proceedings of the 60th Annual Meeting of the Association for Computational Linguistics (Volume 1: Long Papers)*, pages 4310–4330, Dublin, Ireland. Association for Computational Linguistics.

Ilias Chalkidis, Tommaso Pasini, Sheng Zhang, Letizia Tomada, Sebastian Schwemer, and Anders Søgaard. 2022b. FairLex: A multilingual benchmark for evaluating fairness in legal text processing. In *Proceedings of the 60th Annual Meeting of the Association for Computational Linguistics (Volume 1: Long Papers)*, pages 4389–4406, Dublin, Ireland. Association for Computational Linguistics.

Daniel L. Chen and Jess Eagel. 2017. Can machine learning help predict the outcome of asylum adjudications? In *Proceedings of the 16th edition of the International Conference on Articial Intelligence and Law*, pages 237–240, London United Kingdom. ACM.

Jacob Devlin, Ming-Wei Chang, Kenton Lee, and Kristina Toutanova. 2019. BERT: Pre-training of deep bidirectional transformers for language understanding. In *Proceedings of the 2019 Conference of the North American Chapter of the Association for Computational Linguistics: Human Language Technologies, Volume 1 (Long and Short Papers)*, pages 4171–4186, Minneapolis, Minnesota. Association for Computational Linguistics.

Matt Dunn, Levent Sagun, Hale Şirin, and Daniel Chen. 2017. Early predictability of asylum court decisions. In *Proceedings of the 16th edition of the International Conference on Articial Intelligence and Law*, pages 233–236, London United Kingdom. ACM.

Mohamed Elaraby and Diane Litman. 2022. ArgLegalSumm: Improving abstractive summarization of legal documents with argument mining. In *Proceedings of the 29th International Conference on Computational Linguistics*, pages 6187–6194, Gyeongju, Republic of Korea. International Committee on Computational Linguistics.

Suchin Gururangan, Ana Marasović, Swabha Swayamdipta, Kyle Lo, Iz Beltagy, Doug Downey, and Noah A. Smith. 2020. Don't stop pretraining: Adapt language models to domains and tasks. In *Proceedings of the 58th Annual Meeting of the Association for Computational Linguistics*, pages 8342–8360, Online. Association for Computational Linguistics.

Pengcheng He, Jianfeng Gao, and Weizhu Chen. 2023. DeBERTav3: Improving deBERTa using ELECTRA-style pre-training with gradient-disentangled embedding sharing. In *The Eleventh International Conference on Learning Representations*.

Peter Henderson, Mark S. Krass, Lucia Zheng, Neel Guha, Christopher D. Manning, Dan Jurafsky, and Daniel E. Ho. 2022. Pile of law: Learning responsible data filtering from the law and a 256gb open-source legal dataset.

Dan Hendrycks, Collin Burns, Anya Chen, and Spencer Ball. 2021. Cuad: An expert-annotated nlp dataset for legal contract review. In *Proceedings of the Neural Information Processing Systems Track on Datasets and Benchmarks*, volume 1. Curran.

Nils Holzenberger, Andrew Blair-Stanek, and Benjamin Van Durme. 2020. A dataset for statutory reasoning in tax law entailment and question answering. In *Proceedings of the Natural Legal Language Processing Workshop 2020 co-located with the 26th ACM SIGKDD International Conference on Knowledge Discovery & Data Mining (KDD 2020), Virtual Workshop, August 24, 2020*, volume 2645 of *CEUR Workshop Proceedings*, pages 31–38. CEUR-WS.org.

Daniel Martin Katz, Michael J. Bommarito, and Josh Blackman. 2017. A general approach for predicting the behavior of the Supreme Court of the United States. *Plos one*, 12(4):e0174698.

Arshdeep Kaur and Bojan Bozic. 2019. Convolutional neural network-based automatic prediction of judgments of the european court of human rights. In *AICS*, pages 458–469.

Yinhan Liu, Myle Ott, Naman Goyal, Jingfei Du, Mandar Joshi, Danqi Chen, Omer Levy, Mike Lewis, Luke Zettlemoyer, and Veselin Stoyanov. 2019. Roberta: A robustly optimized BERT pretraining approach. *CoRR*, abs/1907.11692.

Andrew D Martin, Kevin M Quinn, Theodore W Ruger, and Pauline T Kim. 2004. Competing approaches to predicting supreme court decision making. *Perspectives on Politics*, 2(4):761–767.

Masha Medvedeva, Michel Vols, and Martijn Wieling. 2020. Using machine learning to predict decisions of the european court of human rights. *Artificial Intelligence and Law*, 28(2):237–266.

Tomas Mikolov, Kai Chen, Greg Corrado, and Jeffrey Dean. 2013. Efficient estimation of word representations in vector space. *arXiv preprint arXiv:1301.3781*.

Sean Rehaag. 2012. Judicial review of refugee determinations: The luck of the draw. *Queen's LJ*, 38:1.

Theodore W. Ruger, Pauline T. Kim, Andrew D. Martin, and Kevin M. Quinn. 2004a. The Supreme Court Forecasting Project: Legal and Political Science Approaches to Predicting Supreme Court Decisionmaking. *Columbia Law Review*, 104(4):1150.

Theodore W Ruger, Pauline T Kim, Andrew D Martin, and Kevin M Quinn. 2004b. The supreme court forecasting project: Legal and political science approaches to predicting supreme court decisionmaking. *Columbia law review*, pages 1150–1210.

Don Tuggener, Pius von Däniken, Thomas Peetz, and Mark Cieliebak. 2020. LEDGAR: A large-scale multi-label corpus for text classification of legal provisions in contracts. In *Proceedings of the Twelfth Language Resources and Evaluation Conference*, pages 1235–1241, Marseille, France. European Language Resources Association.

Samir Undavia, Adam Meyers, and John Ortega. 2018. A Comparative Study of Classifying Legal Documents with Neural Networks. pages 515–522.

Lucia Zheng, Neel Guha, Brandon R. Anderson, Peter Henderson, and Daniel E. Ho. 2021. When does pretraining help? assessing self-supervised learning for law and the casehold dataset. In *Proceedings of the 18th International Conference on Artificial Intelligence and Law*. Association for Computing Machinery.

Haoxi Zhong, Zhipeng Guo, Cunchao Tu, Chaojun Xiao, Zhiyuan Liu, and Maosong Sun. 2018. Legal judgment prediction via topological learning. In *Proceedings of the 2018 Conference on Empirical Methods in Natural Language Processing*, pages 3540–3549, Brussels, Belgium. Association for Computational Linguistics.

A Appendix A: Example of a *Case Cover* (Case #123259)

Immigration and Refugee Board of Canada

Commission de l'immigration et du statut de réfugié du Canada

Refugee Appeal Division

ORG

Section d'appel des réfugiés

RAD File / Dossier de la SAR : TB8-17005

Private Proceeding / Huis clos

Private/Public

Reasons and decision – Motifs et décision

Person who is the subject of the appeal	PERSON XXXX XXXX	**Personne en cause**
Date(s) of hearing	DATE December 15, 2020	**Date(s) de l'audience**
Appeal considered / heard at	LOCATION Toronto, ON	**Appel instruit / entendu à**
Date of decision	DATE December 17, 2020	**Date de la décision**
Panel	PERSON	**Tribunal**
Counsel for the person who is the subject of the appeal		**Conseil de la personne en cause**
Designated representative	N/A	**Représentant(e) désigné(e)**
Counsel for the Minister	N/A	**Conseil du ministre**

RAD.25.02 (April 04, 2019)
Disponible en français

Canada

B Appendix B: Legal Entity Types Description

Type	Description	Examples
LOCATION	cities, countries, regions	"toronto, ontario"
DATE	absolute or relative dates or periods	"june, 4th 1996", "two years"
NORP	adjectives of nationalities, religious, political or ethnic groups or communities	"hutu", "nigerian", "christian"
ORG	tribunals, companies, NGOs	"immigration appeal division", "human rights watch"
CREDIBILITY	mentions of credibility	"lack of evidence", "inconsistencies"
DETERMINATION	outcome of the decision (accept/reject)	"appeal is dismissed", "not a convention refugee"
CLAIMANT_INFO	age, gender, citizenship, occupation	"28 year old", "citizen of Iran", "female"
PROCEDURE	steps in the claim and legal procedure events	"removal order", "sponsorship for application"
DOC_EVIDENCE	pieces of evidence, proofs, supporting documents	"passport", "medical record", "marriage certificate"
EXPLANATION	reasons given by the panel for the determination	"fear of persecution", "no protection by the state"
LEGAL_GROUND	referring to the Convention, refugee status is granted for reasons of race, religion, nationality, membership of a particular social group or political opinion	"homosexual", "christian"
LAW	citations: legislation and international conventions	"section 1(a) of the convention"
LAW_CASE	citations: case law and past decided cases	"xxx v. minister of canada, 1994"
LAW_REPORT	country reports written by NGOs or the United Nations	"amnesty international: police and military torture of women in mexico, 2016"

C Appendix C: Determination Sentences Dataset Split

Because of the dataset imbalance, we chose to oversample the minority class for training. The split is shown in the table below.

Outcome \ Split	Train	Test
Granted	1,064	76
Rejected	1,685	396
Total	**2,749**	**472**

Table 10: Split for determination sentences labeling in number of sentences after oversampling the minority class (granted), used for training – batch size=16, Adam optimizer, 1 epoch

D Appendix D: *Case Cover* Entities Dataset Split

Outcome \ Split	Train	Test
Granted	5,590	1,395
Rejected	14,596	3,651
Total	**20,186**	**5,046**

Table 11: Split for the *Case Cover* Dataset with Outcomes of the Judgments as Labels (Binary Classification Task).

E Appendix E: Hyperparameters used for the Task of Legal Judgment Prediction

We perform experiments on a single GPU and single node/multi-GPU settings. We use a cluster including 38 GPU nodes available, each comprising two 20-core Intel Xeon Cascade Lake CPUs running at 2.4 Ghz, four Nvidia Tesla V100-SMX2-16GB GPUs (640 Tensor cores each), 384 GB of memory per node, and Infiniband interconnect at 100 Gbit/s. Cirrus is an EPSRC UK-Tier 2 HPC supercomputer hosted by EPCC.

For the task of Legal Judgment Prediction on the Determination sentences presented in Table 6, we use the same hyperparameters with all tested models. We use a learning rate of 2.0×10^{-5}, a batch size of 16, a weight decay of 1.8×10^{-2} on one epoch.

For the second experiment on the *Case Cover* Entities (presented in Table 9) the hyperparameters used are detailed in the table below.

Model	LR	Batch	W decay
BERT	1.0×10^{-4}	32	1.6×10^{-2}
RoBERTa	1.0×10^{-3}	8	1.6×10^{-2}
DeBERTav3	5.0×10^{-6}	16	1.8×10^{-2}
LegalBERT	1.1×10^{-5}	4	1.6×10^{-2}
CaseHOLD	2.5×10^{-5}	16	1.0×10^{-2}
Pol	1.0×10^{-6}	16	1.5×10^{-2}
LexLM	1.1×10^{-5}	16	1.8×10^{-2}

Table 12: Hyper-parameters used for training on the *Case Cover* Entities, after performing hyper-parameter search. All implementations use an Adam optimizer and are trained on 3 epochs, except LexLM which is trained on 2 epochs. *LR* is the Learning rate, *Batch* the Batch size, *W decay* the Weight decay.

A Comparative Study of Prompting Strategies for Legal Text Classification

Ali Hakimi Parizi[1*] and **Yuyang Liu**[1*] and **Prudhvi Nokku**[2*]
Sina Gholamian[1*] and **David B. Emerson**[3]
[1]Thomson Reuters Labs, Toronto, Canada
[2]Thomson Reuters Labs, Bangalore, India
[3]Vector Institute, Toronto, Canada
[1,2]{name.surname}@thomsonreuters.com
[3]david.emerson@vectorinstitute.ai

Abstract

In this study, we explore the performance of large language models (LLMs) using different prompt engineering approaches in the context of legal text classification. Prior research has demonstrated that various prompting techniques can improve the performance of a diverse array of tasks done by LLMs. However, in this research, we observe that professional documents, and in particular legal documents, pose unique challenges for LLMs. We experiment with several LLMs and various prompting techniques, including zero/few-shot prompting, prompt ensembling, chain-of-thought, and activation fine-tuning and compare the performance on legal datasets. Although the new generation of LLMs and prompt optimization techniques have been shown to improve generation and understanding of generic tasks, our findings suggest that such improvements may not readily transfer to other domains. Specifically, experiments indicate that not all prompting approaches and models are well-suited for the legal domain which involves complexities such as long documents and domain-specific language.

1 Introduction

Large Language Models (LLMs) have gained significant popularity recently due to their remarkable versatility across a wide range of natural language processing tasks. These models, such as OpenAI's GPT-3 (Brown et al., 2020) and Facebook's OPT (Zhang et al., 2022), have exhibited notable ability to generate coherent and fluent text, resulting in their adaptation in various domains (Artetxe et al., 2022; Xu et al., 2022; Chintagunta et al., 2021). In addition, through prompting, LLMs have demonstrated significant generalizability (Touvron et al., 2023; Wei et al., 2022).

Prompt engineering refers to techniques used to steer LLM generations by providing specific instructions or augmenting a model's input context, which leads to improved responses and better performance on downstream tasks. LLMs have achieved impressive results for a wide variety of tasks, and prior research has shown the effectiveness of different prompt engineering approaches to further improve their performance (van der Meer et al., 2022; Ma et al., 2022; Reif et al., 2022). However, their applicability to specific domains, particularly legal texts, requires more exploration.

Previous research has investigated the potential of various prompting techniques, such as zero- and few-shot prompting (Brown et al., 2020; Agrawal et al., 2022), prompt ensembling (Pitis et al., 2023), chain-of-thought (Wei et al., 2022), and activation fine-tuning (Azaria and Mitchell, 2023; Li and Liang, 2021), in enhancing the performance of LLMs across different tasks, including text-classification. In addition, text-classification is a central focus of parameter efficient finetuning (PEFT) research (Hu et al., 2022; Lester et al., 2021). However, these studies consider general NLP settings rather than the legal domain.

In this paper, we explore various prompting approaches to utilize pre-trained LLMs for legal document classification. The datasets considered here represent a strong test of LLMs' out-of-domain generalization. We begin with zero-shot learning and compare with more advanced approaches such as prompt ensembling and chain-of-thought. Our findings indicate that legal documents present unique challenges for LLMs, such as complex terminologies and long documents, that hinder the transferability of prompting techniques to this domain. Recently, Toma et al. (2023) observed similar findings in leveraging LLMs for medical text.

2 Methodology

2.1 Models

For the experiments, we utilize the OPT family of language models (Zhang et al., 2022). OPT175B

[*]These authors contributed equally to this work.

Proceedings of the Natural Legal Language Processing Workshop 2023, pages 258–265
December 7, 2023

is chosen to represent very large foundation models, and a smaller variant, OPT6.7B, is selected to provide a path to compare the impact of model scale on each prompting approach. The OPT family is chosen because they are fully open-source, come in various sizes, and have shown equivalent capabilities to GPT-3 (Brown et al., 2020). The pre-training data for OPT is drawn from the RoBERTa, The Pile, and PushShift.io Reddit datasets (Zhang et al., 2022). Experiments are conducted using the Kaleidoscope library (Sivaloganathan et al., 2022).

2.2 Datasets

We use two legal classification datasets, ECHR (Chalkidis et al., 2019) and SCOTUS (Chalkidis et al., 2022), both of which are English language datasets. ECHR contains several tasks, one of which is binary classification to determine if a human rights article has been violated. The SCOTUS dataset is a multi-class classification task where Supreme Court case decisions are classified into 14 distinct issue areas. This task is quite challenging as its class distribution is long-tailed. Due to compute and resource limitations, the datasets are randomly down-sampled to 10% and 5% respectively, in a stratified fashion to maintain the original distribution of classes. Additional details are presented in Appendix A.

Since the average token length of SCOTUS documents is substantially larger than the context length of OPT, which is 2048 tokens, each case is first summarized into a smaller paragraph. We use GPT4 (OpenAI, 2023) for this purpose and generate summaries with at most 512 words. Prior to applying this approach to all SCOTUS documents, several summaries were checked for quality and hallucinations. Note that summarization is not necessary for ECHR as its average text length is not higher than the OPT context length.

2.3 Prompt Templates

Each dataset leverages a unique prompt template. For ECHR, we use the prompt template:

> *Complete the sentence with Yes or No*
> **{Few-shot legal case text with label}**
> **{Legal case text to classify}**
> *Has any human rights article or protocol been violated?*

Following (Trautmann et al., 2022), we formulate the prompt as question answering by first providing an instruction and possible answers. The context is then provided, along with the key question to be answered by the LLM. For the SCOTUS dataset, the prompt is structured as follows.

> *Classify the given document with _only one_ label from the following list:*
> **[A list of labels in SCOTUS]**
> **{Few-shot legal case text with label}**
> **{Legal case text to classify}**
> *The label is*

Here, the prompt is formulated as a completion task. We first provide instructions with a set of possible classes and, at the end, provide an unfinished sentence for the LLM to complete. Additional details are presented in Appendix D.

2.4 Prompt Techniques

We investigate four prompting techniques: *Zero-shot & Few-shot*, *Prompt Ensembling*, *Chain-of-Thought (CoT)*, and *Activation Fine-Tuning*. Each approach is reviewed briefly below.

2.4.1 Zero-shot and Few-shot

As observed in Brown et al. (2020); Dong et al. (2023), LLMs trained on massive corpora of texts have shown an ability to perform new tasks from instructions or from a few examples. In zero-shot prompting, the model is tasked with making predictions for a previously unseen problem without training examples, leveraging only prior knowledge obtained during pre-training. While such prompts do not leverage labeled data, they often incorporate task-specific instructions. Few-shot learning offers a middle ground, where the model is provided with a handful of examples ("shots") relevant to the task at hand. Note that few-shot prompting is also often referred to as in-context learning. Effective incorporation of few-shot prompts tends to require models of sufficient size (Kaplan et al., 2020).

2.4.2 Prompt Ensembling

LLMs are known to be sensitive to prompt design, and their task utility can be unpredictable. Ensemble methods have improved deep learning models by pooling classifiers (Ganaie et al., 2022). This has also been successful in prompt-based LLM settings. Pitis et al. (2023) utilized a boosting technique to iteratively construct a group of few-shot prompts of "hard" examples. In this work, we experimented with majority voting classifiers composed of three few-shot prompts.

2.4.3 Chain-of-Thought (CoT)

CoT prompting was initially introduced to elicit internal reasoning in LLMs when generating responses to prompts (Wei et al., 2022). This approach incorporates a series of intermediate examples to steer the LLM to think in a step-by-step manner and, thereby, better achieve the desired outputs. It has been shown to significantly improve multi-step reasoning for LLMs (Yu et al., 2022). In the experiments to follow, we use the zero-shot CoT approach of Kojima et al. (2023). When incorporating few-shot examples, we prepend the CoT prompt with three examples and their labels.

2.4.4 Activation Fine-Tuning

In activation fine-tuning, for each prompt, hidden states for the last non-pad token of the input to the LLM are extracted. Two forms of input to the LLM are considered. In the first, activations are generated by simply passing the case text as input to the LLM. In the second, a three-shot prompt is created as input to generate the activations. This is similar in concept to tuning a classifier on a frozen LM, as is common for models such as BERT (Devlin et al., 2019). In this work, activations from the last feed-forward layer of the transformer are used, along with the label of each sample, to train a small auxiliary feed-forward network. This approach has been effective for challenging classification tasks (Azaria and Mitchell, 2023; Lester et al., 2021). Training details for the classifier are found in Appendix B.

2.5 Prompt Styles

Because OPT models are not instruction finetuned (Chung et al., 2022) or trained for question-answering tasks, we expect completion-type prompts, as discussed in Section 2.3, to perform better than question-answering ones. As such, we also experimented with different prompt styles to evaluate this scenario. The question-answering prompt template for SCOTUS, in which the final completion sentence is removed, is shown below.

> *Can you classify the given "Text" with only one class from the following list?*
> **[A list of labels in SCOTUS]**
> **{Legal case text to classify}**

2.6 Classification Predictions

Predictions are produced by processing responses to the prompts generated by OPT. Without special treatment, the OPT generations do not always match a label from the desired label space. Therefore, to extract classification predictions from the LLMs on these two datasets, the log-likelihood of prompt completions associated with labels in the taxonomy is used. For ECHR, the labels are **Yes** or **No** to indicate if the legal case contains a violation of human rights articles or protocol. Prompts are presented to the OPT models and the probability distribution over the vocabulary for the last token is computed. Since we are only interested in the probabilities of the two classes, we select the one with the highest value after applying softmax. A similar approach is employed for the multi-class SCOTUS setting. Use of the vocabulary probability distribution ensures that the role of hallucinations, a common issue in legal applications, is minimized.

3 Results and Discussion

Table 1 summarizes the experimental results. Additional figures are shown in Appendix C. Across all approaches, prompts and other variables are kept the same to ensure the results are comparable across legal classification tasks. The results are compared with state-of-the-art HIER-BERT (Chalkidis et al., 2019) and Legal-BERT (Chalkidis et al., 2020) models for ECHR and SCOTUS, respectively. These are fully supervised encoder-only transformers, specialized for the target tasks.

In all cases, we observe notable improvements going from zero-shot to few-shot prompting, which implies that more context and task demonstration are quite helpful. However, performance remains well below the supervised approaches. This suggests that the OPT models, despite being large, general purpose language models with similar capabilities to GPT-3, struggle to perform the specialized legal tasks considered here without fine-tuning or domain-adaptation techniques. Results comparing question-answering to completion-style prompts for SCOTUS are shown in Appendix C, Table 3.

Furthermore, we note that performance for CoT is lower than zero-shot prompting. We find that the OPT output/answer generations are not of high quality, and the generations actually add noise to the prompt, likely causing the degradation. This is an interesting finding as it illustrates that CoT improves performance only in cases where the LLM is capable of generating relevant reasoning. There is a growing body of evidence that LLMs whose pre-training corpus meaningfully includes code are

Model	Approach	ECHR						SCOTUS					
		ma-P	ma-R	ma-F1	we-P	we-R	we-F1	ma-P	ma-R	ma-F1	we-P	we-R	we-F1
OPT6.7B	Zero-shot	0.50	0.50	0.43	0.55	0.65	0.54	0.12	0.12	0.07	0.16	0.05	0.05
	Few shot	0.63	0.62	0.55	0.69	0.55	0.55	0.21	0.15	0.14	0.26	0.17	0.15
	Zero-shot + CoT	0.45	0.47	0.44	0.51	0.59	0.53	0.01	0.09	0.01	0.01	0.04	0.02
	Few-shot + CoT	0.46	0.49	0.43	0.52	0.62	0.54	0.01	0.08	0.02	0.03	0.16	0.05
	Few-shot + Ensemble	0.55	0.54	0.54	0.59	0.62	0.60	0.21	0.20	0.16	0.40	0.23	0.19
	Activation finetuning	0.59	0.59	0.59	0.63	0.62	0.62	0.23	0.25	0.23	0.30	0.30	0.29
	Activation finetuning + prompt	**0.69**	**0.67**	**0.68**	**0.72**	**0.73**	**0.72**	**0.42**	**0.51**	**0.44**	**0.58**	**0.61**	**0.58**
OPT175B	Zero-shot	0.33	0.50	0.40	0.43	0.66	0.52	0.07	0.16	0.07	0.09	0.09	0.07
	Few shot	0.61	0.51	0.44	0.62	0.66	0.55	0.32	0.27	0.17	0.56	0.30	0.23
	Zero-shot + CoT	0.44	0.49	0.41	0.51	0.64	0.53	0.11	0.16	0.09	0.14	0.09	0.09
	Few-shot + CoT	0.40	0.49	0.40	0.48	0.64	0.52	0.07	0.10	0.07	0.10	0.14	0.09
	Few-shot + Ensemble	0.61	0.57	0.44	0.68	0.46	0.41	0.11	0.20	0.11	0.15	0.16	0.13
	Activation finetuning	0.68	0.67	0.67	0.71	0.71	0.71	0.11	0.10	0.09	0.30	0.21	0.23
	Activation finetuning + prompt	**0.79**	**0.73**	**0.75**	**0.79**	**0.79**	**0.78**	**0.53**	**0.57**	**0.54**	**0.67**	**0.71**	**0.68**
Supervised	-	0.85	0.78	0.80	-	-	-	-	-	0.66	-	-	-

Table 1: Results from experiments using different prompting techniques. Supervised results are from (Chalkidis et al., 2019) and (Chalkidis et al., 2022) for ECHR and SCOTUS, respectively, using all the available data. The prefixes ma- and we- denote macro and weighted metrics, respectively. R denotes recall and P, precision.

often better at reasoning and responding to CoT prompting (Li et al., 2023; Liang et al., 2022). This may be part of why OPT, which is not explicitly pre-trained on code, does not benefit from CoT prompt structures. It is also possible that reasoning hallucinations degrade the effectiveness of such prompts in this domain. However, qualitative assessments suggest that poor reasoning quality is the major contributing factor.

For OPT6.7B, few-shot learning with ensemble is the best performing approach, excluding activation tuning, for both the ECHR and SCOTUS datasets. For the larger OPT175B model, the results for ensembling are weaker, generally failing to surpass standard few-shot prompting for both datasets. These results suggest that ensembled prompts can be beneficial for this task, but require careful construction and potentially the use of more advanced ensemble approaches.

Activation finetuning shows the best performance among all the methods analyzed. Similar to the findings of Azaria and Mitchell (2023), we observe that the internal states of the pre-trained LLM contain rich information on which to train a classifier. Moreover, few-shot prompting the LLM further improves performance in this context. We see increases in macro-$F1$ percentage points of 9 and 8 for ECHR dataset with OPT6.7B and OPT175B, respectively, by including informative prompts. In the case of SCOTUS, the difference is even more prominent, with 21 and 45 point improvements for the same models.

While the results remain below the fully supervised models for both tasks, only a small proportion of available training data is used and this approach is quite competitive, even for a difficult long-tail classification task. In addition, pure prompting approaches require no task-specific training and activation fine-tuning only trains a small number of parameters. Finally, the activation finetuning results strongly suggest that pre-trained LLMs have the potential to perform these tasks well with proper treatment.

4 Conclusions

In this research, we performed a comparative study of different prompting techniques to assess their utility in the legal domain. The considered prompting techniques are generally helpful, but their applicability to specialized domains requires further exploration, in line with findings for medical texts (Toma et al., 2023). Among the approaches tested, activation finetuning improves performance the most, especially when accompanied by a few-show prompt, even with limited labeled data. For OPT175B, this approach improves the macro-F1 score zero-shot baselines by **35** and **47** points for ECHR and SCOTUS, respectively. Of the pure prompting approaches, few-shot prompts with and without ensembling perform best, while CoT prompting does not work well in this context.

In future work, we plan to explore instruction-tuned LLMs, such as OPT-IML (Iyer et al., 2023), and experiment with PEFT methods (Hu et al., 2022). We are also interested in assessing whether current LLMs exhibit notable biases in their legal decision processes with respect to protected groups (Liang et al., 2022). Finally, we aim to explore how recent advances in reasoning-based prompting can be used to produce good task performance and more interpretable responses (Tian et al., 2023).

Limitations

We have experimented using OPT model variations and several prompting techniques. Our findings might not generalize to other LLMs or other prompting strategies. In addition, we focused on legal domain datasets, and our analysis might not readily transfer to documents from other domains. Foundation models, like OPT, are not instruction fine-tuned, and they may not respond reliably to instruction-style prompts. Therefore, we presume the results we have observed are also limited to the prompt templates that we have leveraged and might not generalize to different prompt templates.

References

Monica Agrawal, Stefan Hegselmann, Hunter Lang, Yoon Kim, and David Sontag. 2022. Large language models are few-shot clinical information extractors. In *Proceedings of the 2022 Conference on Empirical Methods in Natural Language Processing*, pages 1998–2022, Abu Dhabi, United Arab Emirates. Association for Computational Linguistics.

Mikel Artetxe, Shruti Bhosale, Naman Goyal, Todor Mihaylov, Myle Ott, Sam Shleifer, Xi Victoria Lin, Jingfei Du, Srinivasan Iyer, Ramakanth Pasunuru, Giridharan Anantharaman, Xian Li, Shuohui Chen, Halil Akin, Mandeep Baines, Louis Martin, Xing Zhou, Punit Singh Koura, Brian O'Horo, Jeffrey Wang, Luke Zettlemoyer, Mona Diab, Zornitsa Kozareva, and Veselin Stoyanov. 2022. Efficient large scale language modeling with mixtures of experts. In *Proceedings of the 2022 Conference on Empirical Methods in Natural Language Processing*, pages 11699–11732, Abu Dhabi, United Arab Emirates. Association for Computational Linguistics.

Amos Azaria and Tom Mitchell. 2023. The internal state of an llm knows when its lying. *arXiv preprint arXiv:2304.13734*.

Tom Brown, Benjamin Mann, Nick Ryder, Melanie Subbiah, Jared D Kaplan, Prafulla Dhariwal, Arvind Neelakantan, Pranav Shyam, Girish Sastry, Amanda Askell, et al. 2020. Language models are few-shot learners. *Advances in neural information processing systems*, 33:1877–1901.

Ilias Chalkidis, Ion Androutsopoulos, and Nikolaos Aletras. 2019. Neural legal judgment prediction in English. In *Proceedings of the 57th Annual Meeting of the Association for Computational Linguistics*, pages 4317–4323, Florence, Italy. Association for Computational Linguistics.

Ilias Chalkidis, Manos Fergadiotis, Prodromos Malakasiotis, Nikolaos Aletras, and Ion Androutsopoulos. 2020. LEGAL-BERT: The muppets straight out of law school. In *Findings of the Association for Computational Linguistics: EMNLP 2020*, pages 2898–2904, Online. Association for Computational Linguistics.

Ilias Chalkidis, Abhik Jana, Dirk Hartung, Michael Bommarito, Ion Androutsopoulos, Daniel Katz, and Nikolaos Aletras. 2022. LexGLUE: A benchmark dataset for legal language understanding in English. In *Proceedings of the 60th Annual Meeting of the Association for Computational Linguistics (Volume 1: Long Papers)*, pages 4310–4330, Dublin, Ireland. Association for Computational Linguistics.

Bharath Chintagunta, Namit Katariya, Xavier Amatriain, and Anitha Kannan. 2021. Medically aware GPT-3 as a data generator for medical dialogue summarization. In *Proceedings of the Second Workshop on Natural Language Processing for Medical Conversations*, pages 66–76, Online. Association for Computational Linguistics.

Hyung Won Chung, Le Hou, Shayne Longpre, Barret Zoph, Yi Tay, William Fedus, Yunxuan Li, Xuezhi Wang, Mostafa Dehghani, Siddhartha Brahma, Albert Webson, Shixiang Shane Gu, Zhuyun Dai, Mirac Suzgun, Xinyun Chen, Aakanksha Chowdhery, Alex Castro-Ros, Marie Pellat, Kevin Robinson, Dasha Valter, Sharan Narang, Gaurav Mishra, Adams Yu, Vincent Zhao, Yanping Huang, Andrew Dai, Hongkun Yu, Slav Petrov, Ed H. Chi, Jeff Dean, Jacob Devlin, Adam Roberts, Denny Zhou, Quoc V. Le, and Jason Wei. 2022. Scaling instruction-finetuned language models.

Jacob Devlin, Ming-Wei Chang, Kenton Lee, and Kristina Toutanova. 2019. BERT: Pre-training of deep bidirectional transformers for language understanding. In *Proceedings of the 2019 Conference of the North American Chapter of the Association for Computational Linguistics: Human Language Technologies, Volume 1 (Long and Short Papers)*, pages 4171–4186, Minneapolis, Minnesota. Association for Computational Linguistics.

Qingxiu Dong, Lei Li, Damai Dai, Ce Zheng, Zhiyong Wu, Baobao Chang, Xu Sun, Jingjing Xu, Lei Li, and Zhifang Sui. 2023. A survey on in-context learning.

M.A. Ganaie, Minghui Hu, A.K. Malik, M. Tanveer, and P.N. Suganthan. 2022. Ensemble deep learning: A review. *Engineering Applications of Artificial Intelligence*, 115:105151.

Edward J Hu, Yelong Shen, Phillip Wallis, Zeyuan Allen-Zhu, Yuanzhi Li, Shean Wang, Lu Wang, and Weizhu Chen. 2022. LoRA: Low-rank adaptation of large language models. In *International Conference on Learning Representations*.

Srinivasan Iyer, Xi Victoria Lin, Ramakanth Pasunuru, Todor Mihaylov, Daniel Simig, Ping Yu, Kurt Shuster,

Tianlu Wang, Qing Liu, Punit Singh Koura, Xian Li, Brian O'Horo, Gabriel Pereyra, Jeff Wang, Christopher Dewan, Asli Celikyilmaz, Luke Zettlemoyer, and Ves Stoyanov. 2023. Opt-iml: Scaling language model instruction meta learning through the lens of generalization.

Jared Kaplan, Sam McCandlish, Tom Henighan, Tom B Brown, Benjamin Chess, Rewon Child, Scott Gray, Alec Radford, Jeffrey Wu, and Dario Amodei. 2020. Scaling laws for neural language models. *arXiv preprint arXiv:2001.08361*.

Takeshi Kojima, Shixiang Shane Gu, Machel Reid, Yutaka Matsuo, and Yusuke Iwasawa. 2023. Large language models are zero-shot reasoners.

Brian Lester, Rami Al-Rfou, and Noah Constant. 2021. The power of scale for parameter-efficient prompt tuning. In *Proceedings of the 2021 Conference on Empirical Methods in Natural Language Processing*, pages 3045–3059. Association for Computational Linguistics.

Raymond Li, Loubna Ben Allal, Yangtian Zi, Niklas Muennighoff, Denis Kocetkov, Chenghao Mou, Marc Marone, Christopher Akiki, Jia Li, Jenny Chim, Qian Liu, Evgenii Zheltonozhskii, Terry Yue Zhuo, Thomas Wang, Olivier Dehaene, Mishig Davaadorj, Joel Lamy-Poirier, João Monteiro, Oleh Shliazhko, Nicolas Gontier, Nicholas Meade, Armel Zebaze, Ming-Ho Yee, Logesh Kumar Umapathi, Jian Zhu, Benjamin Lipkin, Muhtasham Oblokulov, Zhiruo Wang, Rudra Murthy, Jason Stillerman, Siva Sankalp Patel, Dmitry Abulkhanov, Marco Zocca, Manan Dey, Zhihan Zhang, Nour Fahmy, Urvashi Bhattacharyya, Wenhao Yu, Swayam Singh, Sasha Luccioni, Paulo Villegas, Maxim Kunakov, Fedor Zhdanov, Manuel Romero, Tony Lee, Nadav Timor, Jennifer Ding, Claire Schlesinger, Hailey Schoelkopf, Jan Ebert, Tri Dao, Mayank Mishra, Alex Gu, Jennifer Robinson, Carolyn Jane Anderson, Brendan Dolan-Gavitt, Danish Contractor, Siva Reddy, Daniel Fried, Dzmitry Bahdanau, Yacine Jernite, Carlos Muñoz Ferrandis, Sean Hughes, Thomas Wolf, Arjun Guha, Leandro von Werra, and Harm de Vries. 2023. Starcoder: may the source be with you!

Xiang Lisa Li and Percy Liang. 2021. Prefix-tuning: Optimizing continuous prompts for generation. *Proceedings of the 59th Annual Meeting of the Association for Computational Linguistics and the 11th International Joint Conference on Natural Language Processing (Volume 1: Long Papers)*, abs/2101.00190.

Percy Liang, Rishi Bommasani, Tony Lee, Dimitris Tsipras, Dilara Soylu, Michihiro Yasunaga, Yian Zhang, Deepak Narayanan, Yuhuai Wu, Ananya Kumar, Benjamin Newman, Binhang Yuan, Bobby Yan, Ce Zhang, Christian Cosgrove, Christopher D. Manning, Christopher Ré, Diana Acosta-Navas, Drew A. Hudson, Eric Zelikman, Esin Durmus, Faisal Ladhak, Frieda Rong, Hongyu Ren, Huaxiu Yao, Jue Wang, Keshav Santhanam, Laurel Orr, Lucia Zheng, Mert Yuksekgonul, Mirac Suzgun, Nathan Kim, Neel Guha, Niladri Chatterji, Omar Khattab, Peter Henderson, Qian Huang, Ryan Chi, Sang Michael Xie, Shibani Santurkar, Surya Ganguli, Tatsunori Hashimoto, Thomas Icard, Tianyi Zhang, Vishrav Chaudhary, William Wang, Xuechen Li, Yifan Mai, Yuhui Zhang, and Yuta Koreeda. 2022. Holistic evaluation of language models.

Ruotian Ma, Xin Zhou, Tao Gui, Yiding Tan, Linyang Li, Qi Zhang, and Xuanjing Huang. 2022. Template-free prompt tuning for few-shot NER. In *Proceedings of the 2022 Conference of the North American Chapter of the Association for Computational Linguistics: Human Language Technologies*, pages 5721–5732, Seattle, United States. Association for Computational Linguistics.

OpenAI. 2023. Gpt-4 technical report.

Silviu Pitis, Michael Ruogu Zhang, Andrew Wang, and Jimmy Ba. 2023. Boosted prompt ensembles for large language models. *ArXiv*, abs/2304.05970.

Emily Reif, Daphne Ippolito, Ann Yuan, Andy Coenen, Chris Callison-Burch, and Jason Wei. 2022. A recipe for arbitrary text style transfer with large language models. In *Proceedings of the 60th Annual Meeting of the Association for Computational Linguistics (Volume 2: Short Papers)*, pages 837–848, Dublin, Ireland. Association for Computational Linguistics.

J. Sivaloganathan, M. Coatsworth, J. Willes, M. Choi, and G. Shen. 2022. *Kaleidoscope*. Vector Institute for Artificial Intelligence, Toronto, Canada.

Jacob-Junqi Tian, Omkar Dige, David Emerson, and Faiza Khan Khattak. 2023. Interpretable stereotype identification through reasoning.

Augustin Toma, Patrick R Lawler, Jimmy Ba, Rahul G Krishnan, Barry B Rubin, and Bo Wang. 2023. Clinical camel: An open-source expert-level medical language model with dialogue-based knowledge encoding. *arXiv preprint arXiv:2305.12031*.

Hugo Touvron, Thibaut Lavril, Gautier Izacard, Xavier Martinet, Marie-Anne Lachaux, Timothée Lacroix, Baptiste Rozière, Naman Goyal, Eric Hambro, Faisal Azhar, et al. 2023. LLaMA: Open and efficient foundation language models. *arXiv preprint arXiv:2302.13971*.

Dietrich Trautmann, Alina Petrova, and Frank Schilder. 2022. Legal prompt engineering for multilingual legal judgement prediction. *arXiv preprint arXiv:2212.02199*.

Michiel van der Meer, Myrthe Reuver, Urja Khurana, Lea Krause, and Selene Baez Santamaria. 2022. Will it blend? mixing training paradigms & prompting for argument quality prediction. In *Proceedings of the 9th Workshop on Argument Mining*, pages 95–103, Online and in Gyeongju, Republic of Korea. International Conference on Computational Linguistics.

Jason Wei, Xuezhi Wang, Dale Schuurmans, Maarten Bosma, Ed Chi, Quoc Le, and Denny Zhou. 2022. Chain of thought prompting elicits reasoning in large language models. *arXiv preprint arXiv:2201.11903*.

Hanzi Xu, Slobodan Vucetic, and Wenpeng Yin. 2022. OpenStance: Real-world zero-shot stance detection. In *Proceedings of the 26th Conference on Computational Natural Language Learning (CoNLL)*, pages 314–324, Abu Dhabi, United Arab Emirates (Hybrid). Association for Computational Linguistics.

Fangyi Yu, Lee Quartey, and Frank Schilder. 2022. Legal Prompting: Teaching a Language Model to Think Like a Lawyer. In *Proceedings of the Natural Legal Language Processing Workshop (NLLP)*.

Susan Zhang, Stephen Roller, Naman Goyal, Mikel Artetxe, Moya Chen, Shuohui Chen, Christopher Dewan, Mona Diab, Xian Li, Xi Victoria Lin, et al. 2022. Opt: Open pre-trained transformer language models. *arXiv preprint arXiv:2205.01068*.

A ECHR and SCOTUS Dataset Details

Table 2 presents the details of each dataset after down-sampling. Note that the down-sampling process respected the original train, validation, and test splits, such that no cross-split pollution occurred. The analysis in the table is at the word level, rather than the token level. All text sequences are truncated after tokenization, if required. For ECHR, the task considered is binary classification determining whether a human rights article has been violated based on the provided context. We specifically use the anonymized version of the ECHR dataset. For SCOTUS, the task is to categorize Supreme Court case decisions into one of 14 issue areas. These issue areas include topics such as Criminal Procedure, Civil Rights, and Economic Activity.

Dataset	Train	Val.	Test	Avg. # of Words
ECHR	710	138	299	1947
SCOTUS	250	72	70	10095

Table 2: The number of documents in the ECHR and SCOTUS training, validation, and test datasets. The average number of words are calculated using white-space separation in the test splits for each dataset.

B Activation Fine-Tuning Setup

The same hyperparameters and training procedure are used to train the feed-forward network for both the ECHR and SCOTUS datasets, {*batch_size*: 16, *lr*: 0.0001, *weight_decay*: 0.01, *hidden_size*: 128 *patience*: 3}. In the case of SCOTUS, weighted cross entropy is used to address class imbalance.

C Prompting Strategy Results: Visualization

Figures 1 and 2 provide visualizations of results shown in Table 1 associated with the various prompting strategies discussed in Section 2.4. Solid and dashed lines correspond to macro- and weighted-$F1$ scores, respectively. Horizontal dashed lines in each figure represent the macro-$F1$ scores of HIER-BERT (Chalkidis et al., 2019) for ECHR and Legal-BERT (Chalkidis et al., 2022) for SCOTUS. For the prompt strategies, "Ens." stands for ensembling, "Act." denotes activation, and "FT" is short for finetuning.

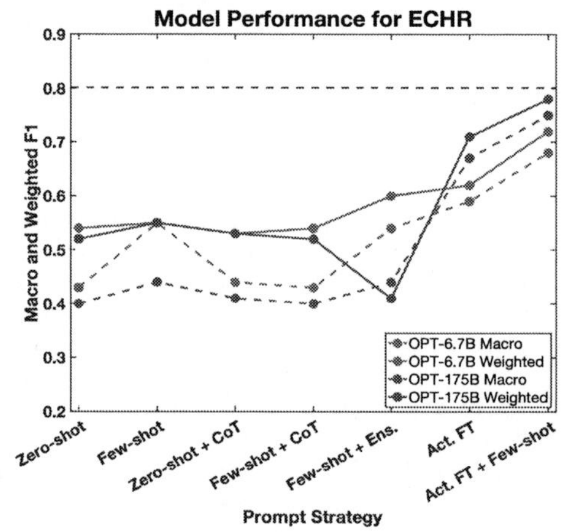

Figure 1: Macro- and weighted-$F1$ scores for the OPT models on the ECHR task. The dashed horizontal line represents the macro-$F1$ score for HIER-BERT in (Chalkidis et al., 2019).

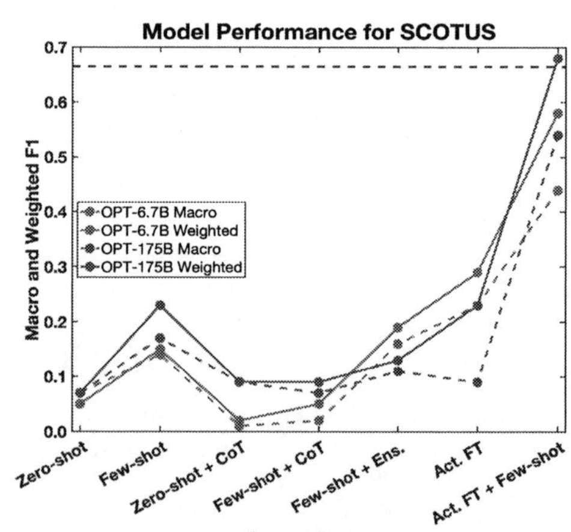

Figure 2: Macro- and weighted-$F1$ scores for the OPT models on the SCOTUS task. The dashed horizontal line represents the macro-$F1$ score for Legal-BERT in (Chalkidis et al., 2022).

Table 3 summarizes the performance differences for prompts following a question-answer or completion-style for the SCOTUS dataset. The results suggest that, when prompting OPT in this domain and potentially other LLMs without special fine-tuning, it is better to formulate the task in a completion-style format rather than a question-answering one. These findings are in line with Touvron et al. (2023) on effective prompt design.

Model	Prompt type	ma-P	ma-R	ma-F1
OPT6.7**B**	Question	0.02	**0.12**	0.03
	Completion	**0.12**	**0.12**	**0.07**
OPT175**B**	Question	0.04	0.13	0.05
	Completion	**0.07**	**0.16**	**0.07**

Table 3: Details of SCOTUS dataset results with different prompt styles in a zero-shot setting. Completion-style prompts perform better for both model sizes.

D Prompt Templates

To illustrate the appearance of the tasks within the context of the prompts, we provide examples of completed prompt templates for ECHR and SCOTUS below. As the few-shot prompts are quite long, only completed zero-shot templates are shown.

Complete the sentence with Yes or No
NORP The applicant, Mr PERSON LOC, is a NORP national who was born on DATE and lives in GPE. From DATE to DATE the applicant was the director general of a NORP limited liability company, ORG (hereinafter "the company"). On DATE ORG of GPE declared the company bankrupt and opened liquidation proceedings. The proceedings were closed on DATE. On DATE ORG of GPE considered a request from ORG to hold the applicant jointly liable for the company's debts because of the company's inability to cover all its debts with its remaining assets. Although duly notified, the applicant was not present at the hearing. ORG request was granted and the applicant was found liable to pay MONEY (RUB, MONEY). On DATE the company officially went into liquidation. The applicant only became aware of the outcome of the proceedings against him in DATE when money was seized from his bank account. The applicant appealed against the decision of ORG of GPE of DATE. The CARDINALth ORG of Appeal considered the appeal on the merits and on DATE discontinued the appeal proceedings. With reference to the position of ORG, the appeal court concluded that it was impossible to adjudicate bankruptcy-related disputes concerning a company that had already gone into liquidation. The operative part of the appeal decision stated that the applicant could file a cassation appeal. On DATE ORG of GPE dismissed a cassation appeal of the applicant
Has any human rights article or protocol been violated?

Can you classify the given "Text" with only one class from the following list? [Attorneys, Civil Rights, Criminal Procedure, Due Process, Economic Activity,Fed Taxation, Federalism, First Amendment, Interstate Relations, Judicial Power, Miscellaneous, Privacy, Unions]
In Kaupp v. Texas, 538 U.S. 626 (2003), the Supreme Court vacated the judgment of the Texas Court of Appeals, holding that Kaupp was arrested within the meaning of the Fourth Amendment before the detectives began to question him. Kaupp, then 17 years old, was implicated in the murder of a 14-year-old girl by the confession of the girl's half brother. Detectives attempted but failed to obtain a warrant to question Kaupp. They instead went to his house at 3 a.m., awakened and handcuffed him, and took him to the sheriff's headquarters, where they advised him of his rights under Miranda v. Arizona, 384 U. S. 436. Once presented with the brother's confession, Kaupp admitted to having a part in the crime. Kaupp moved unsuccessfully to suppress his confession as the fruit of an illegal arrest. On appeal, the Supreme Court held that Kaupp was arrested before he was questioned and that the State did not have probable cause to detain him. The Court found that Kaupp's detention was "in important respects indistinguishable from a traditional arrest" and required probable cause or judicial authorization to be legal. The State's failure to demonstrate that Kaupp's confession was "an act of free will [sufficient] to purge the primary taint of the unlawful invasion" required suppression of the confession. The Supreme Court vacated the judgment of the Texas Court of Appeals and remanded the case for further proceedings consistent with its opinion.

Tracing Influence at Scale: A Contrastive Learning Approach to Linking Public Comments and Regulator Responses

Linzi Xing[†], **Brad Hackinen**[‡], **and Giuseppe Carenini**[†]
† University of British Columbia, Vancouver, Canada
‡ Ivey Business School, London, Canada
{lzxing, carenini}@cs.ubc.ca
bhackinen@ivey.ca

Abstract

U.S. Federal Regulators receive over one million comment letters each year from businesses, interest groups, and members of the public, all advocating for changes to proposed regulations. These comments are believed to have wide-ranging impacts on public policy. However, measuring the impact of specific comments is challenging because regulators are required to respond to comments but they do not have to specify which comments they are addressing. In this paper, we propose a simple yet effective solution[1] to this problem by using an iterative contrastive method to train a neural model aiming for matching text from public comments to responses written by regulators. We demonstrate that our proposal substantially outperforms a set of selected text-matching baselines on a human-annotated test set. Furthermore, it delivers performance comparable to the most advanced gigantic language model (i.e., GPT-4), and is more cost-effective when handling comments and regulator responses matching in larger scale.

1 Introduction

Policymakers rely on information provided by external stakeholders to help design new regulations. For U.S. federal regulators, this process is formalized by the Administrative Procedures Act which requires that whenever an agency is going to make a policy change (known as a "rule"), they must first publish a proposed rule and accept public comment. Then, in the final rule, the agency must respond to comments they received. The number of comments received by regulators has been growing over time, and the federal government now regularly received more than a million comments per year.

Existing research suggest that public comments can have substantial impacts on public policy (Yackee, 2019). However, measuring the influence of individual organizations or tracking patterns of influence over time has been limited by the challenging nature of the data. Both comments and regulator responses are in gigantic scale and take the form of complex natural language text. Prior attempts at large-scale analysis have borrowed insights from the research field of NLP by measuring the lexical overlap between comments and rule text, with researchers assuming that a high degree of overlap is suggestive of influence (Bertrand et al., 2021; Dwidar, 2022; Carpenter et al., 2022) . However, this approach provides at best a noisy measure of influence, which is difficult to verify. Therefore, we aim for pursuing a more precise and efficient measure based on analyzing the regulator's responses to comments and then matching comments to specific responses. Given that some responses are positive, with agencies accepting commenter's suggestions while others are negative, with the agency rejecting the comment, it is very important to link the right comments to the right responses.

In this paper, we propose a simple yet effective iterative contrastive learning paradigm to train a neural-based comment-response matcher in an unsupervised manner. Specifically, we first construct a pseudo training dataset comprising of hard positive and negative samples generated by the inital setup of our proposed comment-response matcher (SBERT (Reimers and Gurevych, 2019) as the backbone). This matcher is then optimized on the obtained training pseudo data and subsequently utilized to generate the hard positive and negative examples for the next iteration. Through empirical evaluation on a human-annotated test set, our proposed comment-response matcher not only surpasses selected unsupervised text-matching benchmarks utilized in previous literature but also achieves comparable performance with the state-of-the-art gigantic language model – GPT-4 (OpenAI, 2023), while remaining more cost-effective to deploy on the full-scale comment-response matching.

[1] https://github.com/bradhackinen/comment_response_linking

Proceedings of the Natural Legal Language Processing Workshop 2023, pages 266–274
December 7, 2023 ©2023 Association for Computational Linguistics

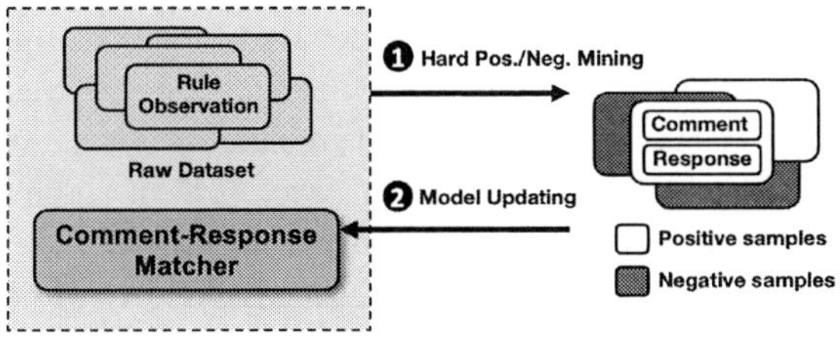

Figure 1: An overview of the iterative training scheme for our proposed comment-response matcher.

2 Comment-Response Matcher

In this paper, we aim to design a text matching model (Section 2.1) that can effectively and efficiently assess the semantic relevance between the public comment text and responses produced by regulators. In essence, given a comment chunk from public $c = \{c_1, \cdots, c_m\}$ and a regulator's response $r = \{r_1, \cdots, r_n\}$, where each c_k is a token in the comment and each r_k is a token in the response, our goal is to learn a function $f : (c, r) \rightarrow s$ that predicts the score s indicating the likelihood that comment c and regulator's response r pertain to the same topic, and that the concern in c is addressed in r.

As illustrated in Figure 1, we employ an iterative contrastive learning paradigm with the training procedure (Section 2.2) consisting of two steps performed alternatingly, namely *hard pos./neg. mining* and *model updating*.

2.1 Model Architecture

Our proposed comment-response matcher functions as a binary classifier essentially comprising two components: a **text encoder** with SBERT[2] (Reimers and Gurevych, 2019) as its underlying structure, followed by a **scoring layer** yielding the likelihood of a pair of comment and response being a match. More formally, given a pair of randomly sampled comment chunk and response c_i and r_j, we first separately acquire the embeddings for these two textual units:

$$v_{c_i} = S\text{-}BERT(c_i), \quad (1)$$

$$v_{r_j} = S\text{-}BERT(r_j) \quad (2)$$

Then the probability of r_j responds to c_i (a match) is computed with the negative exponent of cosine distance between v_{c_i} and v_{r_j}:

$$p(match|v_{c_i}, v_{r_j}) = exp(-\alpha * (1 - v_{c_i} \cdot v_{r_j})) \quad (3)$$

where α serves as a hyper-parameter that controls the decay rate of the matching probability. A greater value of α results in a more pronounced decrease in matching probability when cosine distance increases. Throughout the training process, we optimize the model with cross-entropy loss.

2.2 Training Scheme

Generally, we use contrastive learning paradigm (Hadsell et al., 2006) to train our proposed comment-response matcher. More concretely, we optimize the text encoder in the matcher on selected hard positive and negative samples to effectively capture signals indicating the semantic relevance between public comments and responses from the regulator. This process is therefore arguably conducive to accurately predict whether a comment is discussed in a given response. The training scheme for the matching model spans several iterations, with each iteration consisting of two steps:

-1: Hard Pos./Neg. Mining. As illustrated in Figure 1, our preliminary regulatory data for rulemaking is structured in the form of **rule observations** (§3.1). Each of these rule observations consists of a set of comment chunks and a set of responses associated with a particular rule. As this raw dataset does not have any explicit ground-truth labels about matching between responses and comments within the rule, we make the model training entirely rely on the labels of created pseudo positive and negative comment-responese sample pairs. To do so, we first identify a set of "positive pairs" from the raw data. More specifically, for each response, we find its most similar comment chunk within the same rule observation. This similarity is calculated based on the embeddings of the model's text encoder optimized from the prior iteration. In this way we obtain 11,828 positive comment-response pairs.

In order to improve the robustness and efficiency of model training, within one training step, we first draw a batch of M comment/response strings and then extract hard positive and negative samples associated with strings in the batch. Subsequently, we update the encoder-based matching model on these hard positive/negative samples utilizing in-batch contrastive learning (Wu et al., 2020; Zhou et al., 2022). In practice, we initially apply the match-

[2]We also considered BERT (Devlin et al., 2019), RoBERTa (Liu et al., 2019), Legal-BERT (Chalkidis et al., 2020) and other different versions of SBERT for text encoder, but eventually chose SBERT with version of *multi-qa-mpnet-base-dot-v1* for its observed superior performance.

ing model, derived from the last training iteration, to all comment/response strings, yielding a total of $11,828 \times 2 = 23,656$ embeddings. We then pair each of the M strings in the sampled batch with all embeddings, compute the loss, and generate a loss matrix $l \in \mathbb{R}^{M \times 23656}$. Subsequently, we perform *argmax* on each row of l to identify the response-comment pair corresponding to the maximum loss, ultimately producing M hard positive/negative samples. Each hard positive sample refers to a possibly matched pair which the model struggles to allocate high matching probability to, whereas each hard negative sample refers to a possibly mismatched pair to which the model tends to assign high matching probability.

-2: Model Updating. Once hard positives/negatives for a training step are obtained, in this phase, we update weights of the comment-response matching model by minimizing the cross-entropy loss as described in Section 2.1. This allows us to pull the matched comments and responses closer and push the unmatched ones far apart. The model updated in the current iteration will be fixed and serve as the text encoder to mine hard positive and negative samples again for the next training iteration.

3 Experiments and Analysis

3.1 Experimental Setup

Datasets. As mentioned in §2.2, our preliminary regulatory data for rule-making is structured in the form of rule observations where each rule observation is with a hierarchy depicted as follows:

- **A rule observation** (about one rule document)
  - **A set of comment documents** associated with the rule (Comment A, B, ...)
    - **A set of comment chunks** in Comment A (Comment A-1, A-2, ...)
    - **A set of comment chunks** in Comment B (Comment B-1, B-2, ...)
    - ⋮
  - **A set of regulator's responses** extracted from the rule document (Response A, B, ...)

Textual data in rule observations comes from two main resource: rules published in the Federal Register from 2000-2022, and comments submitted to *regulations.gov* from 2000-2022. As one rule document contains paragraphs other than regulator responses to public comments (e.g., background information, summary of comments), we extract only responses from each rule document using a supervised paragraph classifier developed for another parallel research project. We leverage some external metadata of rules publicly accessible in *federalregister.gov* and *reginfo.gov* to attach comments to the rules downloaded from the different resource. As one comment document can be extensively long, we chop it into a series of comment chunks by grouping adjacent paragraphs in the comment following 1000 token limit. Paragraphs longer than 1000 tokens are deemed as single chunks. After applying some pre-processing constraints (more details in Appendix B), we finally obtain a dataset covers 6,727 rules, 17,452 responses, 10,456 comments chopped into 193,143 comment chunks.

For test data construction, we uniformly (see Appendix B) sample 160 pairs of comment chunk and response from all possible combination in the dataset, and recruite seven students from the law program of our institution to annotate this test set. Annotators were asked to score the relevance of each comment chunk to the accompanying response using a 5-point Likert scale (see Appendix A for detailed annotation instructions). Each sample was assigned to multiple annotators, thus we received 3-5 independent evaluations for each testing pair.

We include more details about our dataset construction pipeline in Appendix B.

Baselines. We compare our proposal with three baseline text matching algorithms (see Figure 2). They are: (1) **Normalized BM25** (Robertson and Zaragoza, 2009), as a widely used term weighting-based ranking model usually applied for information retrieval. We calculate BM25 scores for the corresponding responses and comments tied to the same rule. These scores are then normalized on a per-rule basis; (2) **RoBERTa Score** (Liu et al., 2019), which employs the vanilla $\text{RoBERTa}_{\text{base}}$ as text encoder, transforming both comments chunks and responses into embeddings, which are then used for matching score computing. As we employ the same scoring layer (in Section 2.1), this baseline is essentially equivalent to our proposed matching model in iteration 0; (3) **SBERT Score** (Reimers and Gurevych, 2019), which employs the SBERT (multi-qa-mpnet-base-dot-v1)[3] as text en-

[3]https://huggingface.co/sentence-transformers/multi-qa-mpnet-base-dot-v1

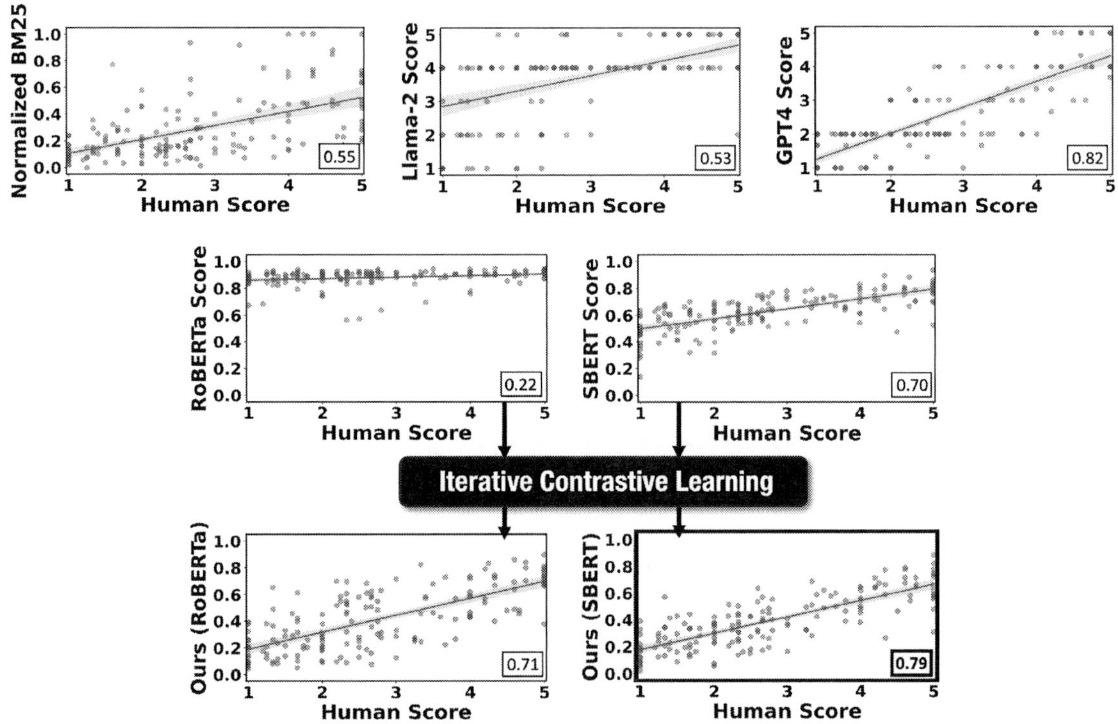

Figure 2: Scatter plots illustrating the correlation between human judgement and seven comment-response matching methods (including Ours (RoBERTa) and Ours (SBERT), which are RoBERTa and SBERT applied our iterative contrastive learning framework) on the 160 test samples. The Pearson's correlations are shown at bottom-right. The best performance achieved by our proposal is highlighted in the bolded box.

coder. The score computing of this baseline is in a manner similar to the RoBERTa Score introduced above; (4) **Llama-2-Chat (70B)** (Touvron et al., 2023), currently the top-performing fundamental gigantic language model within the open-sourced Llama family. We essentially deem it as a human evaluator by providing it with the same guidelines giving to human annotators and then task it to assign a score on the 5-point Likert scale for each pair of comment and response; (5) **GPT-4** (OpenAI, 2023), currently the state-of-the-art gigantic language model, leading in both open-sourced and closed-sourced domains. We prompt it to assign scores for comment-response pairs in the same manner as Llama-2-Chat (70B) introduced above[4].

Implementation Details. As in Section 2.1, we use `SBERT(multi-qa-mpnet-base)` (Reimers and Gurevych, 2019) as the backbone text encoder to demonstrate our proposed comment-response matcher, given its superior performance. However, to validate the model-agnostic nature of our proposed iterative contrastive learning framework, we also test with the vanilla $\texttt{RoBERTa}_{\texttt{base}}$ (Liu et al., 2019) as an alternate backbone text encoder, aiming to discern if improvements brought by the iterative contrastive learning framework extend beyond just one particular text encoder. For both, We take the mean of the contextualized representation of the last hidden layer as text embeddings. For the scoring layer, we set hyper-parameter $\alpha = 50$. For training, we use AdamW (Loshchilov and Hutter, 2017) with with $lr = 1e^{-5}$ and batch size $= 8$. We conduct 5 iterations of model training, with each iteration detailed in §2.2.

3.2 Experimental Results

To investigate how well the baselines and our proposed comment-response matching model align with human judgments, in Figure 2, we use scatter plots to visualize their correlations with human scores, as well as report the Pearson's r correlation score. We can observe that even though GPT-4's predictions show the highest correlation with the 5-point Likert human annotations, our proposed matching model also demonstrates strong performance as ranked in the second place, outperform-

[4]The detailed prompt for Llama-2-Chat (70B) and GPT-4 is in Appendix A.

ing all left baselines by a considerable margin.

More concretely, BM25 tends to underestimate the relevance between comments and responses, assigning low scores to many pairs that humans consider highly relevant in topic. As sharing the same rating scale with human, the predictions of GPT-4 align closely with human judgements, whereas Llama-2-Chat (70B) correlation with human is way less desirable. Interestingly, GPT-4 demonstrates a strong tendency to consistently assign score '2' to samples that humans rated within the range of [1,3], which may indicate that GPT-4 is cautious to determine a comment-response pair as entirely irrelevant. The vanilla RoBERTa without any tuning on our dataset extremely overestimates the relevance between comments and responses by assigning high similarity scores indiscriminately to both matched and unmatched sample pairs. On the other hand, SBERT, being a superior text matching model pre-trained on semantic search as a close analogue to our task, aligns more closely with human judgment, yet the similarity scores it produces for both matched and unmatched samples still fall within a relatively narrow range. When our proposed contrastive learning framework is applied to RoBERTa and SBERT, the correlation of these two base text encoders with human judgments increases from 0.22 and 0.70 to 0.71 and 0.79 respectively, bringing the improved SBERT's performance remarkably close to that of GPT-4 (0.82). It demonstrates the model-agnostic behavior of our iterative contrastive learning framework when effectively interacting with different base encoders. Hence, we believe that with a more advanced base encoder, we could potentially match or even surpass the performance of GPT-4.

To assess the effectiveness of the iterative contrastive learning scheme, Figure 3 showcases the performance of the RoBERTa- and SBERT-based comment-response matchers on the test set across different training iterations applying iterative contrastive learning. We can see the model's performance is improved iteratively across iterations, with the most notable enhancement occurring after the first iteration.

Even though GPT-4 achieves slightly superior correlation with humans in our experiments, from the perspective of real-world application, the cost of deploying the model is also critical. Compared with our SBERT-based matcher, prompting GPT-4 using our designed instruction template incurs

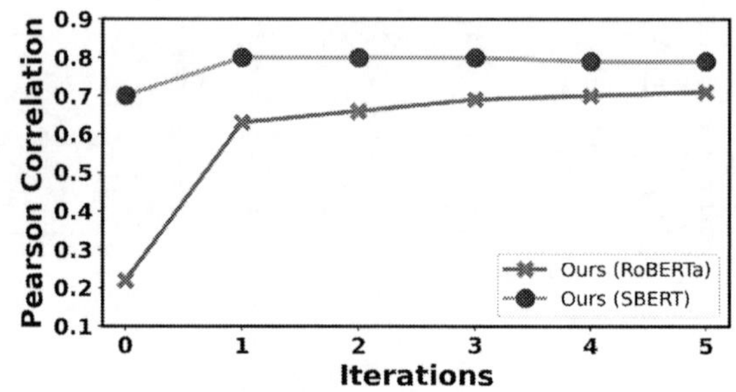

Figure 3: The performance (Pearson's correlation) of the RoBERTa- and SBERT-based comment-response matcher on our test set after each training iteration. "Iteration 0" represents the matcher initialized with $\texttt{RoBERTa}_{\texttt{base}}$ and `SBERT(multi-qa-mpnet-base)`, thus with the correlation score equals to RoBERTa and SBERT score in Figure 2.

an additional cost of \$4.63 on the test set based on its current pricing rate. Given the context that every year U.S. Federal Regulators receive an overwhelming volume of comment letters (usually over one million) from businesses, interest groups, and members of the public, our proposed SBERT-based matcher would be a more feasible option for such practical scenario due to its efficiency and cost-effectiveness.

4 Conclusion

In this paper, we propose a simple yet effective contrastive learning approach following the iterative data construction - model updating training scheme, aiming for automatically matching the responses in policy regulations and relevant comments they respond to. Our empirical study on a real-world test set demonstrates that our proposal outperforms a set of selected benchmarks for text matching in terms of correlation with human annotations, achieves comparable performance but is more cost-effective than the most advanced gigantic large language model (i.e., GPT-4) for comments and regulator responses in larger scale. Our proposed approach can be easily adapted to other text matching applications dealing with text in rather different complexity, such as name matching (Peng et al., 2015), or extended to other more-resourced scenarios like semi-supervised settings, which we will leave as our future work.

5 Limitations

The main limitation of our method is that, while it provides a substantial improvement over BM25 on our task, it is not as accurate as current large language models. It seems reasonable to guess that the cost of employing GPT4 and its successors will decline over time, and at some point, the computational efficiency of our approach may not be so important. Another limitation is that our approach depends on particular aspects of our task that may not be applicable in other domains. Specifically, our unsupervised training method relies on the existence of many groups of responses and comments in the data with the property that positive pairs are only possible within a group. This lets us make good guesses about a subset of the true positive pairs with only a weak model, and generate a large number of true negative pairs by matching strings across groups. However, it is interesting to consider what other tasks and data might have a similar structure.

6 Acknowledgement

We thank the anonymous reviewers for their insightful comments. This research was supported by Social Sciences and Humanities Research Council of Canada (SSHRC).

References

Marianne Bertrand, Matilde Bombardini, Raymond Fisman, Brad Hackinen, and Francesco Trebbi. 2021. Hall of Mirrors: Corporate Philanthropy and Strategic Advocacy*. *The Quarterly Journal of Economics*, 136(4):2413–2465.

Daniel P Carpenter, Angelo Dagonel, Devin Judge-Lord, Christopher T Kenny, Brian Libgober, Steven Rashin, Jacob Waggoner, and Susan Webb Yackee. 2022. Inequality in administrative democracy: Methods and evidence from financial rulemaking.

Ilias Chalkidis, Manos Fergadiotis, Prodromos Malakasiotis, Nikolaos Aletras, and Ion Androutsopoulos. 2020. LEGAL-BERT: The muppets straight out of law school. In *Findings of the Association for Computational Linguistics: EMNLP 2020*, pages 2898–2904, Online. Association for Computational Linguistics.

Jacob Devlin, Ming-Wei Chang, Kenton Lee, and Kristina Toutanova. 2019. BERT: Pre-training of deep bidirectional transformers for language understanding. In *Proceedings of the 2019 Conference of the North American Chapter of the Association for Computational Linguistics: Human Language Technologies, Volume 1 (Long and Short Papers)*, pages 4171–4186, Minneapolis, Minnesota. Association for Computational Linguistics.

Maraam A. Dwidar. 2022. Coalitional lobbying and intersectional representation in american rulemaking. *American Political Science Review*, 116(1):301–321.

R. Hadsell, S. Chopra, and Y. LeCun. 2006. Dimensionality reduction by learning an invariant mapping. In *2006 IEEE Computer Society Conference on Computer Vision and Pattern Recognition (CVPR'06)*, volume 2, pages 1735–1742.

Yinhan Liu, Myle Ott, Naman Goyal, Jingfei Du, Mandar Joshi, Danqi Chen, Omer Levy, Mike Lewis, Luke Zettlemoyer, and Veselin Stoyanov. 2019. Roberta: A robustly optimized BERT pretraining approach. *CoRR*, abs/1907.11692.

Ilya Loshchilov and Frank Hutter. 2017. Decoupled weight decay regularization. In *International Conference on Learning Representations*.

OpenAI. 2023. Gpt-4 technical report.

Nanyun Peng, Mo Yu, and Mark Dredze. 2015. An empirical study of Chinese name matching and applications. In *Proceedings of the 53rd Annual Meeting of the Association for Computational Linguistics and the 7th International Joint Conference on Natural Language Processing (Volume 2: Short Papers)*, pages 377–383, Beijing, China. Association for Computational Linguistics.

Nils Reimers and Iryna Gurevych. 2019. Sentence-BERT: Sentence embeddings using Siamese BERT-networks. In *Proceedings of the 2019 Conference on Empirical Methods in Natural Language Processing and the 9th International Joint Conference on Natural Language Processing (EMNLP-IJCNLP)*, pages 3982–3992, Hong Kong, China. Association for Computational Linguistics.

Stephen Robertson and Hugo Zaragoza. 2009. The probabilistic relevance framework: Bm25 and beyond. *Found. Trends Inf. Retr.*, 3(4):333–389.

Hugo Touvron, Louis Martin, Kevin Stone, Peter Albert, Amjad Almahairi, Yasmine Babaei, Nikolay Bashlykov, Soumya Batra, Prajjwal Bhargava, Shruti Bhosale, Dan Bikel, Lukas Blecher, Cristian Canton Ferrer, Moya Chen, Guillem Cucurull, David Esiobu, Jude Fernandes, Jeremy Fu, Wenyin Fu, Brian Fuller, Cynthia Gao, Vedanuj Goswami, Naman Goyal, Anthony Hartshorn, Saghar Hosseini, Rui Hou, Hakan Inan, Marcin Kardas, Viktor Kerkez, Madian Khabsa, Isabel Kloumann, Artem Korenev, Punit Singh Koura, Marie-Anne Lachaux, Thibaut Lavril, Jenya Lee, Diana Liskovich, Yinghai Lu, Yuning Mao, Xavier Martinet, Todor Mihaylov, Pushkar Mishra, Igor Molybog, Yixin Nie, Andrew Poulton, Jeremy Reizenstein, Rashi Rungta, Kalyan Saladi, Alan Schelten, Ruan Silva, Eric Michael Smith, Ranjan Subramanian, Xiaoqing Ellen Tan, Binh Tang, Ross Taylor, Adina Williams, Jian Xiang Kuan, Puxin Xu, Zheng Yan, Iliyan Zarov, Yuchen Zhang, Angela Fan, Melanie Kambadur, Sharan Narang, Aurelien Rodriguez, Robert Stojnic, Sergey Edunov, and Thomas

Scialom. 2023. Llama 2: Open foundation and fine-tuned chat models.

Chien-Sheng Wu, Steven C.H. Hoi, Richard Socher, and Caiming Xiong. 2020. TOD-BERT: Pre-trained natural language understanding for task-oriented dialogue. In *Proceedings of the 2020 Conference on Empirical Methods in Natural Language Processing (EMNLP)*, pages 917–929, Online. Association for Computational Linguistics.

Linzi Xing and Giuseppe Carenini. 2021. Improving unsupervised dialogue topic segmentation with utterance-pair coherence scoring. In *Proceedings of the 22nd Annual Meeting of the Special Interest Group on Discourse and Dialogue*, pages 167–177, Singapore and Online. Association for Computational Linguistics.

Linzi Xing, Brad Hackinen, Giuseppe Carenini, and Francesco Trebbi. 2020. Improving context modeling in neural topic segmentation. In *Proceedings of the 1st Conference of the Asia-Pacific Chapter of the Association for Computational Linguistics and the 10th International Joint Conference on Natural Language Processing*, pages 626–636, Suzhou, China. Association for Computational Linguistics.

Susan Webb Yackee. 2019. The politics of rulemaking in the united states. *Annual Review of Political Science*, 22(1):37–55.

Zhihan Zhou, Dejiao Zhang, Wei Xiao, Nicholas Dingwall, Xiaofei Ma, Andrew Arnold, and Bing Xiang. 2022. Learning dialogue representations from consecutive utterances. In *Proceedings of the 2022 Conference of the North American Chapter of the Association for Computational Linguistics: Human Language Technologies*, pages 754–768, Seattle, United States. Association for Computational Linguistics.

A Prompt Templates for GPT-4

See next page.

B Details for Regulatory Data Construction

Our data comes from two main sources: Rules published in the *Federal Register* from 2000-2022, downloaded in bulk XML format from govinfo.gov, and all comments submitted to *regulations.gov* from 2000-2022, downloaded via the API. We extracted regulator responses to comments from the rules using a supervised classifier under development for a parallel research project. We extract comment text with the tika parser[5], employing OCR when necessary to extract text from image-only PDFs. The comment text is split into paragraphs, and body paragraphs are identified using a simple rule-based classifier. Finally, we group very short paragraphs (often improperly split by page breaks or other formatting issues) with adjacent paragraphs to form larger comment "chunks" 500-100 characters long. Paragraphs longer than 1000 characters are included as single chunks. Besides this rule-based chunk generation strategy, we believe topic segmentation techniques (Xing et al., 2020; Xing and Carenini, 2021) can potentially lead to comment chunks in better quality if the training data for segmentation in reasonable size is available.

Linking comments to the appropriate rules requires additional data. We collect rule metadata from *federalregister.gov* and *reginfo.gov* and link *regulations.gov* documents to Proposed Rules, and Proposed Rules to Rules using Federal Register document numbers, agency docket identifiers, and Regulation Identification Numbers (RIN). This gives us a database of rules where, for each rule, we can identify the set of comments that the agency would likely be responding to.

The structure of the data is important for our training strategy. Each rule may contain multiple responses, and be linked to multiple comments with several paragraphs each. We can be reasonably confident that each response in a rule is responding to a small number of paragraphs from the linked comments. It is also unlikely that that a given response is related to comment paragraphs from other rules.

When selecting the training data in our iterative algorithm, we restrict our sample to rules with 1-10 comments, and fewer than 1000 unique linked comment paragraphs. We also select at most 10 responses from each rule. This gives us a base sample of 6,727 rules, 17,452 responses, 10,456 linked comments, and 193,143 comment chunks.

To evaluate the quality of the similarity scores learned on the full training set, we used an early iteration of the model to retrieve all pairs with a score greater than 0.1 on a subset of the data. Then we grouped the pairs into bins of width 0.1 by score and kept 10 observations per bin per response. This sampling approach gives us a relatively uniform distribution of match qualities for our test sample. Finally, we sampled 4 random batches of 40 pairs from this binned sample and distributed them to human annotators. The annotators were not shown the scores used to construct the sample.

Our annotators consisted of seven students from the law program of our institution.All of the students had been working with us for several months and were familiar with our data. The annotators were asked to score the relevance of each comment chunk to the accompanying response using a 5-point Likert scale (see Appendix A for the annotation instructions). Each sample was assigned to multiple annotators, and we received 3-5 independent evaluations for each pair.

[5]https://tika.apache.org/0.7/parser.html

Content of Prompt
I will give you a pair of comment-response texts in each turn, you should give a number between 1 and 5. The number should indicate degree of overlap between the topics discussed in the two texts and how likely it is that the agency's response text is intended as a response to the selected comment text: **1 = Incorrect match.** Comment and response text are clearly discussing very different issues. The agency is definitely not responding to this comment text in the response text. **2 = Poor match.** Comment and response text are somewhat related, but appear to be discussing different specific issues. It is unlikely that the agency is responding to this comment text in the response text. **3 = Partial Match.** Comment and response text are discussing related issues but the degree of overlap is either imperfect or somewhat ambiguous. **4 = Good match.** Comment text appears closely related to the agency's response. It is likely that the agency is responding to this comment text. **5 = Perfect match.** Comment text contains the exact argument or information that the agency is responding to in the response text. The agency is definitely responding to this specific comment text. Note: 1. The response text could also be addressing other comments as well. This should not detract from the score. For example, if the regulator is clearly responding to two different comments A and B, and the selected comment text appears to exactly match the summary of comment A, then enter a '5'. 2. Sometimes there is a tension between recognizing that the comment is likely the one being discussed, and whether there is a good topic match. For example, both the comment and response might identify the commenter by name making it clear that this is the correct comment. However, if the topics do not match, the score should still be low (keep in mind this is only a sample of the comment text - it is likely that there is another omitted sample of the comment text that would be a better match). Please give me the answer of the following comment-response pair in such format: number - explanation. ### Comment Text: ... Response Text: ...

Table 1: The prompt templates we applied for the GPT-4 comment-response matching prediction. Text in blue is the content of annotation scheme we also showed to the annotators to label our test data.

Association for Computational Linguistics
209 N. Eighth Street
Stroudsburg, Pennsylvania 18360

ISBN 978-1-7138-8604-4

CURRAN ASSOCIATES INC.
proceedings.com